Review
of
Biblical Literature

2007

Society of Biblical Literature

Review of Biblical Literature _____

Editor
Jan G. van der Watt (South Africa)

Managing Editor
Bob Buller (U.S.A.)

Editorial Board
Yair Hoffman (Israel)
James Alfred Loader (Austria)
William R. G. Loader (Australia)
Ed Noort (The Netherlands)
Manfred Oeming (Germany)
Teresa Okure (Nigeria)
Jonathan L. Reed (U.S.A.)
Thomas Römer (Switzerland)
Angela Standhartinger (Germany)
Joseph Verheyden (Belgium)

Volume 9 (2007)
ISSN 1099-0046

Society of Biblical Literature
825 Houston Mill Road, Suite 350
Atlanta, GA 30329
http://www.sbl-site.org

Typesetting by Lindsay Lingo, The Project Company, Loveland, Colorado

Contents

Index

Editor's Foreword_____

The *Review of Biblical Literature* has established itself internationally as one of the leading review organs for biblical literature and related fields. It has become especially known for the following:

+ The reviews are published in a timely fashion. We normally do not review books older than two years, and we try to place the review within a few months of receiving the book.
+ Longer reviews are published (1,200–1,600 words or even longer), offering a substantial overview of the content of the book as well as a critical evaluation.
+ A wide and comprehensive spectrum of books is reviewed. Books from virtually all important publishers covering the whole range of what may be described as biblical and related literature are reviewed by international peers from basically all the continents. The editorial board overseeing this process consists of leading academics from Australia to America.
+ *RBL* also strives to publish two reviews of some books, a practice that has obvious advantages both for our readers and the authors of books.
+ A very efficient website with excellent search facilities makes access easy. With its substantial archives of reviews, our website is now becoming a very handy and efficient tool for research.

During the past year we focused on two areas, namely, increasing the quality of the reviews and expanding the range of books reviewed. The editorial board tried to increase the quality by asking at least two peers to consider reviewing a particular book before approaching volunteers, except, of course, if a volunteer was in fact a peer. This resulted in the majority of books being reviewed by real peers in the field who were able to form a well-motivated judgment. We also tried to expand the range of books reviewed by requesting books from several publishers (especially from Europe) that usually do not automatically send books for review. Bob Buller is constantly monitoring the situation and oversees the process of inviting as many publishers as possible to have their books reviewed in *RBL*. Our readers can expect to find an increasingly wider range of books being reviewed in *RBL*. This volume also offers a major review by Werner Kelber on orality. The format differs from our normal approach in the sense that not one book is reviewed, but a number of books that appeared on this particular topic are reviewed in relation to one another. By reading this review, our readers will get a good overview of the publications as well as the development of the debate over recent years. (Obviously, the restriction of two years did not apply here).

We are also pleased to learn (through feedback—something that we always welcome and cherish) that the material available on the *RBL* website is of value to a wide variety of readers.

+ Librarians increasingly use the reviews on our website as a guide for ordering books for their libraries.
+ Many colleagues use our reviews as a major research organ as well as to stay up to date on the most recent publications.
+ Academic discussions and contacts are stimulated. Reports of discussions flowing from these reviews are encouraging. We are also encouraged by the fact that *RBL* has become a platform for offering lengthy reviews, fostering discussions between scholars of diverse convictions.

Obviously, we are dependent not only on the publishers supplying books but on literally hundreds of academics who are willing to share their time and expertise with the readership of *RBL*. We would like to thank them all. *RBL* is a group effort in the true sense of the word, with many SBL members joined together to make it the success it is.

What we have in this printed publication is a selection of reviews published on our website during the latter part of 2006 and the first part of 2007. We hope that what we present here will stimulate readers to make even more use of the website. You may access the electronic edition of *RBL* through its own URL (http://www.bookreviews.org) or through the Society of Biblical Literature website (http://sbl-site.org).

I would like to thank Bob Buller and his staff, especially Doug Watson, for doing a superb job in managing the books from the point where they are received to where the reviews are published. Equal appreciation goes to every member of the editorial board who assisted in referring books to peers to review.

We sincerely hope that the selection of reviews presented in this volume will make for enjoyable reading.

Jan van der Watt
RBL General Editor
University of Pretoria
Pretoria
South Africa

ORALITY AND BIBLICAL STUDIES: A REVIEW ESSAY

Werner H. Kelber
Rice University, Houston, Texas

William A. Graham, *Beyond the Written Word: Oral Aspects of Scripture in the History of Religion.* Cambridge: Cambridge University Press, 1987. Pp. xiv + 306. Paper. $32.99. ISBN 978-0521448208.

David M. Carr, *Writing on the Tablet of the Heart: Origins of Scripture and Literature.* Oxford: Oxford University Press, 2005. Pp. xiv + 330. Hardcover. $65.00. ISBN 978-0195172973.

Susan Niditch, *Oral World and Written Word: Ancient Israelite Literature.* Library of Ancient Israel. Louisville: Westminster John Knox, 1996. Pp. xi + 170. Paper. $29.95? ISBN 978-0664227241.

Martin S. Jaffee, *Torah in the Mouth: Writing and Oral Tradition in Palestinian Judaism, 200 BCE–400 CE.* Oxford: Oxford University Press, 2001. Pp. xi + 239. Hardcover. $65.00. ISBN 978-0195140675.

Erhardt Güttgemanns, *Offene Fragen zur Formgeschichte des Evangeliums: Eine methodologische Skizze der Grundlagenproblematik der Form- und Redaktionsgeschichte.* Beiträge zur evangelischen Theologie 54. Munich: Kaiser, 1970. Pp. 280. Translated by William G. Doty as *Candid Questions Concerning Gospel Form Criticism: A Methodological Sketch of the Fundamental Problematics of Form and Redaction Criticism.* Pittsburgh: Pickwick, 1979. Pp. xix + 418. Pp. 280. $25.00. ISBN 978-0915138241.

Richard A. Horsley, with Jonathan A. Draper, *Whoever Hears You Hears Me: Prophets, Performance, and Tradition in Q.* Harrisburg, Pa.: Trinity Press International, 1999. Pp. x + 326. Paper. $39.95. ISBN 978-1563382727.

D. C. Parker, *The Living Text of the Gospels,* by Cambridge: Cambridge University Press, 1997. Pp. xv + 224. Paper. $32.99. ISBN 978-0521599511.

The field of oral traditional literature concerns itself with the study of the compositional, performative, and aesthetic aspects of living oral traditions and texts dependent on them. While oral tradition has long been an issue in biblical studies and in the humanities generally, the subject matter achieved a major impetus through the work of Milman Parry and Albert Lord, two North American classicists whose comparative work on the oral epic traditions of the former Yugoslavia and Homer gained wide attention. By now the field has grown into a scholarship that cuts across a broad spectrum of the humanities and social sciences, bridging national and religious boundaries and encompassing the multicultural body of the human race.

The rediscovery of the oral roots of all verbalization and the deeply influential culture of speech in the Western tradition (and in human culture generally) has in turn generated reflection on our scholarly dealing with texts and exposed a dominantly post-Gutenberg mentality within classical, biblical, and medieval studies. To scholars who are proficient in aspects of oral traditional literature, it is increasingly evident that there is something different about many of our classical Western texts than most of our historical, philological, and literary approaches would let us know. Oral and orally dependent texts, as many of our classical texts are, were tradition bound, variously interfacing with orality, continuously reinventing themselves in variant versions, and deriving meaning from extratextual signifieds no less (or even more) than from internal signification.

The study of orality and texts interfacing with oral verbalization is, therefore, not adequately understood if it is viewed as an embellishment of our prevalent historical, philological paradigm, an addition simply to literary criticism, or something of a mere footnote to the existing body of textual scholarship. More seriously, the exploration of the nature, dynamics, and cultural contexts of the verbal arts seeks to sensitize us to ways in which we tend to impose upon ancient texts a set of rules, methods, and assumptions that we have interiorized from daily reading and writing, revising, and interpreting of mostly printed texts. Today the field frequently referred to as orality-scribality studies challenges us to rethink a set of concepts that we thought we had known for certain, or better perhaps, we had assumed to be assured results of the historical, critical, and/or literary paradigms that required no further critical reflection. Text and intertextuality, author and tradition, reading and writing, original text and variants thereof, memory and imagination, copy and manuscript—central metaphors in Western thinking about the verbal arts—are all affected by the study of oral traditions and a chirographic culture interfacing with them.

The seven books that will be discussed in this review essay have all contributed—from different perspectives—to an understanding of the oral dimension in written texts, and all of them challenge us to be alert to sizeable blind spots in our scholarly paradigm whose methods and sensitivities are largely derived from our continuous working with printed texts.

Although published twenty years ago, William Graham's *Beyond the Written Word* has remained a classic whose significance has only grown over the years. The book does not, strictly speaking, belong to the field of oral traditional literature or orality-scribality studies. But it ranks in its pioneering spirit and intellectual acumen with the pertinent scholarship of Albert Lord, Eric Havelock, and Walter Ong, eminent humanists who have been instrumental in advancing our understanding of the oral component in the verbal arts. Graham is a historian of religion and a specialist in Islamic religious history. But the relevance of his work extends far beyond the history of religion. Biblical scholars, I suspect, have yet to discover the intellectual fecundity of his findings. His prime concern is "scripture," or sacred texts, perceived as a general phenomenon in the major religious traditions and in the popular and scholarly practices of Western modernity. Meticulously researched, internationally documented, and written with a high degree of nuance, the author examines the overwhelmingly oral verbalization of holy writ in Hinduism, recitation and revelation in Muslim faith, and the audible presence and internalization of the biblical word in Christianity. Additionally, he engages principal aspects of scripture in Judaism, Buddhism, and in numerous other religious traditions. In setting the discussion of scripture in this broad comparative context, he is able to expose concepts of the Bible that typify Western modernity. Scripture, he explains, is not primarily a literary genre, something that it has become in large measure in the West, but a phenomenon in the history of religion. That is to say, whereas in Western modernism the relatively recent paradigm for scripture is the tangible document of the print Bible, in most religious traditions, both ancient and contemporary, piety and practice are characterized by a high degree of *scriptural orality*. The latter is the key concept of Graham's study that allows for an understanding of scripture both as written and as oral authority.

Scriptural orality, the author explains, is a dimension that has received little attention not merely because of the ephemeral quality of speech but because modernity in the West has made the printed text the yardstick of civilized culture. Prior to the typographic revolution, the aural character of written texts, vocal reading and voiced texts, recitative and memorial powers dominated Western culture to a degree that is barely imaginable, especially for educated, literate people. To be sure, notions of the heavenly book, Buddhist adoration of physical copies of the *sutras*, veneration of the meticulously copied Torah, reverential treatment of texts of the Qur'an, and the deep respect extended toward illuminated medieval Bibles all testify to the antiquity of the notion of the sacred book. But the sacrality of the written or even printed book was, and still is, in many religious traditions of a piece with its oral uses, be they recitation, preaching, singing, or chanting. In the West, Graham explains, the rapidly disseminated print culture did not immediately displace oral practices and sensibilities. Shifts in the human sensorium, the disappearance of rhetoric from the educational curriculum, and the emergence of the authority of the Bible independent from persons and memory were slow in coming. It has to be remembered, Graham reminds us, that education in Western Europe did not accomplish mass literacy until the nineteenth century. But once the ubiquity of print textuality, combined with general literacy, "became the backbone of modern scholarship" (23), a narrowly culture-bound concept of scripture gained ascendancy that is now shared by many across the spectrum of diverse Jewish and Christian identities: "the literalist's book religion of the Protestant fundamentalist, the conscious or unconscious image of the biblical text in the mind of the average person of whatever religious persuasion, and the liberal scholar's historical-critical understanding of he Bible's genesis are part of the same wider orientation" (48).

Graham exhibits exquisite sensibilities in drawing a vivid picture of the role of the Qur'an in Muslim society. In fact, it was, he writes, his personal experience and study of the oral dimension of the Qur'an that inspired his explorations into the oral aspects of scripture more widely. Such is the intrinsic orality and abiding oral presence of the Qur'an that it can hardly be overstated. From a very early point on, the recitative character of the Qur'an was central to Muslim perception and practice of scripture, and Arabic—rather than vernacular translations—has remained the sacred scriptural language. Perceived as God's *ipsissima vox*, the vocally transmitted text is memorized, internalized, and repeated as divine speech, and it is expected to live on the lips and in the hearts of the faithful. Qur'anic recitation and cantillation manifests itself in a variety of "authentic" versions and covers a range of recitational styles, widely understood to be blessings rather than impediments. By different degrees and in a variety of modes, the public sphere of Muslim societies is scripturally saturated: the virtual omnipresence of qur'anic cantillation, educational memorization, qur'anic enactments at religious events and personal festivities, the use of the Qur'an in worship, and the permeation of religious and traditional scholarly language with the vocabulary and phraseology of the Arabic scripture. It is true, much attention is paid to the material text in the elaborately designed and illuminated copies of holy scripture, but the developed calligraphic art notwithstanding, there always is "functional primacy of the oral text over the written one" (110). The vocal presence of scripture predominates into the present. When in the early twentieth century something of a *textus receptus* was composed, the collaborative work by Muslim scholars was largely based on oral memory traditions—and hailed by Western text-critical scholars as a remarkable feat of a critical edition.

Graham's discussion of Christian scripture focuses on Pachomian monasticism and the Protestant Reformation. In Pachomianism, which served as model for later Christian monastic practice and piety, the centrality of scripture was conspicuous and scriptural presence was primarily an oral and aural one. The minds of the desert monks were disciplined by memorization that facilitated a sustained recitation of texts. Meditation did not mean silent contemplation in the reflective, interiorized sense alone, but an exercise that included recitation *viva voce* as well. Monastic life was truly scriptural life in the sense that it was permeated, paced, and governed by the recited, living words of scripture. Hence, memorization, meditation, and recitation implemented the oral presence of scripture in the Pachomian communities.

The functional orality of Christian scripture, Graham shows, did not end with the waning of the Middle Ages. The Protestant Reformers evidenced profoundly oral sensibilities with respect to scripture. *Sola scriptura* notwithstanding, scripture remained a living presence. Martin Luther, Martin Bucer, John Calvin, and

John Bunyan spoke and wrote a scripturally saturated language, not for the most part for prooftexting purposes but because they were at home in scripture, and scripture in them. Luther, although "the first truly prolific and widely read author of the printed word in the West" (147), was still far from viewing the printed page as silent and standing on its own.

"Does it really matter," Graham asks, "that our modern Western experience of texts may not be normative (and may even be genuinely aberrant) when seen in a larger historical perspective?" Yes, it does, is his emphatic answer, as long as we rely on modern communication standards in dealing with texts that belong to a very different time in history.

The story Graham narrates is both universal and detailed, but never less than absorbing. Scriptural orality expounds a grand vision of the piety and practice of sacred scripture. To the extent that biblical scholars have focused attention on the textual, documentary, and literary history of the Bible, Graham's work merits their close attention. Of particular interest should be the author's understanding of the theology of the biblical Word in the Reformation, a period that was instrumental in shaping the historical-critical paradigm. It is at this point that I wish to add what is not necessarily a corrective to Graham's reading, but a broader hermeneutical, philosophical context in which the Reformers' undoubtedly oral sense of scripture may be viewed. I would claim that the typographic apotheosis of the Bible deeply affected their theological thinking on matters of scriptural authority and tradition, on memory and interpretation. When we think of Luther's rejection of the medieval fourfold sense of scripture in the interest of the one sense, his increasingly high regard for the *sensus literalis*, his repudiation of allegory and all nonliteral senses, his unprecedented elevation of *sola scriptura*, his belief in the Bible's self-interpreting capacity, the steady marginalization of memory, and, perhaps most ominously, his rejection of tradition, this enabling context of biblical learning and interpretation, we observe a reification of the biblical text that was to create a high degree of plausibility for thinking of the Bible as standing on its own.

Carr's exceedingly ambitious *Writing on the Tablet of the Heart* discusses ways in which people in the ancient Near Eastern world produced, worked, and lived with texts, or, more specifically, ways in which writing and literature functioned orally, scribally, memorially in ancient educational contexts. His book is erudite at every step and broadly comparative, building on a stream of North American and international scholarship. The first part commences with the Sumero-Akkadian scribal-educational system of Mesopotamia and its modes of textual production, then turns to Mesopotamian influence on Elam (in what is now Iran), ancient Syria, the Hittite culture in Anatolia (modern Turkey), Canaan and the Phoenician city of Ugarit, and Syro-Palestinian culture. This is followed by a study of Egyptian education and textuality, links between Egyptian and Sumero-Akkadian scribal cultures, and Sumero-Akkadian and Egyptian influences on Israel. This part of the book is concluded with a treatment of the educational curriculum and production of cultural texts in ancient Greece and the epigraphic and literary evidence of education in pre-Hellenistic Israel. A second part commences with an examination of education and textuality in the Eastern Hellenistic world, including Egypt and Hellenistic Judaism, giving special consideration to Qumran as a model of a Second Temple Judaism that had structured communal life apart from the temple. Next, Carr takes up forms of early Jewish textuality and education linked with Sabbath observance at synagogues and no longer directly associated with the temple. The author develops a nuanced treatment of the growing consolidation of Jewish texts into the Torah-Prophets corpus, the forerunner of what came to be the Hebrew Bible. He traces this development to the early second century B.C.E., when Hasmonean policy sought to promote a Hebrew focal point for Jewish identity vis-à-vis the dominant Hellenistic educational system. In short, Carr understands the consolidation of Hebrew Scripture as a phenomenon of cultural resistance. Processes of scriptural solidification, he concludes, tend to be associated with centralized institutions of power, ranging from Mesopotamian kingdoms to the Egyptian monarchy, and from the Athenian democracy to Hasmonean Israel, and all the way to Constantinian Christianity—the rabbinic mishnaic and talmudic scriptural consolidations, I would say, being an exception. Three streams of textual-educational cultures persist into late antiquity: Greek and Latin materials, Christian materials (including the Greek Old and New Testaments), and rabbinic materials (including the Hebrew Bible). All three represented transnational entities, transcending traditional geographical and cultural boundaries.

The ancient writing culture, be it in stone, parchment, or papyrus, manifested itself in different alphabetic systems and cultural contexts. The Sumerian and Akkadian cuneiform script, incised mostly on tablets, featured elite literacy designed to train (mostly) male scribes for administrative and ritual functions. Initially devoted to the genre of lists, it later expanded toward letters, hymns, treatises, and gnomic materials. In Egypt, hieroglyphic inscriptions and cursive chirography served primarily as a means of induction into the sacral, royal bureaucratic elite. Neither in Mesopotamian nor in the Egyptian culture do we recognize an identifiable social institution that was responsible for writing, although a long tradition points to temples as locations for text collections. In ancient Greece, the principal purpose of chirographic activities shifted from the training of a scribal elite toward the formation of an aristocratic class of Greek citizens. Homer now took the place of lexical lists in Mesopotamia and of wisdom instruction in Egypt. In ancient Israel, all literate specialists were officials of some kind: scribes, kings, priests, and administrators. We observe the rise of a still-fluid and growing textual curriculum, with Deuteronomy and the Mosaic Torah at the center of a temple-oriented community governed by priests. The Hellenistic period witnessed a formidable expansion of both production and consumption of texts. Gymnasia became focal points of Hellenistic culture, although literary activities at these places appear to have taken second place to athletics. In the Second Temple period, much of the indigenous textuality, including the pseudepigraphic writings, appear to have had links with the temple and priestly authorities, although in Hellenistic Judaism as in Hellenistic culture generally, the use of writing and texts was no longer the privileged medium of scribal elites. Early Judaism increasingly linked scribal and educational practices with synagogal centers and nonpriestly authorities. While early Christianity rapidly turned to the codex form for Scriptures, using it in largely oral contexts, early Judaism continued to sanctify its Scriptures in scrolls, with the "Oral Torah" coming to play a central role in rabbinic culture.

A signal achievement of Carr's study is the deliberate move away from a paradigm about the ancient verbal arts that is entrenched in typographic and purely textual modes of thinking, and the construction of a model of textual production and appropriation that is firmly situated in historically suitable media contexts. Writing, texts, and literacy, he suggests, have to be understood as core constituents of educational processes. From Mesopotamia to Egypt, and from Israel to Greece and into the Hellenistic period, literacy and education were closely interconnected phenomena. Indeed, literacy and education were virtually synonymous as long as it is understood that neither concept imports what it has come to mean in European and North American cultural history. Concepts derived from the contemporary experience of literacy in the West are too narrowly focused on the rudimentary ability of reading and writing. What mattered most in ancient cultures was a "broader" literacy that went beyond alphabetic competence to include training in and mastery of the tradition. A literate person was not necessarily an alphabetically skilled individual but one knowledgeable in the tradition. Education likewise entailed far more than training in the technology of writing and reading skills. The principal aim of education was the enforcement of a standardized moral, ethnic, and social consciousness, something we might call today the cultural identity of a people. In different words, the central idea of education was socialization into the elite class and increasingly, in the Hellenistic age, into a general citizenship via the (re)inforcement of a core of cultural knowledge. For this process Carr has coined the term *education-enculturation*. Most writing and texts in the ancient world served this educational function of enculturation with the aim of inscribing on people's minds a distinct sense of social, ethical consciousness that would mark them off from others.

Given the fact that much of ancient writing was part of this educational-enculturational project, what was primary was the internalization of texts on people's minds and hearts. This had implications for the social role of scribes. The training of scribes predominantly occurred in family apprenticeship settings or in homes and workshops of master scribes, far less frequently than often assumed in schools run by professional teachers. Ideally, scribal training entailed both alphabetic skills for the purpose of (re)writing the cultural texts and the mental ingestion of these scripted materials. That is to say, scribes were expected to possess or acquire mastery of their core writings by way of memorization and recitation. Our scholarly designation of scribes, connoting strictly writing activities, is thus too limited a term to characterize the professional role and identity of ancient scribes. Memorization, scribality, and recitation were intertwined aspects of the enculturation processes, and scribes were the principal custodians of the authoritative curriculum.

The enculturation model also had implications for the composition and transmission of texts. The notion of scribes copying an extant text or juggling multiple texts that were physically present to them is, for the most part, not a fitting model for the communication dynamics in the ancient world. Undoubtedly, texts were written down, stored, consulted, and also copied. But the core tradition was not primarily carried forward by copying of texts. Rather, scribes who were literate in the core curriculum carried texts as mental templates, using them, recasting them, and/or repeating them. They had ingested the tradition consisting of one or more than one text so as to be able to rewrite the tradition without any need for physical texts. Rewriting texts was a hallmark of enculturation processes. Biblical texts in particular bear clear marks of "recensional" activities that have provided the basis for source and documentary theories. Carr's enculturation model suggests that "editing," "copying" and "revising," "recension," "original version," and "variants," the nomenclature of historical, critical scholarship, seems for the most part ill-suited to come to terms with the transaction of most ancient manuscripts. Biblical texts, along with many other ancient texts that were orally, memorially, and scribally transmitted from generation to generation Carr aptly describes as *long-duration texts*. These were texts in process, representing a fluid, mental, scribal, memorial model of transmission that challenges modern scholarly efforts at retrieving the single, authoritative, or original text.

Carr has given us a strong thesis, a conceptual model that is both comprehensive and thematically focused. Strong theses tend to be risk-taking ventures because they are intrinsically vulnerable to queries from many different angles. Should more allowance be made for processes of faithful copying of texts after all? To balance the picture, should more be said about texts such as economic, agricultural, and military records that were preserved for pragmatic purposes as materials designed for consultation more than enculturation? How can tendencies toward standardization of texts be weighted against tradition in the process of the long-duration texts? The thesis of an early dating of the consolidation of a recognizable body of Jewish texts into the Torah-Prophets corpus in the early second century B.C.E. needs to be balanced with the phenomenon of scriptural multiformity that is manifest in the Dead Sea documents. But then again, biblical studies needs strong theses. In the words of Eldon Epp, "What is needed is a microscope with less power of magnification so that our field of vision is broader." Carr has given us this kind of vision that challenges biblical scholarship to reflect on the phenomenology, use, and formation of biblical texts in broader cultural settings.

Niditch's *Oral World and Written Word in Israelite Literature* is strictly focused on the Hebrew Bible but broadly developed against the background of ancient Near Eastern cultures. While Carr operated with the educational-enculturational model, Niditch uses the notion of an *oral-literate continuum* as explanatory paradigm. Based on this model, she locates the Bible's literature either toward the literate end of the continuum, as in the frequent references to the written Torah, or toward the oral end, as epitomized by Ezekiel's swallowing of the scroll (2:9–3:11), or at oral-literate interfaces, as in frequent examples to write down in order to recite (Exod 17:14–16). Niditch's major objective, therefore, is to illuminate biblical texts according to their location on the sliding scale of oral-scribal communications. It is not that writing played no role in ancient Israel, she explains, but rather that the function of writing and texts was unlike that of modern literacy. The oral-literate continuum model postulates that literacy in ancient Israel and in traditional societies in general ought to be understood in continuity with an oral world. In that sense her model negates the **Great Divide theory** that views oral and scribal dynamics in oppositional terms. In Niditch's understanding, the texts of the Hebrew Bible are variously informed by the aesthetics of orality because the "Israelites lived in an essentially oral world" (44). Written word and oral world, therefore, interact complexly, and the Bible derives much of its force and effect from the dynamics of this oral-literate interplay.

While Niditch takes a cautionary approach with regard to oral compositional processes of Hebrew texts as developed by Parry/Lord, she explores, in chapters 1 and 2, what she calls "traditional Israelite aesthetics" (38). Linguistically, they manifest themselves in stylistic, phraseological, and thematic features such as repetition, recurring formulae, epithets, topoi, conventional scenes, and many more. These features, she explains, are not to be understood merely as rhetorical devices to accommodate audiences, to create strong impressions, or to profile key messages but rather as signifying elements of considerable import in creating meaning. Relying on the work of John M. Foley, she interprets the conventional and stylized patterns as metonymic signifiers that tap into the larger tradition so as to bring it to the hearing of the text. In Foley's words, traditional and conventional language invokes "the ever-impinging presence of the extra-textual, summoned into the process of interpretation" (*Immanent Art*, 45). Obviously, this understanding of the Bible's traditional language is contrary to the work of those modern literary critics who derive meaning strictly from the internal configuration in texts. Traditional Israelite aesthetics as perceived by Niditch (and Foley) evoke a reservoir that is deeper and larger than the particularity of any single text.

In chapters 3 and 4 Niditch examines a wide spectrum of oral-literary relations in a variety of cultural contexts ranging from the Near East and ancient Greece to medieval Europe and early twentieth-century Yugoslavia. These ethnographic parallels serve to place Israel's practice and self-understanding of writing and literacy in historical perspectives. Special attention is given to epigraphic materials, archives, and the material media of communication. Inscriptions on monuments, she states, often fulfill symbolic, religious functions more than providing service to a public readership. For example, the late eighth-century B.C.E. inscription on the wall of the water tunnel connecting old Jerusalem with a spring to the east of the city was intended to commemorate—in the literate mode—the feat of engineering by preserving information that, however, remained inaccessible to the populace. But the inscription also belongs to the genre of graffito that is "the poor man's monument" (55), and hence closer to the oral mode. Archives and libraries (Ugarit, Ebla, Mari, Aššur, Nineveh, Alexandria, Pergamon) appear to be designed for systematic, long-term record keeping in the modern sense. Indeed, in some instances the archival materials give the impression of being marked for identification, consultation, and retrieval, suggesting the beginnings of our cataloguing system. Some archival deposits, however, are more on the order of temporary storage places. Others lack any recognizable systematic ordering or seem to limit access to the elite. Even where archives or libraries are used for purposes of consultation, one must not immediately assume that the archived texts functioned as norms for memory and oral tradition. By no means implausible is the reverse procedure: oral tradition was perceived to be the standard on the basis of which archival texts were subject to rewriting. The writing materials (stone, ostraca [broken sherds], wooden tablets, wax-coated boards, papyrus, parchment, metal, ivory) give evidence of different social circumstances and purposes for writing. Techniques of inscribing on these materials required special scribal training and skills, turning the ancient scribe into "a sort of performer" (75), once again suggesting an intriguing blending of the literary with the oral, performative mode.

In chapter 4 Niditch directs attention to the phenomenon of textual pluriformity as evidenced by the Dead Sea Scrolls and evaluated by Julio Trebolle Barrera, Emanuel Tov, and above all Eugene Ulrich. Quite possibly as late as 135 C.E. scriptures that were eventually going to emanate into the Hebrew Bible manifested hitherto unexpected pluriformity, raising deep questions about the dating of the Masoretic *textus receptus* and the concept both of the "correct," authorized text and "variants." Moving beyond Niditch, I would venture to say that scriptural pluriformity we witness in the Dead Sea Scrolls is a way, perhaps the way, of textual life in the Second Temple period and into the second century C.E. While we have scarcely begun to assimilate the textual evidence that has been generated by the Dead Sea Scrolls, Niditch is surely right in stating that the textual multiformity exhibits "qualities of an oral register" (75).

Attitudes toward writing that are assumed by the Hebrew Bible itself are the main topic of chapters 5–7. On the one hand, writing is infused with numinous and magical qualities: the tablets of stone are written with the finger of God (Exod 31:18), investing them with special powers; the writing of names on sticks (Num 17:2–5; Ezek 37:16–17) serves to symbolize and to effect certain actions; written curses are ritualized and understood to take effect (Num 5:11–31). These and numerous other examples point to the well-known phenomenon of the oral efficaciousness of words. On the other hand, the writing of lists and genealogies, royal annals and letters, certificates and deeds approach the literary function of record keeping, although even these documents have often retained nuances of oral dynamics. Finally, writing self-consciously operates in a dual scribal-oral role, such as the Shema (Deut 6:4–9), which is to be written on doorposts and gates, yet kept in the hearts and recited. No matter at what place of the oral-literate continuum biblical texts come to stand, they are almost always framed or colored by oral dynamics.

In conclusion, Niditch reflects on the implications and applications of her studies. She advocates a reconsideration of major theories about the composition of the Hebrew Bible, foremost among them the documentary hypothesis regarding the pentateuchal sources. That hypothesis, she suggests, "comes from our world and not from that of ancient Israel" (112). At the heart of it is an image like that of "Emperor Claudius of the PBS series, having his various written sources laid out before him as he chooses this verse or that, includes this tale not that, edits, elaborates, all in a library setting" (113). As regards application, Niditch hypothesizes four possible models for the genesis of the Hebrew Bible: texts originated in live performances and were written down via dictation, or orally composed but chirographically "fixed" in the interest of a pan-Israelite identity, or written in oral-traditional style, or written on the basis of an antecedent manuscript tradition. There is no single or simple trajectory that can account for the composition history of the Bible as a whole.

The author is quite right in arguing that all too often we assume that written manuscripts in antiquity operated like our print books. It does make a difference whether we view biblical texts from the vantage point of print-conditioned notions of textuality or in oral-traditional contexts. But my sense is that in her work the line that distinguishes scripturality from orality is anything but clear and often a bit blurred. It may well be appropriate to denounce the Great Divide and opt for oral-scribal interfaces, as most of the seven authors reviewed here are doing. But we will not get around articulating with a degree of precision what meets the definition of orality and of scribality. Still, Niditch has made a bold and admirable effort at stemming the tide of a positively overpowering textual scholarship. Something is announced here and a challenge has been posed that, if pursued further, has a potential for revising substantial aspects of biblical scholarship.

The line of thought inaugurated by Graham and pursued by Carr and Niditch is further extended in Jaffee's work on the *Torah in the Mouth* in rabbinic Judaism. Certainly, oral tradition and Oral Torah have long been an issue in the scholarly discussion of Second Temple and rabbinic Judaism. The Oral Torah has specifically been linked with Pharisaism, while recitation and repetition of tradition are well-established features of rabbinism. Ranging widely from the last centuries of the Second Temple period to the compilation of the Talmud, benefiting from recent orality-scribality studies, and building on a close reading of texts he has developed a coherent and comprehensive view of the oral-literate rabbinic tradition and its perceived relation to the Mosaic Torah.

In the first part Jaffee sketches a broad scenario of the logistics of Second Temple scribalism. Palestinian scribes in that period, he writes, worked and lived with scrolls that functioned less as reference systems for information and more as memory devices for texts often already memorized. As long as the temple existed, most scribes were of priestly descent and closely associated with the central administrative system. No widespread activity of lay scribes is demonstrable. As far as scribal production of scrolls was concerned, Jaffee places heavy emphasis on dictation. Scribal dictation was "a fact of life" so much so that it was fictionalized into a "rhetoric of literary authenticity" (25) that sought to validate texts by reference to the archetypal writing or dictation by revered figures such as Moses, Enoch, and others. Hence, scrolls originated in a human voice and in turn found authentication as aural phenomena in the performative events of recitation. In this culture where scribal products were embedded in orality, scribes enjoyed ample room for creative intervention; textual closure was all but nonexistent. "Scribal orality" (16) is the designation Jaffee uses to capture this Second Temple scribalism in which "the characteristic organ of the literary life was the mouth and the ear, and its main textual reservoir was the memory" (18).

At Qumran Jaffee observes the kind of "orally mediated interpretive tradition" (29) that is generally continuous with the oral-scribal dynamics encountered in Second Temple Judaism elsewhere. Study of the Torah, the central ritual of the community, was practiced as a collective act that required the engagement of the entire assembly. The communally centered textual appropriation proceeded in two stages. In the first stage the sacred text was read or recited aloud, and in a second stage it, or rather its recitation, became a source for explanatory discourse. Both recitation and explication, the central acts of Torah study, were thus delivered orally and apperceived aurally in communal sessions. It was, therefore, not as fixed texts per se that sacred scripture exhibited authority but rather as an "ongoing revelation" (37) that was extended into the present. Texts in this oral-scribal media culture were perceived as both numinous and potential entities. They provided the locus of extraordinary powers, but these were powers that achieved validation in what Jaffee in a particularly felicitous phrase calls "the authoritative oral moment of textual tradition" (38). Put differently, the recitation reinstated the original moment of oral dictation, and the explication activated the texts' full(er) implications. Oral explication and aural appropriation were the norm, while at the same time oral activation remained firmly linked to and grounded in the sacred writings. Importantly, however, there was as yet no attempt in Second Temple communities to reflect on scribal versus oral hermeneutical procedures, let alone to differentiate the written Torah from what would be termed the Oral Torah.

Finally, Jaffee addresses the often stated thesis of a specifically Pharisaic claim on the Oral Torah. His examination of the principal sources—Qumran, early Christian texts, Josephus, rabbinic literature—adduces no evidence that the idea and practice of the Oral Torah originated in pre-70 Pharisaic circles. While the Qumran residents may have entertained tense relations with the "Expounders of Smooth Things"—a possible reference to Pharisees—the Dead Sea scrolls indicate nothing about a Pharisaic concept of tradition/revelation. The ancient sayings Gospel Q and the canonical Gospels have collectively developed a fairly distinct picture of the Pharisees. But apart from the fact that it is a picture drawn up in light of conflictual relations between the Jesus people and the Pharisees, these sources convey little information about the content of the Pharisaic tradition and say nothing about the significance of medium: oral or written. Josephus portrays the Pharisees as a religio-political movement that practiced scrupulous adherence to traditions anchored in the Torah, but he, too, remains silent on the matter of oral versus written transmission. As far as rabbinic literature is concerned, Jaffee expresses a strong caveat against assuming direct social and transmissional continuities between Pharisaism and rabbinism. The most one can say, therefore, is that the Pharisees, like most other scribal communities in the Second Temple period, participated in the prevalent oral-performative activation of texts.

In the second part Jaffee illuminates a rabbinic trajectory toward a gradual coordination of the (mostly) post-70 rabbinic traditions with the Mosaic Torah. It was a move that would culminate in the rise of the Oral Torah, an entity that eventually came to share co-equality with the Written Torah. Following the destruction of Jerusalem and its temple, Judaism found itself in a period of reconstruction seeking to consolidate its identity in the absence of central place. The instructional material that emerged from the early centuries of the Common Era was by and large oral-performative instruction that, transcribed into written form, was finally compiled in the Mishnah and Tosefta. The emergent perception was that the memorially manageable material was transmitted by word of mouth from teacher to disciple and grounded in the personal authority of Hillel and Shammai and their circle of disciples. These two preeminent sages and their disciples were regarded as the authoritative guarantors of the rabbinic tradition. There was no indication in the earlier segments of rabbinic literature that it stemmed from ancient Mosaic origins.

The later rabbinic tradition and especially the more expansive Tosefta, the author explains, exhibit a growing discussion about the relationship between the Mosaic Torah and the rabbinic tradition associated with individual sages. How was the authority of Moses to be understood in relation to the rabbinic teachers, and what was the role of the halakic norms in relation to that of the Mosaic commandments? The underlying issue appears to have been internal rabbinic needs to obtain clarity on the origins, nature, and authority of the halakic tradition. Are rabbinic traditions already anticipated, included even, in the Mosaic revelation? How can the autonomy of the halakic tradition be preserved without undermining scriptural foundations? Several sets of correspondences between the two traditions were suggested, but no unanimity is observable. From the middle of the third century onward, tannaitic exegesis evidences statements to the effect that the rabbinic oral-performative tradition was the work of the same processes that generated Scripture or that in fact the halakic norms issued forth from the mouth of God. The purpose was to bring rabbinic tradition into closer relationship with the Sinaitic revelation. It is a tendency that culminates in the conviction that "two Torahs were given to Israel, one by mouth and one in script" (90).

The tannaitic tendencies to link rabbinic tradition with Mosaic Scripture were further strengthened by the amoraic sages of the third and fourth centuries. Their theories entailed the conviction that the rabbinic oral-performative tradition was by definition torah, that it was exclusively oral in nature, that it constituted an unbroken chain of transmission from Sinai to the present, and that its covenantal efficaciousness hinged on its oral preservation and performance. The "fictionalization of rabbinic oral tradition as Torah in the Mouth" (7) had been accomplished.

Jaffee is at his most astute when he develops a model of *interpenetration or interdependence* of the rabbinic tradition. Irrespective of rabbinic self-definition, his analysis of texts suggests that rabbinic teachers drew on the oral-performative tradition for textual compositions that in turn were subject to reoralization. There was, in short, "a continuous loop of manuscript and performance" (124) that never yields a ground zero on the basis of which "original" instructions or texts are recoverable. Pure oral tradition, uncontaminated by scribality, is as much in doubt as direct intertextuality devoid of oral-performative mediation. For example, the compositional history of the Mishnah cannot be understood as a linearly progressing oral tradition that accomplished its textual breakthrough on the level of mishnaic redaction, but rather as a complex interaction of oral and scribal forces. I suggest that scholars of the Gospels pay particular attention to Jaffee's explanation of the relationship between Mishnah and Tosefta. While the author does not question the toseftan literary closure after the Mishnah, he casts doubt on the compositional explanation of the Tosefta as a literary expansion and interpretation of mishnaic materials. Instead of the widely assumed direct literary relationship, he argues, on the basis of close textual readings, that both Mishnah and Tosefta independently drew on anterior oral-performative traditions. The two literary bodies are thus to be understood as separate "variant formulations" (116) rather than as literary revision of one by the other.

Finally, Jaffee explores possible rationales both for the oral-scribal media interdependency and for the apotheosis of the Oral Torah. As for the former, he points to Greco-Roman rhetorical practice that was devoted to the recycling or transformation of written texts into orally manageable speeches. As far as the elevation of the Oral Torah and the implied suppression of writing was concerned, the author points to the master-disciple relationship and the life-transforming experience of orally performed tradition. The concept arose from the needs of discipleship to legitimate the authority of the sages and to preserve their living instructions.

It is the very substantial achievement of Jaffee to have transposed the often intricate deliberations concerning the nature, function, and media identity of the rabbinic tradition into a new conceptual frame. My questions arise from the second part of the book, which I find not fully coordinated with the first part. Do we really need the model of the Greco-Roman rhetorical education to account for the interdependence of oral and written texts in rabbinic education? Remarkably, many of the features Jaffee has described were likewise observed by Carr and Niditch within the much larger compass of the ancient Near Eastern and Mediterranean verbal arts: oral-scribal interpenetration, scribal orality, the educational locus, the absence of the "original" text, oral implementation of texts, textual variants related to recurring performances, the eminent role of memory, repetition of various kinds—although "repetition" may well be a misnomer in the oral arts. My second question concerns what Jaffee calls the "Ideology of Orality," as in the apotheosis of the Oral Torah. This is an extraordinary feature, unparalleled, as far as I know, in the textual traditions covered by Graham, Carr, and Niditch. Jaffee is surely right in explaining it as a method of rabbinic legitimation that at a later point proved useful as a polemical tool in the amoraic disputes with Christianity. But could we perhaps explore the Oral Torah more deeply from media perspectives, a feature so well developed in the first part of the book? What is happening in a tradition that has become so consciously self-referential that it isolates, identifies, and idealizes one of its media as an entity in its own right?

In turning to the New Testament, and specifically Gospel, scholarship, one remembers that the issue of oral tradition has historically been the pursuit of form criticism. Designed to attend to the orally perceived Synoptic tradition and to oral aspects of New Testament texts in general, the discipline has presided over much, although by no means all, of twentieth-century Gospel studies. Today form criticism is besieged by substantial challenges to its basic premises. The scholar who took the lead in developing a systematically grounded critique of form criticism was Erhardt Güttgemanns. His *Offene Fragen zur Formgeschichte des Evangeliums* (1970) ranks, in my view, among the seminal New Testament works of the twentieth century—not necessarily because of his constructive theses, some of which are questionable or unsustainable, but because of the powerfully analytical force of his criticism. Although translated in an extraordinary labor of professional dedication by William G. Doty under the title *Candid Questions Concerning Gospel Form Criticism* (1979), the work has by and large not been absorbed into the Anglo-American discussion of form criticism, redaction criticism, literary criticism, and orality-literacy studies of the Bible. James Robinson and Helmut Koester, for example, who in the United States were instrumental in espousing the Bultmannian model of form criticism as a methodological basis for Gospel studies and the history of the tradition, have not engaged Güttgemanns's critical objections to the discipline.

Güttgemanns's work must be understood by its location in the history of scholarship of the 1960s and 1970s, when redaction criticism was sharpening interest in the Gospel's relation to tradition and in the internal literary unity of Gospel narrativity. Increasing awareness of the integral narrative form of the Gospel and an understanding of oral dynamics quite different from form-critical assumptions prompted Güttgemanns to raise fundamental questions about the Bultmannian model of an unproblematic and smoothly continuous relationship between oral tradition and Gospel, a model that entailed a trivialization of the difference between oral versus scribal processes. Rigorously systematic and deeply provocative, Güttgemanns challenged the form-critical model of pre-Gospel tradition and the genesis of the Gospel.

What distinguishes *Candid Questions* from a majority of biblical studies is its intense application of linguistic theory and the subjection of the historical-critical model to linguistic scrutiny. "The 'purely historical' is always transmitted by language, and it is only understandable by means of linguistic processes" (3). The motto of the book could well be: we cannot get around the facts of language, because this is all we have. Güttgemanns confronts the reader with the kind of deep linguistic reflection on form-critical premises that one wishes had been undertaken by the founding fathers of the discipline. Uniquely conversant (for a New Testament scholar) in linguistic theory and ranging widely among the works of J. G. Herder, W. von Humboldt, P. Bogatyrev, R. Jakobson, H. Bausinger, L. Lavelle, H. E. Gleason, F. de Saussure, R. H. Robins, A. Martinet, K. Bühler, K. Ammer, and numerous others, the author postulates the essential and functional difference between oral and written language. "Contemporary linguistics considers that between the oral and the written there are *differences on all structural levels*" (197). The thesis of the "structural-functional dissimilarity of 'oral' and ... 'literary' technology" (211) suggested to him that the relation between Gospel and tradition had to be more complex than the form critics had assumed and that the form of Gospel could not be derived genetically from the dynamics and processes inherent in antecedent oral tradition.

Güttgemanns's thesis had profound implications for an understanding of both Gospel and tradition. As for the Gospel, he suggested that we view it as "*an autosemantic language form*, i.e., a language form which in its 'sense' can only be explained through and by means of itself" (307). As for pre-Gospel tradition, it occupies a territory that for the most part escapes our linguistic grasp, "since the evolutionary implications of the [form-critical] method produce only false hopes and scientific phantoms" (311). If oral and written functions of language are different from scribal ones, if the evolutionary model of oral traditions was unprovable, and if the Gospel narrative constituted an integral linguistic, narrative entity, then the form-critical habit of deriving oral units from the written Gospel was problematic in the extreme.

How far Güttgemanns was willing to challenge the form-critical practice of extrapolating assumed oral units from the Gospel narrative can be demonstrated in his handling of Mark's passion-resurrection predictions (8:31; 9:31; 10:33–34). Discussing form-critical theories regarding the pre-Markan status of these formula-like summaries and efforts to arrive at their original form, he concluded that their perfect narrative fit inclines the argument in favor of at least Markan redaction, if not composition. Recognition of the "autosemantic" integrity of the Gospel narrative undercut the form-critical method of identifying detachable Gospel units and using them as building blocks in the reconstruction of the so-called Synoptic tradition.

Still more radically, Güttgemanns struck at the heart of one of form criticism's basic assumptions about the recovery of "the original form"—a thesis programmatically articulated by Bultmann. In this regard, Güttgemanns (204–11) was the first New Testament scholar to appropriate Albert Lord's empirical findings concerning oral performance and written transcription. Based on his fieldwork on the Serbo-Croatian epic tradition, undertaken to illuminate the oral-scribal processes in the Homeric epics, Lord demonstrated that there was no such thing as "the original saying" or "the original form" of a saying. "In a sense each performance is 'an' original, if not 'the' original" (*The Singer of Tales*, 101). Moreover, if there was no such thing as an original form, or, we should say, original performance, then there could not be variants of the assumed original form either. No matter how many, and how many different, oral performances were delivered, each oral rendition was a freshly composed speech act. Güttgemanns concluded that, unless we learn to understand oral speech, tradition, and genres "exclusively in terms of the creative processes of continually new performances," we have not understood the oral legacy of the Gospels (206). An orator in the oral performance medium was not a spokesperson of original forms but a speaker of multiple, authentic performances.

The thesis of the fundamental linguistic differentiation between oral and written communication has played a role in the current Great Divide discussion, but without reflection on Güttgemanns's work. As I pointed out in the part on Niditch's work, we need to come to terms with what constitute oral versus scribal characteristics, even if, and especially if, we increasingly (and rightly) argue in favor of oral-scribal interfaces. Moreover, to the extent that recent performative, receptionist aesthetics perceive the Gospel as oral both in its pretextual tradition and in its scribal manifestation, they appear to view the Gospel simply as an oral variant, as Lord had suggested, or as the culmination of oral drives, as Bultmann had assumed. But that the Gospel was entirely unaffected by the chirographic medium is hardly a plausible proposition. Clearly, the demonstration of oral-scribal interfaces is one thing, but to refrain from drawing precise theoretical distinctions between oral and scribal verbalization is quite another. Regardless of the outcome of that debate, three of Güttgemanns's theses were undoubtedly to the point: the problematic procedure of detaching oral traditions from literary contexts; the inadmissibility of the notion of the single, original rendition; and, consequently, the concept of multiple authentic performances and versions. In retrospect, one wonders whether twentieth-century scholarship on Gospels and tradition would not have developed differently if prior consideration had been given to the Gospels' interior narrative constellation before far-reaching assumptions were made about the history of pre-Gospel traditions. Or, to put the matter differently, would not twentieth-century scholarship on Gospels and tradition have yielded more satisfactory results if early and simultaneous attention had been accorded to oral hermeneutics *and* to Gospel narrativity? Instead, we now look back upon a disquieting history of form criticism's scholarship that focused on oral tradition without an adequate understanding of speech and oral performance, and derived forms of assumed oral speech from Gospel texts without an adequate grasp of Gospel narrativity.

Today, matters of orality and scribality present themselves in a somewhat different light than Güttgemanns had imagined. As most of the authors reviewed in this essay suggest, pure oral tradition, uninfluenced by scribality, is for most an unlikely proposition. Equally important yet not widely recognized, however, is that pure textuality, uninfluenced by oral dynamics and solely relying in rectilinear fashion on another text, is not a widely practiced proposition either. Manifold different oral-scribal interfaces are the rule in the ancient world of manuscript culture. In *Whoever Hears You Hears Me*, Horsley and Draper have provided a challenging test case of the application of an oral lens to the hypothetical text Q. Treating Q (as well as Mark) as an *oral-derived text*, a definition derived from Foley and covering "works that reveal oral traditional features but have reached us only in written form" (*Immanent Art*, 15), the authors institute a major shift in our understanding of the ancient collection of Jesus materials.

The book is motivated as much by recent developments in orality-scribality studies as it is by discomfort with mainstream Q scholarship. In the first five chapters, the authors critically review previous scholarship on Q and lay out the historical, social context of the old Jesus tradition. Both theologically and methodologically, they claim, much of Q scholarship has operated on the basis of an inadequate conceptual apparatus. A certain line of Q studies tended to reach out for universalist categories and/or to opt for an individualist concept of the kingdom, showing scholarly affinities with liberal nineteenth-century theology and its needs to free Jesus from perceived Jewish particularism and to downplay social dynamics altogether. More recent Q studies. committed to a composition and source-critical paradigm, adopted stratigraphic readings of Q that sought to demonstrate a compositional division into an older sapiential and a secondary apocalyptic stage. However, Horsley argues, "[i]f Wisdom appears in 'apocalyptic' or 'prophetic' sayings and 'sapiential' sayings use apocalyptic language against the sages, then the criteria of categorization require critical attention" (74). Instead, Horsley (with Draper) judge Q to be "prophetic throughout" (81). The widely used generic designation of Q as *logoi sophon* is likewise deemed unacceptable because the many and heterogeneous materials referred to as *logoi* in Jewish, Hellenistic-Jewish, and early Christian texts cannot be forced into a single generic category.

A significant feature of the book is its rigorous focus on the social matrix of Q. Firmly locating the ancient hypothetical text in Israel's historical matrix, the authors challenge recent interpretations that postulate Q's rejection of Israel, a thesis that failed to acknowledge the deep roots of the Q sayings and speeches in the Israelite tradition. Among the numerous Israelite references and ideas Horsley identifies in Q are the restoration of the twelve tribes, exposure of the killing of prophets, Jonah's preaching, prophetic laments, Wisdom as sender of prophets, offspring of Abraham, bearing good fruit, the fire of judgment, forty days in the wilderness, indictment of Jerusalem, blessings and woes, and many more. Rather than being in conflict with Israel, Q is positioned at the point of an intra-Jewish crisis between the rulers and the ruled. Growing out of Galilean village communities, the Jesus traditions of Q are said to have taken a stance within Israel's history speaking on behalf of the Galilean and Judean peasantry against Jerusalem governed by Roman power, scribal-Pharisaic representatives, and Galilean rulers. What we find in Q, the authors suggest, adopting the nomenclature of the political scientist and anthropologist James C. Scott, is a classic case of the little or popular tradition pitted against the great or official, Jerusalem-based tradition. In mobilizing both prophetic, revolutionary traditions long operative in Galilee and the overarching themes of the Mosaic covenant and the kingdom of God (not of King David!), Q stands in continuity with and reenacts fundamental values of Israel. In sum, the old Jesus traditions speak for a movement that aspired the renewal (not rejection!) of Israel.

In chapters 6–8 the authors develop a theory of the oral art of verbalization or, one could say, a hermeneutic of oral-derived texts. In broad agreement with a number of recent historical studies, they describe the general lack of literacy, the largely ancillary function of writing and texts in ancient Mediterranean antiquity, and the oral cultivation of ancient Israelite traditions. Writing functioned primarily as an aid to memory and in the service of oral communication. Whether a text existed or not, and whether the genre was poetry, drama, history, or even philosophy, oral transmission and performance were predominant. In ancient Israel, scribal activity worked hand in glove with an intense oral, communal life. By and large, knowledge of scripture was not obtained by reading sacred texts and not necessarily even by listening to them as they were being read aloud. For the most part, scriptural knowledge was acquired by listening to oral recitations in the absence of textual aids because scriptural traditions were an essential part of the oral, communal repertoire. It is in this communications milieu, the authors suggest, that we must imagine the functioning of Q. As oral-derived text, Q originated in oral performance to be sustained in repeated oral recitations. In different words, Q was "a libretto that was regularly performed in the early Jesus movement" (174). By contrast, the authors point out, the International Q Project aimed at controlling and stabilizing the transmission of Jesus materials by securing a, or rather *the* "Q archetype" (J. Robinson).

One of the characteristics of an oral-derived text such as Q (or Mark) is that words relate not intratextually as much as they do in reference to a wider or deeper tradition. Importantly, tradition is perceived here not in terms of transmissional processes but rather as a body of experiences, an orally recited and internalized scriptural heritage, memories, values, symbols, cultural and national identity, and so forth shared by the community. A crucial feature of tradition, perceived thus as a collectively internalized cultural legacy, is *register*, that is, idiomatic modes of verbalization and signification in which different activities, memories, experiences, ideas, and the like take on life. In each instance the register consists not merely of a word or phrase, an idea or concept, but of a wide range of associations that have multiple links with and often deep roots in tradition. To be effective, an oral-derived text uses terms and images that metonymically key into the hearers' register by resonating extratextually with values and experiences that are immanent in tradition. An interpretation of Q will therefore seek to recover the tradition in the context of which Q was heard by summoning the register appropriate to such items as prophetic proclamation of new deliverance, Mosaic covenant renewal, mission and the sending of envoys, arrest of members and trial before authorities, sanctions on discipline and solidarity, consolation in situations of poverty, and so forth. Tradition, this extratextual reservoir of a shared culture, thereby operates as the "enabling referent" (Foley) in the production of meaning.

Following the theoretical part, the authors demonstrate in the remaining chapters (9–14) the oral functioning of key passages in Q. Instead of transmission of isolated sayings addressed to individuals, Q, they argue, functioned as a performance of discourses on issues of communal concern. As far as the actual Q text is concerned, they present the transliterated Greek version accompanied by a translation. Both versions are divided into what are assumed to be speech units that are marked by features characteristic of an oral-derived text: parallel lines; repetition of words, ideas, phrases, and syntactic units; stock images; mnemonic patternings; sound rhythms; paratactic constructions; and many more. Additionally, they divide Q into in stanzas, verses, and lines whereby priority is given to stanzas of which verses and lines are component parts. A crucial aspect of the interpretation depends on recovery of the oral register in order to determine meanings in the performance context. For example, covenantal forms and language, prophetic woes, images and terms such as wilderness, harvest, or sheep among wolves, judgment, and Pharisees summon a larger world of meanings immanent in the tradition. On the whole, the Q discourses are defined as prophetic speech perceived to be spoken through Jesus in the present: "Whoever hears you hears me" (Q 10:16). Through the performance of Q the earthly Jesus (not the exalted Lord!) continues as proclaimer of the kingdom and the renewal of Israel.

The great significance of this study is that if offers its readers a genuinely oral interpretation of a (hypothetical) text based on current theories of orality. Issues of theory and application, performance and format, history and language, social setting and oral aesthetics, register and tradition (perceived as the enabling referent) are unified in a grand theory. I am sure the authors are aware of the irony that their Q text is largely based on the archetype constructed by the International Q project, while all along the premise is that Q as a single text with a single meaning is no longer tenable. I raise a question, moreover, as to the authors' understanding of an oral-derived text. Q, Horsley suggests, is oral in the sense that "scribes are not required for the composition of Q" (294). Foley, however, distinguishes unambiguously oral from oral-derived texts. The latter reveal oral traditional features but are the likely products of literate authorship. I reiterate the question I raised with regard to the composition of the Gospels: Is it plausible to think of the Q composition as having been entirely unaffected by the technology of chirography? Horsley and Draper have pushed our understanding of Q far beyond the limits of the established practices of Q research. In terms of oral aesthetics and hermeneutics, this study is unique in New Testament scholarship. Q in oral performance is not the objectified linguistic artifact of print culture. It is safe to say that biblical scholarship trained in the assumed certainties of strictly textual hermeneutics will find it difficult to acclimatize itself to the open-endedness and polyvalency of an oral hermeneutics.

I have reserved David Parker's *The Living Text of the Gospels* for last because

it articulates matters of ancient scribal life in the intellectually most challenging fashion. Lurking beneath the positively conventional title are theses that, if
pondered thoughtfully, confront the historical, critical paradigm of Gospel scholarship with formidable questions.

The genre of Parker's book is an intriguing one. It presents itself as an introduction to text criticism, but chapter 1 already sets a tone that lets the reader
suspect a deviation from the genre of traditional text-critical handbook. The
author introduces the subject of text criticism by citing the examples of Shakespeare's plays and Mozart's libretto of *Figaro*, this cornerstone of the operatic
repertoire. In Shakespeare's case, many of his early plays exist in a number of different print versions, while the scripts of Mozart's *Figaro* consist of the autograph
and additional performance copies, including the official copy of the court theater
in Vienna. Both the dramatist and the composer instituted changes in rehearsals,
producing differing scripts that later appeared in print format. Which version,
we tend to ask, is the original one? The answer, of course, has to be that there
is no single original script. For Parker, these examples are paradigmatic for the
discipline of text criticism, or rather for the way in which it ought to be recon-
ceptualized. As long as "it is assumed that there *is* an original text, the textual
critic's task is very simple: to recover the original text" (6). This, of course, has
by and large been the basic fascination of the discipline: to sift through multiple
textual versions in order to recover or, as the case may be, reconstruct, the one
fixed point in the tradition, namely the so-called original text. But the quest for
the so-called original text need not be the only objective of text criticism. A different and perhaps more legitimate option, Parker suggests, is to study every scrap of
textual evidence *in its own right and on its own terms* and to evaluate the sum total
of collected texts for the story they tell us about the early scribal tradition. Once
we begin to get a sense of the startling variety of early Jesus traditions and Gospel
variants, the question forces itself upon us: "are the Gospels the kinds of texts that
have originals?" (7). It is a key question Parker's book is wrestling with. Quite
clearly, his book, while principally dealing with text criticism, offers more and
something other than an updated summary of the current state of that discipline.

Chapter 2, still on fairly conventional grounds, discusses the classification of
manuscripts according to materials, script, and contents, as well as translational
versions and patristic citations, and surveys Gospel texts through the centuries
from the earliest scraps of papyrus all the way to the electronic versions in CD-
ROM and diskette format. In chapter 3 Parker sets alongside each other the three
manuscripts versions of Luke 6:1–10 as they exist in Codex Vaticanus (B), Codex
Bezae ((D), and Codex Dionysiou 10 (Ω). A thoughtful examination introduces
the readers into the intricacies of manuscript variation. Many of the variants are
small, minuscule even, yet cumulatively tiny changes can be more significant
than one or two large ones. Can one, should one, favor a particular reading in
view of the variations? The case is dramatized by the fact that "there are as many
differences between D and B in Luke 6.1ff as there are between the two texts in D
of Mark 2.23ff. and Luke 6.1ff" (46).

Chapters 4 and 5, a centerpiece of the book, examines the manuscript evidence of the Lord's Prayer and Jesus' sayings on marriage and divorce, respectively. I limit the review to chapter 5. Sifting through the early manuscript evidence of Jesus' sayings on marriage and divorce, Parker recognizes that the problem is not simply one of explaining the (often redactional) differences between Mark 10, Matt 5 and 19, and Luke 16. There are differences not only between these Gospel versions, as is well known, but within the manuscript tradition of each Gospel. Sometimes the differences among the manuscripts of a single Gospel are greater than those between our printed Gospel texts. Assessment of the full scribal evidence, therefore, confronts us with a quantity and quality of different renditions that go far beyond Markan, Matthean, and Lukan adaptations and are not readily explicable by a single genealogical tree that would take us back to the one root saying: "a single authoritative pronouncement," Parker writes, "is irrecoverable" (183). Perhaps one may add that the project of retrieving the single authoritative saying is not merely fraught with inextricable technical difficulties but, more importantly, incompatible with what appears to be the prevailing spirit of the early scribal tradition.

In chapters 6–10 Parker approaches a series of well-known problems in Gospel studies from the angle of the available scribal evidence. The textually ambiguous story of the woman taken in adultery—sometimes following John 7:52, 7:36, or 21:25, sometimes following Luke 21:38 or 24:53—is judged not to have been part of the oldest textual traditions. However, Parker's point is that its textually inferior status notwithstanding, its existence in the lectionaries of most denominations and in Christian consciousness generally attests to its continuous appeal. The author concludes: "passages do not lose their influence once they have been declared and acknowledged to be spurious" (95). So-called minor agreements between Matthew and Luke versus Mark, always a challenge to the Two-Source Hypothesis, lead Parker to reflect on the quest for a strictly documentary solution to the Synoptic Problem. Advocates of the Two-Source Hypothesis, he observes, tend to envision the compositional history of the Synoptic Gospels "as though it were identical with the publishing of a printed book today" (117). Instead of assuming single-point contacts between two texts (Matthew using Mark and using Q), Parker explores the possibility of "a series of contacts between texts each of which may have changed since the previous contact" (121). The underlying conviction is that the Gospels "were not archives of traditions but living texts" (119). With regard to the issue posed by the ending of Mark, the available evidence suggests that the short ending is "the oldest form of the Gospel" (143). However, its textually superior status has (until recently) not been implemented in our readings of Mark. The fact is that the long ending "has been dominant for the reading of Mark for most of the text's history" (147). Another example Parker examines is Luke 22–24, the concluding chapters of the Gospel that present a known textual conundrum for critics and interpreters alike. Examining the multiple textual versions of these chapters, Parker detects a tendency toward textual growth, frequently marked by harmonization and leading to the gradual loss of distinctly Lukan features. "The Gospel story continues to grow within as well as beyond the canonical pages" (174). In reviewing, finally, the textual history of the Fourth Gospel, Parker finds that there "is no manuscript evidence for either the omission of Chapter 21 or the reversal in order of Chapters 5 and 6" (177), virtual standard assumptions in the commentary literature since Bultmann. Hence to suggest the secondary status of chapter 21 and a reversal in the order of chapters 5 and 6 is to postulate a text for which we lack evidence.

In chapters 11 and 12 Parker expands his focus on successive scribal versions toward the materiality in which they are transmitted, thereby mutating text criticism into media criticism. The early papyrological Jesus traditions were at their most fluid in the first century of their existence: "The further back we go, the greater seems to be the degree of variation" (188). Parker places a high premium on the introduction of the codex because it facilitated *inter alia* comparative Gospel readings that affected textual developments, above all harmonizations. In this sense the materiality of the codex contributed to the character of Gospel versions. What was of the essence of the fifteen hundred years of manuscript tradition was that "every copy is different, both unique and imperfect" (188). It was print culture that conferred an unprecedented authority upon the Bible. However, Parker is quick to remind us that in the desire to print the perfect, the original text, the editors constructed what must be called eclectic text versions, theoretical more than real entities. The author finds it difficult to arrive at a suitable terminology to describe the new vision of the tradition. He opts for a definition of the Gospels as "as a free, or perhaps as a living, text" (200).

It is easy to dismiss Parker for having drawn deeply consequential conclusions on a rather slim evidential basis. But as if to anticipate the charge, he has articulated his defense: "If the degree of variation which we have found were to exist in only one of the passages we have studied, the matter would require a serious evaluation of the nature of the tradition" (198). It is the abiding value of the book that it has contributed to a reevaluation of the discipline of text criticism and to a new view of and, I dare say, attitude toward the (early) Christian tradition. I hope that Parker's studies of the early scribal life of the Jesus tradition can be brought into a fruitful collaboration with orality studies. In view of the theories proposed and evidence produced by Graham, Carr, Niditch, Jaffee, Güttgemanns, and Horsley and Draper, we should not be surprised about variability, multiple originality, and recurring performance in the Jesus tradition as it endeavored to flow with the flux of temporality. These phenomena, while possibly particularly pronounced in the early Jesus tradition, are well-established features of the ancient communications history.

The paradigm of historical, critical scholarship has served as intellectual matrix for biblical scholarship from premodern times throughout the modern period into the present. Our assumptions about the verbal arts are for the most part indebted to and entrenched in his paradigm. It needs to be stated emphatically: the intellectual accomplishments of this paradigm have been incontestably huge, even monumental. More than that: Western modernity is

Mario Liverani
Israel's History and the History of Israel
Translated by Chiara Peri and Philip R. Davies. London: Equinox, 2006. Pp. xx + 427. Hardcover. $60.00. ISBN 1904768768.

Nadav Na'aman
Tel Aviv University, Ramat Aviv, Israel

Histories of Israel have been written ever since the beginning of modern biblical research, and dozens of histories can be found on the library shelves. A few of these works achieved the status of "classics" (e.g., the histories written by Wellhausen, Meyer, Bright, and Noth), widely used by students and scholars; a few others are sometimes cited in scientific literature. Many of these historical works more or less paraphrase the biblical text, reflecting the commonly accepted standards of their time, and describe the Israelite and Judahite histories in a similar way to the Bible.

Since the 1970s, scholarly outlook on the history of Israel has gradually undergone deep changes. Not only has the historicity of the biblical description of the premonarchical period been questioned, but also that of the account of the united monarchy. Scholars questioned the authenticity of the narratives of Saul, David, and Solomon, which for many years were considered a safe point of departure for the reconstruction of the history of Israel. Scholars came to realize that the biblical depiction of the united monarchy cannot serve as a basis for delineating the history of Israel in the tenth century B.C.E., nor can it be used as a point of departure for reconstructing the history of Israel in the ninth–eighth centuries B.C.E. They became increasingly aware of the fact that biblical historiography was written, first of all, in order to convey ideological, religious, and ethical messages and that these considerations strongly influenced the way that the history took shape. Finally, it became clear that biblical historiography was written at a late date (no earlier than the late eighth century B.C.E.) and that parts of it—the extent is debated among scholars—was written in the exilic and postexilic period. The late date in which biblical history was written, as well as its literary and ideological nature and extreme tendentiousness, are serious problems in a source on which to base a history of Israel written to acceptable "Western" standards. As a result, all the histories of Israel written in the past became outdated, and it became imperative to write a new history that would take into account the limitations of the biblical historiography as a historical source, set criteria for using the biblical texts as history, and integrate all the available biblical, ancient Near Eastern, and archaeological data.

It is in this light that the book under review must be considered. Mario Liverani is a prominent leading scholar of the ancient Near East, and he used all his experience, vast knowledge, and skills to write a new kind of history of Israel. To achieve this goal he divided the book into two parts, presenting first what he calls a "normal history" and second an ideologically constructed "invented history." Compared to other histories of Israel, Liverani's "normal history" is relatively thin and minimalist, dismissing a large part of the biblical historiography as nonhistorical. His "invented history" is novel and detailed, discussing systematically and at length the assumed ideological background of the biblical historiography, from the description of the garden of Eden up to the united monarchy, systematically interpreting the literary blocks in this continuum against the background of the exilic and postexilic periods.

Where shall I begin? Missing from the first part (the "normal history') is a discussion on the development of literacy in the kingdoms of Israel and Judah and the earliest possible date in which biblical historiography was written. Nor is the problem of the assumed ancient sources available for the authors mentioned anywhere. Finally, scholars' opinions on the date when the biblical texts were written and on the history of the texts' transmission are not discussed; the dating of the texts is reserved for the "invented history." It goes without saying that the time gap that separates the "event" from when it was first written about is crucial for evaluating a text's historicity. How will a reader who starts reading the first part of the book evaluate Liverani's decisions on the historicity of the textual evidence?

Given the importance of dating the texts, let me start by reviewing the second part of the book, where the problem of dating is discussed in great detail and which is in any case the more original and innovative part of the book. Once the dating of the biblical historiography has been dealt with, I shall address Liverani's judgment of the historicity of the related events as presented in the first part of the book.

The chapters devoted to the "invented history" are characterized by Liverani's conviction that ideology played an exclusive role in the shaping of biblical historiography. According to this line of thought, the shaping of the historical chain of events was dictated mainly by ideological and religious messages formed by the authors of the biblical historiographical works and addressed to the literati and elite of the province of Yehud and of the Babylonian and Egyptian diasporas. Other elements, sometime considered central to the shaping of the biblical historiography, such as oral traditions, literary considerations, and old written sources, played only a minor role in the process of composition and are therefore only marginally dealt with.

According to Liverani, the earlier works of the biblical historiography were composed under the Babylonian Empire, but most of the books of the Torah and Former Prophets were written under the Persian Empire and reflect the ideology of the elite of the returnees to the province of Yehud during the first approximately 150 years of the empire. The three stages in the development of the returnee community in the province of Yehud—the arrival of Zerubbabel in the late sixth century, the arrival of Nehemiah in the mid-fifth century, and the arrival of Ezra in the early fourth century—are the keys to the discussion of the development of the books of the Torah and Former Prophets.

Liverani attributes only the stories of the Primeval History to the time of the Babylonian Empire. Among the compositions written at that time are the story of the flood, the Tower of Babel, the garden of Eden, the table of nations, and the genealogies of the book of Genesis (ch. 12).

The patriarchal stories, in particular those of Abraham, reflect the early stage of the resettlement of the land (ch. 13). The first group of returnees ascribed to a soft ideology, which allowed assimilation and coexistence with the indigenous population of Palestine. Elements such as the migration from Ur of the Chaldeans to Canaan, the promise of numerous descendants, good relations with the local peoples, and marriage with cross-cousins rather than with the inhabitants of the land reflect the reality of the late sixth century. However, some elements in the stories appear quite alien to the community of returnees in the early Persian period. For example, the description of the patriarchs as pastoral nomads moving with their flocks from place to place does not in the least fit the returnees, who were urban and village dwellers. The establishment of some cult places along the hill country and in the Negev (Shechem, Bethel, Hebron, Beersheba), all located outside the borders of Yehud, and the avoidance of Jerusalem, the province's capital, contradict what we would expect from an author whose work is modeled on the community of returnees. Emphasizing the close relations and marriages of the patriarchs with the Arameans of northern Mesopotamia reflects neither the origin of the returnees from south Mesopotamia nor the reality of the Jewish community that lived in Babylonia. These elements are easily explained when we take into consideration a possible long oral tradition from the First Temple period and the availability of early texts that might have dictated the existing shape of the narratives. Side by side with ideology, other elements might have played an important part in shaping the cycle stories and various elements in the stories.

Chapter 14 discusses the exodus, the wandering in the wilderness, and the conquest of Canaan by the twelve tribes under the leadership of Joshua as a prefiguration of the returnees and their alien neighbors in the early Persian period. Liverani realizes that there is an enormous dissonance between the story of the conquest of the vast land of Canaan, including the extermination of its inhabitants, and the peaceful settlement in Yehud of groups of migrants from Babylonia in the late sixth century. He describes the biblical narrative as "a utopian manifesto, intended to support a project of return that never took place in such terms" (272). But how does the "utopian manifesto" of violent conquest and the annihilation of all the inhabitants fit the peaceful, gradual migration in the Persian period? Surprisingly, Liverani does not consider the story in Judg 1—which relates the conquest and inheritance of the tribal territory of Judah in contrast to the failure of the northern tribes to inherit their territories—as an obvious prefiguration of the return to Yehud. The conquest story of the book of Joshua, whose composition clearly predated that of Judg 1, was indeed utopian, but it should be set in the context of the hopes and aspirations of a much earlier period, that of Josiah in the late seventh century.

Liverani considers as fictive the canonical list of six/seven indigenous peoples of Canaan who were exterminated during the conquest. "In their totality, those lists of presumed pre-Israelite peoples of Palestine are built up through completely artificial speculation, with no connection whatsoever (apart from the term 'Canaan') with the historical reality of the time of the archetypical conquest (thirteenth century) or of the resettlement of returnees (fifth century)" (276). In my opinion, the list was fixed in the seventh-century book of Deuteronomy and includes the names of ethnic groups that were memorized in the First Temple oral tradition as the early inhabitants of the land (compare Deut 2:10–12). The names of these vaguely memorized ethnic groups were schematized in a fixed list of six/seven names, in the same way that the list of twelve tribes was fixed. Liverani's observation that "those who do not exist are exterminated—and the fact that they do not exist demonstrates the fact that they have been exterminated" (277), could be correct but applies to the seventh century no less than to the Persian period.

The tradition of the exodus and migration from Egypt to Canaan was always considered very old, since it is explicitly mentioned in the books of the eighth-century prophets Amos and Hosea. Liverani challenges this assumption and suggests interpreting the original tradition as a metaphor of liberation from a foreign power. "There was an agreed 'memory' of the major political phenomenon that had marked the transition from submission to Egypt in the Late Bronze Age to autonomy in Iron Age I" (278). The liberation took place in the land of Canaan, not in Egypt, when the Egyptians withdrew from it in the twelfth century. Unfortunately, Liverani does not discuss the references of Amos (2:10; 3:1; 9:7) and Hosea (2:17; 11:11; 12:10, 14; 13:4), which explicitly state that Israel came out (verb *'lh*) of Egypt, as well as some old summaries of the exodus tradition in the book of Deuteronomy (6:21–23; 26:7–8). He explains the shift in the tradition from an act of liberation to a movement of population from one country to another by reference to the reality of the Assyrian Empire and its mass deportations. The transformation of the tradition took shape in the seventh century, and in the sixth–fifth century the exodus and conquest of Canaan became a prefiguration of the "new exodus" from Babylonia to Palestine (277–80).

The cycle stories of the exodus-wilderness-conquest that followed the patriarchal stories had created a long consecutive history but had the effect of leaving a gap between the occupation of the land and the establishment of the monarchy. Liverani suggests that the author of the stories of the book of Judges had very little information about this period and filled the gap with legendary and folklore stories about military leaders and other figures, most of them reflecting problems of his time, but with bits of traditional narratives (e.g., the story of Abimelech). In his words, the stories of the book of Judges "depict how exilic and post-exilic Israel imagined its formative period in the land of Canaan, transferring values and problems mostly relevant to their own time, though partly based on material that may well have been ancient" (299).

The internal biblical debate on the merits and disadvantages of the monarchy opens the discussion of the united monarchy (ch. 16). Here, too, Liverani allows the possibility that the author had before him a preexilic composition:

Before the priestly solution was reached, creating that "kingdom of priests and holy nation" ... of the priestly author (Exod. 19.6), Deuteronomist historiography needed to revisit the past monarchic history throughout, fully accepting its role and praising its merits as well as condemning its disloyalty. It is probable, but now difficult to prove precisely (without presupposition), that the proto-Deuteronomist school at the court of Josiah judged the monarchy as a positive institution (but attacking the idolatry of individual kings); while the Deuteronomist historiography dating to the exilic period, after the fall of the monarchy, had no qualms about adding passages highly critical of it. (313)

Since almost all the comparisons of the Deuteronomistic history refer to situations and conditions of the early Persian period, it is clear that Liverani dates its composition to this period. For example, he describes the united monarchy as a prototype of the kingdom that should be established by the returnees under Zerubbabel in the late sixth century: "The prototypical kingdom must have been united, and embracing all twelve tribes, all those worshipping the one true God" (314). Nathan's prophecy on the continuity of the dynasty (2 Sam 7:16), and the building of the temple, are set against the early Persian period: "The link between the royal house, the temple, the people and the land was the basis of the project of redemption" (316).

In chapter 17 Liverani suggests that "the architectural elements of the returnees' plans found their clearest expression in the description of the Solomonic temple and palace (1 Kings 6-7)" (327). He makes the suggestion that the Solomonic temple was modeled on the temple of the returnees, while the palace reflected Achaemenid architecture. However, some elements in the temple description do not fit that of the returnees. Most remarkable is the description of the enormous cherubim throne erected in the holy of holies of the First Temple (1 Kgs 6:23–28), as against the kappōret (the "mercy seat'), on the two sides of which two cherubim spread their wings, of the Second Temple. Moreover, some temple appurtenances and vessels, whose manufacture is attributed to Solomon, are mentioned in the histories of several Judahite kings (e.g., 2 Kgs 16:16; 18:16; 24:13; 25:13–17). Finally, the role of Solomon in the cult (1 Kgs 3:4; 8:5, 62–64), and his dismissal of the priest Abiathar (1 Kgs 2:26–27), do not fit the model of the king as depicted in the literature of the early Second Temple period.

The rest of chapters 16–17 is unexceptional. It describes the fading of the hopes for the restoration of a king of the house of David on the throne of Jerusalem, the gradual consolidation of the province of Yehud, with its secular and priestly leadership, and the growth of Jerusalem as the center of cult and government. Expectations once directed to the glorious past were now increasingly directed to the future, and in the visions of the future the God of Israel took the place formerly reserved for the king.

The last chapter of the "invented history" discusses "the invention of the law." Liverani follows the broadly accepted dating of the laws: the Book of the Covenant is premonarchic; the Deuteronomic law is Josianic with postexilic insertions; the

Holiness Code is contemporary with Ezekiel; and the Priestly Code is postexilic, perhaps to be associated with Ezra. He recognizes that the codes contain ancient material but had grown away from the political to become a religious, cultic, and moral model for the community. He illustrates the development of the law by comparing it with ancient Near Eastern codes:

> Unlike ancient Near Eastern society, where a legislative corpus was usually linked to the initiative of the king firmly on the throne (from Ur-Nammu in Ur to Hammurabi in Babylon), the Israelite legislative corpus arose in a different situation: conceived mainly during a (real) period of political destructuring, it was retrojected into another (imaginary) period when the structuring had not yet taken place. The ancient Near Eastern codes had a celebrative purpose, describing how well the current kingdom worked (and therefore how prosperous it was), thanks to the prudent activities of the king in power, while Israelite legislative material had, instead, a prospective function, describing what should be done to achieve prosperity that had not yet been achieved. (344)

Observance of the law held the central place in the life of the community and became the source of self-identification. "National self-identification was perhaps based on less obvious but more important aspects: cooking customs, circumcision, Sabbath observance (and yearly festivities), differences in religious and funerary practices. During the exile period, having lost national political autonomy, all these elements acquired greater importance in corporate self identification" (353). The laws made clear the borders with other, neighboring, ethnic groups. By the time of Ezra in the early fourth century, the formation of ethnic identity of the community was complete, and the foundation myth as described in the Torah and Former Prophets reached its final shape.

As one reads the second part of the book (the "invented history") one becomes aware of the enormous problems entailed in the discussion in the first part (the "normal history"). Liverani dates almost all the biblical historiography to the late exilic and postexilic period, about six to seven hundred years after the transition from the Late Bronze to the Iron Age, the ostensible period of the patriarchs, and about four to five hundred years after the time of the "united monarchy." Yet in his analysis of the sources and the reconstruction of the history, he allows for the possibility that some old, authentic memories have been preserved even for the earliest stages of the history of Israel. This begs the question, What is the basis for such a far-reaching historical reconstruction?

The book is written in an authoritative manner and does not explain the methodological basis for extracting historicity from late, ideologically saturated texts. The lack of criteria for working with the biblical text as history makes it difficult at times to evaluate his historical decisions, and I found only one place where he explicitly explains his methodology. In view of its importance, I cite it here in full:

Concerning the new society of Iron Age I villages, our written sources (the books of Joshua and Judges) come from a historiographical tradition of many centuries later, and thus their reliability is highly dubious.... Given this state of affairs, scholars have taken diametrically opposing positions. Some use the Bible as a historical document, seemingly without questioning its reliability, and suggest that the "period of the Judges" and the "twelve tribe league" were without any doubt historical. Others, facing the enormity of the problems posed by textual tradition and late revisions, prefer to renounce the use of such data and effectively write off the Early Iron Age as a "prehistoric" period.

Nevertheless, the distortions and even inventions we find in the texts with such a long historiographical tradition have motives more consistent with certain elements of tradition than others (i.e., less relevant to the redactors' own problems). Indeed, the typology of distortion and invention is sometimes revealing: a story can be invented using literary or fairy-tale characters and motives (we have several clear examples), while it is difficult to make up a social setting that never existed. We can retroject laws that deal with controversial political decisions or property rights by attributing them to authoritative characters of past history or of myth (again, examples are available), but there is no reason to invent these where neutral or politically irrelevant matters are concerned. Finally, since editorial modification of older texts is difficult and imperfect, it always leaves "fingerprints." Thus, through a critical analysis of later legal and historiographical material, we can manage to salvage some elements of a more ancient historical context. (59)

Applying these criteria to specific issues is not easy and invites criticism. For example, there are some clear examples of making up a social setting that never existed, such as the long isolated wandering as a unified large tribal entity in the desert, the distribution by lot of the entire land among the twelve tribes, or the systems of Levitical and refuge cities. In writing the "normal history," Liverani made hundreds of decisions about the authenticity of the biblical accounts, and readers should therefore read it carefully and form their own judgment on his choices. For scholars who assume that some parts of the biblical historiography were written in the preexilic period and that its author(s) used older sources, making decisions about the historicity of the sources is easier. But Liverani goes into great detail in explaining his reasons for the late dating of the biblical historiography, and readers should judge his historical reconstruction in the light of his dating of the sources.

To close this brief discussion of the "normal history," I cite a short passage in which Liverani explains how the picture of the united monarchy was drawn by a late historiographer on the basis of scanty old accounts:

In discussing the United Monarchy within a historically reliable context ... we mentioned a number of historiographic devices used to turn this into a model kingdom. A number of local wars against small Aramean kingdoms in the north-east may have been magnified in the light of later Israelite-Damascene wars and of the power Damascus had achieved. A number of documents (especially Solomon's "twelve districts") may have been transferred from later administrations or plans (Josiah). A number of buildings (and not only the temple, but also fortified cities) may have been attributed to the most prestigious kings in popular tradition. All that was needed was the addition here and there of an "all Israel" to give the reader the impression of a large and united realm.

Once established, such a model kingdom inevitably became embellished with all sorts of anecdotes or fables, with the leading role played by a king who was brave in battle, or famous and wise, or oppressive. It was easy to decorate details that were otherwise authentic, but far more banal, with colourful fictional features. (315)

Liverani's command of all the disciplines necessary for writing an updated history of Israel produces an original and wholly innovative historical work, unlike any history written until now. He uses the large corpus of ancient Near Eastern texts to illuminate and clarify many biblical issues and analyzes the results of the archaeological excavations and surveys in an effort to determine the rise and decline of the state, the settlement, and the culture of Palestine in the Iron Age and Persian periods. The many tables and figures in the book greatly help the reader to follow the discussions. Throughout his work Liverani presents the developments in Israel and Judah as part of developments in other regions of the Near East. He devotes a detailed chapter to the concept of axial age (ch. 10), demonstrating that the rise of imperial formations in different parts of the world (China, India, Iran, Greece, and Israel) in the sixth century led to the deepening of the role of the individual, signifying a major break with previous ways of life. In another chapter (12) he shows that there was a dramatic demographic decline in large parts of the Near East in the sixth century and that the biblical concept of "an empty land" reflected the marked depletion of population and settlement in that period. No other history of Israel has been written with similar broad outlines and perspective, and it needs a scholar of Liverani's caliber to produce a book of such scope, wide range of topics, and originality.

Finally, the place of ideology, which is so pivotal in the work, must be reevaluated. All scholars agree that ideology and religious beliefs played a major part in the composition of the biblical historiography. But Liverani goes a step further, to suggest that all parts of the history of Israel were written as a kind of prefiguration of the time of the authors, with the aim of shaping the present and conveying messages to the addressed readers. The idea about hidden messages and alluded literary hints encoded in the biblical texts and aimed at the intended readers is quite popular in recent research of the Bible. According to this line of thought, the literati of ancient Israel were extremely sophisticated, possessing a kind of "code" with which they were able to crack the hidden messages and literary allusions produced by other members of the "guild" and to communicate it in a more popular form to the wider audience. In the book under review, this approach was developed to interpret all parts of the biblical historiography as a series of ideological messages intended for the elite of the community of returnees in the early postexilic period. Without denying the centrality of ideology in the composition of biblical historiography, I think that this approach is too one-sided and that other considerations, such as oral tradition, the history of the texts, the sources available to the authors, as well as literary considerations, had an important part in the shaping of biblical historiography. I suggested above a few critical notes on the reconstructed ideological background of some texts, and these notes might easily be multiplied. In my opinion, the emphasis on ideology as an exclusive motive for the composition of biblical historiography, and the accompanying concept of "encoded texts," goes too far and should be treated with caution.

Should the authors of biblical historiography be called "historians" and their works "history"? Did the biblical authors make an effort to assemble all the available sources, verbal and written, and did they utilize them in their own compositions? Liverani does not directly address these questions, but the book as a whole suggests that his answer is clearly no. In my opinion, this issue is the watershed between the so-called "maximalists" and "minimalists," and in this sense Liverani's work should be classified as a kind of minimalism. This does not mean that he shares the other assumptions of "minimalist" scholars. On the contrary, there is an enormous gap between Liverani's work, which rests on the assumption that biblical historiography was written by the descendants of the Jewish community in Babylonia on the basis of its old Judahite roots, and P. R. Davies's book, which rests on the assumption that the history was written by the "ruling caste" of Yehud and its government, which employed a host of scribes to invent a myth of origin so as to create a national identity for the mixed community that the Persians settled in Yehud. Nor is there much in common between Liverani, who dates the biblical historiography to the first half of the Persian period, and N. P. Lemche, who dates it to the Hellenistic period. Similar differences separate conservative and critical "maximalists," and no clear line can be drawn between scholars who support either approach. The only line that can be drawn is between good and bad historians, and both kinds are to be found on either side of the scholarly debate.

In my monograph on biblical historiography (*The Past That Shapes the Present: The Creation of Biblical Historiography in the Late First Temple Period and after the Downfall* [Hebrew] [Jerusalem, 2002]), I devote a chapter to the way the Deuteronomist treated his sources and conclude that he made an effort to assemble as many sources as he could and wrote his work on the basis of these oral and written sources. I therefore regard myself as a "maximalist," but when it comes to the analysis of the biblical texts and reconstructing history, my conclusions are much closer to that of Liverani than to those of conservative "maximalists."

Liverani's book is dense, replete with data relating to all regions of the Near East, covers the history of the lands on both sides of the Jordan for about eight hundred years, and is not easy to read. It is mainly intended for scholars and, in my opinion, is not meant for undergraduate students. The work is stimulating, original in all its parts, and contains many original insights that will no

ELECTRONIC RESOURCES

The Works of Philo: Greek Text with Morphology. Bellingham, Wash.: Logos Bible Software, 2005. CD-ROM. $119.95. ISBN 1577992219.

Torrey Seland, School of Mission and Theology, Stavanger, Norway

HISTORY

This resource is built upon the database compiled by the Norwegian "Philo Concordance Project," which resulted in the publication of the first complete printed concordance of Philo in 2000. The history of this project is long and complicated. It started when Prof. Peder Borgen was at the University of Bergen, Norway, in the early 1970s and at first resulted in a machine-readable text from which a keyword-in–context concordance was produced. In fact, only two or three copies were printed, and when Borgen moved to Trondheim in 1976, he was in charge of one of these. When I became a research fellow in Trondheim in 1983, the concordance comprised several volumes on the bookshelves of Borgen's office and was of great help in my own Philo studies. At the end of the 1980s efforts were made to raise money for the completion of the Philo Concordance Project; happily, the Norwegian Research Council agreed to support this work, and, finally, in 2000 a word index based on the work of the Philo Concordance Project was published by Eerdmans and Brill.[1] A brief but somewhat more detailed history of the project can be read at the beginning of this Logos module and on the homepage of the Philo Concordance Project (http://webster.hibo.no/alu/seksjon/krl/kaare/filon/).

The present Logos Bible Software resource includes the complete works of Philo in Greek, drawn from the same four text editions used to compile the concordance (Cohn and Wendland, Colson, Petit, and Paramelle). The lemmatization and morphology are also supplied as established by the Philo Concordance Project scholars. According to Logos's own presentation in the present edition, however, "The morphological analysis contained in this edition is under revision. Forms that are ambiguous or contextually uncertain are in the process of being reviewed. An updated form of this resource will be made available at no cost via

---

1. Peder Borgen, Kåre Fuglseth, and Roald Skarsten, *The Philo Index: A Complete Greek Word Index to the Writings of Philo of Alexandria* (Grand Rapids: Eerdmans; Leiden: Brill, 2000).

download upon completion of the extended analysis."[2] To my knowledge, no date has been set for this revision.

The purpose of this review is to present the Philo of Alexandria module that goes together with the Logos Bible Software platform (hereafter LBS). It is sold separately but will likely also be included in some of their comprehensive packages. The review, accordingly, will not deal with all the aspects of Logos Bible Software, but primarily with the Philo of Alexandria module and the major program functions associated with it.

Overview of the Resource

The module is called *The Works of Philo: Greek Text with Morphology,* which means that each word occurrence is morphologically tagged. When viewing the text in the LBS platform, one can choose to see only the Greek text or have an interlinear version in which, in addition to the Greek text, one can see the morphology tags and/or the lemma form of the words concerned. The tagging consists of letters and figures that are not that difficult to understand after some use; a tag such as "NNSM" means "noun nominative singular masculine" (a few others are harder to decode). However, one does not need to understand this tagging or even to have it visible on the screen, because when one hovers the mouse arrow over a word, the decoded morphological analysis will be visible at the bottom left side of the LBS screen. Hence, I prefer to use the nonlinear Greek text version only or the Greek text with the lemmas.

The Main Program Functions Associated with the Text Module

In fact, the module as such consists only of the tagged text, in this case a morphologically tagged text. The great profit of having it as a module in a Bible software program platform such as LBS is the possibilities offered of presenting and analyzing the text provided by facilities inherent in the main platform and the possibilities of connecting the Philo text with other modules. When it comes to the LBS platform, I would like to point especially to the following issues to demonstrate what it is like to work with a digitalized text such as this.

Having a morphologically tagged text offers great possibilities when it comes to searching the text for specific forms or word constructions. In LBS one has several ways of searching, from the unspecified to the exact form. The result is nicely listed, and an extract of the paragraph concerned is given. If one then hovers the mouse arrow over the reference, the full paragraph appears in a small pop-up window, and clicking on the reference brings up the full text paragraph concerned in the text window. Searching, for instance, for the verb ἐξαγγέλλω immediately demonstrates that the verb is found two times in the New Testament, twelve times in the LXX, and three times in the works of Philo. One sees

---

2. See http://www.logos.com/products/details/2219.

what verb form is found, and a click brings forth the whole paragraph or verse concerned.

In the LBS one also has the possibility of installing the old English translation of C. D. Yonge. This translation is admittedly old and has its deficiencies,[3] but it nevertheless is of great help in reading the Greek Philo texts. In the LBS the Greek text and the translation can be interlocked; that is, when one scrolls the one, the other follows. In this way one can always have both the Greek text and the translation immediately available on-screen.

Another beneficial aspect of using this module of the Greek text of Philo is the possibility of using the texts in association with various lexica. LBS has several lexica available. If one, for instance, has *A Greek-English Lexicon of the New Testament and Other Early Christian Literature* (3rd ed.; BDAG) in the LBS setup, one can click on a word in the Philonic text and the relevant lexicon entry will immediately pop up. Alternately, one can search the lexicon for a term; a click on a reference to a work of Philo will bring up the full paragraph. Or, one can search BDAG for references to specific passages of Philonic works. However, one needs to have the latest version of this lexicon available; the former BDG version does not have this cross-linking feature included.

The advantages of having these texts of Philo available in their Greek form are great compared to the use of text editions.[4] The many possibilities presented by speedy searches of comparisons or lexical descriptions of the terminology of Philo are something to be highly appreciated. The printed *Philo Index* mentioned above provides only the main form of, for example, a verb and then a list of references where some form of the verb is to be found. In the digitalized version one can perform exact searches. Furthermore, one can easily make up lists of keywords-in-contexts and search across several Greek texts, according to one's specific setup.

Philonic scholars have been greatly helped by the introduction of computers in working with texts such as these. Peder Borgen and his associates initiated this way of working with Philo texts on computers when the use of computers was still something rare in biblical and Philonic studies. The inclusion of their work in the context of software platforms such as Logos Bible Software has demonstrated how future-oriented they were in Bergen in the 1970s. Students of the works of Philo should be grateful for the inclusion of this work in the Logos Bible Software

---

3. On the value of this rather old translation of C. D. Yonge for scholarly work, see the review by David T. Runia, available online at ftp://ftp.lehigh.edu/pub/listserv/ioudaios-review/4.1994/philo.runia.009.

4. After this LBS module was published, there has also been issued a multivolume edition of a key-word-in-context of Philo's works; *see The Complete Works of Philo of Alexandria: A Key-Word-In-Context Concordance* R. Skarsten, P. Borgen og K. Fuglseth. Volume I-VIII (7556 pages). Gorgias Press, New Jersey, USA, 2005.

platform and for the many possibilities of searching, analyzing, and comparing various texts such computer programs represent.

Amos: Hypertext Bible Commentary, by Tim Bulkeley. Auckland: Hypertext Bible Project, 2005. CD-ROM; online at http://hypertextbible.org/amos/. ISBN 0473107147.

Ehud Ben Zvi, University of Alberta, Edmonton, Alberta, Canada

This is the first volume in a new series, the Hypertext Bible Commentary. The series as per its name uses new electronic technologies, online delivery, and particularly hypertextual capabilities to enrich the traditional genre of biblical commentary. The author of this volume has been at the helm of this project and its twin one of developing an online, free biblical encyclopedia, a kind of peer-reviewed Wikipedia (for information on both projects, see http://bible.gen.nz/). Both projects are aimed at the wide, general public that more and more searches for information online. As such, provided that their contents are appropriate, these and similar projects will play a significant, and likely ever-increasing role in the education of the general public on biblical matters. Certainly these are not light matters.

What do readers of this commentary encounter when they turn to it? Many are variants of the same features found in more traditional commentaries. For instance, they find a Hebrew text of Amos and an English translation. The difference is that almost every word in the Hebrew text carries a hyperlink to annotations. For instance, the only word that is not hyperlinked in Amos 1:1 is עַל. But are these annotations always helpful or even necessary? For instance, clicking on יִשְׂרָאֵל in 1:1 brings the following text:

> *yisra'el* Israel. Name of both a people and a state. Jacob, the patriarch was remaned [*sic*] "Israel" after his fight at the Jabbok, and the nation which claims descent from his children are called "Children of Israel" or "Israel". With the separation of the two kingdoms the northern state was called "Israel" and the southern one "Judah".

To be sure, one may argue whether this is a correct place to introduce a sophisticated discussion of the possible (multiple) meanings evoked by the term "Israel" in the world of the book and within the discourse of its intended and primary readerships or not, but I doubt very much that the information given above would help anyone competent enough to read the Hebrew text of Amos. Similarly, clicking on דִּבְרֵי in the same verse brings the following information:

> דבר *dbr* in the piel is the most commonly used word for "speak": Am 3:1, 8 the qal has much the same sense: Am 5:10. *dabar* "word, message, story or business/affair". The usage in Am 1:1 is discussed in the commentary. In the prophets the *dabar* is often the prophet's oracle 3:1; 4:1; 5:1; 7:10 (cf. 7:16; 8:11, 12). In

Amos 3:7 "thing" seems best to describe what God is doing and announcing. The phrase לֹא דָבָר *lo' dabar* in Am 6:13 can either mean "nothing" ('no thing') or refer to a town east Jordan (2 Sam 9:4-5; 17:27).

Leaving aside the problematic wording (*dbr* in the piel is *not* a word but a grammatical concept that can be represented by various words), who requires the basic dictionary entry for this or for that of הָיָה, which is also hyperlinked? More problematic perhaps is the connoted connection between different occurrences of the same term. For instance, why is the reader of בִּימֵי עֻזִּיָּה מֶלֶךְ־יְהוּדָה וּבִימֵי יָרָבְעָם בֶּן־יוֹאָשׁ מֶלֶךְ יִשְׂרָאֵל asked to think of the "Day of the Lord"? Does the author suggest that there is some interpretive link that binds these different instances of the use of יוֹם? If this is the case, then this reviewer for one could not find it in the commentary. It is worth noting that, although the text seems extremely overlinked, some obvious cases in which links would have been helpful for beginners are not present. For instance, there are no links to Moab, Edom, Tyre, and the like, neither in the Hebrew nor the English text.

The commentary includes links to an (incipient?) Bible dictionary and glossary. The Hebrew entries are here offered in transliteration (unlike elsewhere in the commentary). Unlike the usual transliterations, ` = ע and ' = א. For a reason unclear to me, words beginning with ` = ע appear as such, although alphabetically they are located before any other letter (or number; i.e., עַל [= 'al] under ` = ע); however, words beginning with א appear according to "their next letter [sic]," so אַב (= 'ab) appears under "A," as if א were not a letter. (The transliteration of the Hebrew vowel markers is, needless to say, very imprecise—why not use the SBL transliteration system?—and, of course, vowel markers do not constitute a "letter" in Hebrew.)

The English text represents the author's translation. He states that the "translation (the Temporary English Version! TempEV) is highly 'literal', giving the 'flavor' of the Hebrew," and that "it should be read alongside a good recent translation like CEV which gives the sense in contemporary language." The translation is indeed more "literal" than the CEV, but its characterization as "highly literal" is perhaps misleading. For instance, בִּימֵי עֻזִּיָּה מֶלֶךְ־יְהוּדָה is translated as "in the time of Uzziah King of Judah," which is not wrong but not "highly literal" (cf. NRSV, NAB). One may notice that הַחֵלֶק in Amos 7:4 is translated as "the promised land {allotted portion}"; that is, "the portion" is present here only as an explanation, and the translation "abandoning righteousness on the land!" for וּצְדָקָה לָאָרֶץ הִנִּיחוּ is certainly not "highly literal"—surprisingly, the author does provide a more literal translation in his notes on Amos 5:7. More problematic is, in my view, the claim that the translation provides the "flavor" of the Hebrew.

Unlike traditional commentaries, this one includes an audio file with the book of Amos read in Hebrew and in the author's English translation. To include these audio files is probably a good idea, but the Hebrew file contains mistakes (see already Amos 1:4–5). Since there has been for a quite some time a very good audio version of the Hebrew text available on the Internet (and used, e.g., in the Snunit site; see http://kodesh.snunit. k12.il/i/t/ t1501.htm), one wonders why the author did not use it.

Despite its nontraditional form, the commentary includes some "traditional" sections such as a general introduction to the book of Amos, to the prophet, and to the historical setting (of the prophet); a timeline; and some introductory remarks on prophetic literature. It contains a bibliography and a helpful search function. From a contents perspective, this innovative commentary tends to be clearly on the "traditional" side. The basic assumption is that much goes back to Amos, the eighth-century prophet. This is, of course, a legitimate position that is advanced by many in the field, even if not shared by the present reviewer. The author also identifies to a very large extent with the claims advanced by the character Amos in the book and with the other prophets in general, who according to him, "spoke God's message without fear or favor." Debatable or not, this is not an unusual but rather a very "traditional" approach to a prophetic book.

Agreements and disagreements concerning the positions advanced by Bulkeley are only to be expected, cannot be seriously dealt in any review, and above all are not a reason for concern in themselves, the more so in a book aimed at the general public. But the same does not hold true for general matters regarding the presentation advanced in the book. In my opinion, at times it is simply too brief. To illustrate, given the history of interpretation of Amos 2:4–5, is the following all that should be said about this pericope?

> Language and Imagery:
> This oracle against Judah is weak compared with the others - the punishment is described in general terms and briefly "fire on Judah" and "Jerusalem's citadels consumed". The crime too is both less and more precise - no particular acts are mentioned (less precision), but rather unfaithfulness to Adonai and his decrees is condemned (greater precision of the person offended).
>
> Rhetorical effect:
> However, given the context of a Judean prophet addressing an Israelite audience, the effect is startling - perhaps this is why the wording is simple. (Surely a prophet who condemns his own, neighbouring, people must be true!) Following the series of oracles against traditional neighbouring enemies, which surely found a ready audience, this one would raise their appreciation and expectation of Amos still higher....

My main concern here is not necessarily or mainly with what is said, but that *only* this is said. To be sure, any commentary aimed at a large public tends to oversimplify matters, but still it has to convey a sense of the large picture and above all avoid conveying a false sense of closure on matters that are certainly not closed. I tend to think that beginners, and especially beginners, should be made aware that this is the situation. Moreover, attention to the needs of a wide range of readers requires attention to the way in which matters are explained, but not "simplified" contents.

The author's laudable attempt to be easily understood by a wide public led him on occasion to slide into potentially problematic statements. For instance, the commentary to 8:14 (הַנִּשְׁבָּעִים בְּאַשְׁמַת שֹׁמְרוֹן וְאָמְרוּ חֵי אֱלֹהֶיךָ דָּן וְחֵי דֶּרֶךְ בְּאֵר־שָׁבַע וְנָפְלוּ וְלֹא־יָקוּמוּ עוֹד) includes the follow remark, which given the tone of the verse being discussed and the expected readership of the commentary, might lead to misinterpretation:

> In this case all three are references not to other gods, but to the local-ized worship of Adonai. Canaanite religion localized the gods and goddesses so that they became multiple and linked to particular places. This tendency in religious practice perhaps finds expression in popu-lar Catholicism in the difference perceived by the devout between the Blessed Virgin of Guadaloupe and other representations of Jesus' mother.

I am sure that statements that might lead to misinterpretation occur in almost every commentary and that commentaries aimed at a general public may tend to oversimplify matters, but if (a) many more people will read the Hypertext Bible Commentary than the more specialized commentaries that this reviewer and most academics love, and (b) the Hypertext Bible Commentary is going to exert its influence not only over a wider range of people than most commentaries, over people who may not have had any critical education on biblical and cognate matters, and for the most part will exert its influence in a way that is not be medi-ated by academically trained instructors/tutors, then follows (c): a great degree of care for its contents is required. It is from this perspective that I raise questions concerning what I see as potentially misleading oversimplification and the poten-tial impact of remarks expressed in a less than felicitous way.

We all owe a debt of gratitude to Tim Bulkeley for all his work in this impor-tant project. I see this Amos commentary as a version 1.0 that will, I hope, lead to further and better versions in which many of the problems mentioned here will be solved. I am aware that even this version represents an improvement over pre-vious versions (notice, e.g., the wise removal of the term "postmodern" from the title of the series; cf. http://bible.gen.nz/), and I confidently hope that this process will continue and even accelerate.

BIBLICAL THEMES

An Introduction to the Bible, by J. W. Rogerson. Revised edition. London: Equinox, 2005. Pp. xii + 176. Paper. $24.95. ISBN 1845530396.

Pierre Keith, Université Marc Bloch, Strasbourg, France

Dès le premier chapitre, intitulé «qu'est-ce que la Bible ?», l'auteur se met à la disposition d'un lecteur, cultivé, non spécialiste, mais curieux des débats académiques qui, face à la diversité des éditions courantes, peut légitimement s'interroger: «quelle Bible choisir?» La démarche adoptée, pour fournir des critères objectifs, déploie cette question dans une perspective essentiellement diachronique. Dans un souci pédagogique, l'auteur prend appui sur la situation contemporaine, immédiatement accessible, et décrit les éditions modernes de la Bible les plus courantes, disponibles en librairie pour un public anglophone (e.g., AV, RSV, REB, NJB, NRSV, NIV, ESV, GNB). Il rend attentif aux principales différences qui les distinguent pour expliquer ensuite le processus et les facteurs qui sont à l'origine de cette diversité. Chemin faisant, il présente à son lecteur sans en avoir fait le premier objectif de ce chapitre introductif, les principales éditions modernes de la Bible, leurs options et leur public cible, tout en le guidant et en l'accompagnant dans les arcanes des questions historique, linguistique et théologique. Par cette diversité soulignée, l'auteur indique également une réponse possible à la question du chapitre: «qu'est-ce que la Bible?». Il montre de plusieurs manières que la Bible n'est pas un «livre» uniforme, reproduit à l'identique d'une édition à l'autre. Les aspects techniques et les enjeux de la formation et de l'évolution du canon, de l'établissement du texte, de la critique textuelle, de l'alternative entre une traduction basée sur le principe de l'équivalence fonctionnelle ou celui de l'équivalence formelle, sont portés à la connaissance du lecteur dans les limites d'une présentation introductive.

Dans le second chapitre, l'auteur traite la question de la naissance et du développement du matériau dont est constitué une Bible. À partir d'exemples choisis, il introduit son lecteur aux raisonnements spécialistes et explique la genèse des théories contemporaines. Ainsi, parmi d'autres, Jr 27 et le livre d'Esther servent à illustrer le principe d'un processus de composition qui pouvait s'étendre sur plusieurs générations et bénéficier du concours de plusieurs auteurs. L'exemple classique de Gn 6,5 à 9,19 est rappelé pour montrer comment le texte biblique peut être le résultat de la combinaison de sources distinctes à l'origine. Dans le prolongement de cette introduction aux théories et à leurs enjeux, la question est élargie aux procédés de composition en vigueur dans l'Antiquité, au phénomène de la pseudonymie et aux conditions matérielles de la fabrication d'un livre. Dans le même esprit que le premier chapitre, sans entrer dans le détail, l'auteur offre une synthèse riche, alliant une présentation des techniques de composition et abordant succinctement les conséquences herméneutiques des reconstitutions des processus de formation.

Les trois chapitres suivants sont consacrés à la formation des trois grands ensembles dans lesquels les livres de la Bible ont été regroupés, respectivement l'Ancien Testament (34–55), les Apocryphes (deutérocanoniques) (56–72) et le Nouveau Testament (73–100). Dans le chap. 3, l'auteur rend compte de l'importante diversité qui caractérise les écrits rassemblés dans l'Ancien Testament. Il rappelle leurs principales articulations, décrit brièvement pour chaque type littéraire l'environnement historique porteur, et récapitule les débats qui animent les spécialistes au sujet de leurs regroupements. Au chap. 4, une démarche analogue est adoptée pour la présentation des écrits dits «Apocryphes». L'auteur reconnaît l'ambiguïté de ce terme, ainsi p. 72 : «the above heading is at best misleading and at worst nonsense» (voir aussi chap. 1). Il l'entend dans un sens large et regroupe essentiellement sous cet en-tête les écrits de la Bible grecque qui n'ont pas leur correspondant dans la Bible hébraïque. Au chap. 5, l'ordre adopté pour la présentation des écrits qui composent le Nouveau Testament suit une progression chronologique, commençant par les épîtres authentiques de Paul et terminant par un ensemble divers réunissant tout à la fois l'épître de Jude, la seconde de Pierre, la lettre de Jacques et l'épître aux Hébreux. Des questions comme celle du rapport entre les écrits pauliniens et le récit des Actes, ou comme celle de la source Q et de la composition des évangiles synoptiques reçoivent une réponse synthétique, précise et parfaitement informée. Compte tenu de cette qualité qui caractérise l'ensemble du livre de Rogerson, on ne pourra que regretter le traitement superficiel réservé à la formation du Nouveau Testament aux pp. 99s.

D'une certaine manière, on peut dire que le sixième chapitre renoue avec un des fils conducteurs initiaux en expliquant et en déployant un autre facteur qui contribua à la diversité des éditions courantes de la Bible. Dans cette partie consacrée au canon, l'auteur aborde la question du processus de canonisation à partir de ses grandes articulations historiques, et propose de la traiter en tenant compte de ses rapprochements ou non avec le pouvoir. C'est l'occasion de citer les témoignages des rabbins et de la lettre d'Aristée, de consacrer un paragraphe à la Septante, puis un autre à la Vulgate, et de mentionner dans ce cadre le travail d'Origène, de Jérôme, de Théodulf et d'Alcuin. Il montre comment l'idée de canon, si elle répond à une définition précise, n'en est pas moins une réalité en mouvement. Celle-ci comprend: «(a) the belief that sacred writings should have a standard text, (b) the need to establish, in the face of controversy, what writings are authoritative and in what version, (c) the importance of ecclesiastical and political power in promoting canonical processes» (109).

Le septième chapitre ouvre le dossier de la réception de la Bible dans l'occident chrétien et survole l'histoire de son interprétation. Il offre une présentation panoramique de cette histoire, organisée en cinq tableaux, croisant les acteurs, les idées et les circonstances. Une première partie est consacrée à l'Ancien Testament. Elle adopte pour fil conducteur la lecture critique de la Bible et cite dans cette perspective les apports de penseurs tels qu'Augustin, Maimonide, Luther ou Lagrange. La partie suivante, consacrée aux Apocryphes, tout en déplorant le manque d'intérêt des savants pour ces livres, rappelle leur fortune dans les arts, la peinture, la musique ou la littérature. La partie consacrée au Nouveau Testament est très sommaire. En outre, le souci de couvrir 2000 ans de lecture laisse peu de place à la présentation des recherches qui caractérisent la pensée contemporaine. La quête du Jésus historique est limitée à Schweitzer et Dodd, et la *Formgeschichte* réduite à Bultmann. Une partie importante est ensuite consacrée à la lecture fondamentaliste, confrontant la notion de l'infaillibilité de la Bible défendue par différents mouvements à la nécessité d'une approche critique. Une dernière partie, intitulée «développements récents», est consacrée à deux lectures militantes, développées l'une dans le cadre de la théologie de la libération et l'autre dans le sillage des mouvements féministes. En résumé, le septième chapitre de cette introduction à la Bible fixe un certain nombre de repères historiques, et rappelle les circonstances et les enjeux de quelques unes des orientations majeures qui ont nourri ou bouleversé la lecture de la Bible au fil des siècles.

Le dernier chapitre développe des considérations herméneutiques à partir d'une perspective individuelle, sociale et politique. Il cite et commente un grand nombre de passages pour montrer comment la Bible est susceptible d'être utilisée en éthique. Il rappelle à travers cet angle particulier que la Bible est une bibliothèque disponible, dont la lecture est adaptable à chaque génération, pour stimuler en profondeur la pensée et nourrir une réflexion fructueuse sur l'être et la destinée humaine.

L'auteur réussit en 150 pages et 8 chapitres à fournir un dossier introductif complet, abordable pour un public de non-spécialistes, curieux des développements de l'exégèse scientifique moderne. Il présente de façon synthétique les principes généraux et les connaissances de base qui permettront au lecteur de comprendre des études plus approfondies et de tirer un meilleur profit des commentaires bibliques. La riche sélection d'exemples et la profondeur de la réflexion séduira un public averti, de pasteurs, d'agents pastoraux et d'étudiants. Pour qui souhaite prolonger et approfondir ces questions, une information bibliographique est mise à disposition à la fin du livre.

But Is It All True? The Bible and the Question of Truth, edited by Alan G. Padgett and Patrick R. Keifert. Grand Rapids: Eerdmans, 2006. Pp. xii + 175. Paper. $16.00. ISBN 0802863167.

D. A. Carson, Trinity Evangelical Divinity School, Deerfield, Illinois

This book finds its origin in a 1999 colloquium at Luther Seminary. It is dedicated to Donald Juel *in memoriam* (d. 2003), since he helped to organize that colloquium. When he moved to Princeton, the project and the conversation partners "broadened and became more diverse" (12).

The diversity of the book is both its strength and its weakness. The nine contributors include three systematicians, one Old Testament scholar, one professor of biblical theology, two professors of philosophy or philosophical theology, one professor of preaching, and one professor of religion. They lie across a sweep of theological stances as broad as a list of a mere nine essayists allows. The diversity makes for an interesting read if the subject itself is on one's radar screen, but the flip side is that this volume does not as a whole launch a new program or strike out in a new direction. Readers who are already familiar with many of the other contributions of these writers will not find anything very surprising or particularly innovative here (the blurbs on the back cover notwithstanding). The strength of the book is simply the way it brings together in one slim volume some of the diversity views (that we all know are out there) on how the Bible is "true."

Dennis T. Olson ("Truth and Torah: Reflections on Rationality and the Pentateuch" [16–33]) surveys the notion of truth in the Pentateuch. Hebrew אמת ('emet) "signifies both relational trust as well as a more objective testing for truth" (20). This definition, in both its parts, strikes me as odd, focusing as it does on the mental/emotional processes connected with the word rather than on the meaning of the word itself. The word is bound up with reliability or faithfulness, and of course such reliability calls forth "relational trust"—but 'emet surely cannot by said to "signify" relational trust. When what is "reliable" is a report or a prophecy or the like, then surely if it is "reliable" we simply say, in English, that it is true or that it is telling the truth, not that it signifies "a more objective testing for truth." Inevitably we are warned that human beings in the Pentateuch "are given only partial glimpses of the truth of God's promises." Doubtless that statement is true, so true that I know of no one who would question it.

In the shortest contribution of the volume, Nicholas Wolterstorff ("True Words" [34–43]) offers the best opening sentence in the collection: "In the first part of this chapter I will argue that truth is *not* the main issue when we are dealing with Scripture; in the second part I will suggest that truth *is* the main issue" (34). In substance, however, this chapter is very largely a convenient summary of his important book *Divine Discourse: Philosophical Reflections of the Claim that God Speaks* (Cambridge: Cambridge University Press, 1995). Instead of thinking of the Bible in terms of revelation, Wolterstorff proposes thinking of the Bible in terms of speech, that is, as discourse, with a variety of speech-acts possible, and on the assumption of "double-agency discourse" (36). He acknowledges that this biblical speech includes assertions that are true or false, but because of the complexity and diversity of speech forms in the Bible he argues that we need a new and more complex definition of truth. "I suggest that the root notion of truth is that of something's measuring up—that is, measuring up in being or excellence" (42). In this sense, he argues, truth is indeed "the fundamental issue to be raised concerning Scripture. Do the words of Scripture measure up?" (43). The standard by which we measure such "measuring up" is not worked out. What is fairly clear, however, is that Wolterstorff loves to reflect on the many instances where "true" is used in Scripture of something *other* than propositions (e.g., "in the New Testament writings ascribed to John" [42]) and offers almost no reflection on the many instances where "true" and cognates are used in Scripture of propositions.

Ben C. Ollenburger ("Pursing the Truth of Scripture: Reflections on Wolterstorff's *Divine Discourse*" [44–65]) is essentially a critical review. Among Ollenburger's "puzzlements" (his word) in reading *Divine Discourse* are Wolterstorff's "almost exclusive attention to sentences" (50) with almost no reflection on discourse or diverse literary genres and his treatment of authorial intentions (Ollenburger follows Meir Sternberg's distinction between external and internal intentions). Ollenburger has serious reservations about the relationships between the first and second hermeneutics as Wolterstorff constructs them, and he details how none of Wolterstorff's examples of whether Scripture "measures up" is an assertion.

Mark I. Wallace ("The Rule of Love and the Testimony of the Spirit in Contemporary Hermeneutics" [66–85]) says that rule-governed approaches to biblical exegesis and criticism, such as the criterion of dissimilarity or the criterion of multiple attestation, have a certain limited use in making responsible decisions about what is authentic in the Gospels. (He seems unaware of the very substantial discussion on such criteria that has taken place since the work of Norman Perrin a quarter of a century ago.) But the results from such rule-governed approaches "fall short of actually construing the religious truth of the biblical witness—that is, what the Bible means in its fullness and integrity as a compelling theological witness to life's fundamental questions" (69). He therefore promotes Augustine's hermeneutical principle: the aim must be to construe "the meaning of the biblical texts in a manner consistent with a life of charity and other respects" (71). Following an example from Wolterstorff, Wallace asserts that in the light of Augustine's principle, the imprecatory psalms must be taken as negative examples: they are divine speech-acts only in the sense that they are "vivid (if sadly misguided) expressions of pent-up fury against those who make war against God's people" (71). Wallace wants to make Augustine's thought so absolute that it enables us to take steps Augustine would never dream of, including discounting or marginalizing those parts of Scripture that do not contribute to this principle of love as Wallace understands it. With Stephen Davis (see below), Wallace agrees that the Gospel stories purport "to tell us what happened in the life and ministry of Jesus" (75), but the point is surely not the conclusions drawn by "realist theologians" (75) but the manner in which these accounts do or do not contribute to love. Wallace concludes his chapter with one or two examples of "how the love ideal works in an actual reading of the biblical texts," including homosexuality and violence. Regarding the former, he acknowledges "that the Bible is generally negative toward homosexuality" (78) but argues that the love ideal drives us toward full acceptance.

More or less at the other end of the spectrum, Stephen T. Davis, "What Do We Mean When We Say, 'The Bible is True'?" [86–103]) operates out of a broadly confessional evangelical stance. Answers to the question raised by his title, he says, must accomplish three things: they must recognize that human beings are "verbivores," they must explain why Christians read the Bible as opposed to any other book (whether *The Iliad* of *The Koran* [sic] or *The Critique of Pure Reason*), and they "must explain why Christians take the Bible to be normative and authoritative" (87). So what do we mean when we say that the Bible is true? Part of the answer, he argues, is that we commit ourselves to believe its statements, accepting their propositional content, and as a result "trust" them or "lay ourselves open" to them (89). That is surely right, but still slightly shy of the heart of the issue for many Christians: they "accept the propositional content" and lay themselves open to it because they think that such content conforms to reality. Davis goes on to offer useful comments on what "inerrancy" might and might not mean and criticizes Wolterstorff at one or two crucial points (including how Wolterstorff handles the canonical Gospels [97]). His criticism of Mark Wallace is more fundamental (96–101): Wallace's central difficulty is that by elevating an external principle such as Augustine's to absolute control, he has adopted "what is not a characteristic of the Bible but rather a result of an interaction between the Bible and a reader," and as a result this hermeneutic "does little to preserve any sense of the Bible's uniqueness" (97).

Alan G. Padgett ("'I Am the Truth': An Understanding of Truth from Christology for Scripture" [104–14]) announces, "This chapter is about a confession, not a definition" (104). Further:

> I do not seek a definition of truth, although I will mention some in passing. Rather, I want to stand under the truth and receive (understand) what light it brings. I do not seek to define, encompass, and regulate what truth is. Rather, I seek an understanding of truth that implies or suggests many working definitions, spread across many academic disciplines, in whatever art or science we find ourselves at work for the love of truth. I am forced to use the word "understanding" because I think it may be less confusing than other words; but my use of it here is idiosyncratic. By an "understanding of the truth" I mean something less than a theory of truth, less even than a definition of truth. In my work on epistemology I have come to the conclusion that the differing disciplines of academe serve different interests, arise out of different traditions of inquiry, and have different rationalities. (106)

Although that sounds bracingly expansive and inclusive, I am not quite sure how a word such as "understanding" will prove "less confusing" if Padgett's use of it is "idiosyncratic." I would have thought that idiosyncratic usage of a term almost guarantees confusion. Nor am I quite certain why Padgett says he does not seek a definition of truth, when on the next page he proposes his own definition: "To begin with, I will simply propose that we understand truth as *the mediated disclosure of being* (or reality). Sometimes that truth will be mediated through everyday experience, or common sense, sometimes through the specifics of propositions" (106; emphasis original). Padgett says there is a place for "true words"; he has been "impressed by" Alston's realist conception of truth. "We must not … wholly ignore true statements" (109). But this "minimalist-realist" conception of truth must fit "into the larger understanding of truth" that he advances in the rest of this chapter, namely, that Christ is the truth and the Bible is the book of Christ. "This implies that the truth of Scripture is about our relationship with Christ, for a personal truth requires a personal relationship" (111). Thus the Bible is "true when it mediates this personal truth to us" (111). As for "the question of histori-

cal reference," the answer given by theologians as diverse as Ernst Troeltsch and
N. T. Wright must be heeded: at least some "'symbols' or theological truth disclosed in the text demand a real historical event behind them" (112)—although
when the sweep runs from Troeltsch to Wright, I am not sure this is very clarifying. Even Bultmann hung on to his "das."

David Bartlett ("Preaching the Truth" [115–29]) begins well with a question asked by a character in one of Frederick Buechner's novels: "There's just one
reason, you know, why I come dragging in there every Sunday. I want to find out
if the whole thing's true. Just *true*.... That's all. Either it is, or it isn't, and that's the
one question you avoid like death" (115). The six brief sections that follow offer
quasi-independent reflections that circle around the topic but are unlikely to satisfy this Buechner character. For instance, Bartlett tells us that to know truth is to
know God, not to know about God (116). Why the disjunction? The next section
reminds us that Hans Frei suggests we read Scripture best "as a history-like narrative" (118). Frei might well have believed the extratextual referentiality of this
narrative, but "other interpreters of Frei and of Scripture" are happy to disown any
extratextual referentiality in this "history-like narrative," finding it sufficient to
rejoice over "its own internal coherence and power without worrying at all about
its extratextual referents" (118)—an astonishing elitist and intellectualist position
that assumes the Bible tells us we are saved and find fullness of life by entertain-
ing ideas, not by Christ himself. Isn't another word for a "history-like narrative"
without any necessary extratextual referentiality a "novel"? Like Padgett, Bartlett
prefers the path of open-endedness about these things: "My sense is that we neither ignore historical-critical issues nor harp on them" (119). How that will help
the preacher working on next Sunday's sermon, I have no idea. The remaining
sections include some useful asides, while the eight-hundred-pound gorilla in the
room is carefully left unaddressed.

From homiletics to education: Patrick R. Keifert ("Biblical Truth and Theological Education: A Rhetorical Strategy" [130–43]) is the most jargon-filled essay
in the volume. A lot of his focus seems to be bound up with the interactions with
the Bible that take place in the Christian community. At the heart of Keifert's
essay is this: "My initial answer to the question 'When we say that the Bible is
true, what do we mean?' is quite simply this: the Bible is true insofar as it makes
possible the understanding of God truly" (138). The methods "that appreciate
its truthfulness are many. They include ascetic practices such as meditation and
contemplation, singing, dancing, practices of social action on behalf of the vulnerable and poor, and the playful interaction of critical human understanding
with text and tradition" (138). The last line, of course, as Keifert acknowledges,
owes a great deal to Gadamer.

The final essay, by Ellen Charry ("Walking in the Truth: On Knowing God"
[144–69]), is perhaps the most creative contribution of the volume. In one sense,
it does not belong in a volume with the title of this book, for Charry's focus is
on how Scripture functions rather than on what it is. She begins with an overarching survey of two millennia of church history and its three "epistemological

crises": the first was the West's recovery of Aristotle in the twelfth and thirteenth centuries and the move from sapiential theology to theory, the second was the rise of empiricism in the seventeenth century, and the third is the postmodern turn. Much of the rest of this chapter probes these developments in more detail, with reference to specific thinkers and with thoughtful reflection on the theological changes that have ensued. Something can be said for this schema, I am sure, but the exceptions that thoughtful readers will want to mention are so frequent and so powerful that the antithetical nature of Charry's exposition cries out to be challenged. Augustine, for instance, lies at the heart of the "sapiential" period in which, allegedly, all the focus was on the moral-psycho-social ends of truth, truth to make us happy and good, and not a matter of technical skills in the method of disputation, not truth versus error. Yet in his famous Letter 84 to Jerome, Augustine carefully lays out the "truthfulness" of Scripture *not* in sapiential/functional terms, but in terms that insist on its freedom from error, unlike the writings of any other, including Jerome (see 84.3–4). The example of Augustine is easily multiplied. Yet what is attractive about Charry's essay, despite its programmatic oversimplifications, is that because she focuses on what the Bible *can* do in changing people and on its proper functions and transformative power, she exposes the cultural/ ecclesiological/spiritual/moral sterility of approaches to the Bible that are never more than intellectually exciting but that have neither divine authority nor the ring of conscience-binding truth. Unfortunately, because she does not tie her analysis to what the Bible *is* and thus to how she would herself address the controlling subject of this volume under review, she offers little guidance for the way ahead.

In short, this is a useful survey of some of the contemporary options. I cannot bring this review to an end without an amusing observation: without exception, these writers are embarrassed, to a greater or lesser degree, by assertions, by propositions. There are many statements of the sort, "Well, of course, we concede that there are some assertions in Scripture that are either true or untrue, but the really important element in Scripture is Christ as the truth (or the personal nature of truth, or the way Scripture functions to disclose the true God, or whatever)." There was not a single statement of the sort, "Well, of course, Christ is presented as the truth in the Gospel of John, but there are many propositions and assertions not only in John but throughout the Bible that must be thought of as true or false. We cannot long argue about what we mean by saying the Bible is 'true' unless we wrestle with the Bible's countless propositions." In other words, this book abounds in assertions about how unimportant assertions are.

Congress Volume: Leiden, 2004, edited by André Lemaire. Supplements to Vetus Testamentum 109. Leiden: Brill, 2006. Pp. viii + 472. Cloth. $169.00. ISBN 9004149139.

William Johnstone, University of Aberdeen, Aberdeen, Scotland, United Kingdom

This volume contains invited papers read at the plenary sessions of the eighteenth Congress of the International Organization for the Study of the Old Testament, held under the Presidency of Professor Arie van der Kooij in Leiden, 1–6 August 2004. The twenty contributors, drawn from Africa, East Asia, Europe, Israel, and North and South America, fitly represent the world-wide community of Old Testament scholarship; the range of topic and variety of approach illustrate, often brilliantly, the state of the art in many areas of the discipline. "Kaleidoscopic" might be an appropriate descriptor for the collection; this overview will simply follow the sequence of the articles (the rationale for that sequence somewhat eludes this reader: neither alphabetic by author nor grouped by topic, except to a degree in the 67-page appendix on "World Christianity and the Study of the Old Testament," but even there the first of the four contributions, on the ancient Israelite calendars, in its content shows no essential connection with, and shares none of the restrictions perhaps implied by, that heading). All the papers are in English except where otherwise noted.

The Presidential Address, "The City of Babel and Assyrian Imperialism: Genesis 11:1–9 Interpreted in Light of Mesopotamian Sources" (1–17), naturally opens the volume. In it van der Kooij argues, in contrast to many recent interpreters, that the tower—better, city—of Babel story is unitary. Read along with Gen 10:8–12, it marks a sophisticated reflection by the scribal elite in Jerusalem on Neo-Assyrian imperialism, represented above all by the building of the city of Dur-Sharrukin but abandoned on the unexpected death of Sargon II in 705 B.C., as a violation of the divine world order of the dispersion of the human race laid down in primeval times. One of the implications of the argument is the reaffirmation, following the tradition of Abraham Kuenen, the President's pioneering predecessor at Leiden, of the traditional four sources of the Pentateuch; J, to which this material belongs, is now to be dated to the end of the eighth century (E consequently "presumably towards the end of the 7th"). The President thus sets up a fine dialectic with some of the following contributors for whom P represents the earliest transpentateuchal source.

George J. Brooke provides a review of the state of knowledge on "The Twelve Minor Prophets and the Dead Sea Scrolls" (19–43). The Twelve have been somewhat eclipsed in scholarly attention by such "heavyweights" as Deuteronomy and Isaiah; Brooke pleads for an appreciation of them as providing a model of "multiple literary editions" of the biblical text (scribes should be viewed as "active and creative partners in the transmission process"), as well as evidence on the issue of how the Twelve came to be regarded as a unitary collection and for their contribution to the Qumran community's own sense of identity (e.g., withdrawal from the temple; eschatological outlook).

Cécile Dogniez studies the passages on the reconstruction of the temple in the Septuagint version of Zech 1–8 (45–64; in French) and comes to the conclusion that the Septuagint represents a faithful translation of the Hebrew as evidenced by MT with two exceptions, Zech 4:7 (where "heritage" is added) and 8:9 (where the reconstruction of the temple is treated as a fait accompli). In these two passages the text has been interpreted symbolically to suit the needs of its Diaspora audience conscious of its continuing status as the "heritage of the God of Israel" and living in hope of restoration.

Adrian Schenker takes 2 Kgs 23:1–3 (so the title, but 22:20 is added in the body of the article), attested in four forms—MT, the parallel in 2 Chr 34:29–32 (MT and LXX), LXX, and *vetus latina*—as an illustration for the textual history of the books of Kings and considers the implications of that textual history so reconstructed for wider sections of the Hebrew Bible (65–79; in German). The evidence suggests two principal stages in the evolution of the Hebrew text: an earlier version attested by the reconstructed Hebrew *Vorlage* of the original LXX (best preserved in VL, its translation); on this earlier version a later "prae-Massoretic" edition was based. Evidence of similar phenomena in other parts of the Hebrew Bible suggests that the "prae-Massoretic" text was a wide-ranging, officially promulgated, new edition. Schenker attributes it to priestly circles in the Jerusalem temple and dates it to the end of the second century B.C. ("proto-MT" is the text attested by the Dead Sea Scrolls in the first century A.D. [p. 74]). By it, subsequent editions of LXX were in turn corrected.

Zeev Herzog reviews current archaeological research in the Beersheba Valley and its implications for the biblical record (81–102). The "paradigmatic shift" from "biblical" to "social archaeology" as a discipline in its own right is leading to the reassessment of earlier work, especially at Arad and Beersheba itself, pioneered by Yohanan Aharoni. Many of the population changes are to be accounted for by climatic fluctuations: "The [biblical] story of the military conquest of Canaan is bluntly refuted by the archaeology of the Beersheba Valley." Many other long-held views are challenged; for example, "Jerusalem replaced Lachish … as the capital of Judah only in the 8th century"; there was no Kenite high place at Arad, and a temple existed there only for about sixty years during the eighth century, but the reform of the cult evidenced there is indeed probably to be correlated with Hezekiah's reform (2 Kgs 18:4; 2 Chr 31:1).

Matthias Köckert traces the history of the Abraham tradition (103–28; in German), first in a close analysis of those passages outside the Pentateuch where he is named (Ezek 33; Isa 51; 41; 63–64; Neh 9; Josh 24; and Ps 105), which already suggest a lengthy period of development of the tradition spanning from late preexilic times to deep into the Persian period. The Genesis narrative is then analyzed to show that this history is matched by the evolution of the Abraham traditions within the Pentateuch as well. Köckert thus votes for the findings of such as Konrad Schmid, for whom P is the first to provide an integrated history combining the patriarchal narratives with those of the exodus, and E. Blum, who uses the model of *Fortschreibung* rather than that of parallel "sources" to account for the later non-P additions to the P document.

Nadav Na'aman considers the book of Kings as an example of biblical historiography (129–52); although written primarily to convey religious and ideological messages, it is nonetheless based on sources that by analysis can be recovered for the task of critical historiography. By analogy with other ancient Near Eastern cities, it may be assumed that Jerusalem possessed a temple library that provided the main sources (e.g., king lists and chronicles, prophetic stories) for the author of Kings, who "was probably a priest of high degree." He supports the theory of two editions: Dtr[1] at the end of the seventh century, and Dtr[2], an "author of the same ideological school" in the sixth. The latter parts of both histories are also based on the authors' own vivid memories of events and have the stamp of reliability.

Ed Noort writes on the figure Joshua in tradition and history (153–73; in German). The Joshua of the biblical record is a complex figure: middle Palestinian tribal leader, conqueror of the West Bank, distributor of land, and so on. In postbiblical reception history he is given above all the roles of army commander, prophet, teacher of the law, and king. Noort presents examples of reception history above all from Samaritan sources, one of which provides him with the title of his article, "the ravenous wolf," applied to Joshua from Benjamin in Jacob's farewell (Gen 49:27). A key issue both in the biblical record and in later interpretation is the problem posed by the altar constructed by the East Bank tribes in Josh 22: the Samaritan tradition rehabilitates them as coming to Joshua's rescue.

Graham Davies in his article "'God' in Old Testament theology" (175–94) begins with the observation of a shift in interest in writers on Old Testament theology from what is distinctive from other Near Eastern cultures to what is shared but finds that in this shift what is meant by the term "G/god" itself has received insufficient clarification. He limits his study to the three main terms *'l*, *'lwh*, and *'lhym* (terms such as *šdy* are necessarily left out of consideration). The choice of using a generic term for deity in a wide range of biblical material reviewed rather than the proper name may be to avoid the specificity of relationship to Israel and to convey universal nature or general characteristics, although what is conveyed by the name "Yahweh" makes the decisive contribution.

Jean-Marie Husser traces the concept of the *maśkîl*, the sage enlightened on heavenly writings by angelic mediation, in apocalyptic literature from Dan 7–12, through *Enoch* and *Jubilees,* to Qumran (195–213; in French). Three types of heavenly writings are already in evidence in Daniel: the register of works (7:10), the table of destinies (10:21), the list of the elect (12:1). The idea of a body of esoteric knowledge written in the heavens has roots in earlier Hebrew Bible texts (e.g., in the "pattern" of tabernacle revealed to Moses in Exodus and of temple to David in 1 Chronicles) and the ancient Near East. The knowledge transmitted to the *maśkîl* comes to precede and incorporate the law of Moses and lends authority to him, not merely then as expositor but also as initiator, as teacher of "the many," understood as the mass of the faithful in Israel in Dan 11:33; 12:3 and as the initiates of the sect at Qumran.

Carol A. Newsom borrows the title of her article, "Rhyme and Reason: The Historical Résumé in Israelite and Early Jewish Thought" (215–33), from Mark Twain: "history may not repeat itself, but it certainly does rhyme." She offers a response to postmodern claims of the collapse of "the grand narrative" by pointing out the variety of narratives presented in historical résumés, a fundamental "mode of cognition," in the Bible and later literature. As examples she studies contrasting pairs 1 Sam 12 and Josh 24, and Pss 105 and 106, seemingly intentionally collocated; then Ezek 20; followed by further contrasts between Dan 1–6 and 7–12, where (picking up her title) she comments, "the apocalyptic writers perceived … that the rhyme of history facilitates reasoning about the future."

Jean-Marie Auwers, taking Song of Songs as example, finds that the allegorical interpretation of the Bible in the church fathers may still make a contribution to exegesis (235–53; in French). For the fathers, the figurative sense is implicit in the plain meaning (compare the translation technique of LXX and Vulgate: they strive faithfully to convey the obvious sense of the Hebrew, but that plain sense, paradoxically, turns out to be metaphorical). Patristic interpretation is to be found in homilies as well as commentaries; the reader is addressed in dialogue. The eroticism of the Song is precisely intended to engage the reader at multiple levels. Indeterminacy is written into the text (who speaks? who are the speakers?); polyvalency, openness of meaning, is part of the stock-in-trade of modern theories of poetics.

Christo H. J. van der Merwe expounds the contribution that cognitive linguistics can make to biblical interpretation and relates that approach to the developing technology of hypertext (255–80). Cognitive linguistics is defined as the study of "the cognitive processes involved in analyzing and interpreting literary texts, as a particular mode of human communication." The establishment of meaning has moved beyond decoding the correct sense of words in a text to an appreciation that the "entire cognitive environments" of both text and reader are involved. It is in this construal of meaning not just at the word but at the phrase, clause, and text level and as an interactive process that technology has its part to play. Given the nature of the task and the vast amount of information required, the distinction between a dictionary and an encyclopedia now becomes blurred, and the model of linear text bound in a book has to be complemented by that of the networked intertext.

Bernard M. Levinson studies the laws on the manumission of slaves in the Covenant Code in Exod 21, in the Holiness Code in Lev 25, and in Deut 15 (281–324). He defends the traditional critical view of the sequence of these laws, CC-D-H, against proposals to modify that sequence especially in the works of John Van Seters, Sara Japhet, and Jacob Milgrom. He finds in that sequence a model of hermeneutics: the authors of D and H not only receive traditional texts, and must thus be regarded as redactors, but also engage with these sources and with theological authority and daring rearrange, modify, and develop their content.

Johan Yeong-Sik Pahk engages in a thorough review of the meaning of the phrase *dibrê ḥēpeṣ* in Qoh 12:10a (325–53). He argues for the translation "the meaning of reality," not "pleasing words," as by most modern scholars.

Ellen van Wolde expounds what she means by "an integrated approach" in biblical studies, using as illustration the contrasting views of "wisdom" in Job 28 and 38 (355–80). Like van der Merwe above, she wishes to exploit the insights of cognitive linguistics. She uses a biological analogy: the traditional lexical search for the meaning of a word, in this case "wisdom," in its syntagmatic relations within texts may be likened to a "monoculture"; cognitive linguistics offers a complementary approach that is concerned with language not as an autonomous system but as functioning within a culture's whole network of presuppositions and processes of conceptualization, a "biodiversity." In Job 28, taken as Job's last word, where the search for wisdom is contrasted with mining, a monoculture if ever there was one, as can be illustrated from archaeological research in the Arabah, "wisdom" can be reduced to one answer, "the fear of the Lord." By contrast, Job 38, the beginning of God's reply, understood against the immense background of the six levels of Mesopotamian cosmology, appropriately reflects a world of biodiversity.

The appendix (381–448), headed "Session: World Christianity and the Study of the Old Testament," contains four papers. The first of these seems misplaced, as already noted and as is confirmed by fact that the final paper, "responses," is limited to the second and third of these. The second paper begins with an anecdote that seems to indicate that the writer would not in any case wish to be declassified from mainstream Old Testament study to, say, missiology.

The posthumous paper of J. Severino Croatto (†April, 2004) argues (383–400) that Gen 1:14–19 (and many other biblical texts) implies, in conscious resistance to Babylonian influence, the preservation of a solar calendar, against the lunar calendar that now appears to prevail in the Pentateuch, for the fixing of the dates of Sabbaths and festivals on regularly recurring days of the week (cf. evidence from *Jubilees* and Qumran). (His use of the term "counter-text" may account for the relating of his article to the two following.)

André Kabasele Mukenge's article on reading the Bible in the African context (401–18; in French) notes that the "contextual approach" is currently recognized in connection with such movements as "reader-response" criticism. He illustrates what can be meant by this approach by indicating points of contact with African story that can function heuristically to illuminate Old Testament narrative (e.g., the puzzling acceptance or nonacceptance of sacrifice in the Cain and Abel story in Gen 4:1–6) and with linguistic structures that congenially match points of Hebrew grammar and syntax (e.g., the use of the infinitive absolute, *dativus commodi*).

Craig Y. S. Ho employs as his heuristic instrument a Chinese philosophical text and the pervasive Chinese perception on the fundamental importance of food and sex in human existence to investigate the J stories in Genesis by the "cross-textual method" pioneered by his mentor Archie Lee (419–39). "Survival" and "progeny" are the biblical equivalents. He recognizes Gen 15 as suggesting wider elements. He denies, however, that his interpretation is culture-bound.

In his "Responses" to these last two papers (pp. 441–48) John Barton suggests that the historical criticism that evolved in the West need not necessarily be regarded as some kind of cultural imperialism but is, rather, a recognition by Western scholarship itself that the Hebrew Bible belongs to another time and age.

That criticism can be the means of attempting faithfully to interpret the Bible in terms of its own environment. But no interpreter is without culturally imposed presuppositions.

The above has been termed an "overview" rather than a "review." It would be absurdly pretentious for one reader to enter into critical engagement consistently across such a wide-ranging collection, representing as it often does the fruit of long-standing, even lifelong, research by distinguished specialists; it would out of proportion if that reader were to pick out areas of personal interest for special comment. Instead, avoiding even value-judgment adjectives or adverbs, the attempt has been made to summarize objectively, if inadequately, the sometimes highly sophisticated presentations in order to facilitate their entry into debate with specialists in the several areas. Such an account is perhaps the more necessary given the disappointing index provided to the volume, which is confined to references to Bible and other literary sources: there is no biographical note on the contributors, no list of abbreviations, and no author or subject index. Formally drawn up bibliography is confined to the three contributors who have supplied lists of works consulted at the end of their papers. But lack of evaluative comment does not imply lack of interest; this reviewer has often been stretched, frequently enlightened and informed, sometimes delighted, occasionally frustrated (where, precisely, is not a matter of much interest; length of summary is no necessary index of appreciation). In this rich and diverse collection there will be something for everyone.

Theodicy in the World of the Bible: The Goodness of God and the Problem of Evil, edited by Antti Laato and Johannes C. de Moor. Leiden: Brill, 2003. Pp. liv + 834. Cloth. $180.00. ISBN 9004132759.

Lorenzo DiTommaso, Concordia University, Montréal, Quebec

The word "theodicy" was coined by Gottfried Wilhelm Leibniz in his *Essais de théodicée sur la bonté de Dieu, la liberté de l'homme et l'origine du mal* (1710). Over the next three centuries it came to assume several meanings. One of these, the defense of a worldview wherein belief in God can co-exist with reasonable scientific explanations for natural phenomena, has in recent years again become a point of public debate. Traditionally, however, theodicy refers to the attempt to exonerate God of any charge of responsibility for evil or suffering or to explain evil or suffering in a way that effectively demonstrates its ultimate utility. It is with this convention in mind that the editors classify theodicy in its monotheistic contexts (vii–liv). Their taxonomy proceeds from four premises and takes into account R. E. Green's fivefold typology in his article on the subject in the *Encyclopedia of Religion* (ed. M. Eliade; New York, 1987], 14:430–31), and J. H. Charlesworth's eightfold typology in his contribution to this volume. Six categories emerge: (1) retributive theodicy in the framework of covenantal theology, a common perspective in the Hebrew Bible; (2) educative theodicy, whose best example is the book of Job, where suffering serves to instruct or refine an individual; (3) eschatological or recompense theodicy, typical to apocalypticism, which anticipates the end-time redress of perceived imbalances in the present world; (4) deferred theodicy, found mainly in the wisdom tradition and in some of the psalms, where the full understanding of the mystery of the problem of evil comes only in the afterlife; (5) communion theodicy, the idea being that suffering brings persons closer to God, espoused most conspicuously in Isa 52:13–53:12; and (6) human-deterministic theodicy, which holds that humans cannot escape their fate, a view most associated in the Bible with portions of Qoheleth.

The twenty-three core essays in the volume discuss the problem of theodicy in the Bible and related literature. The first section, on the "Ancient Near East," focuses on theodicy in ancient Egyptian (A. Loprieno, 27–56), Akkadian (K. van der Toorn, 57–89), Hittite (H. A. Hoffner, 90–107), and Ugaritic (J. C. de Moor, 108–50) texts. The next section addresses theodicy in the Hebrew Bible, specifically the Pentateuch (C. Houtman, 151–82), the Deuteronomistic History (A. Laato, 183–235), the prophetic literature (J. Crenshaw, 236–55), the Psalms (F. Lindström, 256–303), Job (K.-J. Illman, 304–33), Ruth and Esther (M. C. A. Korpel, 334–50 and 351–74), Qoheleth (A. Schoors, 375–409), Lamentations (J. Renkema, 410–28), and Ezra-Nehemiah and Chronicles (S. Japhet, 429–69). This is followed by papers on theodicy in the early Jewish writings (J. H. Charlesworth, 470–508) and in Sirach (P. C. Beentjes, 509–24), the Wisdom of Solomon (D. Winston, 525–45), the *Psalms of Solomon* (K. Atkinson, 546–75), and Philo (D. T. Runia, 576–604). The next section covers the New Testament (T. Holmén, 605–51) and the book of Revelation (A. Simojoki, 652–84), while the papers of the last section, "Rabbinic Judaism," attend to theodicy in late antique Judaism (J. Neusner, 685–727) and in the Targumim (B. Chilton, 728–52). The collection opens with M. Sarot's "Theodicy and Modernity: An Inquiry into the Historicity of Theodicy" (1–26) and closes with a list of abbreviations and indexes of authors, texts, and subjects (755–830).

This massive volume will serve as the benchmark for the present generation of studies and the foundation for the next. Most of its papers are highly specialized. Others, by virtue of their broad scope, read more as introductory essays. But in almost every instance their quality is excellent, and their arguments are always clearly presented. The last feature is essential to the usefulness of a collection of such vast compass. The four papers on theodicy in the ancient Near Eastern literature, for instance, are richly detailed with passages from primary sources, many of which are transliterated as well as translated. Regardless of one's acquaintance with this literature, the reader is thus able to follow and evaluate the author's line of reasoning at every stage.

Some scholars, however, might consider this volume to be unbalanced. On the one hand, its first two sections contain fourteen papers whose nearly 450 pages exhaustively cover the topic of theodicy in the world of the Hebrew Bible. Even the book of Esther, which famously does not mention the name of God, is accorded a discussion of its theodicy (Korpel's circumvention of this apparent incongruity is intriguing and convincing). On the other hand, given the volume's purpose, perhaps not enough space has been devoted to the topic in its early Jewish and Christian contexts.

For example, although the development of apocalypticism in early Judaism cannot be attributed solely to a concern over the origin of evil, the problem of theodicy does seem, significantly, to stand behind the composition of portions of the early Enoch material, including, as is well known, portions of the Book of the Watchers. Yet this volume cites 1 Enoch only six times and Watchers not once. The book of Daniel exhibits a similarly deep concern with issues of theodicy but also receives scant attention, with only a single page devoted to an analysis of the prayer in Daniel 9 (437). More generally, the question of the potential influence of Zoroastrian dualism on Jewish apocalyptic theodicy calls for more attention than a few summary statements.

Other areas of Second-Temple Judaism are equally overlooked. The Dead Sea texts are hardly uninterested in matters of theodicy, yet only a handful are cited (usually in passing), and most are those that have been familiar to scholarship for decades: the *War Scroll*, the *Hodayot*, *Pesher Habakkuk*, and the *Community Rule*. Even so, this volume lacks a substantive discussion of the tractate on the two spirits in 1QS cols. iii–iv. The sapiential literature receives better treatment, with fine contributions on Sirach, Philo, and the Wisdom of Solomon, and Charlesworth's essay is a thoughtful, articulate appraisal of theodicy in the early Jewish literature. But the enquiry might have been extended to texts such as the 4QMysteries and 4QInstruction, the study of which is currently transforming our understanding of Second Temple wisdom.

New Testament scholars also might be dissatisfied with the depth of the debate. This is not meant as a slight of Holmén's essay, which given its range is necessarily fashioned along the lines of an overview. But one wonders whether the subject warrants the inclusion of a few additional papers, including, most critically, a dedicated examination of theodicy in Paul's theology. Likewise, the inclusion of essays on rabbinic-era Judaism by Neusner and Chilton extends the scope of the volume into late antiquity, but there is virtually no treatment of theodicy in early Christian thought beyond the first century C.E.

These comments should not be taken as a blanket indictment of the present volume, however. The editors selected their contributors well, and, as noted, the quality of the articles is outstanding. As a result, *Theodicy in the World* of the Bible contains much of value for biblical scholars.

Religion and the Self in Antiquity, edited by David Brakke, Michael L. Satlow, and Steven Weitzman. Bloomington: Indiana University Press, 2006. Pp. vi + 268. Paper. $24.95. ISBN 0253217962.

Jan Willem van Henten, University of Amsterdam, Amsterdam, The Netherlands

This attractive collection of essays about the self in ancient religious contexts is the outcome of a conference on "The Religious Self in Antiquity," organized at Indiana University in 2003. The book deals with the early history of the self and the role of religion in this history. The editors' introduction is substantial; it summarizes the essays included in the volume and also discusses various possible approaches to the self in antiquity, building on, among other works, Michel Foucault's famous *Technologies of the Self* (see 2–6). The book has a thematic setup, roughly following the foci of the introduction. Some essays offer a detailed discussion of an aspect, type of source, or author; others describe trends of transformation during various centuries, focusing upon turning points in the early history of the self. Still other contributions deal with the problem of how to retrieve the "real selves" that are, for this period at least, always transmitted to us in socially and textually constructed selves. An important section of the volume concerns "caring for the self" and focuses upon the body, the senses, education, and training.

In the first essay of the book's first part Patricia Cox Miller analyzes an important shift in representations of the self in the period between the third and fifth centuries C.E.: the shift from orientation toward the transcendent divine in the third century, as elaborated by Plotinus and Origen, to the "touch of the real" in the fifth century, which is focused on the material world, because divine power was immanent in this world. Proclus's image of the self as an animated statue and the relic cult are significant elaborations of this self as touched by the real. Saul M. Olyan's search for the elusive self in a selection of passages from the Hebrew Bible (Isa 40–55; Jer 31:27–28; Ezek 47:22–23) leads to the conclusion that self-referential Hebrew Bible passages are conventional constructions, which implies that accessing the self in these passages remains tentative at best. J. Albert Harrill discusses Paul and the slave self in Rom 7. The textual "I" in Rom 7 should be understood in a fictive sense, despite autobiographical interpretations of this chapter since Augustine. Building on Stan Stowers's reading of Romans, Harrill argues that Paul here applies the technique of "speech-in-character" (i.e., inventing the character of a known person or even both the character and the person). This technique was familiar in Greco-Roman discourse. Esther Menn focuses on Queen Esther's prayer in the Septuagint version of Esther. Esther's self-understanding reflects the articulation of Jewish identity in the author's community as a self that is subjected to the Divine King and rejects worldly values (cf. LXX Esth 14:17–18).

Michael L. Satlow studies late ancient Jewish votive inscriptions, which frequently concern commemorations of gifts to synagogues. He demonstrates how these inscriptions suggest that humans can negotiate with God. He also discusses the question why the epigraphic commemoration of votive gifts became usual practice only in the fourth century C.E., despite a long-standing tradition of Jewish votive practices. Peter T. Struck's contribution concerns dream interpretation in Artemidorus. He argues for a divided self in Artemidorus, because the dreaming soul/self stands apart from the dreaming person. The act of dreaming provokes the soul into a dialectics of selfhood and alterity. This "other within" can be called the divine *pneuma* inside the self.

Steven Weitzman opens the second section of the book, which focuses on sensing religious selves, with an essay on sensory reform in Deut 1–11. Building on Stephen Geller's work on Deuteronomy, he argues that these Hebrew Bible chapters call for a set of practices for retraining the senses. Deuteronomy 1–11 instructs its readers to recognize when the senses threaten the relationship with God and to turn to the holy text as the basis of religious experience (e.g., Deut 4:6, 10, 12). Susan Ashbrook Harvey's essay, "Locating the Sensing Body," describes a trend in late ancient Christian sources, including Ephrem, to engage the body as the locus of salvation through actions and sensory awareness. In the fourth century the senses turn into instruments for the self's orientation toward the divine. Georgia Frank studies five biblical characters as recycled in the chanted sermons (*kontakia*) composed by the Christian poet Romanos the Melodist (ca. 485–560). The transformation of these characters in Romanos's liturgical setting helps the self to discern God and requires a re-education of the senses.

The third part of the volume focuses on education. Guy Stroumsa exemplifies the transition from pagan to Christian conceptions of the self with a case study in which he describes two trends of self-orientation: wisdom contemplation of the divine; and Christian spirituality as well as bodily training in imitation of Christ (*askesis*). He argues that in a Christian setting both approaches aim at salvation, not at knowledge per se. Jonathan Schofer's essay analyzes the concern for the body (sexuality, gender, and asceticism) and its role in self-formations in the rabbinic work of *The Fathers according to Rabbi Nathan*. David Brakke analyzes Evagrius of Pontus's work, *Talking Back,* about thoughts and situations that threatened monks. Evagrius settled in the Egyptian desert in 383 C.E. Crucial for Evagrius's representation of the monastic self are the constant external threats by demonic forces that attack the monks during their sensory experiences. This goes against Foucault's model of the self-revealing monastic subject (described in his *Technologies of the Self*). Finally, Edward Watts studies the social location of the student's self in educational contexts as well as Christian religious activities in the schools.

The volume has a broad range, covering Hebrew Bible texts from the sixth century B.C.E. to late ancient and mostly Christian materials. The introduction also compares the essays with another recent volume on the same subject: David Shulman and Guy Stroumsa, eds., *Self and Self-Transformation in the History of Religions* (Oxford: Oxford University Press, 2002). The quality of the individual essays is good, and some contributions are outstanding. The essay by Patricia Cox Miller offers important insights into transformations of the self in Christian learned contexts in the third to the fifth centuries. She also gives a working definition of the self in ancient culture: the self can be identified with the soul as the locus of human identity as long as "soul" is taken as "a placing function that serves to orient the self in a network of relationships that are both material and spiritual" (17). J. Albert Harrill explicitly states what is one of the implications of this volume: there is no term in the ancient sources that covers the modern idea of the self as a unique individual (63). Michael L. Satlow's essay is important, not only because it is the only contribution that concerns documentary texts, but also because it demonstrates that similar transformations of the self can be observed in Jewish and Christian milieus in basically the same period, the fourth and fifth centuries. He connects the votive inscriptions with an important reinterpretation of the synagogue as a holy place, which corresponds with the shift toward "the real" discussed in Cox Miller's contribution. This parallel trend in Jewish and Christian sources in the fourth and fifth centuries is, however, slightly undermined by the non-Jewish votive inscriptions also discussed by Satlow, which are, at least in part, considerably earlier. Do these earlier non-Jewish votive inscriptions show the same trend concerning the self as the later Jewish inscriptions (cf. 100–102)? The volume offers no discussion of "ego documents" such as Perpetua's "diary" in connection with the problem of the "real self," but analyzing the self does lead to another intriguing field of study, the senses and their function, to which the contributions by Weitzman, Frank, Harvey, and Brakke offer important insights. In short, this rich volume about the ancient religious self is highly recommended.

Das Gesetz im frühen Judentum und im Neuen Testament: Festschrift für Christoph Burchard zum 75. Geburtstag, edited by Dieter Sänger and Matthias Konradt. Novum Testamentum et Orbis Antiquus/Studien zur Umwelt des Neuen Testaments 57. Göttingen: Vandenhoeck & Ruprecht, 2006. Pp. 344. Cloth. €99.00. ISBN 3525539584.

William R. G. Loader, Murdoch University, Murdoch, Western Australia

This collection of articles celebrating the seventy-fifth birthday of Christoph Burchard begins with a treatment of the image of the temple in 1 Cor 3:16–17 by Jürgen Becker, which takes us right to the heart of the relationship between early Christianity and the law. Becker argues that these verses stand in some tension with the preceding context and most likely reflect early tradition that will have arisen in the Jerusalem church. He argues the plausibility that the first community experienced the Spirit and that this will have generated the sense that they as a community were the abode of the Spirit and could be described as a temple. Noting that Essenes also spoke in this way, Becker seeks to differentiate the first Christian use from that of the Essenes, arguing that for the Essenes a future cult-based temple remained essential and that they saw themselves performing the functions of atonement, whereas the first Christians came to see Christ as having performed the work of atonement. Becker expresses reservation about the historical viability of alleged statements and actions of Jesus with regard to the temple, including the prediction of its destruction, his action in the temple, and the alleged words about a future temple. At least in relation to the latter, one might find more in common with the Essenes. He emphasizes the break that the image of the community implied, expanding it to include emphasis on Christ's saving work and the sense of the Spirit's presence far from Jerusalem and its temple. He sees this development as having its roots in Jesus' acceptance of sinners and sitting loose to purity issues. While in danger of operating with too narrow a view of the Judaisms of the time, some of which could also celebrate God's presence away from Jerusalem, the essay focuses on a major theme that goes to the heart of Torah in which temple and related requirements are central.

Roland Bergmeier's discussion of Rom 2:12–16, 25–29 about Gentiles fulfilling the law by having it written on one's heart without the written law seeks to reinforce the argument that Paul must mean Christian Gentiles, not Gentiles generally, since that would stand in tension with Paul's statements elsewhere in the context. He nevertheless notes that many coming to the text without that background read it otherwise. That should surely at least give rise to caution. Although arguments from consistency are not invalid and assuming inconsistency should be a last resort, it should never be deemed out of the question, especially in reading Paul. What if there were others like Abraham? Dieter Sänger also focuses on an exegetical crux, arguing for a greater appreciation of the negative role exercised by the *paidagogos* in Paul's argument in Gal 3:24. Also tackling a Pauline crux, Hofius argues for a reading of Paul's statement about "ministry of reconciliation" in 2 Cor 5:19c as a deliberate echo of Ps 77:5, in which the meaning is not that Paul and his colleagues are commissioned with a word of reconciliation but that God has set up this word in their midst as he had earlier set up the law.

Paul's discussion of the law in Rom 7 receives attention in two contributions. Petra von Gmünden contrasts the use of the law in 4 Maccabees and Rom 7, focusing in particular on the use of the prohibition of coveting without object in both. In the former the writer is optimistic that the law enables a person to control dangerous desire both in the area of sexual wrongdoing and, in greater detail, in the area of eating forbidden foods. Paul, by contrast, uses the prohibition negatively, drawing on the popular psychology of counter-suggestivity, to argue that it drives people deeper into the morass of sin. Similarly, his second use of the prohibition in Rom 13:9 does not flow from optimism about fulfilling the commandments as identity markers in protecting the community but functions as part of a summary of what the love that Christ brings achieves. Gerd Theissen addresses Rom 7 in the context of developing the thesis that Romans is not only Paul's letter with the most substance but also his most personal. He argues plausibly that that the rhetorical questions, above all, the criticisms, are real and that Paul is defending himself throughout Romans. In this light he then suggests that his choice of "I" language in Rom 7 is deliberate and, while not autobiographical, does nevertheless reflect his own struggles. To some extent the argument rests on speculation and is difficult to test, but certainly it makes good sense of those few clues that indicate that Paul wrote Romans with an eye to the controversies that surrounded him and that affected him very personally.

Two pieces deal with the theme of Jews and Gentiles within the context of Romans. In his discussion of Rom 11:25–32 Hartwig Thyen argues for an approach that holds together Paul's various approaches and sees in them an affirmation of God's promises reaching their goal not apart from Israel. In his discussion of Rom 15:7–13 Berndt Schaller makes the case for seeing here an important statement that both rounds off the discussion of foods and brings Paul's discourse in the letter to end as it began, with an affirmation of both Jew and Gentile in Christ. Two further works on Paul focus on the kerygmatic statement in 1 Thess 1:9–10, arguing its strongly Jewish background (Gottfried Nebe), and the use of Rom 12:1–2 as a model for understanding quality diaconal care (Renate Kirchhoff). Heinz-Wolfgang Kuhn examines the significance of Qumran parallels for Pauline use of *ekklesia*. He notes that, while there is uncertainty about the term that the Aramaic community would have used, it is likely that the choice of *ekklesia* rather than *synagoge* was taken in Jerusalem by the "Hellenists" as a mark of differentiation and not first under the influence of the LXX.

George Nickelsburg opens up the issue of diverse approaches to the law and to the Deuteronomic theological understanding of history in early Jewish writings. He notes the absence of the scheme and of appeals to Mosaic law in Sirach, 1 Enoch, and Wisdom, in contrast to their prominence elsewhere, including Jubilees, although in a distinctive way that claims a revelatory supplement to the law given through Moses. Such studies are important in helping us recognize the diversity within Judaism and in evaluating the emergence of Jesus and the Christian movement within it and, especially, attitudes toward the Law.

Issues of method are the primary focus of the articles by James Charlesworth and Peter Lampe. The former seeks to develop a taxonomy for determining "influence," direct and indirect, between texts and proposes criteria to sort out what he sees as the frequent confusion. Lampe opens up the issue of rhetorical analysis of Pauline texts, offering a valuable review of development and trends in recent research and proposing new ways forward. This excellent discussion points to the diversity of ancient approaches, which include rhetoric, narrative, and epistolographic analysis. These are neither to be confused nor to be seen primarily in terms of what is written in ancient handbooks, since theory and practice often differed, at times quite deliberately. There are also signs of theorists combining these approaches, especially in narrative or history that includes speeches and letters, where the skill of composing fictive letters in *prosopopoeia* was applied. The likelihood of both epistolary and rhetorical techniques operating simultaneously in Paul's letters is also enhanced if, as seems likely, they were written to be read aloud—also true of the Gospels. Discussion of ancient method is further complicated by the interplay of Jewish rhetorical and epistolary practice and the possibility of distinctively Christian approaches, for instance, in rejecting sophistic techniques of rhetorical manipulation. Reading ancient texts in the light of ancient methods needs also to take into account contemporary rhetorical studies but to be clear about the difference. Oda Wischmeyer's study of James identifies the text as composed for oral communication using the models not of Greek rhetoric but Jewish wisdom literature and deliberately beset with direct personal communication ("Brothers"), which in turn gives structure to the whole, which is deigned for an in-group familiar with both the Old Testament and early Christian epistolary literature.

Matthias Konradt offers a convincing account of the Matthean approach to the law, seeing in the antitheses a contradiction not of Torah but of how Torah was being expounded in the synagogues. He sees Matthew's Gospel as following a consistent line that depicts Jesus as affirming Torah and defining its true interpretation. The reviewer's work on the same theme (*Jesus' Attitude towards the Law*, 137–272), not cited, strongly supports these conclusions. The most provocative thesis, worthy of close consideration, comes in Matthias Klinghardt's proposal that our Gospel of Luke and Acts are an anti-Marcionite redaction of an earlier version that Marcion used and that this accounts for the strong affirmations of the law and of the Old Testament in the redacted works.

ANCIENT NEAR EAST

The Ancient Egyptian Pyramid Texts, by James P. Allen. Society of Biblical Literature Writings from the Ancient World 23. Atlanta: Society of Biblical Literature; Leiden: Brill, 2005. Pp. x + 471. Paper/cloth. $39.95/$199.00. ISBN 1589831829/9004137777.

Youri Volokhine, Université de Genève, Geneva, Switzerland

Les Textes des Pyramides (désormais TP) constituent le plus ancien corpus de textes que l'Egypte ancienne ait livré. Découverts dès 1880 sur les parois des pyramides des souverains des Ve (dès Ounas, vers 2353–2323 av. J.-C.) et VIe dynasties, ensevelies dans les sables de la nécropole de Saqqara, ces textes connaissent depuis lors une aventure éditoriale qui n'est pas terminée. Rappelons-en les étapes. Entre 1882 et 1892, Gaston Maspero, découvreur des pyramides à textes, entreprit sans plus attendre de publier les textes hiérogylphiques qu'il avait mis au jour dans cinq pyramides de Saqqara: Ounas (W); Téti (T); Pépy I (P), Mérenrê (M), et Neferkarê Pépy II (N). C'est ce corpus de cinq textes que le grand philologue Kurt Sethe a réuni dans une édition synoptique en 1908 (*Die altägyptischen Pyramidentexte*), bientôt suivie de plusieurs volumes de traductions et de commentaires, qui constituent l'édition de référence. Cependant, le corpus des TP était loin d'être clos. En effet, Gustave Jéquier, poursuivant les fouilles de Saqqara, mis au jour dans les années 20 une série de tombes qui apportaient non seulement de nouvelles versions, mais qui en outre étaient des pyramides de reines, fait qui démontrait que ces textes n'étaient de toute évidence pas conçus uniquement pour la survie du roi seul: les TP des reines Neith (Nt), Ipou (Ip), et Oudjebten (Oudj) furent publiés par Jéquier entre 1928 et 1935. A cet ensemble s'ajoute encore les TP du roi Aba, qui régna au début de la 1ère Période Intermédiaire. Depuis les années 50, une mission française, dirigée d'abord par Jean Sainte Fare Garnot puis par Jean Leclant, a poursuivi l'étude de la nécropole de Saqqara-sud. Un chantier qui a apporté, et apporte encore, des découvertes sensationnelles. Non seulement des milliers de fragments des TP ont été recueillis, certains replacés sur les parois, d'autres encore à l'étude, mais encore le corpus de textes s'est accru.

En effet, une dizième pyramide à textes a été découverte en 2000 par la Mission archéologique française de Saqqara (Mafs): celle de la reine Ankhesenpépy II (voir: V. Dobrev, A. Labrousse, B. Mathieu, *Bulletin de l'Institut français d'archéologie orientale* 100 [2000]: 275–96). L'année suivante, les égyptologues de la Mafs publient l'édition définitive des TP de Pépy Ier (Chr. Berger, J. Leclant, B. Mathieu, I. Pierre-Croisiau, *Les Textes de la pyramide de Pépy Ier, MIFAO* 118, Le Caire, 2001; une traduction commentée de l'ensemble est annoncée, ainsi qu'un volume paléographique). Les textes de Ankhesenpépy II, qui ne sont sans doute pas encore complets—plusieurs zones du complexe funéraire demandant encore à être dégagées—n'ont pas pu être inclus dans la présente traduction de J. P. Allen (voir dernièrement pour ces textes B. Mathieu, *BIFAO* 105 [2005]: 129–38).

Dans son introduction, J.P. Allen présente la nature des TP (1–14) et l'approche méthodologique appropriée qu'ils réclament. L'auteur expose les principes de lecture qu'il a adopté, c'est-à-dire selon un ordre séquentiel visant à rendre compte par la position dans l'édifice de la nature et de la finalité du texte—une approche du texte qu'il avait lui-même précédemment contribué à établir («Reading a Pyramid», dans *Hommages à Jean Leclant, Bibliothèque d'Etude* 106, IFAO , Le Caire, 1994, 5–28). La précédente monographie de référence consacrée à la traduction des TP était l'œuvre de Raymond Faulkner (*The Ancient Egyptian Pyramid Texts,* Oxford University Press, 1969). Cette traduction suivait encore l'ordre des formules de l'édition synoptique de Kurt Sethe, lequel reprenait et complétait la numérotation de Maspero, une numérotation aujourd'hui obsolète. En effet, cette numérotation ne tenait compte que des éléments en place et/ou accessible. Depuis lors, non seulement des nouveaux textes ont été trouvés, comme nous le rappelions ci-dessus, mais encore de nouvelles portions de textes complétant les formules déjà connues. En outre, la recherche des dernières décennies sur les TP a clairement pu démontrer que la position des textes dans l'appartement funéraire jouait un rôle important pour leur compréhension. En outre, pour rendre compte des différents textes supplémentaires, il importait de reconsidérer la présentation du corpus. C'est ainsi que les archéologues français mirent au point (dès 1975) une nouvelle numérotation fondée sur l'emplacement des textes, ainsi qu'une codification alphabétique pour renvoyer aux éléments pariétaux et à la disposition des textes. C'est ce modèle, suivi par l'auteur, qui préside désormais à la lecture des textes. En fait, les anciens Egyptiens eux-mêmes avaient établi ces principes, dont il s'agit de comprendre l'intelligence: les TP ne sont pas écrits «au hasard» sur les parois; ils suivent une logique. En effet, les dites «formules» (spells) renvoient à des séquences habituellement écrites dans un monogramme commençant par l'indication «récitation/prononcer les paroles» (*dd-mdw*) et inclus dans le signe hiéroglyphique du domaine/chapitre («hout»; cette pratique est observée dès Pépy II). Ces «récitations» réalisent en quelque sorte le figement dans la pierre de la parole du prêtre-ritualiste. Il s'agit donc bel et bien d'une liturgie d'accompagnement, ponctuant et assurant du même coup les étapes d'un processus de revivification funéraire. Les TP révèlent, comme le décrit J.P. Allen, trois groupes majeurs de formules: le *rituels des offrandes,* le *rituel de résurrection,* et le *rituel du matin*. Le *rituel des offrandes* figure toujours sur la paroi nord de la chambre funéraire. Le locuteur/ritualiste présente au défunt des offrandes alimentaires variées, des libations, des encensements. Un *rituel des emblèmes* y est joint, où le bénéficiaire reçoit les *regalia* et les vêtements spécifiques de sa fonction souveraine. L'offrande est souvent décrite comme «l'œil d'Horus», c'est-à-dire l'œil du dieu blessé par Seth mais ensuite guéri, dont la mention fonctionne comme symbole de tout ce qui est préservé et éternellement viable. Le *rituel de résurrection* est inscit sur le mur sud de la chambre funéraire: le défunt se libère de ses attaches corporelles et terrestres pour accèder au monde divin. Le *rituel du matin* reflète les cérémonies entourant le roi rituellement éveillé, habillé, et équipé, durant toute sa vie terrestre palatiale.

La fonction principale des TP est de permettre au défunt de devenir un «akh», c'est-à-dire accéder à un niveau supérieur d'existence. Pour parvenir à cette «transfiguration», tout un appareil est mis à contribution. C'est pour cela que quantité de formules sont de l'ordre de la conjuration, et proviennent manifestement de ces sortes de «grimoires» dans lesquels les ritualistes égyptiens puisèrent, à toute époque, pour prévenir le bénéficiaire du rite de toute attaque nocive. Il semble, effectivement, qu'une partie des formules des TP est issue de textes antérieurs—dont nous n'avons autrement pas de traces. Les TP reflètent une vision du monde et soutiennent une cosmologie tout comme une anthropologie funéraire (à cet égard, les TP sont évidemment une source essentielle pour reconstituer la théologie la plus ancienne de l'Egypte). L'architecture des appartements funéraires réalise une contrepartie de différents lieux du monde où, selon la cosmologie, le Soleil (le dieu solaire Rê) effectue son parcours: un espace dans lequel le défunt s'oriente d'ouest en est, c'est-à-dire de la mort (couchant) vers la vie (levant). Le parcours virtuel part du sarcophage, où le défunt repose, à l'instar du dieu Osiris auquel il est constamment identifié: un sarcophage conçu comme le corps même de la déesse du ciel Nout (le sarcophage devient ainsi un espace de gestation, dont le terme est la vie). Partant de la chambre funéraire, qui correspond à la Douat («l'au-delà»), où les différentes formules d'offrandes lui donnent l'équipement nécessaire, le défunt progresse jusqu'à l'antichambre, qui est la contrepartie de l'horizon «Akhet». Plus à l'est encore, le dit «serdab» (mot arabe traditionnellement utilisé pour ce type de pièce) représente sans doute le point extrême de l'au-delà-Douat, la limite où va poindre le soleil à l'aube, où la vie emerge. C'est un endroit de tous les dangers, qui, par analogie avec le processus humain de la naissance, serait selon Allen celui où «le fœtus doit devenir viable par lui-même» (11). Ayant acquis dans le serdab la capacité vitale, et retournant dans l'antichambre, le roi défunt est désormais un être qui peut se déplacer sans entraves (un *ba*), et qui s'apprête à devenir un être transiguré et lumineux (*akh*). A l'orientation ouest-est succède alors un sens qui conduit du sud au nord. Un circuit qui mènent vers les «étoiles impérissables» du nord du ciel, celles-là même en fonction desquelles étaient orientées les grandes pyramides anépigraphes antérieures. Un mouvement du sud au nord qui, pour Allen, n'est pas non plus sans évoquer celui du Nil.

Après son introduction générale, l'auteur va présenter et traduire les TP res-
pectifs: Ounas (16–64) ; Téti (65–96) ; Pépy Ier (97–207) ; Merenrê (209–37) ;
Pépy II (239–307) ; la reine Neith (309–36); puis les variantes textuelles (337–73).
Les différentes section sont suivies d'un apparat critique assez concis. Il n'y a pas
lieu ici de discuter plus en détails des multiples questions lexicales (voire gram-
maticales) qui ne manquent pas de surgir dans ces textes difficiles. Quant à la
thématique foisonnante, et parfois déroutante pour celui qui n'est pas habitué à
cette phraséologie pharaonique, il serait tout autant impossible d'en détailler ici
le contenu. Contentons-nous de rappeler que la finalité de ces textes est essentiellement d'assurer la survie du défunt dans l'au-delà: cet impératif conditionne
la rédaction des textes, dans lesquels les données mythologiques sont réduites le
plus souvent à l'allusion, et la cosmologie ou l'anthropologie à l'implicite.

Plusieurs concordances détaillées ont été nécessaires pour faciliter le travail
du lecteur; elles figurent en fin de volume. La première (A) établit la correspondance entre les nouveaux numéros attribués aux formules respectives dans
chaque pyramides (soit W1 à W 226 ; T 1à T 304; P1 à P 587/588–589 ; M1a à
M 339; N1a à N 615; Nt 1 à 281) et les numéros des formules selon l'édition de
Sethe (numéro PT/*pyramid texts*). La seconde (B) indique la localisation dans
les diverses pyramides des formules, en suivant la désignation codée établie par
l'équipe française de Saqqara (Mafs). La section (C) indique (en gras) les formules
PT traduites dans le volume (ainsi PT 23 est traduite sous la section W [Ounas]
19, mais se rencontrent aussi en T 23, P 64; M 59, N 115, Nt 57). A cette section
est ajoutée les formules dépourvues de numéro PT, ou pourvue d'un numéro CT
(Textes des Sarcophages, corpus funéraire postérieur). La section (E) signale les
formules absentes de l'édition de Sethe. La section (F) établit la correpsondance
entre les numéros des «Utterance» de R. Faulkner et le présent volume. Enfin, la
section (G) signale la correpondance avec les numéros supplémentaires détermi-
nés par la Mafs. Un glossaire et un index complètent ces index.

Désormais, grâce à cette remarquable contribution de James P. Allen, une
nouvelle étape importante est franchie dans l'histoire de la recherche. Il s'agit en
effet d'une traduction et d'une présentation, non seulement écrite à la lumière
des acquis les plus récents de la philologie, mais encore soutenue par une analyse et une intelligence qui puisent leurs sources dans l'actualité de l'archéologie
des pyramides à textes de l'Ancien Empire. Signalons enfin que l'auteur vient de
publier l'édition longtemps attendue des versions des TP copiées sur les sarcophages du Moyen Empire (James P. Allen, *The Egyptian Coffin Texts, Volume 8.
Middle Kingdom Copies of Pyramid Texts,* OIP 123, Chicago, 2005).

A Passing Power: An Examination of the Sources for the History of Aram-Damas-
cus in the Second Half of the Ninth Century B.C., by Sigurthur Hafthórsson. Coni-
ectanea Biblica: Old Testament Series 54. Stockholm: Almqvist & Wiksell, 2006.
Pp. viii + 304. Paper. $89.50. ISBN 9122021434.

Paul Sanders, St. Stanislas College Delft, Rijswijk, The Netherlands

How much do we know about the history of Aram-Damascus in the second
half of the ninth century B.C.E.? What can we say about the extent of this kingdom and its power over the Aramean and non-Aramean neighbor kingdoms? In
this book, written as his thesis, Hafthórsson carefully scrutinizes not only all the
available textual evidence in Aramaic and Akkadian and in the Hebrew Bible but
also the archaeological data, a source that is often ignored.

In the introductory chapter 1, Hafthórsson makes it abundantly clear that
he is dissatisfied with the uncritical approach of the sources in previous scholarly
research. In the preface he even says: "it is possible to see the present work as
a protest against all the quasi-truths I have experienced in my education." The
need to reevaluate the evidence is clear, but Hafthórsson fails to explain why he
selected this specific period and decided to disregard the following period until
the kingdom's fall in the year 732. As there were more Aramean kingdoms in
the period under discussion, Hafthórsson rightly remarks that epigraphical references to Aram do not necessarily relate to the kingdom centered in Damascus. In
the Akkadian texts, however, the enigmatic expression KUR (*ša*) *imērīšu* ("land
of the donkey driver"?) always refers to the Damascene kingdom.

Chapter 2 gives an extensive overview of previous scholarly literature
about the history of Aram-Damascus in the second half of the ninth century.
In Hafthórsson's view, scholars such as Benjamin Mazar trusted too blindly in
the biblical evidence. Also, most of the theories concerning an alliance of Syrian
states under the supremacy of Aram-Damascus lack a solid basis. However, in
his recent book *The Arameans* (Leuven, 2000), E. Lipiński is more critical. He
expresses well-founded ideas and takes the archaeological material into account.

Because of the danger of harmonizing the sources too readily, Hafthórsson decides to study each source separately to find out what it can contribute
to the whole. In chapter 3 he discusses the relevant texts written in Aramaic.
He argues that the text on the Melqart Stela, found close to Aleppo, cannot be
used as proof that king Bar-hadad of Aram-Damascus, the son of Hazael, had
contacts in the Aleppo region. The text might refer to another Aramean king
called Bar-hadad.

Hafthórsson does not mention a date for the fragments of the ivory plaque
from Arslan Taš. However, as the Damascene king Hazael, the father of Bar-hadad,
was probably the only important Hazael in "that period" (40), the expression "our
lord Hazael" in the inscription would seem to relate to him. The slight uncertainty with regard to the identification pertains also to the expression "our lord
Hazael" in the inscriptions found in Eretria and on Samos. The latter inscriptions
suggest that in the time of Hazael there were contacts between Aram-Damascus

and 'Umqi in northern Syria. Hafthórsson refutes the idea that the expression *mr'n* "our lord" implies that Hazael was the overlord of vassals.

When discussing the much-debated fragments of the monumental stela found at Tel Dan, Hafthórsson notes that their date will become less controversial only when the final reports about the excavations are published. For the moment, however, he assumes that they date from the second half of the ninth century. Hafthórsson expresses some doubt about the position to the left of fragment A, where Biran and Naveh placed fragments B1 and B2, even though most scholars have accepted their arrangement. However, he endorses the view that the fragments belonged to the same stela.

Hafthórsson wants to find out what historical reconstruction can be made when reading A separately from B1/B2, but also when following the arrangement as proposed by Biran and Naveh. He accepts their interpretation of *bytdwd* as "house of David" (= kingdom of Judah) without any discussion and considers their reconstruction of the royal names [*yhw*]*rm* "[Jeho]ram" (king of Israel) and [*'ḥz*]*yhw* "[Ahaz]yahu" (king of Judah) as probable. However, he is certainly right when pointing to the uncertainties surrounding Biran and Naveh's reconstruction. If their attribution of the stela to King Hazael of Aram-Damascus is correct, it seems strange that Hazael, who both in the Old Testament and in the Assyrian texts is described as a usurper, can call his predecessor "my father." However, Hafthórsson notes that the expression "my father" does not necessarily refer to one's biological father. Another problem concerns the death of Jehoram and Ahazyahu. According to Biran and Naveh's reconstruction, Hazael claims to have killed these kings, but the Old Testament says that Jehu killed them (2 Kgs 9:14–27). Hafthórsson regards Wesselius's attribution of the stela to Jehu and Athas's ascription to Bar-hadad as not impossible, but he stresses that if we stick to the authorship of Hazael, the reconstruction of Biran and Naveh could still be correct. The biblical account may not be reliable, as it is "set in a highly ideologised drama of Elisha anointing Jehu as king" (63). Remarkably, however, the beginnings of both Hazael's and Jehu's kingship are seen as interrelated in the Bible (1 Kgs 19:15–18). Of course, the presence of the stela at Tel Dan suggests that the Arameans controlled the site for some time.

The Zakkur Stela, which mentions Bar-hadad the son of Hazael (*brhdd br ḥz'l;* Hafthórsson omits the translation of the following words *mlk 'rm* "king of Aram" [65]), demonstrates the existence of an alliance of several north Syrian and south Anatolian kings under the supremacy of Bar-hadad. The allied forces tried to conquer the north Syrian city of Hazrak, but King Zakkur of Hamath and Luʻaš defeated them. Though Damascus is not mentioned, "Aram" must stand for the kingdom centered in Damascus. It is remarkable that also in the other Aramaic texts Damascus is never mentioned.

Chapter 4 presents and discusses the Assyrian texts that refer to the kingdom of Damascus. They date from the time of Shalmaneser III (858–824) and Adad-nirari III (810–783). However, no references are found from roughly 835 to 805, because then the Assyrians were absent from the west. Hafthórsson fully recognizes that the royal inscriptions were written to magnify the Assyrian king and to present him in a very positive and powerful light. However, when discussing the individual inscriptions, he generally takes the reliability of the information about Aram-Damascus for granted. He assumes that the royal annals must have been written down after the last year recorded there. The Eponym Chronicle is seen as even more honest than the annals, because it reports negative events.

Among the things that we can learn from the Assyrian texts is that in the year 853 the Assyrian army destroyed the city of Qarqar and subsequently defeated an alliance of kingdoms from the west. The fact that the army of king Adad-idri of Aram-Damascus is listed first and the remarkable size of his army clearly both indicate that this kingdom played the leading role in the alliance. It is remarkable that the texts do not refer to a further advance of the Assyrian army to the south. None of the allied kingdoms is said to have surrendered or to have been forced to pay tribute. This means that the Assyrian victory was only small and indecisive. Also, in 845 the Assyrians needed an exceptionally large force to defeat the alliance, which apparently still existed.

After Adad-idri's death, sometime between 845 and 841, King Hazael took the throne of Aram-Damascus. In 841, when he had to defend his country against Assyrian attacks, his army was defeated, but it seems that Damascus was not captured. After the Assyrian campaign, kingdoms in Palestine and Phoenicia had to pay tribute to Assyria.

The texts of Adad-nirari III mention an Aramean king Mari (^{m}ma-ri-i') from Damascus, who, just like King Joash of Israel and other kings in the region, had to pay tribute after a successful Assyrian campaign, possibly in 806 B.C.E. For this later period, the Assyrian texts do not mention any great resistance from the kingdoms of the west. Hafthórsson believes that Mari might be a title of King Bar-hadad, Hazael's son, whose Aramaic name never occurs in the Assyrian texts. Mari could be the Assyrian rendering of Aramaic $mr'y$ "my lord."

In chapter 5 Hafthórsson discusses the passages from the Old Testament that may be relevant for the reconstruction of Aram-Damascus's history in this period. Most of them are found in the books of Kings and Chronicles, but some reliable information may also turn up in passages in the prophetic books. Hafthórsson stresses that it is important to determine the genre of the biblical texts referring to Aram before one establishes the reliability of the information. In the biblical passages we find more legendary descriptions of miracles than in the Assyrian texts discussed in chapter 4, but even texts describing miracles may contain relevant historical information. Also, not only the texts from the Bible but also many Assyrian texts and the text of the Tel Dan stela claim that it was a deity who gave the victories, so the religious element is certainly not confined to the Bible. Hafthórsson assumes that the redactors of the books of Kings probably disposed of older sources with correct information, but he stresses that large parts of the books of Kings were written down several centuries after the events they describe.

Under the legendary passages that lack reliable historical details, Hafthórsson classifies the miraculous story of Samaria's siege and relief in the time of Elisha (2 Kgs 6:24–7:20). However, other texts would seem to provide more reliable information. The assertion that the sinful King Jeroboam II was able to roll back the Arameans to the previous borders seems to have surprised the redactors for theological reasons, which clearly indicates that they regarded this information as correct (2 Kgs 14:23–29). In view of an Assyrian text claiming that Hazael was a usurper ("a son of nobody"), the story about Hazael's coup (2 Kgs 8:7–15) would also seem to go back to a reliable tradition. However, according to the Bible, the name of his predecessor was Ben-hadad, just like his own son and successor, whereas the Assyrian text calls his predecessor Adad-idri. In the case of the early Aramean invasion into Israel during the reign of King Baasha (1 Kgs 14:16–22; 2 Chr 16:1–6), Hafthórsson suggests that the story may be unreliable, as the areas attacked are about the same as in 2 Kgs 15:29, where we find a description of an Aramean attack that took place much later. Although I admit that the information about the battle during Baasha's reign might be incorrect, I do not find the argument against the reliability of the information very convincing.

In his discussion of 1 Kgs 20 and 22, Hafthórsson shows that these sections do not primarily aim at recording battles between Aram and Israel but intend to describe how Yahweh works in history and how he makes his will known through the prophets. Like many other scholars, Hafthórsson doubts whether these texts really describe events that took place during the reign of King Ahab. He devotes a separate discussion to the identity of the Israelite king in these texts, which only rarely mention the name Ahab. All the arguments against the identification with Ahab are listed and weighed carefully. Among the reasons to stick to the identification with Ahab is the fact that 1 Kgs 22 frequently mentions Ahab's contemporary King Jehoshaphat of Judah. It is mainly on the basis of historical details that do not agree with "facts" known from other biblical or Assyrian texts that Hafthórsson prefers to attribute 1 Kgs 20 and 22 to a later period, the time of the Israelite kings Jehoahaz and Joash (see 2 Kgs 13). This means that the Aramean king Ben-hadad mentioned in these passages must be Hazael's son, not his predecessor. Another argument adduced for a later attribution of 1 Kgs 22 is the similarity with the battle reports of 2 Kgs 3:4–27 and 8:28–29. Contrary to Hafthórsson, however, I do not believe that this argument of similarity really reinforces the other arguments. Intertextual links may occur also when comparable events that really took place are described in a similar way.

When trying to establish the historical background of 1 Kgs 20 and 22, Hafthórsson seems to be somewhat unfaithful to his convincing claim that these texts do not intend to describe historical facts. He seems to disregard the possibility that the composers of these texts did not dispose of their own sources but may have created stories intentionally related to the wicked King Ahab, in order to express their theological ideas about Yahweh's intervention and the character of prophecy. Is it not better to assume that these texts are not based on any additional information, neither about the time of Ahab *nor* about the time of Jehoahaz and Joash? Could it not be that the composers of 1 Kgs 22 decided to mention

Ramoth-gilead because they knew it was a disputed city in other periods? In my view, the frequent occurrence of the name Jehoshaphat suggests that the composers consciously attributed the ideological story to the time of Ahab. The reason the text mentions Ahab's name less frequently than Jehoshaphat's name must be due to the Judean background of the text.

Hafthórsson shows that, if we accept all the biblical information as reliable, there must have been at least three kings called Ben-hadad in Aram-Damascus. However, it is possible that the Aramean King Adad-idri, who is mentioned in the Assyrian texts, is erroneously called Ben-hadad in the Bible. The Bible clearly states that Ben-hadad's successor, King Hazael, ruthlessly oppressed the Israelites. He conquered the Transjordanian parts of the kingdom of Israel and even subdued Judah. The oppression continued under his son Ben-hadad, but under Jeroboam II Israel managed to defeat the Arameans and to roll them back. Several passages in the Bible, however, suggest that there were not only wars but also commercial contacts between Aram-Damascus and Israel.

Not being an archaeologist himself, Hafthórsson's discussion of the archaeological evidence in chapter 6 is largely based on descriptions and interpretations by others. However, Hafthórsson is able to judge these interpretations carefully. Unfortunately, it is dubious whether there was an Aramean material culture distinct from neo-Hittite, Israelite, and other material cultures. Another complicating factor is that many sites in the territory of Aram-Damascus have not been excavated. Hafthórsson clearly points out what needs to be done before we can draw more conclusions with regard to the Aramean material culture.

At the site of At-Tall, just north of the Sea of Galilee, a "Bull stela" was found dating from Iron IIB. Stelae with very similar depictions have been found both east of the Sea of Galilee and in southeast Turkey, which is "a clear indication of religious contacts with Syria" (218). However, Hafthórsson cautiously warns that this does not necessarily demonstrate Aramean rule over the site.

According to excavator Avraham Biran, the evidence unearthed at Tel Dan suggests influence from both the south and the northeast. A bronze plaque displays a scene that is reminiscent of scenes of Hittite, Assyrian, and north Syrian origin. However, the finds at the high place are more similar to those in Samaria and Megiddo. Two short inscriptions found at Tel Dan would seem to be in Hebrew and are assumed to be a bit younger than the Tel Dan stela and another Aramaic inscription found there.

A fragmentary Aramaic inscription has been unearthed also at Hazor. The Hebrew inscriptions found there are probably later. According to Israel Finkelstein, the end of stratum IX was due to the destruction by Hazael of Aram-Damascus, not by Ben-hadad, the son of Tab-Rimmon, as Yigal Yadin suggested (see 1 Kgs 15:20). Yadin, however, attributes the destruction at the end of stratum VII to Hazael. Hafthórsson rightly points out that destruction layers may also be due to accidental fires and natural catastrophes. He finds it safest to follow the traditional "high" chronology but stresses that Finkelstein's "low" chronology may not be dismissed out of hand.

Despite the scarcity of inscriptions found in the area disputed by Aram-Damascus and Israel, and despite the doubt concerning their dating, it seems that Aramaic was dominant in the ninth century and Hebrew was used in later centuries. If this conclusion is justified, it would agree perfectly with other indications of a decline of Aram-Damascus at the end of the ninth century. These other indications are: (1) the claim on the Zakkur Stela that Bar-Hadad's siege of Hazrak was unsuccessful; (2) the description of the reign of Jeroboam II in the Old Testament, who is said who have rolled the Arameans back; (3) the references in the texts of the Assyrian king Adad-nirari III to the siege of Damascus and to a huge tribute paid by King Mari of Damascus. According to Hafthórsson, it is absolutely clear that Aram-Damascus bloomed after the twenty-first year of the reign of Shalmaneser III (838 B.C.E.), when his campaigns in the west stopped so he could attend to other matters. However, he is not willing to designate Hazael's kingdom an empire, as others scholars have done. The golden age of Aram-Damascus was over when Adad-nirari III took up new efforts to conquer the west.

This new book offers a wonderful overview of textual and archaeological data relevant for the reconstruction of the history of Aram-Damascus in this specific period. Hafthórsson analyzes the data carefully, which leads to new conclusions and rejections of false truths. It is helpful that the most important Assyrian texts can be found in an appendix. Both the transliteration and the translation have been taken from volume 3 of A. Kirk Grayson, *Royal Inscriptions of Mesopotamia* (Toronto, 1996). Maps, an extensive bibliography, and an index of geographical names conclude the book. Unfortunately, indices of authors, of the kings mentioned in the ancient sources, and of the scriptural references are missing. For the Assyrian, Israelite, and Judean kings mentioned in this book, a complete survey of their supposed years of reign would have been very useful (Hafthórsson follows Donner, *Geschichte des Volkes Israel,* 1995; see p. 4). Illustration 5 (51) could have indicated more clearly where the fragments of the Tel Dan stela were found, and an illustration clarifying the architecture of the so-called *bīt ḫilāni* palace building would have been helpful (188). However, these minor shortcomings do not affect my final judgment. I warmly recommend Hafthórsson's book to all those who want to find out what we really know about the history of Aram-Damascus.

L'homosexualité dans le Proche-Orient ancien et la Bible, by Thomas Römer and Loyse Bonjour. Essais bibliques 37. Geneva: Labor et Fides, 2005. Pp. 117. Paper. €18.00. ISBN 2830911652.

Martti Nissinen, University of Helsinki, Helsinki, Finland

This little book is published as volume 37 of the series Essais bibliques by Labor et Fides, the leading Protestant publishing house of French-speaking Switzerland, which regularly produces books on biblical themes. Apart from academic books, such as the series of commentaries on the books of the Old and New Testament, as well as the recent and very useful textbook *Introduction à l'Ancien*

Testament, edited by Thomas Römer in collaboration with Jean-Daniel Macchi and Christophe Nihan (2004), many works published by Labor et Fides are written for general audiences with an interest in theology and ecclesiastical matters.

Together with Loyse Bonjour, Thomas Römer, the present editor of Essais bibliques, has contributed to the series a volume that, to my knowledge, is the first scholarly introduction to the question of Bible and homosexuality written in French. The book is to be welcomed as filling a significant linguistic gap in the fast-growing literature on what is probably the most hotly debated issue on today's theological and ecclesiastical scene. It is written in a reader-friendly way for an audience not necessarily professionally involved in biblical studies: the reader is provided with basic historical and introductory knowledge on the biblical and ancient Near Eastern texts well known to specialists but necessary for a general readership. Apparently for the same reason, the book quotes only a minimum of other literature, mostly written in French.

Compared with other related works, such as my *Homoeroticism in the Biblical World* (1998) or the flagship of the conservative perspective, Robert Gagnon's *The Bible and Homosexual Practice* (2001), the book of Römer and Bonjour is designed in a different way. Of the total of 107 text pages, some twenty-five pages are dedicated to the ancient Near Eastern material and another twenty-five to Lev 18–20 and Gen 19. More than forty pages deal with David and Jonathan and only eight pages with the New Testament. There is no explanation for this distribution of space, which may strike the reader as strange. The mighty portion of David and Jonathan can be motivated by the desire to demonstrate the approval of a passionate love relationship between two men as an "antidote" to the Levitical and Pauline condemnations. But when it comes to the interpretation of Pauline texts, which in the current Christian debate clearly exceed the importance of the texts of the Hebrew Bible, it is a pity that they play only an ancillary role in the present work.

The first chapter of the book deals with the ancient Near East, focusing not only on Mesopotamian sources but also rather extensively on Egyptian ones. The ancient Near Eastern sources are presented in their proper religious context, which is to be appreciated, even though the recurring concept of "sacred prostitution" should be updated. The authors correctly conclude that the various types of same-sex interaction discernible from this material cannot be taken as documenting homosexuality in the modern sense. It is interesting in any case that a couple of Egyptian texts, as well as some iconographic material, depict a rather intimate relationship between two men without the slightest abhorrence (33–35); unfortunately, the pictures in question are available to the reader only through a weblink.

The discussion on Lev 18–20 in the second chapter is contextualized by the ideology of purity and separation in the Holiness Code, where the condemnation of sexual relations between two male persons is more radical than in Mesopotamian laws: both parties are condemned, irrespective of their social status. Quite interestingly, this radicalization is traced back to the influence of Zoroastrian dualism in the Persian period, on the one hand (45), and to the transcendental-ization of God and the consequent separation of sexuality and religion, on the other hand. Behind this ideological development, however, one finds the patri-archal division between active and passive sexual roles and the concern for male honor, which largely explains the nonmention of sexual relationships between women. In their interpretation of Gen 19, Römer and Bonjour take up the usual (and correct) position that the intended sexual assault in Sodom is about domi-nance and not homosexuality.

The longest chapter of the book, chapter 3, is dedicated to an analysis of the relationship of David and Jonathan as compared to that between Gilgamesh and Enkidu. Antedating the Holiness Code, the David and Jonathan narratives present an entirely different view of an intimate and even erotic relationship between two male figures, which, however, cannot be called "homosexual"; the story is about love, not about sex. A comparison with the Epic of Gilgamesh (which, accord-ing to the authors, may have been known in Palestine when the story of David's rise to the throne was written; cf. the fragment of the epic found in Megiddo) reveals a similar prototype of a heroic and masculine love relationship in which even sexual roles appear to be more flexible than presupposed by the proscrip-tions in Leviticus. The love between the heroes is true love, not just a covenantal relationship. However, it is up to the modern reader to decide to what extent the homoerotic traits of the narratives relate to the modern concept of homosexuality. All this is in line with contemporary scholarship (including my own), which has seen the relationship of David and Jonathan as an example of male bonding not primarily of a sexual nature. It should be noted that Susan Ackerman has chal-lenged this view in her recent book, *When Heroes Love: The Ambiguity of Eros in the Stories of Gilgamesh and David* (New York: Columbia University Press, 2005). Also, Saul M. Olyan leaves the door open for a more sexual interpretation of the relationship of David and Jonathan, with hermeneutical implications similar to those of Römer and Bonjour ("'Surpassing the Love of Women': Another Look at 2 Samuel 1:26 and the Relationship of David and Jonathan," in *Authorizing Mar-riage: Canon, Tradition, and Critique in the Blessing of Same-Sex Unions* [ed. Mark D. Jordan et al.; Princeton: Princeton University Press, 2006], 7–16).

The short chapter on the New Testament, chapter 4, first notes the silence of the Gospels on the matter and then moves to Paul, whose understanding of *physis* embraces the conventional sexual roles as a part of the created order but is not applicable to modern categories of human sexuality. For Paul, sexual acts *para physin* served as an illustration of a voluntary submission to idolatry, but his view of same-sex interaction as comparable to adultery, licentiousness, and excessive use of alcohol has little to contribute to the issue of homosexuality.

Römer and Bonjour's book does not present revolutionary new readings of biblical and other ancient texts but lines up with the majority of today's noncon-servative scholarship, which reads the biblical texts as cultural products, written in a world different from ours and presupposing an understanding of (same-)sex relationships that does not conform to modern presuppositions of what is today anachronistically called (homo)sexuality. Same-sex relationships do not constitute a major issue anywhere in biblical, or even extrabiblical, texts; no text is primarily about legitimizing or condemning same-sex interaction. Eclectic reading of the Bible from the perspective of what is today called homosexuality only makes the reader blind to the fact that the traditional condemnation of sexuality in general is rooted, not primarily in a few selected passages of the Bible, but in the history of the Judeo-Christian civilization, in which sexual acts have most of the time been restricted to the sole purpose of procreation. Attentive reading of the Bible, especially when done against its ancient Near Eastern background, may reveal forms of same-sex relationships—primarily those of David and Jonathan vis-à-vis Gilgamesh and Enkidu—that are neither equivalent to our concept of homosexuality nor directly transferable to the modern Western culture, but may, in spite of this, relativize the understanding of the Bible as strictly condemning all kinds of same-sex interaction. In demonstrating this, and in ending their book with a quotation from Luke 6:37 (cf. Rom 2:1!), Römer and Bonjour render a good service to their readers.

Götterbilder–Gottesbilder–Weltbilder: Polytheismus und Monotheismus in der Welt der Antike, Vol. 1: Ägypten, Mesopotamien, Kleinasien, Syrien, Palästina, edited by Reinhard Gregor Kratz and Hermann Spieckermann. Forschungen zum Alten Testament 2/17. Tübingen: Mohr Siebeck, 2006. Pp. xix + 378. Paper. €69.00. ISBN 3161486730.

Konrad Schmid, University of Zurich, Zurich, Switzerland

I.

Der vorliegende Band, Teil 1 einer zweibändigen Dokumentation, ist aus Vorträgen hervorgegangen, die im Rahmen des Göttinger Graduiertenkollegs „Götterbilder–Gottesbilder–Weltbilder. Polytheismus und Monotheismus in der Welt der Antike" gehalten wurden. Teils entstammen sie einer Ringvorlesung zum gleichnamigen Thema, teils gehen sie auf ein Symposium „Pantheon und Politik. Ihr Zusammenspiel in der orientalischen und klassischen Antike" zurück. Das zweite Thema ist etwas enger gefasst und fokussiert stärker auf das Zusammenspiel von Gottes- und Weltbildern. Die Einleitung macht hinlänglich klar, dass „Gottesbilder ... weder pure Projektionen von Weltbildern noch umgekehrt" (xii) sind, und dass die in der Forschung weiterhin gebräuchliche Terminologie von „Polytheismus und Monotheismus" zwar gewisse Hilfestellungen zur Klassifizierung der untersuchten Phänomene bieten kann, zugleich aber nur „heuristische Funktion" (xv) haben kann. Mit Bedacht ist deshalb auf die weiteren Begriffe „Pantheismus, Monolatrie und Henotheismus" verzichtet worden, „um beim Überblick die Sache nicht komplizierter als unbedingt notwendig zu machen" (xv). Die Beiträge wenden sich in der Regel nicht an ein spezifisches

Fachpublikum, sondern sind für einen beginnenden altertumswissenschaftlichen Diskurs geschrieben. Die Ägyptologin schreibt für den Gräzisten, der Alttestamentler für den Iranisten, die Assyriologin für den Hethitologen.

II.

Der Band wird eröffnet durch drei Beiträge zur ägyptischen Religion: Friedrich Junge, „Unser Land ist der Tempel der Ganzen Welt". Über die Religion der Ägypter und ihre Struktur (3–44); Heike Sternberg-el-Hotabi, „Die Erde entsteht auf deinen Wink". Der naturphilosophische Monotheismus des Echnaton (45–78); Susanne Bickel, Die Verknüpfung von Weltbild und Staatsbild. Aspekte von Politik und Religion in Ägypten (79–99). Friedrich Junge stellt sich die Aufgabe, die „rationale und welterklärende Komponente, sozusagen ihre Dogmatik oder Systematik" zu erheben (5). Er setzt dazu zunächst mit einer Präsentation der Fremdheit der ägyptischen Religion mit ihren eigenwilligen Götterdarstellungen ein, um dann an verschiedenen Texten und Darstellungen die implizite Rationalität des Weltverstehens der ägyptischen Religion herauszuarbeiten. Heike Sternberg-el-Hotabi greift sich gegenüber dieser überblicksartigen und enzyklopädischen Darstellung eine sehr spezifische Epoche der ägyptischen Religion heraus, die für die Monotheismusproblematik von großem Interesse ist, die Zeit Echnatons. Im Anschluss an die Arbeiten von Jan Assmann profiliert sie die „neue" Sonnentheologie um die alleinige Verehrung von Aton in historischer, theologischer und naturphilosophischer Sicht und versucht, ihr religionsgeschichtliches Werden und ihr politisches Scheitern zu plausibilisieren. Susanne Bickel beschreibt die vielfältigen Interaktionen zwischen ägyptischer Weltanschauung und Politik und dem religiösen Symbolsystem und rekonstruiert daraus ein einheitliches Konzept, das sie „Staatsreligion" (97) nennt.

Es folgen drei Beiträge zu den „Religionen in Mesopotamien": Annette Zgoll, Vielfalt der Götter und Einheit des Reiches. Konstanten und Krisen im Spannungsfeld politischer Aktion und Reflexion in der mesopotamischen Geschichte (103–30); Brigitte Groneberg, Aspekte der „Göttlichkeit" in Mesopotamien. Zur Klassifizierung von Göttern und Zwischenwesen (131–66); Astrid Nunn, Kulttopographie und Kultabläufe in mesopotamischen Tempeln: drei Beispiele (167–95). Zgoll entwickelt zunächst „Kategorien der Interferenzen zwischen Götterwelt und Menschenwelt" (107) und illustriert diese an verschiedenen literarischen Zeugnissen der mesopotamischen Kulturen. Im Sinne einer historischen Konkretion wird dann das Lied *nin-me-šara* aus dem 23. Jahrhundert v.Chr. näher besprochen, das die Macht und Prävalenz der Göttin Inana in der damaligen politischen Konstellation beschwört. Groneberg fragt nach der Darstellbarkeit und Konzeptualisierung der Qualität „Göttlichkeit" bei mesopotamischen Göttern und Zwischenwesen, während der Beitrag von Nunn die mesopotamischen Religionsverständnisse von den Kulthandlungen und der Sakralarchitektur beleuchtet.

Die zoroastrische Religion wird durch zwei Beiträge von Philip G. Kreyenbroek (Theological Questions in an Oral Tradition: the Case of Zoroastrianism [199–222]) und Albert de Jong (One Nation under God? The Early Sasanians as Guardians and Destroyers of Holy Sites [223–38]) besprochen. Kreyenbroek entwirft ein diachron gestuftes und bezüglich der häufig an den Zoroastrismus herangetragenen Kategorie des Dualismus differenziertes Bild der zoroastrischen Theologie für die Epoche der *Gathas* sowie die achämenidische und sassanidische Zeit. Ahura Mazda ist zwar der wichtigste Gott bereits in den *Gathas*, doch er ist von ihrerseits mächtigen Funktionsträgern umgeben. Erst in achämenidischer Zeit wird Ahura Mazda zur überragenden Figur, wobei allerdings die Volksfrömmigkeit noch deutlich polytheistische Züge tragen kann. Die Vorstellungen der sassanidischen Epoche dann schließen an die achämenidische Konzeption an, heben allerdings das dualistische Element etwas stärker hervor. Diese letzte vorislamische Epoche Persiens wird näher durch den Aufsatz de Jongs behandelt.

Die verbleibenden sechs Aufsätze des Bandes wenden sich den „Religionen in Kleinasien und Syrien-Palästina" zu: Daniel Schwemer, Das hethitische Reichspantheon. Überlegungen zu Struktur und Genese (241–65); Astrid Nunn, Aspekte der syrischen Religion im 2. Jahrtausend v.Chr.; Hermann Spieckermann, „Des Herrn ist die Erde." Ein Kapitel altsyrisch-kanaanäischer Religionsgeschichte (283–301); Erik Aurelius, „Ich bin der Herr, dein Gott." Israel und sein Gott zwischen Katastrophe und Neuanfang (325–45); Reinhard G. Kratz, „Denn dein ist das Reich." Das Judentum in persischer und hellenistisch-römischer Zeit (347–74). Der Blick bewegt sich dabei weg von den großen Hochkulturen hin zu den kleinen Staaten in der labilen Kontaktzone zwischen Mesopotamien und Ägypten, die in der Antike etwa in dem Maße unbedeutend war, wie sie in der Wirkungsgeschichte umgekehrt an Gewicht gewann und in diesem Band dann auch entsprechend breit behandelt wird. Anhand von Vertragstexten, Opferlisten und des berühmten Felsheiligtums von Yazilikaya versucht Schwemer im Wissen um die Fragmentarität der Quellen (und oft auch der Überbewertung von Yazilikaya) eine Rekonstruktion des hethitischen Pantheons. Quellenmäßig vergleichbar schwierig ist die Beschreibung der syrischen Religion im 2. Jahrtausend v.Chr., die Nunn vor allem mit Blick auf die Totenverehrung vornimmt. Einen sowohl geographisch wie chronologisch weitgespannten Überblick unternimmt Spieckermann mit seiner *tour de force* von Altanatolien bis Griechenland und von Altsyrien bis ins kanaanäische Syrien. Niehr beschreibt die vergleichsweise kleinräumigen religiösen Symbolsysteme der politisch fragmentierten Welt der phönizischen Stadtstaaten, wobei historische Entwicklungen festzustellen sind, namentlich mit dem Beginn der Expansion phönizischer Handelstätigkeit in den gesamten Mittelmeerraum vom 8. Jahrhundert an. Aurelius zeichnet den Weg des Gottesverständnisses im antiken Israel zum Monotheismus hin nach anhand von Texten aus dem Jahrhundert der Zerstörung Jerusalems durch die Babylonier. Er beleuchtet zunächst—mit einem Blick auf den Einfluss der Psalmentheologie— die in den Deuterojesaja-Texten vollzogenen theologischen Transformationen der vorexilischen Prophetentradition, die zur Vorstellung des einen Gottes führten. In einem zweiten Schritt behandelt er den Weg der deuteronomisch-deuterono-

mistischen Tradition zum Monotheismus. Kratz schließlich bespricht in seinem
Beitrag das Judentum in persischer und hellenistisch-römischer Zeit, das seinen
Weg zum Monotheismus bereits gefunden hat und diese Perspektive nun mit
seiner politischen Existenz unter fremder Herrschaft zusammendenken muss.
An den Beispielen der Quellenbestände aus den (mutmaßlichen) Archive in
Jerusalem, Elephantine, Alexandria und Qumran nimmt Kratz vier sich in
geographischer und historischer Hinsicht voneinander unterscheidende Quer-
schnitte der politischen Theologie des antiken Judentums vor.

III.

Im Ablauf gelesen gewinnt man von diesem Band vor allem den Eindruck, hier
werde anhand der Gottesvorstellungen antiker Kulturen eine Religionsgeschichte
der Alten Welt entworfen, deren Kapitel manchmal eher exemplarisch, manchmal eher überblicksartig ausfallen. Der Schluss des Vorworts verspricht den
Leserinnen und Lesern „reiches Material und substantielle Erkenntnisse" (xix).
Das leistet der erste Band (mitsamt dem zweiten [R.G. Kratz, H. Spieckermann,
eds., Götterbilder–Gottesbilder–Weltbilder. Polytheismus und Monotheismus in
der Welt der Antike, Band II: Griechenland und Rom, Judentum, Christentum
und Islam. FAT 2/18, Tübingen: Mohr Siebeck, 2006]) zweifellos, doch ist dieser
Gewinn vermutlich auch die elementarste Grenze der vorliegenden Sammlung.
Die Breite der Beiträge entspricht der Globalität der Fragestellung. Eine Summe
aus dem Gebotenen zu ziehen, bleibt den Leserinnen und Lesern überlassen.
Wenig berücksichtigt sind zudem—bis auf wenige skizzenhafte Andeutungen
im Vorwort—methodische oder systematische Fragen. Angesichts des dreifa-
chen Elements „-bilder" im Titel hätte etwa die Projektionsfrage zur kritischen
Reflexion eingeladen: Wie hilfreich ist die „Bilder"-Metaphorik bei der wissenschaftlichen Erfassung der untersuchten antiken Perspektiven auf Gott, Mensch
und Welt? Doch sollte man einen Sammelband genremäßig nicht wie eine Monographie beurteilen. Die einzelnen Beiträge sind lehrreich zu lesen, bezüglich ihrer
übergreifenden thematischen, kulturwissenschaftlichen, religionsgeschichtlichen
und theologischen Auswertung bleibt der erste (wie der zweite) Band ein gedie-
genes, aber offenes Kunstwerk.

Texts from the Pyramid Age, by Nigel C. Strudwick. Society of Biblical Literature Writings from the Ancient World 16. Atlanta: Society of Biblical Literature; Leiden: Brill, 2005. Pp. xxxvii + 522. Paper/cloth. $39.95/$237.00. ISBN
1589831381/9004130489.

Youri Volokhine, Université de Genève, Geneva, Switzerland

Ce recueil de textes, traduit et présenté par Nigel Strudwick, couvre la
période de l'Ancien Empire égyptien (environ 2700–2170 av. J.-C.); il vise à

refléter autant que possible la grande diversité des catégories de textes qui y sont attestés (à l'exception des textes funéraires issus du corpus des *Textes des Pyramides,* dont une traduction a été publiée récemment dans la même collection: J. Allen, *The Ancient Egyptian Pyramid Texts*). Ce sont donc pas moins de trois cent trente-trois textes et extraits de textes qui sont ici présentés au lecteur, ce qui, à ce jour, fait de ce volume le recueil de traductions le plus complet concernant cette période si faste de l'Egypte ancienne (voir également le précédent et excellent recueil de A. Roccati, *La Littérature historique sous l'Ancien Empire égyptien,* Paris, 1982, qu'il demeure utile de consulter). A quelques menues exceptions, on trouvera traduite l'intégralité des *Urkunden des Alten Reichs* (1933), l'exemplaire édition synoptique de Kurt Sethe (qui réunissait cent soixante-dix-neuf textes hiéroglyphiques en copie manuscrite), que l'A. a largement complété.

Les traductions sont précédées d'une assez longue introduction (1–63), où l'A. précise d'abord ses critères de sélection et de présentation, avant de faire une mise au point rapide sur différentes questions historiques et littéraires, exercice nécessaire à la compréhension de la littérature de l'Ancien Empire.

Les textes traduits ont été réunis dans plusieurs chapitres thématiques (de II à XXI) regroupant chacun une catégorie de textes, respectivement présentées dans l'introduction. Parcourons succinctement cette riche matière, en pointant certains documents présentant un intérêt tout particulier.

Le chapitre «Annales et listes royales» (II) regroupe les textes historiographiques. Ces textes—loin de recouper formellement ce que l'on attendrait d'une historiographie intellectuellement façonnée, dans la pensée occidentale, depuis Thucydide ou Tite-Live (comme le relève l'A. [34])—se présentent pour l'essentiel comme des listes royales, agrémentées de brèves notations cultuelles ou autres. Parmi les textes remarquables, on relèvera notamment la fameuse liste annalistique dite de la «Pierre de Palerme» et de ses fragments associés (n°1 [65–74]; traduction des sections concernant les IV et Ve dynasties), et les annales gravées sur le sarcophage de la reine Ankhesenpépi (n°3 [75–77]). Avec «Textes des temples» (III) , l'A. propose un choix des inscriptions provenant des rares temples préservés de l'Ancien Empire, dont ceux du temple funéraire de Sahourê à Abousir (n°10 [83–86]), ou les extraits du «calendrier des fêtes» du temple de Niouserrê à Abou Gurob (n°11 [86–91]). Les «Décrets royaux» (IV)—des copies sur pierre de règlements administratifs—présentent notamment le décret de Pépi Ier à Dachour (n° 20 [103–5]), les décrets de Pépi Ier, provenant des fouilles de Coptos (n°21–27 [105–15]), et ceux gravés (probablement) sous le règne de Neferkaouhor (n°31–38 [117–23]). Au côté de textes plus ou moins développés, on trouvera également un petit choix de textes courts, d'inscriptions lapidaires, consignés sur des objets divers (statues, vaisselle de pierre, sistre, jarres), rassemblés dans «Objets portant un nom royal» (V, n° 41–47 [129–33]).

Après ces différentes sections consacrées à des textes provenant de la sphère royale, l'A. a regroupé dans plusieurs chapitres distincts les inscriptions privées. Tout d'abord, les «Inscriptions d'expédition» (VI), c'est-à-dire les inscriptions lapidaires laissées par les fonctionnaires en mission (le plus souvent dans des car-rières plus ou moins éloignées de la vallée du Nil): parmi celles-ci, les inscriptions du Ouadi Hammamat, la route vers la Mer Rouge (n° 63–68 [140–45]), et celles des carrières de calcite d'Hatnoub (n°69–73 [145–49]) en Moyenne Egypte. Les «Marques de carriers et textes de phyle» (VII) concernent les différentes inscrip-tions faites par les tailleurs de pierre et par les équipes attelées à la construction des pyramides ou des tombes (n°78–86 [153–60]). Puis, les «Graffiti» (VIII), incluent encore quelques inscriptions que l'A. n'a pu ranger dans les catégories précédentes, dont les inscriptions du Ouadi Helal (région d'El Kab), laissées par les prêtres locaux (n° 88–89 [161]).

Les trois sections suivantes concernent des textes administratifs, juridiques, et des lettres, le plus souvent écrits sur papyrus. Avec les «Textes administra-tifs» (IX), l'A. présente une sélection des textes administratifs issus des papyrus du temple funéraire de Neferirkarê à Abousir (n°90–91 [165–73]). Ces papyrus, exemplairement publiés et commentés par Paule Posener-Kriéger (*Les archives du temple funéraire de Néferirkarê-Kakaï*, Le Caire, 1976), nous introduisent direc-tement à la vie des temples. Un chapitre consacré aux «Lettres» (X) regroupe des textes de nature bien différente: correspondance entre prêtres (n° 92, extraits des documents d'Abousir), protestation adressée à un vizir (n°94), accusation contre un certain Sabni d'Eléphantine (n°96), ou encore «lettre aux morts» (n°101 [182–83]), un genre particulier de texte qui, placé dans les tombes, invoquait l'aide des défunts, dont l'intervention *post-mortem* était requise dans diverses affaires impli-quant des membres de leur famille. L'édition précédente de E. Wente (*Letters from Ancient Egypt*, 1990) est complétée par le n°99 (180–81), extrait de la correspon-dance (sur tablette d'argile) des gouverneurs de l'oasis de Balat (Ayn Asil) (cf. L. Pantalacci, *BIFAO* 98 , 1998, 303–15). Le chapitre «Textes juridiques privés» (XI) présente des contrats et des transactions (par exemple pour un achat de maison, figurant dans les papyrus de Gebelein, n° 102 [185–86]), une dispute pour un héritage à Eléphantine (n° 103 [186–87]), ou des textes juridiques gravés dans des tombes. Parmi ceux-ci, on relèvera particulièrement les contrats passés avec les prêtres funéraires (bloc supposé de la tombe de Kaiemneferet, n° 106 [189–91]), les «décrets» de Metjen (n° 108 [192–94]), concernant ses propriétés funéraires, les inscriptions de la tombe de Nykaiankh (à Tehna) (n°110 [195–99]), détaillant la mise en œuvre du culte funéraire.

Les textes provenant du monde funéraire font encore l'objet de dix chapitres (XII à XXII). Les «Formules d'offrandes et titulatures» (XII) compilent un certain nombre de formules d'offrandes standardisées du type *hétep-di-nésout* («offrande qu'accorde le roi»), occasion de découvrir notamment les titulatures des défunts, ou les noms des fêtes rythmant le calendrier du culte funéraire. Les «Appels aux vivants et mises en garde» (XIII) regroupent les textes où figurent des invoca-tions dirigées à l'égard des visiteurs potentiels, les appelant à faire preuve de piété envers le défunt, en récitant les formules funéraires d'usage, voire les menaçant si, au contraire, ces derniers se montraient impies ou négligents. Les «Inscriptions commémoratives et dédicatoires» (XIV) rassemblent des textes courts, que l'A. a choisi de réunir parce qu'ils commémorent les actes de piété funéraire accomplis par un membre de la famille du défunt. Le chapitre «Textes relatif au paiement des ouvriers et à l'acquisition d'une tombe» (XV) est ensuite consacré à une série d'inscriptions permettant de mieux comprendre comment le projet d'un complexe funéraire privé pouvait être conçu.

Les deux sections suivantes concernant les textes dits «biographiques» (XVI et XVII [260–378]) sont particulièrement développées. L'A. a rassemblé ici les biographies funéraires; ces textes, inscrits dans les tombeaux privés dès l'Ancien Empire, constituent un genre étroitement conditionné par leur finalité, qui consiste à présenter une carrière idéale en vue de la mémoire sociale, indispensable à la survie dans l'au-delà. On peut, tout au long de l'Ancien Empire, suivre l'évolution formelle de ces textes; à la fin de la Ve dynastie, les textes des tombeaux memphites offrent déjà de larges développements. Dès la moitié de la VIe dynastie, les textes accordent une plus large place à la nature (louable) des actions de l'individu vis-à-vis de la société, en parallèle à sa carrière. Il serait vain cependant de chercher dans ces textes «(auto)biographiques», au sein desquels les clichés stylistiques abondent, autre chose qu'une forme standardisée de présentation de l'individu. Il serait vain également d'y rechercher des tentatives d'introspection psychologique dans un sens contemporain; néanmoins, ces textes illustrent comment «l'homme égyptien» se définit en regard de la norme sociale. Certains textes relèvent de la «biographie historique» (ou «événementielle»)—dans laquelle les hauts-faits de la carrière sont consignés—et d'autres se présentent comme des «biographies idéales», soulignant les vertus morales de la personne. Les textes les plus célèbres, relevant du premier genre, sont ceux de Ouni provenant d'Abydos (n° 256 [352–57]) et surtout ceux d'Herkhouf à Qoubbet el-Hawa (n°241 [328–33]), qui relatent sa mission en Afrique, et incluent la copie d'une lettre du jeune roi Pépi Ier, lequel exprime candidement son impatience à voir arriver dans son palais le nain (ou pygmée) que lui ramène l'expédition. Notons que l'A . a séparé les textes selon leur provenance, un chapitre (XVI [261–325]) étant consacré aux «Textes biographiques memphites», où l'on trouvera les textes les plus signifiants des tombes des notables à Saqqara, et un autre aux «Textes biographiques provenant des autres régions» (XVII [327–68]).

Un chapitre est encore tout spécialement dévolu aux «Textes de femmes» (XVIII [379–99])—séparé thématiquement pour corriger, selon l'A., une certaine perspective suivie par plusieurs générations de «male-orientated studies» (50–51)—où l'A. regroupe des inscriptions relatives aux reines, aux princesses, et aux personnes privées. Les scènes des tombes égyptiennes prennent parfois l'apparence de véritables «bandes dessinées»: aussi, l'A. a consacré un chapitre «Textes légendant les scènes figurées dans les tombes» (XIX) dans lequel il présente un choix de légendes de ces scènes «de la vie quotidienne»: scènes de musique, de travaux agricoles, de boucherie, d'artisanat, de bateliers, etc. Une «vie quotidienne» qui, en l'occurrence, devait être envisagée, à l'instar de tous les motifs funéraires, en vue des impératifs de la survie dans l'au-delà. Comme le rappelle l'A. (47), il se trouve que c'est tout spécialement par ces textes que nous avons un accès plus direct à la «parole» des Egyptiens—ce qui n'est pas sans poser nombre de problèmes d'interprétation. Un plus grand choix d'illustrations aurait sans doute été judicieux, tout particulièrement dans ce chapitre où l'image s'avère indispensable pour l'intelligence de la scène (notons que seulement sept figures aux traits sont incluses dans l'ensemble du volume). Enfin, les «Textes divers provenant des tombes» (XX) rassemblent des documents variés (inscriptions sur sarcophage, textes hiératiques peints sur pots (n°325 [426–27]), liste d'offrandes (dont la célèbre stèle de Neferetiabet, n°327 [430–31 et fig. 7]). Un «Addendum» (XXI) ajoute en dernier lieu deux textes récemment découverts (n° 332, tiré de la tombe de Péteti à Giza, et n° 333, texte biographique de Merefnebef à Saqqara).

L'intérêt de ce copieux recueil est de donner une image très précise de la documentation de l'Ancien Empire. Aussi, le lecteur sera-t-il confronté non seulement à des textes d'une importance historique capitale, mais également à des fragments d'inscriptions bien plus modestes. Abordant donc la matière textuelle de la société égyptienne de l'Ancien Empire dans toute sa diversité, ce volume offre un compagnon de travail bienvenu à quiconque s'intéresse à la culture de l'ancienne Egypte.

Le livre se clôt par une liste des sources, une bibliographie, un glossaire et des index. On regrettera cependant l'absence d'un index philologique, qui aurait pu être utile, étant donné qu'un certain nombre de termes sont discutés dans les notes qui suivent les différents chapitres. On trouvera enfin (521–22) une concordance entre le présent ouvrage et le recueil de sources copiées par K. Sethe dans ses *Urkunden I.*

Grâce à ce précieux volume, l'A. a offert au public le recueil le plus complet à ce jour sur les textes de l'Ancien Empire, idéalement présenté, un ouvrage de grande clarté que tout égyptologue consultera également avec profit.

LANGUAGES

The Cambridge Biblical Hebrew Workbook: Introductory Level, by Nava Bergman. New York: Cambridge University Press, 2005. Pp. xiii + 375. Paper. $32.99. ISBN 0521533694.

Joseph Cathey, Dallas Baptist University, Dallas, Texas

Frederick Greenspahn recently pointed out the rationale for the overabundance of Classical Hebrew grammars (see "Why Hebrew Textbooks Are Different from Those for Other Languages" at http://www.sbl-site.org/Article. aspx?ArticleId=420). For those of us who teach Hebrew, the declaration of an excess is nothing new. A cursory examination of current academic publishers yielded no less than twenty Classical Hebrew grammars published in the last decade. For a grammar to be worthy of inclusion upon one's shelf, the presentation of the elements of grammar must somehow offer either a new(er) pedagogy or research into the language itself. Bergman attempts to find a place in today's marketplace by employing not only the traditional tools of Classical Hebrew but also tools of modern language acquisition.

This book is the fruit of many years teaching both Modern and Biblical Hebrew at Göteborg University in Sweden. In essence, this book is the reworked English translation of *Bibelhebreiska för nybörjare: Övningsbok*. Bergman designed the *Workbook* as a part of a comprehensive study-kit that included a textbook, an intermediate workbook, and an audio CD.

The *Workbook* is designed around twenty-eight chapter (or sections) divisions. Bergman does a very good job of elucidating the grammar by selecting passages of different genres of biblical prose. Included are three appendices, the most helpful of which are "Guide to Grammatical Terms"; "Hebrew-English/English-Hebrew Vocabulary"; and "Key to Exercises." One may argue that one of the most helpful portions of a grammar is its answer key. It is pedagogically incumbent upon the professor to provide both exercises and answers so that students may evaluate their progress in real time.

The first twelve chapters of the *Workbook* can stand alone as a type of mini-Hebrew grammar. In these sections Bergman lays out the parameters of basic introduction to the language. She deals with the alphabet, pronunciation, the rules for the *dagesh*, vowels, syllables, *Qere/Kethib*, inseparable prepositions, conjunctions, pronouns, and nouns. Anyone who has taught Biblical Hebrew will find these first twelve chapters familiar in their presentation. However, Bergman adds an element that frankly has been missing for some time to Classical Hebrew grammars. For instance, she introduces the concept of utilizing Hebrew names as a familiar signpost for aid in memorizing vocabulary and grammar. What Bergman seeks to do is integrate Modern Hebrew and/or influences it has had upon the West to help the student not feel so foreign in the quest for a new(er) language. She notes that "Words that can be associated with well-known Hebrew names will be followed by the Hebrew name as pronounced in English in parentheses, preceded by a star symbol" (18).

Commencing in chapter 3 and continuing to the last chapter (ch. 28), the author has a consistent six-point methodology. First, the student is introduced to the main points of grammar. Usually Bergman summarizes each point of grammar with three to four sentences. Second, grammatical cornerstones are concisely presented in shaded boxes in order to highlight their significance. Bergman has set each box in a strategic location in order to hold the student's attention. Third, the grammatical cornerstones often are marked with bold caps print entitled "memorize," suggesting nonnegotiable foundations of Hebrew grammar. Under the heading "Hebrew via Hebrew Names," an elementary reading knowledge is facilitated via familiar Hebrew names. This element is not included in every chapter but is supplied in sixteen of the twenty-five chapters. Fourth, Bergman provides a review and application of the rules in which she elucidates the regular sound changes for newly introduced forms. The fifth point, a word list, is standard among Classical Hebrew grammars. Bergman divides the words into their respective parts of speech (e.g., nouns, pronouns, particles) and provides ancillary endings/spellings as well as a definition. The last point of methodology is the heart of any Classical Hebrew grammar: the exercises. Pedagogically, this part of the grammar is diverse but well thought out. One encounters the typical "fill-in-the-blanks," "translation into Hebrew from English," and "translation from Hebrew into English." In a few of the earlier lessons Bergman emphasizes transliteration. Likewise, she emphasizes in later sections sound-change rules and English-to-Hebrew translations.

In general, one may argue that it is best to shy away for "transliteration" because it does not help the student to actually grasp the language. Essentially, it can be argued that transliteration is only a crutch at best. However, there are those in the field of Classical Hebrew who still employ this teaching methodology, and it is presented well in Bergman's grammar. Her sections on sound changes within the language are quite helpful for students trying to learn a new language for the first time. Bergman notes that this workbook can function as a grammar by itself or supplemented by another grammar. She advises the teacher to "use the (additional grammar) textbook as a source for additional information and complete grammatical charts" (xii). Quite frankly, this suggestion baffles me. If one chose this grammar for the primary textbook, it would seem redundant to have students buy another textbook for the charts. Likewise, not all of Bergman's terms are the same as others within the academic field of Classical Hebrew (e.g., C. L. Seow, *Grammar for Biblical Hebrew*).

Bergman tries valiantly to help the student grasp the meaning of Classical Hebrew. In some measure she succeeds, but in others she falls short of her goal. In the area of verbs, more charts would be very helpful for guiding the student through stem and vowel changes. Bergman goes through the verbal rudiments in paragraph form and refers to appendices, but with today's visual students it would be more helpful for the charts to appear in each chapter. Today's technologically driven students would also benefit from the CD that accompanied the earlier form of this workbook. I believe that the CD along with the workbook would be a boon for students trying to master the language. The CD would reinforce some of Bergman's stronger points, such as the rationale for vowel changes in each of the nouns and verbal stems. While I do not think that Bergman lives up to Greenspahn's challenge, her grammar is not a failure in any sense of the word. Rather, in today's glutted market of Classical Hebrew grammars, many will thrive largely based on teacher/student reception and price competitiveness. It remains to be seen if Bergman can compete with the likes of older standard grammars such as Weingreen's *A Practical Grammar for Classical Hebrew,* Seow's *A Grammar for Biblical Hebrew,* or Kelley's *Biblical Hebrew: An Introductory Grammar.*

Mastering New Testament Greek: Essential Tools for Students, by Thomas A. Robinson. 3rd edition. Peabody, Mass.: Hendrickson, 2007. Pp. ix + 230. Paper. $19.95. ISBN 1565635760.

Robert E. Van Voorst, Western Theological Seminary, Holland, Michigan

For two generations of Greek students, the only published guide to learning New Testament Greek vocabulary was Bruce Metzger's *Lexical Aids for Students of New Testament Greek* (Princeton: self-published, 1946; 3rd ed., Grand Rapids: Baker, 1998). This venerable work lists common New Testament Greek words first by frequency alone, then in a shorter second section by cognate groups alone. Metzger intended that students use both parts in tandem (vii). However, anecdotal evidence suggests that most professors who have adopted this book regularly assign the frequency lists but do not regularly assign the section on cognate groups.

Two books appeared in 1990 to provide a better way to learn Greek vocabulary, with a focus on learning families of words related to a common root, while also taking frequency into account. Thomas Robinson authored *Mastering Greek Vocabulary* (Peabody, Mass.: Hendrickson, 1990; 2nd ed., 1991), and the present reviewer authored *Building Your New Testament Greek Vocabulary* (Grand Rapids: Eerdmans, 1990; SBLRBS 43; 3rd ed., Atlanta: Society of Biblical Literature, 2001). In 1992 a third work appeared, Warren Trenchard's *Student's Complete Vocabulary Guide to the Greek New Testament* (Grand Rapids: Zondervan; 2nd ed. issued in 1998 by the same publisher as *Complete Vocabulary Guide to the Greek New Testament*). Trenchard's work, seeking to be both a vocabulary learning tool and a reference guide, exhaustively lists all New Testament words by frequency alone, all New Testament words that are related by roots, and principal parts for all the verbs found in the New Testament. This work is not as pedagogically oriented as the other books discussed above, suggested by the dropping of the word "Student's" from the title of the new edition. Finally, in 2003 Mark Wilson with Jason Oden authored *Mastering New Testament Greek Vocabulary through Semantic Domains* (Grand Rapids: Kregel). Based on the semantic domain lexicon by Louw and Nida published in 1988 by the United Bible Societies, it lists all New Testament Greek words with a frequency of at least ten into one or more of ninety-three different semantic domains. Together these four recent books have encouraged a significant change in the teaching and learning of New Testament Greek vocabulary.

Now Robinson, of the University of Lethbridge, Alberta, has revised his book and retitled it *Mastering New Testament Greek: Essential Tools for Students*. The material carried over from the first and second editions is presented here largely unrevised. Section 1 is a list of "identical Greek and English words," in which most of the words are, strictly speaking, nearly identical (e.g., ἀπολογία, "apology"). Section 2, the heart of Robinson's book, is a 103-page list of New Testament words listed in their cognate groups, each group with its "root." Many roots have a "memory aid," an English derivative, where possible and appropriate. Also given for each Greek word are an indication of its frequency, its main English meaning, its part of speech, and an indication of how the word relates to its root. Section 3 succinctly explains the main relationships between Greek and English prefixes and suffixes. Section 4 follows this up with a list of "identical" (again, most of them nearly identical) prefixes and suffixes. Section 5, "Derived English Words," briefly explains most of the words given as examples in the "memory aid" parts of the main cognate lists. Section 6, the first new section in this revision, is a "mini Greek/English cognate dictionary" that gives the basic Greek cognate stem, the English basic meaning of the stem, key English cognates, and mnemonic words as a memory aid. Section 7, another new section, is "Prepositions and Cases," which gives helps for learning prepositions. Appendix 1 presents "Grimm's Law," which aids students to understand the phonetic shifts that occur from Greek to English. Appendix 2 presents common pronouns, adjectives, and adverbs. The next section, labeled index 1 and titled "Words Occurring 10–19 Times," lists words of those frequencies without cognates in the Greek New Testament, with their basic English meaning, part of speech, and an indication of how the word relates to its root. Another new part of this book is index 2, a thirty-eight-page list of all possible Greek verb endings, presented in reverse alphabetical order, working from the last letter of the verb ending backward. Robinson explains that it was "compiled solely to make it quick and easy for the reader of a Greek text to identify the ending of a puzzling word" (151). This section also contains a list of all inflected forms of the verb εἰμί in regular alphabetical order and three charts of participle endings, also for help in parsing. Finally, index 3, "Cognate Group Terms," gives page number references to all the words and roots listed in the main section of the book.

This book includes a CD-ROM entitled "Greek Tools" formatted for both Mac OS X and Windows. Both formats install easily and quickly and work well technically. It contains six modules: the first on writing and pronouncing the Greek alphabet; the second on pronouncing key words illustrating the different sounds of Greek; third, an interactive vocabulary review and quiz keyed to three common textbooks (by Mounce, Hewitt, and Wenham); fourth, an interactive exercise reviewing Greek verbs, with emphasis on parsing information; fifth, a "Greek Word Deconstruction" offering parsing analysis of words or word endings the student types in; and sixth, a web-based "Greek Internet Grammar," "intended to provide a non-technical, jargon-free, basic first-year grammar. Simplicity and clarity are our major aims, and diagrams, memory aids and translation tips are included wherever they may help." This module is "under construction," and the CD-ROM program links at the time of this review to http://people.uleth. ca/~robinson/GIG/ GIGindex.html. If this module when finished does indeed offer the equivalent of a good first-year Greek textbook in an interactive, web-based platform, this alone would justify the purchase of the book and make it appealing to many students and professors.

On the whole, this book is well-conceived and well-written. It is printed in a clear, inviting format. Robinson is a seasoned teacher of Koine Greek, and professors and students appreciate his practical approach. Previous editions have demonstrated their worth in many classrooms, and this revision will make *Mastering New Testament Greek* even more useful. The CD-ROM resources, although not tied directly to the sections of the book, will be pedagogically helpful to those in first-year Greek.

Several suggestions can be offered for the next revision of this work. First, it would be helpful to many students if the "Explanation of Greek Prefixes and Suffixes" section and the "Identical Greek/English Prefixes and Suffixes" section were put before the main cognate grouping of Greek words in the present section 2. Learning the basics of word-building before studying the words in cognate groups would be more efficient, and the organization of the book would do well to suggest that order. Second, since index 1 and index 2 are not indices in the common contemporary sense (as is Robinson's index 3), but rather contain material to be studied, these could be renamed appendix 3 and appendix 4. Third, Robinson includes thirty-one words without any cognates in his section 2, "Cognate Groups." These would fit better, at least more consistently and with less puzzlement to the student, in a reworked section presenting all the words without cognates, no matter what their frequency. Fourth, more careful presentation should be made already in section 2 of the different meanings that prepositions have depending on the case they take. For example, it may be ambiguous or confusing to some students to read only that "διά (gen, acc)" mean "through, on account of" (18). Finally, the new title of this revised book claims too much. Although using this book and its CD-ROM carefully will indeed lead the student to "Mastering Greek Vocabulary," which was the title of the first and second editions, it will not lead to "Mastering New Testament Greek," because there is much more to Greek than learning how to write, pronounce, memorize, and understand an extensive Greek vocabulary. Mastery of Greek typically takes more than the first-year study than this book can offer, even when supplemented with the "Greek Internet Grammar."

This volume and CD-ROM have been rather carefully edited and proofread, but some small mistakes, correctable in a second printing, are bound to slip through in a work such as this. On page 5, item 9 should probably read "Prefix, Root, Suffix." On page 7, the introductory paragraph to "Identical Greek/English Words" should note that prepositional prefixes are also included in this list, even though they are not words. On page 11, αὐτός, –η, –ον does not only mean "self," but also commonly "he, she, it" or "same." On page 13, ἐπέρχομαι should be accented on the second syllable. On page 15, γενεαλογέομαι should not have "to" in its definition, so that it will align with the definition of other verbs. Also on page 15, the extra smooth breathing and accent in ἔκγονον needs to be eliminated. On pages 54 and 204, δεκαοκτώ should be spelled as one word. On page 59, the words of the σωζ cognate group should be combined with the words of the σωτηρ cognate group on page 74; the Greek "save," "salvation," "savior," and so forth are true cognates. On page 82, δεξιός could be more helpfully defined as "right (opposite of left)." On page 91, "Copts" and "Greeks" should be italicized.

On page 101, "[δε]" should be added after "[ου]" in the explanation of οὐδέπω. On page 129, the word "different" in the third line from the top needs a parenthesis in front of it. On page 132, the entry for "paternity" should read that it is from the French *paternité* by way of the Latin *paternus*, a cognate to the Greek πατήρ. On page 134, the Greek origin of the first part of "pornographic" is from πόρνη, "prostitute," not (at least etymologically) from "evil." On page 148, in both charts the column heading "original letter" should be omitted. On the "Greek Tools" CD, the second module, which deals with speaking Greek, would be more effective if accents were added to the words for students to notice in reading and pronunciation; they currently have only breathing marks. Pronunciation of the Greek letter χ should be made consistent in that same module; sometimes it is the *ch* sound in the German "machen," sometimes the *k* sound in the English "make." Finally, the sound for the diphthong ευ should be the sound of the *eu* in "feud" rather than the *oo* in "moose." These relatively few mistakes in the book and CD do not diminish its strengths.

On the whole, this revised book is a very good resource for students who are in at least their second semester of New Testament Greek and able to make a shift from learning vocabulary as it is presented in their main textbook to a specialized vocabulary learning book that works with cognates. That the market can support four relatively new books for learning the Greek vocabulary of the New Testament by frequency and cognate is a sign that the in-depth study of New Testament Greek is alive and well and that learning New Testament Greek vocabulary this way is an appealing practice to many. Professors who have adopted, or who are thinking about adopting, a Greek vocabulary learning book combining frequency and cognate should examine the current editions of these four recent books to see which is best for their own courses.

Untersuchungen zur verbalen Valenz im biblischen Hebräisch, by Michael Malessa. Studia Semitica Neerlandica 49. Assen: Van Gorcum, 2006. Pp. xiii + 248. Hardcover. €85.00. ISBN 9023242408.

Christo H. J. van der Merwe, University of Stellenbosch, Stellenbosch, South Africa

This publication is Malessa's doctoral dissertation that he defended in May 2003 at the University of Leiden, with Prof. T Muraoka as his promoter. Malessa's investigation has a clear focus, namely, to describe and explain the formal differences between the complements (Verbergänzungen) of a selection of Biblical Hebrew verbs.

In the first part of chapter 1 Malessa formulates and richly illustrates the problem he investigates, that one and the same verbal lexeme may govern complements of which the formal features differ, but the reason(s) for the differences are not always clear. The different formal features are often listed in lexica. However, the semantic implications of these differences are seldom systematically

treated. Grammars do not pay much attention to the valency patterns of individual verbal lexemes, since they are more interested in the global structure of
the language. Malessa hypothesizes that an empirical investigation of the valency
pattern of specific classes of verbs in terms of a well-justified linguistic model
would help one to identify the syntactic, semantic, and/or historical-linguistic
considerations that account for these differences. In the second part of the chapter, Malessa explains and justifies his theoretical frame of reference, in which the
notions "dependency" and "valency" play a pivotal role. It is clear that he has a
thorough knowledge of the rich tradition of application of these notions to the
description of German. This allows him (1) to enter into a critical discourse with
Wolfgang Richter's use of the notion of "valency" in the description of Biblical
Hebrew, and (2) to formulate his own, but in no way idiosyncratic, set of complements and adjuncts for the description of Biblical Hebrew verbal lexemes.

In chapters 2–6 Malessa addresses the following issues: the different ways
objects are marked in general, for example, sometimes using אֵת־, sometimes
using לְ, and sometimes not using any formal marker (ch. 2); reasons for the similarity in the paradigmatic distribution of בְּ and the "normal" way of marking
objects of some verbs (ch. 3); the implications of the different types of constituents of verbs of observation (ch. 4); the difference between cases where infinite
complements are preceded by לְ and cases where לְ is absent (ch. 5); and the differences in the valency of verbs of speaking, or *verba dicendi* (ch. 6). In chapter 7
Malessa summarizes the findings of his study as far as the syntax, semantics, and
diachronic dimensions of Biblical Hebrew are concerned.

Before empirically investigating all occurrences of eleven frequently occurring lexemes in Genesis to 2 Kings in chapter 2, which provide a representative
sample of lexemes that occur more than fifty times in the Hebrew Bible in 1
Samuel to 2 Kings and a corpus of late Hebrew texts, Malessa points out some lin-
guistic-typological observations important for his analysis, such as that Biblical
Hebrew is a so-called nominative language, the language having a formal object
marker. As in many other languages, the morpheme used for the latter purposes,
אֵת־, is typically the one that marks the constituent with the recipient semantic role. When this morpheme precedes a direct object, it is positively marked,
and when it is not used, the direct object is negatively marked as direct object.
Although the prototypical use of אֵת is that of an "analytic object marker," it
does not mean it cannot fulfill other functions as well (31 n. 31). In his empirical analysis Malessa investigates a range of factors that may have—or have been
claimed to have—a bearing on the use of אֵת־. He then finds the following: (1)
the fronting of an object has no bearing on whether it is marked or not; (2) the
presence or absence of an explicit subject does not have any influence on the
marking of an object; (3) directs objects that do not immediately follow the verb
that governs them because of an intervening other constituent are marked in
significantly more cases than those that immediately follow the verb; (4) direct
objects with the semantic features +human are more often marked by אֵת
than those which have the semantic features –human, +concrete, or –human,

+abstract; and (5) the use of אֶת־ to mark direct objects declined in late Hebrew, its role being taken over by לְ. However, this is not phenomenon that is limited to late Hebrew. The process of using לְ had already started in earlier phases of the language.

In chapter 3 Malessa looks for reasons why a group of verbs in some instances govern objects with the preposition בְּ and in other cases not. He first hypothesizes that the answer lies in the type of activity (Aktionsart) and affectedness of the object and then verifies his hypothesis by illustrating that verbs with the preposition בְּ tend to be durative and that the sentences involved are less transitive than cases without the preposition. In the latter cases, the type of activity tends to be "graduell-terminative," and a higher degree of transitivity is displayed. When applying these insights to verbs of observation (*verba sentiendi*) he finds that in instances where the objects are preceded by בְּ, the verbs are durative with subjects that act intentionally. This is in contrast to cases where בְּ is not used. The activity is inchoative-static or durative, but the subjects do not act intentionally.

Although the findings of chapter 4 may be less definite than those of chapters 2 and 3, Malessa provides valuable evidence as far as the use of infinitives as objects is concerned. He establishes that the use of לְ before the infinitive has no semantic grounds, that the use or nonuse of the preposition is governed by dialectic or stylistic reasons, and that in late Hebrew the infinitive is always used with the preposition לְ.

The difference in the valency patterns of frequently occurring verbs of speaking (*verba dicendi*) is the topic of chapter 6, which investigates reasons why the addressee of the verb אמר is sometimes introduced by אֶל and sometimes by לְ. Refuting some sociolinguistically oriented explanations, Malessa provides convincing evidence that אֶל is used in the earlier phases of Biblical Hebrew predominantly when reference to the addressee does not immediately follow the verb, while לְ occurs primarily when the reference to the addressee immediately follows the verb. The explanation for this phenomenon most probably is the fact that אֶל is semantically more specific than לְ and is less prone to ambiguity than לְ when used later in a clause. In late Hebrew, however, the use of אֶל declined significantly.

In my opinion, Malessa has made a significant contribution to the description of Biblical Hebrew verbal patterns. His work displays a thorough knowledge of current insights in this aspect of Biblical Hebrew. I appreciate the way in which he interacts with the insights of fellow scholars using representative examples from his corpus to confirm or refute proposed solutions. Malessa consistently backs up his own claims with evidence in terms of the distribution of a particular construction. He is also not afraid to point out instances where he is uncertain and that need further investigation. I think this book illustrates the value of taking the valency patterns of verb seriously, and Malessa does this in a scholarly and exemplary way.

ARCHAEOLOGY

Greco-Roman Culture and the Galilee of Jesus, by Mark Chancey. Society for New Testament Studies Monograph Series 134. New York: Cambridge University Press, 2006. Pp. xvii + 283. Hardcover. $90.00. ISBN 0521846471.

Jonathan L. Reed, University of La Verne, La Verne, California

Chancey's most recent book follows his earlier *Myth of a Gentile Galilee* (Cambridge: Cambridge University Press, 2002) in arguing that Galilee was not nearly as Gentile, Hellenized, or Romanized at the time of Jesus as some New Testament scholars would have us believe. Chancey forcefully combines literary and archaeological evidence to show that Galilee was not only overwhelmingly Jewish, but also that it had never been as Hellenized as the coastal cities of Palestine or the Decapolis and would not be subjected to a thorough Roman-styled urbanization until Hadrian's reign, when Roman legions were stationed at nearby Legio. Two important methodological strategies permeate *Greco-Roman Culture and the Galilee of Jesus*. First, the archaeological evidence from Galilee is always situated within the context of developments in neighboring areas and the wider Roman East, which underscores Hellenism's limited penetration in Galilee by the first century C.E. Second, archaeological artifacts are always treated within their chronological framework, resulting in a clear contrast between Antipas's modest urbanization at Sepphoris and Tiberias and their more intensive Roman-styled architecture after the second century C.E. These two criteria, one regional and comparative and the other stratigraphic and chronological, provide the basis for Chancey's critique of much New Testament scholarship on Galilee.

After a brief introduction, the book's argument unfolds in eight chapters. The first four advance the thesis in a more or less historical sequence, from Alexander the Great in the Early Hellenistic period to the Severans in the Late Roman period. "Galilee's Early Encounter with Hellenism" (24–42) stresses the paucity of evidence and that some Hellenistic aspects were mediated through the Hasmoneans; "The Roman Army in Palestine" (43–70) highlights the fact that no Roman forces were permanently stationed in Galilee until well after Jesus' death; "The Introduction of Greco-Roman Architecture" (71–99) describes Galilean urbanization in its infancy under Antipas, who introduced limited aspects of Greco-Roman architecture; and "The Transformation of the Landscape in the Second and Third Centuries CE" (100–121) shows how most evidence for Greco-Roman culture in Galilee dates to after Hadrian, when the entire Levant was thoroughly Romanized. In this latter chapter and throughout, Chancey displays a sophisticated appreciation of the complex relationship between Hellenization and Romanization. To oversimplify his nuanced treatment, Rome was ultimately the vehicle for the Hellenization of Galilee.

Chapters 5–7 then deal with types of evidence, mostly archaeological, and often with a friendly repetition of artifacts that had been previously mentioned in a cursory manner. "The Use of Greek in Jesus' Galilee" (122–65) provides a methodologically sophisticated discussion of the epigraphic evidence and concludes that Greek was quite limited in Galilee; "The Coinage of Galilee" (166–92) contrasts the selective adaptation of Greco-Roman numismatic practices of Antipas with their wholesale adoption in the second–third centuries; and "Greco-Roman Art and the Shifting Limits of Acceptability" (193–220) shows how decorative items from the broader Mediterranean world made some inroads in first-century Galilee, which nevertheless remained, using Steven Fine's term, "anti-idolic."

The book concludes (221–29) with an eye toward the historical Jesus. Even though the extent of Greco-Roman culture is exaggerated by many scholars, Chancey notes that already under Antipas "we see hints of what was later to come" and that Antipas was a "time of transition," with daily reminders of Rome's power, even if indirectly. Thus the study concludes: "Recent scholarship has rightly emphasized that his proclamation of an alternative kingdom, the Kingdom of God, must be understood within the context of a people aware that the imperial shadow that had already fallen on Judea would one day likely cover Galilee as well" (229).

There are two concerns with this otherwise fine book, neither or which undermines its basic thesis. One is that Chancey tends to exaggerate the extent to which advocates of the "maximalist" Greco-Roman Galilee ever formed a scholarly consensus. He does so with an amalgamation of citations from scholars as diverse as Martin Hengel, Howard Clark Kee, and John Dominic Crossan. My own reading of the scholarly majority is different, and I think, in fact, that Chancey emerges from and with this book buttresses the consensus position for a "minimalist" Greco-Roman Galilee at the time of Jesus. In his introduction, Chancey states that "despite occasional claims to the contrary, Galilee's population in the first century was predominantly Jewish, with gentiles only a small minority. Scholars like Eric M. Meyers, E. P. Sanders, and Sean Freyne have long advocated this position, and recent studies by Peter Richardson and Mordechai Aviam, Jonathan L. Reed and myself confirm it" (19). I think those same scholars form a consensus with Chancey that Galilean Jews were minimally Hellenized in the first century and that Greco-Roman style urbanization was only in its infancy under Antipas. A similar conclusion focusing on socioeconomic data, which is beyond the scope of Chancey's examination, has been convincingly articulated by Moren Hørning Jensen's *Herod Antipas in Galilee: The Literary and Archaeological Sources on the Reign of Herod Antipas and its Socio-economic Impact on Galilee* (WUNT 2/215; Tübingen: Mohr Siebeck, 2006).

The second and more troublesome problem is how Chancey juxtaposes archaeological and textual evidence throughout the book. Although archaeology tends to be privileged, often texts and artifacts are fused, especially in the earlier chapters, to write a history of Galilee. The reader is not always sure of the extent to which Chancey trusts Josephus, especially in relation to the archaeological evidence. For example, apparently Tarichaea *did* have an amphitheater, as Josephus says, in spite of the lack of archaeological evidence (97), but apparently the Roman legate Varus *did not* utterly destroy Sepphoris in 4 B.C.E., given the lack of archaeological evidence (83). It is not so much that Chancey is inconsistent, just that the reader is never quite sure what position he takes on some specific passages. His treatment of the New Testament is at times similar, such as when he says "at least one follower of Jesus had a Latin name or nickname, if Acts 1:23 is trusted." Should we? It seems not, given the chapter's conclusion concerning the archaeological absence of Latin in first-century Galilee. Chancey does not always make his positions on textual interpretations clear; perhaps he is simply cautious.

In spite of these concerns, *Greco-Roman Culture and the Galilee of Jesus* is certain to be of enduring value to historical Jesus scholarship. It is well written, clearly organized, and contains a wealth of archaeological evidence with which too many New Testament scholars are still unfamiliar. It also pushes New Testament scholars to examine studies by historians working in the fields of classics and classical archaeology, such as Clifford Ando, Warwick Ball, Jane Webster, and Greg Woolf, whose voices must be heard if trends in the Roman East during the early empire that impact Christian origins are to be understood. Finally, Chancey asks the question in his *Greco-Roman Culture and the Galilee of Jesus* in such a way that should prove fruitful for scholars of Jewish history generally. As he notes in his conclusion, "we scholars have been quicker to recognize the diversity in the *Judaism* of Hellenistic Judaism than in the *Hellenism* of Hellenistic Judaism" (229). That approach bore much fruit as Chancey focused on Galilee in the first century and in light of Roman imperialism.

Herod Antipas in Galilee: The Literary and Archaeological Sources on the Reign of Herod Antipas and Its Socio-economic Impact on Galilee, by Morten Hørning Jensen. Wissenschaftliche Untersuchungen zum Neuen Testament 2/215. Tübingen: Mohr Siebeck, 2006. Pp. xvi + 316. Paper. €59.00. ISBN 3161489675.

Mark A. Chancey, Southern Methodist University, Dallas, Texas

One of the chief insights of the Third Quest for the historical Jesus is that to understand Jesus, one must understand Galilee. Increasingly, scholars have also recognized that to understand Galilee, one most understand the impact of the reign of its Herod Antipas. Despite this insight, however, Herod Antipas has been the object of surprisingly few in-depth examinations. Morten Hørning Jensen's monograph is the first book-length treatment of him to appear in over three decades (the last was Harold W. Hoehner's 1972 *Herod Antipas* [SNTSMS 17; Cambridge: Cambridge University Press, 1972]) and will become a milestone in studies of both Antipas and Galilee.

Jensen's extensive review of not only the pertinent ancient literary sources but also excavation reports sets it apart from earlier discussions of Herod Antipas. He focuses on the socioeconomic condition of early first-century c.e. Galilee, particularly urban-rural relations. He convincingly demonstrates that recent scholarly claims that the reign of Antipas resulted in the impoverishment of the Galilean countryside have little basis in the currently available evidence. His work stands as a particularly significant challenge to studies espousing views of Galilee that are based more on the presuppositions of particular social-scientific models than on careful review of the actual data.

The book is a slightly revised version of Jensen's 2005 Aarhus University dissertation, written under the direction of Per Bilde. It consists of eight chapters, a twenty-five-page bibliography, twenty-nine figures of various types (maps of regions and individual sites; photographs and drawings of coins, structural remains, and other archaeological finds; charts of data), and indices of references to ancient sources, modern authors, and subjects.

Jensen devotes chapters 1 and 2 to the history of scholarship regarding both Antipas and the historical Jesus and to method, describing how his own approach differs from earlier studies. He rightly notes that "Herod Antipas has increasingly become a 'factor of explanation and verification' of the various presentations of his Galilee" (9). Jensen affirms the emerging consensus that "the Galilee of Antipas was *not* as Hellenized as anywhere else in the Roman world" (45). Nonetheless, he argues, "Antipas has emerged as *the* decisive factor of explanation of the socio-economic realities of early-first-century Galilee" (46). Jensen points out that "the different use of [socio-scientific] models seems to predetermine the different views on the urban-rural relationship" (34), contrasting studies that depict harmonious urban-rural relations with those that view those relations as conflicted. In regard to the latter, he points to studies (i.e., those of John Dominic Crossan and Jonathan Reed; Richard A. Horsley; and William E. Arnal) that argue that the ruler's policies—particularly his construction of the cities of Sepphoris and Tiberias, his level of taxation, his minting of coinage, and his purported commercialization of Galilee—created an economic crisis that prompted the activity of Jesus and his movement. He describes his own approach as a "source-oriented method" that examines ancient references to Antipas within their own literary contexts and that interprets archaeological data from Galilee within a larger regional perspective.

Jensen provides a thorough review of the literary evidence regarding Herod Antipas in chapters 3 and 4, discussing not only Josephus and the New Testament but also Nicolaus of Damascus, Strabo, Philo, Tacitus, Justin Martyr, and Dio Cassius. He makes greater use of Josephus scholarship than most other studies of Galilee and carefully differentiates between the emphases of that historian's various works. He argues that Josephus's negative attitude toward Antipas should be understood as part of his larger portrayal of the Herodian dynasty as rulers who were insensitive to Jewish law and tradition: "Josephus wants to present Antipas as another example of a bad Herodian ruler who was not able to safeguard the ancient and stable Jewish way of life" (99). However, despite his negative tone toward Antipas, Josephus provides few specific examples of his tyranny (the execution of Jon the Baptist being an obvious exception). Thus, "*Antipas was by no means remarkable either in deeds or misdeeds*" (100, emphasis original). The ancient sources largely agree in depicting Antipas as having mostly positive relations with both Jerusalem and Rome. Despite the relative stability of his reign, which had no internal uprisings, Antipas never received the title "king" or "ethnarch" from the emperor, a slight that Jensen interprets as evidence of the ruler's mediocrity.

Chapter 5, the longest in the book, reviews the archaeological record, drawing on both published and unpublished information. Jensen carefully sifts through the data for Sepphoris and Tiberias, differentiating the modest early-first-century remains from those of earlier and later periods. For each, the greatest growth occurred in the Middle and Late Roman periods, not the first century c.e. For comparison, he examines several nearby rural sites (Yodefat/Jotapata, Cana, Capernaum, and Gamla, a site in the Golan Heights with historical and cultural connections with Galilee) and neighboring cities (Caesarea Maritima and the Decapolis cities of Hippos, Gadara, and Scythopolis). Far from showing any signs of decline in the decades prior to the First Revolt, the rural communities appear to have been flourishing, with public buildings, upper-class residences, and varied industrial and agricultural activity. The discussion of neighboring cities shows that Sepphoris and Tiberias were modest in comparison, smaller in size, with fewer monumental public buildings. "Antipas, rather than imposing real novelties, brought Galilee up to date with some of the infrastructure already known in the area" (185). Jensen's analysis seriously undermines claims that Antipas's construction programs were massive in scale and led to the economic devastation of Galilean villages by draining away their resources.

Chapter 6 is devoted to an investigation of the coins of Antipas, focusing on their messages (i.e., images and inscriptions) and circulation in comparison with the coins of the Hasmoneans, the procurators, and other Herodian rulers. In line with other studies, he emphasizes the lack of anthropomorphic and zoomorphic imagery on Antipas's coinage as evidence for the ruler's respect for the Jewish prohibition of figural imagery. Jensen's investigation of monetary circulation relies heavily on research by Danny that demonstrates that Antipas minted only a small number of coins. Major changes in the amount of currency in Galilee occurred in the Hasmonean and Middle Roman periods, not the first century c.e.—a fact that weakens assertions that Antipas tried to monetize the economy to facilitate tax collection and debt accumulation.

The final two chapters synthesize Jensen's findings. Antipas, in his estimation, was a "minor Roman client ruler, unremarkable in both successes and failures" (242), "a minor ruler with a moderate impact" (254). Neither the ancient literary sources nor the archaeological data provide clear support for the view that his reign was characterized by economic crisis. Indeed, "it seems indisputable that the rural area was able to sustain its livelihood and even expand it in this period" (247). At least as reflected in the archaeological record, the most significant changes in Galilean society occurred well before and after the reign of Antipas. Thus, hypotheses suggesting that Jesus' activity is best explained as a response to the economic conditions created by Herod Antipas are "too bold and unwarranted. Too much is explained with too little" (259).

My critiques of the book are all minor. More interaction with narrative-critical studies of the Gospels would further strengthen Jensen's consideration of ancient literary references to Herod Antipas. Likewise, his argument for the historicity of Luke's report that Herod Antipas questioned Jesus (23:6–12) would profit from more detail. The overview of the population of Tiberias (136) should be supplemented with Josephus's reference to the massacre of the Greek residents there at the start of the Revolt (*Vita* 67). Lastly, the work exhibits a fair amount of repetition, particularly in its frequent summary sections.

Such criticisms are mere quibbles. This is an important study, one that no scholar writing on the cultural climate of first-century Galilee or the historical Jesus can afford to ignore. It is a fine exemplar of thoroughness and nuance and will quickly become the standard reference work on Herod Antipas's impact on the region. Those who would disagree with Jensen's findings are faced with the daunting task of resifting through the evidence to find support for their own position. The work's significance is broader than Galilean studies, however. It highlights the types of problems that occur when application of theoretical models is not accompanied by extensive review of the actual evidence.

HEBREW BIBLE/OLD TESTAMENT: GENERAL

The Origins of the 'Second' Temple: Persian Imperial Policy and the Rebuilding of Jerusalem, by Diana Edelman. BibleWorld. London: Equinox, 2005. Pp. xvi + 440. Paper. $29.95. ISBN 1845530179.

Albert L. A. Hogeterp, University of Leuven, Leuven, Belgium B-3000

This book by Diana Edelman, senior lecturer in the Department of Biblical Studies at the University of Sheffield, contests a scholarly consensus up to the 1990s that Ezra 1–6, Haggai, and Zechariah can be relied upon for information about the "origins" of the Second Temple. These biblical texts presuppose 515 B.C.E. as the date when the exiles returned to Jerusalem and rebuilt its temple and 445 B.C.E. as the date when Jerusalem became fortified (7–8). According to Edelman's challenging hypothesis, historical priority should instead be accorded to the claim in the book of Nehemiah "that the resettlement of Jerusalem only took place during the governorship of Nehemiah, which began in the twentieth year of Artaxerxes, 444 BCE." Concomitantly, Edelman holds that the rebuilding of the temple and Jerusalem's fortification took place at the same time (8). After a concise introduction (1–12), Edelman elaborates her hypothesis, discussing the literary evidence of Nehemiah, Haggai–Zech 8, and Ezra 1–6 in the respective chapters 1 (13–79), 2 (80–150), and 3 (151–208), while turning more specifically to the archaeological evidence about Yehud's boundaries and its settlement patterns in chapters 4 (209–80) and 5 (281–331). A final, sixth, chapter (332–51) synthesizes insights drawn from the previous chapters.

· Chapter 1, "When Generations Really Count: Dating Zerubbabel and

Nehemiah Using Genealogical Information in the Book of Nehemiah," does a meticulous job of historical identification of generations on the basis of a list of priests and Levites in Neh 12:1–26. The combined reference to Persian military (2:9) and Jewish civil (7:2) appointments in Jerusalem constitutes important evidence for Edelman's hypothesis (26–27). Edelman concludes from the genealogical information and the chronological information in Elephantine papyrus *AP* 30 that Nehemiah belonged to generation 3, while the return from exile under Zerubbabel and Yeshua (generation 2) should be dated around 465 B.C.E. (75). A critical point should be made with regard to Neh 7:6–72. While this genealogical list of returned exiles appears to be less relevant for the discussion (36, 37, 39, 74, 77), Edelman does not give due emphasis to the fact that Neh 7:6–72 and Ezra 2 present parallel versions. The differences—which can be discerned between Ezra 2:2 and Neh 7:7; Ezra 2:10 and Neh 7:15; Ezra 2:17–20 and Neh 7:22-25; Ezra 2:30 having no equivalent in Neh 7:6-73; and Ezra 2:50 and Neh 7:52—need to be accounted for in a discussion about generations starting with the return from exile. This is not to deny the otherwise richly documented character of Edelman's discussion, which pays detailed attention to the ways in which historical information may be derived from both literary and documentary sources, including papyri, inscriptions, coins, and bullae.

Chapter 2, "What's in a Date? The Unreliable Nature of the Dates in Haggai and Zechariah," analyzes Haggai–Zech 8, deferring discussion of Ezra 1–6 to chapter 3 in view of the literary dependence of the latter on the former. Edelman puts the divergent references to the date of the temple-building in the books of Haggai (Hag 1:1, 15; 2:1, 10, 20) and Zechariah (Zech 1:1, 7; 7:1) in perspective. The dating formulae are first compared to Judean, Assyrian, Neo-Babylonian, Persian, Seleucid, and Ptolemaic contexts (82–90). Examples of Persian dating practices include the Behistun inscription, whose English translation is presented in appendix 1 (353–361). Edelman explains the various dates in Haggai and Zechariah in view of prophetic genre conventions (90–106), observing that they deliberately fit "Jeremiah's prophecies in 25.11–12; 27.6–7" (106) and 29:10 (95) about the seventy-year wrath of God against the people of Israel and the land. It may be added here that Dan 9:2 most explicitly refers to Jeremiah's prophecy. The author further reconsiders the "month and day-elements in the date formulae" in Haggai (107–23) and Zech 1–8 (123–31), as well as the "internal organization of Haggai and Zechariah 1–8 as temple-building accounts" (131–39). Edelman concludes that "the dates are secondary and are used in part as a way to interrelate the two texts" (131). She explains the insertion of the seventy-year tradition from the distance in time in the "common collective memory," when the combined edition of Haggai–Zechariah 8 was composed, roughly 325–275 B.C.E. (146).

Chapter 3, "It's All in the Sources: The Historicity of the Account of Temple-Rebuilding in Ezra 1–6," provides new answers to historical problems surrounding the account of Cyrus's commission of rebuilding, the delay in the completion of the temple, and the opposition to the rebuilding of Jerusalem in Ezra 1–6 (154–59). Edelman explains the first two problems in light of the diversity of biblical sources used by the author of Ezra. According to Edelman, these sources are Second Isaiah (Isa 44:28), the books of Chronicles, Jeremiah, Haggai–Zech 8, Nehemiah, and Ezek 40–48, while the Cyrus Cylinder provides further contextual information for Cyrus's policy of religious restoration (163–66 and appendix 2 [362–63]). On the other hand, she contests the scholarly assumption that historical sources underlie Ezra 1:2–5 and the Aramaic documents in Ezra 4:11–16, 17–22; 5:7–17; 6:2–5, 6–12 (180–201), attributing a "later, editorial origin" to the section on opposition to rebuilding in Ezra 4:6–24 (159), and thereby removes the basis for the evaluation of Ezra 1–6 as an independent historical source.

Chapter 4, "Setting the Bounds: The Territory Comprising Yehud under Artaxerxes I in the Mid-Fifth Century BCE," examines the biblical evidence in Neh 3; 7:6–69; and 11:25–35 (210–32), the artifactual evidence of jar stamps (233–38), and the relation between literary and archaeological evidence (238–75). Edelman suggests that the control over the Beersheva Valley and the Negev, exerted by Jerusalem before 586 B.C.E., was reassigned from Edom to Jerusalem by Artaxerxes I as part of the mid-fifth-century redevelopment of the province of Yehud (275–76). According to Edelman, the evidence of Nehemiah does not provide an accurate account of the boundaries of Yehud (233, 275), while the evaluation of archaeological evidence demonstrates the historical unreliability of other prophetic indications, such as in Second Isaiah (276). Yet it is unclear whether and how the supposed ideological motivation and secondary character of Neh 11:25–35 (228–33) could also impact the evaluation of the immediately following section of Neh 12:1–26.

Chapter 5, "Excavating the Past: Settlement Patterns and Military Installations in Persian-Era Yehud," provides an extensive survey of archaeological excavations while still pointing to their limitations as sources of information about the redevelopment of Yehud. The chapter includes a table of settlement patterns, based on Ph.D. theses and publications, many of them from the 1990s up to 2003 (291–310). According to Edelman, the archaeological evidence still allows for the general conclusion that new settlement activity and the establishment of government facilities took place in the Persian period (328–30).

Chapter 6, "Piety or Pragmatism? The Policy of Artaxerxes I for the Development of Yehud," draws the evaluation of literary and artifactual sources together and concludes that the establishment of Jerusalem as a provincial seat, accompanied by new settlement activity, the appointment of a new governor, and the fortification and rebuilding of Jerusalem, including its temple, should be dated to the early reign of Artaxerxes I (465–425 B.C.E.). Edelman observes that pragmatism rather than piety was the motivation of Artaxerxes' policy that made the rebuilding of the temple possible.

Edelman's book provides a major challenge to the scholarly consensus about the "origins" of the Second Temple. It will stimulate much discussion, if only for the need to rethink the historical and literary evaluation of Ezra 1–6 and Haggai–Zech 8, on the one hand, and Nehemiah, on the other. Yet certain questions still remain unanswered by this hypothesis, starting with Edelman's own "open question" about whether Nehemiah succeeded Zerubbabel in office or whether the two "represent the same historical person who has been split into two different people … as a result of the decision to place the rebuilding of the temple almost seventy years earlier than the rebuilding of Jerusalem, for ideological reasons" (351). It further remains unclear why Edelman's interpretation of Neh 2:8 takes the building of the "gates of the fortress of the temple" (*sha'are ha-birah asher-labayit*) to stand for the "the building of a new temple" (345). Edelman's reading depends on an emendation of Neh 2:8, which deems the present text to be the result of "inadvertent scribal error" and supposes that the original reading puts "four major building projects" next to each other (345). Yet the Masoretic Text could presuppose the idea that the gates belonged to fortifications surrounding the temple hill, an idea that 1 Macc 13:52 further attests.

Judah and the Judeans in the Persian Period, edited by Oded Lipschits and Manfred Oeming. Winona Lake, Ind.: Eisenbrauns, 2006. Pp. xxii + 721. Hardcover. $59.50. ISBN 157506104X.

Erhard Gerstenberger, University of Marburg (Emeritus), Marburg, Germany

The Heidelberg symposium of 15–18 July 2003 on "Judah and the Judeans in the Achaemenid Period," sponsored by the University of Tel-Aviv, the "Hochschule für jüdische Studien" at Heidelberg, and Heidelberg University, drew twenty-eight speakers from all over the world, each one a renowned expert in the field, and an unrecorded audience, to represent and discuss most of all the archaeological and historical facts discernable in those "dark" centuries of biblical studies. (The announcement of the event is still available on the Internet; see, e.g., https://listhost.uchicago.edu/pipermail/ane/2003-February/007159.html). This in itself is a very timely and fruitful undertaking, because so many things need to be clarified, particularly since the period of highest literary and theological productivity of the "people of Yahweh"—according to Old Testament scholarship of the past two decades—has been shifting to the postexilic time. Thus far, the parameters of life under Persian imperial rule and their impact on the emerging Jewish community have not yet been sufficiently investigated.

Undoubtedly, the papers given then and presented here in book form do transport a wealth of information, partially correcting and revolutionizing traditional approaches and conclusions in regard to this allegedly "late" period of Old Testament history. What makes the reader wary, however, is the almost complete omission of the spiritual history of the time (e.g., rising or consolidating monotheism; ethical rigorism; approaching apocalypticism; religious community feeling) and the concomitant lack of experts in ancient Iranian religion at the symposium (cf. Michael Stausberg, *Die Religion Zarathushtras* [3 vols.; Stuttgart: Kohlhammer, 2002–2004]; this author has close ties to the University of Heidelberg; Pierre Briant, it seems, had been invited but does not appear in this volume). Besides this, apparently, missing dialogue of Christian theologians with nearby colleagues of the history of religion department, there is remarkably little evidence in the present volume of those illuminating debates among the twenty-eight speakers themselves and with their audience, in spite of the fact that some contributions in paper form exceed considerably (by a factor of five or six!) the supposed oral presentation. (Assuming roughly eight printed pages for a full-sized paper, the twenty-six presentations [two are double authored] of the volume would amount to 224 compared to the actual 687 printed pages. Allowing adequate space to plates, charts, bibliographies, and notes, there still would have been ample opportunity for interaction among the authors).

Yet the work at hand is a very valuable contribution, indeed, to the growing field of Persian studies. There is no stringent compositional order, so I might as well take up the essays in their given sequence. Bob Becking considers the mass deportation to and the uniform return of the Judeans from Babylonia a "historical myth" (12; his essay is entitled "'We All Returned as One!': Critical Notes on the Myth of the Mass Return" [3–18]). Lester L. Grabbe (cf. 531–70 and other publications) as well as a good number of other colleagues would heartily agree (cf. A. E. Knauf [303], also one of the few passages in the whole book to mention a debate at the Heidelberg conference). But the question to what extent any kind of history writing has to be "mythical" or "fictional" in character is hardly touched upon in this volume. Only Hanna Liss (663–90) reflects on this fundamental issue, while Sara Japhet gives it some passing attention (504: "the question of historicity comes forcefully to the fore: how much of the historical picture is determined by historical 'fact' and how much is 'constructed', directed by historical concepts and ideological goals?"). The majority of the contributors (including Grabbe!) seem innocently to believe that we are able to separate neatly between "facts" and "events" and "historical construction." The symposium apparently did not raise such fundamental questions.

The following five papers are concerned with political, administrative, or sociological problems in regard to the province of Yehud. Oded Lipschits investigates "Achaemenid Imperial Policy, Settlement Processes in Palestine, and the Status of Jerusalem in the Middle of the Fifth Century B.C.E." (19–52). The administrative center during the exilic and on into the Persian period had been Mizpah (with the nearby sacred shrine Bethel; see E. A. Knauf, 291–350). It was relocated to Jerusalem (Nehemiah!) not because of imperial Persian needs or interests but solely for the sake of inner-Judean developments (Second Temple; centralized cult). There had been a period of grave tensions between Bethel and Jerusalem, old Judah and old Benjamin tribes (cf. J. Blenkinsopp, 629–45; Y. Amit, 647–61). So, these four contributions (Lipschits; Knauf; Blenkinsopp; Amit) should by all means be studied in concert. The next political-sociological study is on "Constructions of Identity in Postcolonial Yehud" by Jon L. Berquist (53–66). The author succinctly distinguishes traditional constellations of identity formation, then turns to postmodern chaos theories. Emerging patterns of group consciousness are seen as multilayered. "Religion, nationality, and ethnicity are all components of identity—and all of them are simultaneously both imperializing and decolonizing" (63; no one in this volume responds to his collocation). John W. Wright quite reasonably points out, in "Remapping Yehud: The Borders of Yehud and the Genealogies of Chronicles" (67–89), that ancient territorial claims should not necessarily be spelled out by modern national linear frontier demarcations but may include genealogical perspectives as in 1 Chr 1–9 (kinship-patronage type of possessing land). This alert might be quite important for A. Lemaire (413–56). Was there an imperial consciousness in Yehud? (cf. Berquist above). John Kessler argues that the returning "golah" came home as a "charter group" (John Porter, 1965: "The Vertical Mosaic: A Study of Social Class and Power in Canada") deeply tinged by their Babylonian and Persian experience and ready to impose on Jerusalem and Yehud their vision of Yahwism and their allegiance to the Persian rule as well as to the Jewish colonists remaining in Mesopotamia, by alternating means of excluding and including parts of the Judean native population ("Persia's Loyal Yahwists: Power Identity and Ethnicity in Achaemenid Yehud" [91–121]; cf. E. Stern, 199–205). Of course, the homebound Judeans now needed an advocate, but Lisbeth S. Fried dedicates herself only to the semantics of "The 'am hā'āreṣ in Ezra 4:4 and Persian Imperial Administration" (123–45): The term is no reference to the native population, or settlers of the Assyrian period, but indicates only the ruling elite (satrapal officials) installed by the Persians.

Two mainly archaeological presentations follow suit: "The Borders and De Facto Size of Jerusalem in the Persian Period," by David Ussishkin (147–66); and Alexander Fantalkin with Oren Tal, "Redating Lachish Level I: Identifying Achaemenid Imperial Policy at the Southern Frontier of the Fifth Satrapy" (167–97). The first essay makes a strong point for Nehemiah's wall boldly following the wider lines of monarchic eighth/seventh-century B.C. fortifications, thus leaving ample space uninhabited inside Jerusalem. The second seeks to connect the "substantial architectural remains" (167) of level I at Lachish to the increased effort of the Persian military to secure the frontier against Egypt about 400 B.C., a reshuffle of fifty years.

Socioreligious, economic, and literary matters dominate another five-item bunch of essays. Archaeology proves changing cultic patters, says Ephraim Stern in "The Religious Revolution in Persian-Period Judah" (199–205). Typical Judean clay figurines disappear from the scene in the sixth century B.C., ceding all rights to the only cult at Jerusalem. The temple of Mount Gerizim also turned exclusively Yahwistic. Analogous monotheism in Persian religion is not discussed. "Tyrian Trade in Yehud under Artaxerxes I: Real or Fictional? Independent or Crown Endorsed?" is Diana Edelman's contribution. She starts off on a remark in Neh 13:16 about Tyrians in Jerusalem and scrutinizes all kind of texts that might hint at a real trading colony inside Jerusalem in line with Old Assyrian *karum*-settlements in Anatolia. Sometimes she has to admit that the evidence for her case is not too strong, but the effort to discover possible patterns is rewarding. Reinhard G. Kratz, in fact, discovers unexpected religious-literary patterns in the opposition stories about temple reconstructions at Jerusalem (Ezra 1–6) and

Jeb/Elephantine ("The Second Temple of Jeb and of Jerusalem" [247–64]). Both
involve correspondences between local and superior officials betraying a good
amount of "historical fiction" (264; cf. above, paragraph 3). Traditional-minded
scholars, taking 2 Kgs 17 and their Ezra/Nehemiah interpretation as a basis, postulate an eternal antagonism between Jerusalem and Samaria. A good number of
exegetes already tried to relativize this schism. Gary N. Knoppers wants to do justice to the real historical issues ("Revisiting the Samarian Question in the Persian
Period" [265–89]). Using the newest archaeological and epigraphic materials, he
exposes "natural" tensions between the related centers as well as much overlap in
culture and religion. A dialogue between him and E. Stern would be interesting.
The other internal focus of irritation for the Jerusalem community seems to have
been, for more than half a century, the sanctuary at Bethel with its administrative adjunct Mizpah. Ernst Axel Knauf sketches most of all the positive role of
the Benjaminite region, comprising eventually 40 percent of Yehud's population
(Blenkinsopp and Amit emphasize the polemical relationship; cf. 629–61). Knauf
sees Bethel, its sanctuary, and its academy as the main mediator of northern Israelite traditions (cf. Gen 28; 35) on their way into the biblical canon assembled in
Yehud (cf. 318–30: a grandiose synthesis of Bethel's functioning as a catalyst for
Jacob, exodus, and prophetic traditions from 650 to 300 B.C.).

　　Five further studies focus more on outward and neighborly aspects of Yehud's
existence. Raising the question "Cyrus II, Liberator or Conqueror? Ancient Historiography concerning Cyrus in Babylon" (351–72) David Vanderhooft thinks that
Persian propaganda falsifies the great king into an angel of peace. Real history
may have been different in 539 B.C., as, for example, Jer 50–51 or Babylonian readiness for military defense may suggest. M. A. Dandamayev tediously assembles,
mostly from private Babylonian documents, titles and names of higher officials
in Mesopotamia in "Neo-Babylonian and Achaemenid State Administration in
Mesopotamia" (373–98). Laurie E. Pearce discusses some features of about one
hundred new texts from the formerly unknown settlements of āl-Yāhūdu and ālu
ša Našar bearing on Judean or West-Semitic names ("New Evidence for Judeans
in Babylonia" [399–411]). A real first publication is then ventured by André
Lemaire in "New Aramaic Ostraca from Idumea and Their Historical Interpretation" (413–56). One of the great epigraphic experts for this period, Lemaire adds
to his earlier publications a full-fledged edition of thirty new pieces, including
photograph, description of the sherd, transcription, translation, and commentary (420–53), but not without giving a preliminary orientation for evaluating the
scant texts. Some hints at religious practices in Idumea can be gleaned from the
ostraca, perhaps also as to the recognition of Torah (416) and the existence of a
temple of Yahô (417). In the light of this pluralistic picture in Idumea, it is nearly
impossible to understand Lemaire's dating of Old Testament southern traditions
as pre-Idumean, because only then Jerusalem exercised "direct influence" in that
region (419). Bezalel Porten together with Ada Yardeni also have investigated
ostraca of the period, as they have been offered on the antiquities market by the
hundreds ("Social, Economic, and Onomastic Issues in the Aramaic Ostraca of

the Fourth Century B.C.E." [457–88]). They ingeniously organize the extant texts of unknown origin and context into "dossiers," using personal names or subjects as focal points. Thus the accumulated texts, which are mostly very fragmentary, yield much more information than individual pieces can. Of great interest are, of course, theophoric names (cf. 486) and economic activities such as paying or receiving payment, but also linguistic information or dating formulas.

The last batch of eight presentations more or less revolves around biblical texts or topics. Four of them have their focus in Ezra-Nehemiah. This block starts out with Sara Japhet's "Periodization between History and Ideology II: Chronology and Ideology in Ezra-Nehemiah" (491–508; an earlier essay by the author, published in 2003 in a companion volume under the same main title, was dedicated to the Neo-Babylonian period). The authors of the biblical book did not want to give a "historically exact" picture of the postexilic time but structured their narration in analogy to the pattern of the exodus theme. Period 1 comprised return of the captives, settlement, and reconstruction work in Jerusalem, while period 2 was imbued with the consolidation of the community. This means that biblical authors created their own historical reality. Slightly different is the view of Tamara Cohn Eskenazi in "The Missions of Ezra and Nehemiah" (509–29). The main thrust of both leaders' engagement was toward the rights and duties of citizens. An analogous situation may be found in the city of Athens under Pericles. If this analogy holds up, the influence of Persian interests pushing for reforms dissolves in the mist of history. Lester L. Grabbe picks out "The 'Persian Documents' in the Book of Ezra" and poses the question (subtitle): "Are They Authentic?" (531–70). Initially he simply voices exasperation: all the relevant documents look like "Hellenistic forgeries" (531). A closer scrutiny, however, of Ezra 1:2–4; 4:9–16, 17–22; 5:7–17; 6:2–5, 6–12; and 7:12–26 reveals degrees of originality and redactional reworking, summarized in a graded table of historical truthfulness. The letter of Tattenai (Ezra 5:7–17) has "most authentic material," while Ezra 1:2–4 (Cyrus's decree) has the least (563). But what does "authenticity" mean? Can we measure historical truth in percentages? Are not every and all statements about the past by necessity projective or rather retrojective? Nehemiah 9, the great liturgy of penitence leading up to the covenant renewal of Neh 10, is targeted by Manfred Oeming ("'See, We Are Serving Today' [Nehemiah 9:36]: Nehemiah 9 as a Theological Interpretation of the Persian Period"[571–88]; cf. Kessler, 91–121). The prayer, in his view, really is a central confession of faith for the community. Reinterpreting Neh 9:36–10:1, he does away with the age-old translation, making this passage a dire complaint against Persian subjugation and exploitation (the only one in the Hebrew/Aramaic Scriptures!). The expression "We are slaves in the land" (9:36) refers to the service of Yahweh, and the "kings that you placed over us … reign over us with benevolent care" (9:37). The dooming distress (9:37) is attributed solely to disobedience over against Torah. Any body of literature betrays its moorings in that social stratum using the language at hand. In "Sociolinguistics and the Judean Speech Community in the Achaemenid Empire" (589–628), Frank H. Polak skillfully and with good documentation analyzes the changes occurring in classical biblical Hebrew, used mainly in religious contexts, under the influence of vernacular Aramaic: It is Joseph Blenkinsopp's task to illuminate "Benjamin Traditions Read in the Early Persian Period" (629–45) and Yairah Amit's to side up with an exposition of "The Saul Polemic in the Persian Period" (647–61). Both authors are well aware of the historian's predicament of being entangled in his or her own time. Blenkinsopp tries to locate the Benjamin oracle of Deut 33:12: it may not refer to prestate conditions with Gibeon being the chief sanctuary but to the exilic situation, when Bethel became the substitute Yahweh temple (638; no reference to A. E. Knauf). Judges 19–21 with its "war of extermination against Benjamin" (638–43; no reference to A. E. Knauf) bears witness to the hostility between Jerusalem and Benjamin lasting until approximately 450 B.C. Amit, on the other hand, traces late biblical controversies about the first king of Israel from Judg 19–21 (Gibeah!) via Chronicles to the book of Esther. The Chronicler seeks to "diminish Saul's character" by all means (650), while the author of Esther implicitly tries to rehabilitate him in the "virtuous" figures of Esther and Mordecai (654). During the period of Bethel as the main sanctuary there may have been some Benjaminite claim to leadership. Even if not involving direct descendents of Saul's family (their vestiges have been lost in tradition), references to Saul may have served to undergird Benjaminite aspirations (dialogue with Blenkinsopp and Knauf is missing). The very last essay has been written by Hanna Liss (Jewish Institute of Higher Education, Heidelberg) and deals with "The Imaginary Sanctuary: The Priestly Code as an Example of Fictional Literature in the Hebrew Bible" (663–89). Liss is the lone advocate of a fully constructed "history" without ties to real events and circumstances. The Priestly writer's vision of the new temple is a theological concept, using its own parameters of space and time. It does not depend on the real Second Temple, rebuilt under Persian rule. Therefore, she concludes, the P literature must be preexilic. But why this return to fixing literature into a specific historical context?

All in all, the Heidelberg Symposium of 2003 certainly was a very worthwhile undertaking, bequeathing to the interested homebound remnant a veritable treasure of scholarly insights into the most productive period of Old Testament religion. Broadening the interdisciplinary effort to include experts in ancient Iranian religions would be most desirable.

Creation and Destruction: A Reappraisal of the Chaoskampf Theory in the Old Testament, by David Toshio Tsumura. Winona Lake, Ind.: Eisenbrauns, 2005. Pp. xviii + 214. Hardcover. $32.50. ISBN 1575061066.

Michaela Bauks, Universität Koblenz-Landau, Koblenz, Germany

Die vorliegende Studie ist eine sprachlich und bisweilen auch inhaltlich stark überarbeitete Neuausgabe von *The Earth and the Waters in Genesis 1 and 2* (Sheffield 1989; vgl. *JBL* 110, 136ff), die zudem um eine 50seitige Untersuchung zum Chaoskampfmotiv in poetischen Texten ergänzt worden ist. Die wichtige Erkenntnis der ersten, linguistisch angelegten Studie lag darin, dass die Gunkelsche These von der Ableitung des Schöpfungsgeschehens aus einzelnen chaotischen Elementen als falsch dargelegt werden konnte: die umfassenden etymologischen Untersuchungen der Begriffe *tōhû wabōhu, tehôm, 'ed, 'eden* etc. ergaben, dass *tōhû wabōhu* keineswegs eine Bezeichnung für chaotische Materie ist, sondern eine Umschreibung für Leere und unausgefüllten Raum im Sinne eines „noch-nicht" (chap. 1/1) beinhaltet. Auch kann *tehôm* etymologisch nicht mit der babylonischen Göttin Tiamat verwandt sein, sondern ist von akk. *tiamtum/tâmtum* „Meer, Ozean" (vgl. ug. *thm/thmt*; ebl. *ti-ʾà-ma-tum*) abzuleiten, welches keinesorts eine depersonifizierte Göttin umschreibt und ein solches Verständnis folglich auch für Gen 1,2 ausschließt. Auch *'eden* ist nicht etwa von akk. *edinu* „Steppe" abzuleiten, sondern vielmehr verwandt mit *m'dn* „reichlich an Wasser", ein Gebrauch, der in der Biblingue aus Tell Fekheriyeh bzw. in KTU 1.4:V:6–7 belegt ist (p. 116–18). Die sich anschließende syntagmatische Untersuchung von Gen 1,2 und 2,4ff. hat ergeben, dass *'r,* und *tehôm* bzw. *yam* in Gen 1–2 nicht etwa in einem antonymen Verhältnis zueinander stehen, sondern hyponym sind, d.h. einander logisch untergeordnet werden müssen. Die einleitenden Schilderungen des Urstands in Gen 1,1–3 und 2,4b–7 haben dieselbe Grundstruktur (temporal description–setting–event) und bringen semantisch denselben Umstand des Noch-nicht-Sein (not yet productive) zum Ausdruck (58ff.111ff.).

Die Studie läuft auf zwei äußerst bedeutsame Veränderungen im Verständnis der ersten beiden Schöpfungsberichte hinaus:

1. Der erste Schöpfungsbericht ereignet sich nicht in Form einer Schöpfung Gottes auf der Grundlage eines Chaoskampfes. Die Umschreibung des Chaotischen darf lediglich als Beschreibung von Mangel, Leere und Unstrukturiertheit verstanden werden. Diese Ergebnisse hatte ich für meine Doktorarbeit (*Die Welt am Anfang,* WMANT 74, pp. 88, n.149.111–26) als Arbeitshypothese übernommen, hingegen kritisiert, dass Tsumura den abstrakt verstandenenen Aussagegehalts von *tōhû wabōhu* bisweilen zu konkret übersetzte (desert, devastation, an unproductive and unhabited place, 1989, 43.155f) und somit das eigene Untersuchungsergebnis in seiner Bedeutung schmälerte. In der Neuauflage ist die Bedeutung des Nichtigen (nothingness, not yet, p.33f cf. 26f.) stärker hervorgehoben. Desweiteren ergänzt er die Untersuchung von Erde und Wasser um die Bedeutung der *rûaᵃch 'ĕlohîm* im ersten Schöpfungsbericht (pp. 74–76). Er sieht in dieser Wendung weder den agierenden Geist noch einen Wind Gottes, der das Chaos in Schöpfung transformiert, sondern den Atem Gottes, der seinem Sprechen vorangeht als Bild für das In-Aktion-Treten Gottes (vgl. Gen 2,7). Die Vorzüge dieser übrigens in der deutschsprachigen Literatur nicht unbekannten Deutung gegenüber den beiden anderen, die angeblich zu eng mit der Chaosthematik verhaftet wären, ist mir indes nicht klar geworden. M.E. können ebenso die beiden anderen Übersetzungen als Metaphern für das göttliche Agieren dienen (vgl. WMANT 74, pp. 128ff. zur Diskussion).

2. Es lassen sich eine Reihe Hinweise finden, dass Gen 1 und Gen 2 längst nicht so unterschiedlich von dem Urzustand vor der Schöpfung reden, wie es seit

Gunkel immer wieder behauptet wurde. Es stehen sich hier nicht etwa Trocken-
wüste und Überschwemmung gegenüber, sondern beide Berichte fußen auf der
Idee eines alles umspülenden, unterirdischen Urmeeres bzw. eines urzeitlichen
Stromes, die (Yahweh-) Elohim einem Wettergott vergleichbar in Gen 1 unter
Kontrolle bringt bzw. in Gen 2 zur Nutzung bringt. Über diese Funktion hinaus,
übernimmt er, wie in den übrigen altorientalischen Literaturen ein zweiter Gott
tut—oft der Hauptgott der semitischen Panthea—, einen zweiten wichtigen
Aspekt der Schöpfungsordnung: er ist—als der *eine* Gott—Schöpfer und Erhalter
(128f.139f.). Der Problemkreis dreht sich nicht um die Frage des *Wie* der Schöpfung, sondern um das *Dass*.

Soweit zu der überarbeiteten Fassung. Der zweite Teil der Studie widmet sich
neu der Frage, in welchen literarischen Kontexten das Chaoskampfmotiv auftritt.
Tsumura differenziert das Chaoskampfmotiv in zwei unterschiedliche Traditionen: der mesopotamische Typ, wie er am ausführlichsten im Enuma eliš belegt ist
und der kanaanäische Typ, wie er sich im ugaritischen Baal-Zyklus findet. Beide
unterscheiden sich vorrangig darin, dass das Motiv kanaanäischen Ursprungs
nicht an das Schöpfungsthema rückzubinden ist, während Enuma eliš das eine
mit dem anderen verbindet. Ob es sich hier aber lediglich um eine Nebentra-
dition amoritischen (so Durand, MARI 7, 41ff) bzw. nord-mesopotamischen
Ursprungs handelt (Lambert, in Mesopotamia 8, p.64f „Ninurta-Mythology"; vgl.
dazu auch Bauks, WMANT 74, pp. 254ff), die das personifizierte Meer als gegen-
schöpferisches Element beschreiben, gegenüber dem sich ein dem Wettergotttyp
verwandter Gott behaupten muss, stellt Tsumura in Frage (p. 38–41). Das Chaoskampfmotiv im Schöpfungskontext ist seiner Meinung nach in Mesopotamien
von alters her belegbar, ohne dass er in der Bibel Niederschlag gefunden hätte. Es
bleibt also nun die kanaanäische Tradition und ihre Einflüsse auf die biblischen
Poesie zu untersuchen. Tsumura unternimmt dies anhand gängiger Chaoskampf-
beschreibungen, die desöfteren mit der ugaritischen Literatur verglichen worden
sind, wie Ps 18; 29; 46; Hab 3.

Im Anschluss an die Textuntersuchungen kommt Tsumura zu dem äußerst
überraschenden und eigenwilligen Ergebnis, dass es das Chaoskampfmotiv in der
biblischen Literatur insgesamt nicht gibt. Zur Begründung: Er gebietet zum einen
methodische Vorsicht angesichts der formellen Unvergleichbarkeit von epischen
mit prophetischen Texten oder Psalmen (146f.). Auch kritisiert er das Konzept
der Historisierung von kanaanäischen Mythen in den Psalmen (149.163) oder
des übertragenen und metaphorischen Sprachgebrauchs (151) als eine zu vage
Analogie für einen kompetenten Vergleich der Motive. Inhaltlich ist s.E. auch
der Shift von Schöpfung zu Zerstörung in der biblischen Literatur auffällig. Tsumura versucht den jahrhundertealten Irrtum, die Rede vom Chaoskampf oder
Meerkampf auf die biblische Literatur anzuwenden, mit einer zu oberflächli-
chen Betrachtungsweise der Exegeten abzutun, die nicht ausreichend Einflüsse
(influences) von Abhängigkeiten (dependences) und Anspielungen (allusions) zu
unterscheiden vermag. Anhand der Motivkomplexe "Kriegsbeschreibungen als
Sturm oder Flut", "Zerstörung durch Flut oder Meer" sowie der poetischen Aus-

gestaltung dieser Motive mittels Personifizierung und Metaphorisierung versucht er nachzuweisen, dass (nur?) die Israeliten sich der Metaphorisierung der Sprache durchaus bewusst waren und sie bewusst verwendeten, um die Vorrangstellung Yahwes herauszustellen.

Es handelt sich besonders mit dem ersten Teil des Buches ohne jeden Zweifel um eine forschungsrelevante Darstellung, die sich bewußt als eine Weiterführung und Korrektur der Gunkelschen Thesen versteht. Zurecht hebt der Autor hervor, dass Gen 1–2 kein Beispiel für eine biblische Chaoskampfschilderung im Schöpfungskontext bieten und dass die Parallelisierung mit dem mesopotamischen Weltschöpfungsepos einer weitaus umsichtigeren und präziseren Untersuchung bedarf als sie von Exegeten oft geleistet wird. Doch hat die überarbeitete Neufassung die z.T. umfangreichen Arbeiten des letzten Jahrzehnts zum Thema zu wenig und nur sehr ausschnitthaft wahrgenommen, so dass die Schlussfolgerungen sowie die Rekurse auf Gunkel etwas anachronistisch wirken: Denn die Forschung ist längst weiter gegangen. Ebenso anachronistisch wirkt Tsumuras Verdikt, in der biblischen Literatur überhaupt von einen Chaoskampfmotiv sprechen zu wollen. Seine methodischen Bedenken sind grundsätzlich richtig, werden aber insofern *ad absurdum* geführt, als Tsumura für das begrenzte biblische Literaturkorpus eine weitaus strengere Herangehensweise verlangt als er sie für das viel umfassendere und mindestens ebenso disparate altorientalische Quellenmaterial, das er zitiert hat, zulässt. Hier werden in methodologischer Hinsicht zwei unterschiedliche Messlatten angelegt. Zudem stellt er sich zu wenig der Herausforderung, dass jeder Exeget, der die alttestamentliche Traditionsgeschichte in Abhängigkeit zur altorientalischen versteht, übergreifende Pattern bilden muss, welche die thematischen und motivlichen Gemeinsamkeiten zu beschreiben helfen. So ist auch die Rede vom Chaoskampfmotiv als eine Hilfsbezeichnung zu verstehen, die unterschiedliche literarische und thematische Kontexte auf ein verwandtes Thema hin erst untersuchbar macht.

Temples, Tithes and Taxes: The Temple and the Economic Life of Ancient Israel, by Marty E. Stevens. Peabody, Mass.: Hendrickson, 2006. Pp. xi + 209. Paper. $24.95. ISBN 1565639340.

This volume contains many good observations about the economic dimensions of temples in the ancient Near East in the first millennium B.C.E. and raises a number of important issues concerning the economic functions of the temples in Judah during the monarchy and of the temple in Jerusalem in the Persian-Roman periods. The author of the present volume has fifteen years' experience as a certified public accountant, which explains her interest in the topic. She received a Ph.D. in 2002 in the U.S. and now teaches biblical studies at a U.S. seminary. The closing page indicates that the book is intended for pastors and laity, to raise their consciousness that the temple was more than a place of worship; it was the socioeconomic and religious center of ancient Israel. As a modern corollary, it is asserted that a contemporary life of discipleship should not separate the religious from politics, economics, or sociology. There is no clarification as to whether or not the volume stems from her Ph.D. thesis; it is her first book.

The book contains seven chapters. In "Introductory Matters" Stevens provides the nonspecialist reader with what are intended to be helpful explanations of terminology, ancient record-keeping practices, the ancient Israelite economy, a brief history of Israel/Judah, her assumptions and goals, and a guide to foreign words. Her target audience is not stated here, although the two goals from the final page are. These twenty-seven pages will raise a number of red flags for many in the academic community: the term "Israel" is used interchangeably with "Judah"; the historical summary is a paraphrase of the Bible; the author treats the biblical texts as reliable witnesses to historical circumstances underlying the theological interpretation by the authors and editors, although not as inerrant Scripture; and she presents a composite paradigm of how the Jerusalem temple functioned as an institution in the first millennium B.C.E., deliberately commingling information in texts from different time periods in an admittedly "synchronic view." It is hard to see how her former teacher, W. P. Brown, can say that she brings the "judiciousness of a historian" to her analysis (back cover); her rejection of the importance of historical distinctions and the possibility of changes in function and administration within the temple over time is more the mark of a theological approach. Her theological concerns are corroborated by her closing assertion that the temple as a functioning institution (in the kingdom of Judah and later in the religious community of "Israel" until 70 C.E.—my distinction but her timeframe) should inform current Christian views concerning the need not to separate the sacred from the secular.

The focus of chapter 2 (28–59) is temple construction. Here Stevens paraphrases biblical texts relating to the construction of the wilderness tabernacle, the First Temple in Jerusalem, and the Second Temple in Jerusalem, with an excursus on Yahwistic temples outside Jerusalem at Dan, Bethel, Arad, Mount Gerizim, Elephantine, Leontopolis, and sacred sites in the region at Nahariya, Hazor, and Ta'anach. While she often couches her paraphrase by saying that the information she relates is so portrayed in a given book or by a biblical author, there are ample examples where information is presented as historical fact. This is not surprising in light of her straightforward statement of her understanding of the historical nature of biblical texts in chapter 1. This chapter would have benefited the target audience much more had it presented these final-form readings in terms of the ancient literary genre of the temple-building account and if it had raised the possibility that one or more narratives might be examples of ancient utopian literature.

Chapter 3 contains a discussion of temple personnel (64–81). Stevens is comfortable here informing her nonspecialist audience that "a careful reading of the biblical texts, reflective of multiple traditions over several centuries, shows that the distinction between priests and Levites as well as the unilateral association of priests with the authorized worship of YHWH is a post-exilic phenomenon" (66).

This kind of diachronic distinction could have been carried through in all her chapters to reinforce for her audience the complex history of the biblical texts and the likelihood that they reflect multiple views that should not be naively harmonized but respected for their individual integrity. When this is done, we can learn even more about the past by respecting diversity and changes over time.

Stevens makes the useful observation that the office of *sho'er* required accounting skills as well as guarding abilities. What remains uncertain is if every *sho'er* performed both activities, as she concludes, or if there were two types: one whose job was to prevent entry into unauthorized areas and to keep watch over donations left at the gates and doorways; and another who recorded all the donations. Similarly, her recognition that some holders of the office of *sopher* were counters, recorders, ledger-keepers, and enumerators and not merely copyists or dictation transcribers is important, but her conclusion that all *sopherim* functioned in this way, so that the term *sopher* would be best translated "storehouse accountant," is questionable. There is no evidence that *sopherim* worked only in the context of the temple storehouses, although it is also clear that some did, and those who did were effectively "storehouse accountants."

Temple income is the subject of chapter 4 (82–120). Stevens discusses the vital question as to whether the temple in Jerusalem owned land and controlled its production, as did temples in Mesopotamia and Egypt, where irrigation agriculture was practiced and vast acres belonged to temples in both the immediate vicinity and at greater distances, but not apparently in Greece, where agriculture was dependent on rainfall, as in Judah. She wisely seems to conclude that the evidence is insufficient at this point in time to provide an answer. She also emphasizes that the temple in Jerusalem was effectively an agent of the crown and served as the national storage facility for tithes and taxes in kind as well as precious metals, with a royal appointee being present when monies deposited in boxes were counted. She highlights the problem in terminology that suggests differences between tithes, taxes, tribute, and gifts because of the use of distinctive words, namely, the modern problem we have in distinguishing between these. Unfortunately, she fails to distinguish the specific case from the general rule in the case of the Mesopotamian *ilku* labor payment and obligation. This is not a temple tax; it is a royal obligation incumbent on land owners to perform annual free labor for the crown that can, in specific cases, be assigned to a temple. Also, if her analogy between the *shirku* or person donated to the temple in Mesopotamia and the biblical *netinim* is to be upheld, she would need to conclude that the latter were not engaged in cultic service but were a more general physical labor force to be used by the temple as it saw fit, hiring them out or using them to work their own lands. The possibility that the temple in Jerusalem sponsored or used traders is raised on the basis of ancient Near Eastern parallels.

Chapter 5 consists of an examination of temple expenses (121–35). It highlights once again the close connection between the temple and the crown, where the king could appropriate stored foodstuffs and precious metals as necessary to pay government employees and tribute. In Mesopotamia at least, the temple could provide funds to a merchant to ransom someone he discovered during his foreign travels who was a citizen who had become a prisoner of war but did not have sufficient funds to redeem himself. The ideal of the king of Israel and Judah as the champion and provider for the widow, the orphan, and the poor is linked to the same roles assigned to Yahweh in the Psalter, and Stevens concludes that the temple on Zion would have "embodied the graciousness of YHWH by serving as a food pantry for the poor" (134). She cites as support Deut 13:28, which calls for the storage of the tithe in the third year within "your gates" to feed the Levite, *ger*, widow, and orphan. Was this an ideal or a reality? In any event, it is not the temple that would have dispensed the food in this case, since there was only to be one and the food was to remain in the countryside.

In chapter 6 (136–66) Stevens examines the temple's function as a treasury. She rejects the idea that it functioned as a bank because it held deposits by individuals but did not allow others to access them; temples lent their own property, and if they used deposits, they acted as a broker at the direction of the depositor, who maintained the risk of the use. She admits that the earliest evidence for the use of the Jerusalemite temple as a depository is found in the deuterocanonical texts from the Hellenistic period but then seems surprised to find the system "remarkably similar" to the one in Greece. Not coincidentally, it was only in the Hellenistic period that temples in Egypt began making loans to individuals. This is an example of where what are likely diachronic developments are overlooked. Stevens points out that religious vows are strikingly similar to typical ancient Near Eastern loan contracts and that the piel stem of the verb *shalam* means both to "fulfil a vow" to Yahweh and also to "repay a loan." I was surprised that she failed to discuss Lev 27:14–26 in this chapter as a possible use of land as collateral for a temple-sponsored loan, as opposed to one secured from a private, individual lender or as some sort of means of using private land to gain other desired or needed liquid assets from or via the temple.

The final chapter, "Concluding Matters," summarizes the main points made in the earlier chapters. Temples were central collection sites and storage facilities for commodities native to the region. Perishable stocks were used as rations for temple personnel and food supplies for political authorities. Nonperishable surpluses were traded or used in commercial ventures. Credit instruments developed as a means of managing surpluses; loans were made both to peasant farmers needing grain and to merchants seeking an investment opportunity that would hopefully yield a profit. Interest rates were set by temples relative to the market rate. Temples also became central registries for transactions that did not involve temple interests directly because of their literate administrative staff: land sales or leasing contracts, judicial decisions of all kinds and oaths related to commercial contracts. There are hints that the Jerusalem temple engaged in regional trade, assumed fiduciary responsibility for deposits, and made loans of surpluses. Since Stevens notes that "Mesopotamian temple archives are noticeably silent on the topic of land sales" (89), it would have been more accurate to conclude that records of transactions involving lands owned or overseen by temples were kept in temple archives, while private land sales and contracts involving the use or lease of private land were normally kept in private household archives, as evidenced by the Murashu and Elephantine correspondence.

There is a select bibliography, an index of names and subjects, an index of foreign words, and an index of ancient sources. These help make the book user-friendly.

Of Stevens's two stated goals, she accomplishes the first, her desire to make it clear that the temple was more than just a center of worship, but not the corollary of her second, that since religion, politics, economics, and sociology were considered to have been integrated in "ancient Israel," we, or rather "those living a life of discipleship," should adopt the same stance. The latter allegation fails to address the different worldviews that were held when various biblical texts were written and the worldviews current today, presumably the American one in particular. This is a pressing issue needing discussion within church circles: How much of the biblical text is culturally specific, and how much is universal?

While the first goal is accomplished, it comes at an unnecessary cost. There was no need for Stevens to avoid a diachronic reading of the texts because her envisioned audience was comprised of pastors and laity. It is not good to underestimate the ability of nonscholars to "handle" the insights of biblical scholarship. I am left wondering whether she is "sparing" them or whether she is revealing her own convictions that the biblical texts are historical in most of their details, even those relating to the wilderness period and the early monarchy, so no consideration of the date of authorship of these books, the possible sources used in their compositions, or the ideologies that appear to have informed their composition is necessary to understand or work with them. She can read diachronically, so why not do it consistently?

Although the synchronic reading has detracted from the overall success of the volume, scholars who are aware of the pitfalls of such an a-historical approach can still benefit from this volume. It investigates the neglected subject of temple economics in ancient Judah and Yehud, focusing on the temple in Jerusalem, and provides many interesting observations, primarily about the Persian era temple and practices in the Hellenistic period. It is not clear whether we have any reliable information about the monarchic-era temple in the biblical texts, and the likely utopian nature of Ezek 40–48 and Ezra 1–6 highlights the difficulty we encounter in trying to move from the biblical texts to the actual past. The most useful aspect of this volume is the information Stevens has gathered and presented about the functions and practices at temple elsewhere in the ancient Near East, which will undoubtedly stimulate individual reflection and lead to additional publications that will build upon, refine, and correct ideas in the present work.

Ancient Texts for the Study of the Hebrew Bible: A Guide to the Background Litera-ture, by Kenton L. Sparks. Peabody, Mass.: Hendrickson, 2005. Pp. xxxvii + 514. Hardcover. $39.95. ISBN 1565634071.

John L. McLaughlin, University of St. Michael's College, Toronto, Ontario, Canada

This volume fills an important gap in the existing resources for understanding the Hebrew Bible in its ancient Near Eastern context. We have important compendia of a wide range of relevant ancient Near Eastern texts, including the venerable but dated *Ancient Near Eastern Texts Relating to the Old Testament* (*ANET*) and the more recent three-volume *The Context of Scripture* (*COS*), both of which usually include introductions to the specific texts they contain, but these treatments are all too brief. Similarly, one can find anthologies of texts from specific locations that contain fuller discussion of the literature of a specific region. Now this work combines the best of both approaches by providing solid discussions of a wide range of ancient Near Eastern literature relevant to the Hebrew Bible, organized both by genre and by geographic regions.

The book's introduction provides a theoretical basis for what follows with a clear discussion of the comparative analysis of genres. Chapter 1 then considers the archives and libraries of ancient texts discovered in Syria-Palestine, Mesopotamia, Egypt, Anatolia, and Persia. After an orientation to the issues of language, writing, literacy, and textual canonicity, Sparks discusses the location, language, material, types of literature, and date of each find. Chapter 2 moves to wisdom, grouping the regional bodies of literature in terms of "standard" and "speculative" wisdom and providing an overview of the main representatives of each category. Subsequent chapters are devoted in turn to "Hymns, Prayers, and Laments"; "Love Poetry (and Related Texts)"; "Rituals and Incantations"; "Intermediary Texts: Omens and Prophecies"; "Apocalyptic and Related Texts"; "Tales and Novellas"; "Epics and Legends"; "Myth"; "Genealogies, King Lists, and Related Texts"; "Historiography and Royal Inscriptions"; "Law Codes"; "Treaty and Covenant"; and "Epigraphic Sources from Syria-Palestine and Its Environs."

In the preface Sparks outlines how he has structured this material, both within each chapter and in the book as a whole. Since much of the ancient Near Eastern literature was found as part of collections and was copied by trained scribes, he envisions the first two chapters as important for understanding the subsequent genres. Similarly, he discusses historiographies after narrative and chronological genres such as tales, legends, king lists, and the like, since the latter constitute source material used in the production of the former. Each chapter also follows an definite order: a general introduction to the specific genre(s) is followed by discussion of individual examples, with each accompanied by a bibliography comprising (where applicable) texts and translations, and only then scholarly treatments. Specific texts are organized geographically in terms of importance, which is usually Mesopotamia, Egypt, Syria/Palestine, and Hatti (there are occasional deviations when a later region is more significant); on occasion other areas are also included, such as Persia (apocalypses and historiographies) and Greece (apocalypses, genealogies, historiographies, law codes). The individual texts are also organized chronologically within a region, all of which makes it easier to note development and influence from place to place and over time. Each chapter (except the last) ends with "Concluding Observations" that summarize the preceding treatments and usually, but not always, indicate similarities with the Hebrew Bible plus a general bibliography.

It is impossible in a review to even begin to consider in detail the texts dealt with in this book, and more general comments will have to suffice. The range of material covered is comprehensive but not totally inclusive, as Sparks acknowledges. The amount of published comparative material alone, to say nothing of finds yet to be published, is simply too vast to be treated in a single volume. Of course, one could always quibble over an inclusion or omission (e.g., on one occasion when he does assert inclusivity, namely, that there are eight Ugaritic texts mentioning the *marzēaḥ*, Sparks misses *KTU* 4.399), but the selection is generally both judicious and appropriate, with all the major texts one would expect plus important lesser-known examples. At points the volume might benefit from more cross-references among genres, such as with the story of Wenamun; Sparks correctly classifies this as a "tale," but it would be helpful to have a note under "Intermediary Texts" that Wenamun succeeds in his mission when his god possesses a local seer, an instance of ecstatic prophecy. I also missed having "Concluding Observations" in the final chapter relating the inscriptional evidence to the Hebrew Bible. But these are minor points. Overall, the breadth and depth of Sparks's familiarity with these texts and the scholarly interpretation of them is evident on every page. The various bibliographies are up to date as of the book's initial publication, with few gaps. In response to the author's request to be informed of lacunae (xv), he is probably already aware of these recent publications: Gordon J. Hamilton, *The Origins of the West Semitic Alphabet in Egyptian Scripts* (Washington, D.C.: Catholic Biblical Association of America, 2006); and Mark S. Smith, *The Rituals and Myths of the Feast of the Goodly Gods of KTU/CAT 1.23* (Atlanta: Society of Biblical Literature, 2006). A few earlier items that were overlooked include Conrad E. L'Heureux, *Rank among the Canaanite Gods: El, Ba'al and the Repha'im* (HSM 21; Missoula, Mont.: Scholars Press, 1979); John L. McLaughlin, *The Marzēaḥ in the Prophetic Literature: References and Allusions in Light of the Extra-Biblical Evidence* (VTSup 86; Leiden: Brill, 2001), 11–31 (for the Ugaritic *marzēaḥ*); and J. Glen Taylor, "A First and Last Thing to Do in Mourning: *KTU* 1.161 and Some Parallels," in *Ascribe to the Lord: Biblical and Other Studies in Memory of Peter C. Craigie* (ed. Lyle Eslinger and J. Glen Taylor; JSOTSup 67; Sheffield: JSOT Press, 1988), 151–77.

This book is essential for everyone dealing with the Hebrew Bible in its ancient context (its scholarly value is undoubtedly reflected in the fact that it received a second printing the year after its initial appearance). Taken as a whole, it is a thorough introduction to the variety of genres in ancient Near Eastern literature and their relevance for the Hebrew Bible. The chapters can be consulted individually for an orientation to specific literary forms, exemplars from specific locations, or individual texts, as well as for contemporary scholarship on any aspect of the preceding. In short, all future comparative scholarship will take this book as its starting point. The ability to dip into the book for a specific point of reference is greatly enhanced by the six indexes: modern authors; Hebrew Bible and early Jewish literature; ancient Near Eastern sources; English translations found in *ANET*; English translations found in *COS*; museum numbers, textual realia and standard text publications.

Sparks promises a second volume, already underway, dealing more directly with the Hebrew Bible itself. Based on the current work, that book is eagerly awaited.

Old Testament Ethics for the People of God, by Christopher J. H. Wright. Downers Grove, Ill.: InterVarsity Press, 2004. Pp. 520. Hardcover. $30.00. ISBN 0830827781.

Pieter M. Venter, University of Pretoria, Pretoria, South Africa

Christopher Wright began his study on the economic ethics in ancient Israel during the 1970s. His doctoral research was published in 1990 as *God's People in God's Land*. His research continued von Rad's work on Israel's theology of the land, and in his thesis he indicated the strong theological link between land, covenant, and family in ancient Israel's economic structures. His first publication, *Living as the People of God* (1983), was an attempt to set out a way of understanding the ethical thrust of the Old Testament in general terms and to illustrate a suggested method in several applied areas. In the time following he wrote several essays on the subject of Old Testament ethics. These were eventually collected and published as *Walking in the Ways of the Lord* in 1995. In the present work, *Old Testament Ethics for the People of God* (2004), Wright has revised, updated, and expanded his *Living as the People of God*.

The publication is divided into three parts. After an introductory chapter, the first part deals with a structure for Old Testament ethics. The second part addresses several themes in Old Testament ethics, including "ecology and the earth," "economics and the poor," "the land and Christian ethics," "politics and the nations," "justice and righteousness," "law and the legal system," "culture and family," and "the way of the individual." The third part is a new addition to the 1983 book and contains an academic orientation to the discipline of Old Testament ethics. Each chapter includes a list of publications for further reading. Finally, an appendix on the problem of the Canaanites is added. This is followed by extensive indexes of authors quoted, scripture references, and subjects.

Wright's approach to Old Testament ethics can be summarized in his own words as "recognizing the constructive nature of the biblical paradigm, as that which binds together into a coherent structure the various principles or axioms … that we discern in the text" (420). Wright does not use the term "paradigm" in the sense of patterns of ideal behavior but rather as indication of the "total structure of Israel as presented to us in the Old Testament" 368). Aiming at presenting a "comprehensive framework within which Old Testament ethics can be organized and understood" (11), Wright states that "the concept of paradigm includes the isolation and articulation of principles ... not reducible to them alone" (71). In their articulating of a comprehensive corporate response to a wide range of economic, social, and political issues of the day, Israel applied various principles and became a paradigm or model themselves to the nations. They indicated the way God expects society as a whole to operate. Wright's argument is that we should regard Israel and the Old Testament as an ethical paradigm. This would force us constantly to go back to the hard given reality of the text of the Bible itself and imaginatively live with Israel in their world before returning to the equally hard given reality of our own world to discover imaginatively how that paradigm challenges our ethical response here (see 71). The hermeneutics applied to Old Testament ethics, therefore, has the threefold task of getting there (projecting ourselves in the world of Israel of the Old Testament), getting back from there (to respond to what we have been confronted with in our exploration of the biblical world), and answering the question whether and how anything we bring back from the world of Old Testament Israel carries ethical authority in our own day (see ch. 14).

To outline this biblical paradigm, Wright used a triangular structure in his *Living as the People of God.* Convinced that this structure has withstood the test of time, he reuses and expands on this structure in the present work. Israel's worldview can be conceptualized as a triangle of relationships between the three interacting pillars of God, Israel, and the land. The Old Testament's ethical teaching should be examined in terms of these three interrelated angles: theological (God), social (Israel), and economic (the land).

As ethics is fundamentally theological and all ethical issues in the Bible are related to the character, will, actions, and purpose of God, one must start with a basic theology of the Old Testament. Wright uses a traditional schematic approach using themes such as God's identity, actions, words, purpose, and so forth. In chapter 4 he uses the traditional scheme of creation, fall, salvation, and eschatology. As he wants his theological construct to be representative of all the Old Testament, he pays attention to the different literary contexts of the biblical contents (e.g., laws, narratives, and prophetic literature). The sociohistorical context of the biblical literature, however, does not form part of his investigation. This is linked to his basic quest for the ethical authority of the Old Testament for Christians in which he studies the Old Testament in a comprehensive framework that is compatible with the shape of the canon and the covenantal basis of Old Testament theology (20). It is important for Wright to pay attention "to the canonical order of the traditions as found in the Hebrew Bible" (433). Consequently, he works with concepts such as "revelation" and "authority" and the question of the relation between Old and New Testaments. The ethics in the Old Testament is "focused on Jesus in such a way that their authority and ethical relevance is not only sustained, but also enhanced and transformed for those who are 'in Christ'" (470). While one can fully agree with Wright that Old Testament ethics must be related to Old Testament theology, I must unfortunately differ from him that Old Testament theology and eventually biblical theology conceptualized in these terms can be sufficient for writing an Old Testament ethics.

The second pillar in Wright's interacting triangle is the historical and cultural particularity of biblical Israel. Being a different kind of society because their God YHWH was unquestionably a different God, historical Israel articulated a comprehensive corporate response to a wide range of economic, social, and political issues in their day. According to Wright, the whole concrete existence of Israel going through different historical phases is paradigmatic (see 68). As a society, Israel was intended to be a paradigm for the nations. We are therefore not only justified but "indeed expected, to make use of the social patterns, structures and laws of Old Testament Israel to help us in our thinking and choosing in the realm of social ethics in our own world" (74).

Following von Rad and others (e.g., Brueggemann), Wright conceptualizes the third economic angle in terms of "the land." The land as economic angle functions as a gauge that indicates how things are going in the other two angles of Israel's life as a society and their relationship to God. The land as indication of both divine gift and as divine ownership was one of the basic principles that guided Old Testament ethics. As in many other cases, it is especially the Deuteronomistic theology that guides Wright's reflection on this issue, probably as a result of his research for the New International Biblical Commentary on Deuteronomy. In the chapter on culture and family it is interesting to see how the author projects the idea of the land onto the family. The family becomes the shorthand for the extended-family-plus-its-land (see 340).

In the second part of this volume, different ethical themes are addressed using the triangular scheme outlined in the first part. Wright's methodology can be indicated by examples from the first three chapters of this second part. Working with a triangle of relationship between God, humanity, and the created order and focusing exclusively on the creation information in Gen 1 and 2 (not reading them at all as narratives), Wright concludes in chapter 4 that, although ecological ethical issues are not addressed in the Old Testament, ethical implications are articulated there regarding the creation that "do have a far-reaching impact on how biblically sensitive Christians will want to frame their ecological ethics today" (144). In chapter 5 he indicates that the Old Testament's theology of the land and its theology of creation have plenty to contribute to Christian economic ethics. Our ethics in this area "is built around the first principles of creation, the realism of the fall, the paradigmatic detail of Israel's systematic response to economic problems ... and the eschatological hope of a new world that is as certain as God's own character and promise" (180). In chapter 6, on the land and Christian ethics, he adds to the paradigmatic and eschatological methods the typological method borrowed from the New Testament. In the New Testament the land is almost completely absent, and the holiness of the land and all its other attributes "was transferred to Christ himself" (187). Typologically, "we must first recall the *function* of the land in Israel's life and faith, and then ask what aspect of *Christian* life and faith has absorbed or fulfilled that function in the New Testament" (190). To be in Christ is the same as to be in the land. It denotes a status and relationship given by God, a position of inclusion and security in God's family and a commitment to live worthily by fulfilling the practical responsibilities toward those who share the same relationship with you. Reading the Old Testament text literally and according to key words, Wright then presents a case study on the Jubilee indicating the social, economic, and theological angles from which it can be understood ethically. Nearly the same approach is followed in the remaining five chapters of the second part.

The third part consists of three chapters intended for readers interested in studying the theoretical aspect of Old Testament ethics. The first of these sketches some key points in the history of the Christian interpretation of the Old Testament, indicating some representative approaches to the ethical use of the Old Testament. The author refers to Marcion and the Antiochene fathers and even to more recent confessional approaches such as dispensationalism, theonism, and messianic Judaism. The second chapter summarizes the contributions of several scholars to the discipline of Old Testament ethics during the last thirty year, pointing out agreements and differences between scholars and influences they have had on Wright. In the final chapter Wright deals with the problems of methodology, ideology, and authority experienced in this discipline. In his view, the Old Testament "*carries authority for an ethic of gratitude in view of God's actions for Israel in the past, and an ethic of missional intentionality in view of God's purpose for humanity in the future*" (463).

This *magnum opus* can be used as a textbook by students, teachers, and ministers and all who are interested in the relevance of the Old Testament to contemporary ethics. Scholars may disagree on the methods used and especially on the underlying construct of Old Testament/biblical theology used in the work. It is, however, an educational experience to read Wright's nearly lifelong reflection on a discipline that has become increasingly important.

Les systèmes sacrificiels de l'Ancien Testament: Formes et fonctions du culte sacrificiel à Yhwh, by Alfred Marx. Supplements to Vetus Testamentum 105. Leiden: Brill, 2005. Pp. vi + 266. Cloth. $117.00. ISBN 900414286X.

James W. Watts, Syracuse University, Syracuse, New York

Alfred Marx aims to describe sacrifice in the Hebrew Bible in a systematic way without flattening the variety and contradictions within the corpus or ignoring historical changes to the rituals. The major chapters of the book take up, in turn, the terms and categories used for sacrifices in the Hebrew Bible (ch. 1), its descriptions of the kinds of things to be sacrificed (ch. 2), its descriptions of sacrificial rituals (ch. 3), the place and functions attributed by biblical texts to sacrifice (ch. 4), and the changing conceptions of sacrifice in the exilic and Second Temple periods (ch. 5). Marx tries to avoid flattening the diverse data of the Hebrew Bible by dividing chapters 1, 2, and 4 into separate discussions of the information gleaned from the Priestly strand (P) of the Pentateuch, from Ezekiel, and from Chronicles together with Ezra and Nehemiah, preceded first by a review of scattered references in other biblical books. The lack of information about ritual performance in Chronicles and Ezekiel causes him to limit the scope of chapter 3 to scattered texts and P.

As a result, this book provides a very useful catalog of ritual terms, materials and practices that is sensitive to variation between genres and to change over time. On the basis of that catalog, Marx makes some interesting observations and draws some important conclusions about the presentation of sacrifice in the Hebrew Bible.

Let me start with several of Marx's negative conclusions. He observes that the words "giving" and "gift" are very rarely attributed to sacrifice (50–51, 76). The motif of gift therefore cannot be considered a central motif of Israelite sacrifice. Other materials and goods may be given to God but are never sacrificed, which shows that transfer of goods to God is not sacrifice's principal function. Marx is well aware of the economic stakes involved in animal offerings but sees their significance instead in being living foods that sustain life. "Le sacrifice a à faire avec la vie, non avec la richesse" (76).

Neither is sacrifice fundamentally about killing (109–10, 136–38). The actual killing of the animal had little significance within the rituals, so sacrifice cannot be interpreted primarily as a form of violence. Marx notes that the metaphorical application by psalmic and prophetic texts of sacrificial language to the actions of the divine warrior never spills over into descriptions of actual animal offerings. Ritual killing, whether by laity or Levites, is not given a distinct significance. Marx observes, however, that it does mark a turning point in the ritual. As the final act of the presentation rites usually performed by laity before the priests take over, killing and butchering the animal marks the transition from the profane to the sacred realms (110). He also concedes that, in P at least, sacrifice represents the violence inherent in human lives that depend on the death of living things for their sustenance. In P's unique attention to vegetable offerings (Lev 2), Marx sees it anticipating an eschatological time marked by nonviolence (222).

Neither is sacrifice propitiatory in function. The Hebrew Bible rarely portrays sacrifice as a means to appease YHWH's anger or to forestall divine punishment. Prayer and fasting play this role instead. Sacrifices are presented after rescue has been assured, in thanksgiving for deliverance. Marx suggests that the sacrifice at the end of the flood story (Gen 9) presents a paradigm for this understanding of its role (146–48).

In place of these common misperceptions about Israelite sacrifice, Marx argues that the Hebrew Bible presents sacrifice as feudal tribute (50, 77–80, 86–87, 202–4). Sacrifice is a meal offered to YHWH as a sign of homage, expressing deferential submission. The primary function of sacrifice in the Bible is to organize the relationship between Israel and YHWH along feudal lines in which YHWH is the ruler and the Israelites are the subjects. The sovereign owns the land, and the subjects owe him loyalty and rent. Sacrifice is therefore Israel's response to the gifts that YHWH has given them. "Israël ne donne pas, il restitue" (86). But the exchange is uneven, with Israel only giving back a token part of what it has received. An exchange of life circulates between YHWH and Israel, and the fat and blood reserved for YHWH represent the essence of life. Sacrifice portrays YHWH's similarity and difference from humans—similar in consuming the same foods as humans, radically different in receiving portions prohibited to humans (blood and fat). Marx notes that the feudal emphasis appears already in the fact that the first sacrifices mentioned in the Bible are firstborn and firstfruits offerings (Gen 4), emblematic of the theme of feudal obligations that runs throughout the Hebrew Bible. By manifesting this feudal relationship between Israel and YHWH, Marx argues that sacrifice served a properly theological function in ancient Israel by manifesting a God who is both transcendent and near at hand, other and similar, inaccessible and yet familiar (222).

Marx, whose previous book dealt with vegetable offerings (*Les offrandes végétales dans l'Ancien Testament,* 1994), sees P's depiction of vegetarian offerings as a particularly revealing meditation on the feudal theme. Meal offerings represent the minimal needs of life (bread, flour) but also the tribute due a sovereign (80–85). In contrast to meat, cereals and especially bread were the normal food of ancient Israelites. Oil, wine, and honey, on the other hand, characterized festive meals and were also Israel's principal exports. Vegetable offerings could thus represent the land itself. They were not simply substitutes for animal offerings but represented the minimum necessities for life and the characteristic produce of the land. Offering them expressed submission to the divine host. They are what their name indicates, *minḥāh* "tribute."

Marx makes a strong case for a feudal interpretation of sacrifice in the Hebrew Bible. It is a plausible hypothesis for how sacrifice was regarded by ancient Israelites as well, though here the constraints imposed by having only literary evidence recommends caution. Marx begins his book with an optimistic assessment of our ability to understand the meaning of sacrifice as practiced in ancient Israel: "L'Ancien Testament est ainsi l'une des rares sources écrites permettant de connaître de façon précise le fonctionnement du sacrifice et son rôle dans une société antique" (3). Later he qualifies that optimism, noting that it is impossible to determine the importance of sacrifice in ancient Israelite life. One can only summarize the functions attributed to it by the authors of the texts (144–45). Nevertheless, he argues that, although P does not provide a systematic description of the sacrificial cult, it participates "à un système rigoureux, élaboré avec un soin extrême et selon une parfaite logique" (156). Thus, despite the great care with which Marx has tried to distinguish the depiction of sacrifice in different texts and periods, he still presents a synthesis that goes beyond the text's authors to a conception that existed somewhere, in some people's minds, in ancient Israel and Judah. Who conceived of sacrifice in this way, and when, remains unclear.

A second methodological difficulty involves Marx's use of the word "sacrifice" itself. Of course he notes the obvious point that "sacrifice" in the ancient world is not summarized by a singular noun, nor does it describe a single phenomenon but is plural and designated by varied terminology (15). That fact, however, does not stop him at several points from distinguishing what is and is not a sacrifice. Thus, in noting rightly that the sacrificial system represented in the Hebrew Bible changed over time, he observes that some rites became sacrifices that were not such originally (e.g., the Passover rite), new sacrifices were invented (the ḥaṭṭā't and the 'āšām), and others disappeared (libation with wine, absent from Ezek 40–48) (48). He also argues that, while nonliving materials and goods could be donated to YHWH, they were never sacrificed (76). In making these distinctions, Marx is pointing out some real differences in how the texts describe different categories of offerings. He never makes clear, however, what exactly the word "sacrifice" means in this context and why it is particularly helpful for making these distinctions.

The least effective part of this book is the last chapter, which reconstructs the motives behind exilic and postexilic changes in sacrifice. Marx argues that, since the sacrificial cult did not forestall the exile, it would not be restored in exactly the same way as before. The revisions that P and Ezekiel introduce into the rituals were intended to render the cult more effective (211). He also agues that the reestablished cult aimed to integrate new forms of piety that had become popular during the year's of the temple's abandonment. P integrated submission to Torah and the importance of routine purity, while Chronicles gave a central place to the prayer of adoration (218). Here Marx's argument rests on supposition more than evidence. Although the modifications advanced by P and Ezekiel are reasonably clear (in the case of Chronicles, the differences could have more to do with the author's emphasis than with changes in ritual practice), nowhere do our extant texts give direct evidence that such motives lay behind them.

These criticisms aside, this book provides a very helpful catalog of the offerings of Israel as presented by the Hebrew Bible and points out neglected features of that presentation that challenge long-standing stereotypes of how biblical sacrifice works and what it means. It is an important resource for studying biblical rituals and the religious ideas they may reflect.

PENTATEUCH

The Bible with Sources Revealed: A New View into the Five Books of Moses, by Richard Elliott Friedman. San Francisco: HarperSanFrancisco, 2003. Pp. 379, Hardcover, $29.95, ISBN 0060530693.

Christoph Levin, Ludwig-Maximilians-Universität München, Munich, Germany

With this volume, the author of the best-selling introduction *Who Wrote the Bible?* presents a translation of the Torah in which the sources and redactions are typographically indicated. Apart from a few personal idiosyncrasies, Friedman is a supporter of the Documentary Hypothesis in the form that emerged toward the end of the nineteenth century and that was the "customary" hypothesis in pentateuchal research until it was emphatically called in question (in English-language research, first by F. V. Winnett in 1965). Accordingly, Friedman distributes the text between the sources J, E, P, and D. To these are added the redactions: R^{JE} (which fuses J and E into JE), R (which fused JE, P, and D), other independent texts, Gen 14 as a source of its own, Deuteronomy (Dtn), and two redactional layers within Deuteronomy: Dtr1 (from the time of Josiah), and Dtr2 (from exilic times).

The translation takes up almost the whole of the book (33–368). It is supplemented by a brief bibliography (369–79) that refers the reader to other works by Friedman and to select titles on pentateuchal research. Recent German-language exegesis is not taken into account, with the exception of E. Blum, R. Rendtorff (in English translation) and H. H. Schmid, and there is no discussion of even their positions. For Friedman, the Documentary Hypothesis is, essentially speaking, self-evident.

The book begins with a brief introduction in which the Documentary Hypothesis is justified with "seven main arguments" (1–31). These arguments are of varying force. (1) The assertion that the sources can be distinguished according to their position in the history of the Hebrew language is not supported by a single example. This is not by chance. (2) The list of terminology names a number of typical P phrases and D phrases and only four examples from J (8–10). This, too, is not fortuitous. (3) The "consistent content" refers to the revelation of the name for God and otherwise to the provisions for the cult, the cultic personnel, and the numerical system (10–12). Again, P prevails. (4) The narrative flow, on the other hand, is demonstrated mainly on the basis of the non-Priestly text, and from the fused stratum JE at that, not from the sources J and E themselves (13). This argument can also be read as a pointer to a certain weakness in the Documentary Hypothesis. (5) The well known tradition-history connections between the book of Jeremiah and Deuteronomy, between Ezekiel and the Priestly Code, between the book of Hosea and the Elohist, and between the sources for the books of Samuel (the "Court History") and the Yahwist (14–18) are not dependent on the Documentary Hypothesis; they retain their validity even if other hypotheses are adopted. The direction of the dependence is not as certain as Friedman seems to think. For example, it can be shown that P was originally dependent on Ezekiel, not vice versa.

(6) With regard to the historical setting of J, Friedman cites the traditional arguments generally used in localizing this source in Judah. Surprisingly, he dates J as belonging to the period of the divided kingdom, thereby taking too little account of the fact that most of the stories about the patriarchs are set in the northern kingdom of Israel and that the tribes are there presented as a unity, which was no longer the case after Israel and Judah had separated (18ff.). Closer to the customary view is the dating of the Elohist, which is placed in the northern

kingdom of Israel. What is strange is the proposal (21–24) that P should be dated as belonging to the period of Hezekiah (715-687 B.C.E.). Friedman ignores many cogent arguments according to which P did not precede Deuteronomy but succeeded it. On the other hand, as regards the connection between Deuteronomy and Josiah, he follows the generally accepted arguments (24–26). The same is true of the sequence JE–P (24–26ff.). About the relationship of the Elohist to Deuteronomism (which was an important question in earlier research), the reader learns nothing. The Deuteronomistic redaction is presented according to F M. Cross's block model, simply as an undiscussed fact. Other solutions are not mentioned.

(7) No doubt the strongest argument for the Documentary Hypothesis is that of convergence (27–31), and I agree with Friedman "that this hypothesis best accounts for the fact that all this evidence of so many kinds comes together so consistently" (28). But this also is true only with some reservations. It is not without justice that the existence of the source E has been questioned by many scholars since W. Rudolph and P. Volz, *Der Elohist als Erzähler: Ein Irrweg der Pentateuchkritik?* (Giessen, 1933). It is basic for the understanding of biblical literary history that the Supplementary Hypothesis is the "normal hypothesis" (even within the Pentateuch) and that the Documentary Hypothesis (i.e., the fusion of *two* literary sources) is only a notable exception.

The subtitle calls the undertaking "a new look into the five books of Moses." This is not in every respect correct. There were almost from the beginning several comparable presentations of the text differentiated according to sources. An early example was K. D. Ilgen's *Urkunden des Jerusalemischen Tempelarchivs in ihrer Urgestalt* (Halle, 1798). Ilgen presented the sources in German translation, as E. Kautzsch and A. Socin also did later in *Die Genesis mit aeusserer Unterscheidung der Quellenschriften übersetzt* (Freiburg, 1888). The English equivalent was W. E. Addis, *Documents of the Hexateuch* (London, 1892). Another possibility was the edition of the Hebrew text, as in E. Boehmer, *Liber Genesis Pentateuchicus* (Halle, 1860), or the volumes of the famous Polychrome Bible edited by P. Haupt, *The Sacred Books of the Old Testament: A Critical Edition of the Hebrew Text Printed in Colors, with Notes* (Leipzig, 1894, 1896, 1900; the only books of the Pentateuch to appear here were *Genesis,* by C. J. Ball; *Leviticus,* by S. R. Driver and H. A. White; and *Numbers,* by J. A. Paterson.) O. Eißfeldt's German *Hexateuch synopsis* (Leipzig, 1922) had a wide circulation. From a later period A. Campbell and M. O'Brien, *Sources of the Pentateuch: Texts, Introductions, Annotations* (Minneapolis, 1993) deserves mention. In commentaries on Genesis, Exodus, and Numbers, in so far as they include a translation, differentiation according to the sources of the Pentateuch is the rule.

The very authors who offer a version of the pentateuchal sources without a commentary are apt to overvalue the persuasive power of this presentation. The difficulties of the Documentary Hypothesis have seldom been more clearly demonstrated than by Eißfeldt's *Hexateuch synopsis.* It could not have been better invented by the opponents of the hypothesis themselves.

Friedman calls his translation "the largest collection of evidence ever assembled in one place concerning this hypothesis" (i.e., the Documentary Hypothesis). This considerable claim can only relate to the fact that the compilation deviates from earlier work by now including the whole of Leviticus, the law-related parts of Numbers, and the whole of Deuteronomy. Admittedly, the evidential value of this expansion is limited, because a differentiation of sources does not in any case come into question in these texts or—as in the main section of the book of Deuteronomy—is related not to the Documentary Hypothesis but to the redaction history of the Deuteronomistic History.

An erroneous impression is even given when, for example, the whole of Leviticus is assigned without differentiation to the Priestly Code, with the exception of the commandment about booths, Lev 23:39–43, and the mention of the exile at the close of the curse in Lev 26:39–45, both of which are assigned to the redaction R for historical reasons, not literary ones. (The Holiness Code is only referred to in a footnote on p. 218, and then without presenting the reader with a definite opinion.) An over-simplification of this kind gives a false impression of the literary character of the sources. Earlier research never distinguished the sources in as undifferentiated a way as Friedman, and anyone who has eyes to see can perceive even on the basis of the English translation that the simple coherence that Friedman suggests through the typography does not in fact exist.

What is really "new" in Friedman are a number of decisions in which he deviates from the generally received view. On the one hand, these make the book interesting for the discussion, but on the other they are a problem. To take one example, Friedman assumes a separate source for Gen 5:1–28, 30–32; 7:6; 9:28–29; 11:10–26, 32a: the Book of Records. This hypothesis, which is based on Gen 5, can be found in earlier research as well. It is based on the deviating *toledot* formula in Gen 5:1 (*sefer toledot* instead of *toledot*), but Friedman does not define the Book of Records as a source within the framework of P (which would make sense) but as a source *parallel* to P that was only linked to the other sources by R. In this way he destroys a fundamental premise of the Documentary Hypothesis: the genealogical and chronological framework of P. The *toledot* formula usually counts as characteristic of P, but Friedman now assigns it to R (Gen 2:4a; 6:9; 10:1; 11:10, 27; 25:12, 19; 36:1; 37:2a). It is supposed to have been taken over in imitation from the Book of Records. Only 36:9 is left to P, no reason for this being given. In the face of such arbitrary proceedings, academic teaching is better served by a "conventional" account such as those offered by Campbell and O'Brien.

The fact that Friedman has examined the share of R is undoubtedly useful. Earlier the customary procedure was to distribute the text between the sources without any remainder, and this was one of the contestable aspects of the Documentary Hypothesis. But Friedman still underestimates the share of the redaction, and above all he ignores the part of the text that was added only after the fusion of P and J and that can be designated through the siglum R^S (= supplements to the final redaction). There are numerous texts in the Pentateuch to which the proven criteria of source differentiation cannot be applied, because they combine the characteristics of several sources. In such cases it is better to dispense with forced analyses and to accept that these passages already presuppose the redactional combination of the pentateuchal sources. According to my own impression, about a third of the text of the book of Genesis is later than the fusion between P and J (e.g., Gen 14; 15; 20–22*; 34; 38; 46*; 48; 49). In the books Exodus to Numbers, where earlier research already reckoned with extensive revision, the share may well be greater still. We may remember the famous judgment of one of the fathers of the Documentary Hypothesis, A. Kuenen, in his *Historico-Critical Inquiry into the Origin and Composition of the Hexateuch* (London, 1886, 315): "The redaction of the Hexateuch, then, assumes the form of a continuous diaskeue or diorthosis, and the redactor becomes a collective body … including the whole series of his more or less independent followers." Anyone who wishes (and with justice!) to defend the Documentary Hypothesis can do so successfully only if he or she does not ignore the criticism leveled at it during past decades but integrates it.

Cult and Character: Purification Offerings, Day of Atonement, and Theodicy, by Roy E. Gane. Winona Lake, Ind.: Eisenbrauns, 2005. Pp. xxii + 394. Hardcover. $39.50. ISBN 1575061015.

Christian A. Eberhart, Lutheran Theological Seminary, Saskatoon, Saskatchewan, Canada

In *Cult and Character: Purification Offerings, Day of Atonement, and Theodicy*, Roy E. Gane, Professor of Hebrew Bible and Ancient Near Eastern Languages at the Theological Seminary of Andrews University, joins in the ongoing quest for the interpretation of cultic atonement and shows how the Day of Atonement rituals ultimately portray the character of YHWH. Considering recent scholarly claims that all ritual activity is necessarily polyvalent and ambiguous, Gane makes an important contribution by presenting a comprehensive and integrated system of atonement based on meticulous attention to the goals of sacrificial rituals explicitly stated in biblical texts. In doing so he engages in a detailed discussion with past and present research, especially that of Jacob Milgrom. In light of these features and its technical language, the book is primarily targeted at the scholarly community.

Gane's volume is organized in four parts. In part 1, "Ritual, Meaning, and System" (1–42), Gane defines ritual as an activity system that receives its meaning through a goal explicitly assigned to it in the biblical text. This goal is typically a process of transformation "involving interaction with a reality ordinarily inaccessible to the material domain" (15). Gane goes on to outline the entire history of source criticism and diachronic analysis of both the material of Exod 25–Lev 16 that J. Wellhausen identified as priestly codex and the Day of Atonement ritual in Lev 16. Gane concludes that a scholarly consensus regarding the history of composition of these texts has not yet been achieved. By contrast, he provides observations on how the ritual of Lev 16 is functionally integrated into the larger

context of the Pentateuch and argues for its unity. He takes these results to legitimate a synchronic approach to the Day of Atonement rituals as an integrated
system. In the final chapter of part 1, Gane reviews scholarly discussions dealing
with the relationship between the כפר (atonement) processes that occur throughout the year and those of the Day of Atonement.

Entitled "Purification Offerings Performed throughout the Year," part 2 (43–
213) mainly deals with חטאת rituals in Lev 4:1–5:13 and Lev 16. Gane maintains
that the meaning of these rituals is ultimately determined by goals explicitly stated
in the biblical text: as a prerequisite for forgiveness, they purge sin and impurities (hence he follows Milgrom's translation of חטאת as "purification offering").
Gane makes a basic distinction between two kinds of purification offering rituals
depending on where the sacrificial blood is applied: he labels the ritual in Lev
4:22–26 "outer-altar purification offering," and that in Lev 4:3–12 "outer-sanctum
purification offering." After listing all ritual activities of these kinds of sacrifice,
he provides detailed summaries of scholarly discussions of their purposes. Here
he distinguishes himself from most recent scholarship by recognizing that animal
slaughter is not the culmination point of the ritual and that the elaborate blood
application rite, while being the central ritual element of this type of sacrifice,
is not the sole element to constitute its goal. Rather, Gane recognizes that "it is
the entire ritual, including the suet 'debt payment,' that is necessary for achieving
כפר" (67). A much-debated problem in this context is the question if the instructions that officiating priests must eat the meat of certain purification offerings
contribute to the expiatory process as such. Gane affirms this by calling the meat
consumption a "postrequisite" part of expiation through which the priests participate in the process of divine forgiveness. Gane then challenges Milgrom's theory
that the purification offering always purges the altar and/or sanctuary because
sacrificial blood is applied there. He attempts to establish a "revised" interpretation (108) through an extensive and detailed study of כפר formulas and their
prepositions—especially the preposition "from" (מֶן)—describing the objects of
purification (illustrated by a total of twelve tables). He finds that, in the context
of altar consecration, purification offerings do purge the sanctuary; yet in all
other cases he rejects Milgrom's interpretation and arrives at the conclusion that
"purification offerings … remove evil from their offerer(s)" (142). This conclusion becomes the basis of further analysis of the purification offering: Gane goes
on to question Milgrom's theory that the severity of sin or impurity determines
how deeply they penetrate into the sanctuary. Then he develops his own *modus
operandi* of the purification offering (which partially parallels that of N. Zohar):
human defilement is transferred to the sacrificial animal through the hand-leaning gesture. When sacrificial blood is applied at the sanctuary, this defilement is
further transferred to Yhwh (169, 176, 180).

In part 3 (215–302) Gane studies "Phases of כפר." Foundational to this
entire section is his distinction of terms specifying evil. On the one hand, טמאה
refers to physical ritual impurity that results from the general human state of
mortality. On the other hand, Gane carefully distinguishes between פשע and

חטאת, the former defining inexpiable defiant sin, the latter expiable nondefiant sin; finally, the term עון refers to human culpability as the consequence of sin. Gane then determines that different ritual procedures correspond to these expressions of human evil: The purgation of human impurity requires only one outer-altar purification offering, while removal of nondefiant sin requires two phases, accomplished through one purification offering during the year plus corporate purgation through the inner-sanctum purification offering on the Day of Atonement. In addition, the scapegoat is a unique ritual that returns sins and transgressions to Azazel, Yнwн's enemy, who is seen as the source of evil and chaos. Gane thus identifies five individual rituals that form the Day of Atonement complex.

Under the title "Cult and Theodicy," part 4 (303–81) attempts to construct both the profile of Yнwн and the divine-human relationship as they emerge from the interpretation of the purification rituals in parts 1–3. Applying his understanding of two phases of atonement, Gane holds that Israelites need to prove their loyalty to Yнwн twice: throughout the year by following purification rituals and once more on the Day of Atonement by practicing self-denial and abstaining from work. The disloyal are condemned—following talmudic traditions, Gane labels the Day of Atonement "Israel's judgment day" (307). These texts ultimately portray Yнwн as a just king who is responsible for enforcing laws but who also chooses to show mercy when granting forgiveness. The latter, however, can only happen at a price for the divine king: ultimately, Yнwн becomes the bearer of human sin, which is symbolized by the notion that the sanctuary gets defiled through human sin and impurity. Thus an alternative way of describing the purpose of the Day of Atonement is to say that "Yнwн sheds judicial responsibility that he has incurred by forgiving guilty people ... and clears his name of association with those who have been disloyal" (323). Gane concludes part 4 with a chapter devoted to biblical narratives that confirm several aspects of divine justice as they are revealed in ritual texts and a chapter that studies how theodicy is enacted in two Sumerian and Babylonian celebrations. Gane's book includes indexes of modern authors and of Scriptures.

This remarkable resource will easily find its place next to many other established studies on the purification offering and/or ritual atonement, such as those of J. Milgrom, B. Janowski, N. Kiuchi, A. Schenker, B. Schwartz, and N. Zohar. Nonetheless, I would like to offer a few critical comments. First, Gane seems to assume that a synchronic approach in biblical interpretation is only legitimate if the prehistory of a text does not emerge as composite (see 36–37). Modern structuralist exegetes, however, would challenge this point of view and suggest that texts with a complex prehistory can also be interpreted on the level of final redaction. Second, Gane calls the burning rite on the altar of burnt offering "a mandatory payment of an obligation or 'debt' to Yнwн" (66; see also 67, 239). He supports his understanding with scholarship dating from 1862 (Kurtz) and 1925 (Gray), but such scholarly opinions are outdated. A sacrifice is not a payment; this understanding is already contradicted by the fact that every sacrifice is an "offering for YʜᴡH." Third, Gane notes that consumption of sacrificial meat by the officiating priest is a requirement and concludes that it therefore contributes to the overall atonement (92). Yet there is a difference between a ritual activity that, as part of the ritual, is prescribed and thus needs to be carried out by the priest, and the question whether this ritual activity actually contributes toward atonement. Priestly portions are also available from other types of sacrifice (see Lev 7:28–35), even though they do not contribute to their cultic goal. Fourth, Gane's observation has been highlighted above that the atoning effect of the purification offering is not limited to the blood rite, but he does not follow through with it. When discussing the atonement rituals for the parturient woman in Lev 12, Gane understands the atonement formula to refer exclusively to the blood application of the purification offering, even though the text explicitly states (12:7), *and* Gane himself acknowledges (112; see also 119), that atonement is the result of both a burnt offering and a purification offering. He thus neglects the fact that atonement is accomplished through two distinct ritual components: a blood rite and a burning rite. Once this is acknowledged, a basic distinction between their respective effects emerges: blood rites do purge the sanctuary and its components, while burning rites accomplish forgiveness for sins that the offerer bears. Accordingly, table 1 on "Components of Language Governed by כִּפֶּר" (110–11) would more accurately reflect the cultic reality of ritual atonement if it included a column indicating whether atonement is accomplished by blood rites alone (Lev 16:16, 17b, etc.), by combined blood and burning rites (Lev 4:20b, 26b, etc.), or by purification offerings and other offerings (Lev 12:6; 16:33). Later Gane attempts to explain that the combination of a burnt offering and purification offering "amounts to a greater purification offering" (219), but are not the rituals of these different types of sacrifice and the explicit statements of their goals substantially different?

My last criticism pertains to Gane's overall understanding of the purification offering's *modus operandi*. Gane concludes that both the outer-altar and outer-sanctum purification offering as a whole absorb sin and impurity from the offerer (176–78). However, his interpretation leads to several problems, of which I will address here no more than three. First, Gane assumes that the hand-leaning gesture can have two different meanings: while in most types of animal sacrifice it indicates ownership (or the end of ownership, as Gane specifies), it is supposedly only in the context of the outer-altar and outer-sanctum purification offering that this gesture transfers sin to the animal. Such sin transfer is in fact indicated in Lev 16:21 when Aaron leans both hands on the scapegoat. This demonstrates the awareness of the priestly writer(s) that a change in the meaning of similar ritual activity requires explanation. But precisely the lack of any such explanation in the sacrificial rituals of Lev 1–7 should be taken as a signal that one and the same hand-leaning gesture that is performed in an identical fashion for (most) sacrificial animals can hardly have two different meanings. In addition, Gane puts forth the general theory that a purification offering purges the offerer at the moment of physical contact during the hand-leaning gesture. This leads him to interpret the red cow purification offering in an analogous fashion: human defilement from corpse contamination is transferred to the cow when its red ashes are applied to the person. Yet because this reverses the chronological sequence of the red cow ritual, Gane explains that "it is as though this pollution is transmitted back through time and space to the burning of the cow" (183; see 190). How much more straightforward would be the assumption that the red ashes that contain the cow's blood are holy as such and purge the human being by virtue of this holiness? Finally, Gane holds that the bodies of the outer-altar and outer-sanctum purification offering become the vehicle for human sin and impurity. If this were true, how could the suet of such ritually defiled sacrificial animals consequently be offered on the most holy altar as an "offering for Yʜᴡʜ" (קָרְבָּן לַיהוָה, Lev 4:23, 28, 32; 5:11)? Only blemish-free and pure materials are fit for sacrifice. In this context it should be mentioned that the *torah* of the purification offering (Lev 6:17–23) does not describe sacrificial meat and blood as impure, as both Milgrom and Gane claim; rather, the purification offering is explicitly labeled "most holy" (6:18, 22), and the required measures are supposed to prevent the uncontrolled spreading of such ritual holiness.

I offer these comments in the hope of broadening the scholarly perception of atonement that has so far tended to focus on rituals of blood application. Despite these issues I consider Gane's new book stimulating and—considering the complex and technical nature of its subject matter—well-written.

Old Testament Story and Christian Ethics: The Rape of Dinah as a Case Study, by Robin Parry. Paternoster Biblical Monographs. Waynesboro, Ga.: Paternoster, 2004. Pp. xx + 350. Paper. $29.99. ISBN 1842272101.

Yael Shemesh, Bar-Ilan University, Ramat-Gan 52900, Israel

Genesis 34 generates many differences of opinion among its readers and students. Their disagreements about the key question on the plot level—whether it is a story of rape or of seduction—leads to divergent moral evaluations of the characters. Even starting from the assumption that Dinah was raped fails to resolve all of the disagreements. There is still room for questions about the narrator's implicit stand with regard to the massacre of the Shechemites by Dinah's brothers or whether Shechem himself is described as an irremediable villain or in more complex terms.

Robin Parry's book, based on his doctoral dissertation, seeks to clarify these and other questions. The series in which it appears, Paternoster Biblical Monographs, may indicate that the book has not only exegetical but also theological goals. As the author announces in the very first sentence, "this book is an attempt to argue that Old Testament stories are ethically valuable and to set up some guidelines for *Christian* ethical *re*appropriation of such OT narratives" (3, emphasis original).

The overt religious commitment of the author, who sees the Bible as an inspired text that a believing Christian cannot gainsay, may be viewed as an obstacle to objective exegesis. But as many have argued, there really is no such thing as objective exegesis. A commentary from an atheistic perspective or based on a fundamental rejection of the biblical text, too, is tainted by subjectivity. What is more, if we judge by the outcome, Parry's study is balanced and scholarly. Although one may disagree with some of his conclusions, none of them is unreasonable or clearly forced.

Parry's canvas ranges far beyond Gen 34. The first chapter, "Philosophical Reflections on Narrative Ethics" (3–47), deals with philosophical hermeneutics and offers a sympathetic presentation of Paul Ricoeur's theory about the decisive role that stories play in the shaping of individual and communal identity. The second chapter, "Biblical-Theological Reflections on Christian Ethical Appropriation of Old Testament Stories" (48–84), moves from philosophical hermeneutics to theological hermeneutics, with the goal of showing that "story is the context within which Old Testament ethics lives and moves and has its being" (48). To this end, Parry draws on John Barton's three models of biblical ethics: divine commands, natural law, and the imitation of God. Parry maintains that only in the framework of story can these three models find full expression in the Old Testament (53). He sets himself a second goal: "to outline the biblical metanarrative which plays a primary role in the shaping of Christian communal and individual identity" (49).

Part 2 of the book, "The Rape of Dinah as a Case Study," turns to the story of Dinah in the context of Old Testament ethics, on the one hand, and to the ways in which a believing Christian can draw ethical lessons from the story, on the other hand. This part consists of four chapters.

Chapter 3, "A History of the Interpretation of Genesis 34 with Special Reference to Its Use in Ethics" (87–122), is a fascinating journey in the footsteps of exegesis of the story from the second century to the present. Reading the contradictory interpretations, one cannot avoid wondering how the same basic data can be read in such widely varying fashions by different people and what this means for the eternal question of whether one can ever arrive at the "correct" interpretation. For example, some argue that Dinah was seduced rather than raped (e.g., Bechtel); some lay the blame at her door (e.g., Ambrose, *Genesis Rabbah*). Some describe Dinah in a positive fashion and emphasize her guiltlessness (e.g., Philo). Some justify the massacre (e.g., *Jubilees*, the book of Judith, Philo), while others describe it as wicked (e.g., John Calvin, Fewell and Gunn). Some believe that the story portrays Jacob favorably (e.g., Martin Luther, Fewell and Gunn), while others think that he is depicted in an unflattering light (e.g., Sternberg). Finally, some see Hamor as a devoted father (e.g., Sternberg), whereas others argue that he failed in his duty to educate his son (e.g., Luther).

The chapter is also a fine demonstration of how various authors have exploited Dinah's story for political and ideological purposes: *Jubilees* uses it to accent the sinful nature of intermarriage; the *Testament of Levi* utilizes it for a polemic against the Samaritans; and Luther appropriates it to denounce a common phenomenon of his age—the marrying off of prepubescent girls.

Particularly prominent is the use made of the story for gender construction. Parry presents many examples of the phenomenon of blaming the victim, Dinah (and every woman who is raped), and the attempt to use the story to educate the parents of daughters, and daughters themselves, to eschew curiosity, maintain their modesty, and seclude themselves at home. For lack of space, I cite only one example among the many interesting sources presented in the book. In the thirteenth-century English *Ancrene Wisse* (i.e., guidebook for anchoresses), the story of Dinah is cited to justify the seclusion of nuns and as a warning to women not to peak out the window—both to avoid seeing inappropriate things and also to avoid being seen. After all, it was Dinah's curiosity to "visit the daughters of the land" that led to the traumatic results both for her family and for the people of Shechem.

Chapter 4, "An Interpretation of Genesis 34" (123–78), offers a reading of the chapter in its historical and literary context. It examines linguistic, structural, and stylistic questions, analogies and type scenes, and the way in which the narrator shapes the characters. The discussion is balanced, and I found myself agreeing with most of its conclusions, such as that the story is about rape and not seduction; that exogamy is definitely an issue; that Shechem is presented in a complex fashion, so that even though he commits a heinous crime when he rapes Dinah, 34:3, which avers his great love for her, softens the negative judgment against him (*pace* Scholz); and that, from the biblical point of view, marriage to the rapist is a lesser evil for the victim (again, *pace* Scholz), for all that modern readers are horrified by the idea of a woman's marrying her attacker. I should add that even in modern times, in societies that practice abduction-marriage and the abductor rapes his prey, in most cases the latter chooses to marry her kidnapper-rapist (see William G. Lockwood, "Bride Theft and Social Maneuverability in Western Bosnia," *Anthropological Quarterly* 47 [1974]: 254; Brian Stross, "Tzeltal Marriage by Capture," *Anthropological Quarterly* 47 [1974]: 340–42).

The main question raised by Parry has to do with the narrator's attitude toward the massacre. As he shows, the story contains elements that justify it and others that condemn it. Parry believes that the implicit author agrees with Jacob and sees the massacre as an overreaction and immoral deed, even though he also makes an effort to get readers to identify with the brothers' motives.

Chapter 5, "Genesis 34 in Intertextual Communion with the Canon" (179–218), looks at Gen 34 in the light of other biblical stories: Gen 49:5–7, Exod 32, and Num 25 and 31. In Gen 49, the last word in Simeon and Levi's dispute with their father about how they should have acted in Shechem is not given to the brothers (as it is in Gen 34) but to Jacob, who on his deathbed curses them and denounces their violent tempers. In Levi's case, however, the curse turns into a blessing when the members of the tribe of Levi or one of its sons (Phinehas) wreak vengeance out of their zeal for the Lord (Exod 32, Num 25). Parry accepts Gordon J. Wenham's argument that the story of Phinehas in Num 25 is a mirror image of Gen 34 and even adds new elements to Wenham's analogy. But rejecting Wenham's argument that Phinehas's zealous act sheds positive light on Simeon and Levi, Parry sees Num 25 as a corrective to Gen 34: it is because the violence of Levi's descendants derives from their zeal for the Lord (unlike the massacre perpetrated by Simeon and Levi) that the curse is transformed into a blessing; the Levites are indeed scattered among the other tribes, but this is to enable them to fulfill their spiritual mission.

Later in the chapter Parry examines the relations between the patriarchal story in Gen 34, on the one hand, and the Mosaic period and the New Testament, on the other. He enumerates continuities, of which the most important is the vigorous condemnation of rape alongside the rejection of the brothers' exaggerated revenge. But he also finds some discontinuities, notably the attitude toward the Canaanites: *herem*—proscription—was not yet the law at the time of the patriarchs, when peaceful relations with the Canaanites are described as the ideal. Accordingly, he proposes that implied readers have a complex grasp of Gen 34: "They will see in the massacre *at one and the same time* an ethical model to be avoided *and* a partial type of the conquest which is to be approved of" (204, emphasis original).

Chapter 6, "Can Biblical Stories Be Bad for Us? Feminist Hermeneutics and the Rape of Dinah" (219–42), is an interesting attempt to create a dialogue between faith-and-trust exegesis and feminist exegesis, which is at its core a hermeneutics of suspicion. Parry surveys different and contradictory approaches in feminist exegesis and, not surprisingly, feels comfortable with the revisionist line that calls for reinterpreting the Bible in a nonpatriarchal reading, as well as with the integrationist approach that emphasizes that the main message of the Bible is human freedom. His position and analyses are very similar to those of Phyllis Trible in her pioneering article (not cited in the book), "Depatriarchalizing in Biblical Interpretation," *JAAR* 41 (1973): 30–48.

When Parry turns to examining the story of Dinah from a feminist perspective, he does not find any trace of the indictment of the victim that is so common in midrashim and in commentaries. He distinguishes between the fact that the story (like the entire Bible) is patriarchal and the question of whether it means to encourage patriarchalism—which he answers in the negative.

The book concludes with two appendices: "A Discourse Analysis of Genesis 34" (249–92) and "Genesis 49:5–6" (293–97). Personally, I found the first appendix tiresome and technical, with its method detracting from the reading experience, but those who are interested in the method may benefit from it. All readers will certainly do so from the body of this important and engrossing book, which is warmly recommended to anyone interested in biblical narrative in general and in Gen 34 in particular, on the one hand, and to those who are interested in theological hermeneutics and the possibility of interweaving faith and academic scholarship, on the other.

Bible and Midrash: The Story of 'The Wooing of Rebekah' (Gen. 24), by Lieve M.
Teugels. Contributions to Biblical Exegesis and Theology 35. Leuven: Peeters,
2004. Pp. 246. Paper. €32.00. ISBN 9042914262.

Deborah Green, University of Oregon, Eugene, Oregon

Bible and Midrash: The Story of 'The Wooing of Rebekah' (Gen. 24) is, in part,
based on Lieve Teugels's dissertation, which was written in Dutch and defended
in 1994. From the title this reviewer expected a thoroughgoing treatment of
the Rebekah cycle in the Hebrew Bible and midrash but found instead that the
major focus of this work is the methods one might employ to analyze biblical and
midrashic texts. Thus, the Rebekah cycle serves sometimes as a paradigm, at other
times as a frame, for the larger methodological discussions and issues. Although
the book is closely related to her dissertation, Teugels clarifies in her preface that
the book is more of a compilation and revision of several essays connected to the
dissertation that were written "prior to and after" (7) its completion.

The book is divided into two parts: one on the Bible and one on midrash. In
the preliminaries to part 1, Teugels provides what she refers to as a "Colometric
Translation of Genesis 24." The author states that she is presenting the translation according to "Delimitation Criticism"; that is, she is following the traditional
Masoretic accents for her translation. The rationale for this choice is that "the
medieval Tiberian masoretes … did not invent this system but based themselves
on much older traditions and refined them" (13). Part 1 includes six chapters of
varying lengths and subjects. The first two chapters, "Methodological Orientation
and Introduction" and "Events, Plot and Type-Scene in Genesis 24," detail Teugels's methodology for reading biblical texts. In the first chapter she defines the
narratological approach and each of its constituent parts. For example, Teugels
discusses such aspects as the difference between story-time and text-time and
characters and characterization, citing along the way various scholars who have
employed similar literary methods. Among these, Teugels relies heavily on Shlo-
mit Rimmon-Kenan. For those who enjoy discussions of literary method, Teugels
is a gifted explicator. Her points are focused and highly nuanced.

Chapter 2 reviews aspects of the plot and events of the Rebekah narrative
and provides thorough discussion of the betrothal "type scene." As in her first
chapter, Teugels begins theoretically but soon narrows her lens on the Rebekah
narrative and its discrete particulars. Here Teugels turns primarily to Robert Alter
and his use of Buber's and Rosenzweig's conception of *Leitwortstil* to investigate
and compare the key words of Rebekah's betrothal scene with those of the other
matriarchs and patriarchs. Teugels ends this chapter by intimating that, although
divine election (as Westermann argues) is observable throughout the Rebekah
cycle, her overall impression of Gen 24 is closer to Ellen Van Wolde's position
that the cycle emphasizes both human initiative and divine election.

The next chapter entails a brief review of the preceding Genesis chapters (Gen
22–23) in order to provide the literary context for Gen 24. Discussion of these
chapters is necessary for the associations Teugels draws later among Rebekah's

betrothal, her birth narrative, and Sarah's death. The placement of this chapter, its brevity, and the fact that it is missing similar contextual discussion for Gen 25–30 somewhat disrupts the flow of the book and appears rather forced. However, the discussion itself and the connections that Teugels later makes among these events (in chs. 4–6) will be of great interest to students of the Hebrew Bible, as these provide some of Teugels's most interesting insights and opinions.

The heart of the analysis is found in the next three chapters of part 1. In succession, the author presents meticulous analyses of the key words repeated throughout the narrative, other significant repetitions (e.g., of actions and accounts of events), the individual characters and their characterization, the consideration of Rebekah's narrative as part of the matriarchal cycle, and several conclusions. These chapters find Teugels in her element. She provides a careful contextual reading in each of these areas, and her conclusions are prudent, lucid, and persuasive. In particular, her assessment of Abraham's servant as a manipulative "salesman" who selectively chooses his words and which information to impart to Rebekah's family in order to achieve the best result (i.e., Rebekah as wife for Isaac) is convincing and intriguing. The reader will find each of these chapters full of new information presented in a simple and digestible format. Most important, one finishes the biblical section of the book with a fuller picture of the Rebekah narrative rather than the overwrought deconstruction so prevalent today in biblical scholarship. The only point with which some may quibble is Teugels's character analysis of Laban. She insists that Laban's negative portrayal derives from rabbinic commentary on Deut 26:5 which, through a pun on the root 'bd, interprets Laban as the Aramaean who tries to kill Jacob. However, one need only read Gen 25–30 to see that Laban is portrayed as at best a trickster and at worst a mean-spirited father and father-in-law in the biblical text itself. In this light, the language and events of Gen 24 foreshadow the Laban narratives yet to come. But this is a minor point in an otherwise comprehensive and intelligent study.

The second part of the book focuses on the scholarly methods of midrash analysis and relates these to rabbinic interpretations of the Rebekah cycle. Six chapters constitute this section of the book; the first two are theoretical in nature, and the next four explore rabbinic texts. Chapter 7, entitled, "Midrash and the Academic Study of the Bible," seeks to assess how midrash has been used as opposed to how it should be used in Bible criticism. In the course of her analysis, Teugels examines the scholarship of René Bloch and Geza Vermes, who argued that midrash should be considered a literary genre unto itself that could be compared to the literature of the Hebrew Bible, New Testament, rewritten biblical texts, and other early Jewish texts in order to determine the historical development of aggadic traditions and motifs.

In chapter 8, "The Formal Study of Midrash," Teugels seeks to answer the question "What is midrash?" and to develop a definition for the term. The scholarship of Addison Wright, R. Le Déaut, Arnold Goldberg, and Philip Alexander are featured along with nodding references to Daniel Boyarin, Michael Fishbane,

Jacob Neusner, and Gary Porton. Although Teugels is quite taken with Arnold Goldberg's form-analysis approach, she admits that this method leaves out too much. It is difficult to know whether Teugels, following Goldberg, would also omit the *mashal, ma'ase,* legends, and stories that lack reference to biblical verses. One suspects so, since her formal definition is articulated as "rabbinic interpretation of Scripture that bears the lemmatic form" (168). While some might find this definition too narrow, Teugels deserves praise for her efforts to tame this wild beast in definitive terms. This chapter will serve as a good basis for classroom discussion for those students who are just beginning study of midrashic literature—particularly if the argument is compared to one or more of the other methodological constructions.

In the rest of the book Teugels "reads" the rabbinic texts. In chapter 9 three midrashim are analyzed employing Goldberg's form-analysis approach. This technique is problematic in part because it does not address the portion of the lemma left out of the manuscript. As a result, in one case Teugels must reanalyze the midrash to include the second half of the unprinted verse in order to explain correctly the "moves" of the text. This leads one to wonder why she employs Goldberg's method at all, since her own approach in all three cases is superior.

Chapter 10 presents a well-conceived discussion on the connections the rabbis formulate among Rebekah's birth narrative, Isaac's binding, Sarah's death, and the marriage of Isaac and Rebekah. As such, this chapter ties back to the third chapter in which Teugels addressed Gen 22–23. Here Teugels clearly explains the structure of the midrash, explicates the actual text, and then ties this explanation to the overall meaning of the midrash.

Chapters 11 and 12 are two parts of a single topic: "The Virginity of Rebekah in Halakhah and Aggadah." In chapter 11 Teugels first describes the connection of Rebekah to the rabbinic legal category of the *mukat ets* (this is a reference to a virgin whose hymen is considered intact although she has been deflowered by mistake, e.g., by a piece of wood). Again, one may not agree completely with the specifics of Teugels's analysis, but, overall, her descriptions are comprehensible, precise, and useful. The reader not only learns about Rebekah and halakah but also gains perspective on how the rabbis frame their discussions.

In chapter 12 Teugels first addresses the legend of Rebekah's betrothal to Isaac when the matriarch was three years old and then investigates the connection of this story to related matters of halakah. Unfortunately, in this brief chapter the author forgoes the close reading and explication she so generously shared in the previous chapters and instead focuses on the "reception of these issues in feminist interpretation" (220). However, many of the well-known names connected with feminist work on the Talmud and other rabbinic literature are missing. For example, Tal Ilan, Judith Baskin, and Charlotte Fonrobert—to name just a few—are absent. A few other minor disappointments with the book include the many typos and grammatical errors (particularly in the first half of the book), the evident "seams," and some redundancy. Overall, the book leaves the reader wishing to read more of Teugels's own analysis rather than the well-explained methods and analyses of others. These are, however, minor flaws in what is otherwise a most worthwhile addition to the field of literary study of the Bible and rabbinic literature.

The Origin of the Evil Spirits: The Reception of Gen 6.1–4 in Early Jewish Literature, by Archie T. Wright. Wissenschaftliche Untersuchungen zum Neuen Testament 2/198. Tubingen: Mohr Siebeck, 2005. Pp. xvi + 260. Paper. €49.00. ISBN 3161486560.

Grant Macaskill, St. Mary's College, University of St. Andrews, St. Andrews, Scotland

In *The Origin of Evil Spirits,* Archie T. Wright argues that "the non-specificity inherent in the biblical text of Genesis 6.1–4 became the basis for the later emergence of an etiology of evil spirits as Jewish authors engaged with the text. As a result, Genesis 6.1–4, particularly its interpretation in *1 Enoch* 6–16, played an important part in the development of demonology during the 2TP" (1). Wright explores this issue by first examining the ambiguities inherent in the text of Gen 6:1–4, and the various reception histories of this text, and then focusing on chapters 6–16 of the Book of the Watchers and the reception history of the Watcher tradition in the Dead Sea Scrolls. Finally, he examines Philo of Alexandria's interpretations of Gen 6:1–4.

After introducing his thesis (ch. 1) Wright begins his study proper with an overview of previous research into the Book of the Watchers, a chapter that allows him to explore the usual critical discussions of structure, date, authorship, and sources. The bulk of this chapter explores two overlapping issues: the question of sources (29–37); and the question of function (37–47). Previous scholarship is thoroughly and helpfully discussed here, although there is some degree of unavoidable repetition, since the same scholars are discussed in both sections. His conclusions highlight the complexity of the text and the problems associated with it and then foreground his own concern with the centrality of the evil spirits to the story (a concern that does not entirely arise from his study of previous scholarship).

Chapter 3 contains Wright's analysis of the text of Gen 6:1–4 and his discussion of the various strategies of interpretation. The ground is well-trodden, but Wright provides an impressively concise yet thorough examination of the reception history of these verses, ranging through LXX, Dead Sea Scrolls, Targumim, and Midrashim. The result is an important plank in his argument but also a useful study in its own right, one that could prove helpful in a classroom context. He notes that the essential neutrality of the biblical text toward the *bene elohim* tends to be lost in interpretation but not in any consistent way: the ambiguity of words in each verse gave rise to diverse interpretations, possibly by reading them in the light of myths, whether Israelite or foreign. Wright closes this chapter by presenting a translation of the verses in question that reflects this ambiguity, inventively

reinforcing his point and concluding that "it is no surprise that the ancient translators and interpreters had difficulty coming to terms with this passage" (95). In
the midst of these diverse interpretations he argues that "the author of *BW* [Book
of the Watchers] used the Biblical traditions ... to present his interpretation of
Genesis 6.1–4 in light of the emerging demonology and anthropology of 2TP
Judaism" (95).

Chapter 4 examines the reception of the *bene elohim* tradition in the Book
of the Watchers. Beginning with the association of the idea with the language of
"Watchers" and with the "hosts of heaven," Wright goes on to examine closely the
traditions centering on Asa'el and Shemihazah, which concern instruction and
sexual sin, respectively. The chapter contains a helpful refutation of Hanson's link
between Asa'el and the "Azazel" of the scapegoat ritual (Lev 16) as well as a discussion of the similarities with the Prometheus myth. It also has a provocative
discussion of whether inappropriate "marriage" as such is in view in the sexual
sin of the Shemihazah stratum, or merely intercourse. This is largely intended as a
critique of those who have argued that the text contains a veiled polemic directed
against priests engaging in illegitimate marriage. Wright argues that sexual sin
is the main concern and that this is intended as a basis for the appearance of
the monstrous giants and their immortal spirits. His main conclusion is that "the
author of *BW* has interpreted the Genesis 6 story with the Shemihazah tradition
in order to strengthen his view about the existence of evil spirits in his world"
(137).

Chapter 5 explores the rebellion motif in the Book of the Watchers. It is,
Wright argues, unclear as to why the angels rebelled, but their actions have
defiled themselves and, in causing the appearance of the giants whose immortal spirits still plague mankind, have damaged humanity and the earth. In his
discussion of this point, Wright develops the language of "giantology," a notion
of what the giants are (hybrids of heavenly, eternal beings and earthly mortal
ones) that contrasts with the anthropology of the author of Book of the Watchers, in which the "spiritual" aspect of humanity comprises God's image. Both
the notion of evil spirits and that of a spiritual dimension to human anthropology are set in the context of their development during the Second Temple
period. Wright argues that the Book of the Watchers contributes to an etiology of evil spirits, explaining their origin and their relationship to (and impact
upon) the human spirit. As such, it contributes to the developing dualism seen
in later Second Temple Judaism and may, he suggests in a footnote, be responsible for later demonic motifs such as possession and exorcism, so important in
the Gospel traditions.

Chapter 6 examines the reception of the Watcher tradition in the Dead Sea
Scrolls. As with previous chapters, this one is thorough, both in the primary
texts handled and in the treatment of secondary literature. Wright argues that
in the Scrolls we find a development of the anthropology seen in the Book of
the Watchers, where human nature is vulnerable to the impact of the evil spirits
that entered the world through the giants. Thus, the "evil inclination" of humanity

was susceptible to attack by such spirits, and, among other things, this influenced concepts of the role and function of prayer.

Chapter 7 turns to the writings of Philo of Alexandria as a counterpoint to the interpretative strategy of the Book of the Watchers. Wright discusses at some length Philo's concepts of the human soul, including the extent to which the idea is influenced by the Platonic World of Forms. He concludes, "Philo's anthropology incorporates a theory of two souls, one that remains pure in its relationship to the Divine realm; and the other that has relinquished the heavenly quest to pursue the passions of the flesh. Thus, the second type of soul is ineligible to remain in the heavenly realm until it has been purified of the carnal passions" (205). This dimension of Philo's anthropology underlies the study of *De gigantibus*. Wright concludes that Philo identifies the giants "symbolically with the vices of the human body" (217) and relates this to his three-level notion of humanity as earth-born, heaven-born, and God-born. While there may be points of contact between Philo's thought and that represented by the Book of the Watchers (Wright lays these out in a table on pages 216–17), the basic strategy of interpretation of Gen 6:1–4 is radically different, being symbolic rather than etiological. More importantly—and more subtly—Wright sees this difference as resulting from a quite distinct anthropology in Philo, one that fuses Platonic notions with angelology, in that the different kinds of human spirit are related to the angelic realm and to the modes of being of the angels. Interestingly, Wright suggests that Philo may have been aware of the traditions behind the Book of the Watchers and may have sought to correct them.

Essentially, then, Wright argues that the text of Gen 6:1–4 is susceptible to various interpretations and that the author of the Book of the Watchers made use of this vulnerability to develop an etiology of evil spirits, thus providing a textual rationale for the kind of demonology that became increasingly significant in Second Temple Judaism.

This is an important book that ought to feature in any discussion of the Book of the Watchers, of Jewish demonology, and of the interpretation of Gen 6:1–4. These issues have received widespread attention in recent years, thanks to their importance in Gabrielle Boccaccini's *Beyond the Essene Hypothesis: The Parting of the Ways between Qumran and Enochic Judaism* (Grand Rapids: Eerdmans, 1998), which makes the claim that chapters 6–16 of the Book of the Watchers present a distinct concept of the origin of evil. Wright's book is helpful in suggesting that the chapters in question may not so much speak of the origin of evil per se as of the origin of evil spirits. This in itself is an important contribution. In addition, as I have noted throughout this review, the fine detail of the text contains a wealth of helpful analysis.

My one serious criticism is that Wright may have overemphasized his claim for the centrality of the notion of an etiology of evil spirits. He begins his book by noting the complexity of the tradition history of the Book of the Watchers and of scholarly discussions of its function and then essentially makes one function preeminent—thus falling, I think, into the very trap in which he sees others as being caught. A reader knowledgeable of discussions of the Book of the Watchers will often be struck that certain nuances of the text have been glossed over (such as the priestly associations, which are dismissed too easily and without acknowledgement of their importance in Nickelsburg's commentary; G. W. E Nickelsburg, *1 Enoch 1: A Commentary on the Book of 1 Enoch, Chapters 1–36; 81–108* [Hermeneia; Minneapolis: Fortress, 2001], see esp. 230–31]). It would perhaps have been wiser for him to have presented the etiological function of the text as one crucial and undervalued dimension of the text, rather than as *the* hermeneutical key. Nevertheless, this remains an excellent study.

Women, Ideology, and Violence: Critical Theory and the Construction of Gender in the Book of the Covenant and the Deuteronomic Law, by Cheryl B. Anderson. London: T&T Clark, 2005. Pp. x + 148. Paper. $39.95. ISBN 0567082520.

Kune Biezeveld, Leiden University, Leiden, The Netherlands

With this book, which is a revision of her doctoral thesis, Cheryl B. Anderson aims to show the fruitfulness of combining contemporary critical theory, gender theory, and legal theory with the interpretation of biblical texts. Her focus is on the law texts of the Book of the Covenant (BC) and the Deuteronomic Law (DL), which are to be seen in line.

In chapter 1 Anderson accounts for her theoretical choices and methodological considerations. According to contemporary legal theory, laws are to be considered not only in relationship to a society's civil and criminal procedures but as "linguistic frames." Laws both reflect the ideology they are built upon and construct an ideology-loaded identity for the future. This holds true for biblical laws as well. The question is not whether the biblical laws were ever operative; the main point is to reveal the part they had in the construction of an identity that was imposed upon women—and others—from the perspective of free, privileged Israelite males.

Anderson's prime focus is on the construction of gender to which the BC and DL laws contribute, but she pays attention to other identity constructions such as class, race, and nationality as well. By gender she means the oppositional attributes ascribed to men and women in a social system, or, in other words, the "mutually exclusive scripts for being male and female" (7). Seen this way, gender refers to what has become polarized between men and women and leads to a focus on situations or texts where women are treated differently from men.

Based on these theoretical choices, in displaying the BC and DL laws on women in chapter 2, Anderson distinguishes between what she calls "inclusive laws" and "exclusive laws." By "inclusive laws" she means laws in which men and women are both mentioned but treated in the same way. "Exclusive laws" are those laws that (1) especially apply only to women; (2) exclude women; or (3) determine a woman's treatment based on her relationship to a male. This distinction between inclusive and exclusive laws is important for Anderson. What is more, it is her special contribution to the debate on the implications for women of these biblical laws. She criticizes Naomi Steinberg, Carolyn Pressler, and Rhonda Burnette-Bletsch, who are each in her own way involved in this research, for failing to make this distinction (48). They cannot but draw the wrong conclusion by overlooking that not all laws concerning women construct gender but that some do (21).

I have some doubts about the use of gender analysis this way. Not only do I see a kind of anachronism between the modern context in which gender theory has been—and is still being—developed, on the one side, and the clear and open patriarchal context of the biblical laws, on the other. I also question whether the desired results are achieved merely by focusing on texts where women and men are treated differently. As I see it, the real challenge to unveil gender bias lies in so-called inclusive texts. I will come to this later, after first following Anderson's arguments further.

In chapter 3 Anderson aims to show how both the inclusive and exclusive BC and DL laws have their part in the construction of identity. In the case of the inclusive laws, it may concern class identity (being free or being a slave), national identity (being an Israelite or not), and generational identity (being a father/mother in a household or being a child). In the case of the exclusive laws, the focus is on the construction of gender.

Here again I see reason to question this very distinction. It is important, of course, to notice the nuances in the power relations in a societal construction, nuances for which Elisabeth Schüssler Fiorenza coined the term "kyriarchy." Women could also be slave owners, and mothers in Israel had power over their nonadult sons. What is more, women could overpower other women too. Here the term *patriarchy* would be too limited. But, as I see it, in order to stay aware of the fact that at all layers of the power pyramid women are subservient to "their" males, the term patriarchy in its basal meaning will still do. The simple fact that a widow belongs—alongside the orphan and the stranger—to the marginalized has a patriarchal background. By classifying the laws concerning the widow (Exod 22:21–23 [22:22–24]; Deut 24:17–22) under the inclusive laws, Anderson restricts herself in her analysis of their implications for gender construction. In this vein she could not integrate into her own arguments in chapter 2 the gender aspects in terms of the widow and other marginalized, as they are pointed out by others. She could only conclude: "Consequently, the laws taken together construct gender indirectly because the widow cannot inherit her husband's property, a fact that contributes to her economic marginalization. Considered on their own, though, these specific biblical laws do not treat the widow differently than males in these marginalized groups" (30–31). I cannot but see this as a too restrictive analysis in terms of gender construction.

In chapter 4, however, a quite new line of reasoning is taken up. It is introduced by the sentence 'Inclusive laws … are not ostensibly involved in the construction of gender" (77) and is followed by "[A] law can still construct gender differences in spite of the absence of any obvious distinctions" (79–80). Here feminist legal theory is brought in, a theory that enables a more nuanced analysis of gender construction in the law. The question is: Is the law male? This question is to be answered according to three criteria: (1) Does the law systematically favor males and oppress women? (2) Does the law, although neutrally formulated, have a disproportionately negative effect on women? (3) Does the law embody only the male experience?

It is not difficult to imagine that these criteria take away the previously used distinction between inclusive and exclusive laws. Now the financial dependency of married women—and the consequent marginalization of a widow—get their due meaning, just as "inclusively" formulated laws against sorcery and apostasy can now be analyzed in their implications for women. In addition, the "exclusive" laws, which were considered as constructing gender, are seen differently according to this new criteria. Although male authority over women's sexuality earlier was explained as inherent to the patriarchal context, as soon as the women's perspective is brought in the term "violence" comes to mind. Laws such as Deut 22:23–29 actually reflect a rape culture, as Harold Washington suggests. Because of the male perspective in the BC and DL, however, the notion of sexual assault against a female does not explicitly exist.

This new perspective leads to the crux of Anderson's argument. It now becomes clear how she sees that the BC and the DL construct gender. By using the male perspective in a patriarchal context and consequently bypassing the female perspective, a gender script is written that is not only polarizing but inherently contains violence against women. While the subordination of women leads to the repression of the feminine, the consequent construction of masculinity could in this context lead to nothing other than the male dominance with which it all started. As such, says Anderson, this script is a part of—and a legitimacy provider for—Western culture from the first century of the common era until today. My question is: How does one combine this conclusion with chapters 2 and 3?

In the concluding chapter 5, Anderson explicitly takes as context the current rape culture she finds herself living in as feminist/womanist African American female. Here it becomes clear why she declared herself politically motivated in her interest in "defetishizing" the BC and DL laws and the male dominance/female subordination gender paradigm they encode (19–20). She is all too aware of the impact current reading of the Bible can have. The Bible may not be blamed for creating patriarchy, she cedes to Tikva Frymer-Kensky (and on the background undoubtedly Judith Plaskow), but, "The issue in a context of male violence against women is the way in which the Bible has been used historically and is used today to maintain patriarchy's hierarchical ideologies and structures. In this context, biblical interpretation becomes an ethical issue" (113).

Here, as in chapter 4, I feel Anderson's heart beating, and feel connected with her. I regret, however, that she refers here to all new kinds of biblical texts (prophetic and narrative) to illustrate her point. I would have preferred if she had disciplined herself to stay with the BC and DL laws. Related to these texts she has developed her expertise in the legal theories. And, for me, a new look at the arguments of the chapters 2 and 3 from here would have added to the worth of this book.

Anderson has written a thought-provoking book. It was not always easy to read, however, mainly because her own arguments do not always follow clearly from the discussion with others. Sometimes these others fully dominate the text.

In terms of her argument, I agree with the critical approach Anderson has chosen. The biblical laws as the BC and the DL are no innocent texts. One can labor, as many—female and male—scholars do, to point out the positive, distinctive features of these Hebrew laws in terms of the position or treatment of women. This surely makes sense in contexts where the Bible is read as a source for spirituality and moral behavior. In this very context a critical analysis as the one by Anderson will be necessary too, of course. Just because a critical, feminist analysis is needed, however, I would prefer a more balanced approach than Anderson's book in this form presents. On the one side, the reading of the texts deserves a fine-tuned gender analysis in which patriarchy is also seen as a societal structure that enabled "normal" family life and procreation; on the other side, newly developed critical theories are to be seen as contextual theories that are not immediately applicable to texts from a different context. That is, the concept of gender can rise only where patriarchy has become highly criticized or even been abolished as the main societal structure. The ongoing violence against women is one thing; the freeing of the women's body by women themselves is another thing. I would say: let us not overestimate the impact that laws such as the BC and DL still have.

Cult and Character: Purification Offerings, Day of Atonement, and Theodicy, by Roy E. Gane. Winona Lake, Ind.: Eisenbrauns, 2005. Pp. xxii + 394. Hardcover. $44.50. ISBN 1575061015.

Jay Sklar, Covenant Seminary, St. Louis, Missouri

When Roy Gane completed his Ph.D. under Jacob Milgrom, his dissertation focused on the application of systems theory to ancient Israelite, Babylonian, and Hittite festival days. Gane builds upon this work in his most recent volume: *Cult and Character: Purification Offerings, Day of Atonement, and Theodicy*. In *Cult and Character,* Gane uses a combination of in-depth exegesis and systems theory in order to examine and interpret the purification offering. In so doing, he presents a new understanding of the rite and then considers how this understanding provides a window into the character of the Lord. This review will begin with a general overview of the structure of the argument of the book, make general comments on the book as a whole, then turn to consider the various stages of the argument in more detail.

The book consists of eighteen chapters divided into four major sections. In the first section Gane outlines the methodological approach that he will take in interpreting ritual texts (in-depth exegesis and systems theory) and explains why this approach is valid. In the second section he focuses on the חטאת rituals that are performed throughout the year (i.e., not on the Day of Atonement), arguing that the purpose of these offerings is to *cleanse the offerer*—and not the sanctuary—of sin or impurity. He then turns in the third section to focus on the Day of Atonement rituals and how these relate to the חטאת rituals performed throughout the year. He argues that the rituals on the Day of Atonement serve primarily to purge sin and impurity *from the sanctuary* and secondarily from the Israelites. This leads him to an important conclusion: there are two stages of sacrificial כפר, the first stage happening throughout the year (section 2) and the second stage happening on the Day of Atonement (section 3). Finally, Gane turns in the fourth section to consider how his understanding of these rituals informs our understanding of the character of the Lord.

Stylistically, Gane's work as a whole reads well. His writing is clear and the flow of thought easy to follow. (Indeed, the division headings within chapters are robust enough that one can pretty well follow the argument of a chapter from the headings alone.) In terms of subject matter, he is obviously very comfortable with the material and shows great fluency with the secondary literature. Moreover, Gane is to be commended for dealing so thoroughly with matters of methodology (section 1) and for going beyond analysis of the חטאת ritual itself to consider what the implications of this understanding are for matters of theology (section 4). Finally, and perhaps most importantly, Gane's work not only deals very thoroughly with how the חטאת ritual itself is to be understood, but it demonstrates that a prevailing understanding of this ritual is no longer tenable and must be either modified or replaced.

We turn now to consider each of the four sections in more detail, with more attention being given to sections 2 and 3, which contain the heart of Gane's argument. In the first section, then, Gane sets the methodological foundation for his analysis: in-depth exegetical analysis informed by a systems theory approach to rituals. He begins in the first chapter with an explanation of the main presupposition of systems theory, namely, that human activity systems—of which rituals are a part—are designed to accomplish a goal and that it is this goal that in turn defines the meaning of the activities (12–13). Consequently, Gane's "quest for meanings of purification offerings and Day of Atonement rituals will especially focus on isolating and closely examining the language of goals that are indicated by the biblical text" (24). The second chapter then proceeds to argue that the חטאת rituals can be viewed as a system, as can the Day of Atonement ritual.

As a whole, this first section accomplishes its goals quite nicely. On the one hand, it clearly explains what systems theory is and demonstrates why it is a fruitful approach to take. It may briefly be noted in this regard that a systems theory approach shifts the focus of interpreting rituals from their prehistory to the context in which they occur (cf. the shift in linguistics from a diachronic approach in word study methodology to a synchronic approach). On the other hand, it also explains why this method is applicable to the rites that Gane is examining. In particular, Gane marshals several arguments in favor of seeing Lev 16—at least

in the final form of the text—as being integrated in the overall system of Israelite rituals (25–31). Naturally, not all will be interested in a synchronic reading
of these texts. Gane does demonstrate, however, that applying a systems theory
approach to the final form of the text is methodologically viable for the rituals
that he is considering.

In the second section Gane turns to consider חטאת rituals that occur
throughout the year, focusing especially on Lev 4. In keeping with a systems
theory approach, Gane begins by identifying the *goal* of these offerings, addressing the chieftain's offering in particular: "the ritual is to offer a purification
offering to Yhwh that accomplishes purgation on behalf of the chieftain, who has
committed a wrong, so that he may receive forgiveness" (49). (This is especially
important because Milgrom's approach to the purification offering, which emphasizes cleansing of the sanctuary above all else, has tended to place the actual goal
of forgiveness in the background.) With this goal in hand, Gane then proceeds to
an analysis of the individual ritual events and how they accomplish this goal (chs.
3–5; see esp. p. 70).

This leads him to the heart of his work in chapters 6–8. It is helpful to explain
Gane's thesis on the purification offering by setting it in context. One of the most
influential approaches to the purification offering has been that of Milgrom (see
Jacob Milgrom, *Leviticus 1–16* [New York: Doubleday, 1991], 254ff.). In brief,
Milgrom argues that the sin or impurity of the offerer defiles the tabernacle and
that the purification offering serves to cleanse the tabernacle alone. Gane will
agree with Milgrom in part: on certain occasions, such as the Day of Atonement
(Exod 30:10; Lev 16) and the initial consecration of the altar (Exod 29; Lev 8), the
purification offering serves to cleanse the sanctuary and its *sancta*. In all other
instances, however, the purification offering serves to remove sin or impurity
from the offerer (who is defiled), not the *sancta* (which is not defiled). In order to
prove this, he must establish that the offerer is cleansed (ch. 6) and the tabernacle
is not defiled (and thus not cleansed) (ch. 7).

In support of the offerer being cleansed, Gane does a syntactical analysis of
the prepositions that follow כִּפֶּר, in particular the preposition מִן. He notes two
clear instances where the מִן is clearly privative in purification offering contexts,
for example, Lev 12:7: "Then he shall offer it before the Lord and make atonement for her, and she shall be cleansed from the flow of her blood (וְטָהֲרָה מִמְּקֹר
דָּמֶיהָ)" (see also Lev 16:30). Gane then proceeds from these examples to consider
other purification offering passages that use a מִן in the atonement formula and
argues that these passages are likely to be understood in the same way.

It seems clear that Gane has correctly identified the use of מִן as privative in
Lev 12:7 and 16:30 and that this in turn leads to the simple conclusion that the
purification offering does indeed result in sin or impurity being removed from
the offerer. This also means that Milgrom has overstated the case when he says
that the purification offering only cleanses the sanctuary and its *sancta* but never
the offerer. (It may be noted that Milgrom himself states on Lev 12 that "the parturient is purified by the action of both sacrifices" [758], i.e., by the burnt offering

and purification offering. I have been unable to find a place where he reconciles this with his thesis on the purification offering as a whole.) Gane is also correct in pointing out that the purification offering would thus have a similar function in conceptually parallel instances of sin and impurity, such as the leper in Lev 14 or the person suffering from a genital discharge in Lev 15. It is not clear, however, that the מִן must be—or even should be—read privatively in these other instances. This is because these other instances are not syntactically equivalent to 12:7 or 16:30: 12:7 and 16:30 use the מִן in a result clause, while none of the other verses do (this is especially clear from Gane's table on 126). Moreover, translating the מִן privatively in these instances leads to problems with the translation of עַל in verses such as 15:15. (Gane is aware of this problem [139–40], although he does not explain how the עַל should be translated in a sensible way in English if the מִן is privative. It would seem he would have to render: "And the priest will make amends on behalf of the sinner from his sin." Note as well that his appeal to Milgrom's translation of the מִן in Lev 16:16 runs into the same problem, since Milgrom can only translate this way be completing disregarding the עַל.) Nonetheless, these observations do not take away from Gane's overall point that the purification offering cleanses the offerer in these contexts, since this is evident from the functional equivalence of the offerings themselves (whether or not the מִן is privative in all instances; see 115).

Having just argued that the offerer is cleansed by purification offerings that are made throughout the year (ch. 6), Gane now turns to argue that the sanctuary is *not* cleansed by these purification offerings (ch. 7). He begins by noting that *rebellious* sins, which he sees as a more severe category of "intentional" sins, can indeed affect the sanctuary from a distance. In this he agrees with Milgrom. He then points out, however, that Milgrom generalizes from this to conclude that all types of sins and impurities pollute the sanctuary. Gane notes instead that the sins that automatically defile from a distance are all rebellious and not capable of forgiveness through sacrificial expiation. He argues from this that it is incorrect to read *expiable* sins and impurities through the same lens, that is, that these sins and impurities also defile the sanctuary. This also serves to support his overall thesis: the purification offering for inadvertent sin or for impurity cleanses the *sinner,* not the *sanctuary.*

It may be noted that the argument of chapter 7 is primarily negative in orientation. Gane does well to point out that Milgrom is starting with instances of nonexiable sin and then reading instances of expiable sin and impurity through this lens. He is also correct in pointing out that there is "no clear evidence for automatic defilement of the sanctuary by any kind of physical ritual impurity itself" (155). But does this mean that the sanctuary is not cleansed by the purification offering? Two comments may be made at this point. First, it may be noted that Gane himself agrees with Milgrom that the purification of the sanctuary from the people's impurity on the Day of Atonement effectually purifies the people as well (129). This at least allows for the possibility that, even if the purification offerings made throughout the year purify the people, this may in fact be due to the fact that the sanctuary itself is being cleansed. Even more to the point, however, is the fact that the blood of purification offerings clearly does cleanse the *sancta* in at least some instances (Lev 8:15). Gane is aware of this but argues that this is only true in limited cases and not in the purification offerings throughout the year. He thus argues in chapter 8 that the blood of the purification offering is impure (Lev 6:20 [27]) and that it purifies the offerer in that it absorbs evil or impurity from him or her. Why then put it on the altar? "YHWH prefers that evils be acknowledged, brought meekly to the sanctuary, and turned over to him rather than left to run wild and rampage into the sphere of holiness" (179). They will accumulate there, in a way, until the Day of Atonement, when the sanctuary itself is cleansed. This argument, of course, depends on understanding Lev 6:20 (27) to imply that sacrificial blood in these instances is impure, a possible but not necessary conclusion. (See 166 n. 8 for other possibilities; the parallel of 6:21 [28] with 11:31–33 [172] is interesting but not decisive for the simple reason that 11:31–33 is dealing with *unclean* animals, whereas 6:22 [29] explicitly states that the purification offering is *most holy*.) It also leads to the curious position that the blood of the purification offerings made throughout the year *pollute the sanctuary* but that the blood of the purification offering on the Day of Atonement *cleanses the sanctuary* (see ch. 12, esp. 275–76). In any case, it is not clear that Lev 6:20 (27) will bear the weight it must in order to support the argument of this chapter. Indeed, seeing that the most detailed text dealing with a purification offering (Lev 16) makes it clear that the sanctuary is cleansed, and given that Lev 8:15 clearly states that purification offering blood cleanses, the weight of evidence seems to point to a position in between that of Milgrom and Gane: that the purification offering does cleanse the sanctuary but in so doing cleanses the offerer as well.

This leads to his third major section, in which Gane examines the Day of Atonement (Lev 16) in more detail and argues that there are two major phases of sacrificial כפר. The section begins with a very helpful analysis of the purification offerings in Lev 16 and the structure of the chapter as a whole (first half of ch. 10). Gane proceeds from this to spell out more fully his understanding of the differences between the purification offerings performed throughout the year and those carried out on the Day of Atonement. Assuming the arguments of chapters 6 and 7, he argues that there are two main differences: (1) purification offerings throughout the year remove evil from the offerer, whereas the Day of Atonement sacrifices remove evil from the sanctuary (and thus in turn the offerer); (2) purification offerings throughout the year result in purification from ritual impurity or forgiveness of sins, whereas the Day of Atonement sacrifices result in purification from sin. Consequently, cleansing a person from sin "requires two major phases of כפר: First, a [regular] purification offering purges (כפר) the moral evil from the offerer, prerequisite to YHWH's forgiveness (סלח). Second, the corporate purgation (כפר) of the sanctuary on the Day of Atonement results in the moral cleansing (טהר) of the people" (241).

It will be evident from the earlier comments that the first difference Gane has proposed is possible but that the weight of evidence seems to point in the

other direction. As for the second point, it seems difficult to understand how evil
can be removed from the offerer with the purification offerings made throughout
the year and yet for the person not to receive "moral cleansing." In this regard it
may be asked: Is the cleansing (טהר) that results from atonement (כפר) in Lev
16 "*beyond forgiveness*" (234, emphasis original), or is it simply the case that we
are dealing with a *different way* of describing the forgiveness that results from
atonement?

In chapter 12 Gane elaborates upon a point introduced earlier, that there
are two major phases of sacrificial כפר. On the one hand, Gane notes that some
argue for just one phase of sacrificial כפר. By this he means that the purification
offering operates in one consistent way in effecting כפר for the offerer. Representatives here include Hoffmann, Levine, and, of course, Milgrom. Gane begins
his response by reviewing some of the points he has already demonstrated in his
study that undermine Milgrom's thesis (see above; 273–74) and then proceeds
to argue that there are two phases of sacrificial כפר for expiable sins. In the first
phase, sin or impurity is purged (כפר) from the offerer by means of outer-altar
purification offerings, resulting in their forgiveness (סלח). In the second phase,
the "corporate inner-sanctum purification offerings ... on the Day of Atonement
purge (כפר) the sanctuary from ... the physical ritual impurities ... and ... sins
of the Israelites (Lev 16:16, 19), i.e., the same categories of evil that have been
removed from offerers of purification offerings at the sanctuary throughout the
year" (275). As a result, these types of sins—as opposed to wanton sins—are
removed and the offerer is morally pure. In sum, in phase one the offerer is *purified of* impurity or *purified of* and *forgiven for* sin. In phase two the tabernacle is
purified of these same impurities and sins as a result of which Israel as a whole is
morally purified. Gane concludes the chapter by identifying various points where
his approach either avoids difficulties that Milgrom's approach runs into or better
accounts for aspects of the text (277–84).

The strength of this argument of course depends directly on the arguments
advanced in earlier chapters (for which see comments above on section 2). The
conclusion to this chapter does raise some interesting points, some (though not
all) of which might be problematic for Milgrom but none of which are insurmountable to those holding a mediating position between Milgrom and Gane.
Indeed, Gane's comments on the expression "all their sins" in Lev 16:16 could
very well support the view that the sanctuary is indeed cleansed throughout the
year, since they point out that what happens on the Day of Atonement could very
well be redundant, accomplishing the same thing as that which happens throughout the year (277–79). In this regard the atonement that takes place in Lev 16
might be different *in degree* (cf. the cleansing of the leper) though not *in kind* (cf.
Gane's comment on 283–84).

In the fourth section of his work, "Cult and Theodicy," Gane expands on the
conclusions of the earlier chapters and ask in particular, "How does the understanding of the rituals that we have come to help us to understand what these
rituals are meant to communicate?" This part of the work is built on the (proper)

assumption that "ritual states and processes function as dynamic metaphors for factors and interactions involved in the relationship between Yнwн and his people" (305). Consequently, Gane now asks how these rituals reflect and/or contribute to the theology and worldview of an ancient Israelite with reference to their relationship and interaction with the Lord.

In order to answer this question, Gane helpfully uses the metaphor of the Lord as divine and just king and the tabernacle as his royal residence (318–23). This in turn allows him to look to narrative texts in which human kings are involved in matters of justice and to use these texts as a means of shedding further light into the nature of the Lord's just kingship as expressed in the sacrificial cult. If one is persuaded by the arguments of sections 2 and 3, then section 4 will prove a very fruitful field of observations and conclusions. Even if one is not totally persuaded by the earlier arguments, however, Gane's approach in this last section is still tremendously illuminating and promising, since it explores a social relationship within Israel that is analogous to the relationship between Israelites and the Lord (that of citizen to his or her king).

By way of summary then, Gane's work as a whole is clearly written, well researched, and full of insight into the Israelite cult. Most important, it proves well—and it seems unequivocally—that one can no longer argue that the purification offering only cleanses the sanctuary itself (and never the offerer). While this review has raised questions on whether Gane's counterproposal should be adopted, it gratefully acknowledges that Gane has made a very important contribution here and has opened up extremely important avenues for further research and exploration.

FORMER PROPHETS

The Body Royal: The Social Poetics of Kingship in Ancient Israel, by Mark W. Hamilton. Biblical Interpretation Series 78. Leiden: Brill, 2005. Pp. xv + 316. Hardcover. $129.00. ISBN 9004145419.

Markus Saur, Universität Basel, Basel, Switzerland

Das Königtum im antiken Israel ist Gegenstand einer Reihe neuerer Studien, die sich mit literaturwissenschaftlichen, religionsgeschichtlichen und theologischen Fragestellungen im Kontext von König und Königsherrschaft befassen; dieses Interesse am israelitischen Königtum hat seinen Grund in der ausserordentlichen Bedeutung des Königs für Religion und Gesellschaft des antiken Israel. Mark W. Hamiltons Studie gehört zu diesen neueren Arbeiten und reiht sich damit in einen grösseren Forschungskontext ein; der Autor setzt in seiner Untersuchung jedoch einen eigenen Akzent, indem er die Diskussion um das Königtum in Israel mit der Frage nach dem königlichen Körper verknüpft und sich damit einer zentralen Problemstellung der *gender studies* öffnet.

In einem ersten Kapitel („Introduction: The Undiscovered Territory of the

Body" [1–31]) führt Hamilton in die aktuellen Debatten um den Körper ein. Die Zielsetzung seiner Studie ergibt sich aus der in der *gender*-Forschung entwickelten Einsicht in die soziale Konstruktion von Geschlecht und Körper. Gerade im Blick auf den königlichen Körper scheint diese Konstruktion geschlechtlicher und körperlicher Identitäten eine herausragende Rolle zu spielen, so dass die genaue Untersuchung der Darstellungen und Deutungen des königlichen Körpers in den verschiedenen Textbereichen der alttestamentlichen Literatur einen Einblick in die soziale Konstruktion der Geschlechtlichkeit und Körperlichkeit des Königs erlauben dürfte. Die Grundfrage Hamiltons lautet dementsprechend: „[H]ow did Israelites understand the royal body and, by extension, their kings as the model male?" (21).

Den Ausgangspunkt der Textarbeit Hamiltons bilden die Königspsalmen, die in einem zweiten Kapitel behandelt werden ("Creating the Body of the King in the Royal Psalms", [32–82]) und deren zeitliche Entstehung in der vorexilischen Königszeit für Hamilton ein gesichertes Ergebnis der Forschung darstellt. In einem instruktiven Vergleich von Ps 45 mit Hhl 5,10–16 arbeitet Hamilton zunächst die Nähe zwischen König und Gottheit heraus; die Krönungspsalmen Ps 2; 110; 72 und 101 präzisieren diese Nähe vor allem im Blick auf die königliche Ausübung der Gerechtigkeit gegenüber seinen Untertanen. Nach Hamilton wird der König Ps 45 und Ps 2; 110; 72; 101 zufolge aufgrund der Zuschreibungen als ein politischer Körper konstruiert, von dessen Wohlergehen auch das Wohlergehen des Staates als ganzem abhängt.

Im dritten Kapitel („The Royal Body at Work" [83–117]) wird der König im Kontext von Ps 132 als Tempelbauer, von Ps 89; 144 und Jes 38 als Klagender, von Ps 18 als Dankender und von Ps 20; 21 als Krieger dargestellt; auch in diesen Texten werde zum einen die Gottesnähe des Königs unterstrichen, die mit körperlicher Ertüchtigung einhergehe, zum anderen werde vor allem in den Klagetexten die Verletzlichkeit und damit die Menschlichkeit des Königs herausgestellt. Mit dem vierten Kapitel wendet sich Hamilton der erzählenden Literatur zu („Stories of the Coronation of the King" [118–44]); die ‚deuteronomistischen' Texte werden dabei im 8./7. Jh. v. Chr. angesetzt. Die Berichte von der Krönung Sauls, der Erwählung Davids und der Krönung Joaschs bringen Hamilton zufolge die soziale Konstruktion des königlichen Körpers in besonderer Weise zum Ausdruck, denn die gewissermassen biologisch gegebenen körperlichen Vorzüge der Könige werden in diesen Texten zum einen nachhaltig unterstrichen und zum anderen durch die Einsetzungsrituale der Salbung, Akklamation und Präsentation des neuen Königs zu politischen Eigenschaften des Staatswesens transformiert; durch die Verbindung zwischen König und JHWH werde der königliche Körper zudem in der kosmischen Ordnung verankert.

Im fünften Kapitel („While Horse and Hero Fell: Royal Death and Sickness" [145–82]) thematisiert Hamilton den Tod des Königs, der nicht ohne Auswirkungen auf die Natur und das politische Gemeinwesen bleibt; der tote königliche Körper werde in den einschlägigen Texten zu einem Symbol für den potentiellen Tod des ganzen Landes; vor allem die Krönung des Königs mache nach seinem Tod eine sorgfältig ritualisierte Behandlung des gesalbten Körpers nötig. Anschliessend geht Hamilton in einem sechsten Kapitel („The Body of the King in War and Peace" [183–222]) auf den Gefahr bringenden und auf den gefährdeten königlichen Körper ein; in den Saul-David-Erzählungen werde der zukünftige König David als Gefahr für die Feinde dargestellt, während der gegenwärtige König Saul seine körperliche Rolle missbrauche, sich dadurch vor allem selber gefährde und so nicht mehr zur Gefahr für andere werden könne. David dagegen erwachse im weiteren Verlauf der Erzählungen eine echte Gefahr in seinem eigenen Sohn Absalom, der seinem Vater an körperlichen Vorzügen in nichts nachstehe, dem allerdings letztlich die Krönung fehle und der somit keinen erfolgreichen königlichen Körper habe. Neben diesen Berichten von Saul, David und Absalom lassen nach Hamilton auch die Erzählungen von kranken Königen einen Unterschied zwischen den ‚deuteronomistischen' Texten und den Königspsalmen erkennen, die den König—abgesehen von Ps 89—vor allem als Helden sähen.

Im siebten Kapitel („The Body of the Foreign King" [223–65]) wendet sich Hamilton zunächst dem tyrischen König und dessen Darstellung in Ez 28 zu; die anmassende Herausforderung JHWHs seitens des tyrischen Königs lasse letztlich in der Darstellung des Untergangs die Verletzlichkeit und Sterblichkeit des fremden Königs hervortreten. Im Wettstreit mit JHWH zeige sich auch an den Darstellungen der aramäischen und moabitischen Könige das Scheitern des königlichen Körpers in der Form sexueller, politischer und ökonomischer Impotenz und Machtlosigkeit. Nach einer Darstellung der Könige und königlichen Körper der Supermächte Ägypten, Assyrien und Babylonien kommt Hamilton zu dem Ergebnis, dass Israel sich für den fremden König vor allem als militärischen Anführer interessierte, dessen Arme und Beine entweder stark oder schwach, fähig oder hilflos erscheinen, und dass diese fremden Könige zumeist vor dem Hintergrund der judäischen Propaganda—wie etwa in Ps 2—dargestellt werden: Der fremde König ist demnach immer eine potentielle Bedrohung, eine Grösse, die in Wettstreit mit JHWH tritt. Dabei ist nach Hamilton in der Metaphorik eine bemerkenswerte Transformation zu beobachten: „Israelite texts coopt the metaphors of the foreign powers in order to deligitimize them" (265).

Die Ergebnisse seiner Studie fasst Hamilton in Kapitel acht („Conclusions and Implications" [266–74]) zusammen: Der königliche Körper sei als politische und bio-soziale Grösse für den Israeliten ein Zeichen für Männlichkeit, Gesellschaft, Kosmos und JHWH zugleich; in diesem Sinne könne man von einer „social poetics of kingship" (268) sprechen. Im Blick auf das idealisierte, heldenhafte Königsbild der Königspsalmen fragt Hamilton nach der Überzeugungskraft dieser Texte angesichts der oft genug bescheideneren Realität; eine Erklärung liegt wohl in der Nähe zwischen Gott und König, die beide „are on a sliding scale withour clear demarcations between the two" (271).

Die vorliegende Zusammenfassung der Untersuchung kann nur eine Auswahl dessen referieren, was Hamilton erarbeitet hat. Dennoch ergibt sich auch aufgrund dieser Auswahl ein Bild seiner Studie—mit ihren Vorzügen und Problemen. Das grosse Verdienst Hamiltons liegt darin, die einschlägigen Texte des Alten Testaments, die sich mit dem König und insbesondere mit dem Körper des Königs befassen, in einen Zusammenhang zu bringen und auf dieser Grundlage ein Bild der Vorstellungen zu zeichnen, die im antiken Israel einen wesentlichen Teil der Königsideologie ausmachten. Dabei kann Hamilton auf zahlreiche Arbeiten zum Königtum zurückgreifen; seine Verbindung der Frage nach dem Königtum im allgemeinen mit der Problematik der Körperlichkeit des Königs im besonderen führt allerdings einen entscheidenden Schritt weiter als die bisherige Forschung, da vor dem Hintergrund dieser Fragestellung die Texte aus einer eigenen Perspektive gelesen werden, die über konventionelle Lesarten etwa der Königspsalmen oder der Texte aus den Samuel- und Königsbüchern hinausgehen.

Aus dem Blickwinkel der europäischen alttestamentlichen Wissenschaft sei aber doch auch auf einen Sachverhalt hingewiesen, der sich als ein grundsätzliches Problem zwischen deutsch- und französischsprachiger Exegese auf der einen und anglo-amerikanischer Exegese auf der anderen Seite abzuzeichnen scheint: Die Datierungen der Textbereiche gehen deutlich auseinander. Wenn Hamilton die Königspsalmen oder auch das ‚Deuteronomistische Geschichtswerk‘ wie selbstverständlich im 8./7. Jh. v. Chr. ansetzt, so scheint das in seinem Forschungsumfeld die *communis opinio* zu beschreiben. In der gegenwärtigen deutsch- oder französischsprachigen Psalmenexegese (vgl. exemplarisch die Psalmenkommentare der katholischen Exegeten Frank-Lothar Hossfeld und Erich Zenger) und der Forschung zur sogenannten ‚deuteronomistischen‘ Literatur (vgl. exemplarisch die Arbeiten des Lausanner Alttestamentlers Thomas Römer, zuletzt auch in englischer Sprache: „The So-called Deuteronomistic History", 2005) wird dagegen mit guten Gründen auf zumindest exilisch-nachexilische Fortschreibungen und *relectures* dieser Textbereiche verwiesen; ähnliches wird sicher auch von Texten wie Ez 28, dem Bild des tyrischen Königs, zu sagen sein, das im Kontext des Orakels gegen Tyros in Ez 26–28 zu deuten ist—dass dieses Orakel vollumfänglich in das 6. Jh. v. Chr. gehört, wird man angesichts der Anspielungen auf die Eroberung von Tyros durch Alexander den Grossen im Jahre 332 v. Chr. in Ez 26,7–14* nicht behaupten können, vielmehr liegen hier wie auch in Ez 27 und Ez 28 späte, mehrfach überarbeitete Texte vor, die nicht ohne weiteres für die Königskonzeption des 6. Jh. v. Chr. herangezogen werden können. Vor diesem Hintergrund stellt sich die Frage nach der ‚sozialen Poetik des Königtums‘ noch einmal in ganz besonderer Weise, denn wenn bestimmte Textpassagen, die den königlichen Körper und seine Schönheit, seine Kraft und Stärke im Blick haben, womöglich aus einer Zeit stammen, in der es ein politisch-reales Königtum in Israel bzw. Juda gar nicht mehr gab, so muss man auch von einer im Gegensatz zu vorexilischen Zusammenhängen veränderten Kommunikationssituation ausgehen, deren Absicht noch einmal in einem eigenen Schritt zu bedenken und zu erörtern wäre. Diese Frage kann aber nur dann in den Blick kommen, wenn man die Texte nicht *a priori* als bereits in vorexilischer Zeit abgeschlossene Produkte untersucht. Es ist allerdings kein Geheimnis, dass Arbeiten deutsch- und französischsprachiger Exegeten im angelsächsischen Sprachraum mit ähnlichen Anfragen konfrontiert werden—hier liegen offensichtlich ganz grundsätzliche Differenzen und Probleme methodischer Art vor, die in Einzelstudien zu speziellen Themen nicht gelöst werden können; insofern treffen die voranstehenden Anmerkungen zur zeitlichen Ansetzung der Texte und deren Implikationen Hamiltons Studie auch nur am Rande—und sie verringern nicht den Wert einer inhalts- und überaus lehrreichen Arbeit, die zudem in die Form eines sorgfältig edierten, insgesamt xv + 316 Seiten umfassenden Bandes gegossen ist, den ein Literaturverzeichnis sowie Autoren-, Themen- und Textindizes abschliessen.

The So-Called Deuteronomistic History: A Sociological, Historical and Literary Introduction, by Thomas Römer. London: T&T Clark, 2006. Pp. x + 202. Hardcover. $100.00. ISBN 0567040224.

John Van Seters, Waterloo, Ontario, Canada

For some time now there has been a need for an up-to-date, comprehensive treatment of the Deuteronomistic History that both deals with the confusion of recent views in the debate over this corpus of texts from Deuteronomy to 2 Kings and offers a clearly articulated and balanced presentation of its critical analysis as a whole. This little introduction fulfills all of those expectations very well. Thomas Römer has been actively engaged in research and publication in this field for over two decades, and this particular work, which has been in the making for some time, has finally appeared.

After a short introduction for the uninitiated reader or student, followed by a brief survey of the content of the biblical corpus under examination, Römer gives us a concise review of past scholarship on the Deuteronomistic History down to the present state of the discussion, with special focus on the seminal work of Martin Noth and the subsequent reactions and modifications to his work, and in some cases its outright rejection. In his review he examines the key issues of what it means to label this corpus "Deuteronomistic" and whether or not it is appropriate to call it a "history."

With these preliminaries addressed, Römer sets forth his thesis of a Deuteronomistic "school" or "scribal guild" whose work extended from the time of Josiah, through the Babylonian exile, to the restoration in the early Persian period, producing in stages the literary corpus that now makes up the texts of Deuteronomy to 2 Kings in three successive "editions." While the Deuteronomistic ideology originated in the cultic reform of Josiah, each new historical set of circumstances led to modifications in viewpoint that are now reflected in the additional "redactional layers." Römer finds these three successive editorial layers already evident within the centralization law in Deut 12 and sets out to apply this observation to the rest of the Deuteronomistic corpus in the following chapters.

In chapter 4 Römer lays out the social and historical context of the Neo-Assyrian period, which scholars find so strongly reflected in cultural and ideological imitation in parts of Deuteronomy and Joshua, but not in Judges, and in parts of the stories of David and Solomon, as well as the history of the mon- archies down to the time of Josiah. From these clues Römer reconstructs a small Deuteronomistic library collection consisting of a first edition of Deuteronomy, a story of the conquest by Joshua found primarily in Josh 6–12, and a first history of the monarchy from David to Josiah. The function of these works was primarily as propaganda to offer "ideological support for the politics of centralization and for the claim that the kingdom of Judah was the 'real Israel'" after the demise of the northern kingdom.

Likewise, in chapter 5 Römer describes the social and historical conditions of the Neo-Babylonian period and the exile as the context in which he sees the next edition of the Deuteronomistic History. This edition reflects a "mandarin" scribal group of former royal bureaucrats who created an ideology of exile (in contrast to the perspectives of priest and prophet) and who constructed a comprehen- sive history of Israel and Judah from Moses to the end of the monarchy with an attempt to account for the great disaster as divine punishment. This led not only to extensive supplementation of Deuteronomy and Joshua, making them part of the larger history, but also to the creation of the period of the judges out of old northern hero tales to bridge the gap to the time of the monarchy. Key ideologi- cal passages were added at appropriate points of the history but most extensively in Deuteronomy, which were specially made for the audience of the Golah. It is apparently only at this time that the royal edict of Josiah inaugurating cultic reform became the law of Moses against which the whole history of the people was judged. By far the largest bulk of texts that are considered as Deuteronomistic belong to this "edition," with the result that Römer spends much more time in his treatment of texts in this layer.

This leaves a rather brief discussion of the final phase of Deuteronomistic editing in the Persian period, in which the main concerns became separation from "the nations" as ideological segregation from those who did not adhere to the law of Moses, a shift to monotheism in which Israel's God is the only true deity, and the book of the law that became the central focus of religious concern, especially for the Diaspora. This is highlighted in the story of the discovery of the book in 2 Kgs 22 and 23, added to the account of the reform by this late edition. Beyond these Deuteronomistic editions there were other non-Deuteronomistic additions made to the corpus that tended to obscure its role as a history of the people and yield to a wide range of ideological and didactic concerns.

This proposal of a three-stage development of the Deuteronomistic History is presented as a compromise among the various theories, in which the first edi- tion reflects the Cross/Harvard school, which advocates a preexilic first edition, while the major exilic second edition corresponds largely to the original thesis of Noth, and the final postexilic edition emphasizes the DtrN edition of the Smend/ Göttingen school. Yet the problem remains as to whether or not one can convinc- ingly correlate the various strata of the text with the appropriate criteria that are thought to distinguish the different editions. This may be illustrated with a few examples. The first case is the correlation of the first edition of Deuteronomy, reflecting strong Assyrian influence on its use of the covenant/treaty form, with the account of the cultic reform in 2 Kgs 22–23. Römer assigns to this edition 2 Kgs 22:1–7*, 9, 13aα; 23:1, 3-15*, 25aα. This reconstructed account by itself is quite incoherent. It begins, after the introductory formula for Josiah's reign, with the inauguration of a renovation of the temple (vv. 3-7, 9), which is then abruptly interrupted by an assembly of the people to announce a covenant between king and deity that included the people, based on the content of a book (23:1, 3). This presumably correlates with the covenant/treaty language of Deut 13 and 28 that is part of Römer's first edition. The "words of the covenant that were written in this book" (23:3) have reference to "the words of the book of the covenant that were found in the house of Yahweh" that were read out to all the people as a necessary part of the covenant ceremony (v. 2), but Römer relegates the discovery of the book to the third edition, so this verse must not be included in this stage. Römer adds to the exilic edition the account of the consultation of Hulda the prophetess in 22:14–20 but eliminates from it all references to the book as belonging to the third edition; however, this eliminates the motivation for the consultation in the first place. This seems to me a case of special pleading.

The description of the cultic reform in 2 Kgs 23:4–14 seems to be directed primarily at the elimination of all foreign cults and the purification of the worship of Yahweh (see also 22:17), but it does not seem to be specifically concerned with centralization, which may be only a by-product of such activity. What is striking is that the specific language referring to centralization of worship in Deut 12 is not found in this unit, although it certainly occurs elsewhere in Kings. Instead, we have the language of Deut 12:2–3, which is regarded by Römer as belonging to the latest edition. The negative remarks about Solomon in 2 Kgs 23:13 also fit with Römer's second edition of Kings, not his first (see Römer, 151). One could go through the unit and eliminate all of these interconnections as "redactional" additions, but this would make the report of the reform less and less Deuteronomistic. The fracturing of the account in 2 Kgs 22–23 into three strata seems to rest entirely on the need to reflect three editions in this text.

Furthermore, the motivation for the consultation of Hulda, the covenant making, and the reform that follows is a complete enigma without the discovery of the book with its dire threats in the curses of Deut 28 as reflected in 2 Kgs 22:13, but this is attributed to the third edition. Now, Römer is aware of the fact that there are Near Eastern parallels to this feature in the story of finding ancient documents in temples, which are then used to justify royal activity, and he cites some examples of these, although none from the Persian period, which is his date for this episode in Kings. However, he does not cite the best example, the Shabaka Stone, which contains the so-called "Memphite Theology." King Shabaka of the Twenty-Fifth Dynasty (ca. 710 B.C.E.) claims to have found this document in worm-eaten condition, which he then restored and inscribed in stone. It purports to be a very ancient text, "a work of the ancestors," written in very archaic language that scholars for a long time thought was dated to the Old Kingdom but was actually composed in Shabaka's own time. This king clearly intended it to serve his own ideological and propagandist purposes: "in order that his name might endure and his monument last in the House of his father Ptah-South-of-his-Wall throughout eternity" (see M. Lichtheim, *Ancient Egyptian Literature* [Berkeley and Los Angeles: University of California Press, 1975-80], 1:51–57; 3:5). Based on this and other parallels, it makes the best sense to see this "discovery" of the book as belonging to the time of Josiah and used for similar political and religious purposes of his own day. If this is the case, it would largely dissolve all the arguments for a third DtrN edition.

The application of the criteria of Assyriological parallels for dating purposes can be used rather selectively, applied when it is useful or ignored when it is not. Thus Römer advocates an early preexilic version of Joshua in Josh 6–12 because it so nicely corresponds with Assyriological conventions. This also allows him to view this early version of the conquest as quite separate from Deuteronomy, in which Joshua is the successor to Moses. The commissioning of Joshua would then be seen in the account in Josh 5:13–15, a scene that also has its Assyrian parallels. However, in Assyrian texts it does not have the function of investiture but rather serves as a divine revelation given to the king before an important battle, and that is clearly the function in Joshua. On the other hand, Josh 3–4, which deals with the crossing of the Jordan before the beginning of the campaign against Jericho, is a vital component in the whole conquest narrative. As I indicated in my earlier study of the parallels in Assyrian royal inscriptions, which Römer cites ("Joshua's Campaign of Canaan and Near Eastern Historiography," *SJOT* 2 [1990]: 1–12), an account of the crossing of a river at flood stage before the beginning of a campaign is a very frequent component of Assyrian inscriptions. And the crossing of the Jordan in chapters 3–4 is preceded by the mustering of the troops in chapter 1, which takes us back to the actual investiture of Joshua in Deut 31:7–8 as Moses' successor. The parallel Assyrian texts make quite clear that there is no version of the conquest earlier than the one that makes the connection with Deuteronomy and that Römer identifies as the exilic Deuteronomist.

Another significant parallel to Near Eastern texts occurs in the Solomonic account of the building of the temple, which Römer again compares with Assyrian building inscriptions, following the work of Victor Hurowitz (*I Have Built You an Exalted House: Temple Building in the Bible in Light of Mesopotamian and Northwestern Semitic Writings* [JSOTSup 115; Sheffield: Sheffield Academic Press, 1992]), who also concludes that the Assyrian building accounts represent the closest parallels. However, anyone consulting this important collection of texts will discover that it is in fact the Neo-Babylonian period that provides the closest parallels to *temple* building. It was the Babylonian kings who were obsessed with building temples, describing their work in great detail and giving rather scant attention to their palaces, just as in the biblical account in 1 Kgs 5–8, whereas the Assyrian were quite the reverse, with much to say about their palaces but giving little information on temple building. Hurowitz gives only one example of Assyrian temple building (ibid., 76–78), but several by Babylonian kings (ibid., 91–96).

In fact, one can find very many accounts of temple restoration from the Neo-Babylonian period with many features similar to those of the Solomonic temple project. (P.-A. Beaulieu in *The Reign of Nabonidus, King of Babylon 556-539* [YNER 10; New Haven: Yale University Press, 1989], 42, lists seventeen inscriptions that deal with temple building in the time of Nabonidus; for numerous additional examples in the time of Nabopolassar and Nebuchadnezzar, see S. Langdon, *Die Neubabylonischen Königsinschriften* [VAB 4; Leipzig: Hinrich, 1912].)

Another consideration for dating the biblical account of the temple construction to the exilic period is the fact that for Dtr the primary function of the temple is to house the ark, which Dtr regards as a repository for the two tables of the Decalogue. The temple represents the climax of the ark's journey from the wilderness period to the special place in Jerusalem, which is synonymous with the place where the deity has set his name (2 Sam 7:1–13; 1 Kgs 8:6, 9, 15–21). The placing of the ark of the covenant in the temple with great pomp and procession is the direct equivalent of the placing of the gods of the Babylonians in their temples, and in both cases this is followed by much celebration. There is also the same emphasis on the king's piety. It seems to me that the whole point of this elaborate temple-building narrative, in imitation of the Babylonian model, is to articulate an understanding of divine imminence in the words of the Horeb covenant, in contrast to the iconographic representations of Assyria and Babylonia. Consequently, there appears to be little left that one can attribute to the pre-exilic Dtr in Joshua to 2 Kings.

There are still a large number of problems about which there could be endless debate. (1) What is the nature of the sources used by Dtr? Römer mentions "annals" and "chronicles," but Assyrian *annals* record wars of conquest by an imperial power, which is hardly the case for Israel or Judah, and *chronicles* are the invention of the Babylonians in the Neo-Babylonian period. (2) What is the relationship of Deuteronomy and Dtr to the Pentateuch? to the Yahwist? to the Priestly writer? Römer briefly states at the outset where he stands on these questions, but they are still strongly contested issues, and he is very much aware of that fact. (3) Is the work of Dtr a history, and is Greek historiography an appropriate model for comparison? Römer, among others, expresses some reservations about making such comparisons, reservations that I do not share, but he has little reticence about employing what to my mind is the more dubious and highly anachronistic notion of editor or redactor in connection with his Deuteronomistic writers.

The limitations of a review such as this do not allow one to delve into any of these matters. I am merely suggesting that many issues remain on both the larger questions and the smaller details that will require extensive and sustained discussion. Given the great complexity of the biblical text's literary history and the vast accumulation of scholarship with its widespread disagreements, it is little wonder that there is no easy and broad consensus. Nevertheless, these remarks should not detract from the excellence of Römer's book. It remains a very thoughtful and well-informed study that may serve as a good starting point for further discussion on matters such as I have suggested above, and I warmly recommend it to students and scholars as an introduction to this field of study. Unfortunately, the price of the book is way out of line with its modest size and a serious detriment to its academic purpose.

When Heroes Love: The Ambiguity of Eros in the Stories of Gilgamesh and David, by Susan Ackerman. Gender, Theory and Religion. New York: Columbia University Press, 2005. Pp. xvi + 353. Hardcover. $47.50. ISBN 0231132603.

Thomas Römer, University of Lausanne, Lausanne, Switzerland

This very well written and well-documented book offers a new explanation of the heavily disputed erotic components in the relation of Gilgamesh and Enkidu and of David and Jonathan. In an introductory chapter Ackerman warns against an anachronistic use of these stories in the present debate about social acceptation of homosexuality. She adheres to the social constructionist analysis and considers homosexuality as a modern construct of the nineteenth century that cannot apply to the ancient Near East and to the ideology of the biblical writers.

The first major part of her work is then devoted to the epic of Gilgamesh (33–150). Ackerman starts by giving an overview of the content and the formation of the Gilgamesh Epic, emphasizing some differences between the Old Babylonian and the Standard versions (unfortunately, A. George's new critical edition of the epic was printed too late to be used by Ackerman). Then she turns to the question of how to understand the relationship between Gilgamesh and Enkidu. Ackerman enumerates all the possible erotic allusions to this relationship in the different versions of Gilgamesh: the wordplays in the meteor and axe dream accounts; the frequent designation of Gilgamesh and Enkidu as "brothers"; the wrestling account; Gilgamesh's rejection of Ishtar's advances; the deathbed scene in which Enkidu is compared to a bride; and, finally, Gilgamesh's lament over his dead friend. Even if many commentators argue that the relationship between Gilgamesh and Enkidu should not be understood as sexual in nature, for Ackerman "the presence of homoerotic overtones in some of the Epic's descriptions ... seems indisputable" (81).

This, however, raises a problem of interpretation. Given the fact that an egalitarian sexual relationship is not conceivable in the ancient Near East (indeed, each sexual act necessitates an active [the man] and a passive [the woman] partner), how should one understand the epic's homoerotic imagery? Ackerman's answer is to apply van Gennep's and Turner's concept of rites of passage to the Gilgamesh Epic. Rites of passage are necessary to accompany the transition from an earlier social structure to a new structure. This transition is characterized by a liminal state or persona whose most defining characteristic is ambiguity. Indeed, there are many indicators for an understanding of Gilgamesh and Enkidu as liminal characters (e.g., Gilgamesh is two-thirds divine and one-third human; Enkidu stands between animal and human, but he is also on the margin between male and female). Gilgamesh's journey to the end of the world reminds one also of the typically liminal experience of tests and trials. The women of the epic, Shamhat, Ishtar, Siduri (who might be a manifestation of Ishtar), and Utnapishtim's wife, are also liminal characters of a sort. In this interpretation of the epic as reflecting a rite of passage, it is quite logical to find a sexualized relationship between Gilgamesh and Enkidu that does not conform to the Mesopotamian norms of sexuality. The end of the liminal status is described somewhat differently in the Old Babylonian and in the Standard versions. According to the Old Babylonian version, Gilgamesh is urged to reintegrate himself into society by "returning to the normal and normative behaviours of Mesopotamian society" (131). The Standard version, although it does not reject the advice given by Siduri to Gilgamesh, insists on the fact that Gilgamesh is more than a "normal" human and that he can claim some form of eternal life by creating great monuments of civilization.

After this convincing analysis, Ackerman turns to the biblical story about the friendship of David and Jonathan as related in the books of Samuel (153–231). She starts with the scholarly discussion about the historicity of David, heavily criticizing the "revisionist scholars" and arguing that the Tel Dan inscriptions clearly make a strong case for the existence of a tenth-century David. In my opinion, this somewhat passionate statement is not really necessary for Ackerman's demonstration. A presentation about the literary formation of the David story would have been more helpful. In contrast to her discussion of the formation of the Gilgamesh Epic, Ackerman does not give much diachronic indications about the composition of the David story. She mentions only the incorporation of the David material in the "Deuteronomistic History," which she dates, following Cross, at the end of the Judean monarchy. She also distinguishes in the David-Jonathan material a "primary account" and a "variant account."

As in her analysis of the relation between Gilgamesh and Enkidu, Ackerman collects indicators of an eroticized relationship between David and Jonathan, such as the verb חפץ in 1 Sam 19:1, the numerous parallels between Michal and Jonathan, the tender farewell encounter in 1 Sam 20:41–42, the frequent bow-and-arrow references, which "may be a part of the text's homoeroticized imagery" (183), Saul's anger and diatribe against Jonathan in 1 Sam 20:28–29, as well as David's lament over the fallen friend (1 Sam 1:19–27). The story quite often also uses the verb "to love" (אהב), which can nevertheless also be understood in a political sense, as attested by the Near Eastern vassal treaties. Therefore, most commentators argue that the relationship of David and Jonathan cannot be read as sexual in nature, especially since this would contradict the conception of sexuality as expressed elsewhere in the Bible.

To avoid this contradiction Ackerman wonders if the relationship between David and Jonathan should be understood through the concept of liminal characters, as was the case for her interpretation of Gilgamesh and Enkidu. But David and Jonathan appear much less as liminal heroes, even if the narrative of their relation integrates some liminal features. Therefore, Ackerman offers another explanation. Following McCarter, McKenzie, and others, she argues that the David story should be understood as royal propaganda whose function is to legitimate David as the rightful king of Israel and Judah. In this context, the relationship with Jonathan—which supersedes David's marriage with Michal and the "homoeroticized terms that depict David and Jonathan as being like husband and wife, with Jonathan occupying the wifelike role"—furthers "the tradition's goal of affirming David's right to the throne over the claims that might otherwise be advanced on behalf of Saul's descendants" (221–22). For this apologetic reason, the sexual aspects of the story of David and Jonathan were acceptable to the narrators and the audience.

Even if thought-provoking, I find this theory less convincing than Ackerman's analysis of the Gilgamesh Epic. Why not imagine that the authors of the David story knew the Standard version of the Gilgamesh Epic, as Loyse Bonjour and I have argued elsewhere (Thomas Römer and Loyse Bonjour, *L'homosexualité dans le Proche-Orient ancien et la Bible* [Essais bibliques 37; Geneva: Labor et Fides, 2005])? Ackerman never addresses this question. If the authors of the books of Samuel were familiar with the Gilgamesh tradition, and there is little doubt that they were, one could easily argue that they tried to present David as a Hebrew Gilgamesh. This does not speak against the apologetic function of the history of David's rise, but it might provide a better understanding of his relationship with Jonathan. In the end, these remarks do not diminish the high quality of Ackerman's work, which should be read by all biblical and Near Eastern scholars interested in the heroic traditions.

Überlieferungen von Religion und Krieg: Exegetische und religionsgeschichtliche Untersuchungen zu Richter 3–8 und verwandten Texten, by Andreas Scherer. Wissenschaftliche Monographien zum Alten und Neuen Testament 105. Neukirchen-Vluyn: Neukirchener, 2005. Pp. xii + 468. Cloth. €59.00. ISBN 3788720670.

Uwe Becker, Friedrich-Schiller-Universität Jena, Jena, Germany

Mit seiner vorliegenden Bochumer Habilitationsschrift möchte A. Scherer das Verhältnis von Krieg und Religion am Beispiel der Richtererzählungen Jdc 3–8 untersuchen. Dies ist zum einen, wie er in seiner Einführung betont, ein brisantes *religionsgeschichtliches* Thema, zum andern ist damit aber auch das Problem der Entstehung, des traditionsgeschichtlichen Hintergrunds und des Wachstums der Erzählungen angezeigt. „Der dazu erforderliche Arbeitsaufwand nötigt zu einer relativ engen Begrenzung bei der Auswahl der zu behandelnden Texte und drängt mit arbeitsökonomischer Zwangsläufigkeit die religionsgeschichtlichen Anteile meines Buches quantitativ in den Hintergrund" (3). Eigentümlicherweise werden die Jiftach-Geschichte Jdc 10–12, die Simsonerzählung Jdc 13–16 und die sogenannten Anhänge in 17–21 ausgeblendet (vgl. zu Jdc 10–12 die pragmatische Begründung, 21–22), was angesichts der Ausgangsfrage nach dem Verhältnis von

Krieg und Religion ein wenig erstaunt. Das Kapitel Jdc 9 wird exkursartig besprochen.

Die *redaktionsgeschichtlichen* Ergebnisse lassen sich wie folgt zusammenfassen: Der untersuchte Textkomplex Jdc 3,7–8,35 ist Teil einer vom Dtr. entworfenen Geschichtsdarstellung, die Scherer im wesentlichen versteht wie Martin Noth in seinen „Überlieferungsgeschichtlichen Studien" von 1943, nämlich als ein geschlossen komponiertes, von Dtn 1 bis 2 Reg 25 reichendes Werk. Über Noth hinaus rechnet Scherer allerdings mit einer gewissen „innerdtr. Polyphonie" (*passim*). Zur dtr. Richterzeit haben neben dem Kernbestand von Jdc. 3,7–8,35 hinaus auch die Einleitung 2,11ff.*, die Abimelech-Episode Jdc 9, die Jiftach-Erzählung 10,17–12,7* und die zweigeteilte Liste der Kleinen Richter gehört. Vielleicht gehörte auch der ursprüngliche Bestand der Simson-Erzählung Jdc 13–15* hinzu. Die dtr. Anteile der näher untersuchten Erzählungen lassen sich—so Scherer—vor allem aufgrund sprachlicher Kriterien leicht aussondern. Zu ihnen gehört das Beispielstück Jdc 3,7–11, das ganz von Dtr. konstruiert worden ist, der Abschluß der Ehud-Geschichte in 3,30 sowie die (auf älterer Überlieferung beruhende) Schamgar-Notiz 3,31. Die Debora-Erzählung ist mittels 4,1, das Debora-Lied durch den Rahmen 5,1.31b in die dtr. Geschichtsdarstellung integriert worden. „Erst durch die dtr. Rahmenelemente werden die einzelnen Richterepisoden, die sich in ihrer vordtr. Gestalt als *JHWH-Kriegserzählungen* zu erkennen geben, zu paradigmatischen *theologischen Geschichtserzählungen*" (411). Die Richtergestalten erscheinen in dieser „primärdtr." Konzeption als positive Leitfiguren; das Volk hingegen hat versagt, denn seine jeweilige Umkehr war nur von kurzer Dauer. Die dtr. Grunderzählung wurde des weiteren hier und da „in dtr. Geist und in dtr. Sprache"—kaum von ein- und demselben Redaktor—ergänzt, vor allem im Gideon-Zyklus (vgl. Jdc 6,13.14aα, die Prophetenrede 6,7-10 und 8,27aβb).

Nimmt man die spezifisch dtr. Stücke heraus, zeigt sich nach Scherer, daß sich die hauptsächliche Arbeit der Komposition der Kriegserzählung in Jdc. 3–8 wesentlich bereits vor-dtr. Händen verdankt. Scherer kehrt damit im Kern zu der einflußreichen These eines vor-dtn. (!) Retterbuches von Wolfgang Richter zurück („Traditionsgeschichtliche Untersuchungen zum Richterbuch", Bonn 1963), die der Rezensent in seiner eigenen Studie („Richterzeit und Königtum", Berlin 1990) zu widerlegen versucht hat. Anders als W. Richter sieht Scherer aber keine königskritischen Implikationen, denn weder der Gideon-Spruch Jdc 8,22–23 noch die Abimelech-Geschichte waren Teile der alten Sammlung.

Das Debora-Lied ist in seinem Grundbestand „als *JHWH-Kriegsballade mit werbender und mahnender Tendenz* anzusprechen, die später, allerdings noch in vordtr. Zeit, eine *hymnische Redaktion* durchlaufen hat" (414; vgl. schon H.-P. Müller und J.A. Soggin). Die drei Erzählungen Jdc 3,12–30; 4 und 6–8 waren bereits vor-dtr. „literarisch geprägte Größen" (414), die von der gemeinsamen Motivik des JHWH-Krieges geprägt waren. Wenigstens für die Erzählungen Jdc 4 und 6-8 wird man „mit einiger Gewißheit auf einen gemeinsamen Verfasser oder wenigstens auf einen gemeinsamen Verfasserkreis schließen dürfen. Der

JHWH-Krieg ist für diesen Autor nicht ein Element neben anderen, sondern tragendes Motiv seiner Komposition" (414). Typisches Kennzeichen dieses Autors ist die *Übereignungsformel*, die JHWHs Eintreten für Israel veranschaulicht (vgl. Jdc 4,7.9.14; 7.2.7.9.14.15; 8,7) und sich damit charakteristisch von der dtr. Verwendung unterscheidet. Darüber hinaus gibt es weitere verbindende Elemente: zum einen das Aufgebot einer Stämmekoalition (hier begegnet bereits „bedenkenlos und selbstverständlich" [414] der Israel-Name), zum andern das Motiv von der vernichtenden Niederlage des Gegners (Jdc 5,16; 8,10–12). Das Leitmotiv dieser Erzählungen läßt sich denn auch in einem Satz zusammenfassen: „Der Verfasser legt alles Gewicht darauf, die entscheidende Bedeutung JHWHs für den Kriegserfolg herauszustellen. Infolge dessen kommt es zu einer deutlichen Marginalisierung, wenn auch nicht zu einer generellen Nivellierung des menschlichen Anteils am Kriegsgeschehen" (415). Da die Erzählungen jeweils Elemente eines Berufungsformulars enthalten (vgl. Jdc 4,4–9*), kann man den Zyklus nach Ansicht Scherers genauer datieren: Er gehört in die zeitliche Nähe der vorklassischen Nordreichsprophetie. Diese einigermaßen überraschende Frühdatierung hängt im wesentlichen an der literarhistorischen Einordnung der Mose-Berufung, die Scherer in seinem nichtjahwistischen Teil einem Elohisten im 9. Jahrhundert (!) zuweist. In diese Zeit führt nicht nur die Politik eines Elischa, der in seiner Weise die israelitischen Könige bei der Kriegführung unterstützt, sondern auch die Erzählung Jdc 6,25–32, die in die Auseinandersetzung zwischen JHWH und Baal im 9. Jahrhundert verweist. Über *diese* Einordnung ist man indes sowohl aus redaktions- wie religionsgeschichtlichen Gründen mehr als erstaunt. Was die Herkunft der Stoffe angeht, muß man unterscheiden: Die Ehud-Erzählung dürfte dem JHWH-Kriegs-Erzähler bereits in schriftlicher Fassung vorgelegen haben; bei der Komposition der Gideon-Erzähler geht Scherer von einer umfänglichen mündlichen Überlieferungsphase aus.

Die *religionsgeschichtlichen* Ergebnisse der Studie ergeben sich aus den redaktions-geschichtlichen. Der in den alten Erzählungen vorherrschende Zusammenhang von JHWH und Krieg/Gewalt „scheint in der Frühzeit Israels angelegt zu sein" (421). „In Israels Vor- und Frühzeit wurde das Kriegsgeschehen allem Anschein nach als Zusammenwirken JHWHs und seiner Krieger begriffen" (422), wie in Jdc 5* noch erkennbar sei. Im Gefolge der vorklassischen Prophetie kam es dann zur „Wiederbelebung alter JHWH-Kriegstraditionen" (422), d.h. zu einer Zurückdrängung des Synergismus zugunsten der Alleinwirksamkeit JHWHs. Erst in der dtr. Theologie kommt es zu einer kategorial anderen Interpretation: Hier geht es um die *theologische Deutung des Untergangs*; der Krieg wird zu einem „ambivalenten Phänomen" (424).

Die Thesen der Arbeit werfen Fragen in redaktions- wie religionsgeschichtlicher Hinsicht auf, die hier freilich nur angedeutet und nicht näher begründet werden können. Ob sich tatsächlich eine auch redaktionell zusammengebundene *vor-dtr.* Sammlung von Kriegserzählungen ausmachen läßt, scheint mir durch die Arbeit nicht erwiesen zu sein. Gewiß sind gemeinsame *Motive* und *Traditionskomplexe* wahrnehmbar, die auf einen gemeinsamen Hintergrund deuten könnten.

Denn das Motiv der Berufung, das Aufgebot einer Stämmekoalition oder die Übereignungsformel, deren vor-dtr. Herkunft nicht über alle Zweifel erhaben ist, kann eine *literarische* Zusammengehörigkeit kaum beweisen. W. Richter hatte für sein vor-dtn. „Retterbuch" immerhin noch ein festes Rahmenwerk ausmachen können; bei Scherer fällt dies dahin. Damit hängt eine weitere grundsätzliche Frage zusammen. Das methodische Postulat, nur das auf eine (erste) dtr. Hand zurückzuführen, was sich sprachlich eindeutig diesem Literaturbereich zuordnen läßt, ist nicht unproblematisch. Ein beliebiges Beispiel: Daß die Einleitung zur Debora-Geschichte Jdc 4,1–3 im wesentlichen auf Dtr. zurückgeht, ist—da es sich um ein redaktionelles Übergangsstück handelt—offensichtlich. Scherer aber setzt alles daran, hier eine ältere, vordtr. Fassung zu vermuten, die sich freilich nicht analytisch erheben, sondern nur intuitiv vorschlagen läßt (vgl. 88–89). Auch die „900 eisernen Wagen" in 4,3.13, ein offensichtlicher Zusatz, möchte Scherer lieber in seine rekonstruierte alte Vorfassung integrieren, weil—und dies ist das einzige Argument!— in den JHWH-Kriegs-Erzählungen eine „Vorliebe für große Zahlen" (89) zu beobachten sei. Für diese Art der intuitiven Tendenz-Argumentation gibt es eine sehr große Zahl weiterer Beispiele, die hier nicht aufgelistet werden können.

Die redaktions-, traditions- und religionsgeschichtliche Argumentation beruht denn auch im wesentlichen auf einer sehr traditionellen „Beweiskette": auf der Annahme einer elohistischen Quellenschrift aus dem 9. Jahrhundert; auf der These, der Gegensatz JHWH—Baal sei bereits zur Zeit Elijas und Elischas voll ausgeprägt gewesen; auf einem sehr traditionellen Verständnis der Schriftprophetie und ihrer Voraussetzungen.

Man erkennt beinahe auf jeder Seite, daß sich Scherer mit neueren Tendenzen der Spätdatierung alttestamentlicher Texte, ja überhaupt mit neueren Forschungstendenzen im Blick auf die Redaktionsgeschichte der Bücher Gen–2 Reg oder der Einordnung der alttestamentlichen Prophetie nicht anfreunden kann. Die Abwehr exegetischer „Feindbilder" prägt viele Fußnoten. So sind wohl die zahlreichen—leider sehr apodiktischen—Urteile wie „führt in die Irre" (z.B. 376) oder „ist auf jeden Fall zurückzuweisen" (z.B. 372) zu erklären. Freilich ersetzen solche Urteile nicht die Argumentation; man vermißt sie gerade dort, wo die Urteile am schärfsten sind. Stattdessen werden Werke zitiert, deren teils fragile Hypothesen—etwa im Blick auf die Existenz eines Elohisten im 9. Jahrhundert (!)—keineswegs den Stand der Forschung repräsentieren. Daß etwa die Aramaismen im Debora-Lied für die Datierung keine Rolle spielen, damit eine extreme Frühdatierung weiterhin möglich bleibt, sollte man besser nicht mit der Studie von Ian Young („Diversity in Pre-Exilic Hebrew", 1993) begründen. Es geht bei alldem auch nicht um „Modernität" oder „Zeitgemäßheit"—das sind in der Exegese stets schlechte Ratgeber, wohl aber um das Aufnehmen wichtiger Fragen, die sich im Falle der vorliegenden Arbeit sowohl auf die *redaktionsgeschichtlichen* Gegebenheiten als auch auf die *Religionsgeschichte* des antiken Israel beziehen. In der Arbeit erleben längst *ad acta* gelegte literar- und religionsgeschichtliche Modelle, die ja eben auch nur *Hypothesen* mit nicht selten unzureichender

Begründung waren, eine überraschende Wiederauferstehung. Dagegen wäre nichts einzuwenden, wenn die Argumente gegen sämtliche Neuentwicklungen der Forschung wirklich schlagend wären. Nach Meinung des Rezensenten ist das mitnichten der Fall. Im Gegenteil: Unterstützt durch den apologetischen Grundzug, der die Untersuchung von der ersten bis zur letzten Seite prägt, gewinnt man den Eindruck, daß das gesamte Hypothesengebäude sehr schnell ins Wanken gerät, wenn man auch nur einen kleinen Stein—sei es das vor- und frühstaatliche Stämmewesen Israels, sei es der Elohist im 9. Jahrhundert oder anderes—aus dem System herausnimmt. Die gegenwärtigen Anfragen an das überkommene, vor allem vom Alten Testament selbst präsentierte Bild von der Vor- und Frühzeit Israels sind nicht gering zu achten, und diese Anfragen sind auch an die vorliegende Arbeit zu richten.

LATTER PROPHETS

The Prophetic Literature, by Marvin A. Sweeney. Interpreting Biblical Texts. Nashville: Abingdon, 2005. Pp. 240. Paper. $19.00. ISBN 0687008441.

Jacques Vermeylen, Centre d.Études Théologiques et Pastorales, Brussels, Belgium

S'il est l'auteur d'un commentaire des XII prophètes (*The Twelve Prophets* [2 vols.; Collegeville, Minn.: Liturgical Press, 2000]), Marvin A. Sweeney est d'abord un spécialiste du livre d'Isaïe, auquel il a consacré en particulier une monographie remarquée (*Isaiah 1-4 and the Post-Exilic Understanding of the Isaianic Tradition* [BZAW 171; Berlin: de Gruyter, 1988]) et un commentaire (*Isaiah 1-39* [FOTL 16; Grand Rapids: Eerdmans, 1996]). Il était donc particulièrement qualifié pour écrire une introduction générale à la littérature prophétique destinée à un large public cultivé. Contrairement à ce qu'on pourrait croire, la rédaction d'un tel ouvrage, qui doit aller à l'essentiel en peu de pages et faire preuve de pédagogie, requiert une grande maîtrise du sujet.

Le livre est écrit dans un style clair et agréable. Il comporte sept chapitres. Les deux premiers traitent de questions générales: les prophètes dans les Écritures juives et chrétiennes (15–21), puis le monde des prophètes du Proche-Orient ancien et les genres littéraires prophétiques (23–44). Les quatre suivants sont consacrés aux grands recueils des "prophètes postérieurs": Isaïe (45–84), Jérémie (85–125), Ézéchiel (127–64) et le livre des Douze prophètes (165–214). Le dernier chapitre a la forme d'un bref épilogue, qui souligne l'actualité des prophètes de jadis (215–19). Chaque partie se termine par une brève bibliographie, en langue anglaise uniquement. Les notes, qui contiennent surtout des références bibliographiques, sont placées en finale (221–32), ce qui ne facilite pas leur consultation. Le tout est encadré par un double avant-propos (de l'auteur et des éditeurs de la collection, 9–12) et un index thématique (233–40). Il n'y a pas d'index des références bibliques.

La succession des chapitres de l'ouvrage pourrait donner à penser qu'il propose une introduction assez classique à la littérature prophétique. Le chap. 2, par exemple, résume des données qu'on trouve dans d'autres ouvrages; la présentation détaillée (33–42) des genres littéraires reprend en l'adaptant ce que l'auteur avait déjà exposé dans *Isaiah 1–39*. Cette première impression est vite dissipée, car l'auteur s'écarte fréquemment des sentiers battus. Signalons ici quelques-unes de ses préoccupations récurrentes: la volonté de situer les prophètes en général et chaque livre en particulier dans les contextes de la Bible hébraïque, de la LXX et du canon chrétien des Écritures; la proposition d'une lecture cursive des textes, ce qui apparente parfois l'ouvrage à un commentaire très bref de chaque recueil prophétique; le souci d'envisager les textes à la fois sous l'angle historique et sous l'angle synchronique; l'attention aux éléments formels des textes, qui déterminent sa structure (les suscriptions, en particulier, reçoivent une grande importance). Les solutions proposées aux questions classiques sont souvent originales, mais elles reçoivent rarement l'argumentation nécessaire, ce qui s'explique par le format de la collection; pour le Proto-Isaïe et le livre des XII Prophètes, on trouve cette argumentation dans les commentaires écrits par l'auteur.

L'attention précise à la place des recueils prophétiques dans les différents canons des Écritures est, à mon avis, un des points forts de l'ouvrage. Le premier chapitre souligne avec bonheur les logiques théologiques différentes qui traversent l'Ancien Testament (comme préparation du Nouveau) et la Bible hébraïque. La place respective des prophètes est significative. Les *nevi'îm* forment le centre de la *Tanak*, qui n'appelle aucune prolongation. Dans la Bible chrétienne (qui reprend la LXX), en revanche, les prophètes se trouvent en finale du Premier Testament; comme ils annoncent la restauration d'Israël, ils appellent en quelque sorte la venue du Christ. Le Nouveau Testament est d'ailleurs structuré d'une manière analogue; comme la LXX, il comporte quatre parties, dont la dernière (l'Apocalypse de Jean) annonce la seconde venue du Christ (18). Il y a là une intéressante vue d'ensemble sur la Bible chrétienne.

Les relations entre lecture historico-critique et lecture synchronique posent une question fondamentale de méthode. L'exégèse "classique" du XIXe siècle et d'une grande partie du XXe siècle a été largement dominée par les problématiques de l'histoire du texte, et c'est plus récemment que les biblistes ont redécouvert la Bible comme littérature; cette évolution induit une démarche qui part des acquis de la critique historique et s'intéresse ensuite au texte pour lui-même. En bonne logique, cependant, il faut commencer par ce qui est un fait: l'état du texte dans sa forme finale. Ensuite seulement, quand on a exploré la cohérence de ce texte, l'enquête peut se poursuivre au niveau historique. Je reconnais que les nécessités d'une présentation synthétique contraignent parfois à ne pas respecter cet ordre logique. Je crois pourtant que l'auteur aurait eu intérêt à distinguer d'une manière plus claire les deux démarches. Son approche du texte n'est pas vraiment uniforme, mais la manière dont il traite les XII Prophètes est exemplaire. Pour chacun d'entre eux, il commence par préciser le rang qu'il occupe dans la série (Bible hébraïque et LXX); ensuite il relève ce que dit la suscription du livre, ce qui lui permet de dire son point de vue sur la situation historique non seulement du prophète mais aussi du ou des rédacteur(s); il propose une hypothèse sur la structure de l'ouvrage; il termine son exposé avec un rapide survol du texte, en fonction de la structure. Les éléments de type historique sont donc noyés dans un exposé dont la teneur principale est de l'ordre de l'analyse synchronique, et il n'est pas toujours facile de distinguer ce qui relève de la compréhension du texte dans son état final et ce qui relève de l'histoire de sa rédaction.

Sweeney a le souci d'honorer la démarche historico-critique, dont il a lu les travaux. C'est pourtant le parent pauvre de son livre. Les indications qu'il donne sont rudimentaires et n'aident pas vraiment le lecteur à interpréter le texte. Prenons à titre d'exemple Is 1 (54): on y apprend que ce chapitre comprend des matériaux qui remontent au prophète, mais que l'ensemble est organisé en fonction de thèmes qui reviennent aux chap. 55–66. À défaut d'être incontestables, ces propos sont défendables. Il faut cependant se demander à quoi ils sont utiles. On ne sait pas quelles paroles ont été prononcées par le prophète, ni dans quel cadre, en fonction de quelle problématique. Une telle information n'aide guère le lecteur. Pour le livre d'Ézéchiel, Sweeney rejette en quelques phrases l'hypothèse d'une rédaction sacerdotalisante du livre à partir des paroles du prophète lui-même: comme Ézéchiel est à la fois prêtre aaronide et prophète, il n'y a pas de raison de considérer l'apport sacerdotal comme secondaire (132); l'ensemble du livre est donc lu comme l'œuvre du prophète du VIe siècle. La question des rédactions du livre est ainsi réglée d'une manière expéditive, sans faire droit à la grande complexité de la question. Les informations historiques données par l'auteur ne sont pas suffisantes pour saisir la cohérence et la nouveauté de la pensée personnelle d'un Amos, d'un Osée ou d'un Isaïe, par exemple. Je comprends qu'il n'était pas possible de consacrer beaucoup de pages aux questions de *Redaktionsgeschichte,* mais n'aurait-il pas été préférable s'en tenir à une lecture synchronique? Il aurait suffi d'expliquer dans l'introduction que les livres prophétiques sont le produit d'un travail rédactionnel complexe, mais que le format de la collection ne permet pas de traiter ce sujet.

Dans l'ensemble, Sweeney a tendance à minimiser les différences ou les oppositions entre types de prophétisme, entre prophètes et sages, entre prophètes et prêtres. C'est ainsi qu'il voit la qualité de prêtre lévitique comme une clé essentielle de compréhension de Jérémie: elle explique son rôle comme enseignant de la Torah (87), les affinités entre ses "confessions" et certains psaumes (87), la mission qui s'impose à lui depuis sa naissance (96), les visions de l'amandier et du chaudron (96–97), ses discours en forme de sermon lévitique (99), etc. Les observations relevées sont en partie nouvelles et ne manquent pas d'intérêt; elles permettent de comprendre d'une manière cohérente le livre de Jérémie. Valent-elles aussi pour entrer dans la psychologie du prophète, comme le propose Sweeney? C'est beaucoup moins évident. La même remarque vaut pour le sacerdoce aaronide d'Ézéchiel.

Pour déterminer la structure d'une œuvre, Sweeney ne se laisse pas impressionner par les divisions classiques, en partie commandées par des considérations sur l'histoire des recueils. Il accorde une importance essentielle—et excessive, à mon avis—aux titres, au détriment de la cohérence thématique. Cette option le conduit à une fragmentation discutable des livres: le livre de Jérémie compterait 17 sections principales dans la LXX et 21 dans le TM; quant à Ézéchiel, il en compterait 13. De telles divisions obscurcissent la dynamique de chaque ouvrage. Pour le livre d'Isaïe, en revanche, l'auteur privilégie le critère de contenu, ce qui le conduit à placer les césures principales après les chap. 33 et 54; ce choix n'est ni classique ni évident. Cependant les divisions littéraires ne commandent pas, à elles seules, le dynamisme interne des livres bibliques. Ici, Sweeney insiste avec raison sur un mouvement d'ensemble qui marque plusieurs livres prophétiques: chaque recueil part de l'expérience vécue ou annoncée du malheur de Jérusalem (ou d'Israël), il réfléchit sur les causes de ce malheur et, peu à peu, il introduit la perspective d'une restauration.

Il me reste à relever quelques observations pertinentes et souvent neuves, parmi beaucoup d'autres: la correspondance entre les nations énumérées en Is 13–27 et celles qui sont incorporées de force dans l'empire perse (63); le livre d'Isaïe comme réflexion théologique sur la question du mal (82); la correspondance entre l'âge de la première prédication d'Ézéchiel et celui de l'entrée en fonction des prêtres (129); le lien entre la manière dont Ézéchiel dénonce l'idolâtrie à Jérusalem et la déportation des prêtres aaronides (141–42); le cadre extérieur du livre des XII Prophètes formé par le motif du divorce entre YHWH et son peuple (Os 1–3) et la déclaration de Malachie, pour qui YHWH déteste le divorce (167).

L'introduction à la littérature prophétique proposée par Sweeney est, à bien des égards, originale. J'ai souligné l'une ou l'autre de ses faiblesses, mais aussi d'incontestables qualités. En tout cas, elle propose un parcours plein d'intérêt.

Hosea, by Ehud Ben Zvi. Forms of the Old Testament Literature 31A.1. Grand Rapids: Eerdmans, 2005. Pp. xiii + 321. Paper. $55.00. ISBN 080280795X.

Laurie J. Braaten, Judson College, Elgin, Illinois

Ehud Ben Zvi is no stranger to those who read and study prophetic texts. In addition to his monographs and commentaries on individual prophets, he has published numerous articles and essays on prophetic interpretation. His recent work is a welcome addition to Hosea studies.

The volume begins with a brief editorial forward explaining the purpose of the series. Unlike the older form-critical method that focuses on the oral prophetic word behind the text, the Forms of Old Testament Literature series limits its investigation to the literary forms of final written texts. The book begins with a brief introduction to the book of Hosea as a whole (ch. 1). The bulk of the book is chapter 2 (23–317!), which features a section-by-section analysis of every unit (or "Prophetic Reading") in Hosea. Because there are no subsection listings in the table of contents (or section headers at the top of the page), the reader must thumb through these nearly three hundred pages to locate a specific passage. The book concludes with a three-and-a-half page glossary of the genre terms employed in the book. I found it helpful to read this brief glossary before reading the body of the book. Like the other volumes in this series, there are no indices of passages, subjects, or authors. The plan is to print a single index volume when the series is complete (xii). This occasionally presents an inconvenience to the reader who may need to locate a verse referenced in other sections of the book or find a source listed in a bibliography in the beginning of the book but cited again later. As in all the volumes in the series, each larger section and its subunits (in this volume designated respectively by the genre labels "Sets of Prophetic Readings" and "Prophetic Readings") are discussed under the fourfold arrangement of structure, genre, setting, and intention. The bibliographies that follow are extensive—they include many obscure works (including unpublished dissertations)—and show the writer's breadth of knowledge of studies on prophetic literature and Hosea.

In chapter 1 Ben Zvi argues that Hos 1:1 presents the book of Hosea as "A Particular Instance of YHWH's Word." The structure, genre, setting, and intention of the book as a whole are discussed here. Ben Zvi uses the first chapter briefly to define Hosea as an "Authoritative, Ancient Israelite Prophetic Book" (11) that claims to be YHWH's word. As a prophetic book, it contains an introduction (1:1), body (1:1–14:9), and conclusion (14:10), which sets it apart from other prophetic books. The introduction and conclusion provide interpretive keys for the whole book. As an authoritative book it is intended to be read and reread and meditated upon (or studied). In the rereading of the book (or individual readings) various cross-references are found, and multiple meanings emerge, both within a single passage (henceforth "reading") and as readings are (re)read in view of other readings. Ben Zvi emphasizes throughout the book that these cross-references and multiple meanings are construed *by the readers,* since no one can claim access to the original authors' intent (e.g., 255). The conceptual structure of Hosea is governed by a postmonarchic metanarrative of YHWH as faithful patron, Israel as unfaithful client, YHWH as the one who punishes Israel. Due to the deity's love for Israel, however, YHWH will not destroy the people but in the future will bring the relationship to "its proper ideal form" (8–9). The setting of the book is twofold: (1) the world of the book, which is construed by the superscript (Hos 1:1) as eighth-century Israel and Judah (by mention of Kings Uzziah, Jotham, Ahaz, and Hezekiah of Judah and Jeroboam of Israel); and (2) the world of the intended readers, the literati of postmonarchic Yehud. These literati are also the writers of the book, since they are among the very few who can read and write. As members of transtemporal Israel, the literati are the heirs of the temporal Israel of the book. Evidence for this postmonarchic setting includes references to Israel and Judah, the "quasi-messianic" hope for a future Davidic king (Hos 3:5), references to an exile and return portrayed as a reversal of the exodus and a new exodus, and depictions of an idyllic future where a new covenant will be made with Israel and the wild animals (Hos 2:16–23 [14–25], pp. 14–16; Ben Zvi uses the MT verse enumeration, which at several points differs from the LXX system adopted by many translations, e.g., the NRSV; I will supply the NRSV versi-fication in brackets where it differs from the Hebrew). All of these have parallels in Israelite postmonarchic literature, as do a number of key terms and word pairs (17–18). Ben Zvi claims that "[a]s with other prophetic books … the monarchic setting of the world of the book communicates to the postmonarchic readership that some of the events foreseen by the speaker or speakers in the text have come to pass." The partial fulfillment of the threatened destruction fortifies the hope that the promises of salvation will also come to pass (18).

Ben Zvi stresses that the genre of the composition is literary and theological, not historical. The book of Hosea "does not show much interest in historical, par-ticular events" (19; see also 176–77, 242–43, etc.). In the glossary Ben Zvi says, "It is to be stressed that YHWH's word that came to Hosea *signifies* a written book, to be read, reread, and studied" (319, emphasis original). Furthermore, the prophet "Hosea of the book is a literary and ideological character that lives within the world of the book" (6). The contemporary reader should not, therefore, resort to looking for the prophetic word in a reconstruction of historical events not *specifi-cally* mentioned in the text (e.g., 80, 223, 237). All the reader has for certain are readings, found within sets of readings, contained in an authoritative prophetic book. The meaning of the text emerges only as these texts are (re)read.

Ben Zvi declares that the intent of the book is to educate, or socialize the lite-rati and the illiterate majority to whom the literati read the book. "Through their reading and rereading of the book of Hosea, these readers are supposed to learn about YHWH and YHWH's attributes as well as YHWH's relationship to Israel. The book explains YHWH's punishment of Israel in the past and above all com-municates hope by pointing to the ideal future" (19). Since the word of YHWH is a written text, only those who can read have direct access to God's word and mind. As such, the literati become "brokers of divine knowledge." This somewhat likens the worldview of the literati with YHWH's mind, hence the (re)reading of the authoritative text to others reinforces the notion that these illiterate masses should accept the literati's worldview as identical with the deity's (19–20). This places them in the position to fill the role of the wise nonroyal leaders (since the kings are presented as failures in Hosea) until the coming of the ideal Davidic leader (282–83, 286).

The contemporary reader will no doubt want to ponder the sociological implications of this reconstructed setting. In addition, I question why a group's ability to read and write necessitates that their literary production be addressed primarily to their own circle. (This seems somewhat akin to suggesting that Paul wrote his letters primarily to Barnabas, Titus, Luke, and Silas.) In the community memory preserved in the authoritative books, the message or word of YHWH given to the prophets is always directed to those *outside*, not within, the prophetic circle. This is also the case with written documents, whether or not the recipi-ents personally read them (e.g., Jer 29:4–23; 36:1–31; 45:1–5; 51:59–64a; 2 Chr 22:12–15).

In chapter 2 Ben Zvi discusses each unit of Hosea according to his analysis of

the book's structure. He attributes the following structure to the book: (1) introduction (1:1); (2) body (three sets of prophetic readings: A. 1:2–3:5; B. 4:1–11:11;
C. 12:1–14:9 [8]); and (3) conclusion (14:10 [9]). Within each set of readings the
first and last readings function as introductions and conclusions to the whole
set. These prophetic readings are more narrowly defined as didactic prophetic
readings, since their aim is to instruct and socialize the reader by the warnings
and promises given to transtemporal Israel through the example of the monarchic Israel in the world of the book. Each set of readings begins with warnings of
punishment and judgment and ends with promises of restoration. The last reading, Hos 14:2–9 [1–8], is also a fitting conclusion to the body, since it brings the
hope to a high point and grounds Israel's transformation in the healing activity
of YHWH. Ben Zvi notes that since the reader cannot know the intent of the
writer(s) of the book, such structures being a function of the readers' (re)reading
of the book. Therefore, alternative structures are plausible, and Ben Zvi usually
notes the opinions of others in this regard. In addition, these alternative structures are just one aspect of the multivaliancy found in Hosea as the texts are read,
reread, and studied. Ben Zvi gives several examples where multiple interpretations
(or "complementary meanings") of a text might all be construed as valid for the
postmonarchic community that ponders the text's meaning for monarchic Israel
of the book, then considers its function for transhistorical Israel as represented
by their own community (e.g., see the helpful discussion of the problematic Hos
6:1–6, especially pp. 134–35 and 144–45).

Ben Zvi's analysis of the material is impressive. While this is not a full-scale
traditional commentary with textual criticism and philological research, within
the strictures of the assigned format the reader will find a bounty of useful material. While Ben Zvi is clear about his own views, he often respectfully notes
alternative opinions. As mentioned above, each reading is analyzed according
to a fourfold format: structure, genre, setting, and intention. Discussion of individual verses, however, is not necessarily complete or conducted in order in each
of these sections. Furthermore, these headings are not always adequate to bear a
complete discussion of the material in the book, so sometimes it seems that topics
are more or less arbitrarily placed under one of these headings.

Ben Zvi avoids many of the pitfalls that beset the interpretation of Hosea.
Since the author's methodology commends an interpretation of the written text,
it avoids an exposition of the details of the historical prophet's marital life or his
supposed inner turmoil and deep suffering—which has fascinated the (sometimes vivid) imaginations of readers for centuries. Too often the outcome of such
preoccupation has been the construction of a metanarrative with insufficient textual grounding, which becomes, nevertheless, a heuristic guide for interpreting
the text. Indeed, feminist readers have shown how some of these metanarratives
are congruent with—if not constructed by—the patriarchal world of the interpreters. Ben Zvi observes that the "woman of whoredom" is identified with "the
land" in 1:2, which symbolizes an important but often neglected aspect of Hosea's
message. In addition, he recognizes the children (as their names suggest) are

important as symbols of Israel in Hos 1–2. As the "offspring of the land," the "children," or rather their names, take their place as important symbols alongside the feminine imagery in Hos 2–3 (e.g., 36, 64, 68; but see below). Ben Zvi also correctly observes a point missed by some recent interpreters: since the two children are *each* addressed in the plural in Hos 2:3 [1], they function here as the *people*; that is, the text does not depict the prophet addressing his biological children to speak to their biological mother (45–46, 56). If Ben Zvi's emphasis on the prophetic word in this text rather than prophetic biography were heeded, a lot of ink would be spared about "Hosea's treatment" of his "children" and "Gomer" in Hos 2:3–25 [1–23]. Ben Zvi also avoids reference to the so-called Canaanite sex cult in his comments on Hos 1–3 and 4 (114–15, 158–60; cf. 197). Ben Zvi notes that when Canaan is explicitly mentioned in 12:8, it is invoked to illustrate economic wrongdoings, not Canaanite rites (251, 260).

I finds much to commend about this literary approach to Hosea. There can be little doubt that the final form of Hosea was meant to speak to postmonarchic Israel. I question, however, whether the book of Hosea makes or supports all the claims that Ben Zvi suggests. He often lays before the reader the option of reading a section as a postmonarchic text (which, he states, the text *requires* of the reader) or as attesting a historical/oral background in the proclamation of a historical prophet (which, he says, the text does *not* require). Where interpreters find evidence of historical settings in the text (such as a judicial scene or liturgy), Ben Zvi asserts that the text is "evoking" a social setting that it then "defamiliarizes" in favor of the prophetic reading (e.g., 111–12, 136–37, 257–58, 278–80, 30; it should be observed, however, that even traditional form critics have long stressed the unusual ways in which the prophets employ familiar forms and traditions). While I noted above some interpreters' tendencies to construct fictional biographies of the prophet's personal life, I would not advocate abandoning all efforts at historical reconstruction, especially those based upon solid textual clues. So, for example, it could be noted that in the opening of the body of the book the text reads, "The beginning of YHWH's speaking through Hosea" (1:2, my translation). This functions in the following manner: (1) it associates this instance of "YHWH's speaking" (דבר, verbal form) with YHWH's word of 1:1 (דבר, nominal form); (2) it therefore presents 1:2–2:3 [1] as a series of brief events (a marriage and the naming of three children) that are (to use the Ben Zvi's language) "particular instances of YHWH's word" in *history* (and tradition); and (3) implies (by "the beginning of") that the remainder of the book contains similar instances of YHWH's word conveyed through the speaking of "Hosea" in particular historical circumstances. The interpreter may also observe that, since the superscription implies an afterlife of the tradition in the Judean community, these instances of YHWH's word in the book of Hosea are set not only in the life of the prophet but in the (prophetic) community that preserved and expanded the living tradition of Hosea. In other words, I would argue that the book of Hosea contains specific markers that allow the reader to find the prophetic word within a *restrained* reconstruction of events attested by the text. While the newer form-critical method can be heralded as a needed *supplement* to (and corrective to some of the excesses of) the older form-critical method, it would probably be a mistake to consider it as its *replacement*—rumors of its death are, perhaps, premature! It also should be noted that by itself the new form criticism lacks the richness of the "traditional" form criticism. In Hosea Ben Zvi finds basically one form (didactic prophetic reading) and its variant (set of prophetic didactic readings). This means there is also basically one setting and one intention for this genre, as evidenced by Ben Zvi's nearly verbatim opening statements in each of the setting and intention sections throughout the volume.

Likewise, Ben Zvi asserts that when speeches or liturgies are reconstructed from written texts, the depicted events are too brief to be considered historical accounts (280, 301, 311). In the memory of postmonarchic Israel, however, prophets were usually depicted as conveying YHWH's word to their audiences in very brief oracles (e.g., 2 Sam 12:1–15; 1 Kgs 21:15–23; Amos 7:14–17; Jer 7:1–15; 2 Chr 20:15–17; Jon 3:4b) or, less often, in short written documents (e.g., Jer 29:4–23; 45:1–5; 2 Chr 22:12-15). Similarly, the liturgies (or, more accurately, the liturgical readings that belong to a liturgical event) attested in the psalms are often quite brief. I, of course, am not advocating a return to a purely historical analysis of biblical texts or the outdated view that prophets, as "primitives," were capable of making only short speeches (an opinion based on a flawed nineteenth-century anthropology). Rather, I advocate that the multivaliancy of texts can be found not only at the final literary level (*Sitz im Buch*), but also *sometimes* in the settings of the life of the speaker(s).

It should also be noted that, contrary to Ben Zvi's assertions, there are no specific historical markers *within the book of Hosea* that demand of the interpreter a postmonarchic setting. His evidence for a postmonarchic setting for the book of Hosea (see above) has been plausibly interpreted by others as belonging to the monarchic setting(s) suggested by the superscript. It is my contention that there are specific markers for a Yehudian reading for Hosea, but they are found not in Hos 1–14 per se; rather, they are to be located in the literary setting of Hosea in the Book of the Twelve (which dates no earlier than the books of Haggai, Zechariah, and Malachi). This option is not open to Ben Zvi, however, since he excludes the prospect that the Book of the Twelve was constructed to be read as a literary unit (see 6–7, 11, 24, 31; 319). As noted above, it is my contention that the multivaliancy of the text demands that such a postmonarchic reading is not to be considered the only reading.

The text of Hosea is notoriously difficult to understand, so every reader will no doubt have a few disagreements with specific points of Ben Zvi's interpretation. I note one major point where I disagree with Ben Zvi's reading. Despite his concern not to overinterpret the prophet's marital life, Ben Zvi still construes the image of *Israel* as YHWH's bride as a dominant symbol in and interpretive key for the book of Hosea. While one can clearly demonstrate that Israel is presented as a bride in a few verses at the end of Hos 2, and within the five verses of chapter 3, I (and a few others) have plausibly argued that textual evidence for feminine imagery of Israel is completely lacking in Hos 1 and 4–14. (Ben Zvi cites most of these studies, so he is aware of the argument.) Rather than present Israel in *dominantly* feminine imagery, Hosea depicts Israel (who bears a *patriarchal* eponym) more consistently as YHWH's child(ren), usually as a son (e.g., 2:2 [1:11]; 2:6 [4]; 11:1–9; 13:12–13; 14:4 [3] and likely 1:9; 4:6; 5:7; and 9:15). Yet Ben Zvi finds a feminized Israel throughout the book (including 1:2–9 and most of the passages just mentioned), where I find no convincing textual support (e.g., 59, 108, 127, 134, 197, 259, 261, 273, 297–98). Similarly, since the bride imagery does seem to be diverse in a few verses in Hos 2 and 3, it would be helpful if Ben Zvi would explain how the worldview of the text supports such a mixing of imagery. I find a very promising start toward solving this problem, however, in Ben Zvi's proposal that Hos 2 depicts Israel in royal imagery as mediators of YHWH's blessing on the land in (see 76).

Over the centuries, the task of making sense of the book of Hosea has not only been difficult but has also has sparked much controversy in the interpretive communities. Ben Zvi has made an enormous contribution to Hosea studies and the understanding of this enigmatic prophetic book. His readings of Hosea are arguably cutting edge and deserve the careful attention of those who wish to keep current in Hosea studies and recent methods of interpretation. I found here much to employ in my future work. Likewise, as the methods Ben Zvi advocates are further refined by the academy, his work will undoubtedly be viewed as an enduring contribution to this endeavor.

Josiah's Reform and Jeremiah's Scroll: Historical Calamity and Prophetic Response, by Mark Leuchter. Hebrew Bible Monographs 6. Sheffield: Sheffield Phoenix Press, 2006. Pp. x + 206. Hardcover. $85.00. ISBN 1905048319.

K. L. Noll, Brandon University, Brandon, Manitoba, Canada

This monograph is an extensive revision of the author's Ph.D. dissertation. The original dissertation and its transformation were completed at the University of Toronto. The volume includes nine chapters plus an introduction, full bibliography, and indices of authors and Scripture references. The bibliography and footnotes demonstrate the author's thorough familiarity with the history of scholarship, and the work is almost entirely free of typographical errors or other distracting mistakes, making it a pleasure to read. This reviewer is not convinced by the author's hypothesis and will be critical in many instances, but that should not be viewed as condemnation. Leuchter demonstrates mastery of his subdiscipline and is to be commended for his competent scholarship.

Josiah's Reform and Jeremiah's Scroll is the most recent addition in a long line of highly subjective and equally implausible constructions of the "historical Jeremiah." Junkies of the genre will be gratified by the presence of all the usual elements, including rearrangement of the received text, overwrought exegesis of individual passages, and a seemingly arbitrary selection of verses to be regarded as the *ipsissima verba* of the prophet. Leuchter demonstrates awareness of viable alternatives to a quest for a historical prophet, but chooses not to engage those fields of scholarship. The one exception is a brief critique of R. P. Carroll to be discussed below.

The title of the volume aptly summarizes its thesis. In this incarnation, Jeremiah becomes a court prophet in the service of King Josiah. He is an apologist for the newly circulating torah scroll mentioned in 2 Kgs 22. Even the death of Josiah and the failure of his political ambitions apparently does not undermine Jeremiah's Deuteronomistic loyalties, for the prophet begins a campaign against old Jerusalemite "royalism," criticizing the temple complex from a Deuteronomistic perspective and ultimately producing a scroll that is read and rejected by King Jehoiakim.

The thesis is defended in very careful detail through nine chapters that follow a chronological sequence. Chapter 1 invents (the verb has been considered, and it stands) an old tradition of the *zophim,* a group especially associated with Shiloh. These were Mushite tradents who performed the priestly, divinatory, and judicial leadership roles that the biblical Samuel is portrayed as having fulfilled. Chapter 2 attempts to show that Deuteronomy appropriates this tradition and reconfigures it in the service of the state. The old Shilonite *zopheh* becomes Deuteronomy's legal judge (Deut 17:9) equated with the prophet like Moses (18:18), and the office is transferred to the site of the central sanctuary, namely, Josiah's Jerusalem. Chapter 3 rehearses the conventional hypothesis that King Josiah had imperial designs on the Assyrian province to his north, the old kingdom of Samaria-Israel. But, according to Leuchter, a rift emerged between competing scribal groups, one favoring an old Jerusalemite royalism, the other defending an old Ephraimite ideology best preserved in texts such as Amos and Hosea. A mediator was needed.

The role of Jeremiah is constructed in chapters 4 through 9 of the monograph. As a priest from Anathoth, Jeremiah stood within the old Ephraimite stream of Yahwism, and Josiah enlisted Jeremiah to defend the king's appropriation of that tradition. Alas, the northerners of Shiloh and elsewhere were too shrewd to be fooled by Jeremiah's "thinly disguised Josianic propaganda" (74). Jeremiah attempted several rhetorical strategies to win them over, and these are outlined in chapters 4 and 5. First, the prophet painted a rosy picture of restored hope that Josiah's religio-political innovations promised. When this failed, Jeremiah turned to invective, chastising the same audience for lack of fidelity to Yahweh. With the death of Josiah and the collapse of his agenda, Jeremiah reconsidered his allegiance to the royalism within Deuteronomy. At this time, Jeremiah advocated fidelity to Deuteronomy's concept of covenant and did so in opposition to reliance on potentially competing sources of religio-political centrality, such as king, priesthood, or sacred sanctuary. Chapter 6 describes the temple sermon of Jer 7:1–15 as a crucial turning point in Jeremiah's career, and chapter 7 outlines how this new emphasis in the prophet's message brought him into conflict with Josiah's royal heirs.

Chapter 8 constructs the hypothetical *Urrolle* implied by the narrative of Jer

36, identifying passages that derived from Josianic days and other texts Leuchter believes to have been added as part of the "many similar words" mentioned in Jer 36:32. In chapter 9 Leuchter concludes that "we can no longer speak of the prophet Jeremiah as a thinker whose work was brought into the Deuteronomistic fold only by later redactors" (169). Poetry and prose texts of the scroll are permeated with the ideology of Deuteronomy, and this Deuteronomism derives from the prophet himself. As Jeremiah's message evolved, says Leuchter, a new religious ethos evolved as well. From the ashes of Josiah's failed royalism, from the bankruptcy of external symbols such as the temple, and from the construction and then reconstruction of Jeremiah's scroll in emulation of Deuteronomy itself emerged a new idea of scripture as the medium of revelation and covenant. "The prophetic tradition evolves from an emphasis on figures to an emphasis on their written words" (181), and the scroll of Jeremiah thus contributed to "the fundamental ideology of the exilic literary canon and early postexilic Judaism, where Torah would rival and eventually supplant Temple as the defining characteristic of communal and individual identity" (182).

Although Leuchter is a master at constructing a carefully defended, linear argument, his exegesis of Jeremiah depends on a network of implausible assumptions about other biblical texts. For example, Leuchter treats the Former Prophets (and especially Samuel and Kings) as largely accurate accounts of the past, he depends on the minority hypothesis that a Hezekian edition of a Deuteronomistic History existed, and he assumes the equally minority view that a significant part of the Priestly material (including Gen 1) was in existence in the late seventh century b.c.e. Perhaps most egregious is Leuchter's treatment of Deuteronomy. Although Leuchter never summarizes what he believes to have been the content of the Josianic torah scroll, it would seem that the bulk of our received Deuteronomy was part of it, since Leuchter appeals to many sections of Deuteronomy that most exegetes would assign to later redactional stages (e.g., Deut 27). Moreover, Leuchter fails to engage the scholarship that concludes no portion of Deuteronomy was written in the service of King Josiah or any other Judean monarch. For all his creative exegesis about royally appointed Deuteronomistic judges, Leuchter's interpretation is less compelling than Lothar Perlitt's judgment: "Im Dtn findet sich kein entwickelter Staatsgedanke" ("Der Staatsgedanke im Deuteronomium," in *Language, Theology and the Bible: Essays in Honour of James Barr* [ed. S. E. Balentine and J. Barton; Oxford: Clarendon, 1994], 182–98, here 195).

Thus, if one were to accept (as this reviewer does not) a plurality of Leuchter's exegetical conclusions, the portrait of Jeremiah that emerges nevertheless remains implausible as a historical hypothesis. This does not negate the complex exegetical fabric that Leuchter has produced, but the Jeremiah that Leuchter constructs is better viewed as the main character in a late literary fiction dependent on the many texts available from the emerging religious canon of the Persian or early Hellenistic eras. Certainly it is possible that the historical Jeremiah was a spin doctor for a minor king with suicidal illusions of imperial grandeur, but even a sympathetic reading of Leuchter's monograph does not provide much support for the hypothesis. The book reads like a very sophisticated, closely argued, "just so" story.

At the level of exegetical details, Leuchter's thesis rests on decisions that many will find problematic. For example, why prefer MT in places where experts in textual criticism suspect that the Old Greek preserves a superior text (e.g., 22–24 [dealing with 1 Sam 1:1], 148 [treating Jer 8:10b–12])? Why attribute every theological nuance to a competing Yahwistic "tradition" (*passim*)? Why should the absence of a Masoretic *dagesh* in 1 Sam 1:1 be credited with silently preserving historical memory from the early Iron Age (22)? Why treat the obviously late gloss in Jer 10:11 (composed in Aramaic) as though it derives from the historical Jeremiah (142)? Why believe that Deuteronomy's prophet like Moses was intended to be a real public office, when Leuchter himself admits that the criterion for legitimation of this figure in 18:21–22 hopelessly undermines any flesh-and-blood person who attempts to fill that role (45–46)? Above all, why assume, a priori, that "[b]iblical texts were not written casually" but arise from "pressing historical circumstances" (15)? This last question requires serious consideration. I doubt that Leuchter's claim holds for Qoheleth, Job, Song of Songs, or even Genesis or Samuel. Perhaps the case could be made if the thesis is limited to prophetic literature, but if so, Leuchter is obligated to engage competing ideas about prophetic composition, such as the alternative approaches, each far more compelling than Leuchter's, advanced by Philip R. Davies, "'Pen of Iron, Point of Diamond' (Jer 17:1): Prophecy as Writing," in *Writings and Speech in Israelite and Ancient Near Eastern Prophecy* (ed. E. Ben Zvi and M. H. Floyd; Atlanta: Society of Biblical Literature, 2000), 65–81; and Martti Nissinen, "How Prophecy Became Literature," *SJOT* 19 (2005): 153–72.

Perhaps the greatest problem with this very problematic monograph is the methodological assumption on which it rests. Leuchter, like many so-called critical exegetes, believes that it is not a difficult task to peer through a text and into an alleged real world behind that text. But an event or person from a real past need not be the catalyst for the creation of a text. Throughout ancient history, *texts* have generated texts. This is the case whether the text in question describes a person, such as the gnostic Jesus generated from the Synoptic Jesus (who is, himself, an invention from still earlier representations), or describes an event, such as the Trojan War of Dares and Dictys generated from the poetry of Homer and the Epic Cycle (themselves generated from earlier legends). The received form of the book of Jeremiah bears little resemblance to known archives recording prophetic activity in Mari or Neo-Assyria, so it seems more reasonable to search for parallels to Jeremiah's emergence closer to home. In that case, it is worth noting that biblical Balaam bears little resemblance to his namesake at Deir Alla, Daniel is a fictional character, and Malachi is, at best, deeply problematic. Also, nameless prophets were invented for the book of Kings, named prophets were invented by the Chronicler, and even Leuchter believes that the "speeches" of Moses in Deuteronomy have nothing to do with a historical Moses. Throughout the Bible poets emulate other poets, plagiarism is common, conflation frequent, and invention the norm. In the face of these realities, a quest for a historical Jeremiah, like a quest for a historical Jesus, Isaiah, or Moses, is the pursuit of theologians, not historians.

This crippling flaw in Leuchter's method is exposed by Leuchter's engagement with the approach of R. P. Carroll (3–6). Carroll is well known for his thesis that Jeremiah the prophet was invented over time from an original collection of anonymous poetry. In an unfortunate attempt to be clever, Leuchter contends that Carroll deconstructs himself when Carroll admits that his own academic research has undergone discernible evolution but denies us the ability to discern similar stages in the message of an Iron Age prophet. Leuchter writes, "The irony is difficult to ignore" (5). It is not, as a matter of fact, ironic at all. We have at our disposal the published redactions of Carroll's evolving thought, not to mention unpublished writings and eyewitness testimonies concerning the late scholar's thought and activity. This is the very kind of evidence that is lacking in the case of Jeremiah. In its place, as Carroll has demonstrated, we have indisputable textual evidence of supplementary redaction in the book of Jeremiah, as well as the invention of both prophecy and prophets related to this scroll (e.g., Baruch the scribe became, in later times, Baruch the apocalyptic seer). The irony in all of this is that the allegedly antihistorical stance of Carroll displays *greater critical awareness* of the historical realties and complex processes of literary production than does the historical research of Leuchter. One wishes that Leuchter had studied the text of Jeremiah as carefully as had the late and lamented R. P. Carroll.

In sum, this monograph will be hailed as a significant contribution to the quest for the historical Jeremiah only by those predisposed to be convinced by the methodological approach that Leuchter so skillfully employs. For other subdisciplines within Jeremiah research, the monograph will represent the latest very competent installment of a quaint quest for a past that never was.

Isaiah in the New Testament, edited by Steve Moyise and Maarten J. J. Menken. The New Testament and the Scriptures of Israel. London: T&T Clark, 2005. Pp. xii + 217. Paper. $49.95. ISBN 056703030X.

Michael P. Knowles, McMaster Divinity College, Hamilton, Ontario, Canada

Scholarly interest in the subject of biblical intertextuality continues unabated. But the Continuum/T&T Clark series The New Testament and the Scriptures of Israel reverses the usual approach, examining the use of specific canonical documents across a broad spectrum of New Testament material rather than tracing the influence of Hebrew Scripture/Septuagint on a particular New Testament text, writer, or genre. *Isaiah in the New Testament* is the second volume to appear: *The Psalms in the New Testament* was published in 2004, while *Deuteronomy in the New Testament* is forthcoming.

This volume incorporates a brief introduction, followed by eleven commissioned essays. Darrell Hannah's lead article, "Isaiah within Judaism of the Second

Temple Period," summarizes the significance of the Qumran Isaiah discoveries, particularly for questions of text and text-type, then focuses on contemporary readings of three passages in particular. He chronicles messianic interpretations of 11:1–2 ("A shoot will arise from the stump of Jesse...") from Qumran, the Similitudes of Enoch, and *4 Ezra;* traces the influence of 6:1–13 ("In the year that King Uzziah died, I saw the LORD...") in both visionary/apocalyptic and liturgical materials (with specific reference to the *Qedušah* or Trisagion); and discusses messianic and nonmessianic interpretations of "The So-Called Servant Songs" from Isa 42; 49; 50; and 52–53. Notwithstanding the necessary brevity of this treatment, one theme that emerges clearly is the use of Isaiah within Second Temple Judaism to highlight opposition and longing for vindication vis-à-vis the Gentiles.

Turning to the interpretation of specifically Christian texts, Morna Hooker's "Isaiah in Mark's Gospel" discusses quotations and possible allusions in the earliest Gospel, offering an extended critique of the lists provided by appendix 4 of the Nestle-Aland *Novum Testamentum Graece,* 27th edition. By way of direct citation, Isa 40:3 functions positively in Mark's opening verses to undergird the announcement of John the Baptist, whereas key references throughout the remainder of the Gospel highlight the unresponsiveness both of Israel (Mark 4:12; 7:6–7; 11:17; 12:1–12) and of the disciples (9:48), warning of judgment yet to come (13:24–25). How these predominantly negative overtones relate to broader "new exodus" motifs from Isaiah, identified by Watts (*Isaiah's New Exodus and Mark,* 1997) and others, is not made clear.

Christopher Tuckett ("Isaiah in Q") observes that allusions rather than citations predominate in this source. He discusses in particular Q 7:22 (Jesus' description of his ministry in answer to John's disciples), whereby Jesus "implicitly [claims] for himself the role of the figure in Isa. 61:1 who is 'anointed with the Spirit'" [54]; Q 6:20–21 (the Beatitudes, "almost a programmatic summary" of Jesus' teaching [57]); and Q 10:15 (the condemnation of Capernaum). Reiterating proposals from his *Q and the History of Early Christianity: Studies on Q* (1996), Tuckett thus argues for a prophetic and eschatological, rather than predominantly sapiential, Christology in Q.

Richard Beaton expands the narrower focus (on Matt 12:18–21) of his earlier study, *Isaiah's Christ in Matthew's Gospel* (2002), to treat a full range of Isaianic quotations in the First Gospel. Identifying nine of these (1:23; 9:3; 4:15–16; 8:17; 12:18–21; 13:13–15; 15:8–9; 21:13; 24:29), Beaton's sensitive analysis treats a rich panoply of redactional and theological concerns, including transcendent and ethical aspects of Matthean Christology, prophetic critique of Israel's leaders, Gentile salvation, and eschatological fulfilment. Beaton amply succeeds in demonstrating that, far from offering simplistic prooftexts, Matthew's quotations from prophetic literature provide a theologically nuanced lens through which the links between Jesus, the circumstances of his ministry, and the broader contours of salvation history appear.

For Bart Koet, "Isaiah is a key to the understanding of Luke-Acts as a whole"

(80). Treating four references in Luke (Isa 40:3–5; 53:12; 56:7; 61:1–2) and five from the book of Acts (Isa 6:9–10; 49:6; 53:7–8; 55:3; 66:1–2), Koet proposes not only that they buttress "Luke's christological, theological, and ecclesiological substructure" (99) but that references to Isaiah in Luke and Acts, respectively, are intentionally counterbalanced and demonstrate the unity of the two volumes. Even more boldly, he suggests that contemporary legends concerning the martyrdom of Isaiah may provide a model for Luke's depiction of Jesus, although the connection between textual and proposed typological appropriations of the prophet remain unexplored.

Catrin Williams's treatment of "Isaiah in John's Gospel" is more satisfying in this regard. Of John's four direct quotations from Isaiah, the first and last (1:23; 12:38–41) explicitly—and uncharacteristically—name the prophet, with these references serving to frame the Evangelist's depiction of Jesus' public ministry. As distinct from the Synoptic accounts, this Gospel has John the Baptist "make straight" rather than "prepare" the way of the Lord (Isa 40:3) because here the Baptist is a contemporary witness to the Messiah rather than a forerunner. John 6:45 ("And they shall all be taught by God") cites Isa 54:13 (although by no means primarily so, as Williams contends) to the effect that Jesus and his teaching are now the source of divine knowledge. Particularly convincing is the discussion of Isa 53:1 and 6:10 as Johannine *gezerah shewah,* mutually illuminating texts linked by common wording. Thus John 12:38–41 understands Isaiah's temple vision to have revealed the divine glory of either the preexistent or—Williams's preference—the future earthly Messiah. In this sense Isaiah bears personal as well as textual testimony to the Johannine Christ.

Ross Wagner treats "Isaiah in Romans and Galatians," in part summarizing the argument of his 2002 *Heralds of the Good News: Paul and Isaiah 'In Concert' in the Letter to the Romans.* Surveying a multitude of individual passages, Wagner finds that "Paul's understanding of the Gospel … and his decades of labour as apostle to the gentiles … decisively influence his reading of the prophet" (118), even as the message of Isaiah reciprocally illuminates Paul's understanding of apostolic ministry, of Christian mission in general, and of Israel's opposition to it in particular. In each of these respects Isaiah serves for Paul as a witness to divine graciousness, with the present salvation of the Gentiles anticipating future redemption for all Israel.

Florian Wilk concurs as to the interpretive reciprocity of prophetic texts and Pauline self-understanding, although the Corinthian literature that he treats yields only four direct quotations from Isaiah (1 Cor 1:19; 14:21; 15:54; 2 Cor 6:20). He too highlights Paul's concern for the gospel and its proclamation, apostleship, and God's relationship with Israel. However, that his findings are partly based on allusions of varying degrees of probability raises questions of audience reception as well as authorial intent and illustrates the difficulty of establishing a solid evidentiary basis for Paul's scriptural hermeneutic.

"Isaiah in Hebrews," by Cecil McCullough, tackles the difficult question of a citation's original context, arguing that when the writer to the Hebrews puts Isa

8:17–18 (together with other texts) into the mouth of Christ (so Heb 2:13), he has in mind the whole of Isa 6–9 and in particular the putatively Isaianic theme of "perseverance in faith" (165–67). Despite McCullough's careful nuancing of the parallels, surely this is overreading, a case of reading the interests of the receptor text back onto the source of the quotation. But that the writer to the Hebrews did something very similar with his own christological reading of Isa 53:12 in Heb 9:28 seems clear (168–71). When New Testament authors take liberties with sacred texts, New Testament scholars are at liberty only to contemplate their methods, not—even unintentionally!—to imitate them.

First Peter provides a plentiful mine of scriptural references, among which Steve Moyise examines six from Isaiah, concentrating initially on similarities and differences between the respective texts. These cite well-known sources of Christian *testimonia*, among them the foundation stone/cornerstone/stone of stumbling passages from Isa 8; 28; and Ps 118; as well as Isa 40; and the "Suffering Servant" motif from Isa 53. Moyise highlights the fact that from the perspective of 1 Peter, reappropriation of these prophetic texts gives evidence not of Christian exegetical practice but of inquiry and exegesis on the part of the prophets themselves, as they sought to understand their own testimony to the future Christ (1 Pet 1:10–12).

Drawing on the work of J. Fekkes (*Isaiah and Prophetic Traditions in the Book of Revelation: Visionary Antecedents and their Development*, 1993), David Mathewson considers the allusive interplay between Isaiah and the book of Revelation. That delineating the limits of intertextuality may also prove *elusive* is highlighted by Mathewson's assertion that "it is doubtful whether discussion of Isaiah in Revelation can be limited only to what can be proven to lie within the author's conscious intention" (189). Following Fekkes, he adopts the thematic categories of "Visionary Experience and Language" (e.g., Isa 6:2–3 in Rev 4:8); "Christological Titles and Descriptions" (especially "the root of David," from Isa 11:10, and various iterations of "the first and the last" from Isa 44:6); "Eschatological Judgement" (concerning the "Day of the Lord" and the fate of the enemies of God's people); and "Eschatological Salvation" (with particular reference to the new heaven, new earth, and new Jerusalem of Rev 21–22). The volume concludes with three indices: "Quotations and Allusions–New Testament Order"; "Quotations and Allusions–Isaiah Order"; and "Modern Authors."

This volume illustrates both the promise and the challenges of the critical approach in question. On the one hand, these studies provide a comprehensive introduction to the *Rezeptionsgeschichte* of the book of Isaiah in early Christian texts. The footnotes offer a wealth of references to further secondary literature. Yet the broader problematic of distinguishing between citations, allusions, and echoes is left largely unaddressed (although Moyise ably tackles this question in "Intertextuality and the Study of the Old Testament in the New," in *The Old Testament in the New Testament: Essays in Honour of J. L. North* [ed. S. Moyise; JSNTSup 189; Sheffield: Sheffield Academic Press, 2000], 14–41). Different essays have clearly differing estimations of the importance of text-type for a particular biblical author. There is a range of opinions as to whether textual references imply an interest in the prophet himself. Not surprisingly, there is a similar breadth of opinion as to the relevance of original context for the receptor text. From this it will be obvious that the editors have not sought to impose any methodological or theological uniformity on the various contributors. Although each essay stands solidly on its own merits, some degree of interaction among them (e.g., between Q and Matthew or Luke with reference to Isa 61, or comparing the various Pauline epistles) would have added further depth to the discussion. By the same token, whereas these essays trace lines of continuity between Jewish and (Jewish-?)Christian interpretations of Isaiah, an intriguing question remains as to what the early church made of other contemporary readings (highlighted by Hannah's introductory article) that focused on vindication of the faithful in the face of (Gentile!) opposition.

While questions of synthesis or integration are thus left for readers to decide, it is immensely helpful to have such a focused compendium delineating the influence of a particular biblical text on the thinking of the early church. Perhaps this and companion volumes will add further impetus to the resurgent interest in Christian *testimonia* lists, given, for instance, the appearance of Isa 40 in all four Gospels, 1 Corinthians, and 1 Peter; the influence of Isa 49 in Acts, Galatians, 2 Corinthians, and Revelation; or the references to Isa 53 in Matthew, Luke, John, Acts, Romans, Hebrews, 1 Peter, and possibly 2 Corinthians as well.

The Message of Isaiah 40–55: A Literary-Theological Commentary, by John Goldingay. London: T&T Clark, 2005. Pp. xi + 578. Hardcover. $89.95. ISBN 0567030385.

Jacques Vermeylen, Université Catholique de Lille, Lille, France

Ce volumineux commentaire est le fruit d'une dizaine d'années de recherche et d'écriture. À vrai dire, l'intérêt de John Goldingay pour Isaïe 40–55 est encore plus ancien, comme l'attestent plusieurs articles (à partir de 1976) et une étude sur les poèmes du Serviteur (*God's Prophet, God's Servant*; Paternoster: Exeter, 1984). Après avoir enseigné à Nottingham, l'auteur est aujourd'hui professeur au Fuller Theological Seminary. Il est bien connu pour son commentaire du livre de Daniel, paru dans la série «Word Biblical Commentary» (Dallas, TX, 1989), son commentaire du livre d'Isaïe publié dans la collection «New International Biblical Commentary» (Hendrickson: Peabody, MA, 2001) et son *Old Testament Theology*, dont seule la première partie est parue à ce jour (*Israel's Gospel*; Downers Grove, IL, 2003).

Comme l'auteur l'explique dans la préface (vii), le manuscrit était originellement destiné à la série «International Critical Commentary», mais il était beaucoup trop long pour cette publication, si bien qu'il fut décidé de lui réserver les éléments les plus techniques (critique textuelle, discussions sur l'histoire du texte, etc.) et de faire paraître à part les éléments de commentaire théologique.

C'est cette seconde publication, destinée à un large public cultivé, qui est ici recensée.

L'ouvrage s'ouvre par une courte introduction (3–7) destinée à le situer dans le contexte de l'exégèse contemporaine de Is 40–55. Ce texte ne doit pas être considéré comme un message théologique intemporel (approche pré-moderne) ni comme l'œuvre homogène d'un auteur anonyme du vıᵉ siècle, à étudier indépendamment des chap. 1 à 39 (approche moderne). Le point de vue adopté est celui de l'exégèse post-moderne, qui s'efforce de comprendre le texte dans son contexte littéraire—celui du livre d'Isaïe comme ensemble—tout en sachant qu'il a été produit par un ou plusieurs auteurs à l'époque exilique ou au-delà. Plus précisément, le texte porte la marque d'un prophète-poète qu'on appellera «Deutéro-Isaïe». Le chap. 40 ne porte aucun titre et n'est pas le début d'un livre, mais si les chap. 34–39 forment un élément de transition, il fait passer subitement le lecteur de la cour de Jérusalem à la cour céleste, du récit d'événements terrestres à un drame qui se situe sur un tout autre plan. Par ailleurs, ce chap. 40 est à la fois parallèle et en opposition avec la scène de la vocation d'Isaïe au chap. 6 : là, YHWH disait «ce peuple», ici, il dit «mon peuple».

Le commentaire lui-même s'étend sur 550 pages. C'est dire s'il est ample et détaillé! Le sous-titre de l'ouvrage le qualifie de «littéraire» et «théologique», ce qui correspond exactement à son double point de vue. «Littéraire», il s'efforce de suivre les méandres de la pensée exprimée par le texte et en relève la qualité poétique; il montre comment les idées ne se développent pas selon une logique cartésienne, mais plutôt en spirale (131, etc.). «Théologique», il s'intéresse à l'image de Dieu que celui-ci suggère, mais aussi à sa portée christologique ou à ses échos dans diverses traditions chrétiennes. L'exposé suit le texte verset par verset et parfois presque mot par mot; il se veut paisible, nuancé et positif: jamais il ne discute telle ou telle position, mais il suit son chemin en proposant une interprétation aussi cohérente que possible. Assez souvent, il cite l'opinion d'autres commentateurs, soit pour la reprendre à son compte, soit pour proposer plusieurs variantes dans la lecture. À l'opposé de tout dogmatisme, il aime souligner diverses possibilités de sens. Pour l'identification du mystérieux Serviteur de YHWH dont parle 42,1–4, par exemple, il propose quatre solutions, en montrant chaque fois les avantages et les inconvénients (150–52); un peu plus loin, il montre que l'anonymité de la même figure peut revêtir quatre significations (153–54). La section 52,13–53,12 fait l'objet d'un long développement (473–88, plus le commentaire proprement dit), justifié par le destin exceptionnel de ce passage et ses échos dans le Nouveau Testament. Les mots les plus importants font l'objet d'un exposé plus ou moins développé. À défaut d'une lecture vraiment nouvelle du texte, qu'on chercherait en vain dans ce commentaire en définitive assez classique, on y trouvera comme une synthèse des meilleurs travaux antérieurs. Le tout est solide et bien écrit. C'est, à mon avis, le commentaire le plus complet et le plus équilibré proposé aujourd'hui à un lectorat non spécialisé, en vue de la prédication ou du travail pastoral par exemple. Il n'est pas destiné à la lecture continue, mais plutôt à la consultation.

Après la fin du commentaire, l'ouvrage ne propose malheureusement aucune forme de synthèse ou de conclusion générale. Il comporte, en revanche, une bibliographie (559–63), un très utile index thématique, dans lequel figurent les principaux mots hébreux (565–72) et enfin un index des auteurs modernes (573–78).

The Message of Isaiah 40–55 est donc un ouvrage d'excellente qualité, qui rendra de grands services. Qu'il me soit cependant permis de formuler ici quelques questions, voire quelques réserves, en attendant la publication—imminente, au moment où j'écris ces lignes—du commentaire jumeau (en deux volumes) du même auteur dans la collection «International Critical Commentary». On y trouvera sans doute réponse à certaines de mes remarques.

Tout d'abord, le commentaire suit le texte biblique pas à pas, mais il ne donne guère de vue d'ensemble, si bien que la dynamique des seize chapitres reste obscure. Je dois évidemment aussitôt nuancer ce jugement: la table des matières (v–vi) propose un découpage caractéristique du texte, et l'exposé de chaque nouvelle section s'ouvre par une courte introduction destinée à établir des liens avec ce qui précède et à proposer les grandes articulations du texte concerné. Il n'empêche: le lecteur risque de se perdre dans ce qui ressemble à un labyrinthe. J'ajoute que le découpage proposé manque d'évidence; peut-être répond-il à la nécessité de traiter des sections de longueur raisonnable plus qu'à la prise en compte de critères thématiques ou littéraires. Ainsi, s'il est vrai que Cyrus n'est mentionné comme tel qu'en 44,28 et 45,1, il ne me paraît pas justifié d'isoler sous le titre «YHWH's work with Cyrus» la section 44,24–48,22, alors que cette œuvre est déjà un thème récurrent à partir de 41,2 (85). Du point de vue littéraire, il aurait été utile de mettre en évidence la correspondance entre 40,1–11 et 55,9–13, qui encadrent l'ensemble du texte concerné, ou encore les césures marquées par les chants de louange à la fin de plusieurs sections ou sous-sections (42,10–13; 44,23; 48,20–21; 49,13; 52,9–12).

Ma deuxième perplexité concerne la déclaration faite dès le point de départ: c'est dans le cadre littéraire du livre d'Isaïe qu'il faut interpréter les chap. 40–55 (3). Je pense, en effet, que cette option s'impose: il n'y a qu'un seul livre d'Isaïe, placé tout entier sous le signe du prophète du VIᵉ siècle, et cela quelle que soit son histoire littéraire. Goldingay n'est pas insensible à cette réalité, et l'opposition qu'il relève entre Is 6 et Is 40,1–11 (5–6) en témoigne. Au fil du commentaire, cependant, le Deuxième Isaïe est considéré comme un autre prophète, et le lien dynamique avec les chap. 1 à 39 n'est pas vraiment privilégié par rapport à d'autres liens. Par exemple, la formule finale de 40,5 («Car la bouche de YHWH a parlé») est identique à celle de 1,20, ce qui fait des vv. 1–5 un nouveau discours inaugural, parallèle à celui qui ouvrait le livre entier; l'auteur note la reprise de plusieurs thèmes (9), mais pas celle de la formule finale, et il n'en tire aucune conclusion. En définitive, le commentaire de Goldingay ne serait pas très différent si Is 40–55 formait un ouvrage indépendant.

Ce qui précède est lié à une troisième question, à propos de la méthode. D'un côté, Is 40–55 est lu d'un point de vue qui me semble avant tout synchronique: Goldingay ne distingue pas ce qui appartiendrait à l'auteur principal du texte et des éléments d'une autre origine; même le cas des sections souvent tenues pour secondaires, comme celles qui parlent de la fabrication des idoles (41,6–7; 44,9–20; 46,5–8) n'est pas envisagé. D'un autre côté, le commentaire est émaillé de brèves considérations sur l'origine du texte: ce sont les exilés qui sont encouragés (11), le thème des relations d'Alliance est typique du vɪᵉ siècle (12), 40,3–5 annonce le retour des déportés depuis Babylone (22); etc. De toute manière, ce n'est plus le prophète Isaïe, mais un autre prophète qui s'exprime (5). Ici, Goldingay quitte l'exégèse synchronique pour s'intéresser à l'histoire. Je pense que les deux démarches sont également nécessaires, mais qu'il y a grand intérêt à ne pas les mélanger. D'un point de vue strictement littéraire, l'ensemble du livre—les chap. 40–55 y compris—doit se lire dans le contexte du ministère d'Isaïe, prophète de Jérusalem au vɪɪɪᵉ siècle. D'un point de vue historique, il est difficile de tenir ces mêmes chapitres pour une œuvre homogène, et on ne peut faire l'économie d'une enquête minutieuse sur le cadre de chaque élément comme sur l'histoire de la formation du recueil. J'ai l'impression que Goldingay se situe quelque part entre les deux univers, ce qui l'empêche d'aller jusqu'au bout de chacune des deux logiques.

Goldingay a choisi de réserver les débats pour le double volume de la collection «International Critical Commentary». Cet ouvrage-ci s'adresse à un autre public, et il est adapté à son but: proposer à un grand nombre l'accès à une lecture riche d'un texte difficile.

Die Propheten Nahum, Habakuk, Zephanja, by Lothar Perlitt. Das Alte Testament Deutsch 25.1. Göttingen: Vandenhoeck & Ruprecht, 2004. Pp. xvi + 148. Paper. €26.90. ISBN 3525512287.

Anselm C. Hagedorn, Humboldt-Universität zu Berlin, Berlin, Germany

This commentary on Nahum, Habakkuk, and Zephaniah by Lothar Perlitt replaces the older volume written by Karl Elliger (first published in 1949) in the same series. It is the first German commentary on these three notoriously difficult Minor Prophets to appear in a long time, and it offers a straightforward and lucid interpretation. Right from the beginning Perlitt argues against current scholarly trends to see the individual prophetic books simply as part of a larger redactional corpus called the Book of the Twelve. In classic German literary-critical fashion, he proceeds compellingly to uncover the message (Or, shall one say, *ipsissima verba*?) of each individual prophet in his historical setting. He is convinced that, without a personal and historical kernel of each book, there would have been no need for wider redactions or additions. Perlitt is certainly right to be cautious with regard to far-reaching redactional hypothesis, but, unfortunately, he does not offer a detailed discussion of the arguments. Especially considering the intended readership of his commentary—(German) theologians, according to the author's preface—one would have wished for more than simply a few quotations from the works by E. Ben-Zvi and B. A. Jones. Furthermore, in those instances where there is clear indication of redactional activity beyond the individual books (cf. Zeph 1:7 and Hab 2:20; Zech 2:17 and Nah 1:7; Zeph 1:15b and Hab 3:16), the reader searches in vain for philological or literary-critical arguments against such an intended redaction.

Throughout his commentary Perlitt assumes that the words of the individual seventh-century prophet were supplemented by a process of literary continuation (*Fortschreibung*), which should not be confused with "redaction," that continued until the fourth century B.C.E. Here one is able to discover the literary and innerbiblical reception history of biblical prophecy. The introduction to the commentary on each individual prophetic book contains a paragraph about the person of the prophet, his time, his, message, and, finally, his book. Taking the paucity of information we have about almost any Minor Prophet, these passages are necessarily short and simply rephrase material from the books themselves.

The original prophecy of Nahum is dated after the fall of Thebes (663 B.C.E.) and before the fall of Nineveh. Perlitt finds fragments of words spoken by Nahum in 1:9, 12, 13; 2:1*, 4–11*; 3:1–17*. Everything else is attributed to secondary additions that finally resulted in the eschatological message of the book. It is difficult to argue for a planned redaction of the book, since such a process would probably have eliminated such confusing passages as 1:10–11. In the course of his detailed analysis of the book, Perlitt is able to show that Nahum wrote in a highly developed poetic language but offered only a fairly bland theology. With his message he sought to offer support for Judah in the light of Assyrian domination.

As for the book of Habakkuk, Perlitt distinguishes three different compositions with their own literary origins: 1:2–2:5; 2:6–20; 3:1–19. Only in 1:5–11* (a passage described as military poetry) and in the single woe oracles in 2:6b, 9, 12* does Perlitt find authentic words of the prophet. Due to the mention of the Chaldeans in 1:6, the prophecy is dated to 600 B.C.E. As was the case with Nahum, all other parts of the book are regarded as additions by the circles responsible for transmitting the original book. Again, the literary activity continued until the fourth century. Unfortunately, neither in the chapter on Nahum nor in that on Habakkuk does Perlitt look at the evidence from Qumran in great detail; this might have been useful especially for the interpretation of the setting of Hab 3.

For his interpretation of Zephaniah, Perlitt follows the date given in the secondary but historically reliable superscription in 1:1 and places the prophet in Jerusalem around 630 B.C.E. As such, Zephaniah critiqued—in a style close to Hosea—the syncretism before Josiah's reform. As is common in the exegesis of Zephaniah, the words of the prophet are found in chapter 1. Here the passages dealing with the day of the Lord are seen as an important feature of the composition of Zephaniah but are not the starting point of his prophecy. Zephaniah 2:4–15 and 3:1–20 are seen as two further compositions that have their own literary history. The closure of the book is classified as a collection of late postexilic literary continuations that are not simply additions but also corrections of older material in Zephaniah. For Perlitt, the end of Zephaniah reads more like an anthology; even parallels to Mic 4:6–7 in Zeph 3:18–19 are explained in this way.

Throughout the book Perlitt offers an excellent close reading of the individual passages in their context of the Hebrew Bible; the many insights one gains from a careful reading of his work are too numerous to be recounted here. However, not everyone will agree with the "fragmentary-hypothesis" that he uses to explain the literary growth of the individual books. Especially in the exegesis of Zephaniah recent redactional models such as the Book of the Four should have been at least mentioned. If Perlitt wants to stress the individuality of each prophetic book, he should possibly also allow for such individual books to be fitted in a larger literary context .

All these criticisms aside, Lothar Perlitt has written a lucid and highly useful commentary that will become an indispensable tool for any serious study of the books of Nahum, Habakkuk, and Zephaniah.

Micha, by Helmut Utzschneider. Zürcher Bibelkommentare. Zürich: Theologischer Verlag Zürich, 2005. Pp. 175. Paper. €25.00. ISBN 3290173682.

Klaus-Peter Adam, Philipps-University Marburg, Marburg, Germany

This commentary on the book of Micah is based on the assumption that the book named after the prophet Micah is to be understood within the framework of ancient drama (11). Correspondingly, the author's focus is on the "dramatic aesthetics" of the book of Micah, while he also examines its "theological intention" (11). Utzschneider's interpretation is based on the assumption that, although a dramatic side text indicating the way in which the text is to be read is missing in the manuscripts, the main text implicitly contains all the information necessary in order to understand the current text as a characteristic drama.

This dramatic setting of the prophet Micah is seen in the so-called *lexis*, understood in an Aristotelian sense (12). Utzschneider assumes a sequel of several forms of appearances on stage; that is, speeches in the text are seen in different episodes, such as a monologue in 3:1–8 or a dialogue with text-internal and with text-external figures in 4:1–5; 7:8. The speaker's self-address with "I" or with "you," according to Utzschneider, suggests a scenic setting of the figures of a theater play (12). Listeners and/or readers are called upon to imagine the person talking and thus—at least on the level of the recipient's imagination—the *dramatis personae* become visible. The *opsis* then creates a visual and an auditive space in the reader's imagination. This is the decisive factor for a separation of single scenes. The larger units within the plot are (again with Aristotle) to be understood as the acts. A separated time frame exists within the context of the book. Everything that forms Micah's past also belongs to the past of the readers and listeners, and the future to which Micah relates, likewise, is the future of the audience (13).

According to Utzschneider, the spatial arrangement of the prophetic book

may be reconstructed, if it is seen within the book's presupposed dramatic setting. The drama as it is written in the book of Micah makes use of two special
effects. First, the drama brings a figure's imaginative perspective into play. The
scene changes virtually to another area away from the current scene when the
figure takes the perspective of a person looking from a wall into another place
(*Teichoskopy*). That which takes place in a distant country is then reported out of
the perspective of a watchman from the top of a wall. A further special effect that
is part of the dramatic technique of the book of Micah is the soliloquies in which
figures talk over their inner thoughts and partly also explain their motivations for
certain actions (14). While Utzschneider does not necessarily assume a performance of the book of Micah as a play, he focuses on the aspects of performance of
the current text of Micah (15), suggesting a loud recitation of the texts and, more
important, the imagination of the play as a scenic performance in the recipients'
minds.

Naturally, Utzschneider's emphasis on the dramatic character of the book of
Micah implies less interest in its literary development and its redaction history.
Instead, this commentary focuses largely on the biblical text in its current form
and limits itself to a description of the main developments within a redaction history and within a literary history of the prophetic book.

Understanding Micah as an essentially dramatic text leads to a structural
analysis in which Utzschneider suggests reading the book as a bipartite drama:
1:2–5:14 and 6:1–7:20 form two acts, both of which show a clear-cut plot (16).
The first act, 1:2–5:14, describes the future history of Israel and Judah, portrayed
from the perspective of Micah at the end of the eighth century B.C.E. This is why
Utzschneider calls this act "Micah's journey into time," in which the prophet
recalls the distant future times from an eighth-century perspective.

This first act consists of six scenes. In the first, 1:2–7, YHWH predicts
the destruction of Samaria and Jerusalem. In the second scene (1:8–2:5) the
destruction of the cities in the land of Judah and the deportation are reported.
The judgment oracle against Jerusalem is affirmed (1:16), especially against
the city's wealthy inhabitants (2:1–5). The text alludes to Judah's destruction
in 701. The fact that Jerusalem was spared seduces Micah's critics in the third
scene (2:6–13) to reject his judgment oracle. Micah stands up against a false
prophet who predicts the return of Judah from the exile. In the fourth scene
(3:1–4:7) Micah presents in two judgment speeches the situation before the
destruction of Jerusalem, criticizing again the citizens of Jerusalem for neglect-
ing the law and the city's leaders for their willingness to accept bribes. Micah
ends with the announcement of the destruction of the sanctuary of Zion in
the far distant future (4:1–7). This last scene forms a contrast to the judgment
scenes in 3:1–12: Zion will become a universal center of law and prophecy. The
fifth scene (4:8–5:3) is set in a different epoch, in 587/586. While Jerusalem is
destroyed and its population exiled, a future royal ruler is expected to rise from
Bethlehem. The closing sixth scene (5:4–14) alludes to this ruler's reign, only
described roughly.

The second act of the drama of Micah follows the logic and the framework of a lawsuit between God and his people and is thus fundamentally different from the historical reflection given in the book's first part. The forensic character is indicated by the Hebrew term *rîb* (6:1–2; 7:9), which provides the key word for understanding this scene. In the second scene (6:9–16), a punitive lawsuit trial takes place in which God accuses the city and the people. The third scene (7:1–7) shows the lament and the prophet on the wall, who sees the announced punishment as it happens and implores YHWH as savior. In the final fourth scene (7:8–20) the formerly accused city confesses her misdeeds, asks God for forgiveness, and is absolved. According to Utzschneider, both of these two acts contain a plot. While the first tells a future-related history, the second follows the several stations of the *rîb*.

As to the literary growth and the redaction history of the book of Micah, traditions within the first literary stage of the prophet at the end of the eighth and the beginning of the seventh century are to be seen in the judgment against Zion in 3:12 (which Jer 26:18 connects to the time of Hezekiah, while this is not suggested for 3:1–11). Utzschneider does not ascribe 3:1–11 to Micah as a historical figure but takes it to be written after the destruction of Jerusalem, since it is close to Jeremiah's temple speech (Jer 7;26). The poem about the cities' fall in 1:10–16 and the judgment oracles in 2:1–5 and 2:8–9 allude to the social situation of the eighth century. The oracle of woe in Mic 2:1 claims that the loss of the Judean cities was the fault of Jerusalem's nobles, and 2:6–8 focuses on the discussion whether Micah and his expectation of the end of Jerusalem (1:12; 2:1–3) were correct.

Thus, according to Utzschneider, only passages from the current prophetic text must be dated to the eighth century, while he ascribes 2:6–12 to the time of Jeremiah. A first version of Micah 1:10–5:3 dates from the exilic or early postexilic times at the end of the sixth/beginning of the fifth century. The introductory scene (1:2–7) dates from this same period, so the destruction of Samaria is thus portrayed only as a past event.

Scenes 1–5 contain older materials that were collected but can be traced back to exilic times. The sixth scene (5:4–14, esp. 5:9-13 and possibly 14) partly refers to Deuteronomy and late parts of Zechariah and is thus to be dated later. The Zion oracle of 4:1–5 and the oracle of the return of the exiled (4:6–7), according to Utzschneider, are to be dated (with B. M. Zapff) to the third century B.C.E. (as is the parallel in Isa 2:2–4). For the second act in Mic 6:1–7:7, a date in the fifth–fourth century is suggested.

As to the date of Micah's composition within the Book of the Twelve, Utzschneider takes the prophet Micah as an independent literary unit, over against, for example, A. Schart, who argued that Micah never existed as an independent book but was a complement to a two-prophet book consisting of the writings of Hosea and Amos. *Pace* B. M. Zapff, Utzschneider suggests the idea of a secondary literary layer of ongoing writing (*Fortschreibungsschicht*) in Mic 2:12–13; 4:6–7; 5:6–7; 7:4b; 7:8–20. The redactors of this secondary literary layer wrote in the third century B.C.E., creating the book of Micah's bipartite structure, with reference to Nah 1:2–8; they also wrote the Jonah psalm in Jon 2.

This commentary offers interesting insights into the book of Micah on the basis of a discussion of current research on Micah. It is especially helpful that the author carefully considers the book's structure within its textual units. If Utzschneider's suggested reading as a prophetic drama is correct, it is most helpful for an understanding of Micah that his analysis connects textual signals in the text to units used in a performance. For example, the fifth scene in 4:8–5:3 describing the decline of the old Jerusalem and the rise of a new ruler is understood as a sequel of acts in which the different *dramatis personae* appear on stage. Micah 4:8 is understood as a first appearance framing the others (*Rahmenauftritt*), in which the new rulership for the daughter Zion is announced. The three appearances on stage in 4:9–10, 11–13, 14 are added with the formula "now" or "and now." Each of these is opened with a typical act during a siege, offering a picture of the siege, while the prophetic message about the messianic ruler from Bethlehem that forms again part of the appearances on stage that frame the other appearances (*Rahmenauftritt*) in 5:1–3 closes with "*for now*" in 5:3b (Eng. 5:4b). The topic of the whole scene is the future royal reign over the daughter of Zion (4:8). These insights as to the structure of the prophetic book and its units are most valuable.

One of the most interesting concerns of this commentary, unfolded systematically by its author, is the dramatic character of Micah and of prophetic books in general. Whether and to what extent such a dramatic reading is in fact suggested for these prophetic writings is, however, yet to be discussed. Thus far scholars have only reluctantly addressed such an interpretation of the biblical prophetic writings in analogy to Greek drama. Most prominently, this attempt was previously undertaken by Klaus Baltzer for an interpretation of Deutero-Isaiah. This overall suggestion for a new understanding that is likewise suggested by Utzschneider needs further thorough reflection. In order to prove the close relation of biblical prophecy to ancient Greek drama, a number of questions must be considered, such as when and how the dramatic reading was used, which dramatic texts served as models for the biblical texts, and how we should imagine the form of their performance. Also, the time when this dramatic understanding of Judean prophetic writings was of importance and how the specific mode of performance might have shaped the form of the prophetic books should be subject to further reflection. A general enquiry of Greek influence in the Hebrew Bible may thus be necessary. Since theater buildings are lacking in Hellenistic Judah, it remains at least doubtful whether the prophetic writings were in fact performed on stage or, more likely, performed in a dramatic reading. A more in-depth investigation on the influence of dramatic speech and performance in Judah is thus needed.

Even though the commentary does not deal with these questions comprehensively and instead focuses on the text of Micah understood as a dramatic reading, Utzschneider provides a most stimulating attempt. This well-structured and most readable commentary is an important achievement of the current research on the prophetic book of Micah.

Between Fear and Freedom: Essays on the Interpretation of Jeremiah 30–31, by Bob Becking. Oudtestamentische Studiën 51. Leiden: Brill, 2004. Pp. x + 342. Cloth. $131.00. ISBN 9004141189.

Donald C. Raney II, MidAmerica Christian University, Oklahoma City, Oklahoma

Brill has a well-deserved reputation for providing biblical scholars with high-quality research across the entire spectrum of texts and approaches within the field of biblical studies. The latest addition to their Old Testament Studies series certainly continues that legacy. In *Between Fear and Freedom: Essays on the Interpretation of Jeremiah 30–31,* Bob Becking examines Jeremiah's so-called "book of consolation" using a variety of methods, including syntactical analysis, source-critical investigation, and comparative study of language, motifs, and themes with ancient rabbinic and ancient Near Eastern texts. These once-separate essays have been woven together into a well-documented unit that presents the reader with a significant contribution to the field of Jeremiah studies.

As an overarching interpretive method, Becking has sought to join Barton's call for literary competence with Talstra's approach that emphasizes the role of the reader. He seeks to accomplish this through both careful syntactical and literary analysis and engagement with other readers both ancient and modern. In his dialogue with other readers, however, Becking is not interested in reader-response but focuses on the history of interpretation. Although Becking does not seem to achieve the level of methodological purity he seeks (if such is even possible), his approach does provide the reader with a multifaceted view of his chosen text.

The starting point and central issue for Becking is the question of whether one can read these chapters as a coherent whole. According to Becking, a problem of coherence arises due to thematic dissimilarities. Within these two chapters descriptions of punishment and suffering are placed alongside promises of hope and comfort. Such dissimilarities have led many scholars to question the unit's coherence and to develop proposals concerning its redaction history. Yet Becking notes syntactic similarities throughout the unit and illustrates its essential literary unity.

The first three chapters lay the foundation for his study by surveying the text of Jer 30–31 in search of macro structures. Becking presents the reader with a survey of previous proposals concerning the composition of these chapters, including those of Sweeney, Bozak, Kidner, Brueggemann, and Holladay. He then includes a lengthy series of detailed charts containing extensive exegetical notes that provide excellent reference material. After carefully examining textual variations between the MT and LXX Vorlage, Becking determines that the Hebrew text is preferable, since it does not seem to be an abridgement of the Greek and since it is impossible to decide which is original. According to Becking, most of the deviations are either forms of linguistic exegesis or minor content variants, with no evidence of interpretative or theological tendencies being evident. His analysis also led him to divide the text into ten subcantos that coincide with the Hebrew *petuhah* and *setumah*. By drawing attention to certain poetic features, such as particles, prophetic formulae, and parallelism, Becking further divides these sub-cantos into a total of twenty-one canticles. Five of the subcantos are examined in chapters 4–8.

In each of these five subcantos, and implicitly in the five not examined, Becking points to a double thematic pattern that he refers to as Transformation I and II. The first part of each subcanto forms the first Transformation, which looks into past history and focuses on the distress of the people. Transformation II makes up the second part of each subcanto and looks with hope to the future. Since these Transformations make up a pattern that is consistent across the extent of this unit, one does not need to turn to redaction criticism to explain the different views. Also, since this pattern is thematic, it points to certain theological conclusions on the part of the author. Primary among these is the presentation of God, not as paradoxically or capriciously punishing and comforting but as passionately involved in the life of His people, changing plans and actions as he responds to human actions. This is a God who willingly enters covenants with humanity and who can re-create those covenants as required in order to restore cosmic order and bring new life.

This message is most clearly demonstrated in chapter 5, in which Becking analyzes Jer 30:12–17 and the issue of divine changeability. Whereas other scholars have noted the inconsistencies in God's attitudes and behavior as evidence of layers and redaction, Becking utilizes extrabiblical sources to argue clearly that these shifts are part of the writer's intent. Rather than seeing paradox, Becking sees the concept of divine changeability as a *force majeure* within these chapters. In the single idea that may alter God's course, the writer helps his audience cope with a past and present of suffering while simultaneously providing hope for a better future.

Professor Becking has given biblical scholars a significant work that presents the complexity and richness of Hebrew poetry in though-provoking ways In addition, the numerous charts of exegetical notes as well as the extensive bibliography could serve well as a reference or instructional tool for graduate students. Yet while Becking has made a significant contribution in his inclusion of comparisons with other ancient texts, there is a noticeable lack of discussion of how these two chapters relate to the rest of the book of Jeremiah, particularly given the content of Jer 29 and 32. In addition, while his step-by-step investigation has shed valuable light on the individual parts, more attention could be given to pulling the parts together for the reader to show the art side of the hermeneutical process. Finally, Becking's admittedly short side trip into redaction history in the concluding chapter seems to detract somewhat from the primary focus. This is particularly evident in his position that these chapters were not authored by the "original Jeremiah" but by an unknown prophet living near the end of the Babylonian exile. Such a conclusion needs additional discussion, since the conceptual coherence that lies at the heart of Becking's work could equally be attributed to a prophet living in Jerusalem during time of the fall of the city. Overall, however, Becking is to be highly commended for providing such a thoroughly documented and comprehensively presented exegesis of Jeremiah's book of consolation in a way that does serve as fertile soil for theological reflection. The depth of analysis as well as the wealth of new insights makes this a significant contribution to the study of ancient Israel's prophetic literature.

"As Those Who Are Taught": The Interpretation of Isaiah from the LXX to the SBL, edited by Claire Mathews McGinnis and Patricia K. Tull. Society of Biblical Literature Symposium Series 27. Atlanta: Society of Biblical Literature; Leiden: Brill, 2006. Pp. xii + 342. Paper/cloth. $39.95/$150.00. ISBN 1589831039/9004130411.

Michael Tilly, Johannes Gutenberg-Universität, Mainz, Germany

Der vorliegende umfangreiche Band enthält 15 wissenschaftliche Beiträge zu unterschiedlichen Aspekten der Wirkung und Auslegung des biblischen Jesajabuches in Geschichte und Gegenwart. In ihrem einführenden Beitrag (1–27) gehen die Herausgeberinnen auf die Entstehung und Programmatik der Aufsatzsammlung ein und bieten eine knappe Zusammenfassung wesentlicher Inhalte und Thesen der einzelnen Arbeiten im Kontext der gegenwärtigen Jesajaforschung.

In den beiden ersten Beiträgen geht es um die griechische Jesajaübersetzung. David A. Baer (29–47) beschäftigt sich mit der deutenden Übertragung von Jes 1–12 in der Septuaginta. Diese Übersetzung zeige sowohl eine gleichsam „nationalistische" Tendenz als auch ein generelles Verständnis der Prophetie Jesajas als vorzeitiger Ankündigung aktueller Vorgänge und Ereignisse: „The translator of Greek Isaiah reads the Hebrew *Vorlage* as a text to be mined for insight into the future of Israel and the predicament of the contemporary Diaspora community" (46). Auch Arie van der Kooij (49–68) behandelt Beipiele für den interpretierenden Charakter der Septuaginta zum Jesajabuch. Zum einen weise die griechische Version der „Modepredigt" Jes 3,18–23 sachliche Eigentümlichkeiten aus dem akkulturierten ptolemäisch-ägyptischen Milieu auf, zum anderen verdeutlichten insbesondere die antiken Übersetzungen von Jes 24–27 ein Bemühen um Betonung der gruppenspezifischen Aktualität der prophetischen Botschaft. George J. Brookes (69–85) Beitrag zu den Jesajamanuskripten und -kommentaren aus Qumran lenkt die Aufmerksamkeit vor allem auf ihre Textgestalt, die das Alter und die Zuverlässigkeit der masoretischen Texttradition bezeuge, aber auch einige Rückschlüsse auf die Bewertung und Bedeutung des Jesajabuches in der Geschichte der (seines Erachtens deutlich konturierten) essenischen Gemeinschaft erlaube.

J. Ross Wagner (87–105) fragt nach der Deutung und Funktion des Jesajabuches im Kontext des paulinischen Schrifttums. In Röm 10,19–21; 11,8; 15,9–12 verknüpfe der Heidenapostel Zitate aus und Anspielungen auf Jesaja und Dtn 29–32, um hierdurch die Gemeinschaft von Juden und Heiden in Christus in begründender Weise zu deuten und sie heilsgeschichtlich zu verankern. Catrin H. Williams (107–24) untersucht die christologische Bedeutung der Bezugnahmen auf Jesaja im vierten Evangelium. Die Rahmung der johanneischen Darstellung des öffentlichen Wirkens Jesu durch explizite Jesajazitate sei „to bring to the surface a sustained christological reflection on a series of related Isaianic passages" (122–23). Die Prophetie Jesajas sei von Johannes als ein proleptisches Zeugnis des Auftretens und des Geschickes Jesu verstanden worden: „It is because Isaiah is perceived as having beheld God`s glory in Jesus long beforehand that he becomes a key witness in John`s Gospel" (123). Jan Fekkes III. (125–43) führt anhand der (zumeist impliziten) Bezugnahmen auf Jesaja in der Johannesoffenbarung den Nachweis, daß der antike Seher sich und sein literarisches Werk in die prophetische Tradition stellte.

Der Schwerpunkt des auslegungsgeschichtlich orientierten Beitrags von J. David Cassel (145–69) liegt auf der patristischen Jesajaexegese: „For the church fathers, Isaiah`s prophecy was a powerful prediction of the future glory of Christ and his saving acts" (146). C. verdeutlicht insbesondere den prägenden Einfluss der hermeneutischen Voraussetzungen und Methoden der hellenistisch-römischen Textauslegungstradition auf die frühchristlichen Autoren. Robert A. Harris (171–87) stellt mit den Kommentaren der mittelalterlichen jüdischen Exegeten Joseph Kara und Eliezer von Beaugency zu Jes 1–12 zwei Werke vor, die weniger die traditionellen (auf Formen des Analogieschlusses und der Allegorese beruhenden) Schriftauslegungsregeln des Midraschs zur Anwendung brachten als—ganz in der Tradition Raschis—im 12. Jahrhundert die exegetische Erhellung der Bedeutung des hebräischen Prophetentextes mittels textlogischer und grammatischer Erläuterungen anstrebten. Mit der Deutung von Jes 52,13–53,12 in Eliezer Aschkenasis „Ma'ase Adonai" (Venedig 1583), eines Kommentars zu den narrativen Partien der Tora, befaßt sich der Beitrag von Alan Cooper (189–200). Von besonderem Interesse in dem Werk des frühneuzeitlichen rabbinischen Exegeten aus Saloniki seien der Aufweis einer engen Beziehung der literarischen Gestalt und des Schicksals Hiobs mit dem leidenden Gottesknecht Jesajas und der Versuch, in beiden biblischen Büchern Reflexe einer Glaubenskrise der Exilsgemeinde zu suchen.

Amy Plantinga Pauw (201–21) untersucht Jean Calvins Jesajakommentar und seine Predigten über Jesajatexte. Zwar habe auch der Genfer Reformator das christliche Alte Testament im Fluchtpunkt des Christusgeschehens betrachtet und ausgelegt, doch sei ihm eine undifferenzierte christologische Deutung des gesamten Jesajabuches weder als sachgemäß noch als „erbaulich" erschienen: „Edifying exegesis for Calvin did not have to center around finding overt references to Christ in the Hebrew prophets" (221). Gary Stansell (223–42) stellt die ausführlich kommentierte Jesajaübersetzung des Bibeltheologen und Bischofs Robert Lowth (1710–1787) vor. Vor allem L.s Bemühen um eine sachgemäße Erschließung der Sprachgestalt des hebräischen Prophetenbuches sei bis heute von großer Aktualität (241). Marvin A. Sweeney (243–61) gelangt nach einem umfassenden Durchgang durch die Jesajaforschung zwischen 1780 und 1890 zu dem Schluß, daß Bernhard Duhms wegweisende Arbeit „largely represents the merging consensus of nineteenth-century critical scholarship concerning the composition of the book of Isaiah" (245). Roy F. Melugin (263–78) bietet einen konzisen Überblick über die historisch-kritische (Deutero-)Jesajaforschung im 20. Jahrhundert, wobei er insbesondere das Verhältnis zwischen synchron und diachron orientierten Zugangsweisen in den Blick nimmt. An diesen Punkt knüpft auch der letzte Beitrag des Bandes (279–314) an. Patricia K. Tull skizziert die Vielfalt der methodischen Ansätze der Jesajaforschung der letzten drei Dekaden, die in ihrer Heterogenität, insbesondere im Hinblick auf Fragen der Kohärenz der prophetischen Schrift, die Vielschichtigkeit des biblischen Prophetenbuches widerspiegelt. Beigegeben sind Verzeichnisse der biblischen und außerbiblischen Quellen (317–34) und Namen (335–42).

Die Beiträges des vorliegenden Bandes überzeugen durch ihr durchweg hohes exegetisches und philologisches Niveau. In ihrer Gesamtheit ermöglichen sie einen instruktiven Überblick über den gegenwärtigen Diskussionsstand der Jesajaforschung und über die Wirkungsgeschichte des Jesajabuches im Judentum und im Christentum. Hierbei werden die unterschiedlichen Funktionen der Schriftauslegung in der langen Geschichte beider Religionen deutlich. Daneben stößt man immer wieder auf hochinteressante Einzelbeobachtungen, die eine weitere Beschäftigung mit Aspekten der Auslegung und Applikation des Prophetenbuches provozieren.

Provocation and Punishment: The Anger of God in the Book of Jeremiah and Deuteronomistic Theology, by Samantha Joo. Beihefte zur Zeitschrift für die alttestamentliche Wissenschaft 361. Berlin: de Gruyter, 2006. Pp. xiii + 320. Cloth. $118.00. ISBN 3110189941.

Mark Leuchter, Hebrew College, Newton, Massachusetts

This book is based on the author's 2003 doctoral dissertation completed under the direction of David Wright at Brandeis University. Joo has taken upon herself the task of examining the literary contexts of the Hebrew word הכעיס as it appears throughout "Deuteronomistic" literature. Joo aligns herself with a well-established scholarly tradition concerning the Deuteronomistic History (often known as the "Cross school") by identifying these works primarily as a pre-exilic Dtr1 and an exilic Dtr2 and by focusing on several key passages in the book of Jeremiah. It is clear from the proceedings of recent SBL conferences and a variety of publications that other models regarding the redaction of the book of Kings and the orchestration of the book of Jeremiah have emerged alongside that of the Cross school, but even if one prefers those alternatives, the implications of Joo's careful analysis remain pertinent for any literary consideration of the text.

The book is divided into six parts. Following a brief introduction to the problem of the divine-wrath dynamic, part 1 considers various forms of the root כעס and its function within the redactional matrix of Dtr1. This section of the book focuses upon the dynastic curses associated with the limited dynasties of Jeroboam, Baasha, and Omri, with a short discussion of the function of הכעיס in Deut 32 (a chart on 41 summarizes these passages and their features). Joo concludes that the word הכעיס functions as a redactional "pivot" term, defining historical events such as the fall of the northern dynasties in terms of conformity with divine will. Part 2 goes on to consider the term in the second redactional level (Dtr2), which considers a wider variety of texts rather than the more limited dynastic evaluations of the Dtr1 material. In this section Joo looks at Deut 4:25–28; 9:18–20; 31:27–29; Judg 2:11–16; 1 Kgs 14:15–16a; 16:7; 2 Kgs 17:7–23a; 21:2–15; 22:16–17; and 23:19–20, 26–27 (summary chart on 68–69). Joo concludes that the appearance of the term הכעיס in Dtr2 attempts to recognize the divine role in punishment but also to exonerate YHWH from direct blame, stating that "the late redactors mitigate God's involvement by 1) making the punishment correspond more to the sin … 2) using divine anger either as motivation … instrument … or the agent of the destruction … and 3) constructing the punishment out of the people's own 'evil'" (115).

Part 3 then engages what Joo defines as "Non-Deuteronomic Attestations of הכעיס," looking at the term's function in Hosea, Ezekiel, and Third Isaiah as well as in Pss 78 and 106 and 2 Chr 28. These texts, according to Joo, exhibit certain commonalities regarding the role of divine provocation and punishment, but with less consistency than that which emerges in her examination of Dtr1 and Dtr2. This section is particularly significant as it demonstrates that, in contrast to these other works, the Deuteronomistic/Jeremianic material evidence a conscious attempt to develop the theme of provocation into a systematic interpretation of history. As such, they represent a more cohesive line of argumentation and stand in a special relationship to each other.

What follows in part 4 is "the heart of the present study" (155): an examination of the term הכעיס in the book of Jeremiah. This (relatively concise) examination focuses of a few highly significant passages in the book: 7:16–20; 8:18–23; 11:17; 25:1–14; 32:26–35; and 44:1–14 (summary chart on 158–59). Joo devotes considerable attention to these passages and, while identifying different genres, redactional layers, and sources, still manages to discern a basic and consistent theme regarding the appearance of הכעיס in these different contexts, concluding that, more than Dtr1 or Dtr2, the redactional use of הכעיס in Jeremiah attempts to ascribe even greater culpability to the people in the meting out of divine punishment ("God is only the Hermes of the punishment…. the punishment is directly the result of the people's sins…. the people self-destruct" [233]). Part 5 constitutes a brief conclusion to the entire study where Joo notes that Dtr2's more direct attribution of YHWH's mastery over historical events (inspired by the destruction of Jerusalem in 587 B.C.E.) was subsequently interpreted by the redactors of Jeremiah as not simply evidence of divine wrath but of human provocation, further amplifying the role of the nation in their own punishment.

Some of Joo's presuppositions regarding the relative dating of certain texts are open to debate; two examples will suffice. Joo's treats the anti-Manasseh passage in 2 Kgs 21:2–15 as a Dtr2 text (104–9), and while she admits that several layers of redaction are evident in the text, "in the final form, הכעיס does function as the pivot to the punishment in which God is the primary executor" (104). This observation is no doubt correct, but Joo's discussion does not consider whether any material involving this provocation language may be attributable to a writer earlier than Dtr2. Indeed, as many commentators have noted, a preexilic stratum is discernible within this passage, and the appearance of the כעס terminology in 2 Kgs 21:6 may derive from Dtr1. Joo's argument regarding the Dtr2 usage of כעס terminology in 2 Kgs 21:15 (a verse many would agree derives from Dtr2) reinforces her position, but a more detailed discussion of the passage's disparate layers may have yielded a more compelling argument in this case. The recent work of Francesca Stavrakopoulou (*King Manasseh and Child Sacrifice: Biblical Distortions of Historical Realities* [BZAW 338; Berlin: de Gruyter, 2004], 15–119) indicates that the matter of Manasseh's presentation in various strata of the book of Kings is one of significant complexity; discussing only the final form of 2 Kgs 21:2–15 obscures important valences in the text.

One might also question Joo's conclusion that the function of הכעיס in Jeremiah is evidence that the redaction of Jeremiah is subsequent to that of Dtr2, since several studies of Jeremiah see Dtr2 as dependent on a fairly mature form of that prophetic corpus as a source for ideas and scribal methods. Recent essays by Baruch Halpern ("Why Manasseh Is Blamed for the Babylonian Exile: The Evolution of a Biblical Tradition," *VT* 48 [1998]: 511–14) and Richard E. Friedman ("The Deuteronomistic School," in *Fortunate the Eyes That See* [Festschrift for D. N. Friedman; Grand Rapids: Eerdmans, 1995], 70–80) suggest Dtr2's reliance upon the Jeremiah tradition, a view supported in the concluding chapter of the present writer's own study (*The Polemics of Exile in Jeremiah 26–45* [Cambridge: Cambridge University Press, forthcoming]). These different understandings (notably, *within* the Cross school of thought) regarding redactional sequences in the Deuteronomistic and Jeremiah literature do not nullify Joo's observation of the provocation/punishment themes in these respective works, but they suggest that the differences may not strictly be a matter of linear progression from one to the other.

The formatting and copyediting of the book are periodically problematic. Joo's footnote discussions are often overwhelming and sometimes unnecessarily detailed. Several pages are almost entirely dominated by the footnotes, and this might interfere with the reader's digestion of the book's main analysis and argument. Some of Joo's insights within the notes might have been worked into the main text and could have stimulated some additional fruitful discussion. The page layout involving the analysis of various passages is sometimes difficult to follow, and several mistakes have eluded the copyeditor's eye. In these cases, Joo could have been better assisted by the English editors at BZAW.

Nevertheless, the aforementioned problems are by no means insurmountable, and they do not overshadow the merits of the book. Joo does not attempt to reinvent the wheel (advocates of the dual-redaction theory have long noted that Dtr2 possesses a theology of history adjusted from that of Dtr1) but rather to elucidate the shape of one of its treads with respect to the הכעיס terminology. The close attention paid to the term הכעיס reveals organizational strategies that arise from conscious design and purpose. Scholars who see little redactional consistency in or a connection between the texts Joo identifies as part of the Deuteronomistic History or within the book of Jeremiah must reckon with Joo's discussion, since she makes clear that at least in the case of the term הכעיס a coherent development of thought may be discerned within these works. While current scholarly dissatisfaction with older understandings of the Deuteronomistic historiography may be justified, variations on the dual-redaction theory of the Cross school are still worthy of consideration, and new contributions are valuable. Joo's book should stimulate discussion among scholars who endeavor to identify an ideological evolution in the preexilic and exilic layers of the Deuteronomistic literature.

WRITINGS

The Discourse of Wealth and Poverty in the Book of Proverbs, by Timothy J. Sandoval. Biblical Interpretation Series 77. Leiden: Brill, 2005. Pp. xvi + 234. Hardcover. $99.00. ISBN 9004144927.

James Alfred Loader, Institut für Alttestamentliche Wissenschaft und Biblische Archäologie, Universität Wien, Wien, Austria

Dass dieser Band eine leicht überarbeitete Fassung einer an der Emory Universität eingereichten Dissertation ist, teilt der Verfasser gleich am Anfang (xi) mit. Aber auch ohne die Auskünfte der vorgefügten Anerkennungsworte sollte es jedem klar sein, dass wir hier die Gattung der Universitätsdissertation vor uns haben. Die stringente Organisation der Kapitel bietet dafür ein typisches Beispiel. Voran geht eine Einführung, in der die Untersuchung gerechtfertigt wird („Why This Text?") und deren theoretischen Grundlagen dargelegt werden, hier auf „Metapher" und „Diskurs" fokussiert, wobei der Verfasser sich dem Ricœur'schen Ansatz sehr verpflichtet zeigt. Die obligatorische aber nützliche Forschungsübersicht zum Thema „Reichtum und Armut im Sprüchebuch" (Kap. 2) leitet zur Darlegung der eigentlichen Forschung über. Diese ist sich in drei Kapitel zu den vom Verfasser in den Sprüchen erkannten „Diskursen" von Reichtum und Armut gegliedert: der Diskurs von Reichtum und Armut in Spr. 1–9 (Kap. 3), die beiden Diskurse von der „Tugend der Weisheit" und von der „Sozialen Gerechtigkeit" in Spr. 10–31 (Kap. 4), der Diskurs von „sozialer Wahrnehmung" in Spr. 10–31 unter Berücksichtigung der vom Verfasser so genannten „Gestalt" der Sprüche (Kap. 5). Es folgt die übliche Zusammenfassung der Ergebnisse, hier allerdings eine „Konklusion" (Kap. 6), die wiederum aus „Konklusionen" schöpft, die gewissenhaft am Ende von jedem Kapitel außer dem vorletzten (und sogar von Unterabschnitten, 141) rekapitulieren, was bereits wiederholt in den jeweiligen Ausführungen selbst gesagt worden war. Darüber hinaus bietet das letzte Kapitel vorsichtig und etwas unverbindlich anmutend auch eine denkbare sozialgeschichtliche Situierung des

Sprüchebuches—was freilich nicht als „Schlussfolgerung" aus dem in den früheren Kapiteln Ausgeführten angesehen werden kann.

Reichtum und Armut im Sprüchebuch ist kein neues Thema. Seit den sechziger Jahren (etwa die kurzen Studien von F. C. Fensham 1962 oder T. Donald 1964) über Studien wie von B. W. Kovaks 1974 und B. V. Malchow 1982 bis in die neunziger Jahre (etwa die längeren Untersuchungen von R. N. Whybray 1990, R. Van Leeuwen 1992 und H. C. Washington 1994) wurde das Thema mehrmals behandelt. Davon gibt der Verfasser selbst einen guten Überblick (29ff.), wobei er seinen eigenen Beitrag durchwegs sehr bewusst von allen anderen absetzt. Während die unterschiedlichen Gesichtspunkte, die zur Reichtum-Armut-Thematik im Buch vorkommen, nach Sandoval entweder den unterschiedlichen und komplizierten Realitätswahrnehmungen der Weisen oder einer geschichtlichen Entwicklung oder divergierenden sozialhistorischen Situationen zuzuschreiben seien, meint er, eine viel größere Kohärenz in den Aussagen des Buches sehen zu können. Das argumentiert er mit seiner These der „Diskurse" im Sprüchebuch.

Sandoval nennt den (Sub-)Diskurs von Reichtum und Armut in vor allem Spr. 10–31, aber auch in Kap. 1–9, den „Diskurs von der Tugend der Weisheit". Nach ihm bietet dieser umfangreichste der drei von ihm identifizierten Diskurse das Motiv des Reichtums als Symbol des Guten, um damit den Hörer vom Wert der Weisheit zu überzeugen. Mit seinen typischen Vokabeln der Wurzeln 'šr, hwn, mcswr und rjš soll dieser Diskurs als Motivation für den Jüngling dienen, den Weg der Weisheit zu wählen.

Ebenfalls findet der Verfasser den (Sub-)Diskurs von sozialer Gerechtigkeit hauptsächlich in Kap. 10–31, aber auch in Kap. 1–9. Hier seien die eigentümlichen Vokabel dl, 'nj und 'bjwn, die für eine Darstellung eines Ethos von Barmherzigkeit gegenüber den sozialökonomisch Schwachen verwendet werden. Bei diesem „particular economic ethic" könnte die von Sandoval unterschätzte Frage gestellt werden, ob es wirklich soziale Gerechtigkeit ist oder ob es nicht nur einen ökonomischen status quo, „der doch ein Herz hat", anerkennt. Obwohl keineswegs unwichtig, kann diese Sicht aber hier dahingestellt bleiben, weil sie die bloße Existenz eines solchen Diskurses nicht anzweifelt und weil es nicht in der Absicht des Verfassers liegt, mehr als eine Beschreibung zu bieten, wie dieses Ethos ausschaut. Die Tatsache, dass er ganz am Ende seiner Arbeit (211) nebenbei „evaluiert", dass das Sprüchebuch zutiefst konservativ bleibt, verändert daran nichts.

Der Dritte (Sub)-Diskurs heißt „der Diskurs von sozialer Wahrnehmung". Auch hier kann man die Benennung hinterfragen, da dieser Diskurs nach dem Verfasser selbst eigentlich nichts „wahrnimmt", sondern vielmehr die Folgen übermäßigen Reichtums kommentiert und kritisiert oder die sozialen Konsequenzen der Armut evaluiert (208).

Die drei Diskurse überschneiden einander teilweise, aber das Wichtige ist nach Sandoval, dass man erkennt, wie die Aussagen des Sprüchebuches zu Reichtum und Armut einander beeinflussen und ergänzen, so dass ein komplexes Gefüge entsteht. Damit ist dem Kern der Hauptthese nahe gekommen: Angesichts dieser Aufeinanderbezogenheit gäbe es eine Einheit im übergreifenden

Hauptdiskurs zu Reichtum und Armut des Sprüchebuches. Meiner Meinung nach artikuliert der Verfasser mit diesem Gedanken sowohl seine Stärke als auch seine Schwäche. Zunächst ist es ihm gelungen, die Diskurse im Buch nachzuweisen. Obwohl sich nicht jeder mit dem Begriff der Diskursanalyse als (nur) soziali-deologischer Forschung (20) wohl fühlen wird, ist diese Perspektive in der Linie Bakhtins durchaus legitim. Sie wird von Sandoval als wertvoll dargestellt. Seinen positiven Beitrag sieht dieser Rezensent vor allem darin, dass der Verfasser auf der Ebene des *Buches,* d.h. der redaktionell zu Ende geführten Sprüchesammlung, nachgewiesen hat, wie verschiedene, teils auseinanderstrebende Dimensionen der Reichtums- und Armutsthematik einander begrenzen und daher beeinflussen. Nachvollziehbar ist das im Lichte seiner Argumentation aufgrund des Prologs. In einer eingehenden Diskussion (45ff.), auf die er immer wieder zurückkommt, entwickelt er die Sicht, dass der Prolog als „hermeneutischer Schlüssel" eine Ein-ladung darstellt, das ganze Buch auf seinen Tropengehalt zu befragen, sprich: eine symbolische Auslegung zu bevorzugen.

Aber dabei kehrt er auch, obwohl er das nicht will, zu viel unter den Teppich. Immer wieder wendet er sich gegen eine „übermäßig literalistische" („overly literalistic") Auslegung. Damit ist gemeint, dass sowohl die Lehrdichtungen in Kap. 1–9 als auch die einfachen Sprüche ab Kap. 10, die zum Diskurs von Reich-tum und Armut gehören, auf ihren bildlichen Sinn befragt werden sollen, da sie „generell bildlich funktionieren" („generally function figuratively" [118]). Dabei ist der Verfasser immer wieder darum bemüht, zu versichern, dass er nicht jede „buchstäbliche" („literal") Interpretation ablehnt und dass solche Auffassungen „gewissermaßen wahr" oder „denkbar" seien, aber dieses Geständnis spielt keine Rolle, sein einseitiges Treiben der „übertragenen" Leseweise zu mäßigen. Daher überrascht es nicht, dass einige Bedenken sich hinsichtlich der Durchführung seines eigenen Diskurses hervordrängen.

Zum einen wäre zu fragen, wie eine Interpretation „übermäßig literalistisch" ist. Der ständig wiederholte Einwand setzt voraus, dass es eine *weniger* buchstäbli-che Interpretation gibt. Wie sieht diese aus und wie ist die These davon berührt? Der Verfasser räumt dem Literalsinn von Reichtum- und Armut-Sprüchen immer wieder ein gewisses Recht ein,[1] aber das bleibt praktisch wirkungslos und scheint nur als rhetorische Absicherung zugegeben zu sein. Es kann aber sein, dass die angebliche Kohärenz seiner Diskurse bei einer alternativen Lesestrategie weniger überzeugend erscheint.

Sandoval scheint mir weiters eine gute Illustration zu bieten, dass *verschie-dene* Lesungen eines geschichteten Buches wie Sprüche nicht nur möglich,

---

1. Der Verfasser selbst interpretiert etwa Aussagen über Waagschalen und Gewichte (Spr. 11,1; 16,11; 20,10.23) recht „literalistisch"; vgl. 143–44, wobei unklar bleibt, warum man nicht auch bei anderen ohne den „Schlüssel" der metaphorischen Interpretation auskommen kann. Einfache Gerechtigkeit und „fairness" im Handel und beim Gericht sind ja auch durchaus moralische Werte.

sondern auch nötig sind. Wiewohl es verständlich ist, dass eine Dissertation sich zu „verschiedenen Lesearten" bekennt, aber doch nur eine bevorzugt, zeigt der Autor dennoch, dass eine generell „bildliche" Lesestrategie nur auf einer Ebene funktionieren kann. Das Ignorieren der hinter der letzten Textgestalt stehenden Dimensionen führt zu Problemen auf allen Textebenen, einschließlich der „End-gestalt" (was immer das auch sein mag). Davon spricht der dritte Problemenkreis, der sich hier meldet.

Fraglich ist nämlich besonders die Unterbewertung des Tun-Ergehen-Zusam-menhangs (Sandoval spricht am liebsten vom „wisdom prosperity axiom", also vom Weisheit-Wohlstand-Axiom), die ein Hauptmerkmal der Dissertation aus-macht. Obwohl ein solcher Versuch dort verständlich ist, wo man die Diskurse möglichst kohärent vorstellen will, vermag der Verfasser damit nicht zu überzeu-gen. Immer wieder gibt er zu, dass „etwas" in dieser Kausalitätsauffassung steckt, nur um sie dann als zu buchstäblich und nicht „ganz" richtig herunter zu spielen. Die Schwäche dieser schwammigen Sicht ist z.B. gut in der Diskussion von Spr. 11,4 und 28 (163–64) zu beobachten. Dass der Tun-Ergehen-Zusammenhang der israelitischen Weisen generell—und nicht nur der Redaktoren des vorliegen-den Buches—„am besten als Konstruktion einer symbolischen Weltanschauung" zu interpretieren ist, die empirisch nicht verifizierbar ist und nie so gemeint war (205–6), wird keineswegs nachgewiesen, sondern ist eine unbegründete Annahme. Das dürfte von der These bedingt worden sein, dass weniger Diskre-panzen und Spannungen im Buch vorkämen denn normalerweise gedacht. Aber damit wird eine Schwierigkeit gerade herbeigeführt. So wäre die Entstehung einer Glaubenskrise und der Theodizeefrage unverständlich. Dieses Glaubensringen mit der empirischen Realität ist nur dort begreiflich, wo gerade die Diskrepanz, die Sandoval elegant wegerklärt, eine empirisch erfahrbare Realität ist. Die von ihm behauptete „Kohärenz" der Sprüche ist nur um den Preis eines lückenlosen Systems, in dem alles passt, zu haben. Aber eben das verursacht die Theodizee-krise.

Der Autor besteht immer wieder darauf, dass Reichtum und Wohlfahrt posi-tiv sind (z.B. 118, wo freilich seine Formulierung bei der Frage welche Kapitel des Sprüchebuches nun die „späteren" seien, verwirrend ist). Allerdings wird er nie müde, sie als „mindere Güter" („lesser goods") abzuqualifizieren, und zwar solche, die nie mit einem fundamentaleren Gut, Weisheit, verwechselt werden sollten. Dazu dienen seine eingehend dargelegten metaphorischen Interpreta-tionen. Aber wer bestreitet das? Sogar Vertreter der alten „eudämonistischen" Auffassung von Sprüchen leugnen nicht, dass der Wert der Weisheit überragend ist. Der Wert der Wohlfahrt ist, dass sie den Wert der Weisheit *demonstriert*. Um ein Beispiel hervor zu heben: es ist nicht so „klar", dass die Faulheit-Fleiß-Aus-sagen eher etwas über Tugend als über den Ursprung von Reichtum und Armut sagen (138ff.). Der Faule (etwa Spr. 10,26) wird getadelt, *weil* er das Erringen von Erfolg frustriert. Man erkennt die Untugend bzw. Tugend gerade an ihren Folgen, wobei eine Aufteilung zwischen „höheren" und „niedrigeren" Werten nicht vom Text her gerechtfertigt werden kann. Nach Sandoval selbst ist Reichtum ein „motivierendes Symbol", dem er sogar zwei ganze Abschnitte widmet (71–101). Dann bedeutet das logisch, dass der „höhere" Wert an sich nicht für überzeugungsfähig gehalten wird, sondern erst mit Hilfe eines „niedrig" genannten, aber erst wirklich wertvollen Wertes attraktiv gemacht werden soll. Was für ein „moral value" wäre das?

Dass es sich um eine typische Dissertation handelt, spürt man sofort am Übereifer, sicher zu stellen, dass Leser und Leserinnen die Argumentführung integriert und deren Teile eng zusammenhängend empfinden. Das sind sie auch. Der Verfasser hätte sich die Mühe ersparen können, ständig zu deklarieren, was er jetzt vorhat, dies dann auszuführen, und schließlich wiederholt kundzutun, was er früher eigentlich gemacht hat (wobei sein Lieblingsverb, „intimate", ein Manierismus ist).

Das Buch leidet unter vielen orthographischen Inkonsequenzen, Rechtschreibfehlern, englischen Sprach- und Formulierungsfehlern und schlampigen Wiedergaben von deutschen Wörtern und Namen (z.B. 102, 150, 173, 229), die man in der *Biblical Interpretation Series* nicht erwartet. Aber weder das noch die Bedenkungen, die die Ausführungen Sandovals aufrufen, heben auf, dass er eine wertvolle Monographie vorgelegt hat. Einmal wegen der zwar für diesen Rezensenten einseitigen, aber dennoch durchaus möglichen Darlegung einer rhetorischen Lesung auf der Ebene des durchkomponierten Buches, und zum anderen wegen seiner eingehenden Einzelexegese. Eben in diesen oft reichlich mit Literaturangaben und Sonderauseinandersetzungen versehenen Ausführungen wird der an Sprüchen interessierten Leserschaft viel Wertvolles geboten.

Surrendering Retribution in the Psalms: Response to Violence in the Individual Complaints, by David G. Firth. Paternoster Biblical Monographs. Waynesboro, Ga.: Paternoster, 2005. Pp. xviii + 154. Paper. $29.99. ISBN 184227337X.

Brian D. Russell, Asbury Theological Seminary–Florida, Orlando, Florida

David Firth is both an academic biblical scholar and a practitioner with extensive pastoral experience in his native Australia and service as a missionary in South Africa and Zimbabwe. He currently serves as Old Testament Tutor at Cliff's College in the United Kingdom. *Surrendering Retribution in the Psalms: Responses to Violence in the Individual Complaints* is a slightly revised form of his doctoral thesis submitted in 1996 to the University of Pretoria.

If Firth's work in South Africa during the waning years of apartheid and subsequent move to majority rule serves as a fitting contextual impetus for this investigation, then the presence and persistence of violence around the world demonstrates the timelessness of the themes raised in his work. In the face of violence, Firth asks, "What does the Psalter teach about violence and the human response to it?" After narrowing his focus to the individual lament psalms, Firth formulates the following thesis: these psalms present a consistent theology of the rejection of all forms of human violence as an appropriate response to external violence. No human has a right to initiate violence, since to do such is to usurp the prerogatives of God, in whom alone abides the right to violence. Although the psalms do recognize the reality and threat of violence in the world, the right to respond to violence with violence is a right handed back to God in the context of worship.

Surrendering Retribution in the Psalms includes five chapters. After an introduction in which Firth's thesis and methodology are made evident, Firth presents an intensive study of individual laments within the Psalter that reflect a response to violence. Firth offers detailed exegesis of thirteen psalms, which he divides into three groups: psalms of false accusation (7; 17; 109; 139), prayers for protection (3; 27; 35; 55; 56; 64; 143), and psalms of sickness (38; 69). The middle three chapters follow this outline. A conclusion summarizes the findings of the research and reflects on its implications for the study of the Psalter as well as for additional research.

In the Introductory chapter, Firth discusses the nature of violence. He defines violence as "an unnecessary use of force" (4). Assuming this definition, he describes three overlapping spheres in which violence occurs: physical; psychological; and structural. Physical violence is the use of unnecessary force directly against a person or persons. Psychological violence is the application of unnecessary force against individuals in a nonphysical manner in a way that affects a person's peace. The threat of physical violence is a key element of psychological violence. Structural violence is unnecessary force directed at the underlying structures that give a society order and well-being.

In order to study the interplay between violence and retribution in the Psalter, Firth applies a form-critical method to the Psalter in order to isolate psalms of the individual that describe acts of violence. Form criticism is merely the jumping-off point for Firth. His actual exegesis focuses on the final form of the text regardless of its prehistory and is informed by questions of the canonical shaping of the Psalter. When Firth reads the Psalter, he is more sympathetic to newer canonical ways of reading the psalms than to attempts to reconstruct the original cultic settings of individual psalms. Firth's basic exegetical method contains four movements: review of form-critical issues; analysis of the rhetorical structure of each psalm; a description of the nature of the violence reported by the psalmist; and the psalmist's response to the violence.

Chapter 2 studies the psalms of false accusation (7; 17; 109; 139). Here and throughout Firth's exegesis is sound and penetrating. In this group of psalms, Firth demonstrates that psychological violence is the most prominent. In each case the psalmist responds to the violence by pleading his or her case to God and relinquishing the right to respond or judge to God alone. Firth argues that this has implications for a canonical reading of Psalter. Since the cult is no longer the primary context for these psalms, they can now function as model prayers for worshipers in a variety of contexts.

Chapter 3 investigates the prayers for protection by individuals (3; 27; 35; 55; 56; 64;143). This is the largest section of the book. Despite the diversity in settings, these psalms contain a number of common threads. Psychological violence is again the most common form of violence manifested in the prayers. The threat posed to the psalmist is almost always physical, with the threat of death looming in many of the prayers. Yet again the psalmist's request for retribution is to God alone. Moreover, in no case is the requested vengeance in excess of the actual threat to the psalmist. This leads to one of Firth's key findings in this study: requests for retribution were governed by the *lex talionis*.

Chapter 4 examines the psalms of sickness (38; 69). The findings are similar to those of the previous two chapters. These particular psalms, however, implicitly confirm Firth's argument that only violence initiated by God is just. Both contain confessions of guilt. Since the sickness is assumed to have come from God, this confession of guilt tends to confirm that all violence initiated by God is just. These prayers also confirm Firth's contention that all violence initiated by others is unjust.

Chapter 5 offers concluding remarks to the study. Firth reiterates his thesis that the only fitting response by an individual to violence is the presentation of one's case to God and allowing God to serve as the judge.

Firth's work is well written and serves to illuminate an understudied facet of the Psalter. His argumentation is clear, and his exegesis offers deep insight into the meaning of each psalm that he studies both as a discrete prayer and as part of a larger canonical conversation within the Psalter. His combination of insights from both form criticism and more recent canonical studies demonstrates the importance and promise of using multiple approaches in tandem.

One principal weakness in the study is Firth's decision against updating his work. Although he suggests that his work remains unchallenged by recent studies, it is also true that scholars working on the Psalter have turned their attention in recent years to the vast numbers of laments. Firth's bibliography is current to the early 1990s. As such, he has missed the opportunity to place his work into a more contemporary context.

Second, by limiting his study to one narrowly conceived genre, it is difficult to assess the broader theological implications of his conclusions. Furthermore, it would have been interesting for Firth to have placed his conclusions into conversation with other voices in the Psalter and then also to have brought his conclusions into dialogue with marginalized persons working in situations where they are victimized by violence.

Surrendering Retribution in the Psalms is an important addition to our understanding of the theology and composition of the Psalter. Moreover, its conclusions provide resources for ethical reflection by Christians in the modern world where violence continues to plague humanity.

Song of Songs, by J. Cheryl Exum. Old Testament Library. Louisville: Westminster John Knox, 2005. Pp. xxiii + 263. Hardcover. $39.95. ISBN 0664221904.

Christoph Uehlinger, University of Zurich, Zurich, Switzerland

The Song of Songs is seductive poetry, making it hard for readers to resist its exuberant unfolding of pleasure, desire, and erotic fantasy displayed in a multi-sensual atmosphere. J. Cheryl Exum has authored a truly seductive commentary on the Song in turn, a piece so splendidly written that this reader often found it difficult not to succumb to it either. Since succumbing is, however, not the sort of things one is meant to do as a reviewer, and since Exum's commentary is first of all an eminent piece of critical scholarship, I shall accommodate to academic conventions and serve the legitimate expectations other readers may have when they turn to a review such as this. As it happens, Exum's book has already been praised by two other, more timely critics (Athalya Brenner and Mark McEntire; see http://bookreviews.org/bookdetail.asp?TitleId=4959&CodePage=4959). My comments shall therefore concentrate on aspects not touched upon or less developed by these predecessors. As Exum herself states with fully justified self-confidence, "the present commentary is the first to examine systematically gender differences and the role they play in the presentation of the relationship between the lovers in the Song" (81), and this is one major reason why her book makes such inspiring reading.

As usual with commentaries published in the OTL series, this one comes with a substantial introduction (1–86) and a commentary section proper (87–263), which follows the standard format of the series: translation, philological notes with references to textual variants or alternative translations, and an exegetical verse-by-verse commentary exposing the meaning (or, in this instance, several layers of meaning) a careful reader may discover in this stunning lyric collection. The main parts of the book are preceded by a list of abbreviations (vii–ix) and select bibliography listing twenty-three commentaries in series, fifty-three other books and monographs as well as approximately 250 articles and chapters in books (xi–xxii)—an ample if not exhaustive bibliography (see below). There is no foreword, where readers usually get an idea about an author's social and scholarly location and academic affiliation beyond dustjacket information.

1.

The introduction includes the following seven sections:
A Love Poem (1–2)
Love and Death (2–3)
Controlling Poetic Strategies (3–13)
Gendered Love-Talk and the Relation of the Sexes (13–28)
Poetic Composition and Style (28–47)
The Song of Songs and Its World (47–73)
The Song of Songs and Its Readers (73–86)

These superscriptions reveal the main axis of Exum's approach. She explores the Song of Songs essentially as lyric poetry, subtle and even sublime literature, as it were, a literary work of art parts of which were probably once sung and possibly performed but which has come down to us as literature and, after all, a book in the Bible.

Among the many issues Exum develops in her introduction, one may single out the following ones, which are more original, characteristic, or particularly well argued and make this commentary an outstanding contribution to modern scholarship on the Song: For Exum, the Song of Songs is a lyric poem about erotic love and sexual desire (1). A major key to its understanding is 8:6, which declares that love is as strong as death. "The proof is the poem. Perhaps all literature is a defense against mortality; certainly the Song of Songs is.... Real lovers die, but the love that is celebrated here lives on, preserved on the page. It still seems fresh and alive centuries after it was written down, because it is love in progress, not a story about famous lovers of the past" (3). Among the controlling poetic strategies, there is the illusion of immediacy: "By presenting the lovers in the act of addressing each other, the poem gives us the impression that we are overhearing them and observing their love unfold" (4). It conjures up the beloved as if by incantation: "The lovers are always present for each other because they are always speaking or being spoken about.... Throughout the Song, speech embodies desire by calling bodies into being and playing with their disappearance in an infinite deferral of presence" (6–7). At the same time, the poem requires and implicitly invites its readers. It is so conceived that readers may feel well when looking at the love play that unfolds along the individual speeches. Who are the lovers we are looking at? Exum thinks they are two "archetypal lovers" rather than identifiable individuals, composite figures who change their guise according to various contexts and circumstances. Still, "the lovers seem to take on distinct personalities as we get to know them.... They are consistent in the way they each talk about their love and in the way love makes them behave ... and this encourages us to feel we know them and enables us to build a picture of them" (8–9). The special art of the poem reflects itself in the way the lovers are designed as plausible, consistent, authentic, and "believable female and male characters" (66), while still remaining universal figures who represent all lovers of any time and place. Among the special features of the Song's poetry is its unfolding of love in progress, blurring distinctions between anticipation and enjoyment, seeking and finding, desire and fulfillment of love without ever letting the play come to a definite closure. According to Exum, "its resistance to closure is perhaps the Song's most important strategy for immortalizing love" (12).

Section 4, addressing the issue of gendered love-talk, includes among the most original and sensitive pages of this commentary. Exum reminds us that we are dealing with love poetry,

> where the boundaries between the conventional and unconventional are unpre-
> dictable, and not with a description of actual gender relations of a particular

time and place. The Song of Songs is a priceless resource not so much for what it tells us about relations between the sexes in ancient Israel, for it tells us very little, but for what it reveals about the construction of desire in ancient Israelite culture.... Because we possess the Song of Songs, we know that a romantic vision of love was available in ancient Israel, a vision that recognized both desire and sexual pleasure as mutual and that viewed positively a woman actively seeking to gratify her desire. (13).[1]

Exum further notes "the poet's remarkable sensitivity to differences between women and men—differences that, in turn, reflect cultural assumptions about gender differences and roles" (14). For instance, the man constructs the woman through the *gaze*, whereas she constructs him primarily through the *voice*;[2] she quotes him speaking to her (2:10–14; 5:2), but he never quotes her. Her condition is repeatedly characterized in the Song as *lovesickness*. He rather thinks of their mutual passion in terms of conquest, capturing, and being captured or *awestruck*; she, in turn, would go so far as to surrender, which he never does. He would also *take* love and consume it (although "he takes what he desires only by invitation" [27]), whereas she, while occasionally tasting sweet fruit as well (2:3; 5:13, 16), is more prepared to *offer* her gardenly pleasures, and the imagery of her speech is generally more relational than his. Exum further notes that "only the woman is concerned with self-description" (22), something the man apparently does not need to do. Hence "it appears that, in ancient Israelite culture as in many others, autonomy is part of the dynamic of male eroticism.... She is not in awe of him; she is in need of him" (15). While any of these statements would require detailed cross-checking, the case is well-taken and on the whole very convincing.

Section 5 provides more technical discussions such as one is used to in commentaries on biblical books: manuscript tradition, poetic features, voice identification, structure and composition, anthology of discrete poems versus unified work, multiple versus single authorship. Following Fox, Murphy, and others, Exum stresses the Song's overall coherence, which in her opinion makes it unnecessary to posit an editor but allows us to speak of a real author, regardless the fact that we should not think of an individual inventing all the poems by himself. "Whether commentators see the whole or only the parts when they read the Song may be largely a matter of temperament.... The present commentary assumes that only by reading it as a whole can we do justice to its poetic accomplishment" (37).

Section 6 on "The Song of Songs and Its World" is the longest, which is due mainly to extensive quotes from Egyptian and Mesopotamian texts. These allow

---

1. As it will become clear below, I have some doubts as to just how unpredictable the boundaries of convention are in this poem, and I am not quite sure that I understand what Exum means when using the phrase "ancient Israel."

2. Still, "she too owns the gaze" (5:10–16), and this is "an extraordinary feature of the Song, for traditionally women are looked at and men do the looking" (20).

readers to get a sense of both similarities and differences between quite different literary corpuses. Although not necessarily the most original part of Exum's
introduction (she acknowledges Fox's discussion, unsurpassed in this reviewer's
opinion, of the Egyptian collections and their relationship to the biblical Song),
these pages provide a well-informed state-of-the-art account. Exum's reading
of texts from neighboring cultures is generally as careful as with biblical texts,
though legitimately less detailed and based on translations. It allows her to define
distinct literary profiles of the various compositions referred to. "Perhaps the
most remarkable difference between our one example from ancient Israel and the
other surviving love poems from the ancient Near East is that the Egyptian and
Mesopotamian love poetry deals with a wider range of situations and emotions,
and offers a more multifaceted vision of love, than the Song of Songs" (63). This
impression may be essentially due to the fact that we know but *one* single collection of love poetry from the Bible, as opposed to several from neighboring
cultures.

Curiously enough, Exum does not discuss Greek or Roman love poetry from
Sappho to Ovid, nor does she show particular interest in Arabic love poetry,
medieval to contemporary. These materials have been repeatedly brought into
the discussion of the Song by scholars who prefer to enlarge a debate that often
tends to remain too narrowly Egypt-cum-Mesopotamia-focused. The more one
considers the Song to be a relatively late work, composed in the late Persian or
early Hellenistic period, one should consider the fact that its "world," in the sense
of the world that produced it, must have differed considerably from that of late
third-millennium or early second-millennium Mesopotamian writers. At this
juncture, however, Exum's option to read the Song as universally pertinent love
poetry while at the same time considering it in historical terms as a testimony of
"ancient Israelite culture" betrays its limitations and perhaps a real contradiction.

Taken as a whole, Exum's introduction has the laudable effect of laying open
much of her interpretative premises and assumptions. As a rule, they are well
argued and presented in a style that tries to avoid normative reading instructions
but leaves room for several alternatives. Among these, I would mention one that,
in my opinion, does not get a fair enough trial in Exum's commentary. As many
(probably most) commentators before her, Exum considers 8:6 to be some sort
of a climactic statement toward the end of the poem (3), so there must be progression (5). She recognizes that repetition, echoes, interlacing patterns, and the
like have a cumulative effect, which she would describe as "a gradual unfolding
and a denouement" (12). The Song, in her opinion, "far from being structure-
less ... offers a superabundance of structural clues" (37). At one point she even
finds it conceivable that the dialogue format of the Song reflects actual performance (4). Further on Exum acknowledges "the powerful readerly tendency to
read sequentially and to make sense of a literary work as a whole; in other words,
to read for the plot" (42). However, she rejects herself what she considers too
linear a reading and with it any dramatic approach to the interpretation of the
Song of Songs, claiming that dramatic theories inevitably must provide their plot

from outside the textual world. At this point, and strangely enough, her generally pluralistic and nonexclusive approach to interpretation becomes normative in its overconfident rejection of two readerly options that both can claim a long history among attentive readers: the recognition that the male voice in the Song may actually not represent a single character but two different speakers (a king and an outside lover) belonging to different social environments; and the hypothesis that the redactional arrangement of the individual poems may well reflect a progressive plot insofar as the girl from the very beginning is described as being taken into the loving company of the king and the daughters of Jerusalem (probably concubines and other women inhabiting the women's quarter of the royal palace) but regularly escapes from that world in order to find another lover in a less formal and otherwise luxurious environment. This is not the place to develop any further such a reading hypothesis, which makes sense of many features in the text, such as what one might call the "Solomonic plot" unfolding from 1:1 to 8:11–12, and stresses nuances in gender perspectives that clearly go beyond a mere male/female dichotomy (curiously enough, Exum is aware of but does not really explore the gender dimension involved in the girl's brothers' and mother's role).[3] Suffice it to say that Exum does not seem to have put the plot hypothesis to a real test, as against her own preferred option, and I found her rejection of what I consider a valid alternative both surprisingly superficial and disappointingly dogmatic. Resisting readers will of course recognize that there is some fundamental tension between a three-character plot, on the one hand, and Exum's tendency to universalize love as displayed by the Song (heteronormative love, after all) and to range it under the "romance" umbrella, on the other—a rubric, by the way, that I doubt is as culturally innocent and may be as easily universalized as Exum wants us to believe.

2.

The commentary section divides the Song into ten subunits of very different length. A glance at the following table of contents confirms that Exum's main interests are neither in exposing a subtle overall composition nor identifying and connecting a series of well-balanced units and even less an implied narrative subtext with a real plot:

1:1   Superscription
1:2–4   The Voice of Desire
1:5–2:7   A Dialogue about Love

---

3. But see Erich Bosshard-Nepustil, "Zu Struktur und Sachprofil des Hohenlieds," *BN* 81 (1996): 45–71; Christoph Uehlinger, "Das Hohelied—Anthologie oder Dramaturgie?" *Welt und Umwelt der Bibel* 6 (fasc. 21, 3/2001), 34-39; idem, "Cantique des Cantiques," in *Introduction à l'Ancien Testament* (ed. Thomas Römer, Jean-Daniel Macchi, and Christophe Nihan; Genève: Labor et Fides, 2004), 530–43.

Readers will probably agree that this table of contents does not exactly reflect what one would call a well-conceived, structurally coherent and aesthetically pleasant literary work of art. How would anyone imagine making music of such an uninspiring sequence of just speech and talk?

Still, initial perplexity rapidly vanishes once one enters the commentary proper. There is much insight to be gained from many detailed (but never too long) discussions, including such issues as who kisses whom in the Hebrew Bible and under what circumstances (93). There obviously are a number of instances where any critical reader will contest details of translation. I am unconvinced, for instance, that once one has recognized how problematic it is to render *nepeš* with "soul," one should simply go on perpetuating the problem. To Exum "soul" seems "especially appropriate, since it has an English equivalent in such expressions of total devotion as to love someone with all one's soul, or with all one's heart" (106–7). But in modern use the heart has largely outruled the soul in matters of passion, and there would thus be good reasons to look for alternative and more sensual translations of *nepeš*. The Song of Songs is rightly famed for its imagery, and hence it matters how one translates metaphors and what meaning one constructs for them. Generally speaking, Exum favors a delicate approach that aims at not pressing the similes too much. She privileges open translations that hint at a semantic field rather than narrow lexematic precision. Regarding the metaphor "Your eyes are doves" (1:15), for instance, it is enough for her to recall that "the dove was used as a symbol of love in the ancient Near East" and that it attained a special status as love bird in ancient and modern love poetry "for the range of romantic images it conveys by its aspect, movement, and behavior, as well as its association with the love goddess and with spring" (112). Keel, whose inspiring work on metaphors and similes in the Song is acknowledged by Exum, would tend to be significantly more specific and stress the dove's *function* as a messenger of amorous sentiments.

One feature found particularly helpful and actually illuminating the whole commentary section is Exum's recurrent use of straightforward questions involving the reader's imagination to participate: "Where does she want to be kissed?" (93 on 1:2); "Who then is the 'we'?" (95); "Might the other women … be present in the king's chamber?" (96); "How are the women of Jerusalem looking at her? With disdain? With envy? With fear? … Moreover, why does she tell them she is lovely? Can they not see it?" (103–4 all on 1:4). Reading both the poem and the commentary side by side, readers are thus invited to give their opinions. They are conceived as true partners who should have an essential share in a common interpretative undertaking (see 82–86 on "Privileging the Reader").

Could such an attitude be overstretched at times to the extent that it favors arbitrary or even meaningless reading options? As someone trained in the German-speaking tradition of biblical exegesis, I was surprised by the liberty this commentary may occasionally take with issues that are considered basic and essential ones in German exegesis. "Would knowing when it was written help us understand the poem? Probably not very much" (67) is a rather startling statement for someone who takes profound interest in the *history* of cultures. On a different level, I find it rather strange to read that "Hebrew ḥăbaṣṣelet is surely not a rose (which did not grow in Israel in biblical times)" (113, undoubtedly correct) alongside the following translation of 2:1: "I am a rose of Sharon, a lily of the valleys" (98). Exum justifies her option for the familiar by the subterfuge that "a rose by any other name would smell as sweet" (113), but why should we give precedence to smell over other aspects of the flowers involved, and how far should we go in de-contextualizing the Song? As for the other flower, Exum notes that "šôšannâ has been variously identified as a lily (*Lilium candidum,* which has large white flowers, or *Lilium chalcedonicum,* with red flowers), the lotus (*Nymphaea lotus*), or the water lily (*Nymphaea caerulea*). The narcissus, chamomile, crowfoot, sea daffodil, sternbergia, yellow flag iris, and blue hyacinth are also candidates" (113–14). Not surprisingly, her commentary leaves the issue undecided, but the translation cannot and once more returns to the conventional and familiar, however wrong that may be in this particular instance. Part of a justification for such an open approach to imagery, symbolism, and metaphor is given in the introduction, where Exum writes that her observations "are not intended to explain the meaning of the images in any definitive sense, for it is not the case that there is only one correct way to approach them.… Images are matched in some way to their referents and are not interchangeable.… But what exactly the images are meant to convey is not always apparent. Words and images are never simply denotative, and in poetry they are excessively connotative" (19). Still, the world reflected in the Song, as imaginary as it may be, is a culturally peculiar one, shaped by geographical, cultural, social, and historical context, experience, and imagination. I would maintain that these contexts deserve to be acknowledged in their own right as precisely as possible, however reader-friendly a scholarly commentary wants to be. The problem of decontextualization that underlies any universalizing reading strategy is a serious one and ultimately relates to the ethics of interpretation. While I cannot imagine that this problem could not have occurred to such a sensitive and resistant reader as J. Cheryl Exum, I am surprised to find her commentary insufficiently affected by the issue.

3.

A cursory examination of the bibliography cited may explain two major characteristics of Exum's work. To begin with, most secondary literature cited comes from the English-speaking world, most notably North American and English

authors; there are a few titles each in French and German, but it is obvious that
Exum addresses the Song of Songs well within an Anglo-American scholarly
discourse and shows little interest in a number of questions that German scholarship, for better or for worse, has long been preoccupied with (form criticism,
literary criticism in the sense of *Literarkritik,* questions of origin, date, *Sitz im
Leben,* etc.). More important in my opinion is the fact that no commentary on
the Song of Songs has ever been so sensitive to various forms of resistant reading,
that is, interpretations that aim at unveiling the hidden premises of heteronormative ideologies of sex and gender. Such ideologies, characteristic of any patriarchal
society and culture, run as a subtext throughout the Song, disguised as they are
by such truly remarkable features as stunning lyrics, erotic exuberance, the fact
that a woman is (one of) the Song's main protagonist(s), the presence of female
speakers in general, a distinctive female perspective on human love and sexuality, and so forth. These and other features have led a number of commentators,
feminist and traditionalist alike, to consider the possibility of female authorship.
Exum discusses the issue but considers the solution unlikely—there is more to
social history than is sometimes acknowledged.

Exum's bibliography and introduction cites numerous articles published
within the last twenty-five years and informed by feminist and queer criticism,
ideology criticism, or psychoanalysis. Not surprisingly, they warn readers from
too easily succumbing to the charms of all this sublime poetry. Their authors,
generally less inhibited than ecclesiastical scholars, have raised important new
questions about the Song: Does it allow for sexist, voyeuristic, pornographic,
or even perverse readings? How does it relate to and what does it tell us about
the (cultural) history of sexuality and erotic desire? Exum's is to my knowledge
the first commentary published in one of the major Hebrew Bible (or Old Testament) commentary series that gives ample room for such questions to be asked
alongside the more conventional ones in one of those well-established hardbound
series, which display all but the characteristics of a "marginal" or "alternative"
scholarly milieu.[4] It would have been thrilling to put her insights into dialogue
with recent research on homosexuality in the Bible and the ancient Near East.[5]
This may be the subject for another celebration, just as "It remains for future
study to construct the history of gender ideology in Song of Songs interpretation

---

4. "One person's erotic look may be another person's voyeuristic gaze. Moreover, one
might, for any number of reasons, want to resist the Song's invitation to look, or one might
choose to look differently, or even perversely.… Readers of this commentary … will decide for
themselves how they feel about looking, both the characters' looking and their own looking at
the characters in this love poem" (24).

5. See especially Martti Nissinen, *Homoeroticism in the Biblical World: A Historical Per-
spective* (Minneapolis: Fortress, 1998); Daniel Boyarin, "Are There Any Jews in 'The History of
Sexuality'?" *Journal of the History of Sexuality* 5.3 (1995): 333–55; Thomas Römer and Loyse
Bonjour, *L'homosexualité dans le Proche-Orient ancien et la Bible* (Essais bibliques; Genève:
Labor et Fides), 2005.

by examining how and to what extent commentators reinscribe the gender ideology of the text or how they read sexual stereotypes of their times and their own culturally conditioned gender biases back into the biblical text" (83).

To sum up, Exum's commentary offers much food for thought because it differs in more than one respect from conventional scholarship on the Song. As someone who is more acquainted with the *mores* of Continental European exegesis, which is culturally more traditional in its approach to biblical literature despite (or because of?) greater confidence put in the interpretative potential of the so-called historical-critical method, I have found much to be learned in this book while taking great pleasure when reading it. I am sure many other professional and nonprofessional readers will share that experience and will find this a sophisticated, imaginative, and truly inspiring commentary too.

Konzeptionen des Königtums Gottes im Psalter: Untersuchungen zu Komposition und Redaktion der theokratischen Bücher IV–V im Psalter, by Martin Leuenberger. Abhandlungen zur Theologie des Alten und Neuen Testaments 83. Zurich: Theologischer Verlag, 2004. Pp. x + 466. Hardcover. €40.00. ISBN 3290172740.

Philippus J. Botha, University of Pretoria, Pretoria, South Africa

This book, published in 2004, is a slightly reworked version of a thesis submitted in the Faculty of Theology at the University of Zurich in 2003. As the title aptly states, it is primarily an investigation of the composition and redaction of Pss 90–150. The author endeavors to investigate how the individual psalms in books 4 and 5 of the Psalter were selected, edited, and arranged and how knowledge of this process can help us to understand the growth of the Psalter as a whole. In his view, changing perspectives on the kingdom of Yhwh have played a decisive role in the process of composing and editing the Psalter. The method the author chose for this investigation is that of redaction history, but then with the incorporation of a conceptual investigation. He argues that a diachronic investigation of the development of concepts can help to render compositional and redaction-historical hypotheses more plausible.

The thesis for this investigation is that the final form of the Psalter is the result of a process in which the concept of the kingdom of God as it is presented in the so-called "messianic" psalms (Pss 2–89) was critically assessed and adapted through various stages to form the "theocratic" perspective found in books 4–5 (Pss 90–150) and, consequently, in the Psalter as a whole. The two classical *Gattungen* that have a direct bearing on kingship, namely, the royal psalms and the Yhwh-*malak* psalms, immediately come to mind as representatives of different perspectives on the kingdom of God, namely, a Davidic-earthly concept of kingship and a concept of kingship in which Yhwh himself takes over the role of the earthly king. The paradigm shift between these two kinds of psalms (as manifested in Pss 2 and 97 as representatives of the two kinds) is interpreted theological-historically. For the investigation of books 4 and 5, the concept of the kingdom of God is differentiated on different levels: in terms of the domains of cosmos/nature, the nations, Zion/Judah, and the contrast between groups designated as the righteous and the wicked.

The author senses a general process of widening of the temporal and spatial horizons of Yhwh's kingship in the last two books of the Psalter, a process that begins in the Yhwh-*malak* Psalms and that reaches a climax in Ps 145 before being rounded off in the final Hallel by the exploding universal praise in Ps 150. Yhwh's acts of saving is expanded in these books from individual Israelites and groups of Israelites to all peoples, so that his reign is described as manifested in his care for all living beings.

Before turning to the investigation of books 4 and 5 proper, the author revisits the work done during the past two decades (especially Wilson, Hossfeld and Zenger, and Millard) on the composition and redaction of the Psalter. The editorial differences between books 1–3, on the one hand, and books 4–5, on the other, are pointed out and are described as two distinct segments of the Psalter. On pages 93–123 the reader is provided with an invaluable overview of the current state of research into the composition of books 1–3, in which the groups of Pss 3–14, 15–24, 25–34, 35–41, 42–49, 51–72, 73–83, and 84–89 are shown to be arranged generally in concentric groups or otherwise meaningful arrangements around the concept of kingship, moving from the divinely ordained universal reign of the Davidic king to the shattering of this utopia in Ps 89.

The state of research on the editing of book 4 is also reviewed and described as consisting of three composition-segments: Pss 90–92; 93–100; and 101–106. The book as a whole is described as reflecting a fundamental reworking of the historical crises of the exile (217), ending with an important supplication for the manifestation of God's kingship in 106:47. The hope for a restitution of Davidic kingship is abandoned and a return made to the kingship of Yhwh that has manifested itself since creation. Psalms 93–100 are shown to be arranged concentrically around Ps 97 in terms of quite a number of common aspects. A priestly view of the kingship of Yhwh seems to dominate in the psalms of this group. Psalms 101–106 are shown to have been originally devised as the conclusion of a four-part integrated book (books 1–4; Pss 2–106) in which the idea of a theocracy served as the guiding principle (261). The collection of Pss 2–89 in which (Davidic) kingship seems to have been the guiding editorial principle was first expanded into the (priestly) collection of 2–100, which developed into the basically theocratic collection of 2–106, constituting the first four books of the Psalter.

According to the author, book 5 of the Psalter is more closely connected to book 4 than it is to books 1–3. The composition of this book is shown to have developed (broadly speaking) in three stages: Pss 107–118 (which grew out of the combination of 107, 108–110, and 111–118) were added to the existing Pss 2–106 to serve as an expansion of the idea of a theocracy encapsulating all peoples; this was then edited with the addition of 119, 120–134 and 135–136 to refine the concept of theocracy;, finally, it was expanded by the addition of 137, 138–145, and 146–150. In this part of the Psalter Yhwh is constantly represented as king, especially in the places where compositional units were merged. This concept is represented less strongly in 120–134, although the members of this group are said to stand on the same foundation. The important conceptions that represent the kingship of Yhwh in this book of the Psalter seem to be the spatial-temporal range of his reign, the opposition between righteous and wicked, and, especially, themes expressing deliverance.

The investigation concludes with a prospect of research themes that could develop from this investigation. Two of these are a synchronic comparison of the concept of the kingdom of Yhwh as it has been described here in the Psalms and in other (late) Old Testament corpora of texts, and a comparison between this concept and the concept of the kingdom of God as it is found in the core of the preaching of the historical Jesus in the Gospels.

Apart from the four main parts, each with three to four chapters (the introduction, a comparison between books 1–3 and 4–5 of the Psalter, the conceptual development of book 4, and the conceptual development of book 5), there is an overview of the results, a very representative bibliography of about fifty pages, and an index of references to the Old Testament, apocryphal and pseudepigraphic works, Qumran literature, texts from the New Testament, and others.

This volume provides a masterful overview of research on the editing of the Psalter, and I have little doubt that the author has correctly identified the most important concept that played a role in the selection and arrangement of psalms to form compositional groups and eventually the Psalter as a whole. His explanation of the development of this concept of the reign of Yhwh through Davidic kings to become the idea of a universal kingdom of God is very plausible.

The book contains detailed discussions of the editing of certain individual psalms from books 4 and 5, although not every psalm could be investigated in the same detail. One can obviously also not expect to find a critical discussion of every point of view already expressed in recent research in a book that covers such a comprehensive subject; the most important opinions are merely mentioned in footnotes. But in my view this book does indeed break new ground and deserves to be described as enhancing not only our collective knowledge of the editing of the Psalter but also of the development of an important concept in the theology of the Psalms and the Old Testament that seems also to have dominated in the preaching of Jesus.

Daniel: Kapitel 1,1–4,34, by Klaus Koch. Biblischer Kommentar Altes Testament 22.1. Neukirchen-Vluyn: Neukirchener, 2005. Pp. viii + 463. Cloth. €109.00. ISBN 3788707887.

John J. Collins, Yale University, New Haven, Connecticut

This volume brings together the first six fascicles of Koch's monumental commentary on Daniel. The first fascicle appeared in 1986. In the preface we are informed that Martin Rösel, who has already been cooperating with Koch on the text of Daniel, will co-author future fascicles. Even if this accelerates publication, it will be a long time before this commentary is completed.

But on the evidence thus far available, it is worth the wait. This is the most detailed, thorough, even exhaustive commentary ever attempted on Daniel, perhaps on any book of the Hebrew Bible. Koch brings a rare combination of skills to the task. He begins with a text-linguistic analysis that deals with the surface of the text, the structure of sentences, and the division of units. This includes discussion of the unity of the text. Koch is not averse to recognizing redactional elements, but he is much more restrained than many of his German compatriots and is acutely aware that modern Western logic may not be attuned to the compositional devices of the text. This text-linguistic analysis leads into form-critical analysis, of which he has long been a master. The verse-by-verse commentary pays extensive attention to ancient Near Eastern traditions that may be viewed as parallels or sources for Daniel. Finally, he provides lengthy discussions of the theology of the book, especially of its theology of history. The commentary is richly informed by the history of interpretation, both Jewish and Christian.

Positions taken on major issues include the following. Chapter 1 was originally composed in Aramaic and translated into Hebrew, but not by the author of chapters 8–12, since the Hebrew is different. Aramaic composition has been proposed before, but never so well supported, by the demonstration of Aramaisms in the text. Chapter 1 was originally written as an introduction only to the first six chapters. Like the other Aramaic tales, it reflects good knowledge of imperial bureaucracy, but there are significantly more Persian than Akkadian loanwords. While the history is inaccurate, Koch is at pains to show that the author was not cavalier about history but worked carefully from the sources available to him, especially Chronicles. He also drew on the Hellenistic Babylonian history of Berossus, or perhaps on one of its sources. Daniel's refusal of the king's food was not based on Levitical law, which does not regard Gentile wine as impure and uses the word טמא rather than גאל for defilement.

In chapter 2, Koch argues that the schema of four metals was derived from a Persian source on which Hesiod also drew. The sequence of four kingdoms, including Media, was also of Persian origin. This position is controversial. The extant Persian sources that speak of a sequence of four metals date from the early medieval period. Neither the four metals nor the four kingdoms are found in the Achaemenid inscriptions. Nonetheless, Koch makes a good circumstantial case. Hesiod was evidently adapting a schema, and the inclusion of Media in the sequence strongly suggests an ultimate Persian source. This position will continue to be disputed, but Koch provides a more extensive discussion of the Persian sources than any previous commentary. He contends that the apocalyptic view of history, as evidenced here, is by no means a denial and that the sharp contrast between the kingdom of God and the human kingdoms is an aberration of twentieth-century Christian theology.

In chapter 3 he finds parallels for the fiery furnace in the story of Phalaris, the tyrant of Sicily, who roasted his victims in a metal bull, and in references to a similar contraption in Carthage. Whether these stories are immediately relevant to Daniel or not, they show that the idea of punishment by roasting was not uniquely Jewish. Koch interprets the statement of the Jewish youths that they will not worship the image even if their God does not deliver them in light of the story of Job and the affirmation of fidelity regardless of reward. He provides full commentary on the apocryphal additions in chapter 3. Here his most noteworthy contribution is his acceptance of the authenticity of the Aramaic text of these stories found in the medieval Chronicle of Jerahmeel. The prayer of Azariah that the death of the youths be accepted in lieu of sacrifice bespeaks not the spiritualization of the cult but the atoning power of martyrdom.

In chapter 4 Koch engages in extensive comparison of the Old Greek and Masoretic texts. He shares the view that neither one is based on the other but that they are variants of a common textual tradition, with distinct theological emphases. He argues that this story was originally based on the Harran inscriptions of Nabonidus. The Prayer of Nabonidus from Qumran is an independent witness to this traditional story. The iconography of Nabonidus sheds light on some puzzling aspects of the biblical text, such as the mention of bands of iron and bronze, which reflect the staves depicted on the inscriptions, and the mention of sun and moon in the tree in the Old Greek version.

Since this is a work in progress, there is no introduction to pull together an overview of the commentary. A few themes are clear. The prominence of Persian loanwords, and motifs, points to an origin in the eastern Diaspora. Only in chapter 4 are Babylonian themes more prominent. All these tales reflect a vigorous political theology. They also show a vigorous engagement with history, even though they are now known to be historically inaccurate.

In much of this, Koch agrees with my own commentary in the Hermeneia series, which was published after his first fascicle but before the second. I also argued for an Aramaic original of chapter 1 and for Persian influence on the theme of four kingdoms depicted as metals and for origin of these tales in circles familiar with the imperial court in the eastern Diaspora. Many of these issues are expounded in greater detail by Koch, and he also provides an extensive text-linguistic analysis. Inevitably we disagree on some details. Koch is inclined to restore a reference to a beast in the Prayer of Nabonidus and also to see a reference to dreaming in the second column. I do not find a secure basis for either of these points. I am less confident than he is about the authenticity of the medieval Aramaic text of the prayers in chapter 3. I agree that it is an important textual witness and should be taken seriously, but I suspect that it depends on a Hebrew original, although the evidence is slight. Koch has far lengthier discussions of the theology of history than I do, reflecting in large part a debate in Germany in the 1970s.

The interpretation of Daniel is ambiguous at many points. All one can ask of a commentary is that it be thorough and learned. By any criterion, Koch's commentary is an outstanding achievement.

When a commentary like this is published gradually over many years, there are some unfortunate side effects. It is inevitable that the frame of the discussion shifts somewhat over the years. An author might change his or her mind on some issues, and the discontinuity is greater should a new author take over the project. Ideally, it would be good to see Klaus Koch provide at least a synthesis of his views on Daniel as a whole. This volume, no more than one third of the whole commentary, whets the appetite, but it also stands as a monument to one of the great commentators on the book of Daniel.

"Wer eine Grube gräbt...": *Der Tun-Ergehen-Zusammenhang und sein Wandel in der alttestamentlichen Weisheitsliteratur*, by Georg Freuling. Wissenschaftliche Monographien zum Alten und Neuen Testament 102. Neukirchen-Vluyn: Neukirchener, 2004. Pp. viii + 301. Cloth. €49.90. ISBN 3788720077.

Beat Weber, Theologisches Seminar Bienenberg (Liestal), Linden, Switzerland

Bei der vorzustellenden Monographie handelt es sich um eine für die Veröffentlichung geringfügig überarbeitete Doktoraldissertation, die von der Evangelisch-Theologischen Fakultät der Rheinischen Friedrich-Wilhelms-Universität Bonn angenommen wurde. Wie der Untertitel anzeigt, geht es um die Bestimmung der grundlegenden Vorstellung des sogenannten „Tun-Ergehen-Zusammenhangs" (TEZ) im Zusammenhang der alttestamentllichen Weisheitsliteratur.

In der vorangestellten Einleitung gibt der Verfasser einen Überblick über den bisherigen Stand der Forschung. Dabei werden den Studien von Kurt Koch, namentlich dessen Aufsatz „Gibt es ein Vergeltungsdogma im Alten Testament?" (1955), besondere Aufmerksamkeit geschenkt. Unter Aufnahme von Überlegungen von Johannes Pedersen prägte Koch den Begriff der „schicksalswirkenden Tatsphäre", die er insofern grundsätzlich theologisch qualifizierte, als in allen alttestamentlichen Traditionsbereichen das Zustandekommen des Zusammenhangs von Tun und Ergehen mit dem Handeln JHWHs verbunden wird. Hat sich das Verständnis eines TEZ in der alttestamentlichen Weisheit seither geradezu als „klassisch" etabliert, so geht es Freuling in seiner Untersuchung um eine präzise Erfassung bzw. Feinabstimmung dieser Vorstellung im Rahmen des alttestamentlich-weisheitlichen Schrifttums. Dazu werden die einschlägigen Aussagen in Proverbia, ausgewählte Psalmen, Hiob und Kohelet einer eingehenden Analyse unterzogen.

Das erste Hauptkapitel beschäftigt sich mit den Proverbia, und zwar zunächst mit der älteren Spruchweisheit (Prov 10–29), anschliessend mit den als jünger geltenden Lehrreden (Prov 1–9). Als „Zwischenergebnis" hält der Verfasser fest, dass in den Lehrreden zwar eine stärkere theologische Reflexion greifbar wird, im Blick auf die untersuchte Thematik aber zwischen beiden Teilen weithin Übereinstimmung herrscht und lediglich Akzentverschiebungen vorliegen.

Festzuhalten ist, dass rechtes und verkehrtes Verhalten häufig auf ihren Gemeinschaftsbezug hin bedacht werden. Vorherrschend ist dabei eine „pädagogische Intention": In Sentenzen wie Lehrreden äussert sich das Bemühen, den Menschen zu einer heilvollen Lebensorientierung anzuleiten. Auch wenn bereits die ältere Weisheit um widersprüchliche Erfahrung weiss, gilt der Grundsatz: „es wird *gelehrt*, nicht *problematisiert!*" (104; Kursivsetzung GF). Dabei kann der TEZ mit und ohne eine Reflexion auf die Teilhabe JHWHs entfaltet werden (tendenziell sind gute Taten und heilvolles Ergehen stärker mit dem Wirken Gottes verbunden als die Kehrseite). Die Wirksamkeit Gottes und die Eigendynamik menschlichen Tuns sind nicht als alternativ, sondern als koexistent zu fassen: Beide Aspekte konvergieren, ohne einander auszuschliessen. Was den Geltungsbereich des Zusammenhangs von Tun und Ergehen betrifft, ist von der Vorstellung eines starren Ordnungsdenkens Abstand zu nehmen (keine „Zwangsläufigkeit", kein „Naturgesetz"). Ebenso ist die Redeweise Kochs von der „schicksalswirkenden Tatsphäre" aufgrund unzureichender Implikationen aufzugeben und beim offeneren und sachgemässeren Begriff des TEZ zu bleiben.

Im zweiten Hauptkapitel analysiert Freuling die als weisheitlich geltenden Psalmen 37, 49 und 73, in Problematisierungen des TEZ greifbar werden. Ps 37 reagiert auf die Erfahrung, dass es dem Frevler nicht immer entsprechend seinem Tun ergeht. Allerdings stellt sich das Wohlergehen des Frevlers aus Sicht des Psalmisten als vorübergehendes Problem dar, so dass nicht der TEZ an sich, sondern die Haltung derer problematisiert wird, denen das Gebahren der Gottlosen zur Anfechtung wird. Dies geschieht unter starker Betonung der Initiative JHWHs für die Seinen.

Ps 49 liegt eine Konfrontation mit den von Glück begünstigten, negativ charakterisierten Reichen zugrunde. Ihr „Vorteil" erfährt angesichts des Todes eine völlige Einnivellierung. Die Gemeinschaft und Nähe zu Gott erweist sich dagegen als über die Todesgrenze hinaus bleibend, wodurch der innerweltliche TEZ gleichsam überschritten wird.

In Ps 73 gesteht der Betende die Anfechtung ein, in die er aufgrund der Erfahrung einer (scheinbaren) Umkehrung des TEZ geraten ist: Den Frevlern geht es gut, und die Gerechten (zu denen er sich rechnet) müssen leiden. Ein Tempelbesuch und die Einsicht in das Ende der Frevler führt zu einem Perspektivenwechsel: Der Blick auf das Wohlergehen der Frevler löst sich durch die Gewissheit der Gottesnähe.

Im Hiobbuch wird am Geschick Hiobs in paradigmatischer Weise eine grundsätzliche Infragestellung des TEZ ansichtig. In der Rahmenerzählung ordnet sich Hiob der Souveränität JHWHs unter: Er ist es, der gibt und nimmt (1,21); von ihm ist entsprechend Gutes wie Böses anzunehmen (2,10). In der Hiobdichtung zeigt sich dann ein Mensch, der gegen sein Geschick aufbegehrt. Die Freunde sind dabei nicht einfach als Dogmatiker eines starren TEZ zu (dis)qualifizieren, zumal sie sich diesbezüglich durchaus als „flexibel" erweisen und Hiob nicht von vornherein zum Frevler stempeln. Die von ihnen geforderte Unterwerfung eröffnet für Hiob allerdings keine heilvolle Perspektive, zumal er Gott als Feind erlebt und sich gegenüber ihm beharrlich als gerecht behauptet. Im Verlauf des Dialogs verschieben sich die Konturen dahin, dass aus der Sicht der

Freunde Hiob aufgrund seines Geschicks als Frevler zu gelten hat. Die Freunde wie auch Hiob selber fixieren sich in je eigener Weise auf den TEZ, ohne dass es zu einer „Lösung" kommt. Die Elihu-Reden bereiten den Paradigmen-Wechsel vor, der zu neuem Erfahren und Verstehen führt: „Gott offenbart sich zuletzt als Schöpfer, vor dem sich Hiob schliesslich wieder einfinden kann, ohne auf seiner Gemeinschaftstreue *ihm* gegenüber zu beharren ... Einher geht eine Flexibilisierung des Zusammenhangs von Tun und Ergehen: Unheilvolles Ergehen wird als eine Möglichkeit des erzieherisch wirkenden Schöpfergottes begriffen, der dem Menschen darüber eine heilvolle Lebensperspektive bewahrt" (274).

Die Perspektive im Buch Kohelet ist insofern nochmals anders, als die genannte Thematik in einer grundsätzlichen und umfassenden Perspektive („alles, was unter der Sonne geschieht") wahrgenommen und beurteilt wird. Die Faktizität der Vergänglichkeit und des Todes, Kontingenzerfahrungen sowie die Einsicht in die Unverfügbarkeit der Zeit(en) führen nicht nur zu einer Problematisierung des TEZ, sondern auch zu einer Relativierung der Weisheit an sich. Die Aporien des Lebens bringen zwar Aufweichungen, aber nicht eine grundsätzliche Bestreitung des TEZ. Gott bleibt im Regiment, auch wenn die Möglichkeit sein Walten zu verstehen, nicht gegeben ist. Für den Menschen gilt, sich der Gottesfurcht zu befleissigen, die Begrenztheit anzunehmen und in Gelassenheit sowie unter Auskostung der geschenkten Freuden zu leben.

Als Ertrag der Studie ergibt sich, dass der TEZ die biblisch-weisheitliche Weltsicht grundiert. Das gilt zunächst für die Proverbia, wo dieser eine Basisorientierung abgibt und zu einer Pädagogik gelingenden Lebens umgemünzt wird. Dies gilt aber auch für die anderen Texte, welche widersprüchliche Erfahrungen dazu ungleich stärker voraussetzen, bedenken und damit den TEZ neu konfigurieren oder gar relativieren. Es ist daher nach Freuling verfehlt, von einer *grundsätzlichen* Krise oder gar einem Scheitern der Weisheit bzw. des TEZ zu sprechen. Seine Studie ergibt vielmehr ein subtiles Geflecht von Kontinuität und Diskontinuitäten. Das weisheitliche Denken macht denn auch keiner pessimistischen Weltsicht Platz, sondern erweist sich über lange Zeiten hinweg als kreativ und flexibel insofern, als auch „Grenzen der Weisheit" erkannt, integriert und zur Lebensbewältigung fruchtbar gemacht werden. Die dabei gemachten Grenzerfahrungen führen darüber hinaus zu weiterführenden theologischen wie lebensdienlichen Einsichten.

Auch bei da und dort abweichenden Texteinschätzungen und theologischen Gewichtungen im Einzelnen vermag der Gesamtduktus dieser Monographie, die sorgfältig und umsichtig erarbeitet wurde, zu überzeugen. Damit liegt eine gewichtige Studie für eine Strömung im alten Israel vor, die das Leben und Denken in dieser Zeit (und darüber hinaus) nachhaltig prägte. Namentlich der theologische Ertrag ist ebenso beachtlich wie begrüssenswert. Er bietet eine hilfreiche Basis und Vorarbeit für die Erarbeitung des Teilbereichs der Weisheit im Rahmen einer alttestamentlichen Theologie bzw. Biblischen Theologie des Alten Testaments. Dem Band ist eine gute Aufnahme und weite Verbreitung zu wünschen.

Cantos and Strophes in Biblical Hebrew Poetry: With Special Reference to the First Book of the Psalter, by Pieter van der Lugt. Oudtestamentische studiën 53. Leiden: Brill, 2006. Pp. xv + 581. Cloth. $270.00. ISBN 9004148396.

Josef M. Oesch, University of Innsbruck, Innsbruck, Austria

Nach den grundlegenden Arbeiten im 18. Jh. von R. Lowth zu den Elementen der hebräischen Poesie haben J. L. Saalschütz und Friedrich Köster im 19. Jh. die entscheidenden Anstöße gegeben, auch die strophischen Strukturen der poetischen Texte genauer zu untersuchen. Diese Forschungsrichtung wurde zuerst hauptsächlich—wenn auch kontrovers—von deutschsprachigen, im 20. Jh. dann zunehmend von englisch- und französischsprachigen Autorinnen und Autoren vorangetrieben und in den Niederlanden in unseren Zeiten vor allem von zahlreichen Bibelwissenschaftlerinnen und Bibel-wissenschaftlern der so genannten „Kampener Schule" intensiv und auf hohem Niveau weitergetrieben. An wichtigen einschlägigen Veröffentlichungen seien hier neben zahlreichen Einzelstudien z.B. zu Dtn 32 und Gen 49 der grundlegende Artikel von M. C. A. Korpel und J. de Moor, „Fundamentals of Ugaritic and Hebrew Poetry"(in W. van der Meer u.a., (ed.), *The Structural Analysis of Biblical and Canaanite Poetry* (JSOTS 74), Sheffield 1988 [Erstveröffentlichung 1986], 1–61), deren umfangreiche Monographie *The Structure of Classical Hebrew Poetry: Isaiah 40–55* (OTS 41, Leiden 1998 = SHP) und die Studien von Pieter van der Lugt (PvL) angeführt. Deren erste ist die 1980 erschienene Dissertation über die strophischen Strukturen in der hebräischen Poesie anhand der Psalmen (*Strofische structuren in de bijbels-hebreeuwse poëzie: De geschiedenis van het onderzoek en een bijdrage tot de theorievorming omtrent de strofenbouw van de Psalmen,* Kampen 1980); 1995 folgte die umfangreiche Studie zur poetischen Struktur des Ijobbuches, in der er eine Skizze der biblischen Poesie („Design of Biblical Poetry") entwickelte und in deren Anwendung er zu einer ganz neuen Sicht des Buchganzen gelangte (*Rhetorical Criticism and the Poetry of the Book of Job,* OTS 32, Leiden 1995).[1] In den im Prinzip gleichen methodischen Schritten untersucht er im Mittelteil seiner neuesten Veröffentlichung die ersten 41 Psalmen (93–418), dem eine umfangreiche Forschungsgeschichte vom 19. Jh. an zur strophischen Struktur der Psalmen vorangeht (1–92) und auf den eine umfangreichere Skizze der biblischen Poesie folgt (419–566).

Trotz der gemeinsamen Herkunft aus der „Kampener Schule" unterscheiden sich die methodischen Textzugriffe von de Moor/Korpel und PvL grundlegend. Beiden ist zwar gemeinsam, dass das masoretische Verssystem in den Ergebnissen der poetologischen Analysen weitgehend Berücksichtigung findet. Doch bei Ersteren entspricht dies ihrem methodologischen Ausgangspunkt, wonach vorerst in der Bestimmung der poetischen Elemente „feet", „cola", „verse-line",

---

1. Vgl. dazu die Rezensionen von H. Strauß in ThLZ 121 (1996) 350–51 und von W. H. Irwin in CBQ 58 (1996) 730–32.

„strophes", „canticles" und in der Untersuchung der Makrostruktur von den in der Textgeschichte überlieferten Daten auszugehen ist, wenn diese Daten auch nicht ohne kritische Prüfung zu übernehmen seien (vgl. z.B. zur Behandlung der Akzente SHP 11 und allgemein die Durchführung in Jes 40–55). Dazu gehören nicht nur die Akzente, Verseinteilungen und die Petucha-/Setumagliederung der masoretischen Tradition, sondern auch die entsprechenden Daten der ältesten Kodizes der griechischen und syrischen Übersetzungen. Im Gegensatz dazu geht PvL vom Textganzen aus, konkret also zumeist von der überlieferten Größe „Psalm". Sie zerlegt er in einer „rhetorical analysis" nach inhaltlichen und formalen Kriterien in ihre größeren und kleineren Einheiten „cantos", „sub-cantos", „canticles", „strophes" und „cola". Als Grund für diesen unterschiedlichen Zugang nennt PvL den Umstand, dass der Weg von Unten nach Oben einer der Gründe sei, warum soviel Verwirrung („confusion") in der Frage der Länge eines colons und der Struktur einer „Hebrew poetic line" herrscht (73).[2] Wenn man aber von Oben her, von der Makrostruktur des ‚poem' ausgehe, d.h. vom Aufbau der ‚cantos' und – gegebenenfalls der ‚canticles', könne man oft relativ einfach die strophische Struktur bestimmen, die wiederum Angaben zum Aufbau und der Abgrenzung der „verse-line" gibt. Von daher sei dann das Problem der Länge der „cola" sekundär.[3]

Im konkreten Vorgehen der Analyse der einzelnen Psalmen fragt PvL demnach zuerst nach dem Gedankengang („thought content, the thematic flow of a specific composition"; 74) entsprechend dem rhetorischen Aufbau des Gedichts.[4] Die Beschreibung der logischen Gliederung des Inhalts kann allerdings die Struktur der „cantos" (und „canticles") nur eingeschränkt begründen. Sie muss ergänzt werden durch formale Untersuchungen der „transition markers", der „verbal repetitions" und der „quantitative structural aspects" der Makrostruktur (77).

Diesen Linien folgt die Präsentation der Erforschung der einzelnen Psalmen. Zuerst wird ein formalisierter Überblick über die Struktur des Psalms geboten (z.B. 5.5 > 1.2.2 | 2.2.1 zu Ps 8), dann der mit Großschreibungen, Unterstreichungen und gliedernden Strichen in Umschrift geschriebene Text (in Umschrift). Darauf folgt der meist kurze Abschnitt „Text" zu textkritischen Fragen, ein Abschnitt „Content", zwei weitere zu den „Transition markers" und

---

2. Sonst spricht PvL von „verse-line". Das dürfte auch hier gemeint sein.

3. „Having established the macrostructure of a poem, i.e. the framework of the cantos (and as the case may be the canticles), one can often relatively easily determine its strophic structure in the proper sense. The strophic structure in its turn also gives an indication with regard to the composition and division of the poetic verselines. From this perspective, the problem of the lenght of the cola is of ‚secondary' importance" (73). PvL setzt sich darin ausdrücklich vom Zugang von J.de Moor/M.C.A. Korpel ab (73 Anm. 9).

4. Grundlage dieser rhetorischen Analysen sind die Ausführungen PvLs in seiner Dissertation 1980 und die Einführung in die Rhetorik von Roland Meynet, *Rhetorical Analysis: An Introduction to Biblical Rhetoric*, JSOTS 256, Sheffield 1998, französische Originalfassung Paris 1989.

„Verbal repetitions in strophic perspective" auf den verschiedenen Ebenen des Aufbaus, die als formale Gliederungskriterien im Gesamtaufbau dienen. Neu gegenüber der Gliederung in der Ijobuntersuchung folgt darauf ein Abschnitt „Quantitative structural aspects", in welchem die unterschiedlichen Zahlen und Zahlenkombinationen auf der Ebene der Wörter, Kola, Verszeilen und höheren Kompositionseinheiten sowie deren Funktionen im Ganzen besprochen wird.[5] Drei weitere Abschnitt enthalten „Various divisions" mit einem formalisierten Überblick über die wichtigsten alternativen Gliederungsvorschläge, „Comments and summary" mit einer die formalen Elemente einbindenden inhaltlichen Besprechung der Ergebnisse, und eine Bibliographie zu jedem Psalm.

Auf eine kuriose Art kommt in diesem reich mit Informationen und Anregungen versehenen Hauptteil der Studie eine Problematik des gewählten methodologischen Ansatzes zum Vorschein. Dreimal übernimmt PvL nämlich nicht die im Codex Leningradensis überlieferte Einteilung in die Psalmen. Entsprechend der LXX und dem akrostichischen Aufbau liest er Ps 9–10 als einen Psalm.[6] Im Gegenzug teilt er die Psalmen 7 und 40 auf je zwei Einheiten auf. In Ps 40 fasst er die vv2–13 und 14–18 je zu einem Psalm zusammen und kann sich dabei zwar auf kein Zeugnis aus der Textgeschichte, aber auf andere Kommentatoren wie Zenner, Herkenne, Kraft und Ravasi berufen, die diese Abgrenzung ebenfalls vertreten. In Ps 7 nimmt er den Einschnitt in v9 vor, und zwar nach v9a (vv2–9A; 9B–18), und setzt sich dabei nicht nur gegen die gesamte Kollegenschaft und die Textüberlieferung hinweg, sondern sogar gegen die gut bezeugte Versabgrenzung. Darin kommt nicht nur eine mutige, auf den ersten Blick vielleicht bestechende Entscheidung, sondern auch ein methodologisches Problem zum Vorschein. Denn welchen Sinn macht eine Auslegung von Psalmen, die nach dem Ausweis der Textgeschichte nie als solche gelesen wurden, wenn damit nicht der Anspruch erhoben wird, dass dies „ursprünglich" zwei Liedeinheiten waren? Aber genügen für eine solche Annahme ein schwieriger Textbestand und einige Kriterien der „Rhetorical Analysis"? Der eingeschlagene methodische Ansatz vom Ganzen zu den Teilen wird sich das Ganze von irgendwoher—wenn auch nicht unkritisch—geben lassen müssen und ist methodologisch überfordert, wenn er das Ganze selber konstituieren muss.

Auf den Teil der „Rhetorical Analysis" der ersten 42 Psalmen folgt ein formalisierter Überblick über die Verszeilen, „cantos" und Psalmen mit Refrain im

---

5. Den vorsichtigen Einbezug dieser Daten halte ich für sehr wertvoll, wenn daraus nicht vorschnell Schlüsse auf die Auslegung gezogen werden. Vgl. dazu die Ausführungen PdLs 84–87 und z.B. zu Ps 23.

6. Auch Ps 42–43 liest PvL (gegen LXX) als einen Psalm. Weitere Veränderungen in der Abgrenzung der Psalmen nimmt er aber nicht vor, sodass er am Schluss wieder auf die Zahl von 150 Psalmen kommt. Musste das sein? In der jüdischen Tradition sind recht unterschiedliche Zählungen von 147 bis 170 Psalmen belegt, sodass auch die Zählung von 149 Psalmen in der Tradition noch Platz gefunden hätte (EncJud 13[1971] 1306).

After a translation and some text-critical remarks affecting the interpretation of the text, a structural analysis of the psalm is proposed. This proposal attempts to account for both the strong thematic link between verse 8 ("No one can ransom himself") and verse 16 ("God will ransom me") and the quasi-repetition of verse 13 in verse 21. After the remarkably long call for attention (vv. 2–5), the psalm should be divided in three parts, Delkurt argues. Verses 8 and 13 constitute the respective cores of the first two parts (6–10/11–15), whereas the final part (16–21) opens and closes with the counterparts of those central verses of the two preceding parts. This results in a clear structure …A… / …B… / A'…B', which is attractive in its elegance and does justice to the text's meaning structure. The next thirty-eight pages of this study consist of a straightforward verse-by-verse commentary in which Delkurt presents his interpretation of the psalm. In short, he argues that the psalm is concerned with the question of whether the rich have the possibility of escaping their descent into Sheol after death by paying God ransom money in a cultic setting. The psalmist maintains that even the largest sum of money cannot influence one's fate after death and that all people share the same destiny: dying without taking anything of one's wealth or fame. In the final part, the biblical author provides a positive answer to the question of human fate: only God can take one from Sheol, securing the community between God and human after death (v. 16), and hence there is no need to envy the rich (vv. 17–21).

Given this interpretation of Ps 49, Delkurt goes on to compare the psalm with two other psalms with which it is often mentioned together: 37 and 73. Although these psalms all have a sapiential background and deal with theodicy, they differ considerably. Most important, Pss 37 and 73 are concerned with the problem of retribution, while Ps 49 does not address that issue at all. Psalm 37 expresses the belief that the apparent injustice of righteous people suffering and sinners prospering will be repaired before death, whereas Ps 73 leaves open the possibility of a restoration to justice also after death. Psalms 49 and 73 thus share the conviction of the existence of life after death and of a God being able to interfere in one's postmortem fate. Delkurt argues that Ps 49 was acquainted with ideas about afterlife and took them one step further in addressing the question of how people could or could not influence their fate in this afterlife. Contrary to what is usually held to be the case, Delkurt therefore considers Ps 49 to be younger than Ps 73.

In the final chapter of this monograph, Delkurt deals briefly with the book of Qoheleth, in particular with its understanding of death. Qoheleth's only certainty, Delkurt argues, is the temporality of everything and the impossibility for humans to obtain any permanent gain. Although Qoheleth does not deal with the question of the (im)possibility of influencing the course of the afterlife with gifts to God as Ps 49 does, it does warn readers against trying to use God as it pleases them (Qoh 4:17). This and other relations between Ps 49 and Qoheleth lead Delkurt to conclude that both texts must have originated in the same period and milieu. Both react against a misinterpretation in the sapiential tradition, thinking that everything is understandable and explainable through the *Tun-Ergehen-Zusammenhang*. Both Ps 49 and Qoheleth maintain the inscrutability of God and the human obligation to open oneself to God's giving acts, since eventually a person's fate is solely in God's hands.

In his discussion Delkurt repeatedly identifies specific circles and their practices in reaction to which the views in Ps 49 and Qoheleth would have been expressed. Psalm 49:8–10, for example, would have been directed against a specific cultic practice in which the rich tried to influence God with numerous or frequent gifts, "which for certain circles of the people had become the standard practice" (41). Similarly, both Ps 49 and Qoheleth would have been written with particular postexilic circles in mind that no longer accepted limits of knowledge that earlier generations accepted, by claiming insight into the mysteries of the world or even in God's acts (100–101). Due to a lack of any external evidence, however, those identifications remain interesting hypotheses at best. It is very hard to identify accepted practices or schools of thought solely on the basis of the views of their alleged opponents, especially when the latter do not explicitly address their adversaries. In my view, it is more sound methodologically to conclude that the biblical authors might have reacted against certain contemporary ideas but without identifying those ideas with specific sapiential circles. Without claiming that the authors of Ps 49 and Qoheleth fell into the straw-man fallacy, it is perfectly feasible that they wanted to oppose particular views that were going around, without having specific groups of people in mind.

Delkurt's very specific interpretation of the text's adversaries is closely related to his literal reading of a number of Hebrew terms, such as כפר, פדה, and פדיון in the context of Ps 49:8–9. All these terms are read by Delkurt in their literal and concrete meaning of "(paying) ransom money," even though they are not used in their usual context of interpersonal relations but in the context of the relation between humans and God. Although this reading cannot be excluded, it would require the support of more texts testifying to this specific cultic practice. In my opinion, it would be better to read the terms as metaphors designating human actions toward God that are similar in intention to the payment of ransom money. As Delkurt has correctly remarked, the term כפר is regularly used in a figurative way, as are פדה and פדיון. This is also the way in which they should be read here.

The work has a clear outline and reaches the goals set out by the author, even though, on the basis of the introduction, I had expected a more extensive comparison between Ps 49 and Qoheleth. Moreover, it is written in a clear and succinct style and has only a few typographical errors. In a following edition of the work, the following could be corrected: לקה for לקח (10); "ihre Gräber" for "Gräber" (translation of the reconstructed קברם, 17, correctly on 15); B" for B' (23); עזה for עשה (104). Although הטת אזנים (27) is morphologically correct, one would have expected a perfect form to refer to the expression, in line with the author's own practice elsewhere in the book and with general scholarly practice in biblical studies.

In conclusion, this book adds an interesting voice in the discussion on the emergence of the belief in life after death, even though I doubt that the different positions in the development of that belief can be ascribed to different groups or circles in the way Delkurt has done.

APOCRYPHAL/DEUTEROCANNONICAL AND OTHER JEWISH WRITINGS

Philo's Flaccus: The First Pogrom: Introduction, Translation and Commentary, by Pieter W. van der Horst. Philo of Alexandria Commentary Series 2. Atlanta: Society of Biblical Literature, 2005. Pp. xii + 277. Paper. $29.95. ISBN 1589831888.

René Bloch, University of Lausanne, Lausanne, Switzerland

Pieter W. van der Horst, dem man schon so manches wichtige Werk zum Judentum in griechisch-römischer Zeit zu verdanken hat, hat eine Ausgabe von Philos *In Flaccum* vorgelegt, die höchsten Ansprüchen genügt: Eine exzellente Übersetzung und ein überaus wertvoller Kommentar erleichtern künftig den Zugang zu diesem „exceptional work" (van der Horsts letztes Wort im Kommentar). Van der Horst verzichtet auf eine neue Edition des griechischen Texts und verweist auf diejenige von Reiter in Cohn-Wendland (1915); dass dieser Ausgabe (bzw. generell dieser Kommentar-Serie zu Philo) kein griechischer Text beiliegt, mag man bedauern, der Autor nimmt aber im Kommentar immer wieder philologische Fragestellungen auf und kommt auch im Laufe der Übersetzung vereinzelt auf textkritische Probleme zu sprechen. Es ist nicht zuletzt die philologische Souveränität van der Horsts, welche diese Ausgabe zu einem Genuss macht: Jede Partikel ist vom Übersetzer sorgfältig abgewogen worden, sprachliche Finessen (z.B. Alliterationen) werden in der englischen Wiedergabe nachgeahmt, um dem Original möglichst gerecht zu werden. Der im Kommentarteil immer wieder beigezogene Vergleich mit früheren Übersetzungen stellt sich zudem als sehr fruchtbar heraus.

Philos Schrift *In Flaccum* ist nicht leicht zu werten. Zwar handelt es sich um eine von Philos sogenannt politischen Schriften, aber vor allem gegen Ende der Abhandlung überwiegen die fiktiven und theologischen Elemente (insbesondere in Bezug auf Flaccus' Reue über seine Taten) derart offensichtlich, dass man dem Text, was die Wahrhaftigkeit des Erzählten anbelangt, mit einer gewissen Distanz begegnen muss. Philos *In Flaccum,* die einzige erhaltene Quelle über die Ereignisse des Jahres 38 n.Chr., ist nicht zuletzt eine Art Theodizee (p. 2), im Rahmen derer der Autor für sich selbst, noch mehr aber wohl für andere Juden, die nach dem Geschehenen den Glauben an Gott verloren hatten (*Legat.* 3), nach Erklärungen sucht. Andererseits hat van der Horst sicher auch recht, wenn er festhält, dass Philon „sich lächerlich gemacht hätte" (12), wenn er seinen Zeitgenossen einen mehrheitlich unhistorischen Bericht über die Geschehnisse des Jahres 38 n.Chr. vorgelegt hätte. Für die Figur des Flaccus aber (sicher weit weniger für die Ereignisse insgesamt) ist dieser Philo-Traktat ein nur eingeschränkt als Geschichtsschreibung zu verwertendes Werk. Entsprechend offen bleibt die Interpretation von Flaccus' Motivationen und Handlungen (in jüngerer Zeit wichtig v.a. Erich S. Gruen, *Diaspora: Jews amidst Greeks and Romans*, 2002, 54–66).

In seiner informativen Einführung (1–53) geht van der Horst zuerst dem Aufbau, Inhalt, dem historischen Kontext der Schrift (mit einem Exkurs über Flaccus: 34–38) sowie, sehr knapp, der Textüberlieferung nach. Die Stoßrichtungen der bisherigen Forschung, von Delauney (1867) bis Gruen (2002), werden kritisch zusammengefasst (38–49). Die Heftigkeit des antijüdischen Pogroms erklärt sich nach van der Horst zu einem nicht geringen Grad durch die v.a. in Ägypten entstandene antijüdische Literatur, die er ausführlich zusammenfasst (25–32). Was letztlich, neben antijüdischen Vorurteilen, das Pogrom auslöste, bleibt eine schwierige Frage: die Nähe der Juden zu Rom, der halb-autonome Status der Juden in Alexandrien, dann der dortige Besuch des jüdischen Königs Agrippa—dies sind wahrscheinliche politische Gründe für den Ausbruch der antijüdischen Gewalt (33).

Man kann Philos *In Flaccum* aus ganz verschiedenen Blickwinkeln lesen: als theologischen Traktat, als historisches Drama, als politisches Pamphlet, als Quelle über einen römischen Präfekten Der Text ist aber oft auch ein wertvoller Beleg in Bezug auf Realia des griechisch-römischen Judentums. Und auch in dieser Hinsicht überzeugt der Kommentar vollends: Der Leser findet wertvolle und stets auf dem neusten Stand der Forschung dargelegte Informationen etwa zur Synagoge (134, 146–47) oder zum Theater in Alexandrien (133). Die klassische Frage, ob die Juden Alexandriens über das Bürgerrecht verfügten, verneint van der Horst (153–54, 236, er folgt dabei v.a. Smallwood und Delia, nicht aber Philo [§172]).

Van der Horsts Kommentar, der erste in englischer Sprache seit demjenigen von Box (H. Box, *Philonis Alexandrini In Flaccum*, London 1939), ist ganz und gar gelungen. Man trifft hier auf einen Kommentator, der alles daran tut, dem Text gerecht zu werden, der im Übrigen aber auch vor Kritik gegenüber dem Autor nicht zurückschreckt (243: „Philo could better have left out this lame §187"). Man ist froh, über diese neue Ausgabe verfügen zu können.

Jewish Literature between the Bible and the Mishnah, by George W. E. Nickelsburg. 2nd edition. Minneapolis: Fortress, 2005. Pp. xxiii + 445 + CD-ROM. Paper. $29.00. ISBN 0800637798.

Kenneth Pomykala, Calvin College, Grand Rapids, Michigan

The literature of early Judaism constitutes a vast, diverse landscape of documents representing different genres, ideas, situations, and movements, along with a host of intersecting pathways between them. Any interpreter of this literature—especially the beginning interpreter—needs a clear, comprehensive, and reasonably detailed map to navigate the complex terrain and the associated network of connections. For a generation such a map was available in the first edition of *Jewish Literature between the Bible and the Mishnah*, published in 1981. Yet as Nickelsburg observes, the last two and a half decades have seen the "geometric increase" of scholarship on early Jewish literature and the publication of the entire Qumran corpus (xi), developments that made a new edition of his handbook necessary. The result is an updated and expanded map that students of Second Temple literature will be grateful to have as they venture out on their own.

Nickelsburg organizes his revised volume along the same lines as the first edition—chronologically (for the most part). Accordingly, in the prologue he sets the historical stage by reviewing the crucial sixth-century B.C.E. events of exile, return, and dispersion. This leads to the subject of his first chapter, "Tales from the Dispersion," where he treats Dan 1–6, additions to Daniel, 1 Esd 3–4, Tobit, and the Epistle of Jeremiah. Here and throughout the volume Nickelsburg follows a similar procedure for each document treated: he offers a fairly thorough summary of its contents, highlighting key ideas and themes; explains matters of literary structure and genre; sets the work within its historical context; deals with major interpretive questions; and observes how the document relates to other Second Temple texts. Moreover, in the copious endnotes for each chapter, Nickelsburg interacts with an impressive array of scholarly works on the literature, many produced in the years since his first edition. Finally, each chapter concludes with a bibliography that lists critical editions, translations, and significant studies for each document considered.

Chapter 2, "Palestine in the Wake of Alexander the Great," begins with a brief historical overview and covers the early Enochic works (1 En. 72–82; 1 En. 1–36) and the Wisdom of Ben Sira. Chapter 4 is devoted to works emanating from the turbulent years of 175–164 B.C.E., that is, from the Hellenistic reform through the Maccabean revolt: the Book of Jubilees, the Testament of Moses, Dan 7–12, and 1 En. 85–95. Chapter 4 considers texts associated with the Hasmoneans and their opponents: Baruch, Judith, 1 and 2 Maccabees, and 1 En. 92–105.

In the next two chapters Nickelsburg departs from the chronological scheme, with chapter 5 dedicated to literature from Qumran and chapter 6 to Jewish texts of Egyptian provenance. Nickelsburg reviews a hefty sample of Qumran literature—both sectarian and nonsectarian, including all the major rules and legal works, several pesharim, liturgical works, a sapiential work, and others. With regard to writings from Egypt, he includes, among others, the Septuagint, Sibylline Oracles 3, the Wisdom of Solomon, and Philo. Then returning to the chronological framework, chapter 7 deals with the Romans and Herodians, treating the Psalms of Solomon, the Testament of Moses revised, 1 En. 37–71, and 4 Maccabees. Chapter 8 turns to the period of the Jewish Revolt (66–70 C.E.) and its aftermath, discussing Pseudo-Philo, responses to the destruction of Jerusalem (4 Ezra, 2 Baruch, Apocalypse of Abraham), and Josephus. In a final chapter, Nickelsburg takes up texts of disputed provenance, such as the Testaments of the Twelve Patriarchs, the Testament of Job, and Joseph and Aseneth.

Nickelsburg explains that he has revised his earlier volume in three ways. First, additional texts are covered: newly included are sections on books from the Apocrypha absent from the first edition, many new Qumran texts, the Septuagint,

Philo, and Josephus. Second, Nickelsburg took account of the scholarship produced in the last twenty-five years, documenting and in some cases revising his interpretations, as well as expanding the bibliography. Third, he omitted his original chapter "The Exposition of Israel's Scriptures," largely replacing it with the final chapter on texts of disputed provenance. A CD-ROM with the complete text of this volume, along with photos and links to other resources, is also included. Beyond these changes, however, this revised volume is significantly longer than the first—partly due to the additional texts but also due to the expanded discussion of documents. Noteworthy in this regard is the increased attention to feminist issues and scholarship as they bear on texts such as Susanna, Judith, and *Joseph and Aseneth*. The resulting volume is therefore more comprehensive in both breadth and depth. On the other hand, given his broader coverage of the literature, I wondered why the revised volume dropped *3 Baruch* from the texts responding to the destruction of Jerusalem in 70 C.E.

With regard to the arrangement of the volume, Nickelsburg retains the chronological format of the original because of his conviction—proper, in my judgment—that the literature is rooted in the historical and cultural setting from which it emerged. This arrangement also allows him to offer brief but helpful surveys of the historical context before discussing the relevant texts. Then again, fitting all the Second Temple literature into a chronological framework is problematic due to the uncertain provenance of many books. Nickelsburg addresses the problem by conceding the difficulty and grouping works of uncertain provenance in his final chapter. Also, however, he removes the Qumran texts from the chapter in the first edition on the Hasmoneans and their opponents and places them in a separate chapter. While this is understandable, since not all the Qumran texts can be assigned to the Hasmonean period or dated at all, for that matter, it does tend to segregate the Qumran texts—especially the nonsectarian and precursor texts—from the broader chronological framework. Nevertheless, Nickelsburg's comments about how specific Qumran texts fit into their historical context compensate for this organizational choice. Similarly, grouping texts from Egyptian Judaism from various periods into one chapter lends itself to isolating them from broader trends in early Judaism. In the end, however, there is no neat solution to the question of arrangement, and Nickelsburg's approach is probably the best one possible, given his basic commitment to historical context.

Finally, let me note some key features typical of Nickelsburg's discussion throughout the volume. First, he regularly cites source material in the Hebrew Bible for the language and ideas found in early Jewish texts, thus illustrating how these texts have both carried on and adapted the biblical tradition. Second, Nickelsburg consistently observes interconnections between different literary works. For example, in his section on the *Genesis Apocryphon,* Nickelsburg concludes by assessing its relationship to ideas found in the Enochic corpus, to *Jubilees,* and to the Qumran community (176–77). As a scholar deeply familiar with the entirety of Second Temple literature, Nickelsburg excels at highlighting similarities and differences between the documents. As a result, individual texts are located within the network of ideas and movements present during the period. Third, Nickelsburg offers judicious interpretations of the texts, gauging the probabilities and possibilities on the basis of textual evidence and scholarly interpretations. Nor is he afraid to concede that he does not know how to decide some questions, as for example in his treatment of *Joseph and Aseneth* (337). Perhaps the only weakness in the volume is the newly added section on Philo. In view of the size of Philo's corpus, Nickelsburg decided to focus on Philo's life and context and to deal only generally with his writings. What he says here is fine, but it forms too sparse of an introduction to Philonic texts. A fuller overview of these texts—or at least of the types of texts—along with several examples would have been helpful.

In the end, however, maybe the most important feature of this revised volume is something it shares with the first: it serves not only as an introduction to the early Jewish writings and their interpretation but as a point of departure for more detailed study and investigation. Nickelsburg explains that this was his intent: "To some extent I intend this as a prolegomenon for the study of the exegetical *details*" (3), and in this he has succeeded. Ultimately, then, not only does Nickelsburg give us an updated and expanded map of the landscape of early Jewish literature; more important, he invites us to come visit.

Fallen Angels and the History of Judaism and Christianity: The Reception of Enochic Literature, by Annette Yoshiko Reed. New York: Cambridge University Press, 2006. Pp. xii + 318. Hardcover. $75.00. ISBN 0521853788.

Siam Bhayro, University of Cambridge, Cambridge, United Kingdom

As the title suggests, the author of this revised doctoral dissertation lacks nothing in ambition. The aim is a comparative analysis of the reception, in various Jewish and Christian traditions, of the "distinctive treatment of the fallen angels as corrupting teachers of humankind" (5) as told in the Enochic narrative of the Book of Watchers (hereafter BW; i.e. *1 En.* 1–36). The author further states that the reception history of this aspect of BW "provides a lens through which to examine broader issues" (2), including the early history of Jewish-Christian relations and ideas concerning the origin of evil.

In order to accomplish this, the author would have to come to terms with both the vast and rapidly expanding array of sources on BW and the not insignificant amount of literature associated with the various subsequent Jewish and Christian corpora in which the Enochic traditions manifest. The former is accomplished in the first two chapters, which deal specifically with BW and its context. The latter is accomplished in the following five chapters, which examine BW traditions in prerabbinic Judaism, rabbinic Judaism, and Christianity, as far as the early Middle Ages. On the whole, and considering the magnitude of the project, the author does very well, managing to produce a good synthesis of the various sources and providing a well-informed and erudite piece of scholarship that is a pleasure to read.

The content of the latter chapters could perhaps have been strengthened in two respects. First of all, on a number of occasions throughout the book Reed mentions the canonicity of *1 Enoch* within the Ethiopian Church, mostly as part of her general argument against sidelining the text as sectarian (e.g., 276). Beyond this, however, very little is made of the reception history of the Enochic traditions within the Ethiopian context, perhaps due to the comparatively small number of secondary sources available on this subject. Still, considering the importance of the Ethiopian tradition to Reed's general argument, this is a significant gap in coverage. R. W. Cowley refers to a number of Ethiopic manuscripts containing commentaries on *1 Enoch* (*Ethiopian Biblical Interpretation* [Cambridge: Cambridge University Press, 1988], 436, 457), and, moving beyond exegesis, there are clear examples of Enochic traditions manifesting in later Ethiopian texts, such as the reference to Noah's face shining (*1 En.* 106:1–5 with the Chronicle of Johannes IV, f. 111vb; for an English translation, see B. Tafla, *A Chronicle of Emperor Yohannes IV [1872–89]* (Wiesbaden: Steiner, 1977], 33). Indeed, Reed's decision to ignore the Ethiopian chronicles is in marked contrast to the attention given to the Byzantine chronicles.

Second, Reed discusses the angelic name Azael in relation to the Aramaic incantation texts (252). With the recent increase in the number of such texts in publication, it is clear that they represent an important archive that cannot be ignored. It is, therefore, a shame that Reed neglects to mention the appearance of Shemihazah in another Aramaic incantation text (J. A. Montgomery, "A Magical Bowl-Text and the Original Script of the Manichaeans," *JAOS* 32 [1912]: 434–38, esp. 435). Considered in the light of Montgomery's comment, "I have found a number of connections between the bowl-texts and Ethiopic angelology" (436–37), Reed's decision not to investigate this corpus further could be significant.

Furthermore, Reed's bibliography on the incantation texts is out of date. This is unfortunate, as the most recently published occurrence of Azael in a bowl text (M163:18) is found in a text that not only concurs more with the Enochic traditions than the examples that she cites (252), but also invokes the Holy Trinity in conjunction with the Lord of hosts (M163:29). This could have proved useful in the context of her discussion on the early relationship between Judaism and Christianity (for M163, see D. Levene, *A Corpus of Magic Bowls* [London: Kegan Paul, 2003], 120–38).

In her analyses of the subsequent corpora, Reed sets herself an almost impossible task, and, obviously, she has had to prioritize in terms of coverage. Perhaps she could have made more of the two areas just highlighted, but she has done a remarkable job all the same.

Regarding the analysis of BW and particularly *1 En.* 6–11, I have three specific comments. First, Reed states, "While describing the proliferation of human wickedness that prompted God *to cleanse the earth with the Flood,* Genesis recounts," followed by a quote from Gen 6:1–4 (5, emphasis added). Of course, the problem here is that, as has already been discussed by Van Ruiten, these verses in Genesis have nothing to do with the following flood story. Indeed, Gen

6:1–4 and 6:5–8:19 are two distinct literary units, and their subsequent association, which makes the actions of the sons of God a wicked act and part of the
rationale for the flood, is a very distinct, but secondary, line of exegesis (J. Van
Ruiten, "The Flood Story in the Book of Jubilees," in *Interpretations of the Flood*
[ed. F. García Martínez and G. P. Luttikhuizen; Leiden: Brill, 1998], 79–81). Furthermore, as has been discussed by the present reviewer, the idea that the flood
is sent to cleanse the earth is also secondary and Enochic (*1 En.* 10:20–22) and
contrary to the biblical narrative (S. Bhayro, *The Shemihazah and Asael Narrative
of 1 Enoch 6–11* [Münster: Ugarit-Verlag, 2005], 243, 258–59).

Second, Reed states that BW "appears to integrate at least five *originally independent* units into the larger narrative framework" (24, emphasis added). Now, it
is true that scholars divide BW into four or five units, but the use of the phrase
"originally independent" troubles me. For instance, the first unit of BW is the
introduction (*1 En.* 1–5), which was clearly composed as an introduction for BW
(see G. W. E. Nickelsburg, *1 Enoch 1* [Minneapolis: Fortress, 2001], 132). Furthermore, *1 En.* 12–16 was composed with reference to *1 En.* 6–11, *1 En.* 17–19
developed a theme raised in *1 En.* 12–16, and *1 En.* 20–36 expanded yet again on
the section it follows (Nickelsburg, *1 Enoch 1*, 25, 229–30, 290, etc.; Reed herself
clearly is aware of this [e.g., 26]). In other words, can any of these units truly be
said to have been "originally independent"?

Finally, Reed's treatment of the chapter divisions in *1 En.* 6–11 also causes
concern. The wider context is the recognition that *1 En.* 6–11 is a composite narrative with several strata. Rather than try to unravel the various strands, Reed
chooses to consider the narrative as it now stands, to "discern an attempt to interweave the various strands into a meaningful whole through the imposition of a
literary structure, however loose" (29). This, in itself, is a good idea, but it should
not be done at the exclusion of previous attempts to unravel the strands. Thus,
in describing what she regards as "three descriptions of the Watchers' transgressions, each with a different focus" (27), she states that the first is found in *1 En.*
6–7, the second in *1 En.* 8, and the third in *1 En.* 9, each concluding with an
account of violence followed by the cry of the oppressed (*1 En.* 7:4–6; 8:4; 9:9–10,
respectively). This approach to the chapter divisions then continues through the
author's analysis (30–34).

The problem here is that most analyses of this passage have rightly suggested,
for example, that the cry of the earth in *1 En.* 7:6 leads straight into the cry of
humankind in *1 En.* 8:4, with the intervening material being an obvious insertion
[e.g., Nickelsburg, *1 Enoch 1*, 165]. In discussing her "three descriptions," Reed
neglects the issue of how and why one strand (to continue her very useful metaphor) was effectively cut. In other words, any attempt to draw conclusions from
how a text has been interwoven, which ignores the composition of the various
strands, is extremely problematic. Reed's apparent willingness to do this, coupled
with a result that fits in so conveniently with the chapter divisions, comes across
as too simplistic.

To be fair, Reed does explain very clearly her reasons for doing this (26–

27), including an important discussion of the shortcomings of source-critical and form-critical analyses. At this point, however, her criticism that previous scholars, by performing such analyses, "tacitly dismiss the redacted product as a muddled combination and conflation of originally coherent 'legends'" (26) does seem rather harsh on pretty much every other scholar who has published in this field and perhaps betrays an attempt to justify her own neglect of this approach, as well as her call "to move beyond questions about the origins of its composite parts, to consider also the purpose and effect of their present arrangement" (27). The present reviewer doubts whether one can truly appreciate the purpose and effect of their present arrangement without first understanding how they were thus arranged. This is something I attempted to do in my own monograph (Bhayro, *The Shemihazah and Asael Narrative of 1 Enoch 6–11*), and it is perhaps unfortunate, for both the author and the present reviewer, that our books appeared simultaneously.

Despite these very finite reservations, this is a worthwhile book, and there is much to be gained from Reed's synthesis. As stated above, this book lacks nothing in ambition. For the most part, it succeeds and is a most welcome addition to Enochic scholarship

Concordance du Siracide: Grec II et Sacra Parallela, by Jean-Marie Auwers with Églantine Proksch-Strajtmann. Cahiers de la Revue Biblique 58. Paris: Gabalda, 2005. Pp. 92. Paper. €25.00. ISBN 285021159x.

Jeremy Corley, Ushaw College, Durham, United Kingdom

This volume makes a contribution to research into the complex textual situation of the apocryphal/deuterocanonical book of Sirach. Among Second Temple Jewish writings, the textual problems for the Wisdom of Ben Sira are notoriously complex. Although the earliest surviving Hebrew manuscript (the Masada scroll, with much of 39:27–44:17) was copied about a century after the work's composition, the six medieval Hebrew manuscripts from the Cairo Genizah contain many corruptions and additions. Similarly, whereas the basic text of the grandson's Greek translation is preserved in the major uncial manuscripts (Sinaiticus, Vaticanus, and Alexandrinus), later Sirach manuscripts contain an amplified text form known as Greek II. Some of the additions in Greek II arose as pious glosses, such as 20:32: "Better unwearied patience in seeking the Lord than being a masterless charioteer of one's own life" (all translations my own). By way of contrast, other Greek II verses may in fact represent Ben Sira's original thought, such as 1:21: "The fear of the Lord drives away sins, and where it remains, it will turn away all anger."

The text of Greek II, previously confined to the critical apparatus in Alfred Rahlfs's *Septuaginta* (Stuttgart: Deutsche Bibelgesellschaft, 1979), appears in smaller type within the main text of the critical edition of Sirach edited by Joseph Ziegler, *Sapientia Iesu Filii Sirach* (Septuaginta 12/2; Göttingen: Vandenhoeck &

Ruprecht, 1965). Up until now, however, no concordance has taken full notice of the vocabulary of Greek II, since only thirteen cola (or stichoi) from ten verses were listed in Edwin Hatch and Henry A. Redpath, *A Concordance to the Septuagint and the Other Greek Versions of the Old Testament (Including the Apocryphal Books)* (2 vols.; Oxford: Clarendon, 1897). The situation was partly remedied in Hatch and Redpath's 1906 *Supplement,* which included thirty-four cola from twenty-one verses of Greek II, as Auwers and Proksch-Strajtmann note (9).

To remedy this omission properly, the volume under review provides a full concordance to the extra 135 cola in Ziegler's Greek text, plus twenty-eight cola attributed to Sirach in the *Sacra Parallela* of John Damascene. As a result, this concordance lists 456 words, of which (as noted here, 87–88) thirty-two are unique to Sirach within the LXX and twenty-six are unmentioned in Hatch and Redpath's 1906 *Supplement.* Of the words listed in the concordance, only two are human names, Adam (16:16b, according to a conjectural emendation) and Pharaoh (16:15a). The concordance lists in italics important Greek variants, especially from the Origenic and Lucianic witnesses. Where a corresponding Hebrew text, often dubbed Hebrew II, appears in the Cairo Genizah manuscripts (e.g., 11:15–16; 16:15–16), the concordance mentions the relevant Hebrew word, while a helpful Hebrew-Greek index appears in an appendix (89–92). These Hebrew equivalents are taken from the text edition by Pancratius C. Beentjes, *The Book of Ben Sira in Hebrew* (VTSup 68; Leiden: Brill, 1997), now available in paperback from the Society of Biblical Literature.

For the twenty-eight Greek cola of the *Sacra Parallela* of John Damascene (here marked *SP*), the concordance relies on the text presented in Otto Wahl, *Der Sirach-Text der Sacra Parallela* (FB 16; Würzburg: Echter, 1974). Of these twenty-eight cola, eighteen are identified as glosses on Sirach passages (including fifteen attested in the Latin tradition), while ten are unidentified in Sirach (see editors' list, 10–11). These ten "unidentified citations" are less clearly connected with the book of Sirach and may derive from other sources; for instance, saying 5 ("Idleness is the mother of famine and the beginning of thieving") is based on Tob 4:13. Indeed, some of these aphorisms seem to derive from Greek secular writings. Saying 3 ("Continual dripping hollows out rock") resembles an aphorism already found in fifth-century B.C.E. sources (Choerilus 10; Acusilaus 4J), while different versions of this proverb appear in later Greco-Roman authors (Plutarch, *Lib. ed.* 4.2D; Lucretius 1.314; Ovid, *Ars* 1.476; Seneca, *Nat.* 4B.3.4).

In the volume's introduction, the editors outline previous research into the text of Greek II. In particular, they note the index of Greek II vocabulary presented as an appendix in Christian Wagner, *Die Septuaginta-Hapaxlegomena im Buch Jesus Sirach* (BZAW 282; Berlin: de Gruyter, 1999), 413–16. Wagner's monograph discusses a total of 273 septuagintal *hapax legomena*: eighteen from the Greek prologue; 232 from Greek I; twenty-seven from Greek II. Included in his work (328–48) is a discussion of twenty-seven septuagintal *hapax legomena* from Greek II (= twenty-three new words plus four words found also in Greek I). Indeed, Wagner (331) notes a gloss not in the concordance, since Ziegler's apparatus lists a variant to 23:4a: "O Almighty Lord of your eternally begotten creation." This gloss may be of some interest, since it employs two words found elsewhere only once in Greek II, namely, "almighty" (*pantokratōr*, 24:24c) and "eternally begotten" (*aeigenēs*, 24:18d).

From the concordance the reader can gain an interesting perspective on the theological tendencies of Greek II. For instance, belief in the afterlife (probably absent from Ben Sira's original Hebrew text) is attested by the occurrence of "immortality" (*athanasia*) in 19:19b: "Those doing what pleases him [= the Lord] will enjoy the fruits of the tree of immortality." The doctrine of the afterlife may also be implied in 2:9c: "For his recompense is an everlasting gift with joy." The emphasis on the fear of the Lord, elaborated from Greek I, appears in an aphorism occurring twice in Greek II, although with a different word order (10:21a; 19:18a): "The fear of the Lord is the beginning of acceptance [by him]." Elsewhere in Greek II the phrase "fear of the Lord" appears three times (1:12c; 21a; 25:12a), while the term "life" (*zōē*) appears six times (plus two variants). Religious exhortations also characterize Greek II, as in 13:14bc: "In all your life love the Lord, and invoke him for your salvation." For further discussion of the special vocabulary of Greek II, see Jean-Marie Auwers, "L'apport du texte long du Siracide au lexique du grec biblique," in *Interpreting Translation: Studies on the LXX and Ezekiel in Honour of Johan Lust* (ed. Florentino García Martínez and Marc Vervenne; BETL 192; Leuven: Peeters, 2005), 33–44.

All in all, this volume (entirely in Greek and French) will be a valuable reference work for advanced students of the Septuagint (especially Sirach) and of patristic lexicography. It will serve as a useful supplement to Hatch and Redpath's *Concordance to the Septuagint.* Such detailed work will surely be a helpful tool for scholars attempting to unravel the origin of the Greek II textual tradition of the book of Sirach.

SEPTUAGINT

Les deux visages d'Élie: Texte massorétique et Septante dans l'histoire la plus ancienne du texte de 1 Rois 17–18, by Philippe Hugo. Orbis Biblicus et Orientalis 217. Fribourg: Academic; Göttingen: Vandenhoeck & Ruprecht, 2006. Pp. xxii + 389. Cloth. €84.00. ISBN 3525530137.

Graeme Auld, University of Edinburgh, Edinburgh, Scotland

This closely argued yet clearly presented monograph is a lightly revised version of a doctoral dissertation supervised by Adrian Schenker and presented in Fribourg in 2005. With its substantial statement of method and its close attention to a manageable sample of connected text, it furnishes two sorts of support for Professor Schenker's own briefer overview of the earliest textual history of the books of Kings published in 2004 (*Älteste Textgeschichte der Königsbücher: Die hebräische Vorlage der ursprüngliche Septuaginta als älteste Textform der Königs-*

bücher, OBO 199). Hugo's substantial opening chapter (5–125), some third of the whole text, reviews the place of LXX in the study of the history of the text of Kings against a broad background and concludes by proposing six methodological criteria for a comparison of MT and LXX in Kings. The following major discussions apply these criteria to Elijah's raising of the child; details relating to the portrait of Elijah earlier in 1 Kgs 17; the sacrifice on Mount Carmel and the issue of Ahab and idolatry in 1 Kgs 18; and the schema command/execution in twenty-three portions of the Elijah cycle. General conclusions are quickly drawn (323–30): in a few trifling cases, LXX is secondary, but overall MT, with its view of Elijah and the theology of prophetism, with its portrait of Ahab, with its characterization of idolatry, and with its additional characteristics of "Deuteronomistic" type, represents a second edition of the Hebrew text underlying LXX. Two confirmatory appendices handle the prophetic condemnation of Ahab and the story of Naboth's vineyard in MT and LXX of 1 Kgs 20–21.

The Greek Bible has assured status as the principal witness to the text of the Old Testament alongside the Hebrew, but its attestation is much more varied than that of MT. Hugo reviews this diversity and the reasons for it, from early Jewish revisions to Christian recensions. He gives his own account of the more general hypotheses associated with de Lagarde, Barthélemy, Cross, Talmon, and Tov, before concentrating on the books of Reigns or Kingdoms. Here he briefly introduces the late-nineteenth-century giants: Wellhausen, Field, Ceriani, Vercellone, Driver, Silberstein, and Mez. Closer attention is paid to Rahlfs's study of Lucian's recension (LXXL) of the books of Kings (1911) and to Thackeray's delimitation of five sections in "The Greek Translation of the Four Books of Kings" (*JTS* 8 [1907]); then Hugo proceeds to explore the significance of the Qumran scrolls. Already the preliminary evaluation of 4QSama-b-c by Cross in the 1950s proved as important for our assessment of LXX as for the Qumran fragments themselves.

The fact that, where OG and MT diverge, the texts found close to the Dead Sea share more readings with the best witnesses to the Old Greek than with the Masoretic Text served to confirm that OG had rendered a text different from proto-MT. Text-critical research on Samuel and Kings in the last half-century has sought on that basis to clarify the history and interrelationships of the several Greek witnesses. Among these, LXXB and LXXL are the privileged witnesses to the early LXX of Kingdoms, LXXB in sections α, ββ, and γγ, and LXXL in sections βγ and γδ of 1–4 Kingdoms, as identified by Barthélemy, following Mez, Rahlfs, and Thackeray.

Two continuing issues bring the agenda up to date. The Greek witness to an older Hebrew, however privileged, was also a translation, and that makes it crucial to evaluate the literalness of that rendering. Yet strictly the issue of literalness is relevant only at the level of the word or short phrase. In many biblical books, including Samuel-Kings or Kingdoms, the divergences are not restricted to matters of wording: larger units of text are present in this witness but absent in that, or appear in different positions. And this has to subvert the traditional operational priority of textual criticism over literary criticism. If in such books the Hebrew text underlying OG was likely to have been more original than proto-MT, then the principal goals of textual criticism could no longer be limited to improving MT or reconstituting the text underlying MT. The majority of twentieth-century commentaries on Kings have ignored the implications of the positive evaluation in the nineteenth century by Thenius and Wellhausen of the testimony of LXX and the Qumran discoveries in the mid-twentieth century alike. Equally, several recent detailed studies of 3 Kgdms 2–11 and 17–18 (1 Kgs 2–11; 17–18) have wholly prescinded from detailed comparison with MT. Where detailed comparative studies have been undertaken by major scholars, some of these (Wevers, Gooding, van Keulen, Talshir) have largely or wholly given the priority to MT and found LXX "midrashic." Others (Bogaert, Shenkel, Trebolle Barrera, Schenker) have found the LXX *Vorlage* (supported by the Old Latin) to be witness to the oldest Hebrew text. The third option (MT and LXX *Vorlage* as two secondary and parallel revisions) he finds followed by Bösenecker, Stipp, Polak, and Auld (somewhat to the surprise of this reader!). Hugo sensibly finds the third option the least likely as a global account, although possibly helpful for the later stages of textual transmission, and sets out to put the seniority of the *Vorlage* of the LXX to the test.

His first major worked example concerns the reviving of the widow's child (1 Kgs 17:17–24), where there are three significant differences between MT and LXX: the terms in which Elijah calls out to Yahweh (20); what he does to the child (21); and whether divine response (22) is only suggested (LXX) or fully stated (MT). To refocus the discourse away from divine to prophetic action, Hugo argues that the editor responsible for the OG version would have had to suppress the explicit statement that Yahweh heard the voice of his prophet and replace (clear) insufflation with (opaque) measuring oneself over. Better the conclusion that MT has insisted that the action was divine, with prophetic action become intercession. MT is more like Ezek 37 than at first apparent (155).

The second major example concerns the sacrifice on Carmel. Thiel and Schenker had already studied 18:21–40 in similar fashion but with diametrically opposed results (214). The reader of LXX deduces that only one altar was used and then reused by Elijah. MT was concerned to protect Elijah from any suggestion of either reusing an altar of Baal or building a fresh altar outside Jerusalem and implies that what Elijah repairs is a former Yahweh-altar. Hugo notes (242) that the mention of the offering of the sacrifice in verse 36 (MT) echoes verse 29 (MT and LXX). Far from being a narrative incoherence, this repeated temporal indication encases the section that relates the healing/restoration of the altar (vv. 30–35). Hugo understands from this *inclusio* that, for MT, the central scene of the pericope unfolds wholly during the liturgy of the offering of the evening sacrifice at the temple of Jerusalem. The perfect contemporaneity of the restoration of the altar by Elijah, then of his sacrifice, with the liturgy of the temple is a supplementary argument for manifesting that these actions are not situated in opposition to the Deuteronomic commandment of cultic centralization. MT thus manifests the unity of a profound theological conception. Well and good, perhaps. But this phrase for the celebration of the evening offering appears unique to these two verses, and there is no explicit mention of Jerusalem. Hugo offers no defense of his suggestion that the terminology used was uniquely Jerusalemite.

It would have been interesting to see fuller comment on the reading mechanism involved in some of the cases where the Hebrew text apparently underlying OG had looked very similar or was in fact identical to the consonants of MT. At 18:4, "exterminate" in MT (הכרית) is stronger in sense than "strike down" in LXX (<הכות), yet graphically similar. Ahab's tears (18:45, OG) probably attest ויבך rather than וירכב (MT). Ahab weeping had proved open to different interpretations: the Old Latin specified that is was "for joy" that he had wept. His riding (MT) is more logical, but does that imply more original? Then חרמי in איש חרמי (20:42) is read adjectivally in OG but as noun with suffix in MT. How do what Hugo calls "authentic variant" and what we might call expected reading relate? Had the different readings contributed to the larger-scale divergences or been influenced by them?

As Hugo reports, the case for the greater antiquity of the proto-Masoretic text of Kings is advanced in commentary after commentary—and largely because most textual divergences, when viewed in and for themselves, do remain open to different explanations, and MT continues to receive the benefit of the doubt. The pioneering work of Thenius and Wellhausen has not been followed up, and the few monographs on the Septuagint of these books have concentrated on synchronic readings of some chapters rather than comparative evaluations. Schenker and Trebolle have been rather isolated voices. At the very least, Hugo deserves appreciation for putting the other side of the case—not in any selective way but by means of point-by-point comparison of MT and OG throughout two chapters of Kings. And to this reader it appears that he has in fact mounted a compelling defense of two propositions. One is the priority of the Hebrew *Vorlage* of OG over MT in many of the cases where they differ. The other is that most of these new readings in MT are not individual, separate adjustments to the older text: taken together, they represent nothing less than a fresh edition of the books of Kings. What we need now is a thorough review of theories of the development of the books of Kings based not on MT but on the Hebrew *Vorlage* of OG.

HEBREW BIBLE/OLD TESTAMENT THEOLOGY

Encounters with Biblical Theology, by John J. Collins. Minneapolis: Fortress, 2005. Pp. ix + 243. Paper. $22.00. ISBN 0800637690.

James A. Sanders, Ancient Biblical Manuscript Center, Claremont, California

John Collins has become one of the most interesting and trustworthy observers of the current field of pre-Christian biblical studies. (See his more recent *The Bible since Babel*, 2006, for a critique of the various subdisciplines today in critical study of the Bible.) Here he offers fifteen studies about what has been happening (and not happening) in the area of biblical theology. Each had been published earlier, most during the last quarter of the last century, five more recently. An Irish Catholic with no personal investment in defending any particular view of "Scripture" (as Catholics prefer to call the Christian double-Testament Bible, but without the "sole authority" Protestants invest in it), Collins is an astute observer of serious efforts to make theological sense of the Bible. He has critiqued such efforts without attempting himself to do a biblical theology.

"If ... everyone has a power-seeking agenda (the thesis of Stanley Fish in *The Trouble with Principle,* 1999), then it is better to have these agendas out in the open" (37). This Collins attempts as well as anyone in the field today. "Biblical theology" at the mid-twentieth century was an effort to base a generally accepted theology of the Bible on the work of biblical criticism. The effort by and large failed, as heralded by Brevard Childs's *Biblical Theology in Crisis* (1970). Childs cited, among other things, the format of *The Interpreter's Bible* (1951–57) as an indication of its failure, with its commentary bifurcated into "exegesis" and "exposition" of each passage, one rarely relating to the other. Biblical criticism as an Enlightenment method of historical/literary study of the Bible has created an arena for conversation and dialogue across the spectrum of the individual scholars' personal faith commitments but has failed to provide a firm base for a generally accepted biblical theology.

The Society of Biblical Literature (SBL) was founded under the leadership of Prof. Philip Schaff of Union Seminary in New York in 1880 to sponsor and organize critical study of the Bible and soon attracted Protestant scholars of the Bible of differing faith stances; some Jewish scholars later joined the Society, along with a few adventurous Catholic students of philology and archaeology of the Bible. It attracted anyone who was committed, for the conversations, not to a faith position but to open, critical study of the histories of the formation and transmission of the text of the various parts of the Bible. As the modernist-fundamentalist controversies of the latter part of the nineteenth century subsided, the SBL attracted increasing numbers of those who subscribed to critical study of Scripture no matter how they spent their weekends.

By the end of the Scopes Trial in Dayton, Tennessee, in 1925, most seminaries of most denominations included critical study of the Bible in their curricula, including the Presbyterian denomination that had in 1893 condemned a Union scholar as a heretic for teaching the Bible by the historical-critical method instead of through the prism of the Westminster Confession. Then when Pope Pius XII promulgated the *Divino Afflante Spiritu* encyclical in 1943, Catholic scholars were free to study Scripture critically without restraint and joined the SBL freely, some eventually becoming officers of the Society. The Catholic Biblical Association (CBA) was founded in 1936 in anticipation of the *Divino* but "in a context of faith." Actually, the SBL and the CBA are now in essence parallel groups, with the CBA open to non-Catholic membership, so that the "context of faith" is clearly subordinate to critical study of the Bible. (The present writer, a member of both societies, was among a few non-Catholics invited to participate in a symposium held in the Vatican in 1999 sponsored by the Holy Office on "The Bible in the Church" and the only one invited to read a paper; see *L'interpretazione della bibbia nella chiesa,* Libreria Editrice Vaticana [2001], 121–43)

When one steps into such gatherings, especially the SBL, one is expected to set aside his or her faith commitment and to dialogue on the basis of critical study of the Bible only. The minutes and records of the SBL meetings in the 1890s offer not a hint of the modernist-fundamentalist controversies raging outside the meetings but inside Union Seminary itself, where they were held (see Ernest Saunders's *Searching the Scriptures: A History of the Society of Biblical Literature, 1880-1980* [1983]; and see my "The Bible at Union: 1835 to the Present," *Union Seminary Quarterly Review* 52/3–4 [1998]: 123–30). When, as late as 2004, a resolution was circulated within the SBL that in essence criticized politicized "faith-based" stances of the current federal government, 44 percent, nearly half, of the membership rejected it as irrelevant to the business of the Society, and it was dropped. Clearly, the Society still cherishes its commitment to critical study of Scripture as well as its own "irrelevance" to current theological and political issues.

The issue here is whether biblical theology in any guise can be done solely on the basis of biblical criticism. The answer would be yes, if one deals simply with what the texts "meant" in terms of ancient beliefs and belief systems, but probably no, if one insists on it being relevant to life today, that is, what it "means." The former would, however, be "a history of religions" treatise and not "a biblical theology." "Theological language is an integral part of the biblical material and should not be simply bypassed"(23), but while it must be dealt with in a history of religions approach, doing so is, nonetheless, not necessarily part of "a biblical theology." Even the text critic knows that God language in certain passages may determine the critically most responsible text to establish. If one dealt only with what the texts meant, there would be "theologies" to treat that are sometimes in conflict, but this would indeed be a history of religions approach. Collins's conclusion about whether a critical biblical theology is even possible he sums up thus: "It is my thesis that there is a legitimate enterprise that goes beyond the simple description of what was thought and believed..., while stopping short of the projection of faith into facts" (23). With this the reviewer is in hearty agreement (as Collins notes on 72), but I would go further to assert that the biblical exegete has an obligation to make his or her critical findings accessible to lay readers for whom they would not otherwise be available.

After treating some recent efforts at doing biblical theology Collins groups the fifteen studies under four headings: those that treat of theoretical issues involved in the enterprise; topics in the Pentateuch (e.g., the binding of Isaac, the exodus; 47–88); wisdom and biblical theology (wisdom was essentially ignored in the "biblical theology movement"; 91–126); wisdom and apocalyptic literature (129–66); and Christian adaptations of Jewish traditions (specifically, the concepts of messiah and of monotheism; 169–89).

Brevard Childs opted for the faith horn of the dilemma by taking an explicitly confessional starting point for his efforts to read the Bible "in canonical context." The result has been a construct based on the extrinsic concept of "canon" imposed from without (25). Using that construct, Childs has been quite successful in keeping a Reformed theology of the Word alive into the beginning of the twenty-first century. Norman Gottwald avoided Childs's "mystification of the text" by a rigorous sociological approach, which guards against the disinterest of secular critics, who tend to bracket the theological dimension of the biblical text. Walter Brueggemann has essentially avoided it by applying his teacher James Muilenburg's "rhetorical criticism" to the task, which becomes a testimony of many, even contradictory, facets to belief in Yahweh. Jon Levinson, who objects to any kind of biblical theology based on historical criticism, nonetheless admires Childs's confessional approach, although he cannot subscribe to it. Levinson feels that criticism, which provides a common base for dialogue on the historical and philological levels, cannot nonetheless provide common ground for a biblical theology.

Collins, in a particularly perceptive study of the similarities and distinctions between biblical theology and the history of religions approaches, treats the widespread influence of Gerhard von Rad's view of the centrality of early recitals (which the latter first called creeds) of the Mosaic/exodus and Davidic/royal covenants in the Torah and the Prophets. Collins notes that von Rad's was a largely history of religions approach in the guise of biblical theology. Collins counters Childs's exclusively confessional approach (which has the merit of being quite clear about which horn of the dilemma he chooses), saying that in combination with a sociohistorical perspective the ongoing quest for a "biblical theology" can be fruitful, if not claimed as the only approach. It is at this point that Collins shows appreciation for what my students and I have been doing over the years in focusing on canon as function—the phenomenon of repetition/recitation of certain central traditions, like that of the exodus but others as well, in ever-changing sociohistorical contexts—and the use of comparative midrash and the "hermeneutic triangle" to discern how the multivalency of a tradition worked, in later biblical and nonbiblical works, well into rabbinic and Christian literature.[1]

In a daring treatise on "the politics of biblical interpretation," Collins treats the uses and abuses of the basic biblical narrative to support modern political stances. He notes that William F. Albright, the great archaeologist and philologist of the early part of the last century, took the biblical story as "a master narrative" and compared it to the American master narrative. The biblical story put "the

---

1. In rebuttal he rightly shows how James Barr has misunderstood my interest in canon, which is sharply different from that of Childs (27, 31, 32, 72–74, 79). (Collins, incidentally, seems to fail to note the importance of the recital of the exodus traditions in 1 Sam 12:6–8 and its important function in the passage that marked the fateful transition to monarchy in Israel [73–76].)

coming of Christianity as the climax of antiquity and the rise of (biblical) Israel as an essential step toward that goal." In so doing Albright noted that "a people of markedly inferior type would vanish before a people of superior potentialities since there is a point beyond which racial mixture cannot go without disaster" (39). The American master narrative almost obliterated Native Americans in this country and helped create the racism that rallied even nonslaveholders to the Southern cause, first of slavery and then of post-emancipation segregation and repression. Albright, with his master narrative, increasingly became a supporter of Zionism. His was an organismic view of history in which evolutionary providence was on the side of the Jews; it was a goal-oriented view of history (38–49).

Collins then treats three theories advanced in the wake of Albright's stance: Norman Gottwald's, Israel Finkelstein's, and Keith Whitelam's. Gottwald's reconstruction of the history of Israel was part and parcel of the liberationist movements of the third quarter of the twentieth century, for which he saw Israel's story as model; in doing so, Gottwald never questioned Israel's right to the land nor acknowledged modern Palestinians' claims. While Finkelstein has seen no hard evidence of a foreign (Israelite) culture intruding on that of the Canaanites in the "settlement" period, he nonetheless used his findings to support Israel's claim to the land. Whitelam has been the clearest in questioning Albright's use of a biblical master narrative to make modern political decisions, but Collins notes that Whitelam has done nothing himself to offer a Palestinian history of the area. Nor has anyone, but it is doubtful that any attempt to do so would meet with anything but disdain from modern Jews or Christians in the West.

Now that we are in a more or less postmodern period one wonders if objective historical scholarship is even possible. Collins holds out the possibility that some measure of objectivity is possible if we are willing to recognize and acknowledge data that do not fit ideological presuppositions. When there is lack of sufficient evidence, he points out, even widely accepted theories eventually fall of their own weight, like Albright's and Gottwald's. Progress becomes possible when new data are made available. Collins concludes by noting that truth demands listening to "voices from the margins, to the Others of history who appear only as foil" in master narratives (44).[2] It may be that hearing those voices can come only from engaging in dialogue while doing criticism, and criticism must always be in revision and correction (43).[3]

---

2. Listening to the foils and the "others" in biblical narratives has been a major component of this writer's hermeneutic of biblical narratives as a whole. See, e.g., Sanders, *God Has a Story Too* (Fortress, 1979), especially "The New History: Joseph Our Brother" (41–56), in which the Joseph story is retold from the viewpoint of the brothers, and "What Happened at Nazareth?" in which Luke 4:16–30 is reread from the viewpoint of the Nazareth congregation (67–79).

3. See my proposal in "The Impact of the Judaean Desert Scrolls on Biblical Studies: Scripture in the First Century," in *The Hebrew Bible and Qumran* (ed. J. H. Charlesworth; BIBAL, 2000), 29–42, esp. 42. It is necessary to remember that the observer is a part of the observed in human endeavor, and the most effective way to make progress in the quest for truth is through

This is one of the more poignant of Collins's observations: the very nature of criticism is its constant need for revision and correction. And yet each generation or school of thought wants to think it has found enduring solutions to the problems addressed. Even postmodernists seem to think they have found either the way or the wall of "reality." When and if humans arrive at a measure of humility in their quests, the fruits of criticism may indeed become the steps needed to progress to the goals the Bible sets, especially the monotheism that would at least prevent demonizing the "others" in any age.

Collins's treatment of wisdom in the Bible is insightful for the whole task of biblical study. "The task of modern exegesis may fairly be described as that of showing the relevance of the ancient biblical material to the universal, contemporary human experience" (104). That task embraces all the biblical material, not just wisdom. However, the wisdom tradition may be of particular interest to the exegete insofar as it provides an explicit precedent for the correlation of revelation and experience within the biblical corpus. Collins claims that wisdom in the Bible provides a base for natural theology. He offers four theses by which to express the significance of wisdom in the theological enterprise: wisdom is an integral part of the Bible; it articulates the religious dimension of universal human experience; it attempts (particularly in the later literature) to relate that experience to Israel's specific traditions; and elements of natural theology can be found within the wisdom the Bible espouses (93). Wisdom teaches and shows the limits of human experience, indeed human finitude. But it also points to a kind of cosmic order, and from this arose attempts at correlating wisdom to Israel's specifically apocalyptic traditions.

Collins, however, objects to the observation some have made of the influence of wisdom thinking on the prophets. In this he follows James Crenshaw's critique of the work, for example, of Samuel Terrien in this regard (103). However, wisdom vocabulary and rhetoric are clearly discernible in Amos's oracles, and when one asks where the prophet got his subversive hermeneutic, turning the exodus story on its head by insisting that, while Yahweh was the God of Israel's story he was also the God of the stories of Israel's enemies (Amos 9:7), wisdom can supply the answer. According to Amos, Yahweh was the judge of Israel and of all her neighbors (1:3–3:2). Where better might Amos have learned the "blasphemy" with which he was charged than from the wisdom traditions in the town of Tekoa that produced the likes of the wise woman of Tekoa (2 Sam 14)? Whence did Amos, in the middle of the eighth-century B.C.E., perceive such

---

"dialogue between differing confessional and professional points of view and between differing hermeneutics addressing the same issues. Critique of one position by another should have as its purpose not to demolish the other, but to correct and strengthen it for the sake of dialogue, the kind of dialogue that is now essential more than ever before to the success of the human enterprise. We need each other" (42). See also Sanders, "Lecture canonique," in *Guide des nouvelles lectures de la Bible* (ed. Andre Lacocque; Paris, Bayard, 2005), 67–93.

an international dimension to Israel's national deity? Amos in effect challenged the official master narrative by denying the nationalist exclusivity of the story. Amos need not have presented an integrated view of how to combine wisdom and prophecy in order to have learned, even as a child, the essential element of wisdom—its international and common-human dimension—from the same circles in Tekoa as Joab's co-conspirator.

The tension that Collins observes in the Bible between universalism and particularism is that they rest on quite different presuppositions and "can never be fully reconciled" (126). I am not sure. Where did the monotheizing dimension so poignantly shown in the canonical process come from? The prophetic insistence on Yahweh being Israel's judge as well as her redeemer and sustainer, which became an integral part eventually of the biblical story but which was resisted until utter calamity had to be explained in the exile, probably came from the wisdom traditions that developed parallel to the national traditions. Reconciling "different presuppositions" would not be a hindrance when it became increasingly important to see Yahweh as considerably more than the early national traditions allowed. The latter alone did not provide the explanation necessary when disaster occurred, but the prophets did provide the perspective needed—the reason canonically speaking the great prophets became an integral part of the larger Torah story. But where did they get the perspective? Undoubtedly from those who thought outside the box of the national-identity traditions, seeing God as creator of all as well as Israel's deity.

To make such observations does not eliminate the differences between the universalism of wisdom and the particularism of the "master narrative." The Bible itself, however, provides the frame for the dialogue that exists between them. Have modern students of the Bible learned what Amos apparently learned before he preached at Bethel? Not all, as evidenced in some recent very polytheistic "Christian" denunciations of Allah! The monotheizing process that the Bible launched is clearly not yet complete! But the Bible above all else is a dialogical literature, with many points of view about God and most all else, which also provides a kind of model for the ever-changing contours of criticism itself.[4]

Collins in this collection of essays has pulled together some of his most trenchant studies of efforts made in the last century toward biblical theology. It is a felicitous voice here at the beginning of this century, urging sanity and a measure of humility in efforts to make current sense of what these ancient texts were all about and why we still bother to probe into what they might mean for us today. As new generations come along with their fresh approaches and methods, Collins's voice can help to guide new efforts to seek viable ways to bring the biblical past into the present in ever-changing contemporary and responsible terms.

---

4. See my *Torah and Canon* (2nd ed.; Eugene Ore.: Cascade, 2005), 136–41.

Inspiration and Incarnation: Evangelicals and the Problem of the Old Testament, by Peter Enns. Grand Rapids: Baker, 2005. Pp. 197. Paper. $17.99. ISBN 0801027306.

Joel B. Green, Asbury Theological Seminary, Wilmore, Kentucky

While teaching in Berkeley, California, I periodically witnessed sometimes debilitating social and religious crises among our new students. Our seminary was located south of the campus of the University of California, Berkeley, and diagonally across from Peoples' Park, infamous for its role in the heyday of the free speech movement of the late 1960s and 1970s, more recently the center of the homeless population of North Alameda County. A number of our students came from racially homogeneous enclaves in small towns, areas of social and political conservativism. If for no other reason than this tectonic shift of context, the first weeks of the seminary experience could be stressful as a host of taken-for-granteds were called into question and theological categories were reshaped. Because Enns, a professor at Westminster Theological Seminary, concerns himself here with similar crises of dislocation, memories of those days came to me as I read this book. In this case, however, the impetus comes not from physical relocation but from the face-off of traditional evangelical views of Scripture and critical study of the Old Testament. Claiming that the theological implications for evangelicals of critical biblical studies have received little attention, Enns sets out "(1) to bring together a variety of data that biblical scholars work with every day for readers who do not have firsthand familiarity with these data and (2) to look at these data with a clear view toward discussing their implications for an evangelical doctrine of Scripture" (9).

The "problem of the Old Testament" to which Enns addresses himself is actually threefold: (1) the uniqueness of the Old Testament, given its many parallels among Israel's ancient neighbors; (2) the integrity of the Old Testament's message, given its self-evident theological diversity; and (3) the interpretive challenges presented by the use of the Old Testament by New Testament writers, who seem little concerned with issues of "context" so central to biblical studies in the past three centuries. Obviously writing for newcomers to biblical studies, Enns exhibits extraordinary patience as he walks his readers through numerous examples of these phenomena. Enns's authorial audience is comprised, moreover, of novices to academic study of the Bible who come to the task with a high view of scripture. For them he demonstrates continued respect, even pastoral care, in his writing. Convinced that doctrine ought to account for available evidence, he urges that the question is not *whether* but *how* the Bible is God's word. His solution to the problem is to adopt what he calls an "incarnational analogy," which allows for and takes seriously the character of the biblical materials as fully at home in the ancient world. That this book is oriented toward beginners is highlighted by the inclusion of a glossary of key terms (e.g., "Dead Sea Scrolls," "Mishnah," "Septuagint") and introductory bibliographies.

For those familiar with the general tenor of biblical studies in the past couple of centuries, the issues Enns raises hold few surprises. With regard to parallels with Near Eastern literature, for example, he introduces such texts as *Enuma Elish,* the Epic of Gilgamesh, the Code of Hammurabi, and Hittite suzerainty treaties, as well as a number of relevant inscriptions. The nature of his thesis comes to the fore, then, as he allows those parallels to surface questions about the Old Testament, in this case especially about the uniqueness of Yahweh's revelation to Israel and the nature of Old Testament myth and historiography. His responses focus on taking seriously the connectedness of the biblical materials to their social-historical environments both as a prophylactic against assessing those materials according to modern standards and interests and as a boon to grasping the significance of these texts as divine self-disclosure in the particularity of the ancient world.

With regard to the other two "problems"—that is, theological diversity and the use of the Old Testament by New Testament writers—Enns works similarly on two fronts. Having outlined the nature of the question through a series of exemplars, he first indicates why typical responses to the issues fall short, usually either because they allow doctrine to trump data or because they refuse to struggle with the implications of the data for a theology of Scripture. Second, he develops his own response in ways I might characterize as programmatic rather than exhaustive, humble rather than dogmatic. That is, Enns works to point the way forward in ways that welcome others to join the conversation. Theological diversity, then, is a function of divine accommodation that eschews any facile claims of scriptural unity. On this, Enns finds helpful a more traditionally Jewish approach to the problem of diversity, one that seeks less to resolve diversity than to explore points of tension and to engage them in conversation. Enns then shows that the distinguishing characteristic of New Testament exegesis of the Old Testament is not methodological (since New Testament writers employed interpretive methods at home in the Second Temple period) but hermeneutical. He develops this hermeneutic in "christotelic" and "ecclesiotelic" terms and argues that contemporary ecclesially located exegesis can and ought to embrace and practice this hermeneutic.

Clearly, Enns's book will be most useful in the context out of and for which it was written, where critical biblical studies stands in tension with conservative-minded students. Beyond the confines of conservative Christianity, his work is helpful for the way it urges conversation about the implications of biblical studies for doctrinal issues, not least for theologies of Scripture. Perhaps even more global in importance is his suggestion that "we should think of biblical interpretation more as a path to walk than a fortress to be defended" (162). This is counsel appropriate to most anyone.

Erzähldiskurs und Redepragmatik im Alten Testament: Unterwegs zu einer performativen Theologie der Bibel, by Christof Hardmeier. Forschungen zum Alten Testament 46. Tübingen: Mohr Siebeck, 2005. Pp. viii + 444. Cloth. €89.00. ISBN 3161487729.

Jean Louis Ska, Pontifical Biblical Institute, Rome, Italy

Recueillant seize articles publiés entre 1981 et 2005, parfois dans des revues à diffusion limitée, Ch. Hardmeier met à la disposition des lecteurs une série de travaux qui ont tous trait, d'une manière ou d'une autre, au thème fondamental de l'interaction entre le texte et ses destinataires. L'A. parle de *Redepragmatik*, ce qui équivaut à *pragmalinguistique*. La méthode prônée ici est beaucoup plus liée au texte et à ses composantes que le *Reader-Response Criticism* qui connaît un grand succès aux Etats-Unis (voir surtout Stanley Fish, *Is There a Text in This Class? The Authority of Interpretive Communities* [Cambridge: Harvard University Press, 1983, ²2003]; il faudrait aussi citer les noms de Wolfgang Iser et Umberto Eco). Mais, comme nous le verrons, notre auteur choisit une direction différente.

Au point de départ de la recherche de Ch. Harmeier, nous trouvons en effet une insistance sur la proclamation de la «parole», et nous retrouvons ici l'écho de nombreuses publications du monde protestant allemand de ces cinquante dernières années et même de l'herméneutique existentielle d'un Rudolf Bultmann, tout comme une certaine aversion envers la métaphysique et la théologie systématique. L'oralité est donc plus importante que l'écriture, car même les textes écrits étaient destinés à être lus en public. La mise par écrit ne met pas fin à la transmission orale, loin de là. L'A. cite Aleida et Jan Assmann, mais un lecteur de langue anglaise pensera certainement à Susan Niditch, *Oral World and Written Word: Ancient Israelite Literature* (Library of Ancient Israel; Louisville: Westminster John Knox, 1996). Voir aussi, sur l'état de la question, le livre récent de David M. Carr, *Writing on the Tablet of the Heart. Origins of Scripture and Literature* (Oxford: University Press, 2005). De cette insistance sur la parole, sa proclamation et la réponse existentielle et responsable des «auditeurs» *coram deo* dérive l'intérêt pour le langage «performatif» (John L. Austin).

Dans son introduction, l'A. nous décrit d'abord l'itinéraire académique qui l'a mené à ses recherches actuelles. La plupart des noms qui balisent cet itinéraire sont mieux connus en Allemagne qu'ailleurs et ceci permet de mieux comprendre certains traits du volume que nous présentons. Citons au moins les noms de Dietrich Bonhoeffer, Gerhard Ebeling, Eberhard Jüngel, Ludwig Wittgenstein, John L. Austin, Hans Walter Wolff et James Barr. L'A. citera souvent Ernst Fuchs pour qui le but de la théologie est de contrôler et discuter ce que nous disons à propos de la révélation divine dans notre langage humain. L'A. propose, au terme de son itinéraire, une «herméneutique de la lecture circonspecte» («Lesehermeneutik der Behutsamkeit»). Les textes prophétiques ont surtout retenu son attention, mais il s'est également intéressé aux textes narratifs. Pour de plus amples informations sur sa méthode, l'A. renvoie à une publication en quatre volumes intitulée *Textwelten der Bibel entdecken: Grundfragen und Verfahren einer textpragmatis-*

chen Literaturwissenschaft der Bibel, Textpragmatische Studien zur Literatur- und Kulturgeschichte der Hebräischen Bibel I–II (Gütersloh: Gütersloher Verlagshaus, 2003–2004). Deux volumes ont déjà paru et deux sont en préparation. Une image, employée par l'A., explique la méthode mieux que de longs développements: les textes sont semblables à des partitions de musique. Il faut qu'elles soient jouées ou chantées pour devenir véritablement de la musique. En d'autres termes, le texte n'existe que dans l'acte de la lecture. Sinon, il reste lettre morte.

L'introduction, après ce résumé de l'itinéraire académique de l'A., contient aussi un résumé des seize articles repris dans ce volume; trois sont en anglais et les autres en allemand. L'A. s'attache à montrer en particulier comment sa méthode peut aider à découvrir l'arrière-fond littéraire et sociologique de l'utilisation des textes. En second lieu, elle permet de mieux comprendre certains aspects de l'histoire de la littérature, en particuliers le phénomène de relecture, réactualisation et intertextualité. Les articles sont regroupés en quatre sections.

Dans la première série, nous trouvons quatre articles sur les différents aspects et les fonctions des narrations bibliques. 1. «Erzählen – Erzählung – Erzählgemeinschaft. Zur Rezeption von Abrahamserzählungen in der Exilsprophetie». Le rôle des figures d'Abraham et de Sara dans la prophétie exilique, selon cette étude, n'est pas lié aux seuls faits ou aux seules «vérités» rationnelles que l'on peut en tirer. Le sens vient de la narration elle-même, de l'acte de raconter, de la lecture «participée» (50). Au sens propre, on ne peut pas «expliquer» un récit, on ne peut que le raconter à nouveau ou continuer à le raconter. Le récit ne communique pas des «vérités», mais invite d'abord à partager une expérience. 2. «Old Testament Exegesis and Linguistic Narrative Research». L'A. aborde quelques questions de méthode, puis il applique ces principes à Amos 7,10–17. Ce récit invite le lecteur à s'identifier avec le courageux prophète qui conteste la «raison d'État». 3. «„Stark wie der Tod ist die Liebe". Der Mensch und sein Tod in den Schriften des Alten Testaments». Le problème de la mort est envisagé à partir de trois textes: 2 Sam 12,15–25; Gn 3; Ps 90, Ct 8,6. L'article se termine par un plaidoyer contre toute instrumentalisation ou manipulation de la mort.

La deuxième série contient quatre articles consacrés à la *tora* dans le Deutéronome. C'est en effet uniquement dans le Deutéronome que la Bible définit ce qu'est la *tora*. En deux mots, la *tora* est un enseignement performatif qui rend ses auditeurs (le peuple d'Israël) responsables *coram deo*. Cet enseignement est d'abord proclamé avant d'être mis par écrit (31,9), pour être proclamé à nouveau (31,10–13). 1. «„Geschichten" und „Geschichte" in der hebräischen Bibel. Zur Tora-Form von Geschichtstheologie im Kulturwissenchaftlichen Kontext». Au cours d'une analyse de Dt 2,26–36 et 9,1–6 (épisode de Sihon), puis de 3,21–22 (instruction de Josué), l'A. analyse les concepts narratifs utilisés par les discours sur la *tora* et il réfléchit sur le mode d'envisager l'historiographie dans l'histoire deutéronomiste. 2. «Das Sch^ema Jisra'el in Dtn 6,4 im Rahmen der Beziehungstheologie der deuteronomistischen Tora». Certains aspects particuliers de Dt 6,4 entraînent une actualisation «performative» de la théophanie de l'Horeb durant l'assemblée dans les plaines de Moab. Cette actualisation se résume en un appel à la loyauté envers Yhwh seul. 3. «Die Weisheit der Tora (Dtn 4,5–8). Respekt und Loyalität gegenüber Jhwh allein und die Befolgung seiner Gebote—ein performatives Lehren und Lernen». La «pédagogie de la mémoire» est au centre de cette étude sur le langage métaphorique de l'alliance et sa fonction performative. 4. «Wirtschaftliche Prosperität und Gottesvergessenheit. Die theologische Dimension wirtschaftlicher Leistungskraft nach Dtn 8». à propos de Dt 8,7–18, l'A. discute le problème de l'économie de marché, du néo-libéralisme et de la relation entre religion et économie. Il préconise une économie de la *Nachhaltigkeit* («économie de la longue échéance») dans le cadre d'une théologie de la création et de l'économie mondiale.

Dans la troisième partie, le lecteur trouvera des études sur le discours pragmatique dans la prophétie et le psautier. Sont exclus de ce volume tous les articles sur Jérémie et sur l'histoire deutéronomiste. 1. «Jesajas Verkündigungsabsicht und Jahwes Verstockungsauftrag in Jes 6». L'A. affronte le thème de l'endurcissement du cœur (Is 6,9–10) dans le cadre de la vision d'Isaïe (6,1–10) et du «Denkschrift», c'est-à-dire du «Mémoire d'Isaïe» (Is 6,1–8,18). En conclusion, l'endurcissement du cœur est une façon d'annoncer, après une série d'échecs, que l'effet négatif des prophéties sur leur auditoire était prévu dès le début. Is 6,9–10 est donc un *vaticinum ex eventu*. 2. «Verkündigung und Schrift bei Jesaja. Zur Enstehung der Schriftenprophetie als Oppositionsliteratur im alten Israel». Quand et pourquoi la prophétie s'est-elle servie de l'écriture? Is 8,16–18, texte à interpréter comme colophon du «Mémoire d'Isaïe» (Is 6–8), contient aussi une réflexion *a posteriori* qui permet de mieux comprendre le présent et de s'orienter en vue du futur. C'est le rejet de la prophétie orale qui a conduit à la rédaction des oracles en vue d'une lecture postérieure. 3. «Die judäische Unheilsprophetie als Antwort auf eine gesellschafts- und Normenwandel im Israel des 8. Jh. v. Chr.». La prophétie de jugement en Juda au 8ème siècle, qui fait l'objet de ce troisième article, est connue pour l'importance qu'elle accorde à la critique de la société. Ici encore, l'A. passe assez vite aux problèmes d'actualisation de cette critique sociale pour montrer la pertinence de cette problématique aujourd'hui, en particulier en ce qui concerne les rapports avec le Tiers-Monde. Il conteste aussi la séparation trop nette entre un monde religieux et un monde profane, une culture gréco-romaine (séculaire, profane, parfois anticléricale) et une culture judéo-chrétienne qui survivrait seulement dans les églises et dans le judaïsme. 4. «Die Propheten Micha und Jesaja im Spiegel von Jer 26 und 2 Reg 18–20. Zur Prophetierezeption in der nach-josianischen Zeit». L'A. reprend dans cet article la problématique des récits prophétiques de Jr 26 et 2 Rois 18–19. Dans quels milieux ces récits ont-ils été transmis? Autre question importante: pourquoi l'histoire deutéronomiste ne parle-t-elle pas des prophètes, sauf d'Isaïe? Pour l'A. l'élite de Jérusalem s'est divisée au temps de Sédécias au sujet des prophéties négatives de Jérémie et d'Ézéchiel. 2 Rois 18–19 est écrit par les ennemis mortels de Jérémie, les «faucons», partisans de la révolte de Sédécias, qui mettent dans la bouche du généralissime de l'armée babylonienne certains propos de leur adversaire (Jérémie) pour le disqualifier. Ces partisans de Sédécias font confiance à l'Égypte et s'appuient la théologie de

Sion propre à Isaïe. De l'autre côté l'on retrouve la famille des Safanides et Jérémie, c'est-à-dire le parti des «colombes», pro-babylonien. Les circonstances de ces récits sont le retrait temporaire de l'armée babylonienne en 588, dû à une montée de l'armée égyptienne. Pour les partisans de Sédécias, la catastrophe est liée uniquement au problème de la centralisation du culte introduite par la réforme de Josias. Peut-être les auteurs de l'histoire deutéronomiste sont-ils à chercher dans les meurtriers de Guedalias qui espéraient en une restauration de la dynastie de David. Pour ces auteurs, les modèles sont Ézéchias et Josias. D'où l'exclusion des prophètes de malheur et de leur critique sociale. L'histoire deutéronomiste aurait cependant été conçue plus tard par un groupe revenu d'Égypte (Jr 44,14.28; cf. Dt 2,16). Il s'agit certainement d'une hypothèse très intéressante. 5. «„Geschwiegen habe ich seit langem ... wie die gebärende schreie ich jetzt". Zur Komposition und Geschichtstheologie von Jes 42,14–44,23». La prédication du second Isaïe, selon cette étude, est une méditation sur les chances de salut offertes par l'histoire. 6. «„Denn im Tod ist kein Gedenken an dich" (Psalm 6,6). Der Tod des Menschen—Gottes Tod?». Les Ps 6, 30, 88 présentent des cas extrêmes où la communication est interrompue par la mort. L'A. y examine en particulier la fonction performative de la «louange» (*toda*).

Dans la quatrième partie nous retrouvons des articles sur le thème traité dans l'introduction, et donc des études plus théoriques. 1. «Systematische Elemente der Theo-logie in der Hebräischen Bibel. Das Loben Gottes—ein Kristallisationsmoment biblischer Theologie». L'exégèse du Ps 30 et de la fonction performative de la louange (*toda*) conduit à examiner à nouveau la fonction de la mémoire, comme dans le Deutéronome et l'histoire deutéronomiste. 2. «Bibel-Reading AND Critical Thinking». Ici, l'A. recueille les fruits de son travail sur la *tora*. Comment prendre une bonne décision? L'examen de Dt 1,19–46 («mauvaise décision») et de Dt 2,26–36 («mauvaise décision d'un adversaire d'Israël») aboutit aux réflexions de Dt 9,1–6 sur les conditions de la conquête. 3. «New Relations between Systematic Theology and Exegesis and the Perspective on Practical Theology and Ethics». Le thème de ces pages est le dialogue entre l'exégèse vétérotestamentaire et les autres disciplines théologiques. Le point de départ est Ex 3,14. Puis l'A. interroge Job pour constater que le discours de la théodicée est conduit *ad absurdum*. Il parle enfin de la solidarité éthique dans la *tora* deutéronomique.

Le volume contient une liste des références aux premières publications des articles, une bibliographie, et divers index (auteurs, mots hébreux, citations bibliques, index thématique). L'impression générale, après la lecture des ces articles souvent très denses où les questions méthodologiques et exégétiques sont mêlées à des questions d'actualisation, est certes positive. Le plaidoyer de l'A. en faveur d'une exégèse plus «performative» mérite d'être entendu. Par ailleurs, l'A. ne nous en voudra pas de faire trois observations d'ensemble car il est impossible de discuter dans le détail les résultats de recherches menées depuis plus de trente ans par un expert en la matière. (1) Le terme «performatif» est sans doute employé à bon escient dans la plupart des cas. Il n'est pas sûr cependant qu'il puisse être toujours appliqué à ce qu'il conviendrait peut-être d'appeler une exégèse de la réponse du lecteur ou de son rôle actif dans la lecture. Cela vaut en particulier pour la lecture des récits, des psaumes, ou même de Dt 6,4. La rhétorique du Deutéronome a souvent été étudiée, tout comme les stratégies mises en œuvre pour «impliquer» le destinataire. Nous pensons en particulier à Timothy A. Lenchak, *«Choose Life!»: A Rhetorical-Critical Investigation of Deuteronomy 28,69–30,20* (AnBib 129; Rome: Biblical Institute Press, 1993), ou, sur le rôle spécifique de l'écriture dans le Deutéronome, Jean-Pierre Sonnet, *The Book within the Book. Writing in Deuteronomy* (Biblical Interpretation; Leiden: Brill, 1997). Ces auteurs offrent des réponses différenciées au problème traité ici. (2). Ici comme ailleurs, il me semble que la bibliographie est souvent limitée aux ouvrages en allemand (et encore…). On y trouve, si j'ai bien compté, une vingtaine de titres en anglais (un peu plus d'un par page dans une bibliographie de quinze pages) et trois en français (*graeca sunt, non leguntur?*). Certains seront surpris de voir que l'A. discute de narrativité sans citer Robert Alter, Meir Sternberg et son *drama of reading,* ou Hans Frei et sa célèbre formule: «the narrative is the meaning» (Hans Wilhelm Frei, *The Eclipse of Biblical Narrative: A Study in Eighteenth and Nineteenth Century Hermeneutics* [New Haven: Yale University Press, [3]1978] 270). À propos du discours performatif, il semble méconnaître Andreas Wagner, *Sprechakte und Sprechaktanalyse im Alten Testament: Untersuchungen im biblischen Hebräisch an der Nahtstelle zwischen Handlungsebene und Grammatik* (BZAW 253; Berlin: de Gruyter, 1997). Certes, il faut juger les études de l'A. d'abord en fonction de ses propres critères et de son propre contexte. Il n'en reste pas moins vrai que la résonance de cette publication dépendra en partie de cette particularité. (3) Pour reprendre une formule du regretté Luis Alonso Schökel, les études recueillies dans ce volume parlent beaucoup—et très bien—de musicologie, mais on y entend peut-être pas assez souvent jouer de la musique. En d'autres termes, il existe une certaine disproportion, sans doute voulue, entre la théorie et la pratique, entre l'effort méthodologique et ses résultats. Mais ce qui peut apparaître comme un défaut aux yeux de certains sera probablement vu comme un point fort par d'autres. Chacun, en fin de compte, y trouvera son bien et c'est bien sûr l'essentiel.

JUDAISM: GENERAL

Questions and Answers: Intellectual Foundations of Judaism, by Jacob Neusner. Peabody, Mass.: Hendrickson, 2005. Pp. xxvi + 254. Paper. $19.95. ISBN 1565638654.

Arian Verheij, University of Amsterdam, Amsterdam, The Netherlands

This book offers less than its broad subtitle would suggest. First, Judaism is understood here in the specific sense of rabbinic Judaism; second, Judaism's intellectual foundations are found exclusively in early rabbinic literature. The discussion of these foundations, finally, is focused so as to be of interest to New

Testament students. As the author puts it: "I focus not on rabbinic Judaism through the ages, but only upon aspects that interest New Testament studies. I address the frequently asked questions about rabbinic Judaism most likely to confront New Testament students as they seek a context for the life and teachings of Jesus, his disciples and apostles" (xxiii). Only the ten final pages address some issues of modern-day Judaism and Christianity.

The author is well aware of one problem inherent in his focus on the New Testament and early Christianity: the chronological gap between the writings of the New Testament, on the one hand, and the rather much later rabbinic literature, on the other (a problem that affects the famous New Testament commentary by Strack-Billerbeck as well). His answer, basically, is that both bodies of literature deal in part with the same subject matter: "facts of the Gospels and Paul's letters and the rabbinic writings intersect" (xxiv). So, even if "not synchronically," still "in logic ... the two approaches each appeal to the same received revelation, each in accord with its own system and logic" (xxiv). This is an essentially ahistorical point of departure that determines the outlook of the work as a whole.

Using the question-and-answer (Q&A) method—a genre familiar to modern readers, much used in the computer industry (FAQ), and alluding to the rabbinic tradition of *She'elot u-Teshuvot*—Neusner covers a variety of topics, ranging in eight parts from "Defining Rabbinic Judaism" (1); through its sources: "Scripture and Midrash" (2), "Law (Halakah)" (3), and "Lore (Aggadah)" (4); via the two main aspects of its "Theology": "Aggadah" (5) and "Halakah" (6); to the "Social Doctrines of Rabbinic Judaism" (7) and, finally, "Rabbinic Judaism and Christianity: Points of Intersection of Two Coordinate Scriptural Systems" (8). Part 5 is the largest, covering some seventy pages. Each part consists of one or several clusters of questions (there are forty-six numbered sections, containing 207 unnumbered questions and answers). As the author points out, the material was gleaned from decades of lectures given in numerous institutions of Christian education—with the addition of "a few questions I wish that people *would* ask" (xxv). The answers are of varying length, ranging from one brief paragraph to several pages, and many of them are illustrated with quotations from rabbinic literature, mainly the Mishnah. The straightforwardness of the Q&A method is highlighted by the author's own perspective on this book: "My job is to get things straight and make them clear" (xxv), spelling out "simple answers to basic questions of fact" (xxiii).

Asking good questions is always of the highest importance, and questions of fact are among the best. But the questions asked in this book do not always meet that standard. Some of them do, such as: "What is *Pirqé Avot* and how does it relate to the Mishna?" (60), "What are the 613 commandments?" (184), or "What was the role of the family in rabbinic Judaism?" (191). Others do not, such as: "How did Scripture's power exert itself through proof texts?" (233) or "What kind of actions does God really admire?" (203). The question "What was the relationship between Judaism and ancient Israel" (5, in the section on the "Early Stages of Judaism") is too vague and indeed too idealistic to be taken seriously in this particular wording. Likewise, the problem whether "rabbinic Judaism and Christianity meet at prayer? How does Matthew 6:9-10 compare with the Qaddish," along with its very brief answer, is less than satisfactorily put and addressed (32). A few more questions, randomly picked, may illustrate the theological tendency of the book. "What explains the prosperity of the wicked and the suffering of the righteous?" (122); "How is suffering part of God's plan?" (125); "Why is resurrection a logical necessity of monotheism?" (151); "How did purity represent a position in the contest between life and death?" (175). Questions of fact in the area covered by a book such as the present one should have strong historical overtones, and so should their answers. Now, even if Neusner offers a handy introduction to the rabbinic literature, he does so focusing on its canon without going very much into its historic context. The sages Gamaliel and Hillel are mentioned; Shammai, Yehudah ha-Nasi, Yohanan ben Zakkai, and others are not.

The book has indexes on subjects (lacking an entry on the five hermeneutical rules governing the Bavli, 69) and passages from the Bible and rabbinic literature. There is no bibliography. The works cited (and mentioned at the end of separate sections) are almost exclusively Neusner's own publications and translations.

On the whole, and this would be the present reviewer's main objection, the character of the book is theological rather than critical. It testifies to the author's impressive knowledge of rabbinical Judaism, but it appears to serve mainly as an expression of his theological views, based exclusively on (his own reading of) rabbinic literature. It is obvious that the book was written with the best of intentions, and it certainly will promote understanding of Judaism among Christians—for the latter's own benefit, to be sure, as they are made to recognize the Jewish origin of their faith, or at least the common ground they share with it. But this is not enough to justify the claim that the book presents (the) "intellectual foundations of Judaism."

Purity, Sacrifice, and the Temple: Symbolism and Supersessionism in the Study of Ancient Judaism, by Jonathan Klawans. New York: Oxford University Press, 2005. Pp. x + 372. Hardcover. $55.00. ISBN 0195162633.

Ayse Tuzlak, University of Calgary, Calgary, Alberta, Canada

In this important book, Jonathan Klawans demonstrates that scholars have treated the subject of sacrifice with an embarrassing lack of rigor. Klawans argues that in the study of sacrifice, for all its popularity over the past two hundred years, our discipline's misplaced obsession with origins is still unquestioningly accepted. As a result, even the most careful scholars still harbor some evolutionist assumptions about sacrifice that would not be tolerated in discussions of other religious phenomena.

Purity, Sacrifice, and the Temple has two stated goals. First, Klawans wants to examine concepts of sacrifice in Israelite religion and ancient Judaism without falling prey to supersessionist assumptions. These assumptions, Klawans maintains, mar the scholarship of historians of all religious persuasions. The Christian tradition teaches that animal sacrifice has been superseded by the death of Jesus, while Judaism takes as axiomatic that animal sacrifice was replaced by prayer and Torah study after the destruction of the Second Temple. (Reformed Judaism goes on to assert that this is a good thing that need never be "changed back.") For Christianity, and for liberal strains of Judaism, animal sacrifice is assumed to be barbaric and outmoded, a transitional phase in God's plan for the world. Since even Christian and Jewish scholars betray a lack of sympathy for the sacrificial practices of their spiritual ancestors, secular scholars find no reason to take it seriously at all: nothing in our culture provides any compelling reason to support animal sacrifice, even in an abstract way.

One of the most startling revelations that Klawans's book provides is that no emic study of Israelite sacrifice has been written since, well, perhaps since Leviticus, but at the very least since Maimonides. Instead of engaging with the already-developed sacrificial system of ancient Israel within its social and literary context, modern scholars have constantly tried to dig back through prehistory to find the beginnings of sacrificial practice everywhere, collapsing Greco-Roman, Israelite, and Vedic materials into some prehistoric "Big Bang." Perhaps there is nothing wrong with this approach in and of itself, but Klawans argues that no one has taken any *other* approach to sacrifice since William Robertson Smith wrote *The Religion of the Semites* in 1889. Klawans points out that not every book on Jewish circumcision searches for the origins of all body modifications across all cultures. Why is sacrifice in particular treated in this way? In a thoughtful aside, Klawans ventures some possible answers to that question, suggesting that many post-industrial writers and readers feel a deep-rooted anxiety about environmental degradation, animal abuse, capitalist excess, and consumerism. Those anxieties leak into their analysis, just as Victorian obsessions with sex can be detected in innumerable books about phallic cults.

Klawans is not the first to make at least some of these observations. For a generation now, historians have been aware that sacrifice is often yoked into the service of totalizing, reductionistic theories about religion. (René Girard is singled out by Klawans for particularly brutal critique, although no author before Mary Douglas—and only a few after her—come off especially well in his review of the literature.) For much of his career, Jonathan Z. Smith has deplored the strong antiritual bias that plagues the academic study of religion. Sacrifice is often imagined to be the most wasteful, violent, and meaningless example of ancient rituals, which are already "mechanical" and "empty." This is an argument that Klawans uses to good effect and with due respect to those who made it before him.

Purity, Sacrifice, and the Temple goes further, however, arguing that criticisms of sacrifice in modern scholarship arise out of stubborn, and surprisingly consistent, misreadings of ancient texts. Scholars who see sacrifice in terms of divine food (following Robertson Smith), or gift exchange (following Mauss), or the management of violence within a society (following Girard), simply cannot justify any of those perspectives from within the biblical or rabbinic traditions: the original texts never interpret what they are doing in those terms. Freudians and neo-Freudians, like Girard, get around this problem by claiming to "read between the lines" in order to find the "unconscious motivations" of the text. Klawans has no patience for this approach. I think this is unfortunate, since reading against the grain can be a very productive hermeneutical strategy, as can be seen in the work of scholars who seek to understand minority viewpoints on, say, heresy or gender. Nevertheless, I agree with him when he says that sacrificial texts are frequently read with a peculiar lack of charity and with an aggressive theoretical agenda.

The second goal of Klawans's book is, unfortunately, not pursued very effectively after the first chapter. Klawans makes the case that, for the Israelites, purity and sacrifice were intimately connected. The rules for one depend on the rules for the other, and discussions of the two concepts always appear together in biblical ritual material. Thanks to Mary Douglas, ritual purity is now taken seriously in biblical studies. No historian will dismiss Leviticus as a primitive attempt at legislating hygiene after reading *Purity and Danger,* and even those who do not apply purity law in their own religious lives will generally admit that Israelite legal codes served a genuinely useful social and symbolic function. Klawans seems to want modern scholarly interest in, and respect for, ritual purity to "spill over" into analyses of sacrifice, and he spends much time in this book expressing his frustration with the authors who have tried (and, in his opinion, failed) to treat sacrificial practice fairly.

The rest of Klawans's book is made up of case studies. In order to break free of evolutionist assumptions, he treats his material thematically rather than chronologically, which serves his argument well. The only chronological division occurs between the two halves of the book, the first of which deals with biblical sources and the second with late antique material. Within those sections he treats sacrifice and purity in light of broad themes such as prophecy, cosmos, and priesthood, with a final chapter on the way these ideas were addressed in early Christian texts.

Some of these chapters are very strong. I was impressed by Klawans's treatment of prophetic indictments of sacrifice within the Hebrew Bible, so often used by Christian apologists as a stick with which to beat Judaism, and also used by modern Jews to justify liturgical and theological reforms that exclude sacrifice even from the text of prayers. The academic left has traditionally defended the position that a person can be a fervent patriot even as she critiques a governmental policy with which she disagrees. It is an argument that has a special urgency in today's political climate, and it is a shame that the same logic is so rarely applied to the Jews who loved their temple but hated the hypocrites who, in their view, misunderstood or abused it. At the end of the book, Klawans claims that Jesus and Paul were no different from these other Jews. The antipriestly and antitemple material in the New Testament is all late (Revelation and Hebrews) and unconcerned with the historical Jesus.

Other parts of the book were less successful. The fourth chapter contains a lengthy argument about angelology and Platonism whose relevance was not entirely clear to me. In this chapter Klawans points out that talk of the "spiritualization" of the Jerusalem temple is often code for the dismissal of the *actual* temple as irrelevant (what Jonathan Z. Smith might call transforming "symbol" into "*mere* symbol," and a point to which Klawans himself returns in the final chapter of his book). Indeed this is an important concern. But the fine distinctions Klawans draws between "heavenly temples" and "heavenly cities with temples in them" seem to have little to do with purity and even less to do with sacrifice. There is certainly a kind of supersessionism implicit in the vocabulary used to discuss mystics' visions of celestial temples, and no doubt that bias in the literature deserves its own study, but it did not fit well with the rest of this book.

This reviewer found Klawans's overarching argument very persuasive, but it would have been much more so if the author had paid closer attention to the texts themselves. Klawans's analyses often seemed rushed. The reader is frequently provided with a string of references in parentheses, followed by a blunt conclusion and a blanket condemnation of two hundred years of scholarship. For all his concern about taking priestly material seriously, it felt as though Klawans spent little time on the Torah; Leviticus is frequently invoked but rarely analyzed, while Numbers makes almost no appearance in the text at all. Josephus is covered in three pages, Philo in seven, the *Temple Scroll* in six. One of the things that made Douglas's work so great was her minute attention to detail. Even those who disagree with her cannot fail to be impressed at the questions she puts to her texts, word by painstaking word. There is very little of that sort of close reading in *Purity, Sacrifice, and the Temple.*

That being said, there is much in this book to consider, and much to admire. Many of Klawans's arguments are very subtle, and a short review cannot do justice to them all. He introduced me to ideas that I had never considered before: the predication of the sacrificial system upon ownership and property; the importance of the selection of an animal from a flock; the role of the metaphor of fire and consumption in descriptions of God; and the concept of "economic purity," to name only a few. Even the ideas that have common currency in biblical studies are addressed in creative and refreshing ways here: the differences between ritual and moral purity; the roles of prophets and priests; the differences between Qumran and Jerusalem. However, I could not help but wish that each chapter of this book were a book of its own, so that Klawans could allow the texts to make their own case for the importance of sacrifice, purity, and temple worship. So much rich and fascinating material is glossed or left out, particularly among late antique sources, which are too often treated superficially. It is my hope that the observations that Klawans makes here are expanded into more books soon, both by Klawans himself and by other scholars who realize the importance of what he is saying.

Jewish Martyrs in the Pagan and Christian Worlds, by Shmuel Shepkaru. New York: Cambridge University Press, 2006. Pp. xii + 414. Hardcover. $70.00. ISBN 0521842816.

Daniel R. Schwartz, The Hebrew University of Jerusalem, Jerusalem, Israel

Wherever and whenever religious persecution raises the possibility of martyrdom, or later observers discuss such places and times, the propriety of martyrdom is typically a topic in dispute, according to the relative value different believers or observers ascribe to religion, on the one hand, and human life, on the other. Historical studies of Jewish martyrdom, accordingly, frequently focus on analyzing such disputes and the reasons that might account for them. There is a good bit of this in Shepkaru's study. However, because it "attempts to provide a linear history of martyrdom that stretches from the Hellenistic period to the dawn of the modern era" (3), it is subject to a tendency to characterize each separate period more or less monolithically, but also differently from those adjacent to it, thus allowing for interesting differences from one period to the next.

This broad but heavily documented study presents in its ten chapters a five-part reconstruction of the history of martyrdom among the Jews: there was (contrary to scholarly consensus) little interest in martyrdom in the pre-Roman period (ch. 1); interest in it grew greatly, and under Roman influence, in the first century (ch. 2); the rabbis, in the next few centuries, had serious reservations about it and attempted to limit it, thus distancing themselves from Christian enthusiasm for martyrdom (ch. 3); and so it was only thereafter, in the face of persecutions in the Byzantine period and especially in medieval Europe, that Jewish martyrdom really took off (chs. 4–9). Finally, according to some brief and explicitly preliminary observations, the Holocaust and post-Holocaust periods are to be characterized as backing away from martyrdom and toward life, if only to spite Hitler (ch. 10).

This is a very attractive theory, organizing a large quantity of texts and other data. And there is a lot to it. If we focus on the first three stages delineated above, which are of the most interest to the readers of *RBL* and the ones in which the present reviewer is most competent—although it is to the fourth stage that Shepkaru devotes the most space—we may note that, in rejecting the general consensus that the Jewish martyrological tradition began in the Hellenistic period, Shepkaru is right to play down the evidence for it in Daniel (where the persecuted heroes hope to survive, and do) and 1 Maccabees (where martyrs get only minor attention and function as foils for the real heroes—soldiers), thus leaving 2 Maccabees quite isolated. Similarly, he is right to juxtapose first-century evidence such as that of Philo, Josephus, and 4 Maccabees as evidence for a heavy concentration of martyrological interest in first-century Judaism. Finally, concerning the third stage, Shepkaru quite rightly points to some rabbinic texts that indicate both doubts about the propriety of martyrdom or the fact that Jews in fact avoided it; thus, for a prime example, the rabbis' well-known decision, at the time of the Hadrianic persecutions, to mandate martyrdom only if the Romans required Jews to violate three cardinal prohibitions dovetailed nicely with the fact that the Romans did not impose such demands.

However, it is also the case that any attempt to put together a neat theory requires some interpretations, and decisions, that are open to debate. Here are a few. (1) Concerning Daniel, the fact that those Jews who defied the royal decrees hoped nonetheless to survive, and did, should not, I believe, be allowed to set aside their willingness to die, which is the prime element of martyrology.

(2) Shepkaru's attempt not only to underline how little echo 2 Maccabees found in ancient Judaism but also to belittle the book's interest in martyrdom leads him to suggest (as others before him) that chapters 6–7 are a late interpolation. Without opening up that discussion in detail, we may note that there is little basis for his claim that "Chapters 6 and 7 display a digression from the constant praising of the book's militant hero, Judas Maccabee, and his successful campaigns on behalf of Judaism" (25–26); in fact, prior to chapter 8 Judas is mentioned only once in the Epitomator's preface (2:19) and in a proleptic reference at 5:27, where he is no more than a pious and vegetarian refugee.

(3) Again, it seems difficult to justify Shepkaru's insistence (22–24) that the youths of chapter 7 are to be understood as dying on account of their own, personal sins, and hence to be distinguished from martyrs, since the latter are supposed to be "innocent sacrifices who bring salvation to others." Whatever one thinks of the latter as a sine qua non of martyrdom, such a personal interpretation of the sins mentioned in 2 Macc 7 ignores the fact that, as 8:3–5 shows, the youths' deaths were indeed functional for the whole Jewish community.

(4) Concerning the first century, Shepkaru views the surge in Jewish interest in martyrdom as a Jewish response to Roman models. But given the fact that Philo, Josephus, and the author of 4 Maccabees all wrote in Greek, it is surprising that Shepkaru gives no attention to such classical Greek exemplars as Socrates and Antigone—who already seem to have influenced 2 Maccabees. Doing so would reopen the question of continuity between the Hellenistic period (2 Maccabees) and the first century.

(5) In this connection, we might consider not only books but also real life: Shepkaru notes well that Josephus reports the death of priests serving in the temple in 63 B.C.E. who were killed because they refused to abandon the divine service when the temple was invaded by Pompey's men and their Jewish allies. As literature, this is late first century C.E. and fits Shepkaru's thesis fine. But as an event—documented, as Josephus notes (*Ant.* 14.68, cited at p. 46), by several writers of the first century B.C.E.—the priests' behavior must have drawn upon notions as early as that and also contributed something of its own to the Jewish martyrological tradition; to infer from Josephus's emphasis on non-Jewish witnesses that Jewish martyrological behavior was in fact unusual (46) seems to me to be somewhat overdone.

(6) Finally, concerning the rabbinic period too, the picture seems to be more nuanced than what a linear history can easily allow; Shepkaru himself notes, at the outset of chapter 3, that "early rabbinic texts present the greatest challenge to [his]

methodology of linear history" (66). Indeed, his chapter begins with a lengthy discussion of the great exemplars of rabbinic martyrdom. Nevertheless, it ends, as the thesis requires, by positing an antimartyrological swing of the rabbinic pendulum, presented as a reaction against Christian enthusiasm for martyrdom (97–106). This is problematic in and of itself, because it should require some explanation as to why Jews chose sometimes to distance themselves from Christianity by avoiding what Christians do, and sometimes, as in the Middle Ages, by competing with them so as to do it just as well or better. Moreover, it is problematic because it requires some one-sided use of texts. Two examples: (a) it is quite difficult to accept Shepkaru's remark that "Even R. Akiba showed no desire to become a martyr" (98), which hardly fits the central rabbinic account of his death in *b. Ber.* 61b, a text that Shepkaru studied, accordingly, not in this part of chapter 3, but rather in the first part, which is dedicated to the opposite attitude; (b) when Shepkaru twice cites (98, 100) the story in *Gen. Rab.* 82:8 about two rabbinical students who changed their garb so as to avoid arrest by the Romans, using it quite properly as evidence for avoidance of martyrdom, he neglects to note that the story goes on to show, quite pointedly, that the two were weak students who did not recall their master's teachings. So while this story tells us about Jews who avoided martyrdom, it hardly recommends that. When we add to this the fact that the sentence that Shepkaru depends upon in explaining that they avoided martyrdom "because consciously killing oneself was considered unnatural even on behalf of the Law" does not appear in most manuscripts and is, accordingly, left out of the text in its standard critical edition (ed. Theodor-Albeck, 985), it seems that it is actually the avoidance of martyrdom that this rabbinic story is condemning or, at least, presenting as problematic.

In sum, this is a very challenging book, one that attempts to make sense out of large dossiers of variegated material. As all such surveys and syntheses, it runs the risk of flattening out evidence, of making too much fit in too well. Nevertheless, if historians are to do their job, they must not only collect scattered data but also strive to make history meaningful by discovering its major trends and lines of development. Shepkaru's is a very serious attempt to do this for Jewish martyrdom. Anyone who wants to make sense of the history of Jewish martyrdom, even if he or she will do it differently, such as by beginning the continuous tradition in the Hellenistic period and not inserting the early rabbinic turnabout, will have to do so vis-à-vis this volume.

"Kein Knochen soll gebrochen werden": Studien zu Bedeutung und Funktion des Pesachfests in Texten des frühen Judentums und im Johannesevangelium, by Christine Schlund. Wissenschaftliche Monographien zum Alten und Neuen Testament 107. Neukirchen-Vluyn: Neukirchener, 2005. Pp. xiii + 254. Cloth. €39.90. ISBN 3788720875.

Craig R. Koester, Luther Seminary, St. Paul, Minnesota

This is a revised dissertation that was accepted by the faculty at the Humboldt University in Berlin. It is an important contribution to the discussion about the meaning of the death of Jesus in Johannine theology—a topic that has generated lively discussion in Germany and warrants renewed consideration among English-speaking scholars. Schlund's basic question concerns the implications of Jewish Passover traditions for the interpretation of John. The Fourth Evangelist gives prominence to these traditions, noting three Passovers in the course of Jesus' ministry and placing the crucifixion on the day of preparation for the third Passover. Many interpreters assume that John's passion narrative depicts the crucified Jesus as a Passover lamb and assume that this means that his death atones for sin. The way Jesus is introduced as "the Lamb of God who takes away the sin of the world" in John 1:29 seems to invite this interpretation. The problem is that Jewish traditions do not suggest that the lambs sacrificed at Passover provided atonement for sin. If atonement was not a part of the Passover tradition, then is it appropriate to argue that Jesus' death at Passover is an atoning sacrifice? Her consideration of the problem has three parts: (1) a consideration of Jewish Passover traditions; (2) a discussion of the Passover traditions in John and Paul; and (3) some comments on Christian traditions of the second to fourth centuries A.D.

The study of Jewish traditions begins with the Scriptures, especially in their LXX form. Schlund finds using the LXX helpful because the translators had to interpret the Hebrew texts for the Greek-speaking world. The LXX shows an interplay between text and cultural context. Moreover, the LXX was widely used by Jewish and Christian writers, so that the interpretations formed by the translators contributed to the later shaping of the tradition. The principal Passover passage is Exod 12, which emphasizes that the Passover festival commemorates the way God protected the people of Israel from the destroyer. The slaying of the lamb was not understood in the ordinary categories of cult sacrifice. A passage in Ezek 45:18–20 does refer to smearing blood of a sin offering on the doorposts of the temple in a manner reminiscent of the Passover and comments about the Passover celebration follow in 45:21, but this does not seem to have led to a common tradition about Passover lambs being used to make atonement. Passages in other biblical texts sometimes relate purity or holiness to the Passover but assume that these are the conditions required for someone to participate. There is no suggestion that the Passover sacrifice purifies people or makes them holy. Rather, people are to purify themselves before the Passover, and those who are unclean are not to participate.

Philo interprets the tradition in two ways: (1) he identifies Israel's movement out of Egypt with the upward movement of the soul through wisdom; (2) Passover helps to make the Israelites a people. Josephus also thinks of the Passover as something central to Jewish identity. The book of *Jubilees* develops the theme of divine protection by depicting Passover as the time when God preserved Israel from the power of the demonic figure Mastema. *Jubilees* also regards the festival as constitutive for Jewish community life. Therefore, the dominant aspects of the Jewish tradition are that Passover commemorates divine preservation of Israel and grounds Jewish communal identity. The Passover requires purity for those participating, but it does not make people clean.

The Passover plays an important role in the passion narrative in John. The timing of Jesus' death is coordinated with the Passover sacrifice in John 19:13–16. Some have argued that the peculiar idea that the sponge with sour wine was placed on hyssop in 19:29—rather than on a reed, as in the Synoptics—recalls the use of hyssop to smear the lamb's blood in Exod 12:22. Schlund finds this unlikely. Many find a stronger link to the Passover tradition in the Evangelist's observation that Jesus' legs were not broken, followed by a comment that scripture said, "None of his bones shall be broken." This was written about the animal sacrificed for Passover (Exod 12:46; Num 9:12), but in Ps 34:20 the same thing was said about God preserving a righteous sufferer, without a Passover connection. Schlund thinks it likely that the Gospel refers to Passover at this point, given the Passover context in John. Nevertheless, she argues that this does not determine what Jesus' death means. In *Jub.* 49:13, for example, the fact that the Passover lamb's bones were not broken anticipates the way God would preserve the people of Israel. Where cleansing is mentioned in John's Passover context, it is part of the preparations for the festival, not a cleansing from sin by means of the Passover sacrifice (John 11:55; 18:28).

Schlund relates John's theology in part to the Passover theme of divine protection. Before his death, Jesus prays that God will protect his followers from the evil one (17:11–15), says that those who follow him preserve their souls for eternal life (12:25), and promises to keep them from destruction (6:39). To belong to Jesus is to be protected by him (10:28), for through his death he casts out the ruler of this world (12:27–33). Connections are also made with the Passover emphasis on community. The fruit of Jesus' death includes the gathering of the Greeks into the people of God (10:16; 12:20–21), so that Jesus' death, like the Passover, is central to the formation of a community. Schlund maintains that the cleansing reflected in the foot washing belongs to the preparation for the Passover and that it does not point to a cleansing from sin achieved through Jesus' death.

The study is detailed and contains a great deal of useful material, but several comments can be made. Schlund argues that calling Jesus "the Lamb of God who takes away the sin of the world" has nothing to do with Passover (1:29). She recognizes that later interpreters related the imagery to the Passover lamb, but she does not think this fits the Gospel itself. Many will find this unpersuasive. The opening chapters refer to the temple cleansing and to Moses lifting up the serpent on the pole in ways that anticipate the passion, making it highly likely that the lamb imagery does so as well. Introducing Jesus as the Lamb at the beginning of the Gospel anticipates his death as the Passover sacrifice at the end of the Gospel.

Schlund has clearly shown that Jewish traditions concerning the Passover did not depict the lamb as an atoning sacrifice—something many interpreters of John have overlooked. Nevertheless, the Fourth Evangelist frequently transforms the traditions he receives in order to give them new meanings. His theology is not controlled by the earlier categories related to Passover. Schlund is certainly correct that the death of Jesus can be related to protection from evil and to the establishment of a community. At the same time, it can also be related to the removal of sin, and if the Passover traditions shape John's interpretation of Jesus' death, his interpretation of Jesus' death in turn reshapes his understanding of the Passover. Schlund's careful study provides a wealth of material for continued discussion of John's interpretation of Jesus' death. Even those who disagree with some of her conclusions will find her questions challenging and her case well-argued, instructive, and worth careful study. This is a welcome addition to recent literature on the Fourth Gospel and its theology.

The Cambridge History of Judaism: The Late Roman-Rabbinic Period, edited by Steven Katz. Cambridge History of Judaism 4. New York: Cambridge University Press, 2006. Pp. xxvii + 1135. Cloth. $200.00, ISBN 0521772486.

Marvin A. Sweeney, Claremont School of Theology and Claremont Graduate University, Claremont, California

This magisterial volume, edited by Steven T. Katz, presents forty major essays that provide state-of-the-art discussion of the various aspects relevant to the study of Judaism in the rabbinic period during the latter period of Roman antiquity. As part of his general introduction to the work which provides the reader with an overview of all of the essays in the volume, Katz indicates that the essays were sent to outside reviewers for evaluation to ensure full coverage of the topic in question. Although encyclopedic, many essays also present original views.

Seth Schwartz's survey of political, social, and economic life in the land of Israel, 66–235 C.E.., raises questions concerning the full destruction of the Jewish population of Judah in the immediate aftermath of the Bar Kokhba revolt. Four scholars cover the Diaspora from 66 to 235 C.E. Allen Kerkslager treats the Jews of Egypt and Cyrenaica with a special emphasis on the failed 116–117 revolt against Rome. Claudia Seltzer treats the Jews in Carthage and western North Africa with a brief review of archeological/inscriptional and literary evidence. Paul Trebilco treats the Jews in Asia Minor with emphases on synagogue structures and the diversity of communities. David Goodblatt treats the Jews of Babylonia with brief indications of Jewish self-government, including consideration of the origins of the office of exilarch, under Parthian rule. Miriam Pucci ben Zeev treats the Diaspora Jewish revolt against Rome in 116–117 with a special interest in the interrelationship of uprisings throughout the empire. Hanan Eshel provides a masterful treatment of the Bar Kokhba revolt with special emphasis on archeological data.

Amnon Linder takes up the legal status of Jews in the Roman Empire during the pagan and Christian periods, including the freedom to manage local affairs and obligations to the state. Eric M. Myers treats Jewish art and architecture in the land of Israel from 70 to 235 C.E., including synagogues, private and public spaces, tombs, and the like. Robert Goldenberg treats the meaning and consequences of the destruction of the Jerusalem temple by emphasizing the shift from an ethnic to a religious community in the Roman world. Hayim Lapin treats the origins and development of the rabbinic movement in the land of Israel and emphasizes the early social marginalization of the rabbis as they transformed the cultural identity of Jews. James A. Sanders describes the canonical process of the formation of the Jewish Bible. Peter Richardson discusses the beginnings of Christian anti-Judaism from 70 through 235 C.E. by emphasizing that anti-Judaism appears especially in the urban areas and in the western empire, particularly among Christian communities that had been Jewish. Editor Katz presents an important treatment of the rabbinic response to Christianity with special emphasis on the blessing of the sectarians or heretics, which is intended to bring apostate Jews back to Judaism rather than simply to ban them.

David Kraemer provides a discussion of the Mishnah that undercuts the popular notion that it functions as commentary on Bible while nevertheless emphasizing its use of biblical language and concepts. Paul Mandel's discussion of the Tosefta emphasizes its oral character during the process of transmission. Jay M. Harris discusses Midrash Halakah, with many examples to illustrate its methods and concerns. Moshe Bar-Asher's treatment of Mishnaic Hebrew traces its linguistic growth from biblical Hebrew and its relations with Aramaic, Greek, and Latin.

David Goodblatt provides an overview discussion of the political and social history of Jews in the land of Israel from 235 to 638 C.E., with an emphasis on the transition from the Patriarchate to the Rabbinate. Joshua J. Schwartz discusses material remains from the land of Israel during the same period with emphasis on everyday life in both rural and urban settings. Yohanan Breuer discusses the development of Aramaic in late antiquity as a vernacular and literary language, with extensive treatment of rabbinic sources in Aramaic. Two scholars treat the Diaspora from 235 to 638 C.E. Leonard V. Rutgers treats the Jews of Italy, noting the relatively late rabbinic influence, while Scott Bradbury treats the Jews of Spain from its origins through King Sisebut's decree that all Jews convert to Christianity in 416 (*sic,* read 614) and its aftermath in the Visigoth period. Lee I. Levine masterfully treats Jewish art and architecture in late antiquity with copious photographs and illustrations. Joseph Tabory treats Jewish festivals in late antiquity as the formative era in the history of Jewish observance. Reuven Kimelman addresses Jewish prayer in late antiquity, providing a comprehensive discussion of the synagogue, rabbinic liturgy, and the question of emperor worship and divine sovereignty in the world.

Michael L. Satlow discusses rabbinic views on marriage, sexuality, and the family by emphasizing the developing view of the sanctity of marriage in late antiquity and the paucity of evidence as to how families actually functioned. Tal Ilan treats women in Jewish life and law by emphasizing how women gradually disappeared from rabbinic study by the time the Mishnah was completed. David Novack treats Gentiles in rabbinic thought from biblical through talmudic times, emphasizing that a Jew who sins is still a Jew and the conversion of a Gentile is permanent. Leib Moscovitz treats the formation and character of the Jerusalem Talmud by emphasizing its less-developed character in relation to the Babylonian Talmud. Avigdor Shinan treats the late midrashic, paytanic, and targumic literature in relation to their presentations of haggadic and halakic traditions and concerns. Michael D. Schwartz presents a timely discussion of Jewish magic in late antiquity in relation to folklore traditions, amulets, the *hekhalot* literature, and so forth. Eli Yassif discusses Jewish folk literature in late antiquity, with special emphasis on the biographical legend so common in rabbinic literature, magic, fables, and humoristic tales. Rachel Elior presents a state-of-the-art discussion of early forms of Jewish mysticism, with emphasis on the priestly origins of the works, Qumran literature, liturgical dimensions, and the *hekhalot* tradition.

Isaiah M. Gafni discusses the political, social, and economic history of Babylonian Jewry from 224 to 638 C.E., with particular emphasis on the origins of the office of exilarch and the poll tax in the third century and their development through the end of Sassanian rule. David Goodblatt discusses the history of the Babylonian rabbinic academies by emphasizing that the earlier Amoraic manifestations were hardly as institutionalized as the Gaonic academies of the later Islamic period. Richard Kalmin discusses the formation and character of the Babylonian Talmud by arguing for the possibility of recovering earlier traditions within the final, edited edition of the work. Hanina Ben-Menahem discusses talmudic law from a juridical perspective as a dynamic, diverse, and developing system of social organization and regulation. Marc Hirsch discusses the theology of learning in rabbinic thought that emphasizes the innate power of Torah that demands prudent use of its powers. Editor Katz provides an informative overview discussion of humanity, sin, and redemption in rabbinic Judaism that should be read by all in the field of religious studies. Reuven Kimelman discusses the rabbinic theology of the physical, including blessings, the body and soul, resurrection, and covenant and election, in an essay that should also be read by all in the field of religious studies.

Paula Fredriksen and Oded Irshai discuss the polemics and policies of Christian anti-Judaism from the second century on that examines the charge that Jews played some role in pagan persecution of Christians and the vehemence expressed by Christians against Jews upon ascending to power. Steven Bowman's discussion of Jews in Byzantium treats archaeological and demographic patterns and stresses that Justinian's war against Jews was part of a larger effort to recover parts of the empire lost to invaders. Lawrence H. Schiffman examines messianism and apocalypticism in rabbinic texts in relation to both the restoration of Israelite independence and the utopian perfection of society. An appendix by Alfredo Mordechai Rabello succinctly examines Justinian and the revision of Jewish legal status as the last Roman attempt to construct a legislative assault on the Jews with consequences for Jewish life through medieval and modern times. Each essay includes essential bibliography. A full subject index concludes the volume.

This is an essential and well-executed reference work on rabbinic Judaism that must be included in all research and teaching libraries.

JUDAISM: DEAD SEA SCROLLS

Women in the Damascus Document, by Cecilia Wassen. Society of Biblical Literature Academia Biblica 21. Atlanta: Society of Biblical Literature; Leiden: Brill, 2005. Pp. xiv + 257. Paper/cloth. $39.95/$137.00, ISBN 1589831683/900413770X.

Devorah Dimant, University of Haifa, Haifa, Israel

This volume is a Ph.D. dissertation analyzing one aspect of the *Damascus Document.* Partly known from several leaves of two Genizah manuscripts (=CD), ten fragmentary copies of this work were later discovered among the scrolls from Qumran. The *Damascus Document* is therefore recognized as one of the literary products of the community related to the Qumran scrolls. The full publication of Cave 4 copies by Joseph Baumgarten ten years ago permitted a fresh examination of this unique work, and several studies on specific aspects of the *Damascus Document* have been produced. The present volume belongs to this type of study, addressing the issue of women. The choice of this theme determined the major concern of the volume, namely, analysis of the halakic laws and the communal rule set out on pages IX–XVI of the Genizah version and in various passages from the Qumran copies. The author should be complimented on her concise and clear exposition. Besides succinct and well-informed introductions, the analyses of the pertinent text units are properly organized with comments, surveys of scholarly discussions, and useful conclusions. The volume renders a valuable service to students of the Scrolls and helps to focus the discussion on several important issues.

In a short introduction (1–17) the author explains her reasons for adopting the approach developed recently chiefly by Charlotte Hempel, namely, the division of the legal material in the *Damascus Document* into two types: (1) halakic laws, assembled in CD IX–XII, 18 and various passages from other Qumran copies and compared with the *Temple Scroll* and other Qumran documents; and (2) community ruling, found in CD XII, 20–XVI and compared with similar material of the *Rule of the Community* and the *Rule of the Congregation* (1QSa). Such a division is certainly justified by the distinct literary character and content of each type of material, and it has been generally accepted for many years. Regrettably, Wassen also embraces, albeit with some modification, the more controversial part of Hempel's analysis, her chronological interpretation of these literary data (of which more will be said below).

The second chapter (19–44) offers a survey of scholarly opinions on the literary character of the *Damascus Document.* Wassen favors the approach that detects several literary layers in the *Damascus Document,* represented in research mainly by the work of Jerome Murphy-O'Connor and Philip Davies. This has an important bearing on Wassen's approach and conclusion. No one will deny that the *Damascus Document* reworks a variety of sources. However, the existence of literary layers and redactors (cf., e.g., 126–27) is disputable. It is regrettable that Wassen did not consider more seriously the view, expressed in print by the present reviewer (briefly mentioned by Wassen on 32), that in its present form the *Damascus Document* displays a single overall framework.

The first substantial chapter (45–106) deals with the halakic material. Labeled by Wassen "The Early Law Code," it discusses the various halakic laws pertaining to women, such as cases of *zavah, nidah,* and childbirth; *sotah* and intercourse with slave women; marital arrangements; women's oaths and the like. Not surprisingly, Wassen concludes this part with the statement that the halakic laws in the *Damascus Document* "display an androcentric perspective, whereby women are viewed as other than male.… This perspective parallels the general tendency in biblical literature" (102–3). But she notes that on three issues the *Damascus Document* halakah "constitutes a clear improvement of women's legal position compared to biblical law": men are allowed to annul women's oaths only when the oaths may lead to transgression; the application of the ordeal of *sotah* is more difficult; and the inspection of a bride under suspicion not being a virgin is conducted before rather than after the wedding. However, as noted by Wassen herself, in regard to the second and third issues a more lenient approach to women is evinced in rabbinic halakah as well (64–65, 85–86). Therefore, the "improvement," in Wassen's terms, of women's status in Qumran halakah may reflect an earlier, more general halakic development in early Second Temple times, not a specific feature of the Qumran group or a parent circle. As for the oath, Wassen herself observes elsewhere (121) that it is based on a gender-inclusive understanding of the biblical law, as is the prohibition to marry a niece (CD V, 7–11). Consequently, the law of oath does not aim at "improving" women's status but at the application of a certain exegetical rule. Wassen briefly discusses items concerning women in the so-called Catalogue of Transgressors, found in 4Q270 2 i 16–19; ii 15–17 (pp. 107–12), and reaches similar conclusions. Yet this catalogue is sprinkled with sectarian terms and occurs in a sectarian context (cf. below).

In a separate chapter (113–29) Wassen discusses two laws pertaining to women in the admonition section: the prohibition of polygamy and marrying a niece; and defilement through menstrual blood (CD VII, 7–11, 20–21). She rightly concludes (128) that the marital laws in this section distinguished the community that practiced them from Israel at large. This approach, and the specific style and terminology of these laws, reveals the restrictive and separatist character typical of the Qumran community.

In the largest chapter (31–205) Wassen discusses the various rulings concerning women incorporated into the communal rule of the *Damascus Document.* She stresses the extensive control by the Examiner over the life of the community and the families therein, and in her conclusion she likens this system to a family, a simile used, in fact, by Josephus to describe the Essene community (*War* 2.120). Yet some particular facets of the community that emerge from Wassen's analysis merit special attention. The first is that there was a measure of equality between men and women within the communal structure. Such an equality is implied, for instance, in the initiation into the community (155–56) and in the equal education enjoyed by both boys and girls (CD XIII, 17–18; see the discussion on pp. 165–66). Based on her analysis of the terms "fathers" and "mothers" in 4Q270 7 i 13–15, another significant fact transpires from Wassen's discussion, namely, that women performed leading roles in the community (184–88). Here Wassen proposes an interesting interpretation of the term *rwqmh* (= "embroidery"), which the "mothers" are said not to possess (4Q270 7 i 14–15). Making the connection with the mystical embroidered cords given to the daughters of Job, according to *T. Job* 46:7, Wassen suggests that *rwqmh* designates specific garments that functioned in some sort of mystical activity within the Qumran community (194–96).

To conclude, I should point out that the overall picture drawn by this volume has important consequences. Significant is the fact that the halakic section represents the traditional, more "androcendric" view, while the communal rule shows tendencies toward some improvement of women's position. In itself this is an important conclusion that carries several implications meriting further study in the wider context of the sectarian organization system. However, interpreting these literary data in chronological terms, attributing the halakic laws to a different, earlier priestly group, is to miss the particular character of the sources. First, the halakic law of the *Damascus Document* is sprinkled with specific sectarian terminology, a fact that points to a sectarian adaptation of this material. Second, several sections pertaining to halakah (e.g., the Catalogue of Transgressors; see above) are sectarian even by content. In several places Wassen herself admits the separatist and sectarian character of a given halakah (e.g., the marital laws in the admonition section; see above). In addition, the definition of certain sectarian passages as "interpolation" (e.g., 126–27 in CD VII, 6–9) by a sectarian redactor is open to criticism. The accumulating effect of these aspects of the halakah point to their sectarian nature. They belie the label "general" given to the halakic section, as opposed to the communal law. The literary character and genre of the halakic section in CD may represent early literary conventions applied to halakic materials as such. Perhaps they stem from the main halakic tradition, based on biblical law and adhered to by all the groups active in Israel in Second Temple times. The distinction between the various groups resided in the interpretation of this major halakic tradition, hence in its practical application, but not in its essential character. What we really have in the halakic section of the CD, as well as in other halakic material from Qumran, is the specifically sectarian adaptation of the "general" halakah, an adaptation effected by particular interpretation of the biblical law and by the use of sectarian terminology.

Thus, there is no room to interpret these literary data in historical and chronological terms and to deduce from them the existence of a "pre-Qumranic" group different from the Qumran community. If there was such a "pre-Qumranic" group, and I believe there was, its existence must be argued on the basis of other types of evidence.

JUDAISM: RABBINIC AND MEDIEVAL

From Sermon to Commentary: Expounding the Bible in Talmudic Babylonia, by Eliezar Segal. Studies in Christianity and Judaism/Études sur le christianisme et le judaïsme 17. Waterloo, Ont.: Wilfrid Laurier University Press, 2005. Pp. vii + 164. Hardcover. $49.95. ISBN 0889204829.

Joshua Schwartz, Bar Ilan University, Ramat-Gan, Israel

Those of us who studied Talmud (and always the Babylonian Talmud) at various levels in *yeshivot* were accustomed to glossing over, or skipping entirely, those sections of the Babylonian Talmud being studied that dealt with haggadah, the component of rabbinic literature that relates to the Bible from a nonlegal standpoint, as opposed to those that dealt with halakah, or legal discourse. "We, in our generation, are not capable of understanding these haggadic traditions," our rabbis would tell us, "and best not to waste time on them when we should be studying important legal issues." This seemed to be a polite way of stating that many of these haggadic traditions in the Babylonian Talmud seemed to be superfluous, cryptic, capricious, and often seemingly the least likely of imaginable interpretations of a biblical word or verse, even if we were not really expecting to find there *peshat* or the simple meaning of the text. The author of this review was often much perturbed by this attitude. If it was possible to dissect and analyze complex halakic questions, why was this not possible in matters of haggadah? And when it was done, why was the analysis so unfulfilling?

The fact is, though, that our teachers were right, even if they did not know why. Eliezer Segal is hardly the first to deal with this issue from an academic perspective, but he does provide in this short work an explanation that traces the roots and development of haggadic midrash in the Babylonian Talmud, shedding further light on the distinctive traits of this haggadic midrash and helping one to understand these traditions, or at least why they often seem to make no sense. While his study should be defined as "tentative" and "prolegomena," I cannot imagine going back to deal with the haggadah of the Babylonian Talmud without reference to his work.

It has long been noted that a superior rendering of traditions that focuses on the interpretation and homiletical exposition of biblical texts is found in the Palestinian haggadic tradition. The seeming inferiority of the Babylonian Talmud in haggadah[1] has been explained in terms of psychological or cultural factors.

---

1. Obviously, sweeping generalizations should be avoided, and Segal is well-aware of the work of scholars who find literary sophistication in haggadic passages of the Babylonian Talmud. However, Segal also points out that these passages tend to be narratives, whether legendary anecdotes regarding talmudic sages or of biblical figures and episodes associated with them. Segal makes reference to the work of Jonah Fraenkel, Ofrah Meir, and Jeffrey I. Rubenstein (2).

One of the more common explanations relates to the supposed different political and cultural realties of Babylonia and the Land of Israel. The continued polemical barrage of assaults on the religious values of the Palestinian Jewish community, which were often rooted in claims and counterclaims concerning the understanding of the Bible, resulted in the development of synagogue sermons on biblical portions aimed at lifting morale as well as providing ideological weapons to defend the beleaguered faith. The insularity and relative autonomy of Babylonian Jewry did not prove a fertile environment for midrashic preaching. Segal sees the Babylonian community as less insular, having to face also ideological enemies, and he prefers to account for the differences between the vibrant haggadah of the Land of Israel and the much less vibrant haggadah of Babylonia in terms of the different types of literary corpus that formed the basis for both haggadic literatures as well as the institutional settings in which both midrashic traditions were created.

The distinction between the two types, and consequently the understanding of the haggadah in the Babylonian Talmud, is the result of the fact that haggadic midrash was created in the synagogue, whereas the Talmud was created in the academy (3). The synagogue's ambience provided for interplay between the rabbi and the living community, which finds its literary expression in the sermon. The ambience of the academy was characterized by theoretical study and scholarly interpretation. For the preacher, biblical verses were used to further the literary and ideological objectives of a sermon; for the talmudic scholar, the goal of intellectual activity vis-à-vis the Bible was the elucidation of the text. The explanations in the Palestinian synagogue were often homiletical with the intent of providing some type of ethical or religious lesson. In transition from synagogue to academy, the sources and their framework often became skewered. Homilies were transformed into exegesis, and often very bad exegesis at that.

Segal has long been aware of this pattern, which he discovered in earlier work (*The Babylonian Esther Midrash: A Critical Commentary* [BJS 210; Atlanta: Scholars Press, 1994]). However, since those initial investigations related to a single block of text (*b. Megillah* 10b–17a), and might not represent Babylonian haggadah in general, he decided to perform a similar analysis of a different corpus of Babylonian haggadah. This time Segal has chosen to study traditions attributed to the first-generation Babylonian Amoraim, Rav and Samuel, and particularly the formal pattern: "Rav and Samuel—One says x and one says y."

After explaining all of the above to the reader, Segal proceeds to examine thirty-two passages of haggadic nature from the Babylonian Talmud introduced by the formula just cited (9–128). In respect to each passage he poses the following questions: How does the interpretation function as exegesis (if at all!)? How might the interpretation have been (originally) incorporated in a homiletical discourse preached at the synagogue? Are there similar interpretations in the Palestinian midrashic corpus, and, if so, how do they rate as exegeses or homilies? Are there grounds for supposing that one version might have evolved out of the other or that both might be variants of a common prototype? Finally, are there ideological, hermeneutical, literary, or other factors that would account for the differences?

His conclusions are quite interesting, sometimes more so for what is missing (129–39). Most of the thirty-two traditions have parallels in the Palestinian traditions, even when the scriptural texts were from works that were not central to the liturgy of the synagogue. The bulk of the exegeses were also quite exegetically unsatisfying and rarely contributed to our understanding of the subtleties of Scripture (and thus providing much [apologetic] work for the traditional commentators of the Talmud), and quite a few fall into the category of midrashic name etymologies, which are not unusual and are also quite unsatisfying.

The Palestinian traditions are intertextual, based on encounters between two or more verses, and central to their liturgical background and the liturgical practice of linking pentateuchal readings on Sabbaths and festivals to related passages in the Prophets. The Palestinian parallels are often also incorporated into rhetorical structures, most commonly *petihtot* proems but also closing perorations or other elements. The intertextuality of the Palestinian version often inspired novel interpretations, usually as the result of the interplay between the verses. The Babylonian versions often interpreted isolated verses, without reference to the intertextual cross-fertilization. Is it any wonder, then, that the Babylonian versions often seemed so strange? On top of this, the Babylonian haggadic versions being incorporated in the Talmud, whose interests and methodologies were halakic, were often subject to the dialectics of inappropriate halakic discourse.

Essentially, what the "editors" of the Babylonian Talmud seemed to have done was to blur the borders and distinctions between exegesis and homiletics. What made sense in homiletical discourse became often incomprehensible as exegesis. Unfortunately, as Segal points out, this blurring became quite rampant in Jewish scriptural studies through subsequent generations. The ancient preachers in the synagogues had utilized homiletic manipulations for their own rhetorical purposes but never had any intention of turning it into authoritative philological exegesis. The blurring of literary genres resulted in the indiscriminating reader being unable to appreciate the beauty of the homily, on the one hand, and to the mindless acceptance of outrageous or indefensible readings of the Bible, on the other. Those somewhat more discriminating might even develop disdain for the misguided rabbis who fostered such exegeses. Ultimately, rhetorical devices of ancient Jewish preachers coalesced into exegesis that might even become presented as historical fact and as religiously obligatory interpretation, and questioning them became tantamount to repudiating ancestral tradition.

This brings us back to the *yeshiva*. We teachers and students who were unaware of literary genres, blurred or otherwise, were perhaps much better served at that time by skipping the midrashic haggadah of the Babylonian Talmud. However, all who would seek to understand the haggadah of the Babylonian Talmud, as well as its relation to Palestinian tradition, would be very well served by reading this book and the other studies of Eliezer Segal.

Trajectories in Near Eastern Apocalyptic: A Postrabbinic Jewish Apocalypse Reader, by John C. Reeves. Atlanta: Society of Biblical Literature; Leiden: Brill, 2005. Pp. xvi + 262. Paper/cloth. $29.95/$134.00. ISBN 1589831020/9004130950.

Lorenzo DiTommaso, Concordia University, Montréal, Quebec, Canada

John C. Reeves's fine reader serves two useful functions. First, it provides introductions to and translations of a broad selection of medieval Jewish apocalyptic literature, primarily from the last half of the first millennium. Second, it should put to rest the tired proposition that the mainstream production of Jewish apocalyptica had run its course after the failure of Bar Kokhba and that the sole heir to Second Temple apocalypticism was *merkavah* mysticism.

Reeves's general introduction (1–25) is welcome. Although analogues exist in modern Hebrew, the only other recent overview in English is Moshe Idel's contribution to the *Encyclopedia of Apocalypticism*.[1] Before this we need to go back to Moses Buttenweiser's *Outline of the Neo-Hebraic Literature*, published in 1901.[2]

The translations appear in part 1, "A Gallery of Jewish Apocalypses" (a misleading title, since not all the texts are apocalypses). The section begins with the two compositions perhaps most familiar to scholars of biblical apocrypha. The first is the *Sefer Elijah* (29–39), the base text for which Reeves draws from Buttenweiser's *Die hebräische Elias-Apocalypse* (Leipzig, 1897), with variants from the version printed in the third volume of A. Jellinek, *Bet ha-Midrasch* (Leipzig, 1853–77). The second is the *Sefer Zerubbabel* (40–66), a version of which is embedded in the *Chronicles of Yeraḥmeel* of Oxford, cod. Heb. d.11 (no. 2797). Reeves's translation relies mainly on a study of this manuscript, via the transcriptions of I. Lévy, *RÉJ* 68 (1914), and A. Yassif, *Sefer ha-Zikronot hu' Divrey ha-Yamim le-Yeraḥmeʾel* (Tel-Aviv, 2001), and in consultation with other Oxford manuscript copies, several print editions, and manuscripts from the Cairo Genizah.

Next is a synoptic version of *Pirqe de-Rabbi Eliezar* §30 (67–75), presented with four parallel columns of the Hebrew text: two print versions, one from 1544 and reproduced in L. Zunz and Ch. Albeck, *Haderashot be-Yisrael* (2nd ed.; Jerusalem, 1954), the other included in M. Higger, *Halakhot va-aggadot* (New York, 1933); plus two manuscript versions, Hebrew Union College codd. 75 and 2043. After this are sections on groups of compositions associated with a person or motif. The R. Šimʿōn b. Yoḥai complex (76–105) features the *Secrets* and the *Prayer* of the rabbi, with the translations based on texts in *Bet ha-Midrasch III* and *IV*. The "Apocalypses featuring 'Ten Signs'" (106–32) include the *'Otot* of R.

---

1. "Jewish Apocalypticism: 670–1670," *Apocalypticism in Western History and Culture* (vol. 2 of *The Encyclopedia of Apocalypticism*; ed. B. McGinn; New York Continuum, 2000), 204–37.

2. (Cincinnati: Jennings & Pye). According to its preface, this short tract (45 pages) was originally composed for the *Jewish Encyclopedia* but endured editorial alterations of the sort that its author was obliged to disavow it and publish his original study in book form.

Šimʿōn b. Yoḥai (from a Genizah manuscript published by A. Marmorstein in *RÉJ* 52 (1906)), the *Ten Signs* (*apud* Higger), the *'Otot Ha-Mašiaḥ* (from *Bet ha-Midrasch II*), and *Ten Further Things Pertaining to the Days of the Messiah* (Oxford cod. Heb. d.11 again, *apud* Yassif, *Sefer ha-Zikronot*).

The gallery concludes with translations of the Responsum of R. Hai Gaon on Redemption (133–43), *apud* the text of Y. Even-Shmuel, *Midreshey Ge'ullah* (2nd ed.; Jerusalem, 1954), and the *'Aggadat ha- Mašiaḥ* (144–48), the *Pirqe (Pereq) Mašiaḥ* (149–71), and the end of the *Midrash Wa-Yosha'* (172–76), from *Bet ha-Midrasch III, VI,* and *I,* respectively.

Part 2 is devoted to "Thematic Excursuses." Here we encounter sections on "Metatron as Apocalyptic Persona" (179–86), "The Eschatological Appearance of the Staff of Moses" (187–99), and the "People of Moses" (200–224). The book ends with a bibliography and thorough indexes of the ancient sources, ancient and medieval authors and commentators, and modern authors.

The quality of the translations is excellent. Reeves's prose is lean and uncluttered, and in the places where he introduces or explains a text, his points are clear. The nearly one thousand citations from the Hebrew Bible are, on the basis of a small sample drawn for verification, identified with precision. The typescript appears to have been proofread with great care.

An attention to detail characterizes the book and increases its utility. Its footnotes, a genuine pleasure to read, are a mine of valuable data and demonstrate Reeves's familiarity with the texts and knowledge of their broader contexts. He takes the trouble to list the manuscript evidence and print history for most of his selections, including copies identified through his examination of manuscript catalogues, and in several places employs unedited manuscripts for his translations. These features, as well as the thematic excursuses, render the book suitable for advanced research, a quality not normally associated with anthologies of this type.

Certain aspects of the book are open to question. Reeves admits that the limitations of scope did not permit the investigation of several important themes, such as the relationship between his selections and the Karaite apocalypses or the *hekhalot* material. Also excluded are translations of anything from the vast corpus of late antique and early medieval Daniel apocalyptica on the grounds that its complete extent remains unknown.[3] From one perspective these are the correct decisions, and the book is more focused because of them. Yet the omission of any discussion of the Daniel complex restricts Reeves's evaluation of the subject matter, particularly regarding its shared elements with Christian and Islamic apocalyptic literature, which in turn would have informed, among other things, his structural comparison of the nature and order of the material in medieval

---

3. The publication date of Reeves's book indicates that he could not have known of the existence of this reviewer's volume, *The Book of Daniel and the Apocryphal Daniel Literature* (SVTP 20; Leiden: Brill, 2005), which identifies and discusses many of these texts.

Christian, Jewish, and Islamic texts (17–24). Also missing is a sense of the book's importance within the context of the history of the understanding of postrabbinic Jewish apocalypticism.

Neither objection, however, obscures the fact that *Trajectories in Near Eastern Apocalyptic* is a wonderful collection that fills a specific, obvious need. For a long time Anglophone scholars wishing to read many of these medieval Jewish apocalyptica have been frustrated by outdated or unavailable translations. This is no longer the case, and we must thank Reeves for his excellent work.

Households, Sects, and the Origins of Rabbinic Judaism, by Alexei M. Sivertsev. Supplements to the Journal for the Study of Judaism 102. Leiden: Brill, 2005. Pp. viii + 301. Hardcover. $136.00. ISBN 9004144471.

Gary Porton, University of Illinois, Urbana, Illinois

Sivertsev's study argues that the family was the basic social unit within Judaism from the biblical to the rabbinic periods. He notes that in "Ancient Israel and the early Second Temple period" scribal schools trained professional bureaucrats. However, "a good deal of education took place within informal and often family-based circles, including those of scribes and priests.... The family was perceived as a locus of knowledge transmission far beyond elementary education" (5). Sivertsev sees the rabbis' disciple circles as the new feature of rabbinic Judaism that most separates it from the earlier periods. Like many before him, he believes that the creation of circles of master-disciples developed from Greco-Roman models of education, and he draws parallels between the rabbinic schools and the Hellenistic academies (10–11).

Sivertsev claims that family life, household activities, and household functions were "religiously meaningful loci of sanctity" for a variety of religious groups from the biblical through the early rabbinic periods. "By meticulously observing halakhic regulations pertaining to everyday household activities these groups tried to achieve religious ideals of purity, piety, and ultimately, holiness and salvation" (17). He suggests that the rise of the disciple circles was "a great paradigmatic shift in the discourse of holiness," which "occurred when new associations of like-minded adult individuals began to sideline more traditional kinship groups in their capacity as 'sacred communities.'" The "new holiness projects" that developed at that time had to "either accommodate both social types or deny religious validity to one of them" (17).

One of his more interesting and challenging suggestions it that the Jewish sects that developed during the Hellenistic period were "essentially alliances of individual families bound together by their common understanding of Torah. Jewish law took its form within the family setting and was often indistinguishable from the ancestral practices of individual households" (20–21). In addition, he reads the *Damascus Covenant* from Qumran in terms of family holiness (101–8), which is different from the *Community Rule,* which he argues placed the community, not the family, as the locus of holiness (132–40). Sivertsev argues that at Qumran we find evidence of both models, holiness centered in family and holiness centered in community, overlapping. He believes that the family-centered modes of Judaism continued into the rabbinic period and formed the basis of the universal teachings of rabbinic Judaism. The rabbis attempted to integrate the family into their project of holiness by legislating for them. Family life was religiously meaningful, and the newly emerging rabbis often created their halakah around the setting, practice, and functions of the family (211–74).

Sivertsev has written an interesting and important book. Clearly, within the biblical text the family unit plays a central role, from the patriarchal narratives through the priestly and Levitical families and culminating in the royal dynasties. While the prophets seem not to be centered around family relationships, one could argue, and I assume Sivertsev would, that the individual prophets got the main elements of their messages from the "traditions of their family." The only clear example of nonfamily units are the prophetic bands to which Elisha and Elijah belonged and the assumed groups of followers-disciples of the literary prophets, from which we have a few names but few other details. Sivertsev has pointed to an obvious social reality, and his work forces us to think with greater seriousness about the ancient family as a source of teachings, traditions, and laws.

The book is well-written and the arguments clearly stated. However, one is not always convinced that Sivertsev has offered the only, or best, explanation for the evidence he discusses. The family unit is clearly important in the marriage regulations in Ezra-Nehemiah, and priestly genealogies focus on family lineage. Nehemiah does place his brother in charge of Jerusalem. At the same time, I am not convinced of the fact that children and women, along with men, gathering to hear the reading of the Torah points to the centrality of family. Just as likely, the author wishes to make it clear that everyone must hear the reading of the Torah of Moses, and no point regarding family is intended at all. Similarly, the fact that Nehemiah mentions his brothers and servants as his supporters need not be taken literally as referring to his family's household, nor does the fact that Nehemiah placed men as guards in front of their houses necessarily support a claim for the importance of the family unit.

The Hellenistic period clearly continues the centrality of family—the Tobiads, the Oniads, and the Herodians all could have easily had family traditions upon which they based their understandings of the proper ways to structure the Jewish community and engage in public life. Sivertsev's reading of Tobit is interesting and important. However, his claim that family is crucial to *Jubilees* because the laws first originated with the patriarchal families and then became written on the heavenly tablets, although accurate, misses one of the major points of *Jubilees*, that the laws of Exodus and Numbers go back to the patriarchal period. Thus, they have always been part of Judaism; they were not practiced only from Sinai forward.

Sivertsev's literal reading of the "traditions of the fathers" as the origin of

Pharisaic law and Sadducean traditions is problematic. While it is possible that some Pharisees taught laws and interpretations that were traditions in their families, the "traditions of the fathers" most likely does not refer literally to the fathers of the various families of the early Pharisees. It more likely is a literary phrase referring to the fact that the traditions and interpretations are quite old. Also, Sivertsev does not explain how several families who agreed on the interpretations and laws they taught and shared joined together to form "groups," such as the Pharisees and Sadducees. These are recognized groups of people who are called by the same nomenclature in Josephus, the New Testament, and the rabbinic texts. Each document deals with the "groups" differently, focusing on different traits. What the various "families" had in common is not clear, nor is it obvious why like-minded families would have joined together to form a "sect." How much would they have to agree upon to be a group? How would they function when a particular tradition was not in every family or when various families had differing laws and rituals?

In contrast to these problems in the discussion of the Pharisees and Sadducees, Sivertsev's discussion of the *Damascus Covenant* and the *Community Rule* is fascinating; in fact, his treatment of all of the Qumran texts presents new ways of reading the sect, its origins, and its history. While again, one can accuse him of overreading or taking some phrase too literally, this discussion deserves serious attention by specialists in the field.

Sivertsev argues that early rabbinic laws were merely individual traditions that the rabbis, over time, taught as Torah for the whole community. To support this claim, he points to a few tannaitic passages in which a rabbi states that he learned something from his father or saw his father do something in a particular way. He does note that most of these sages come out of priestly families, which would have been a natural locus for family traditions. However, he finds other instances, such as the Gamaliel corpus and the "case stories" of early sages that he says point to family traditions. But it is not at all clear why Sivertsev dismisses the relevance of the fact that Gamaliel was a patriarch. The old argument that the Gamaliel stories are different because they stem from the patriarch's traditions could explain the phenomenon as well as Sivertsev's analysis. Finally, Sivertsev's demonstration that much of early rabbinic law attempts to legislate the family setting, a point, as he notes, others have made before him, is interesting in light of his larger analysis.

Sivertsev's suggestions about the early rabbinic traditions are interesting but also not fully convincing. We do have a *few* texts in which sages refer to their families' practices, but those are the exception. The Gamaliel material is noted for the fact that it is so different from the other materials in the tannaitic collections. In addition, a good deal of scholarship has convincingly demonstrated that the Mishnah's Yavnean traditions tend to talk about and develop themes attributed to pre-70 rabbinic masters, and the Ushan strata takes up and develops both the substance and the legal theories of the laws from Yavneh. The Mishnah thus comprises a cogent and evolving legal system, not merely a listing of practices that individual rabbis knew from their families. While it is possible, perhaps even likely, that there were instances in which a rabbi might have seen, known, or learned a certain approach from his father or that family traditions were brought into the study house, the evidence before us, even the material Sivertsev presents, suggests this was a small percentage of the tannaitic materials we have before us. The vast majority of the evidence from Mishnah-Tosefta suggests that the sages developed specific legal theories on topics that they chose to talk about because those topics allowed them to explore philosophical and theological issues they thought were important. While Sivertsev is correct that the rabbis often discussed their specific issues in the contexts of homes, villages, and farms, it is not clear to me what other settings were available to them that could provide the realia around which they could build their legal theories or express their theological assumptions. Within the early rabbinic world, the family thus is only as important as we would expect it to be.

The texts Sivertsev cites and the arguments he puts forth need to be taken into consideration by anyone who wishes to understand the development of Judaism from Ezra-Nehemiah through the rabbinic period. While one can argue with specific points and readings throughout Sivertsev's study, his reminder that the family was a source of Jewish tradition, customs, interpretations, and laws is an important fact that many often overlook. Sivertsev has produced an important work that should be read and discussed by large numbers of scholars. We can all learn from Sivertsev's arguments and suggestions.

Rereading the Mishnah: A New Approach to Ancient Jewish Texts, by Judith Hauptman. Texts and Studies in Ancient Judaism 109. Tubingen: Mohr Siebeck, 2005. Pp. xi + 285. Hardcover. €84.00. ISBN 3161487133.

Joshua Schwartz, Bar-Ilan University, Ramat-Gan, Israel

Judith Hauptman has long been studying the relationship between Mishnah and Tosefta and the history of their origins and composition. These issues, of course, have long been studied by scholars and before that even by talmudic commentators. The first to attempt to comment on the relationship between Mishnah and Tosefta in a (somewhat) systematic manner was the tenth-century Babylonian Gaon Sherira. Sherira theorized that after Rabbi Judah the Prince had composed the Mishnah, his younger colleague Rabbi Hiyya explained its principles and rules in a work that came to be known as Tosefta (14–15). Sherira Gaon's theory remained unchallenged for many centuries, whether among medieval commentators of the Talmud or among scholars. While scholarship has at times modified or fine-tuned various aspects of it, the core assumption remains: the Mishnah is earlier and the Tosefta is later, and the Tosefta, as Jacob Neusner put it in his systematic study of both Mishnah and Tosefta, rests upon the Mishnah and was its first commentary, amplification, and extension (16).

Hauptman was bothered by a number of problems in this accepted theory: the Tosefta's comments on Mishnah often appear in a different order from the

Mishnah; the Tosefta often presents a topic that appeared in the Mishnah in a totally different manner, making it hard to consider it a response; and the Tosefta often has nothing to say about many topics in the Mishnah that cry out for explanation. Moreover, often the Tosefta seems not to be commenting on the Mishnah, but rather the Mishnah seems to be rewriting, reworking, and modifying the Tosefta.

All this lead Hauptman to the realization that Tosefta was not a commentary on our Mishnah but rather on an earlier collection of Mishnaic material that the author, in the spirit of New Testament scholarship, calls "ur-Mishnah," and that the Tosefta was a commentary on this earlier text (which the author can uncover only as snippets when cited by Tosefta). The present-day Mishnah, according to all this, is an amalgam of the two older texts, the ur-Mishnah and the Tosefta, and was produced by the redactor of the Mishnah early in the third century, for reasons unknown to us today, to reflect his own teaching. The redactor frequently reshapes and compacts Tosefta material to reflect his own thinking (17–24). Moreover, working backwards, if the Tosefta can be regarded as the basis for the Mishnah, the redaction of the Mishnah can now be understood in new and different ways. Hauptman is not alone in claiming the Tosefta as the basis for Mishnah, and the primacy of Tosefta to Mishnah in certain instances has been postulated by other scholars such as Shama Friedman,[1] but Hauptman is the first and the only scholar to present it all as "global theory" (x), and it is this theory that Hauptman offers to the reader in the present volume.

The book has seven chapters: (1) "Rethinking the Relationship between the Mishnah and the Tosefta"; (2) "The Tosefta as a Commentary on an Early Mishnah"; (3) "Rewriting the Tosefta's Halakic Paragraphs for Inclusion in the Mishnah"; (4) "Condensing Aggadah"; (5) "Editing for Ease of Memory"; (6) "From Tosefta to Mishnah to Talmud"; (7) "A New Model of the Mishnah-Tosefta Relationship." The five essential points of the book are: (1) the Tosefta existed as a collection prior to our Mishnah and is a commentary on an early Mishnah, the ur-Mishnah; (2) the redactor of the Mishnah rewrites paragraphs and chapters of the Tosefta in accordance with his own halakhic approach; (3) the redactor compresses lengthy aggadic excurses of Tosefta sometimes to the extent that the Mishnah cannot be understood; (4) the redactor introduces mnemonic devices into the text, superimposing structure, a point made by Jacob Neusner long ago, although without accepting the priority of Tosefta as Hauptman does; (5) the Tosefta passages, already altered by the redactor for inclusion in the Mishnah, continued to evolve after incorporation into the Talmud (29–30). The bulk of the book consists of examples and analysis to prove these points. Obvious constraints of space force us to make do with an example or two.

---

1. See, e.g., Shama Friedman, "The Primacy of Tosefta to Mishnah in Synoptic Parallels," in *Introducing Tosefta: Textual, Intratextual and Intertextual Studies* (ed. Harry Fox and Tirzah Meacham; Hoboken, N.J., 1999), 99–122.

The first example relates to the "Tosefta's stringent stand on dogs and the Mishnah's more liberal one" (34–36). We read (in both sources in the author's translation) in *m. Baba Qamma* 7:7: "One may not raise small cattle in the land of Israel.... One may raise a dog only if he ties it with a chain." *Tosefta Baba Qamma* 8:17 reads: "Even though they have said: 'One may not raise dogs in a settled area,' but one may raise them in towns which are near the frontier. By day one ties them up on iron chains, but one unties them at night. R. Liezer says: one who raises dogs is like one who raises pigs." Hauptman's first point is that the Tosefta cannot be citing *our* Mishnah, because that source allows dogs to be raised in any area, as long as they are chained, but the Tosefta categorically forbids dogs to be raised in settled areas, even if chained. They may be raised only in "frontier" areas or in border towns. Thus, the Tosefta is undoubtedly quoting the ur-Mishnah, which represented a stringent view vis-à-vis settled areas. The redactor of the Mishnah took the point about chains, originally pertaining only to the "frontier," and transferred it to all types of settlements and areas, representing a more canine-friendly view. Thus, instead of seeing the Tosefta as commentary, perhaps too general and somewhat unclear, regarding dogs, we now have a chronologically developed formulation regarding the attitude to dogs in these sources and in Jewish society. Why these changes in attitude came about, however, is clearly not the business nor the problem of the author, although it would have been helpful if she integrated the view of Rabbi (E)liezer into her explanation of the textual development. If she is correct, however, in her Talmudics, some of the relevant canine issues of social history and material culture might have to be revised. [2] What is missing, though, is proof of the elusive ur-Mishnah and its supposedly "ur-stringent" view on raising dogs.

The second example we shall cite is a case of the redactor of the Mishnah compressing lengthy aggadic sections of the Tosefta (148–50). *Mishnah Yoma* 3:10 mentions a number of temple benefactors who merit praise and among them "Niqanor for whose gates miracles were performed." There is no mention here of what those miracles were. *Mishnah Middot* 2:3 also refers to Niqanor's gates and states that to help people remember the miracles related to the gates, without indicating what these miracles were, these gates remained their original copper (or brass) and were not coated with gold, as the other gates of the temple *azarah* complex were. *Tosefta Yoma* 3:8, however, provides a very lengthy and detailed

---

2. On dogs in ancient Jewish society, as well as on the sources presented by Hauptman, see Joshua Schwartz, "Dogs in Jewish Society in the Second Temple Period and in the Mishnah and Talmud Period," *JJS* 55 (2004): 246–77. See also idem, "Dogs in Ancient Jewish Rural Society," in *The Rural Landscape of Ancient Israel* (ed. A.M. Maeir, S. Dar, and Z. Safrai; BAR International Series 1121; Oxford: Archaeopress, 2003), 127–36; idem, "Dogs and Cats in Jewish Society in the Second Temple, Mishnah and Talmud Periods," in *Proceedings of the Twelfth World Jewish Congress, Division B, History of the Jewish People* (2000), 25*–34*; and idem, "Dog, 'Water' and Wall," *SJOT* 14 (2000): 101–16.

description of the obscure, aggadic allusions of the Mishnah. Some of those scholars who considered the Tosefta to be late tended to discount the relevance and, needless to say, historicity of the Tosefta tradition and sought explanations for the Mishnah reference in other types of early literature from 1 and 2 Maccabees to Josephus.[3] If the miracle traditions are early, perhaps even stemming from the ur-Mishnah, they take on more potential relevance for the study of the Jerusalem temple and its courts. Why the redactor of the Mishnah should have sought to hide all this from the reader is anybody's guess, and Hauptman's suggestion that the redactor left just enough to pique the curiosity of the reader and send him to read the Tosefta is not entirely convincing.

Hauptman's (re)reading of Mishnah and Tosefta not only offers new understanding regarding the development of these texts and their meaning but, as shown above, has great relevance for any scholar who might use Mishnah-Tosefta in studies ranging from social history to realia to ancient economics and much more. Making sense of the literary and subsequently the halakhic development of the building blocks of this literature is a *sine qua non* for the study of Mishnah-Tosefta for any purpose whatsoever. However, in spite of the importance and potential of Hauptman's reading and theory, a number of general issues still seemed problematic to this reviewer.

The first certainly relates to the elusive ur-Mishnah, which at best can be found only in Hauptman's reading of the Tosefta and whose existence requires a certain leap of academic faith that will undoubtedly not be accepted by all. The second relates to her somewhat too light dismissal of orality theory, which might be relevant to the study of the interrelationship of Mishnah and Tosefta (28–29). Hauptman admits that, in the view of orality critics, her "textual dependency" might seem outdated and make no sense. Orality scholars claim that scribes had access to pools of material and could draw upon them at will. According to this view, the micro-study of differences and similarities between Mishnah and Tosefta is superfluous. "I do not dismiss the findings of orality theory," states Hauptman, "but hold that they need to be applied with care to Mishnah and Tosefta studies." Indeed! But, as Hauptman mentions, referring to the work of Martin Jaffee, not every apparent borrowing is indeed such, throwing the potential wrench into the workings of her system.[4] Orality theory might not provide a satisfactory model for similarities or differences between Mishnah and Tosefta, but it does make a logical case for a reality different from that postulated by the author, and both theories rest on much that cannot be proven. From a literary point of view, it should also be remembered that text citation in the ancient world was probably a little less stringent than in our academic one, providing another caveat in relation to the author's close readings.

3. See, e.g., Joshua Schwartz, "Once More on the Nicanor Gate," *HUCA* 62 (1991): 245–84.

4. Martin S. Jaffee, *Torah in the Mouth: Writing and Oral Tradition in Palestine, 200 BCE-400 CE* (Oxford: Oxford University Press, 2001).

In spite of the few problems just mentioned above, Hauptman has provided the reader with a work of importance, offering a stratagem for (re)reading the Mishnah and Tosefta. Whether or not one agrees with her views regarding their genesis and development as collections or accepts the readings and interpretations of the sources she presents, she has opened the door to vast new interpretations of rabbinic literature.

JUDAISM AND CHRISTIANITY

Encountering the Rest of God: How Jesus Came toPersonify the Sabbath, by Henry Sturcke. Zürich: Theologischer Verlag Zürich, 2005. Pp. 393. Paper. €34.50. ISBN 3290173518.

Boris Repschinski, Leopold Franzens Universität, Innsbruck, Austria

The so-called parting of the ways between Judaism and early Christianity enjoys intense discussion among scholars. In this context, the dissertation of Henry Sturcke, submitted to the theological faculty of the University of Zurich and directed by Jean Zumstein, is a most welcome addition, because if focuses on a very particular topic that nevertheless is one of the central issues in the debate. Sturcke's question concerns the development of the abandonment of the Sabbath among Christians in favor of the celebration of the first day of the week as the Lord's Day. Sturcke is well aware that this was probably not a linear process and that different communities dealt in different ways with the Sabbath. However, as the title suggests, Sturcke is convinced that the roots of the abandonment of the Sabbath as the day of rest lie in the words and deeds of Jesus that might be interpreted as critical of the Sabbath.

The study is divided into seven chapters. The first chapter is an introduction that lays out the subject of inquiry and provides a brief history of research on various aspects of the Sabbath. It then lays out the structure and method of the book and ends with Sturcke's main thesis. He aims to show that there is no single reason for the abandonment of the Sabbath observance, since this could not account for the diversity of early Christianity. Instead, he suggests a process that was catalyzed by the advent of the Gentile mission, the cooling of ardor of the first generations of Christians, and the impossibility of returning to Sabbath observance when the need for more structured worship made itself felt (36).

The second chapter traces the Sabbath in the Old Testament and intertestamental Judaism and then in the Roman world. In the latter part Sturcke also refers to attitudes toward Judaism occasioned by Sabbath observance, as well as to proselytes and Godfearers in the synagogue. Interestingly, Sturcke does not explicitly differentiate between Palestinian and Diaspora Judaism, probably rightly so, since there is little indication that Sabbath observance differed greatly between them.

The third chapter is at the same time the first chapter dealing explicitly with a New Testament text, namely, Gal 4:8–11. While Paul competes with missionaries who try to convince the Galatians to be more observant with regard to Torah and mentions circumcision as a point of contention, Sturcke argues that Sabbath observance was also at stake, since 4:10 mentions the observance of certain times. This implies not only a Pauline mission that did not include a Sabbath observance but also that Paul was not interested in religiously significant times at all but lived in the "last days, when the coming of Christ had changed the very quality of time" (136).

In the next chapter Sturcke examines the attitude of Jesus toward the Sabbath by way of the three Synoptic accounts of the gleaning of grain on a Sabbath. Sturcke's rationale for selecting this pericope is the absence of a healing miracle, which accompanies other Sabbath controversies. The story allows for a much clearer assessment of the issues at stake with regard to the Sabbath. Sturcke first examines Mark's version of the story and then compares the attitude found here to some of the other references in the Gospel. Unsurprisingly, Sturcke concludes that, while Mark describes a Jesus who comes into conflict with some of the expectations about Sabbath observance, there is no clear indication that the community behind the Gospel did or did not observe the Sabbath. What is clear, however, is its subordination to the authority of Jesus. Sturcke's treatment of the Lukan and Matthean versions comes to similar results. However, Sturcke also observes that in Matthew the authority of Jesus alone did not suffice to resolve the problem. Yet on the question whether Matthew's group was observant, Sturcke waxes, to my mind unnecessarily so. Finally, in this chapter the traditions behind the Markan story are studied, with the aim of suggesting some probabilities concerning Jesus' own attitude toward the Sabbath. Here Sturcke observes that Jesus probably subordinated the Sabbath to the dawning of the kingdom of God.

The fifth chapter turns toward the Gospel of John in the examination of the two healing miracles in John 5 and 9. Again Sturcke finds no definite indication either way as to the actual observance of the Sabbath in the Johannine community. He takes the *heos arti* in 5:17 as ambivalent. However, he also points out that the separation between Judaism and Christianity in the Gospel seems so far ahead that a dialogue with the synagogue had ceased.

In a sixth chapter Sturcke turns to further writings, among them extracanonical Christian literature. He looks at Heb 4:9, the *Epistle of Barnabas,* and the *Gospel of Thomas.* He observes how the link between weekly Sabbath observance and entry into the divine Sabbath is broken in Hebrews and the confession of Christ takes the place of weekly Sabbath observance. The *Epistle of Barnabas* takes over the entirety of the scriptures and the covenant as exclusive property of the Christians (301). This means that the Sabbath is to be observed, with the caveat that this is only truly possible for those consecrated and justified by God. Sturcke's very sensible and careful examination of logion 27 of the *Gospel of Thomas* leads him to state that the most we can say is that it subordinates Sabbath observance to specific soteriological concerns.

The seventh chapter provides a conclusion that in a first step summarizes the results of the study so far, then attempts an all-too-brief historical reconstruction of the Sabbath question in early Christianity, and finally moves on to some hermeneutical observations that prepare for the application of the question of Sabbath observance to contemporary worship practice. The volume concludes with a bibliography and an index of ancient literature.

Sturcke's book is well written. It provides excellent summaries of his findings at the end of each section, is carefully edited, and does not contain too many tedious repetitions. The amount of secondary literature Sturcke has worked through is quite admirable, and he is conversant not just with the English but also with the German and French literature on the subject. His analyses are always careful. He achieves a good representation of the diverse attitudes toward the Sabbath and succeeds in showing that this diversity in ancient Christianity does not allow for the general statement that most early Christians observed the Sabbath. He is also careful in his assessment of the details still recoverable with regard to community practice, even if the historical reconstruction at the end goes a little beyond the evidence of his individual analyses. This book is balanced and makes good sense. Therefore, it can be recommended to all interested in early Christian worship and history.

Jünger und Brüder: Studien zum Differenzierungsprozess von Kirche und Judentum, by Walther Bindermann. Münster: LIT, 2005. Pp. 505. Paper. €39.90. ISBN 3825886824.

Wolfgang Kraus, Universität des Saarlandes, Saarbrücken, Germany

Die Untersuchung von Walter Bindemann Jünger und Brüder ist dem Differenzierungsprozess von Kirche und Judentum im 1. Jh. mit einem Ausblick auf das 2. Jh. gewidmet. Dabei versucht Bindemann anhand des Begriffspaares „Jünger" und „Brüder" ein detailliertes Bild zu entwickeln, das die Gestaltwerdung und Identitätsfindung der Kirche nachzeichnet. Er geht davon aus, dass es sich dabei um eine „Entwicklungskurve mit dramatischen Wendungen" handelt (442).

Doch nicht nur die Beziehung kirchlicher Gruppierungen zum Judentum, sondern auch der „Diversifizierungsprozess" innerhalb der frühchristlichen Bewegung lässt sich nach Bindemann mit dem gewählten Begriffspaar näher bestimmen (443). Zusammengefasst ergibt sich:

> Aus jüdisch-christlichen Anfängen heraus entwickeln sich Gruppen, die sich aber schnell für ehemalige Heiden öffnen. Dies geht Hand in Hand mit der Absage an Tempelkult, Gesetzesfrömmigkeit und Beschneidung. Andere jüdisch-christliche Gruppen bleiben im Synagogalverband und verhalten sich tora-treu; vom *mainstream*-Judentum unterscheidet sie ihre messianische Frömmigkeit, die in Jesus den Messias Israels sieht, seine Auferstehung verkündet und auf seine Wiederkunft wartet. Diese Gruppen der „Brüder" und „Jünger" haben sich nicht unabhängig voneinander herausgebildet und entwickelt, sondern in

Interaktion miteinander. ... Dieser Prozeß war nicht nur ein „innerkirchlicher",
sondern reflektiert auch die Differenzierung von Kirche und Judentum in neutestamentlicher Zeit. ... Mit den „Jüngern" bildet sich am Rand des synagogalen
Judentums eine neue religiöse Gemeinschaft, die schon bald nicht mehr jüdisch
ist. Sie hat ihre jüdischen Wurzeln nicht verleugnet, sich aber kultkritisch verhalten und für ehemalige Heiden geöffnet. So läßt sich anhand des Begriffspaares
„Jünger"–„Brüder" und seiner Entwicklungsgeschichte die Differenzierung von
Kirche und Synagoge im 1. Jahrhundert sowie die Diversifizierung der frühchristlichen Bewegung verfolgen. In einer relativ klar abgrenzbaren Periode
zwischen 40 und 90 u. Z. markieren die beiden Termini die Grenzlinie zwischen
intra- und extra-synagogalem Judentum. (442–43)

Bindemann setzt nach einer Einleitung, die eine (sehr) knappe Übersicht
zur Forschungslage hinsichtlich der Begriffe Jünger und Brüder enthält (9–14),
mit der These ein: „Die Differenzierung von Jüngern und Brüdern stellt über
einen längeren Zeitraum das Zentrum frühkirchlicher Entwicklung und Iden-
titätsbildung dar" (16, im Original kursiv). Er geht dann, angefangen von der
Apostelgeschichte (Kap. 2), die meisten der neutestamentlichen Schriften durch
und überprüft sie auf ihre Verwendung der beiden Begriffe (Kap. 3: Lk; Kap. 4:
Mk; Kap 5: vormk Tradition und Q; Kap. 6: Mt; Kap. 7: Joh; Kap. 8: 1–3Joh; Kap.
9: 1Kor, 1Thess, Gal, Röm; Kap. 10: Jak, Hebr, Offb; Kap. 11: Schriften des 2. Jh.).
Kap. 12 bietet eine Rekonstruktion der geschichtlichen Entwicklung anhand der
gewonnen Ergebnisse (442–60) und das Schluss-Kap. 13 enthält hermeneutische
Überlegungen, etwa welche Relevanz die frühchristlichen Differenzierungspro-
zesse für die heutige Verkündigung haben, und wie die Kirche heute mit ihrem
jüdischen Erbe umgehen kann (460–72).

Um das Ergebnis meiner Lektüre gleich zu benennen: Bindemann hat mit
seiner Arbeit ein wichtiges Problemfeld neutestamentlicher Forschung bearbeitet.
Er hat gezeigt, dass der Umgang mit den Begriffen „Brüder" und „Jünger" im NT
differenziert zu beurteilen ist. Dabei hat er an vielen Stellen zu Differenzierungen
geführt, die bisher so nicht gesehen wurden. Insofern leistet seine Arbeit für die
weitere Forschung einen wichtigen Beitrag. Bindemann sieht dabei richtig, dass
bei dem Prozess, der schließlich zum faktischen Getrenntsein von Kirche und
Judentum führte, Kräfte auf beiden Seiten am Werk waren: Ausgrenzung und
Selbstabgrenzung.

Ich bin jedoch nicht davon überzeugt, dass man anhand der beiden Begriffe
eine Geschichte des „partings of the ways between Christianity and Judaism"
schreiben kann. Hierzu ist der Gebrauch der beiden Begriffe m.E. nicht eindeutig genug und es müssten außerdem andere „significant terms" (8) einbezogen
oder wenigstens in Relation dazu gesetzt werden (etwa die Begriffe *ekklesia* [*tou
theou*] oder *sperma Abraam* und deren Relevanz hinsichtlich des Selbstverständ-
nisses frühchristlicher Gemeinden). Damit soll die exegetische Detailarbeit von
Bindemann nicht geschmälert werden. Für einen Gesamtentwurf reicht m.E. die
terminologische Basis nicht aus. Man würde—setzte man den Gebrauch von Jün-

gern und Brüdern in Relation zu anderen ,significant terms'—dann womöglich feststellen, dass der Gebrauch der beiden von Bindemann untersuchten Begriffe *einen* Aspekt darstellt, dem jedoch andere an die Seite gestellt werden müssen. Das Gesamtbild würde sich dann jedoch m.E. verändern.

Es ist im Rahmen dieser Rezension nicht möglich, umfassend zu argumentieren, es können nur auf unterschiedlichen Ebenen einige Punkte exemplarisch genannt werden, die mir die These von Bindemann als fragwürdig erscheinen lassen:

1. Bindemann beginnt seine Analysen mit einem umfassenden Statement, das durch einen Verweis auf die Arbeit von P. R. Trebilco untermauert wird und das in Variationen die ganze Arbeit durchzieht: „Die christliche Kirche gewann ihre Identität durch Abgrenzung vom synagogalen Judentum" (7). Diese Abgrenzung war „die logische Konsequenz aus dem Bekenntnis zum gekreuzigten Jesus als Messias" (7). Bindemann schließt sein Arbeit mit einem Rekurs auf eben diesen Sachverhalt ab (Kap. 12, 442–60). Mir scheinen hier drei Aspekte problematisch:

(a) So wie Bindemann dafür votiert, bei der Verwendung der Begriffe Jünger und Brüder zu differenzieren, so muss das auch bei dem Begriff „synagogales Judentum" vollzogen werden. Es erscheint mir nicht möglich, diesen Begriff als Gegenbegriff zu den „christlichen" Gruppierungen für das Judentum im 1. Jh. so pauschal zu verwenden. Dies gilt insbesondere für die Zeit, in der der Tempel noch stand, aber auch zunächst noch für die Zeit des sich formierenden Judentums nach 70 n.Chr. Zwar spricht Bindemann durchaus auch von der „Diversität" des antiken Judentums (455–56). Er wendet diese Erkenntnis m.E. jedoch nicht durchgehend bei seiner Analyse der neutestamentlichen Schriften an.

(b) Das Bekenntnis zu Jesus von Nazaret als Messias ist unbestreitbar ein Grunddatum und zentrales Unterscheidungsmerkmal christlicher von anderen religiösen Gruppierungen. Ob jedoch das Bekenntnis zum „gekreuzigten Jesus als Messias" als „logische Konsequenz" die Trennung der Jesusanhänger vom Judentum nach sich ziehen muss, scheint mir aufgrund der Variabilität des frühjüdischen Messiasverständnisses, aufgrund geschichtlicher Tatbestände im Frühjudentum und aufgrund der unterschiedlichen Positionen innerhalb des NT noch nicht ausgemacht. Es müssen (1) weitere Faktoren hinzukommen, etwa die Aufnahme von Unbeschnittenen in die Gemeinschaft und deren Gleichstellung, oder die Ablehnung bestimmter Regelungen, die als Minimalforderungen der Tora angesehen wurden, oder eine Exklusivität der Tora-Anweisungen, wie sie der Jesus des Mt vornimmt usw. Und (2) erfolgt die Trennung nicht pauschal vom Judentum, sondern hat es jeweils mit bestimmten Ausprägungen von Judentum zu tun.

(c) Die „Abgrenzung vom synagogalen Judentum"—wenn man denn den Begriff überhaupt verwenden will—ist ein wichtiger, vermutlich entscheidender, aber sicher nicht der einzige Faktor, der zur christlichen Identitätsgewinnung beitrug. 1Kor, 1Thess, Lk und Apg—um eine Auswahl zu nennen—zeigen, wie die Absetzung von der nicht-jüdischen Umwelt teilweise unter Aufnahme jüdischer

Positionen erfolgt ist (vgl. etwa die Areopagrede und wie dort nichtjüdische von jüdischen Traditionselementen her verarbeitet werden).

2. In Kap. 5 (182–91) diskutiert Bindemann auf wenigen Seiten (182–86) die Herkunft des Jünger-Begriffes. Bindemann geht dabei m.E. viel zu schnell davon aus, dass der Jüngerbegriff „seine Prägung in ‚Lehrstreitigkeiten' zwischen pro-synagogalen jüdischen Christen und torakritischen jüdischen Christen" erhalten habe (185). Die Möglichkeit, dass hierin die Schicksalsgemeinschaft zwischen dem irdischen Jesus und seinen Nachfolgern zum Ausdruck kommt, wird nicht erwogen. Arbeiten, die in diese Richtung argumentieren (etwa von Freyne und Riesner), werden ohne intensive Diskussion abgelehnt (10–11). Die These, dass „das Jünger-Konzept des Matthäus in messiasgläubigen Kreisen des hellenistischen Diasporajudentums entstanden" sei (239 Fn. 491) und deshalb die „Öffnung zu Heiden" nahegelegen habe, wird dagegen weder in Kap. 2 noch später ausreichend begründet. Außerdem spricht die Tatsache, dass auch die Anhänger von Johannes d.T. als *mathetai* bezeichnet werden, dagegen, das Aufkommen dieser Terminologie nicht in Palästina, sondern nur „am Rande des hellenistischen Diasporajudentums" für denkbar zu erachten (184).

3. Bindemann geht davon aus, dass sich im Mt-Ev trotz des „deutlich jüdisch-christlichen Hintergrund[es]" ein „starkes Auseinander-Driften von christlicher Gemeinde und synagogalen Judentum" spiegele (191). „Die ‚Jünger' befinden sich eindeutig außerhalb der Synagoge und im Gegenüber zu ihr", wenngleich Bindemann die Entscheidung, „ob christlicher Messias-Glaube nicht doch als eine Version des Judentums möglich" sei, als noch nicht gefallen ansieht (191).

Ob die Gemeinde des Matthäus wirklich die Trennung vom sog. „synagogalen Judentum" bereits hinter sich hat, ist in der Tat derzeit umstritten (vgl. etwa die Aufstellung bei M. Vahrenhorst, Ihr sollt überhaupt nicht schwören, WMANT 95, 2005, 4, und die gängigen Positionen, die dort S. 6–16 diskutiert werden). Die bei Vahrenhorst genannten Argumente scheinen dafür zu sprechen, das Mt-Ev innerhalb „eines differenziert zu sehenden Judentums" zu verorten (Vahrenhorst, 16). Dann aber würde das Jünger-Konzept des Mt gerade nicht Ausdruck dafür sein, dass es für die matthäischen Gemeindeglieder „*in* der Synagoge keinen Ort und keine Identität mehr gab" (238, kursiv im Original), vielmehr wäre sein Konzept als eine konkrete Position innerhalb des sich formierenden Judentums nach 70 n.Chr. zu verstehen. Es wäre dann zu überlegen, ob für das Mt-Ev die Bezeichnung „Judenchristen", die auch Bindemann für messiasgläubige Gruppen der frühchristlichen Bewegung ablehnt (443), nicht durch „jesuanische/christliche Juden" ersetzt werden sollte, anstatt durch „jüdische Christen". Sollte man nicht analog zu „pharisäischen Juden", „sadduzäischen Juden", „essenischen Juden", „hellenistischen Juden" usw. auch für die matth. Gemeinde sachgemäß von „jesuanischen/christlichen Juden" sprechen?

4. Dass Paulus den Begriff *mathetes* nicht benutzt (367), ist in der Tat auffällig. Dass es dafür jedoch „nur eine befriedigende Erklärung" gäbe, nämlich dass „der Terminus als frühchristliche Gruppenbezeichnung" zur Zeit der Abfassung der Paulusbriefe noch nicht existierte, und Paulus deshalb noch gar nicht „zwi-

schen Jüngern und Brüdern differenzieren" konnte (367), scheint mir eine petitio principii. Die Erklärung, wonach das Kreuz Christi „den Bruder zum Bruder gemacht" hat (9–10, Zitat von U. Wilckens, vgl. aber immerhin Röm 8,29, wo christologisch argumentiert wird) reicht in der Tat nicht aus. Aber ist die Rede von den Brüdern bei Paulus nicht hinreichend dadurch zu begründen, dass er die Gemeindeglieder unterschiedslos als „Söhne/Kinder Gottes" bzw. als „Nachkommenschaft Abrahams" ansieht? (Vgl. auch hier vom Kontext her Röm 8,14ff.29.) Und ist der Verzicht auf den Begriff Jünger bei Paulus nicht hinreichend damit zu erklären, dass dieser seinen Ursprung bei den Anhängern des irdischen Jesus hat (so auch die These von Sean Freyne) und Paulus eben nicht an solche, sondern an Glaubende der zweiten Generation und dazu an Gemeinden in der Diaspora schreibt? Gerade die Tatsache, dass die Evangelien die Jesusgeschichte transparent für ihre jeweilige Gegenwart erzählen (richtig Bindemann 17ff.193.449 u.ö.), könnte eine hinreichende Begründung dafür sein, warum hier der Begriff des Jüngers in den Evangelien die dominante Rolle erhält, und warum es nicht darum geht, durch „Brüder" bzw. „Jünger" unterschiedliche Konzepte (ältere und jüngere) mit differenten Frömmigkeitsprofilen von einander zu unterscheiden (Bindemann spricht hinsichtlich der Apg sogar von „Konfessionen", 22ff. Zur Charakterisierung dieser beiden Konzepte in der Apg s. bes. 39.62–63). Die Verwendung des Begriffes „Brüder" bei Paulus lässt m.E. keine Zuspitzung auf ein bestimmtes Frömmigkeitsprofil (etwa gesetzestreue sog. Judenchristen) zu (vgl. dagegen z.B. 1Thess 4,10.13; 5,12.14.25–27 und erneut Röm 8,29, unabhängig davon, ob Paulus hier ein „Überlieferungsstück jüdischer Herkunft" [so Bindemann 399] oder nicht verarbeitet hat).

Walter Bindemann hat mit seiner Arbeit auf ein wichtiges Problemfeld hingewiesen. Weitere Forschung muss sich jedoch noch einmal mit der traditionsgeschichtlichen Herkunft des Begriffes Jünger beschäftigen. Dabei wird es u.a. darum gehen, anhand der inzwischen gewonnenen differenzierten Sicht des antiken Judentums bezüglich der in K. H. Rengstorfs Artikel im ThWNT vorliegenden traditionsgeschichtlichen Einschätzungen, über die auch Bindemann nicht hinausführt, weiter zu kommen.

GRECO-ROMAN WORLD AND HELLENISM

Heraclitus: Homeric Problems, edited by Donald A. Russell and David Konstan. Society of Biblical Literature Writings from the Greco-Roman World 14. Atlanta: Society of Biblical Literature; Leiden: Brill, 2005. Pp. xxx + 144. Paper/cloth. $20.95/$107.00. ISBN 1589831225/9004130829.

Dennis R. Macdonald, Claremont School of Theology, Claremont, California

How I wish that this book had been available twenty years ago when I began investigating Homeric influence on early Christian narratives! We who have labored with previous editions of Heraclitus's *Homeric Problems* can attest that his Greek is difficult, his commentary often elliptical and technical, and the sheer bulk of scholarly attention to Homer and Stoicism daunting. It has taken the collaboration of two internationally recognized authorities to offer this slim but important vade mecum edition, with a useful introduction, the Greek text with philological notes, an *en face* English translation with notes for citations and brief commentary, a select bibliography, and two indexes: "Nominum et Rerum" and "Locorum."

The introduction treats the following topics: "Name and Date" (ca. 100 c.e.), "The Beginnings of Allegory," "The Authority of Homer," "The Nature of Allegory," "Approaches to Myth," "Plato's Attack on Homer and Its Aftermath," "The Varieties of Allegory," "Allegory and Literary Criticism," "Heraclitus's Treatise," and "Text and Translation." Particularly noteworthy is the discussion of allegory in the context of ancient literary criticism, where Russell and Konstan elsewhere have made significant contributions.

Heraclitus set out to rescue Homer from the charge of impiety that was popular in classical antiquity ever since Socrates' objections in Plato's *Republic* (though Socrates was by no means the first to vilify Homer's Olympians). This review cannot to justice to the significance of this publication; I will limit my response to its relevance to students of Hellenistic Judaism and early Christianity.

Perhaps the most obvious payoff is for scholars of Jewish and Christian allegorists of the Bible, such as Philo and Origen, who allegorized to account for difficult content in the lxx much as Heraclitus did for Homer. They, too, would cite a text, identify a problem, cite a countervailing text, or promote a philosophically or morally acceptable *sensus plenior*, a "fuller meaning," valuable ore buried below the noxious topsoil. Heraclitus not only amply illustrates this method of interpretation, but he provides the critical vocabulary and rhetorical sleights-of-hand that make such readings of difficult texts compelling, at least to some ancient readers. Students of early Christian apologists will find that Heraclitus deals with several ethical problems in Homer that the likes of Justin Martyr, Clement of Alexandria, and Tatian denounced. Scholars invested in understanding early Christian attitudes toward sexuality may benefit from comparing Paul's denunciations of homoeroticism with Heraclitus's insistence that, when it comes to morality, Plato has no room to boast: "Plato's dialogues … are disgraced through and through by pederasty: there is not a passage which does not show the man bursting with desire for a male partner" (76.15). Heraclitus's extended treatment of the matter fills forty lines of text.

These and many other benefits await the reader of this volume, but there are two in addition that point the way to promising research on the New Testament. First, both at the beginning and at the end of his work this contemporary of the Evangelists (ca. 100 c.e.) reveals Homer's importance for elite Greek males.

> From the very first age of life, the foolishness of infants just beginning to learn
> is nurtured on the teaching given in his school. One might almost say that his
> poems are our baby clothes, and we nourish our minds by draughts of his milk.

He stands at our side as we each grow up and shares our youth as we gradually come to manhood; when we are mature, his presence within us is at its prime; and even in old age, we never weary of him. When we stop, we thirst to begin him again. In a word, the only end of Homer for human beings is the end of life. (1.5–7)

The author returns to this theme at the end by imagining the ignorance that would reign if people followed Plato's advice in banning Homer.

Can Homer, the great hierophant of heaven and of the gods, who opened up for human souls the untrodden and closed paths to heaven, deserve to be condemned as impious? Were this vile and unholy verdict to be given and his poems destroyed, dumb ignorance would spread across the world; no help would come to the band of little children who drink in wisdom first from Homer, as they do their nurses' milk; nor would boys and younger men or the older generation that has passed its prime any longer have pleasure. Life's tongue would be ripped out; it would all dwell in dumb silence. (76.1–5)

This paean to the poet par excellence stands in stark contrast to the near silence about Homer in New Testament scholarship. If we are to understand the literary context of Greek Christians in the early Roman Empire, we cannot afford to ban Homer from our exegetical republic!

Second, Heraclitus's *Homeric Problems* also provides a magnificent example of how interpreters who were looking for a *sensus plenior* in a text went about doing so. The most common of his strategies was to examine Homeric names and epithets for clues. By my count there are over thirty significant names and ten significant epithets. For example, Aphrodite is taken to mean "folly" (*aphrosynē*), Charis "grace," Proteus "first person," Hades "invisibility" (*a-idēs*), Cocytus "lamentation," Helius "sun," Hera "air" (*aēr*), Leto "forgetfulness" (*lēthō*), Posidon "drink" (*posis*), Rhea "flowing," Mnemosyne "memory," Thetis "laying down" (*thesis*), and, of course, Zeus "life" (*zēn*). Many of these forced etymologies are common, but many are not and are used to justify elaborate allegorical readings.

In *Christianizing Homer* I argued for a similar strategy in the *Acts of Andrew*, where significant names are used to notify the reader that these named characters emulate personalities from Greek mythology, often from the Homeric epics (*Christianizing Homer: "The Odyssey," Plato, and "The Acts of Andrew"* [New York: Oxford University Press, 1994]). For example, Varianus, "fickle," emulates Zeus, who changed his shape to sleep with mortals; Callisto, "most beautiful," plays a role similar to Aphrodite; Lesbius, "goblet," calls to mind Dionysus; Alcman evokes Heracles, Nicolaus of Sparta suggests Menelaus of Sparta, the son of Alcmene; Trophime, "suckled," is Atalanta, who was nursed by a wolf; Callisutus, "most beautiful," is Gangymede; Anthimus, "blossoms," is Orpheus; Philopater, "father-lover," is Orests; Calliope, "beautiful singer," is Circe; and, ironically, Antiphanes, "inconspicuous," is Heracles. Even the name of the hero is significant: Andreas, "courage." Place names, too, may carry significance: Myrmidonia is the land of Achilles' Myrmidons, and Patras, the location of Andrew's death, allows for play on the famous phrase in the *Odyssey: eis patrida gaian,* "to his homeland." Once the reader recognizes this strategy, she should be alert to deeper narrative ambitions.

Significant names also appear in the Gospel of Mark, although their significance lies primarily in the contribution the name makes to the narrative itself: Barabbas, "son of the Father," a roguish alternative to the Son of God; Judas, "Jew"; and Joseph of Arimathea, "excellent discipleship" (*ari-matheia*). I also suspect that the combination of name and epithet, Mary the Magdalene, has double significance: Mary is the name of Jesus' mother, who is not on hand to care for her dying son, and Magdalene, from Magdala, "tower," may point to Hector's wife Andromache, who watches her husband die from Troy's tower (*pyrgos*). There is one instance where a significant name in Homer may influence the characterization of an unnamed character: Euyclia, "renowned far and wide," was famous for recognizing the identity of her lord from the scar on his leg that she saw while washing his feet. The unnamed woman who anointed Jesus for his burial will have far-flung renown for having done so.

Significant names are even more impressive in Luke-Acts. Cleopas, *kleo-pas,* "all fame," is one of two disciples who recognizes Jesus on the road to Emmaus; the name Eurycleia is a compound of *kleos* and *eury;* she was one of Odysseus's faithful servants, another of whom was Eumaeus. Stephen, "wreath," evokes Achilles, whose head Athena "wreathed [*estephan*]" with radiance; Lydia from Lydia is a Christian Maenad, like the Lydian women who compose the chorus in Euripides' *Bacchae;* Eutychus, "lucky," is luckier than "unfortunately Elpenor," who fell to his death in the *Odyssey;* Dionysius and Damaris evoke Dionysus and his wife (*damar*) Ariadne, famous heroes of Athens; Scevas, "lefty," evokes the ambidextrous Asteropaeus, and so on. Uses of significant names likewise are common in Greek and Latin novels, where the authors are free to create names for the fictional characters they have created.

Heraclitus's *Homeric Problems* dramatically underscores a popular ancient strategy for detecting in narratives embedded and disguised meanings: the etymologies of significant names and distinctive epithets. Just as Heraclitus, Philo, and other allegorists forced their etymologies on Homer and the Bible, many ancient authors sprinkled their narratives with characters bearing significant names and traits to prod their readers to look for *sensus plenior.*

The role of significant names is but one example of how this accessible presentation of Heraclitus's Greek and Russell's and Konstan's brilliant English translation will provide insights into how readers contemporary with the Evangelists read sacred narratives, whether Homer or the Bible. It also may provide new insights into how ancient authors composed for their more perceptive and curious readers.

Building Jewish in the Roman East, by Peter Richardson. Waco, Tex.: Baylor University Press, 2004. Pp. xxii + 413 +52 plates. Paper. $39.95. ISBN 1932792015.

Byron McCane, Wofford College, Spartanburg, South Carolina

Most of the essays that make up the chapters in this rich volume have already been presented or published elsewhere, but the world of biblical scholarship can be grateful that they are updated and re-presented together here. As a collection they are more clearly visible as a coherent body of work that spans a remarkably broad chronological, geographical, and methodological range. This is, in other words, a serious book for serious readers.

Chapter 1, "Religion and Architecture in the Eastern Mediterranean," makes up all of part 1 and sets Jewish building practices within the broader context of society, culture, religion, and architecture during the Late Hellenistic and Early Roman periods. Richardson reaffirms the basic methodological principle that historical reconstructions are to be based upon both textual and material evidence. In addition, his wide experience in architecture—including several years of professional practice, along with travels in Central and South America—gives him an uncommonly keen eye for reading material remains. An illustrative example is this remark from page 13: "Religious convictions and expressions were just as deeply interwoven into the fabric of small villages such as Macha Picchu or Cana, as they were woven into the urban fabric of large cities such as Mexico City or Corinth."

On this foundation, the essays in part 2 (chs. 2–6) explore towns and villages in the Lower Galilee, with particular focus upon Cana, Yodefat, and Capernaum. Chapter 2, "Jesus and Palestinian Social Protest," surveys various forms of social protest in Early Roman Galilee and argues that the historical Jesus probably did not support the form chosen by *lestai,* or "bandits." Chapter 3 describes the production of a PBS documentary on Yodefat. While the information about AutoCAD and DTM may not be of interest to many biblical scholars, the chapter does include the important observation that, at Yodefat at least, the Early Roman period was characterized by general economic expansion and growth and not by the increasing concentration of wealth in the hands of a few. Chapter 4, "Khirbet Qana (and Other Villages) as a Context for Jesus," reviews archaeological data from several Galilean villages to show (among other conclusions) that such villages were generally more conservative religiously than larger urban areas were. While social and economic differences between villages are evident, it is nonetheless possible to speak of a "common Judaism" in all of them. In chapter 5, "First Century Houses and Q's Setting," the archaeological data is joined with textual evidence from Q to make the case that "the Lower Galilee is the most logical, if not the only, choice" for the location of the Q communities (90). Here Richardson classifies three kinds of village housing: terraced houses (on hillsides), central courtyard houses (on level areas), and small houses without courtyards (on the perimeter). Chapter 6, "What Has Cana to do with Capernaum?" examines Johannine literary sources for indications that Cana might have been both a center of early Christian traditions and a center for activity of the historical Jesus.

Part 3 (chs. 7–12) concentrates upon larger public structures, particularly synagogues and churches, and especially their similarities with voluntary associations. Chapter 7, "Pre-70 Synagogues as *Collegia*," locates the origins of the synagogue in the social phenomenon of Roman voluntary associations. A particular feature of this chapter is a careful reconstruction of the inscription from the "synagogue of the Herodians" (*CIJ* 173). The fact that "first-century BCE synagogues in Rome were dedicated to some of the leading protagonists for Judaism" (132) supports Richardson's argument that the synagogue arose in the milieu of *collegia* in the Diaspora. Chapter 8, "Architectural Transitions from Synagogues and House Churches to Purpose-Built Churches," argues that the Roman basilica was a basic architectural model, first for synagogues and later for churches. Chapter 9, "Philo and Eusebius on Monasteries and Monasticism," surveys important archaeological data on early Christian monasteries in Egypt, but the attempt to connect the first-century Jewish Therapeutae with late ancient Christian monasticism is not convincing. Chapter 10, "Jewish Voluntary Associations in Egypt," reviews archaeological and textual evidence for the Leontopolis temple and the Therapeutae, arguing that equality between men and women in these groups was caused by their assimilation to Egyptian culture. Chapters 11 and 12 continue the argument that synagogues developed out of the Roman phenomenon of voluntary associations, largely reprising the contents of chapters 7–10.

Part 4, "Judea and Jerusalem," concentrates especially upon Herod's temple in Jerusalem. Chapter 13, "Law and Piety in Herod's Architecture," situates the temple within the context of Herod's wide-ranging building activity. From this perspective Herod appears to have employed public structures as political devices and yet to have done so in a way that evinced a not-too-strict Jewish piety. Like Paul and Hillel, Richardson argues, Herod's Jewish piety was genuine but generally accommodating toward the wider Hellenistic world. This chapter, like most of the chapters in part 4, is richly filled with important archaeological and architectural details. Chapter 14, "Why Turn the Tables? Jesus' Protest in the Temple Precincts," argues that Jesus' action in the temple was motivated by his "hostility to the use of Tyrian shekels to pay Temple dues" (251). Chapter 15, "Josephus, Nicolas of Damascus, and Herod's Building Program," compares Josephus's descriptions of Herod's buildings with archaeological evidence and concludes that the descriptions in *War* were based largely on Josephus's personal observations but that *Antiquities* probably made more extensive use of literary sources such as Nicolas of Damascus. Chapter 16, "Origins, Innovations, and Significance of Herod's Temple," combines a close reading of literary texts, archaeology, and architecture to emphasize the high degree of creative innovation in Herod's design of the temple. Richardson observes that "both Jews and Christians have taken his form of the Temple to be so normative that his [Herod's] vision of the proper arrangements has been read back into earlier periods and his innovations overlooked" (298). Chapter 17, "Herod's Temple Architecture and Jerusalem's Tombs," explores architectural similarities between the temple and the Akeldama tombs, which were located within sight of the temple. Chapter 18, "The James Ossuary's Decoration and Social Setting," may be the most comprehensive appraisal of this artifact currently in print, although for some reason it continues to hold out the (most unlikely, in the light of recent indictments) possibility that the inscription might be genuine.

Part 5, "Conclusion," consists of just chapter 19, appropriately titled "Building Jewish in the Roman East." This closing essay constellates each of the major themes of the book, showing both what was typical and what was distinctive about Jewish-built structures in the eastern Roman Empire. It concludes with the observation that, if the use of this material evidence leads to a deeper understanding of early Judaism and Christianity, "it will have been worth all the effort in finding the material evidence and listening carefully to it" (345).

It is the obligation of a reviewer to make some critical comment, so it can be pointed out that it might not be quite appropriate to suggest (as Richardson does on page 57) that the street plans of Early Roman villages such as Capernaum, Yodefat, Gamla, and Cana might be a "modified Hippodamian plan." These sites are better described as organic in their layout, since their patterns of settlement and construction appear to have been driven much more by topography and environment than by planning.

Because the material in these essays is wide-ranging, sophisticated, and detailed, they will be of interest to both textual scholars and archaeologists. But this book can also be used with undergraduates as well, because no essay is inordinately long and the writing style is consistently clear and interesting. This book is, in sum, a remarkable achievement: sophisticated in ways that will satisfy the specialist and accessible in ways that will attract a student. Most of all, it shows that the benefits that do repay the effort—both physical and mental—to find and listen to the material evidence.

Leaving the Fold: Apostates and Defectors in Antiquity, by Stephen G. Wilson. Minneapolis: Fortress, 2005. Pp. xvii + 158. Hardcover. $25.00. ISBN 0800636759.

David Redelings, Bethel University, San Diego, California

Stephen G. Wilson's new book is appropriately titled *Leaving the Fold: Apostates and Defectors in Antiquity*. This sociological study is a comparative examination of apostasy from Judaism, apostasy from Christianity, and defection from pagan schools of philosophy. The book focuses on the period between the time of the Maccabean revolt and the time of Julian the Apostate.

Wilson's declared purpose is to correct ancient misrepresentations about apostasy that arose from the hostility of ancient writers. He says that apostasy has been largely suppressed from the record, which was written by the apostates' critics. In his view, for example, Jewish accounts of apostasy regularly underplayed its actual extent and offered simplistic assessments of its character. Similarly, he

argues that ecclesiastical writers like Eusebius wrote apostates out of the historical record. However, Wilson's concerns must be tempered by consideration of
counterexamples. Early Jewish Christians such as Paul were considered apostate
by leading Jewish authorities, yet Christians are well represented in the historical
record. It is likewise of note that Irenaeus wrote extensively about certain heretics, so that apostates are sometimes described at length by their opponents.
But despite such exceptions, Wilson has a case for saying that the voices of those
considered apostates are underrepresented in the historical record. His plan is to
correct the false perspectives that result by trying to see apostasy "from the point
of view of the apostate" (2).

Wilson treats apostasy and defection as a social phenomenon characterized
by the separation of some members from a religious or philosophical community with characteristic teachings and practices. He does not evaluate apostates
from the perspective of a particular religion but from a nonreligious perspective. It is this sociological perspective that encourages a comparison of apostasy
from different religious and philosophical groups. Because of this perspective,
and because apostasy does not always involve conversion to another faith, Wilson
treats apostasy separately from the phenomenon of religious conversion. Noting
that there are already several sociological studies of conversion, Wilson intends
this book to instead be a study of apostasy. As converts are largely ignored, the
focus is on people who leave a religious community without joining another,
which is to say, apostates who are individualistic. As ancient apostasy is a new
field of sociological study, Wilson judiciously issues his book only as "a start" that
gathers "a broad range of evidence" (ix).

Wilson's first chapter establishes many foundational ideas for the book. He
provides a carefully nuanced discussion of terminology and concepts that are relevant to the project. He ultimately adopts for this book one definition for both
defector and apostate: "those who considered themselves, or were considered
by others, to have abandoned the main practices and/or beliefs of their religious
community" (22). He distinguishes these people from dissidents who remain
within the community. Consequently, he further defines apostates as "those
whose assimilationist tendencies finally took them beyond the limits of their
community (22). Apostates are implicitly defined as community minorities.

Wilson's treatment of all kinds of apostasy as a single phenomenon provokes
a concern that differences between various kinds of apostasy might be inadver-
tently and systematically ignored. For example, how far is it true that leaving one
religion or philosophical school is the same as leaving any other, if the respective religions or philosophies have fundamentally different ideas and beliefs and
communities? To use a modern example, how far can those who left the Heaven's
Gate cult (even before their radical call to mass suicide) be understood the same
as those who have dropped the Jewish or Christian faith of their parents? Or to
use an example from antiquity, how far is leaving the school of the Pythagoreans really the same phenomenon as leaving Judaism? Similarly, if we may here
consider apostasy resulting from religious conversion, was Jewish conversion to

paganism at the time of the Maccabees (yielding to pressures for assimilation to paganism) really the same phenomenon as pagan conversion to Judaism in that same social context? Granted, there are characteristics that are identical for all kinds of apostasy, but are there also equal or greater differences, even differences in social consequences, which are obscured by treating all apostasy identically? How far is apostasy really a single phenomenon, even a single social phenomenon, when it refers to different individuals who apostatize from a single faith for widely different reasons and purposes? What is lost by treating apostasy for the pursuit of wealth and power or for a life of moral squalor on the same level as apostasy out of sincere and blameless conviction? As becomes evident later in the book, Wilson is too careful a historian not to be aware of the variety of motives that lead to apostasy. However, his methodology raises concerns at the outset that his collection of evidence is too selective, skewing the conclusions that either he or his collection of evidence may suggest. The project would benefit by comparison with perspectives that do not treat all apostasy as a single phenomenon.

Wilson's second chapter discusses Jewish apostates. He begins with the limited literary evidence and supplements this with the more limited epigraphic evidence. The evidence is covered sequentially, one source at a time, which makes for a slow read but allows for a far clearer historical analysis of each source. Literary evidences of Jewish apostasy that are discussed include: Menelaus's apostasy as recounted in the Maccabean literature, Jewish apostasy in Alexandria as recounted in 3 Maccabees, the apostasy of Antiochus of Antioch as recounted by Josephus, the apostasy of Dositheus recounted in 3 Maccabees, the probable apostasy of Tiberius Julius Alexander (nephew of Philo) as reported by Josephus, the views of Philo on apostasy, reports of Jewish defections by Suetonius, talmudic accounts of Elisha ben Abuyah, critiques of other Jews by the Dead Sea Scrolls, and the apostasy (as seen by Jewish leaders in Jerusalem) of Paul.

Epigraphic evidences of Jewish apostasy form the next long list of sources. Wilson's discussions include: former Jews in Smyrna during the reign of Hadrian, a third-century B.C.E. inscription in Oropus of a stela set up in the temple of Amphiaraos by a Jewish slave named Moschos, several second-century B.C.E. inscriptions at a temple of the god Pan in el-Kanais, a second-century B.C.E. inscription of a donor to a Dionysus festival from Jerusalem, a first-century C.E. inscription in Gorgippia referring to three pagan gods, a first-century C.E. inscription in Cyrene by Eleazer that is a dedication to a god, a first-century C.E. inscription in Acmonia by Julia Severa, a few fourth-century C.E. Christian inscriptions from North Africa that have Jewish names such as Mose and Sabbatiolus. and a fourth-century Christian inscription from Italy of a Jew renamed Peter. Wilson has provided a diverse and important collection of evidence.

There are omissions in Wilson's collection of evidence that apparently arise from his adopted definition of *apostasy* as a characteristic only of minorities in any community. This redefinition is a potentially misleading shift from the historic use of the concept of *apostasy*, since that concept has regularly been used also to describe community majorities and their leaders. The prophet Jeremiah, for example, says in a general address to the house of Israel, "your apostasies will teach you" (Jer 2:12 LXX). Similarly, later Jewish minorities sometimes accused the majority of the Jewish community, or their leaders, of apostasy. Wilson notes briefly, for example, the charges of Jewish apostasy that are made by the Qumran documents. Qumran is a case where a minority regards itself as conservators of ancient practice against the historically recent deviations or assimilation of a religious majority. Likewise, although it implies a claim that the nation is apostate, there is no discussion of John the Baptist's call for Jewish repentance and purification by baptism or of the Baptist's pronouncements of impending divine judgment, despite the evidence from both Josephus and the Gospels regarding the Baptist's popularity and influence. Similarly, no coverage is given to New Testament claims that Jesus called for Jewish repentance and purification by baptism or of Jesus' own pronouncements of coming divine judgment, which indicate that he made a charge of apostasy against the nation. Likewise omitted is Paul's claim that the majority of Israel had turned from God as in the time of Elijah (Rom 11:1–8). The assumption that apostates are not a community majority also may explain Wilson's neglect to mention the deep split between Pharisees and Sadducees, since he implicitly assumes that the community majority is a unified group. A different impression is given by the Mishnah's later pronouncement against the Sadducees, "These are they which have no share in the world to come: he that says that there is no resurrection of the dead" (*m. Sanh.* 10:1). Wilson makes no claim to be comprehensive, but his selection of evidence about apostate minorities alone, omitting charges of majority apostasy, may lead to skewed conclusions or cause readers to confuse apostasy understood in its historical usage with apostasy as an accusation made only against religious minorities.

In the third chapter Wilson discusses the evidence for Christian apostates, based in this case solely on the more abundant literary evidence. He begins with the New Testament, claiming that its evidence for apostasy is slight because of "the absence of accepted orthodoxies and established boundaries" (66). This characterization is surprising, since there are few new religious movements that lack knowledge of what makes them distinctive. In this case, the necessity to repent of sins and be purified by baptism and to follow the messenger foretold by John the Baptist, along with the implicit requirement not to follow pagan belief, were boundaries that were understood from the very beginning. Additional community boundaries for Jesus' followers were given in Jesus' teaching. Nevertheless, some issues were formally decided later, as Wilson indicates.

Perhaps the most important New Testament accusation of apostasy from the Christian faith is Paul's controversy with those Jewish Christians who required Gentiles to follow the law of Moses and to be circumcised. Wilson characterizes Gal 4:8–10 as an appeal by Paul not to return to paganism and concludes that Paul is "somewhat hysterical." A more coherent reading is that Paul is addressing former pagans, many of whom had become Jewish proselytes before they became Christians, and that Paul is appealing to them not to become full Jewish converts. Under this reading, Paul believes that such conversion (including the rite of circumcision) will undermine the reason for Jesus' crucifixion, as well as invalidating the main reason that Paul had been "persecuted for the cross of Christ" (Gal 6:12) for so many years.

Wilson continues discussions of Christian apostates in 1 Pet 2:20–21; 1 Tim 4:1–3; 1:19–20; 1 Cor 5:1–5; Heb 6; 10; and Rev 2, concentrating mostly on Jewish-Christian relations. He does not discuss the defection of Jesus' disciples in John 6 as a historical possibility, nor does he discuss the defection in 1 John 4 by those prophets who denied the human Jesus. Wilson next discusses *Hermas*, Pliny the Younger's letter to Trajan, the *Martyrdom of Polycarp*, Cyprian's *De Lapsis*, Barnabas, Justin's *Dialogue with Trypho* and *Apology*, the *Apocalypse of Peter*, Lucian's *Peregrinus*, Porphery's *Against the Christians*, Pseudo-Cyprian's *Carmen ad Senatorum*, Julian the Apostate's *Epistles* and *Against the Galileans*, and Libanius's *Orationes*.

In the fourth chapter Wilson describes defectors from philosophical schools (including philosophy of medical practice) but offers no significant evidence for defectors from pagan religion. Wilson discusses pagan defectors connected with the following: the Pythagoreans, the medical school of the Alexandrian physician Herophilus, an inscription from the temple of Zeus in Sardis, the execution of Flavius Clemens and the exile of Domitilla (as described by Dio Cassius), the case of Epicurus and Timocrates (as described by Diogenes Laertius), and Antiochus of Ascalon.

Joining the category of pagan defectors from philosophical schools to the category of religious apostates is somewhat problematic, as Wilson acknowledges, and cannot fill the gap left by ignoring conversions from paganism. The evidence for defectors from pagan philosophical schools comprises less than a tenth of Wilson's book. The paucity of evidence itself suggests that the category of philosophical school defection does not really belong with the category of religious apostasy. Although Wilson earlier discussed Paul's conversion to Christianity and in this chapter discusses the possible conversion of Flavius Clemens and Domitilla from paganism, he does not discuss other cases of converts. Yet this is where far more cases of defection from pagan religion would be found, due to the many proselytes and converts in the ancient world who adopted Judaism or Christianity. Wilson notes the popular accusation of atheism that is made against Christians but does not discuss that charge against Polycarp by the crowds present at his execution. Since atheism is an accusation also made centuries beforehand at the trial of Socrates, this suggests that some pagans thought leaving paganism was an impiety justifying execution. This indicates that Jews, and certainly proselytes to Judaism, were also sometimes in a precarious position in pagan cities, a conclusion supported by the wide hostility against Jews in the Diaspora, such as the first-century riots in Alexandria. This pagan conception of impiety is also seen in the book of Acts, where Christians anger pagans in Ephesus by persuading people not to serve idols of the goddess Artemis. While there is some merit in initially limiting discussion to defection that is not conversion, in this case the stricture eliminates too much significant evidence. Furthermore, since Wilson includes defection from philosophical schools, it is not clear why he does not discuss cases of defection from other kinds of communities, such as political and military alliances or tribal groups, since these groups were often united by religious practice in ancient societies.

In his concluding chapter Wilson reflects on J. G. Barclay's work on apostate Jews and then looks to sociological studies of modern apostasy by David Bromley and Stuart Wright for potential insights into ancient apostasy. Drawing from this work, Wilson then suggests that apostates could be categorized into three groups: gradual defectors, precipitate defectors, and antagonistic apostates. Alternatively, he suggests they could be categorized by the inner motivations for apostasy: social and family ties, former lifestyle, intellectual doubts, or avoidance of social oppression. He denies the practical significance of the claim that Jewish apostates were still Jews. In closing, he notes that the "sheer range and variety of defectors" is "striking." He concludes that the social boundaries that define apostasy and deviance are often rather ambiguous.

The strength of this book lies in the impressive variety of sources that Wilson has gathered, his detailed description of that evidence, and his usually insightful historical analysis of the sources. It is not a book to be neglected in research. The book is short enough to be used as one of several texts for a course, but because of its pioneering and specialized nature, and its selective gathering of evidence, it would be best suited for use with texts giving complementary perspectives in an advanced course.

To Caesar What Is Caesar's: Tribute, Taxes, and Imperial Administration in Early Roman Palestine 63 B.C.E.–70 C.E., by Fabian E. Udoh. Brown Judaic Studies 343 Providence, R.I.: Brown Judaic Studies, 2005.Pp. xiii + 350. Cloth. $44.95. ISBN 1930675259.

Daniel Schowalter, Carthage College, Kenosha, Wisconsin

The fundamental point of Fabian Udoh's book is that most modern interpreters of the economic situation in Palestine during the early Roman period go far beyond the evidence to develop theories about the oppressive weight of taxation and tributes paid to the empire and its representatives in the region. If sustained, this corrective is extremely important, since economic oppression has become a standard starting point for many scholars seeking the "historical Jesus" and the origins of Christianity. In order to support this important challenge, the author provides a thorough consideration of the relevant ancient evidence and presents the results in a format of six chapters and an epilogue. The approach is chronological, with the exception of chapter 6, which seems to be less connected to the overall work (see below).

The first chapter considers Roman tribute in Jewish Palestine under Pompey (63–47 B.C.E.). The evidence presented indicates that Pompey did demand tribute from the Jewish state but does not allow certainty regarding the nature and amount of that tribute. Further, Udoh feels that the unsettled nature of the military and political hierarchy of Roman Palestine—and the empire in general—at this time made it impossible for tribute to be collected in a systematic and consistent way. As a result, contributions to the Romans during this period tended to take the form of unofficial or "irregular" exactions by magistrates and/or generals who happened to be in the region. The foremost example is the looting of the temple in Jerusalem (54 B.C.E.) by M. Licinius Crassus, who used the proceeds to finance his ill-fated Parthian campaign.

Chapter 2 examines the favors granted to the Jewish state by Julius Caesar in gratitude for support during his Alexandrian War (47 B.C.E.). These favors, later confirmed by the Senate, were two-edged in that the restoration of authority (for Hyrcanus) and territory (especially the port of Joppa) brought with it the establishment of tributes to be paid to Rome. Evidence for these decrees comes from citation of *senatus consulta* by Josephus. There has been significant discussion on the authenticity and reliability of Josephus's presentation of these documents, and Udoh works through them carefully to glean the most accurate information.

Leadership in the eastern provinces by Cassius and Antony forms the context for the third chapter. After participating in the assassination of Julius Caesar, Cassius and Brutus came east and prepared to defend themselves against those who would avenge Caesar's death. They used harsh methods to raise troops and funds in numerous places. For Udoh, Cassius's exaction of 700 talents of silver from the Jewish cities in 43 B.C.E. is seen as part of this larger strategy, rather than action targeted at the Jews alone. He also comments that it is difficult to assess the impact of this demand for tribute without knowledge of "the total revenue of the territory" or a sense of what they would have been expected to pay before and after 43. Reports of Marc Antony's reorganization of the east highlight both his beneficence in redressing the wrongs imposed on the region by Cassius (Josephus) and his greed and avarice in continuing the oppressive policies (Appian). Udoh again urges caution in forming conclusions based on this conflicting testimony, especially since Appian also speaks of Antony's concessions for the abused territories. He points out that Antony is remembered for trying to return to the policy of toleration for and tribute from the Jewish state established by Julius Caesar.

Chapter 4, dealing with Herodian taxation, is by far the longest chapter in the book and reads as the strongest reaction to modern scholarly approaches to the subject. This more nuanced approach to Herod and his reign follows on the work of Peter Richardson and others, but it is focused on what can and cannot be concluded about Herod's social and economic policies. Udoh argues that a conclusion about whether Herod "did or did not impoverish his kingdom through excessive taxation can be reached not by references to one-sided remarks by Josephus but rather by a comprehensive examination of the evidence at our disposal" (117). Of course, the works of Josephus are an important part of that evidence, but Udoh points out that Josephus comments not only on Herod's oppressiveness but also on "the prosperity of his realm" (190). This is not an attempt to rehabilitate Herod but rather a caution against "erroneous" interpretation (184), "arbitrary" selection of parallels (160), imaginative applications of tribute payments (119), and even "fantastic speculation" about the impact of Herod's building program (189). In short, Udoh suggests that the "widespread and persistent" view that Herod "spent himself to bankruptcy and taxed his subjects to 'helpless poverty'" is not sustained by the available evidence (115).

The same kind of warning is found in chapter 5, which considers the taxation of Judea under the governors. Conflicting ancient reports and diverse scholarly opinion on the place of the census, the role of the *denarius* in the Judean economy, and the payment of tribute "in kind" rather than with cash make it impossible to speak with "dogmatic certitude" about how economic policy affected the population and contributed to the Jewish revolt in 66 C.E. (243). This analysis includes a rejection of the idea that New Testament references can be used as "historical information about taxation in Jewish Palestine during Jesus' lifetime" (236).

Chapter 6 consists of a very thorough discussion of tithes in the Second Temple period. While interesting and informative, the chapter is somewhat difficult to connect to the broader approach and argument of the book. The discussion of tithes leads away from interaction with the Roman world to a focus on evidence from the Jewish Bible, Apocrypha, pseudepigrapha, and rabbinic material. The connection to the broader project is that tithing is often cited as yet another financial demand made on the people of Judea in the first century. Once again, Udoh reminds us that we have conflicting evidence on the details of that system and are not in a position to determine the extent to which it might have contributed to any supposed oppression.

Udoh's epilogue traces the scholarly history of using economic or social-historical approaches to analyze the New Testament material and the historical Jesus. He describes these practices as fundamentally theological in spite of their attempts to use "historical" methodologies. Udoh provides a convincing case that it is theological presupposition rather than careful analysis of the facts that supports the view of Jesus' ministry as a revolutionary response to an oppressive economic system. "The general view that excessive taxation of the Jewish state in the early Roman period was the cause of observable economic depravity in the first century C.E. is not supported by the evidence" (285).

Throughout the book Udoh highlights aspects of the evidence that do not often receive due consideration. A good example is his discussion of how Caesar's grant of Roman citizenship to Herod's father Antipater impacts the question of whether or not the Jewish state paid tribute to Rome. While most modern commentators include one or more forms of tribute in their listing of taxes for Herod's kingdom, Udoh argues that there is no conclusive evidence to support this position. Furthermore, he cites very strong circumstantial evidence that Herod's status as a Roman citizen and a "friend and ally of the Roman people" meant that he was immune from taxation. This immunity apparently continued to the next generation. "Rome, I have argued, derived no direct taxes from Herod's kingdom,

or portions of it, while the territory was governed by Herod and his descendants"
(180).

Udoh's work features careful reading and rereading of the literary evidence
for tribute and taxation in early Roman Palestine. His approach to the ancient
authors is for the most part even-handed and includes appropriate doses of skepticism about their motivations and tendencies. Given the heavy use of Josephus
in these chapters, the book would have benefited from a more comprehensive
discussion about his accuracy and reliability. In a few cases, Udoh does raise
questions about Josephus's testimony (e.g., Udoh offers "some corrective" to the
claim that Herod was "procurator of all Syria" [149]), but in general Josephus is
treated as a reliable witness to the events described even when those events took
place long before his time.

Overall, this study shows the importance of careful analysis of a broad
spectrum of evidence and thereby calls into question the tendency to develop
sweeping sociological conclusions about first-century Judea or the early Jesus
movement based on a limited view of that evidence. Given the popularity and
influence of the notion that Jesus' ministry responded to a particular set of
oppressive socioeconomic circumstances, Udoh's attempt to reexamine the evidence for those circumstances deserves careful attention.

*Götterbilder–Gottesbilder–Weltbilder: Polytheismus und Monotheismus in der
Welt der Antike, Vol. 2: Griechenland und Rom, Judentum, Christentum und Islam*,
edited by Reinhard Gregor Kratz and Hermann Spieckermann. Forschungen
zum Alten Testament 2/18. Tübingen: Mohr Siebeck, 2006. Pp. vii + 335. Paper.
€59.00. ISBN 3161488075.

Konrad Schmid, University of Zurich, Zurich, Switzerland

I.

Der zweite Band der zweibändigen Dokumentation aus Vorträgen, die im
Rahmen des Göttinger Graduiertenkollegs „Götterbilder–Gottesbilder–Weltbilder. Polytheismus und Monotheismus in der Welt der Antike" gehalten wurden, ist
offenbar vor allem aus buchtechnischen Gründen vom ersten Band (R. G. Kratz,
H. Spieckermann [eds.] Götterbilder–Gottesbilder–Weltbilder. Polytheismus und
Monotheismus in der Welt der Antike, Band I: Ägypten, Mesopotamien, Persien,
Kleinasien, Syrien, Palästina. FAT 2/17, Tübingen: Mohr Siebeck, 2006) getrennt
worden. Er enthält kein eigenes Vorwort, sondern stellt wiederum jeweils 2–5
thematisch verwandte Beiträge zu Gruppen zusammen („Griechisch-römische
Religion"; „Urchristliche Religion"; „Rabbinisches Judentum"; „Islamische Reli-
gion"; „Die christliche Religion im Orient"). Beschlossen wird der Band durch
zwei kulturübergreifend ausgerichtete Beiträge, die als „Nachwort" eine weitere
Gruppe bilden.

II.

Der Abschnitt zur „[g]riechisch-römische[n] Religion" wird durch drei gräzistische Beiträge eröffnet: Walter Burkert, Mythen–Tempel–Götterbilder. Von der Nahöstlichen Koiné zur griechischen Gestaltung (3–20); Heinz-Günther Nesselrath, Die Griechen und ihre Götter (21–44); ders., Tempel, Riten und Orakel. Die Stellung der Religion im Leben der Griechen (45–67). Burkert beschreibt für verschiedene Aspekte griechischer Religiosität (religiöse Überlieferungen, sakrale Architektur und Ikonographie) deren Teilhabe an der „nahöstlich-mediterrane[n] Koiné" (3) und ihre Besonderheit in diesem Rahmen. Bemerkenswert sind seine Hinweise zur kulturgeschichtlichen Parallelität der Götterkritik von Xenophanes und Heraklit mit der persischen Religiosität und ihrer Konzentration auf Ahura Mazda (18–19). Nesselrath zeichnet einerseits die Vielfalt und innere Logik des griechischen Pantheons nach und lenkt in seinem zweiten Beitrag andererseits den Blick von der „Gottes-" bzw. „Götterlehre" auf die praktischen Vollzüge der griechischen Religion. Der erste der beiden latinistischen Beiträge von Dorothee Gall (Aspekte römischer Religiosität. Iuppiter optimus maximus [69–92]) rückt zunächst das Vorurteil der grundsätzlichen Inferiorität der römischen gegenüber der griechischen Religion zurecht und akzentuiert dann deren Eigenheit vor allem anhand ihres *numen*-Charakters, der sie weitgehend resistent gegen die anthropomorphe Vorstellung einer Götterfamilie sein ließ, wie sie in der griechischen Religiosität zelebriert werden konnte. Götter werden nicht in erster Linie personal konzipiert, sondern als Wirkmächte. Anhand des Kultes des römischen Iuppiter optimus maximus illustriert Gall eine wesentliche Transformationsgestalt dieser römischen *numen*-Religiosität. Der zweite latinistische Beitrag von Ulrich Schmitzler (Friede auf Erden? Latinistische Erwägungen zur *pax Augusta* [93–111]) ergänzt die von Gall verfolgte Perspektive um den politischen Aspekt römischer Theologie.

Der zweite Abschnitt des Buches widmet sich der „[u]rchristliche[n] Religion" und enthält zwei Aufsätze von Reinhard Feldmeier („Abba, Vater, alles ist dir möglich". Das Gottesbild der synoptischen Evangelien [115–33]; „Der das Nichtseiende ruft, dass es sei". Gott bei Paulus [135–49]). Der erste fragt nach dem Gottesbild der synoptischen Evangelien und transformiert diese Frage, angesichts des auffälligen Zurücktretens Gottes als *dramatis persona* in den Evangelien, sogleich in diejenige nach dem Bild des „Gottessohnes", das Feldmeier anhand verschiedener Merkmale eindringlich niedrigkeitstheologisch beschreibt. Der zweite Beitrag ist gewissermaßen ein paulinisches Komplement dazu, das ebenfalls dezidiert theologisch argumentiert und nachweist, wie bei Paulus klassische Begriffe der griechischen Gotteslehre soteriologisch uminterpretiert werden. Gottes Wesen wird durch sein Wirken beschrieben.

Das „[r]abbinische[] Judentum" wird durch einen Beitrag von Hans-Jürgen Becker abgedeckt (Einheit und Namen Gottes im rabbinischen Judentum [153–87]). Becker zeigt auf, dass die Rabbinen nicht an einem theoretischen Monotheismus interessiert waren, sondern an der Alleinwirksamkeit Gottes, die sie aber sehr vielgestaltig wahrnehmen und interpretieren konnten, wie sich nicht zuletzt an der Vorstellung der Vielzahl der göttlichen Namen ablesen lässt.

Die „[i]slamische[] Religion" wird durch drei sich ergänzende und fortsetzende Beiträge von Tilman Nagel behandelt (Schöpfung und Kosmos im Koran [191–209]; Die Anthropologie des Islams [211–26]; Die muslimische Glaubensgemeinschaft als die Verwirklichung des göttlichen Willens auf Erden [227–40]). Der Kosmos ist „ein von Allah souverän gestalteter Prozess, in den auch der Mensch ganz und gar einbezogen ist" (207); entsprechend tritt das kosmologische Interesse an der Schöpfung im Koran ganz zurück, er enthält keinen Schöpfungsbericht. Der Mensch allerdings hat eine Sonderstellung im Koran, die sich seiner partiellen Geistbegabung, seiner „Gläubigkeit" (216) verdankt. Sie befähigt ihn, die menschliche Geschöpflichkeit in Dankbarkeit zu erkennen, nicht aber, die Schöpfung und das Handeln Gottes insgesamt zu durchschauen. Die soziologische Seite des Islam besteht darin, „für den Fortbestand der von Mohammed gegründeten ‚besten Gemeinschaft' zu sorgen" (231).

Zwei Aufsätze von Martin Tamcke erhellen die Stellung des Christentums im Orient (Im Schatten von Schah und Kaliph. Christsein östlich der griechisch-römischen Welt [243–61]; Zwischen Größenwahn und Minderwertigkeitsgefühl. Christsein im Haus des Islam [263–76]).

Zwei eher theoretisch ausgerichtete Aufsätze beschließen den Band. Andreas Bendlin (Nicht der Eine, nicht die vielen. Zur Pragmatik religiösen Verhaltens in einer polytheistischen Gesellschaft am Beispiel Roms [279–311]) versucht, die innere Logik religiöser Rituale in polytheistischen Kontexten zu erfassen. Es zeigt sich dabei, dass Polytheismen nicht nur Selektionen erlauben, sondern nachgerade hervorbringen. Verehrung gilt „nicht de[m] Eine[n], nicht d[en] vielen", der Kult ist vielmehr in eine komplexe soziale Wirklichkeit der religiösen Subjekte eingebunden und bezieht seine Logik von dort her.

Der Beitrag von Jan Assmann schließlich (Gottesbilder–Menschenbilder: anthropologische Konsequenzen des Monotheismus [313–29]) wendet sich dem Menschenbild des Monotheismus zu. Er bespricht dabei die Konzeptionen von Schrift und Bund, Reue und Martyrium, die allesamt Zeichen und Äußerungen einer fundamentalen „Exkarnation" sind, die sich von der Durchsetzung der monotheistischen Idee her ergeben: Der Monotheismus treibt einen Keil zwischen Gott und die Welt, zwischen den Schöpfer und die Schöpfung, der die Religion nicht mehr (nur) Interpretation, sondern Regulativ der Welt sein lässt.

III.

Der zweite Band bietet wie der erste „reiches Material und substantielle Erkenntnisse (Vorwort zu Band I, xix). Ebenso wie bei Band I wiederholt sich für den Leser dieser umfassenden Publikation das strukturelle Problem des Verhältnisses von Polytheismus und Monotheismus, von Vielfalt und Einheit, noch einmal auf der über diese Phänomene reflektierenden Ebene: Was ist nun dieses religionsgeschichtliche Material zu synthetisieren und zu interpretieren? Einzelne Beiträge wie diejenige von Walter Burkert oder Dorothee Gall verfolgen bereits von sich aus kulturübergreifende Perspektiven, andere, wie diejenigen von Andreas Bendlin oder Jan Assmann, überspannen verschiedene wissenschaftliche Disziplinen, doch für das meiste andere Dargebotene ist nun die Mitarbeit des Lesers gefragt. Auch das Vorwort hält fest: „Auf diesem Fundament kann man gut weiterbauen" (ebd.). Doch es ist hier noch einiges zu leisten, bis auf diesem Fundament ein Haus entstehen kann (was die beiden Bände sich wohlgemerkt auch nicht vorgenommen haben). Besonders arbeitsreich und in der interdisziplinären Vermittlung schwierig, aber auch besonders vielversprechend dürfte—neben dem Versuch einer weitergreifenden kulturwissenschaftlichen Synthese—dabei der Einbezug theologischer Argumentationsarbeit, wie sie etwa in den Aufsätzen Feldmeiers erkennbar wird, in die weiteren altertumswissenschaftliche Diskurse sein. Es käme jedenfalls einer Verkürzung der Problemstellung zu Polytheismus und Monotheismus gleich, wenn die religionswissenschaftliche Untersuchung der entsprechenden Konzeptionen ohne theologisches Problembewusstsein auszukommen meinte.

NEW TESTAMENT: GENERAL

A Critical Introduction to the New Testament: Interpreting the Message and Meaning of Jesus Christ, by Carl R. Holladay. Nashville: Abingdon, 2005. Pp. xxii + 609 [expanded CD-ROM version included]. Hardcover. $49.00. ISBN 0687085691.

Jan G. van der Watt, University of Pretoria, Pretoria, South Africa 0043

Several noteworthy introductions to the New Testament have appeared recently, each one aiming at introducing the reader to the books of the New Testament on different levels. Although the different introductions deal with the same basic material, each one has its own unique characteristics. This is also true of Holladay's critical introduction.

Scanning the book for the first time left the impression that much thought has gone into both the content and the presentation of the material. The first unique feature that immediately catches the eye is the expanded CD version that comes with the book. Holladay distinguishes between the Standard Version (the printed text) and the Expanded CD Version. These should be used in tandem. Where there is expanded material available on the CD, it is clearly indicated in bold letters in the Standard Version. The CD not only contains the full text but adds the additional material on the pages indicated in the Standard Version. More technical material, such as primary references, more detailed discussions and debates, additional diagrams and illustrations, are available on the CD. Detailed annotations and footnotes on the CD also enrich the available material. In his own words, Holladay remarks that adding a CD "represents the changing face of academic publishing" and represents a "bold editorial move by Abingdon" (5). Of course, this is not the first time this concept has been used, especially not in works of a more popular nature. The drawback is that one does not always have a computer at hand to run the CD when reading the book. It is thus a matter of convenience. However, those who are interested in the additional material will take the trouble to consult the CD. At least one has the material available if it is needed. Fortunately, Abingdon and Holladay made sure that the CD is user-friendly, the result being that all of the material on it is easily accessible. There are various ways of finding the material on the CD, and the software interface runs effectively and quickly. It is even possible to copy text from the CD to a word processor. History will show whether this approach of enriching a printed version with technology (who knows what the future might hold) is viable and sustainable. I believe history's judgment will be positive, which means that the shelf life of Holladay's work will be significantly increased if he (or his students) continue to update the material on the CD. The cost of changing CDs is significantly lower than publishing new editions, not to mention the technical ease with which it can be done. I therefore regard this effort as successful and expect it to be copied by others, especially in works offering an overview of large bodies of material.

Holladay's aim with this book is to introduce multiple audiences to the writings of the New Testament, including readers with little or no previous knowledge of these writings. It should, however, also appeal to more advanced readers without "boring" them with generally known information. This is, of course, a challenging endeavor and requires a delicate balancing act. Enough substantial information should be offered to help the novice to build a proper and sound frame of reference and simultaneously to broaden and enrich the existing frames of reference of the more experienced reader. Holladay uses his thorough and long experience as university lecturer to address this problem. He embeds the content of the different books of the New Testament in the existing critical discussions about those books. That is why the title of the book includes the words *Critical Introduction*. The word "critical" refers to a reflective discussion of the interpretative issues related to the different dimensions of the text of the New Testament. Part of this presentation is also a thorough engagement with the reception history of these books through the centuries. How this material is presented is, of course, important. It should not create the impression that it is an elementary "popular" book so that the already "initiated" become disinterested and do not want to read further; it should also not have such a high "academic feeling" that "first readers" are scared away. An important question is therefore whether this book succeeded in keeping this delicate balance.

The answer is positive; in fact, this seems to be one of the strengths of this introduction. There are several reasons why I believe this to be so. The language and level of discussion is not overwhelming. It is reader-friendly, and one is not bombarded with theological jargon. Even more important, the flow of ideas is clear and crisp. Every theologian knows that each issue of the New Testament can be problematized to the level of a dissertation. The challenge is to extract the essence in each case without falling into the trap of oversimplifying matters. The student must be given a solid and trustworthy framework of information that would facilitate and help to integrate further reading.

I read Holladay's introduction in this light and was impressed by his ability to present material in a digestible way without being too simplistic or elementary. In general, I would say that the information in this introduction is representative of current debates and views on the subject (with a few exceptions). The concept of expanding the material on a CD-ROM, of course, helps to accommodate the more informed reader.

The clear, systematic presentation of the material, enriched with diagrams, adds to the positive reading experience and will benefit the reader in absorbing and retaining the information. Overall I am of the opinion that this insightful work benefits from Holladay's understanding of the needs and expectations of students of the New Testament gained through years spent as a lecturer in the subject.

The book is presented in seven parts, each part consisting of individual chapters. The presentation of material broadly follows the canonical sequence of the books of the New Testament, with some issues discussed at the beginning and conclusion of the book.

Part 1 ("Theology and Scripture") deals with the New Testament as theological writings and with some canonical issues related to the New Testament. There is a reflection on the nature of theology, and the process of doing theology is consequently seen as the means though which the content of one's faith is formulated. This process includes a diversity of elements, including engaging with ancient authoritative texts and traditions and recognizing the distinctive roles of interpreters (as groups or individuals). Doing theology is aimed at making sense of, and giving formal expression to, how "God is at work in Christ" and how this should be understood and experienced in a specific context (19). Holladay thus outlines the theoretical framework within which he presents his material in the rest of the book. The material of the New Testament is not only "history" that must be described as past events. Of course, it is also that and must be understood within its proper historical, social, and literary contexts. However, these texts are also read and interpreted, not only by the first readers, but subsequently by many generations of scholars and otherwise "involved" readers. This interest in the history of reception of the New Testament becomes apparent in the discussions of the way in which the relevant material was treated throughout history. The content of the New Testament and the process of interpreting these texts are linked, not only as a punctuating event but also as a continuing process. Holladay also points out that the figure of Jesus is the primary catalyst for early Christian theological reflection and should therefore be taken seriously in doing theology. The events surrounding Jesus (including his ministry, sudden and unexpected death, and living presence afterwards with his followers) triggered and determined the nature, content, and intensity of subsequent theological discussion and reflection. The essence of Christian theological reflection remains the interpretation of what God has done in Christ.

Obviously, the writings of the New Testament are not studied out of curiosity but because they have canonical status for Christians. Some texts are thus defined as more important than others and form an authoritative basis for formulating Christian tradition. Holladay gives a historical overview of the process of canonization and positions his material within this framework, giving special attention to the general arrangement of the different books of the New Testament.

Parts 2–6 systematically deal with the writings of the New Testament more or less in canonical order (the order of Paul's letters are a bit different from their order in the Bible). The basic pattern of the different chapters is the same, obviously taking the differences in nature of the writings into account. "Discussing the Gospels" (part 2) includes chapters on relating the Gospels to each other and to Jesus. In the part on Paul, the question of reading the Pauline letters is addressed. Paul's letters are positioned within the framework of ancient letters, and the structure and chronology of these letters are discussed.

The treatment of the different books of the New Testament should be especially noted. The older atomic approach of first dealing with introductory questions, followed by exegesis and discussions of some critical problems, continuing to the theology of that particular book, is long gone. The circular interrelatedness of all these issues is now acknowledged. Holladay's book is a very good example of how the different issues related to interpreting the New Testament are interwoven. Strong emphasis falls on the content of each book. This forms the core of each discussion. I regard this as a strong point of this introduction. The book is not intended to replace the text of the New Testament. Rather, a reading of the primary texts will be complemented by the material presented in this book. The arguments are not developed from specific set of hypotheses or theories but are essentially developed from material flowing from the text of the New Testament itself. The reader is constantly reminded of the primary sources behind the discussions and is forced back to these primary sources. This results in an introduction into the New Testament as document and not into secondary theories about the New Testament; the latter is not neglected, but it does not dominate. The content is not discussed in a vacuum or in an ahistorical and abstract way. It is embedded into the sociohistorical and literary framework pertinent to that particular book. Disputed or unresolved issues in debates about a particular book are given due attention, although not in tiresome detail. In this way "introductory or related critical issues," exegesis, and theology merge well. The reader is left with a more holistic and much more digestible picture of each book. The various elements make sense in relation to and in light of one another. This illustrates to the reader how the dating of a book interrelates to the view of who the author could have been and how the historical, theological, ethical, or social material in the books could be interpreted or how one's view about the issues in the text itself can guide one in determining the date or possible authorship. By interrelating these different aspects, a more coherent picture of what is going on in a particular book of the New Testament emerges.

Obviously, there are some critical elements one should be aware of. The articles do bear clear evidence of Holladay's preferences, but this also contributes to the unique nature of the book. He does not approach the material in a stereotypical manner but rather takes his own avenues into the discussions, based on the content or message of each book. How this relates to the religious convictions of the author and original readers is considered. This means that different present-day readers might react differently, feeling that this or that should have received more emphasis or should have been more prominent or that other material received too much attention. This is natural, and the advantage lies therein that this book will stimulate further discussions. The book does not give the impression of giving final solutions, although the chapters are written in a positive and affirmative style. It is not as if Holladay is a "floating theologian" who does not know what his views are.

Another important issue is, of course, the bibliographies and indexes. There is a very useful index at the back of the printed edition, and search possibilities on the CD are also available. As far as the bibliography is concerned, the question is whether the novice is referred to books that will help him or her to effectively build up a solid working knowledge of that particular book or only guided in a specific direction. Is the reader referred to standard works in that particular field? The criterion here is not how many books are mentioned but rather which books are mentioned. One can continue ad infinitum adding more and more titles. The secret to success is adding the correct titles. Here I also feel that Holladay did a good job. Here and there I missed a book that I would regard as standard, but, as I said, drawing the boundaries of what to include and what not to include is not easy. I do, however, have one point of criticism. There is too little mention of books outside of the English circle. There are some references to works in other languages, but then only to translations. I do have sympathy with the fact that the intended readership would most probably not have language skills in German or French and that mentioning these works would just seem like window dressing. On the other hand, I think the impression should not be created that scholarship can do without these works. This would be a major mistake.

In conclusion, what is my overall impression? I will definitely add this book to the list of prescribed books for my students and will encourage them to use the CD. I think Holladay has done teachers and prospective students of the New Testament a big favor in making such a well written, clearly planned, and thorough but not overwhelming introduction available.

Reading with Anthropology: Exhibiting Aspects of New Testament Religion, by Louise J. Lawrence. Waynesboro, Ga.: Paternoster, 2005. Pp. xix + 212. Paper. $22.99. ISBN 1842273752.

David F. Watson, United Theological Seminary, Trotwood, OH 45426

Over the last two decades a significant body of literature has developed bringing social-scientific research, and particularly cultural anthropology, into dialogue with New Testament criticism. Much of this work has focused on the values of honor and shame and associated cultural practices within the first-century Mediterranean world. In *Reading with Anthropology: Exhibiting Aspects of New Testament Religion,* Louise J. Lawrence takes the anthropological approach to the study of the Bible in new and interesting directions and thereby makes an original and valuable contribution.

The book is conceived on the model of a museum exhibit, "a carefully designed selection of objects for consumption by viewers" (xii). In particular, it "presents a series of 'exhibits' of selected scriptural texts and materials drawn from anthropological sources" (xii). As the "curator," Lawrence has shaped the exhibit in keeping with her own creative ideas and interests. She notes, "In any museum the viewer is to a certain extent at the mercy of the choices made by the curator" (xii). As a book, however, her work involves significantly more commentary on the "exhibits" than one might expect to find in an actual museum, and she therefore guides their interpretation more thoroughly than one would typically expect from a curator. The guidance that she provides is informed largely by postcolonial and feminist approaches to anthropology and New Testament criticism.

There are two major sections of this book. "Part I: Reading with Anthropology" comprises the first two chapters. The first chapter provides a brief overview of the use of anthropology and other forms of social-scientific criticism by biblical scholars. As the author notes, this overview is not comprehensive, but it does give one a sense of some of the more significant past and present discussions of social-scientific biblical interpretation.

In the second chapter Lawrence shows that anthropology can illuminate faith claims and contribute to theological inquiry. She provides several examples of scholars who have brought anthropology and Christian theology into dialogue with one another. In particular, she focuses on missionary Charles Kraft and theologian Douglas Davies, both of whom are also anthropologists. She then introduces two concepts, "Embodiment" and "Humans as Ceremonial Animals," that play into much of the discussion that follows in later chapters. She proposes that these two concepts help to illuminate faith and theology not from the traditional philosophical perspective but through investigation of "rituals and bodily performances" that are "powerful mediums of the sacred" (31).

"Part II: Exhibiting Aspects of Scriptural Religion" comprises the remaining eight chapters. Each chapter except for the final one focuses on a particular "exhibit." In "Exhibit 1. Reading with Religious Practitioners" the author uses cross-cultural comparison with shamans and shaman healers to discuss the depictions of Jesus in Mark and Luke. She argues that Mark's Jesus offers important parallels with the shaman (individualistic, trance-led, impulsive), while Luke's Jesus correlates more closely with the shaman healer (group-oriented, ritual-led, with more formal training).

In "Exhibit 2. Reading with Tricksters" the author uses the cross-cultural figure of the "trickster" to illuminate the portrayal of Jesus in the Fourth Gospel. She argues that the trickster gives voice to the perspectives of individuals and communities who are oppressed by institutionalized power structures. John's Jesus, like other tricksters, crosses cultural boundaries, disrupts established norms, and challenges structures of authority. For the Johannine community, the members of which experienced dislocation from the wider culture, Jesus helped to carve out new "liminal" social space with its own social structures and norms of behavior.

Lawrence again takes up the theme of resistance to domination in "Exhibit 3. Reading with Rituals of Resistance," this time discussing ways in which "willing deaths" can provide such resistance. Biblical figures that play into this discussion include the Maccabean martyrs, Jesus, and the martyrs of Revelation. Lawrence argues that willing deaths can function as rituals of resistance in circumstances in which martyrs accept the violence that their oppressors inflict upon them but simultaneously reject "the efficacy of that domination by commentary on the failings of the oppressors" (77).

"Exhibit 4. Reading with Women's Religions" builds upon the work of Susan Sered (*Priestess, Mother, Sacred Sister: Religions Dominated by Women*), who has identified and studied twelve religious traditions in which women play prominent roles. Lawrence looks at these religions alongside "early Christianity" (including the Jesus movement, the Pauline churches, the Gospels, 1 Peter, and the Pastoral Epistles). She holds that early on Christian communities exhibited characteristics found in religions in which women play prominent roles (e.g., emphasis on solidarity, the alleviation of suffering, and maternal images). As Christianity developed, however, it came to emphasize respect for authority, subservience, and hierarchical patterns.

In "Exhibit 5. Reading with Poetry" the author uses ethnographic studies of bedouin society in which poetry and song provide "culturally acceptable avenues for expression of individual sentiments that often contradict the status quo" (150). Such songs and poems are discussed in relation to the Song of Songs (an odd text in a work on New Testament religion). She argues that, while the Song should not be considered a revolutionary text from a feminist perspective, it does give voice to individual feelings that are in some ways contradictory to the expectations of the ethics of the dominant culture.

"Exhibit 6. Reading with Communities of Goods" involves a discussion of three communities that practice the sharing of possessions: the early Christian community portrayed in Acts, the Qumran community, and the Hutterites. Lawrence discusses in this chapter "virtuoso religion," in which a community establishes strict boundaries of thought and action so as to engrain deeply within its members proper moral vision and behavior. In the groups discussed in this chapter, the sharing of economic resources is part of a larger vision of moral behavior that is inscribed through virtuosity.

"Exhibit 7. Reading with Food and Memory" discusses modern anthropological work on the Greek island of Kalymos in connection with Paul's account of the Lord's Supper in 1 Corinthians. A particular concern in this chapter is to demonstrate the ways in which food, as a means of forming group identity and evoking social memory, can overcome social divisions.

The work's final chapter, "Exiting an Exhibition," provides a brief summary conclusion and a final reflection on the ways in which anthropology can help us to engage those who are culturally different from us.

This book is both informative and provocative. The author, who writes in a lively style, clearly knows the field of anthropology quite well. Further, while she obviously sees many benefits of a comparative anthropological approach to the study of the Bible, she is also aware of the weaknesses of such an approach. For example, she cautions against the pitfall of "parallelomania," the identification of cross-cultural parallels without sufficient attention to the differences that may exist between the paralleled elements (42).

An interesting aspect of this book is that, while much contemporary social-scientific New Testament criticism stresses the adherence of individuals to the norms of their social groups, Lawrence emphasizes the "consciousness, agency and creativity of the individuals presented in the Bible" (191). Although she recognizes that individuals are strongly influenced by "social habits" (191), on several occasions she criticizes "cultural scripts" according to which human beings always function in keeping with established cultural patterns. In pushing for greater clarity on the issue of individual agency, Lawrence's work promises to open interesting channels of dialogue regarding the ways in which ancient Mediterranean people understood themselves in relation to their in-groups and cultural norms.

Some of the cross-cultural comparisons she makes are more helpful than others. For example, her discussion of the relationship between food, social memory, and identity provides rich insight into the social dynamics at work in the Corinthian church. Conversely, her analysis of John's Jesus in light of the "trickster" figure is less illuminating. While John's Jesus does engage in some of the behavior that Lawrence identifies with cross-cultural representations of trick-sters (e.g., he is a "boundary crosser" who performs miracles), it is harder to find clear instances in which he is deceptive of or "tricks" those around him. Of the presentations of Jesus in the four canonical Gospels, John's Jesus is the most out-spoken and forthright about his identity and mission.

This is not the only instance in which the method, which involves the quest for comparative cultural elements, takes precedence over the biblical text that the comparison is supposed to illuminate. Rather than exhibiting aspects of New Testament religion, as the title suggests, this book primarily exhibits aspects of comparative anthropology. The texts often serve the method, rather than the method functioning to illuminate the texts. This work is not primarily an exercise in biblical exegesis but a means of showcasing a particular approach to the study of the New Testament. Hence the book's strength lies in the author's command of the method and relevant literature, but it is not as strong in its treatment of the biblical texts themselves.

These issues aside, Lawrence knowledgeably introduces a comparative anthropological approach to the study of the Bible. This book is accessible enough to serve as a useful introduction, yet it is broad enough in the range of scholarship it covers to be helpful even to scholars who have some knowledge of anthropology.

The Child-Parent Relationship in the New Testament and Its Environment, by Peter Balla. Peabody, Mass.: Hendrickson, 2003. Pp. xii + 279. Paper. $29.95. ISBN 1598560344.

Reidar Aasgaard, University of Oslo, Oslo, Norway N-0315

Within the last decades there has been a marked growth of interest in the study of family and family roles within the biblical world, and much work has been done, for example, on gender issues and social relationships such as slave–master and client–patron. Surprisingly, the family as a totality and some of its most central roles, particularly siblings, parents, and children, have until recently received less attention. Within the last decade, however, a number of scholars have studied these matters more closely. As for the place of children, important contributions have been made within the classical field by scholars such as B. Rawson (2003) and C. Laes (2006) and within the New Testament and early Christian field by P. Müller (1992), W. A. Strange (1996), and O. M. Bakke (2005).

In *The Child-Parent Relationship in the New Testament and its Environment* Peter Balla, chairperson of the New Testament department at the Karoli Gaspar Reformed University in Budapest, directs attention to parent–child relations in the New Testament and views these relations in the light of general attitudes in antiquity. He does not deal with the matter in full breadth but limits his discussion to the rights and duties of children (particularly grown-up children) toward parents. This is, in his opinion, a "from below" perspective that has been much neglected within scholarship.

Balla calls attention to two central features in the New Testament material, the contrast (1) between the early Jesus-followers' break with their families and the social stability reflected in the household codes of the late New Testament letters, and (2) between the call in the Gospels to "honor" one's parents and to "leave" or "hate" them. Balla's aim is to account for these seemingly contradictory features. Modern scholarship has frequently portrayed the early Christians as being in conflict with their social milieus, particularly their families of origin, and has presented the Christian groups, with the strong and close relations among their members, as a substitute for the loss of one's family of origin. Balla's main point is that this conflict is very much exaggerated: the early Christians were all along—not least motivated by Jesus' own attitudes—taken up with preserving the old social structures and thus of honoring their parents. Sayings about "leaving" or "hating" parents were very much hyperbolic expressions with parallels in classical, non-Christian material. The function of such sayings was to underscore the radical character of loyalty toward Christ: honoring God had higher priority than honoring parents. But it was only in extreme cases that such priorities collided,

since living up to current expectations about honoring parents also meant showing due honor to God.

In the first three chapters Balla investigates the non-Christian material. Chapter 1 (6–40) surveys classical Greek sources such as Plato, Aristotle, the tragedies,
laws, and inscriptions, while chapter 2 (41–79) deals with Greek and Latin sources
from Hellenistic and Roman imperial times, for example, Cicero, Cynic and Stoic
material, and papyri letters. In chapter 3 (80–111) Balla turns to Jewish literature
from Hellenistic and early Roman times, particularly Philo, but also to Josephus,
Qumran, and the Old Testament apocryphal and pseudepigraphal works.

Balla follows a fairly similar procedure within each of these chapters. First he
addresses a number of conditions that were significant in shaping parent–child
relations: the family hierarchy, the strong position of the *paterfamilias*, gender
differences, social inequalities, marriage structures, and inheritance rules. Then
he describes the norms children were expected to live up to: they should honor
and obey parents, learn from them, take care of them in their old age, provide a
worthy burial, and secure their posthumous reputation. These obligations were
justified in a variety of ways: out of respect for the gods/God and the laws of society, in that they were ethical or given by nature, or as a return for parents' services
during childhood. Within Judaism the commandment to honor parents had a
central position, with its promise that one's "days may be long in the land."

Importantly, Balla also pays attention to the limits set in the sources with
regard to children's loyalty toward their parents. Such limits were that the gods/
God and their will ranked above parents and their will, that philosophy could
take precedence over them (the Pythagoreans), and that parents were to be dis-
obeyed when they were mentally unaccountable or behaved ethically or socially
irresponsibly. For Jewish converts, the obligation to the Torah was also expected
to have priority. In spite of some differences among cultural traditions, similarities in views on this were clearly the most prominent, however.

In chapters 4–6 Balla deals with the New Testament material. His intention
is to explore early Christian views on parent–child relations and to clarify how
these views agreed with, or deviated from, general attitudes in antiquity. His
main conclusion is that early Christian attitudes—from Jesus, via the Gospels and
Paul, and to the post-Pauline letters—were in keeping with conventional ideas
on parent–child relations: they had the same emphasis on children's obedience
toward parents and the same limitations as were current in antiquity. Although
Balla concurs with Gerd Theissen that there existed two main forms of Christian
lifestyles, the one represented by wandering charismatics, the other by believers
belonging to established communities, both "types" of early Christians shared the
ideal of honoring one's parents. Conflicts between this ideal and the call to follow
Jesus would only occur in extreme situations and did not even then deviate from
attitudes generally accepted in antiquity.

In chapter 4 (114–56) Balla discusses the most central parent–child passages
in the Gospels, though without basing his analyses on some established view
about the relations among these writings or whether their material can be traced

back to the historical Jesus. Balla first deals with passages common to all the Synoptics, then to two of them, then each Gospel's special material, and finally the Gospel of John; all the way his focus is on texts in which parent–child relations are of a concrete nature. He sorts the material into two main categories: passages that speak about honoring parents, and passages dealing with familial tensions. As for the former, in his opinion they show that Jesus and the early Christians reflected current attitudes, in keeping with the commandment of the Decalogue. As for the latter passages, Balla holds that they do depict conflicts not following from the Christian message itself but from how Christians were met by their families. The language of these passages has a radical stamp (e.g., "Let the dead bury their own dead"), since it reflects a calling taking place in "the last days." However, this language is meant to be interpreted not literally but as a pointed way of expressing the will of God. According to Balla, such sayings may also have been aimed at a limited group of disciples, namely, those who traveled about with Jesus.

Chapter 5 (157–201) deals with the letters of Paul and the Pauline tradition. As with the Gospels, Balla here too approaches the material as expressing common and general views among the early Christians; consequently, he puts little emphasis on distinguishing between authentic and nonauthentic Pauline material. First Balla addresses passages dealing with parent–child relations in a concrete sense (e.g., the household codes) and then passages in which they are dealt with in a figurative sense (e.g., God and Paul as "fathers"). In Balla's view, this material likewise reflects conventional ideas about parent–child relations. However, the texts appear to attach less weight to giving detailed advice on the matter or to the obligation to honor one's forefathers (in accordance with Jewish skepticism). The letters are also to a lesser degree than the Gospels affected by tensions of loyalty between God and one's parents. According to Balla, this reflects the fact that the addressees of these letters lived in stable families and established religious groups and that they both internally and *ad extra* wished to show that Christians represented an honorable way of living.

In chapter 6 (202–28) Balla presents a more summary survey of the rest of the New Testament. Within these writings, figurative parent–child language occurs far more often than concrete language (particularly in Hebrews, James, 1 Peter, and 1–3 John). In a concrete sense, parent–child relations are most frequently spoken of in Acts and Hebrews. In both types of language, however, current attitudes on parent–child relations are reflected. Neither in these writings does any conflict arise between loyalty toward God and toward parents; here too such allegiances are seen as two sides of the same coin.

Finally (229–32), Balla briefly summarizes his findings and adds copious indexes and a bibliography (233–79). The latter include many non-English contributions but also betrays a few surprising lacunae.

Balla has provided a very valuable contribution to the issue of children in the New Testament. With his broad presentation of classical material, his analyses of the New Testament material, and his nuanced discussions with other scholars, he has argued convincingly in favor of his main thesis: early Christians very much remained faithful to their families of origin. Thus he has succeed at least initially in adjusting the picture that has been formed within scholarship of strong tensions, conflicts, and breaches.

The way Balla approaches parts of his material, is problematic, however. Since he deals with much of the material almost disconnected from its tradition-historical and redaction-critical context, that is, he sees it as an expression of general early Christian attitudes, nuances in the material are covered up, particularly differences among the Gospels. In this way he is able to present his view clearly, but he also becomes repetitive and in his one-sidedness makes himself vulnerable to criticism. Since he fails to analyze the figurative use of parent–child language in the Gospels, he also loses some of the dynamics between concrete and figurative usages (e.g., Matt 23:8–9). On several occasions Balla deals with text-critical issues, but he often gives it more space than required, considering the slight outcome of his discussions. In addition, the classical texts are sometimes fragmentarily presented, and some Greek quotations should have been translated.

In his study of parent–child relations in the New Testament, Balla manages to deal with the material in both depth and breadth, which is of much value, given the many brief and/or rather specialized studies that have been produced thus far. His sociohistorical approach, with extensive use of non-Christian material, also proves very fruitful. The attention he pays in his analyses to the limitations of children's responsibilities toward parents also serves to gainsay the frequent stereotype of the all-powerful antique parent (i.e., father) figure. Finally, his basic perspective, namely, to view the New Testament material from the angle of the child, is of special merit. In this, his work places itself within a larger critical-hermeneutical tradition in which liberation theological thinking is in the process of gaining a good foothold in the study of this major, yet marginalized, group of human beings in the ancient world. It is promising that it now appears to have become the children's turn within biblical scholarship. They have been ignored for too long.

Performing the Gospel: Orality, Memory, and Mark: Essays Dedicated to Werner Kelber, edited by Richard A. Horsley, Jonathan A. Draper, and John Miles Foley. Minneapolis: Fortress, 2006. Pp. xvi + 239. Hardcover. $35.00. ISBN 080063828X.

Alan Kirk, James Madison University, Harrisonburg, Virginia

This volume takes its point of departure from Werner Kelber's pioneering work on the orality/writing problematic, in particular as this impinges upon Gospels scholarship. In aggregate the essays are a measure of the uneven but steady progress Kelber's work has made in a field in significant respects still guided by the cognitive habits of print culture.

Fittingly placed at the beginning, Holly Hearon's essay surveys some of the leading applications of orality approaches within contemporary Gospels scholarship. Prominent among these are attempts to redescribe the dynamics of written texts in terms of a cultural environment characterized by pervasive orality, an environment, that is, where texts would have been enacted and appropriated orally and aurally. Judging from her survey, however, it appears that a number of studies have tended to marginalize textuality in favor of orality, in other words, to dissolve the written texts and their literary relationships into oral processes. This hardly seems an adequate reception of Kelber's work, which has always taken the phenomenology of the written text seriously and whose dominant concern has been to explore the *interface* of the oral and written mediums. Hearon, in fact, recognizes this problem and calls for new studies that will focus upon "the complexity of the relationship" between the orality and writing in early Christianity.

The work of Kelber on the Gospels has been paralleled by Martin Jaffee's analyses of oral tradition and writing in rabbinic Judaism, and those studying the history of the gospel tradition have much to learn from him. Here Jaffee argues that the rabbis' conception of their oral tradition as revelation, that is, "Oral Torah," functioned rhetorically to define the boundaries of the rabbinic circle and to distinguish its members as an elite within Israel. The effect, moreover, was partial absorption in rabbinic rhetoric of undisciplined Jews (male Jews not belonging to the study circles and hence less observant) and Jewish women to the category of Gentiles, all marked by their common consignment to a position outside the privileged circle of revelation. This rhetoric, Jaffee argues further, was gendered, with masculine qualities predicated of the discipleship circles in their cultivation of Oral Torah and feminine qualities of persons excluded from those circles, in effect a symbolic extension of the general exclusion of women from Torah-study to all categories of persons ignorant of Oral Torah. Jaffee's depiction of oral tradition in this particular case undergirding claims to elite status is a salutary corrective to the tendency one occasionally encounters in Gospels studies to view orality as intrinsically egalitarian.

Jonathan Draper focuses upon the oral/written interface in a Zulu prophetic community that coalesced around the prophet George Khambule (1884–1949), which though largely illiterate left behind hundreds of handwritten pages of their prophetic oracles. These materials bring to light the ways in which oral dynamics impinge upon the manuscript medium. The oracles, although committed to writing, clearly continued to function in various performance settings and, moreover, came to display the multiformity emblematic of oral tradition. Responding to Kelber's call for attention to the mnemonics and social dynamics of transmission, Draper observes that it is through performance that these oracles undergo formalization and "pass into the memory of the community." Although Draper is duly cautious about drawing hasty analogies, it is clear that contemporary case studies such as these cast light on the intersection of oral tradition, writing, and memory in the early Jesus communities.

This volume is particularly notable for a contribution from Jan Assmann, the leading theorist on cultural memory, many of the leading features of which he sketches out in this essay. Memory is a social phenomenon; shared memories are the basis for belonging to communities. By the same token, it is the basis for culture and the reproduction of cultural identity, crucial to which is the formation and transmission of tradition. Tradition, in other words, must be understood within the framework of cultural memory dynamics. Those familiar with Assmann's work will be particularly intrigued by the phenomenological parallel he postulates as existing between tradition and the morphological transformation across time of the material artifacts of culture. This may offer a fresh approach to the problem of stability and transformation in the Synoptic tradition. The essay concludes with an analysis of canonization as a protracted cultural memory process. Assmann's discussion on this point seems particularly pertinent to contemporary debates about the significance of the variability that is found in the early manuscript tradition of the Gospels.

Memory is likewise the subject of John Miles Foley's essay, "Memory in Oral Tradition." Taking an emic approach, Foley surveys conceptions of memory's connection to oral-traditional performance as these are found in oral-derived texts from the Anglo Saxon, South Slavic, and ancient Greek cultural spheres. In all three cases memory is understood not as wooden reproduction of material memorized by rote but as a dynamic ("kinetic"), cued enactment of the oral-traditional repertoire of the culture to create a particular performance of tradition. Because enacted in performance, memory is socially produced; it "requires an audience of co-rememberers," and performance can be viewed as a collective "rite of remembering." As in Assmann's essay, we see here a convergence between memory theory and studies of tradition that seems in turn to have applicability to classic problems in the history of the Gospel tradition.

Ellen Aitken's contribution is a focused assessment of how the representation of Jesus as a performer, that is, interpreter of scripture, as in the Emmaus episode of Luke 24, is in important respects analogous to conventional depictions of the ritually present hero authoritatively reinterpreting tradition in Greek hero cult. "In the Gospel of Luke," she concludes, "is embedded a conceptualization of the performance of scripture in which 'correct' interpretation is available through cult practices that activate the presence of Jesus." This in turn makes it possible to reconstruct settings of early Christian performance of tradition—ritual settings in which the voice of Jesus merges with the voice of the performer.

The question of the origins of the Gospel canon is picked up again by Jens Schröter. Schröter locates its emergence in the second-century enterprise of securing identity by establishing the connection of foundational traditions to the authoritative past, in his own words, in the drive "to preserve the tie between Christian faith and its origins." The Gospels historicized tradition within the framework of written narratives of Jesus' earthly activity. The boundaries between the written and oral tradition, however, remained indistinct and porous. The result was that early and late forms of the tradition came to be transmitted together and multiformity characteristic of the written Gospel tradition itself. As attested by Papias, this period was already marked by the attempt to link the written Gospels to the apostles. The concern to repel heretical movements emerged as a subsequent factor and one that served largely to refine the criteria for inclusion, the major one remaining the postulated tie to the beginnings of the Christian tradition.

The Gospel of Mark, in Gospels scholarship a preferred site for examining the problem of orality and writing, is the subject of essays by Vernon Robbins and Whitney Shiner. Robbins has long argued that orality and writing in the ancient world need to be assessed in terms of their interaction in what was a "rhetorical culture." Here he compares how the three Synoptic Gospels respectively represent the appropriation of "the writings," that is, scriptures, in Jesus' reported speech. Mark's virtually seamless voicing of scriptural quotation within the recitational flow of the narrator's or Jesus' speech most closely approximates to the dynamics of oral performance, while Matthew and Luke's tendency to bring the scriptures into Jesus' speeches as formally marked and distinct quotations is more self-consciously literary, a separation of the written from the oral.

In the ancient world, memory was central both to composition and oral delivery of written texts. Authors brought together and organized their materials initially in memory. Likewise, written texts were largely performed from memory, and accordingly written compositions were organized to cue their memorial reproduction. Taking note of these realities, Whitney Shiner develops an account of Mark as a product of memorative compositional techniques. Shiner breaks new ground here. While Jocelyn Penny Small and others have established that ancient composition largely proceeded in this manner, Shiner works out in detail how this might plausibly have occurred in a particular case, namely, the Gospel of Mark.

The volume concludes with an essay by Richard Horsley that is notable for its integration of memory approaches with Foley's discussion of oral-traditional referentiality—oral-traditional performances as enactments of an encompassing cultural repertoire. Horsley argues that the depiction of Jesus in the Gospel tradition and in particular the Gospel of Mark is embedded in Israelite cultural memory, in particular popular memory of epic figures such as Moses and Elijah, who led resistance to oppressive rulers. In its framing of the present in terms of the salient past, that is, in its constitutive alignment of Jesus and his activities with archetypal persons and narratives of Israel's epic past, the Gospel tradition is in fact itself the product of social and cultural memory dynamics. As such it delivers historical insight into the origins of the Jesus movement, namely, that the Jesus movement itself originated in local contexts in which popular memory of the salient past provided the cognitive frameworks for understanding contemporary conditions and the scripts for mobilizing resistance and renewal movements.

This volume attests to the vitality of the scholarly tradition inaugurated by Werner Kelber and in particular to its capacity to connect with important developments elsewhere in the social sciences and humanities. This augurs well for the continuing expansion of its influence in Gospels scholarship.

Picturing Christian Witness: New Testament Images of Disciples in Mission, by
Stanley H. Skreslet. Grand Rapids: Eerdmans, 2006. Pp. xv + 263. Paper. $24.00.
ISBN 0802829562.

Dirk G. van der Merwe, University of South Africa, Pretoria, South Africa

Stanley Skreslet has contributed a superb piece of work to the discipline of
missiology. This fine book, *Picturing Christian Witness,* is a feast that stimulates a
Christian's imagination, faith, and care for others. Skreslet states explicitly, right
at the beginning, that his approach in this book is grounded in his own experience as an interpreter of mission (ix). When reading this book, the reader gets
the impression that Skreslet himself wants to sit next to you and say, "Come let us
read together and allow me to explain and show you...," just like what Phillip did
in Acts with the Ethiopian (Acts 8:26–35).

Skreslet's approach in this book is fresh and unique, with sound exegeses of
the New Testament text that approach mission as Christian witness from different
perspectives that complement one another. The author's intention with this book
was to discover a fresh way, from the perspective of the New Testament, to inform
contemporary thinking about mission theology by stimulating the renewal of
mission imagery. In both the academy and his ministry he consistently found that
image-language often permeated and shaped what we think about evangelization
and witness.

He justified this approach by the current crisis felt in the field of missiology.
It was in ecumenical circles that hard questions have been raised about past missionary attitudes toward non-Western cultures and religions. As a result, many of
the images used by previous generations to portray Christian missionary action
seem, according to him, inadequate today. Skreslet points out how attempts have
been made to renew missionary imagery. He briefly reviews several of these
studies and points out how a certain kind of methodology has taken hold. This
methodology tended to proceed in a negative manner by recommending images
and metaphors that correct or compensate for particular errors felt in current
mission theology and practice. Therefore, his purpose in this book was to do
something quite different.

His initial point of departure is the missionary roles assumed by the apostolic-
era disciples of Jesus. His focal enquiry comes from the New Testament, for it is,
according to him, the most complete and sometimes the only source for much of
what is known about the activities of Jesus' first disciples. He substantiates this
with a reference to Mark 1:17, where Jesus handed to his disciples a symbolic
task for the future: "I will make you fish for people" (NRSV). The reason why he
decided to focus on Jesus' disciples in the New Testament rather than on Jesus
himself or the church as a corporate body is that it holds several advantages. For
instance, it offers many examples of ordinary people from a variety of ethnic and
cultural backgrounds who were involved in mission. They are described as participating in different kinds of communities and social circumstances. While some
of these people had been specifically called, and to a certain extent trained, to

continue Jesus' mission, many others appear to have been more spontaneously moved to share their faith.

For Skreslet, five different patterns of Christian witness emerged out of his exegetical analyses. These different patterns, which complement one another, are constituted from the different genres in the New Testament. In each case a distinctive kind of action performed by a follower or followers of Jesus defined the image under discussion in that particular pattern.

In the first pattern mission is looked at as an act of announcing good news. In this approach the verbal aspect of Christian outreach predominates. Announcers of good news are proclaimers of a message they consider to be of paramount importance. For Skreslet, the ones most often shown exercising this ministry in the New Testament are the highest-profile members of the emerging Christian community. They were widely acknowledged within the early church to be its most influential leaders.

The second kind of missionary action takes place when Christ is shared with family members and friends. This image pays special attention to more common forms of interpersonal communication. Christian witness here rather takes the form of conversation within families and visits to neighbors. To share Christ with close relatives does not mean primarily to transmit information to others about Christ or the Christian religion. Instead, it involves introducing his presence where he is not yet known, sometimes by word but just as often by deeds.

The third *pat*tern concerns how time and again in the New Testament the good news is shown crossing substantial boundaries of social difference. What is evident here is the universal character of Christian witness. This image of mission pictures the scenario in which the spiritual aspirations of others receive courteous respect and in which invitations to explain the basis of Christian faith are extended to would-be interpreters of the gospel. The interpreter is a facilitating figure who enables communication to take place across the dividing lines of cultural blinkeredness. Once contact has been made and the gospel becomes intelligible to these hearers, the need for cross-cultural interpretation diminishes. Eventually the interpreter is made redundant and then may disappear altogether.

Shepherding is the fourth pattern. In contrast to the three previous approaches, missionary shepherds seek out lost and disoriented sheep. Their attention is not focused on that part of the flock already safely established but on other folds as yet cut off from the experience of Christian community. Missionary shepherding requires one to stretch the traditional limits of pastoral care.

The last pattern concerns the cooperative nature of Christian mission. This pattern emerges clearly in the concepts of planting and building. Both define metaphorically the heart of what Paul understood to be his own missionary identity. He concentrated his efforts on the substructures of evangelism, where critical supports for the future must be laid. Throughout his ministry Paul was committed to a methodology of mission that emphasized the building-up of the Christian community. The first step for him was to act in a positive fashion by laying solid foundations and planting carefully.

In his attempt to discuss mission in the New Testament, Skreslet also effectively portrays what he discovered exegetically. He incorporates illustrations into each of his discussions on the various patterns of mission. As representations of ideas and metaphors, these pictures are meant to exhibit and make more transparent what he considers to be the most crucial theological issues raised by this series of New Testament mission images.

The illustrations included in this study have been drawn from a variety of cultural contexts and, in time, range from the pre-Constantinian period of the church right up to the late twentieth century. Throughout history and across an expanding cluster of cultural matrices, Christians have been persistent in their efforts to reinterpret and reappropriate the New Testament story of mission for themselves. Apart from the few secular scenes displayed, the illustrations show how a global sample of these interpreters of mission within the church has attempted to portray that story visually in terms that made sense in their own times and places.

Skreslet's study of mission images also considers the manner in which a given image is likely to impact viewers and readers. Some of the images appeal especially to human emotions. The most poignant of these are the ones that move or strongly motivate and so engender a deeper commitment to missionary action. Other images stimulate more rational forms of cognition. This conveys new and compelling insights about the basis, forms, or purposes of Christian mission. As these different stories are allowed to interpret each other, the image at stake begins to acquire new textures and potential meaning. Another stratum of signification is made possible when more than one mission image is considered at a time. A situation of interplay develops among the images, similar to the functioning of single images as narrative intersections, but on a larger scale. In such a case, new aspects of meaning may be produced that lie beyond the capacity of anyone image to capture or convey.

In my opinion, the most important contribution of *Picturing Christian Witness* is that Skreslet has put forward an argument in support of an expansive definition of Christian mission, one that cannot be reduced to a single idea or task. The contours of the big picture that emerge here, when a group of images is viewed as a whole, defines mission fundamentally in terms of several actions: announcing good news, sharing Christ with friends, interpreting, shepherding, and planting/building. The fact that these are multiple actions, not one, that are described serially rather than hierarchically means that no single approach has been allowed to monopolize the discussion of Christian missionary vocation.

The only point of critique is that Skreslet overwhelmingly emphasizes witness and very rarely introduces service. This is, for instance, apparent from the table of contents: "*Announcing* the Good News"; "*Sharing* Christ with Friends"; "*Interpreting* the Gospel" (cf. also "*Shepherding*" and "*Building* and *Planting*"). Also, his definition of mission on page 27 proves this verdict: "acting in the name of Jesus Christ with the intention of communicating or demonstrating to others something substantive about the Good News that defines the believing fellowship of the church. At the center of this Good News is a *message* about what God has done for all humanity through the life, death, and resurrection of Jesus Christ and a *commitment to live* in ways that publicly affirm the transforming power of God's love."

This book is well written, logically organized, and copiously illustrated. It is systematic in its presentation and guides the reader continuously in expectation. It is a book that can be used widely in didactic environments such as Bible schools teaching on mission and theological seminaries. The freshness of this new approach to missiology will stimulate readers to rethink the epistemology of mission and to re-engage in the "great commission" of Jesus Christ. Skreslet certainly succeeded through the multiple images and metaphors used in the book to merge biblical theology, missiology, spirituality, and discipleship.

Hearing the Old Testament in the New Testament, edited by Stanley Porter. McMaster New Testament Studies. Grand Rapids: Eerdmans, 2006. Pp. xiii + 316. Paper. $29.00. ISBN 0802828469.

Gert J. Steyn, University of Pretoria, Pretoria, South Africa

The field of study that occupies itself with researching the occurrence, use, and interpretation of "the Old Testament" in "the New Testament" continues to share the center stage of biblical scholarship. Developments and discoveries regarding the text of the Old Testament and the rhetoric employed by ancient authors, as well as better insight into the intercultural interface of the first century C.E., assist in a better understanding of early Christian hermeneutics. Stanley Porter's collection of essays *Hearing the Old Testament in the New Testament* certainly is a welcome compendium of the latest viewpoints in this regard and makes an invaluable contribution on several aspects in this complex field, although "The final word is far from having been said on such an important topic" (vii).

The book consists of twelve essays that are neatly wrapped by the first essay, an introduction written by the editor himself, and the last essay, a response written by Andreas J. Köstenberger. The list of contributing authors reads almost like a "Who's Who" of North American scholars in this field and includes prominent and well-known names, not least that of Porter himself. The volume is the eighth in the McMaster New Testament Studies series and a publication of the papers that were read during the 2003 H. H. Bingham Colloquium in New Testament at McMaster Divinity College in Hamilton, Ontario, Canada.

The opening essay, "Introduction: The Use of the Old Testament in the New Testament," by Stanley Porter, presents a useful overview and summary of the essays. It provides the reader with the thread that holds the essays together. Apart from the methodological issues, the contributions deal with the corpus of New Testament literature, roughly in its canonical sequence. This in itself makes this collection a handy introductory textbook to all those interested in the field.

The second essay, by Dennis L. Stamps, focuses on "The Use of the Old

Testament in the New Testament as a Rhetorical Device: A Methodological Proposal." It is an important, clear, and well-structured contribution that certainly should form the basis for students and scholars who embark on this field. Stamps draws attention to terminological issues, hermeneutics, and theological questions in the first part of his essay. An extremely important aspect that he quite rightly points out when discussing the issue of a still-open canon is the question about "what textual tradition the NT writers used when citing their sacred Scriptures" (12)—a point that is also later highlighted by McLay in the next essay. It has become more and more critical, in my opinion, that scholars establish the possible *Vorlage* of citations first before all sorts of assumptions are made about the author's adaptation and interpretation of such a citation in its newly applied context. It is appropriate that Stamps's point of entry into the methodology highlights this aspect as well. Furthermore, the confusion about what exactly is meant by "citation" is discussed. The author again highlights another important aspect, namely, that there should also be space to discuss "the way OT themes, characters, stories, and the like are utilized without any direct citation or verbal allusions" (13). "What one means by Judaism" (14) is another key issue regarding the use of terminology. The conclusion is that "scholars would enhance the study of NT use of the OT by being more precise in defining their terms" (15). When it comes to the hermeneutics, "one needs to look at historical factors, literary dimensions, and interpretative issues" (16), which are spelled out in more detail. In dealing with the theological questions, Stamps again emphasizes the aspect of "the variety of OT texts the NT writers use" (22). However, looking at the terminology, hermeneutics, and theological issues is not enough, as they are linked and interwoven (23). In the second major part of his essay, Stamps highlights the use of the Old Testament as a rhetorical device and defines rhetoric for the purposes of this study "as the ways and means employed in a text to persuade and the effect(s) of those ways and means" (26). Using rhetoric in this intertextual field of studies "expands the appreciation of the nature of a quotation to include its persuasive effect" (35). In the third major part of his essay, Stamps concludes with the question about how people hear the Old Testament in the New Testament today.

The third essay, on "Biblical Texts and the Scriptures for the New Testament Church," is written by R. Timothy McLay, the same author of the excellent introductory work on *The Use of the Septuagint in New Testament Research* (Grand Rapids, 2003). Building and expanding on what Stamps pointed out regarding the importance of establishing the version that the New Testament writers used, McLay uses the well-known example of Heb 1:6, which has received attention by a number of scholars during the last few years (Steyn, Karrer, etc.). McLay's main point is, quite rightly, "that there was a canon in the making" (41) and that there "are a wide variety of textual variants, ranging from single words or morphemes to whole sentences and paragraphs, when one compares the ancient texts for any book of Scripture" (44). This is aptly illustrated by in a meticulous exposition of the different versions of Heb 1:6 that were in circulation: "the OG, 4QDeutq, MT, and Odes 2:43/Heb 1:6 represent four separate and distinct ways that the biblical text was transmitted and that they all were regarded as Scripture" (55). But apart from the "pluriformity of the Scriptures that were available to the NT writers" (58), also "multiple literary editions and revisions" were reasons "why the text exhibited significant differences when read by first-century Christians" (55). This essay is a must for anyone wanting to become acquainted with the field of the use of the Old Testament in the New Testament in order to gain a grasp of what a number of Septuagint scholars in particular pointed out the last few decades, namely, a text theory of a multiplicity of texts.

The fourth essay, written by Michael P. Knowles, has the Gospel of Matthew in view and is entitled: "Scripture, History, Messiah: Scriptural Fulfillment and the Fullness of Time in Matthew's Gospel." The author's question boils down to: "How does Jesus himself employ Scripture in this Gospel, and how does his methodology compare to that which the narrative assigns to the evangelist?" (62). He opens his study by looking briefly at the citation formulae ("It is written" and "Have you not/never read?"), then pays attention to the nonformulaic references, as "it is possible to overemphasize the importance of explicit formula citations" (66). Some principles that govern the use of Scripture in Matthew's Gospel include messianic exegesis (*to* the Messiah, but also *by* the Messiah), that it is foundationally authoritative and univocal in its prophetic testimony (69). One major example discussed is Matt 5 (Isa 61 LXX), but the essay abides with comparative material, including examples and a discussion on messianic exegesis in Second temple Judaism. A useful table consisting of the Matthean passages with their cited texts and the themes is presented (76–77). Matthew's Gospel has a "seemingly seamless coordination of text and history" and represents the final outcome of a multidirectional hermeneutic (82). The gist of the essay can be stated as formulated by the editor: Knowles points out that Matthew "weaves together a variety of references from a range of sources to create a seamless theological and narrative fabric" (3).

The fifth essay, by Craig. A. Evans, is entitled "The Beginning of the Good News and the Fulfillment of Scripture in the Gospel of Mark." Evans points out that it can be deceiving to assume that Mark has little interest in the Old Testament and that the Gospel should be examined without comparisons to the other Gospels in this regard. After presenting an overview that lists "some twenty quotations or obvious allusions" and referring to all three major text types represented in Mark's quotations and allusions, Evans states that "Not only does the Markan evangelist make use of all parts of Scripture and all major text types; the evangelist also incorporates quotations of or allusions to Scripture at key points in his narrative" (85). Evans then focuses on Christology and prophecy in a Roman context and proposes that the newly installed emperor Vespasian was seen as the fulfillment of prophecy and the world's savior—a position that was challenged by Mark (93). It is Jesus, not Vespasian, who is the fulfillment of prophecy. The value of this essay is thus found, on the one hand, in picturing the historical setting of the Markan Gospel and, on the other hand, in proposing that the viewpoint of

Vespasian as the new "son of God" was challenged by Mark, who indicated that "the good news begins with Jesus Christ, the true Son of God" (103).

The sixth essay, by Stanley E. Porter, deals with Luke-Acts and is entitled "Scripture Justifies Mission: The Use of the Old Testament in Luke-Acts." It is a daunting task to discuss within the limitations of an essay the use of Scripture in Luke-Acts, not only because it comprises of almost a third of the entire New Testament but also because of Luke's use of Mark and his literary and artistic abilities to use broader motifs from his Scriptures when writing his story about Jesus and the early Christian origins. Porter should be congratulated for presenting an apt overview that carefully selects the main (programmatic) texts in both works (Luke 4 and Acts 2). After presenting a brief research survey, Porter deals with these passages. He scrutinizes the form and meaning of the Isa 61 quotation in Luke 4, asks whether Jesus uttered those words, and deals with the implications of Luke 4:18–19 as programmatic for Jesus' mission and the purpose of Luke's Gospel. Hereafter, the three quotations in Acts 2:14–36 are discussed. Their textual problems and theological significance receive attention, before the author discusses its implications as programmatic for the purpose of Acts. Porter's argument is that an exposition of these two key passages "outlines the major themes of the Gospel and Acts and provides a programmatic statement for determining the purpose of each work, as well as unifying them around these common themes" (4). This certainly undergirds the position of continuity between these two works.

The seventh essay moves on to the Gospel of John: "'They Saw His Glory and Spoke of Him': The Gospel of John and the Old Testament," by Paul Miller. The author's train of thought is that "Christological function determines form" and that "John's use of Scripture was guided by his Christology" (128). It is thus Miller's intention to indicate "that Christ was John's primary hermeneutical principle in whose light the Scriptures of Israel were to be properly construed" (128). Miller focuses on John's hermeneutics, "seeing" in the Fourth Gospel vision and witness—pointing to four representative witnesses, with Moses as the most prominent Old Testament figure in the Gospel—after which he discusses the uniqueness of John's use of the Old Testament witnesses. He asks whether Scripture is a "sign" and proceeds to the issue of John and the Old Testament today.

The eighth essay, by James W. Aageson, concentrates on the four major Pauline Letters: "Written Also for Our Sake: Paul's Use of Scripture in the Four Major Epistles, with a Study of 1 Corinthians 10." The author points to the five major areas of investigation in scholarship on the use of Scripture in the four major Pauline epistles: textual traditions, comparison with that of other Jewish interpreters, Christian *testimonia,* and the relation to larger Old Testament contexts and intertextuality. His intention is to focus on the latter two. After discussing intertextuality and innerbiblical exegesis, he addresses echoes and allusions, then finally uses 1 Cor 10 as an example. Aageson's conclusion is that Paul's use of Scripture was a dynamic work in progress. "He was an interpreter who rethought the Jewish Scriptures and their meaning in the new theological world of an increasingly Gentile church" (180).

The ninth essay also focuses on the Pauline literature. Sylvia C. Keesmaat entitled her contribution "In the Face of the Empire: Paul's Use of Scripture in the Shorter Epistles" and deals with Ephesians, Philippians, Colossians, 1 and 2 Thessalonians, and Philemon. All of these, she assumes, were written by Paul, though she does not supply any reasons for her assumption. These "shorter epistles" are viewed against the backdrop of the Roman Empire. She uses a narrative approach and ends with "Reading Our Story."

The tenth essay, entitled "Job as Exemplar in the Epistle of James," was written by Kurt Anders Richardson. The author's approach is "(i) to review the kind of sapiential prophet Job's book portrays him to be, (ii) to analyze his role in James, and (iii) to offer some conclusions that present the complementarity of Job's prophetic wisdom with the wisdom of Job extolled throughout James" (214). This essay provides an interesting perspective on hearing the Old Testament in the New. By looking through the window of Jas 5:10–11, Job's role in James "is that of an exemplar (ὑπόδειγμα), one to imitate, to emulate" (219).

The eleventh essay, by Andreas J. Köstenberger, puts the spotlight on the remaining New Testament literature, which includes Hebrews and Revelation, probably the most difficult books of the New Testament in this kind of intertextual study. His contribution is entitled "The Use of Scripture in the Pastoral and General Epistles and the Book of Revelation." He defends the Pauline authorship of the Pastorals and points to the fact that "Overall, references to the OT are comparatively infrequent" (231). After discussing the clusters of references in 1 and 2 Timothy (there are no Old Testament references in Titus), Köstenberger turns to a discussion of the General Epistles. Among these, the author quite rightly points out that "It is clearly impossible in the space allotted to provide a full treatment of the use of the OT in the book of Hebrews" (239). The fact that Hebrews (and the same is true for Revelation) does not receive any dedicated attention is probably the main weakness of this collection of essays. Given the fact that Hebrews contains the longest and the most quotations from all the New Testament books, it leaves a visible gap—but one that is at least recognized. Regarding Jude, Köstenberger notes that "Jude's midrashic method evinces a certain affinity with the *pesher* exegesis practiced at Qumran" (243). This observation certainly highlights the work of scholars such as E. Earle Ellis in the past and should make modern-day scholars aware that there is still much to be done when it comes to comparative studies on Jewish exegetical methods between the Dead Sea Scrolls and that of the New Testament writers. Köstenberger then discusses 1 Peter and compares 2 Pet 2:1–3:3 with Jude 4–19. "The solitary reference in the Johannine epistles is the reference to Cain" (249). When it comes to the discussion of Revelation and its close to four hundred Old Testament references, the situation is similar to that of Hebrews. Köstenberger concludes that the reader becomes aware of "a remarkable variety in which the NT writers used Israel's Scriptures" and "reflects the variety of scriptural uses in the larger Jewish world" The situation regarding the use of the Old Testament in these particular New Testament books and, may I add, *all* the New Testament writings discussed in this collection, can be summarized by the following statement by Köstenberger: "It appears that the use of the OT by a given NT writer depended upon a variety of factors, which included the type of polemic in which he wished to engage, his own command of Scripture and the scriptural literacy prevalent among his audience, his genre of writing, and other factors" (252).

Andreas J. Köstenberger also wrote the last essay: "Hearing the Old Testament in the New: A Response." It serves as a conclusion to the collection of papers, as a critical response to each of these contributions, and as an indication of where further research is needed. One might not always agree with the positions taken, but they are formulated in a reflective, honest, and critical manner. The author is certainly right that these papers "make an important contribution to the ongoing discussion of the complex and multifaceted issues surrounding the NT use of the OT" (293).

Apart from the invaluable information regarding secondary sources in the footnotes, also indices of modern authors and ancient sources are attached, which greatly enhance the usability of the book. *Hearing the Old Testament in the New Testament* is highly recommended for students, pastors, and scholars. Those working in the field will no doubt use this work for many years to come.

Hearing the Old Testament in the New Testament, edited by Stanley E. Porter. McMaster New Testament Studies. Grand Rapids: Eerdmans, 2006. Pp. xiii + 316. Paper. $29.00. ISBN 0802828469.

Michael Labahn, K.U. Leuven, Leuven, Belgium

Der Herausgeber Stanley E. Porter, bekannt durch seine editorische Tätigkeit wie durch seine Publikationen zur Fragestellung, versammelt in „Hearing the Old Testament in the New Testament" die Vorträge des 9. H.H. Bingham Colloquium in New Testament von 2003. Das Kolloquium wendet sich an Studierende und an Laien, so dass auch der Sammelband wissenschaftlich abgesichert ein breites Publikum im Blick hat.

Auf die Einleitung des Herausgebers folgt der Beitrag „The Use of the Old Testament in the New Testament as Rhetorical Device: A Methodological Proposal" (9–37) von *D. L. Stamps*. Stamps fordert zu Recht größere definitorische Klarheit und methodische Präzision. Sein eigener Ansatz erweitert die Diskussion um die Schriftrezeption um eine hermeneutische Variante aus der oralen Kultur: der rhetorischen Fragestellung. Er liest damit die neutestamentliche Schriftrezeption vor ihrem hellenistischen Hintergrund, in dem die Verwendung autoritativer Texte zur Klärung und Unterstützung eigener Argumentation in der Rhetorik, definiert als „the ways and means employed in a text to persuade and the effect(s) of those ways and means" (26), eine beachtenswerte Rolle spielt. Diese persuasorische Funktion gehört nach Stamps in die Auseinandersetzung des frühen Christentums mit seiner antiken Mitwelt hinein, wo sie der Stabilisierung der eigenen Identität dient. Stamps betrachtet seine Studie als Impuls für weitere Forschungen und Konkretisierungen, die sich vor dem Hintergrund dieses Beitrages als vielversprechend erweisen können.

Dem noch Klärungen suchenden Problem, was für die frühchristliche Literatur „Schrift" und „Kanon" ist, widmet sich *R. T. McLay* in „Biblical Texts and the Scriptures for the New Testament Church" (38–58). „Kanon" und „Schrift" sind zu unterscheiden, wobei weder für die zeitgenössischen jüdischen noch die neutestamentlichen Schriften fest umrissen ist, welche Schriften zur „Schrift" gerechnet werden. So ist auch der Terminus „biblical text" undeutlich, da auch eine Anzahl unterschiedlicher Texte dieser Schriften in unterschiedlicher Sprache in Nutzung waren—als Beispieltext wird die Schriftrezeption von Hebr 1,6 vorgeführt, die belegt, wie unterschiedlich angenommene Prätexte überliefert werden. Man wird m.E. gegenüber weitreichender Kenntnis hebräischer oder gar aramäischer Texte in den frühchristlichen Abfassungs- oder Adressatengemeinden skeptisch sein müssen ebenso wie gegenüber zu weitgehender Infragestellung des zeitgenössischen Grundkonsenses darüber, was zu „Kanon" und „Schrift" gerechnet wird. Hinter die Einsicht gewisser Offenheit und Vielfalt ist allerdings nicht zurückzuschreiten.

Der matthäischen Schriftrezeption (vgl. den wichtigen Band von M. J. J. Menken, Matthew's Bible, BETL 173, 2004) widmet sich *M. P. Knowles* in „Scripture, History, Messiah: Scriptual Fulfillment and the Fullness of Time in Matthew's Gospel" (59–82). Der Verfasser stellt die vorherrschende Konzentration auf die Erfüllungszitate zur Erhebung der matthäischen Intertextualität in Frage. Sein Argument, dass in den durch „es steht geschrieben..." eingeleiteten Texten Jesus selbst zu Wort komme, ist m.E. sachlich am kreativen Umgang Jesu mit der Schrift (vgl. Lk/Q 7,22–23; Labahn, The Significance of Signs in Luke 7:22–23 in the Light of Isaiah 61 and the Messianic Apocalypse, in: Evans [Hg.], From Prophecy to Testament, 2004, 146–68) gemessen strittig und im Rahmen textzentrierter Exegese methodisch problematisch. Dies erkennt auch Knowles, wenn er sich den nicht-formalen Referenzen stellt, bei denen das historische Urteil nachvollziehbarer ist. Im Rahmen seiner Argumentation wäre jedoch die Fokussierung auf Jesus als narrativer Autorität im Text aussichtsreicher, die interessante These zu illustrieren, dass die Variationen im matthäischen Schriftgebrauch „demonstrate the correlation of Scripture as a whole with the revelatory reality that the Messiah represents. ... both Scriptures and Messiah are viewed as hermeneutically entire and complete, both in themselves and in relation to the other" (80).

Herausfordernd und anregend ist die These von *C. A. Evans* in „The Beginning of the Good News and The fulfillment of Scripture in the Gospel of Mark" (83–103), dass das markinische Portrait von Jesus als Gottessohn auf Gerüchte im Römischen Reich reagiere, Vespasian erfülle jüdische Prophezeiungen als neuer Sohn Gottes. Dass wenigstens *rezeptionsorientiert* die markinische Sohn-Gottes-Christologie im Horizont der Propaganda römischer Kaiser gelesen werden kann, wird durch diesen Beitrag mit weiteren Beobachtungen untermauert, wenngleich mit Blick auf den Verfasser des Markusevangeliums die Feststellung einer direkten Relation Rückfragen aufwirft.

Der Essay „Scripture Justifies Mission: The Use of the Old Testament in Luke-Acts" (104–26) von S. E. *Porter* widmet sich den Zitaten in Lk 4,18–19 (Jes 61,1–2) und in Apg 2,14–36 (Joel 2,28–32; Ps 16,8–11; 110,1), deren Bedeutung innerhalb der *plots* jeweils signifikant markiert ist. Seine Analyse zeigt in bedenkenswerter Weise die programmatische Bedeutung der Zitate für die Entwicklung der Grundthemen in den jeweiligen Schriften, aber auch, dass beide AT-Referenzen eine Kohäsion von beiden lukanischen Werken entwickeln: „these two sets of themes from Luke and Acts can be brought together to show a continuity between Luke and Acts around their common theology" (125).

Dem komplexen Schriftgebrauch des vierten Evangeliums widmet sich *P. Miller* „‚They Saw His Glory and Spoke of Him': The Gospel of John and the Old Testament" (127–51). Die christologische Frage nach Jesus beschäftigte das frühe Christentum in einem komplexen Interpretationsprozess, der nicht zuletzt durch Auslegung der Schriften betrieben wurde. In diesem Kontext betont Miller mit Recht die christologische Konzentration der johanneischen Schriftauslegung, die den alttestamentlichen Verfassern eine Kenntnis des göttlichen Logos zutraut: „*Scripture is the enduring record of those who saw the activity of the divine Logos prior to its appearance in Jesus and then testified to what they had seen*" (134)—ein m.E. wichtiges Motiv johanneischer Schriftrezeption (vgl. Labahn, Jesus und die Autorität der Schrift im Johannesevangelium, in: Labahn, Scholtissek, Strotmann [Hgg.], Israel und seine Heilstraditionen im Johannesevangelium. FG Beutler SJ, 2004, 185–206).

In „Written Also for Our Sake: Paul's Use of Scripture in the Four Major Epistles, with a Study of 1 Corinthians 10" (152–81) stellt *J. W. Aageson* zunächst die Fragestellungen der bisherigen Forschung vor; dem Problem des alttestamentlichen Kontexts der paulinischen Argumentation und Schriftauslegung als Intertextualität und innerbiblischen Exegese wird in Konzentration auf 1Kor 10,1–33 nachgegangen. Ergebnis ist, dass Paulus nicht nur ein dynamischer Denker, sondern sein Schriftverständnis dynamisch qualifiziert ist, da Paulus Schrift als „inspiration for life and a basis for interpretation and religious argumentation, as well as an expression of the will of God" begreift (155); in solcher Dynamik ist paulinische Schriftauslegung nicht nur christologisch, sondern auch ekklesiologisch orientiert.

Sylvia C. Keesmaat widmet sich im Beitrag „In the Face of the Empire: Paul's Use of Scripture in the Shorter Epistles" (182–212) den kürzeren Briefen, die Paulus zugeschrieben werden, mit der Globalthese, dass sich in ihnen die paulinische Schriftrezeption mit dem römischen Imperium auseinandersetzt; mehrheitlich werden Anspielungen besprochen, die, wie die Adam-Rezeption, Rückfragen provozieren. Die Anwendung narrativer Methodik verspricht interessante Ergebnisse, erfordert aber methodische Reflexion in Bezug auf den Gegenstand. Die Grenze der Überzeugungskraft des Essays liegt auch darin, ob man alle genannten Briefe Paulus zuschreiben kann. Kritisch ist dies zu vermerken, da es sich nicht nur um die Diskussion von Einleitungsfragen handelt, sondern da neben der im Beitrag vorrausgesetzten Einheitlichkeit des Verfassers auch die der Adressatensituation und der Themen problematisch ist.

Einen beachtenswerten Weg beschreitet *K .A. Richardson*, wenn er in „Job as Exemplar in the Epistle of James" (213–29) die Aufnahme Hiobs und der Hiob-tradition in Jak 5,10–11 als Beispiel für frühchristliche Schriftrezeption analysiert. Die Figur des Hiob fügt sich in die Pragmatik des Jakobusbriefes ein, da der den Propheten nahegestellte Hiob als Beispiel eines gerechten Reichen, aber auch als Beispiel von Ausdauer und Geduld in Versuchung fungiert.

Mit dem Ziel inhaltlicher Geschlossenheit fügt sich der Beitrag von *A. J. Köstenberger* „The Use of Scripture in the Pastoral and General Epistles and the Book of Revelation" (230–54) an. Diese notwendig summarischen Ausführun-gen können kaum der für das Verstehen insbesondere des Hebräerbriefs oder der Apokalypse grundlegenden Schriftrezeption in ihrem Facettenreichtum gerecht werden, geben dem Lesern aber eine hilfreiche Orientierung, auch wenn man wiederum fragen muss, ob die Pastoralbriefe unterschiedlos dem paulinischen Schriftgebrauch zuzuordnen sind.

Den Abschluss bildet *A. J. Köstenberger* „Hearing the Old Testament in the New: A Response" (255–94), der detaillierte Rückfragen an die Beiträge stellt und so die Adressaten dieser Sammlung zum Weiterdenken anregt—eine mutige Entscheidung, die damit ernst macht, dass Interpretation ein dynamischer Vor-gang ist, der sich in Diskussion und Gespräch zu bewähren hat. Insofern sind die weiterführenden Fragen nicht nur hilfreiche Impulse, sondern auch ihrerseits kritischen Rückfragen auszusetzen; um nur zwei Punkte zu nennen: die autoren-zentrierte Perspektive von K. wird m.E. schon durch die Adressatenorientierung neutestamentlicher Schriften selbst um die Rezipientenorientierung erweitert. Überschneidungen und/oder Anknüpfung an Sprache und Motive der hellenis-tischen Umwelt fordern, die literarischen und religiösen Sinnbildungen dieser Mitwelt ernst zu nehmen, zumal zeitgenössische „Jewish conventions" unter hel-lenistischem Einfluss stehen.

Das Spiel neutestamentlicher Autoren und Schriften mit alttestamentlichen Prätexten erfreut sich seit Jahren eines beachtlichen Interesses. So stellt sich jeweils die Frage, welchen Fortschritt neue Publikationen zum Thema bringen. Der Titel lässt erwarten, dass die antike Medienwelt zwischen Mündlichkeit und Schriftlichkeit in ihrer Bedeutung für das spezifische Feld intertextueller Studien fruchtbar gemacht wird: *Hearing* the Old Testament. Solche Erwartung wird im Beitrag von *Stamps* erfüllt, der sich mit der rhetorischen Funktion der Rezeptio-nen beschäftigt. Für andere Beiträge ist das „Hören" eine Metapher für die jeweils spezifische Form der analysierten Rezeption, deren Dynamik dieser Sammelband auch gerade dort, wo er kritische Rückfragen provoziert, erweist. Darin bieten die unterschiedlichen Beiträge in der Regel neue Perspektiven und/ oder ver-tiefen bekannte Fragestellungen. Durch die Fokussierung auf Studierende und Laien kann man auch fragen, ob die Literatur- und Methodendiskussion nicht zu sehr auf die Englisch-sprachige Literatur begrenzt ist, aber dies ändert nichts an der Empfehlung des Bandes zur Lektüre und Auseinandersetzung um die neutestamentliche Schriftrezeption, die Impulse von ihm erhält. Der durch ein einfangreiches Stellenregister benutzerfreundlich erschlossene Sammelband wird sich seinen Platz in der wissenschaftlichen Diskussion um die Rezeption alttestamentlicher Schriften im Neuen Testament erobern und die Forschung trotz genannter Bedenken befruchten.

An Introduction to the New Testament, by D. A. Carson and Douglas J. Moo. 2nd edition. Grand Rapids: Zondervan, 2005. Pp. 781. Hardcover. $39.99. ISBN 0310238595.

John Paul Heil, Catholic University of America, Washington, District of Columbia

This volume claims to be a "special introduction" to the writings of the New Testament. It is a "special" introduction in the sense that its primary focus is on such traditional historical issues as authorship, date, sources, purpose, destination, and so forth. It is thus not as concerned as other New Testament introductions with issues more directly related to exegesis, such as literary form, rhetorical criticism, and historical parallels. It does, however, contain a brief summary of the content of each New Testament document, a brief account of current studies on it, and its theological contribution to the canon.

First- and second-year students of seminaries and theological colleges are the intended readers for this introduction. An effort has been made to limit its length in order to enhance its value as a textbook for classroom use. Nevertheless, the book is quite substantial, containing 781 pages. The detail of its discussions and nature as a "special introduction" would seem to render it more suitable for graduate rather than undergraduate students.

The book is an updated revision of an earlier version published in 1992 by Carson, Moo, and Leon Morris. Carson and Moo divided the chapters originally written by Morris between them for this new edition, as well as revised and updated their own work. In this new volume the chapter on Paul contains an analysis of the current debate on the "new perspective." A new preliminary chapter provides a brief history explaining how Christians moved from the reading of the first hand-written documents of the New Testament to contemporary study of the New Testament. The treatment of "pseudonymity" has been removed from the chapter on the Pastoral Epistles, expanded, and placed within a new, separate chapter on New Testament letters. More substantial summaries of the content of each New Testament document have been added to this new version, along with brief discussions of more recent literary and social-science methods.

There are a total of twenty-six chapters. An introductory chapter entitled "Thinking about the Study of the New Testament" is followed by a chapter on the Synoptic Gospels. In the next twenty-three chapters each New Testament document is discussed in its canonical order. In addition to the new chapter on New Testament letters, there is a separate chapter entitled "Paul: Apostle and Theologian." The final chapter is devoted to the canon of the New Testament. Each of the chapters dealing with the New Testament writings contain sections on content, author, provenance, date, destination, purpose, text, adoption into the canon, the writing in recent studies, and the contribution of the writing.

Although both authors admit to being evangelical, they have tried to remain as unbiased and objective as possible. They present a sampling of the various viewpoints in the current literature, sometimes trying to suggest a fresh way of looking at an issue. But they tend to argue, often in new ways and with new evidence, for more traditional stances on issues of authorship and date. They generally date the New Testament writings as early as possible. Further, with good reasoning they totally reject pseudonymity as a solution to questions of authorship in the New Testament.

Indeed, in this reviewer's opinion, the section on pseudonymity and pseudepigraphy (337–50) is one of the more enlightening and convincing discussions in the book. They perceptively point out that, although there certainly were pseudonymous writings circulating at the time of the New Testament, none were letters. The authors thus maintain that the historical Paul, in one way or another, that is, with perhaps varying degrees of collaboration with others, is the "author" of all of the letters attributed to him. Similarly, Peter is the author of both letters attributed to him, despite their quite different characters. James, the brother of Jesus and leader of the Jerusalem community, is the author of the letter attributed to him, and so forth.

With regard to the view of some scholars that the original audiences of the New Testament writings would have known which ones were pseudonymous and fully understood this, so that they were not in any way deceived, the authors conclude: "In short, the search for parallels to justify the view that the intended readers of some New Testament documents would have understood them to be pseudonymous, so that no deception took place, has proved a failure. The hard evidence demands that we conclude either that some New Testament documents are pseudonymous and that the real authors intended to deceive their readers, or that the real authors intended to speak the truth and that pseudonymity is not attested in the New Testament" (350). This conclusion about no pseudonymity in the New Testament is supported by other recent discussions that were not yet available to the authors. For example, Terry L. Wilder writes: "Though the case against the traditional authorship of some of the disputed Pauline letters is sometimes strong, several scholars today believe that no pseudonymous works exist in the New Testament. Scholars hold this view with good reason because (a) the greatest weakness of pseudepigraphic theories is the number of assumptions upon which they rest, and (b) they have been encouraged by recent studies which focus on Paul's use of a secretary, a co-author, and tradition when writing his letters. A resort to pseudonymity is not necessary" (*Pseudonymity, the New Testament and Deception: An Inquiry into Intention and Reception* [Lanham, Md.: University Press of America, 2004], 265 n. 52). Likewise, Ben Witherington notes that, "although there may be pseudepigrapha within the New Testament, the burden of proof falls squarely on the shoulders of those who make that claim" (*Letters and Homilies for Hellenized Christians Volume 1: A Socio-rhetorical Commentary on Titus, 1–2 Timothy and 1–3 John* [Downers Grove, Ill.: InterVarsity Press, 2006], 38).

Another noteworthy feature of this new edition is the section on the "New Perspective" in understanding Paul's relation to Judaism (375–85). Central to this new viewpoint, initiated by E. P. Sanders in 1977 and furthered since by James D. G. Dunn and others, is the soteriological notion of "covenantal nomism." According to this notion, God has chosen Israel, and Jews at the time of Paul believed that that gracious choice was the basis for their salvation. They did not have to keep the law to be saved; they were already saved. They obeyed the law in order to maintain their covenantal status. After pointing out several problems with "covenantal nomism," the authors conclude with their own views that in Paul there is "a key antithesis between human doing and human believing as the means of accessing God's salvation" and "that, contrary to advocates of the new perspective, justification by faith was an important component of Paul's gospel from the beginning" (385).

This reviewer finds most of the argumentation for the more conservative and traditional views quite balanced, fair, and judicious. Indeed, their views seem to be in accord with an apparent trend in recent New Testament research that is at least open to if not supportive of many of these views on historical issues. There are a few points with which to quibble: the authors hold that Philemon, Colossians, and Ephesians were most likely written from a Roman imprisonment. However, it may be more likely that they were written and sent together from a Caesarean imprisonment, all three carried and delivered by Tychicus, as argued persuasively by Bo Reicke, E. Earle Ellis, and others. The view of this introduction that the apostle John authored both the Gospel of John and the book of Revelation may be the most questionable. To be sure, the authors make a valiant argument for at least a possibility of this, but the question remains: Although it may be possible, is it likely?

For the most part this introduction is very up-to-date on recent research. But since it was published in 2005, it was not able to take advantage of significant recent work on some important issues, such as that of the situation at Colossae (see Allan R. Bevere, *Sharing in the Inheritance: Identity and the Moral Life in Colossians* [JSNTSup 226; London: Sheffield Academic Press, 2003]; Michael Dübbers, *Christologie und Existenz im Kolosserbrief: Exegetische und semantische Untersuchungen zur Intention des Kolosserbriefes* [WUNT 2/191; Tübingen: Mohr Siebeck, 2005]; Ian K. Smith, *Heavenly Perspective: A Study of the Apostle Paul's Response to a Jewish Mystical Movement at Colossae* [LNTS 326; London: T&T Clark, 2006]).

This "special introduction" can be highly recommended. With its very careful, keenly nuanced, and extensively researched discussions, it may well be considered "special" in a way not originally intended by its authors. It deserves to be read not just by students but by all scholars of the New Testament. It will prove to be welcome support for those tending toward more traditional views on historical issues involving the writings of the New Testament. While it may not convince others, it may require them to reconsider, refine, and redefend their views.

NEW TESTAMENT AND CHRISTIAN ORIGINS

Le Mouvement de Jésus: Histoire sociale d'une révolution des valeurs, by Gerd Theissen. Translated by Joseph Hoffmann. Paris: Cerf, 2006. Pp. 364. Paper. €35.00. ISBN 2204080438.

Odette Mainville, Université de Montréal, Montréal, Québec, Canada

Dans cette monographie G. Theissen n'aborde pas un sujet nouveau mais reprend et enrichit l'étude intitulée *Soziologie der Jesusbewegung* (trad. française: *Le Christianisme de Jésus: Ses origines sociales en Palestine*), qu'il avait rédigée en 1977. Cette étude s'inscrivait alors dans les tout débuts de la recherche socio-historique sur le christianisme primitif. Le présent ouvrage en conserve la thèse de base et les grands axes de développement.

La thèse principale se déploie en quatre volets ainsi résumés: (1) dans les débuts du christianisme primitif, il y avait des charismatiques itinérants, préconisant une éthique radicale; (2) ces derniers faisaient partie d'un mouvement de renouveau, intérieur au judaïsme, suscité par Jésus; (3) leur apparition était en réponse à une crise émanant de la société judéo-palestinienne; (4) ils réagissaient à cette crise en proposant une vision d'amour et de réconciliation. Le mouvement de Jésus, que l'auteur limite à l'espace syro-palestinien, entre les années 30–70, s'enracinait encore plus profondément à l'intérieur du judaïsme que ne l'avaient fait les mouvements antérieurs simplement parce qu'il avait appris des expériences et des échecs de ces mouvements.

Dans la partie introductive, l'auteur annonce quatre types d'analyse pour une sociologie adéquate du mouvement de Jésus: analyse des rôles, qui examine les comportements typiques des personnes au sein du mouvement; analyse du groupe, qui se concentre sur la spécificité de l'ensemble du mouvement; analyse sociale, qui prend en compte le contexte social dans son ensemble; analyse des idées et des valeurs, qui s'intéresse aux concepts et aux intentions du mouvement dans leurs portées sociales. Du point de vue méthodologique, la démarche fonctionne à partir de trois procédures différentes: (1) les procédures constructives, qui cherchent à exploiter les données concernant les personnes (origine, biens, statut) et les groupes (programmes, formes d'organisation et comportements); (2) les procédures analytiques à partir de textes qui, indirectement, laissent transpirer des données sociologiques (par ex. les normes et les règles); (3) les procédures comparatives qui prennent en compte des mouvements analogues intraculturels ou interculturels. Les sources littéraires sur lesquelles s'appuient les analyses sont d'abord les évangiles synoptiques, les lettres authentiques de Paul, les Actes des

Apôtres, mais aussi des écrits du début du christianisme (la Didachè, l'Évangile de Thomas, Flavius Josèphe et Philon d'Alexandrie, etc.).

L'étude se divise en quatre chapitres correspondant respectivement au déploiement des quatre volets de la thèse évoqués ci-dessus. Le premier s'intitule «Un mouvement de marginaux et de charismatiques itinérants. Analyse des rôles du mouvement Jésus». «Charismatique» fait ici référence à «un don d'exercer une autorité sans s'appuyer sur des institutions et des rôles prédonnés» (37). Le chapitre répertorie trois types de rôles complémentaires. Le premier, dit charismatique 'primaire', est assumé par Jésus de Nazareth, porteur d'une espérance. Ce rôle se cristallise autour du titre de Fils de l'homme, le seul que Jésus se serait lui-même appliqué. Dans son propre langage, le titre n'aurait cependant fait référence qu'à sa condition d'homme. Il aurait acquis sa transcendance dans le mouvement de Jésus, qui en fait alors une sorte de passerelle entre l'homme de Nazareth et le Christ ressuscité. Le mouvement lui confère une charge christologique polyvalente qui permet de faire endosser diverses fonctions à Jésus: Messie, Fils de Dieu, Seigneur. «L'expression *Fils de l'Homme* unit les deux: énoncés d'exaltation et énoncés d'abaissement» (102). Le deuxième type de rôle concerne celui des charismatiques 'secondaires', composés de ceux qui prennent à leur compte, dans la continuité, l'enseignement de Jésus. Tout comme ce fut le cas du rôle de Jésus, le leur ne correspondait à aucune forme de vie institutionnalisée. Un troisième rôle, celui des charismatiques 'tertiaires', désignant ceux qui apportent leur soutien aux charismatiques secondaires. Ce rôle correspond, en fait, à la contribution des communautés locales de sympathisants sédentaires. Ces derniers, vivant en symbiose avec les charismatiques itinérants, sont à la fois le terreau fertile et le lieu de censure de leurs enseignements doctrinaux et éthiques.

Le deuxième chapitre, intitulé «Le mouvement de Jésus: un mouvement millénariste. Analyse de groupe du mouvement de Jésus», fait ressortir la spécificité du mouvement de Jésus par rapport aux autres mouvements juifs. Tandis que ces derniers s'opposaient de diverses manières à l'occupant romain, celui de Jésus préconisait un renouveau intérieur, visant la transformation de l'ensemble de la société, voire du monde entier; transformation désignée par la métaphore du «Règne de Dieu». Le mouvement est millénariste, non pas tant du fait qu'il annonce un règne de mille ans—cela viendra plus tard avec l'Apocalypse—, mais bien du fait que dans la foulée du changement fondamental qu'entraînera à l'établissement du Règne de Dieu, les souverains actuels perdront leur influence et leur pouvoir.

Le troisième chapitre, le plus imposant, intitulé «La crise de la société juive, terreau du mouvement Jésus. Analyse sociale du mouvement Jésus», porte l'attention sur la condition de crise prévalant dans la société judéo-palestinienne. Il fait ressortir comment la domination romaine et ses répercussions sur la configuration sociale, politique et économique de la Palestine engendrent une véritable crise d'identité au sein du peuple juif. Le facteur religieux, le véritable phare sur toute la vie du peuple, conduit alors à une double canalisation de la crise: par la radicalisation des normes et dans la projection eschatologique. En ce qui concerne la radicalisation des normes, trop exigeante, elle eut pour effet de créer des schismes à l'intérieur même du judaïsme, le reste élu lui-même ne parvenant à y satisfaire. Il devenait, de toute manière, quasi impossible d'identifier ce véritable reste; situation qui ouvrait à l'éventualité que tout homme puisse avoir part à Israël. «De même que la démarcation interculturelle conduisait de façon nécessaire au schisme intra-culturel, de même le processus schismatique préparait l'universalisation du judaïsme. Cette percée se produisit dans le mouvement de Jésus» (270).

Les tensions et les changements sociaux avaient donc engendré une situation révolutionnaire. Le mouvement de Jésus serait né de cette crise. Et comme l'exprime l'auteur, s'il faut distinguer, dans la sociologie des religions, entre les théories de l'intégration et les théories du conflit, c'est la théologie du conflit qui est la plus appropriée pour interpréter le mouvement de Jésus.

Le quatrième chapitre s'intitule «La vision sociale du mouvement de Jésus. Analyse des idées». Il fait bien voir que, même si le mouvement de Jésus s'inscrit dans le grand remous révolutionnaire marquant le monde judéo-palestinien, les moyens préconisés se démarquent nettement de ceux des autres mouvements. La société juive, elle, est prête à l'insurrection pour défendre ses valeurs fondamentales, plus particulièrement la vénération du Dieu unique dans le temple de Jérusalem, menacée par les velléités romaines d'imposer le culte de l'empereur; le mouvement de Jésus, lui, propose une révolution, non pas militaire mais des valeurs et des attitudes. Cette révolution se présente dans le cadre du 'mythe' de l'irruption du Règne de Dieu. Mythe qui prend deux formes dans le mouvement de Jésus: l'attente eschatologique qui anticipe dans le présent les événements déterminants de l'avenir; le récit christologique qui déplace le regard vers l'arrière, sur ce que Jésus a été et fait et interprète le présent à partir de la croix et de Pâques.

La lecture du développement des hypothèses, si fascinante soit-elle, occulte néanmoins une pratique de Theissen, laquelle utilise souvent sans discernement des données post-pascales, nivelant ainsi les distinctions qui devraient s'imposer entre l'histoire et la théologie. L'auteur défend cette pratique (24), la jugeant acceptable si elle s'en tient aux traditions cadrant au monde syro-palestinien de la première moitié du 1er siècle. Il s'explique: «Si nous présupposons l'authenticité d'une tradition, nous pouvons admettre que ses témoins ont modelé leur vie en accord avec la tradition. Si nous plaçons l'origine de la tradition dans le mouvement de Jésus postérieur à Pâques, nous pouvons présupposer que ses témoins ont modelé cette tradition en accord avec leur vie» (24).

Malgré ce bémol, l'ouvrage s'avère de très grande valeur. Il tire sa force de la mise à profit d'une érudition remarquable de l'auteur en ce qui a trait aux divers contextes, historique, social, culturel, économique et religieux, et du maniement habile des jeux interactifs entre ces contextes. Ses argumentations tissent une trame harmonieuse se déployant du début à la fin comme dans l'arrangement réussi des parties d'une grande mosaïque. Il s'agit donc d'une œuvre d'une réelle maturité, une incontournable pour la recherche socio-critique des débuts du christianisme, qui couronne trois décennies de recherche de G. Theissen.

Religious Rivalries in the Early Roman Empire and the Rise of Christianity, edited by Leif E. Vaage. Studies in Christianity and Judaism/Études sur le christianisme et judaïsm 18. Waterloo, Ont.: Wilfrid Laurier University Press, 2006. Pp. xvi + 324. Hardcover. $85.00. ISBN 0889204497.

Joseph Verheyden, University of Leuven, Leuven, Belgium

Under the overall title of "Religious Rivalries" this book brings together twelve essays that all deal with one or another aspect of the religious, and by extension the wider socioeconomic and political, context in which Christianity was shaped and first developed. The essays, some written already back in 1999, are divided into three parts: "Rivalries?"; "Mission?"; and "Rise?" The question mark in each title indicates that the authors are well aware that each of these concepts is in itself problematical or should be problematized in order to avoid misusing them.

Part 1 consists of five essays. By way of introduction to the volume, Leif E. Vaage ("Ancient Religious Rivalries and the Struggle for Success") offers a critical reflection on the basic models that lie behind Edward Gibbon's ("providential history" and the "inherent superiority of Christian teaching and doctrine"), Adolf von Harnack's ("mission and expansion"), and Arthur Darby Nock's ("conversion") reconstructions of the earliest history of Christianity. Vaage has doubts about all three of these models and points out that the situation must have been far more complex than these scholars assumed it to be. He argues that for a very long time the kerygma remained unappealing to the larger and better part of society. "Mission" even appears to be a relatively recent category for describing Christianity's earliest initiatives to reach out to the outer world. And "conversion" may well be too fuzzy a category that, moreover, does not take into account the impact of social and political factors in the process.

The concept of "rivalry" itself is further nuanced, and complicated, in the other essays of this first part. Philip A. Harland ("The Declining *Polis*? Religious Rivalries in Ancient Civic Context") draws attention to the very dynamic character of social and religious life in the "pagan" *polis* long after Christianity had begun to look for its place in the picture. Stephen G. Wilson ("Rivalry and Defection") surveys a number of interesting cases of defection from each of the three religious traditions, thus offering some sort of prelude to his recent book on apostasy in the ancient world. Defection may have been caused by the missionary zeal of others, but the evidence shows that this conclusion cannot be generalized. "The reasons given for defection are quite varied, ranging through hostile pressure, career advancement, social attachments, prior religious experience, and intellectual doubt: a rich enough array to alert us to the manifold circumstances and motives that could prompt people to change their religious allegiance" (71). Reena Basser ("Is the Pagan Fair Fairly Dangerous? Jewish-Pagan Relations in Antiquity") examines the concerns of and cautions formulated by the rabbis about participating or even becoming involved, however loosely, in pagan festivals. The threat of idolatry was of course a primary factor for this concern, but the evidence also shows that not infrequently it was balanced to some degree by economic necessity, as can be derived from some sections in the Tosefta qualifying or modifying the strictures of Mishnah in this respect. In a contribution of a more methodological character ("My Rival, My Fellow: Conceptual and Methodological Prolegomena to Mapping Inter-Religious Relations in 2nd- and 3rd-Century CE Levantine Society Using the Evidence of Early Rabbinic Texts"), Jack N. Lightstone deals with much the same sources and issues as Basser, wondering whether religious rivalry was always that strict and concluding that it can by no means constitute the whole picture but that there is also some evidence of a more cooperative or at least a more pragmatic attitude.

Part 2 contains three essays. Terence L. Donaldson ("'The Field God Has Assigned': Geography and Mission in Paul") examines Paul's missionary work and reaches the (negative) conclusion that the apostle had no sense of being on a missionary task. Consequently, Paul can be said to have been instrumental in spreading Christianity in the very first decades of its existence, but he did not in any way "found" a missionary movement. Once Christianity had been brought to the great cities of the Eastern Mediterranean, it would further develop in more informal and spontaneous ways and not through an "official" mission of the church (137). Steve Mason ("The *Contra Apionem* in Social and Literary Context: An Invitation to Judean Philosophy") argues that Flavius Josephus, on the other hand, was well aware of his "missionary" or propagandistic task while in Rome. One might get the impression that the concepts of "mission" and "missionary" are used in a somewhat too narrow sense in the first and in a somewhat too loose sense in the second of these two essays. Roger Beck ("On Becoming a Mithraist: New Evidence for the Propagation of the Mysteries") adds a third "untypical" approach when examining how a largely nonmissionary movement as Mithraism nevertheless succeeded to survive and even to attract new members. Beck studies in particular the Virunum bronze plaque that was discovered and published in the early 1990s, a membership list of a Mithraic cult association that seems to have been supplemented over a number of years.

Part 3 centers on the concept of the "rise" of a movement, in particular of Christianity, as this has been analyzed by Rodney Stark in his monograph *The Rise of Christianity*. Adele Reinhartz ("Rodney Stark and 'The Mission to the Jews'") looks for evidence of Christian mission to the Jews on the terms of Stark's model of an ongoing successful mission to the Diaspora Jews and finds this evidence lacking, at least for what the Fourth Gospel shows us. John's community was not a uniformly Jewish one; there is no evidence that the Jewish part in it kept growing after a certain point in time; and it cannot be ascertained that it solely consisted of Diaspora Jews (211). Steven C. Muir ("'Look How They Love One Another': Early Christian and Pagan Care for the Sick and Other Charity") takes issue with Stark's fourth chapter about the impact of health care and other charity practices on the development of Christianity and notes that the Christian attitude in this respect may after all not have been so revolutionary and innovative. What distinguished Christian charity from pagan initiatives, however, was

its well-organized and institutionalized character over against the more individual approach in pagan circles, where much depended on the goodwill of a
private benefactor (231). The volume concludes with two more essays by Beck
and Vaage. Beck ("The Religious Market of the Roman Empire: Rodney Stark and
Christianity's Pagan Competition") modifies Stark's presentation of Christianity's
triumph and success by also adding the pagan side. There were other traders on
the market as well, and they used partly the same methods (the mystery cults)
and partly developed methods of their own (often through the initiative or under
the auspices of the emperor). Vaage ("Why Christianity Succeeded [in] the
Roman Empire") takes a different path. He does not question the fact that sociological factors did contribute to the spread of Christianity but argues that these
factors have a role to play only in a "historical script" that is shaped by the continual resistance of Christianity to Roman rule. It was a battle between an earthly
empire and a heavenly kingdom for a hegemony that is ruled and sanctioned by
utterly different means. Rivalry thus becomes a far more complex entity than that
of "market mechanisms," more complex indeed to the degree that it was built in
a major way by borrowing the language of (imperial) power from the opponent.
Or, as Vaage, paraphrasing Richard Horsley, puts it: "My proposal is quite simple,
if far-reaching: earliest Christianity was inherently an imperial religion, which is
to say, a social movement decisively shaped by the political culture of the Roman
Empire under whose aegis it first came into being" (277).

This is a fine collection of essays that is daring in the choice of its topic and
in its purpose and refreshingly innovating in some of its conclusions, but also
moderately critical of approaches that tend to be too one-sidedly focused on sociological factors to explain the growth of a new religion.

*Los comienzos del cristianismo: IV Simposio Internacional del Grupo Europeo de
Investigación Interdisciplinar sobre los Orígenes del Cristianismo (G.E.R.I.C.O.),*
edited by Santiago Guijarro. Bibliotheca Salmanticensis Estudios 284. Salamanca: Universidad Pontificia Salamanca, 2006. Pp. 254. Cloth. €16.00. ISBN
8472996980.

Juan Chapa, Universidad de Navarra, Navarra, Spain

Were Christians from the first generation faithful to their founder? To what
extent did they continue to follow Jesus' teaching? Was there any rupture between
Jesus and his disciples? These are some of the questions which were discussed
at the congress organized by the group GERICO in Salamanca in June 2005. In
spite of the title, which is rather generic (resulting perhaps from the diversity of
approaches, topics, and methodologies), the specific topic of the congress was
continuity and discontinuity between Jesus and the first generation of disciples.
It followed discussions from previous GERICO congresses on the principles,
sources, and study methods of Christian origins.

The volume consists of thirteen papers (in Spanish, English, Italian, German, and French), preceded by a brief introduction by S. Guijarro and summaries in Spanish and English. Works cited in each paper are collected and listed alphabetically as bibliography.

Not all the papers deal with the topic of continuity/discontinuity. The first of them, by J. Schröter, considers various aspects related to the historical Jesus and Galilee as a separate environment within Israel. The second one, by W. Stegemann, looks at the nature of the Gospel of Mark in relation to modern research on the historical Jesus to claim that the Evangelist transformed the mythical story of Jesus the Son of God into history. The author's conclusion is that Mark must be interpreted as a foundational legend for the collective identity of Mark's Christian readers.

The paper by A. Destro and M. Pesce goes directly to the topic of the congress. It studies continuity and discontinuity between Jesus and his followers from the point of view of cultural forms or religious practices that made contact with the divine world possible. It specifically examines and compares supernatural experiences in Jesus (baptism, temptations, and transfiguration) with those of his followers (Acts, Paul, and the Johannine communities) to show the elements of continuity/discontinuity in terms of cultural mechanisms rather than in terms of content.

The following three papers have in common their attempt to define some of the features that may have characterized Jesus' first followers in places directly related to Christian origins. S. Guijarro, from the analyses of the Galilean controversies (Mark 2:1–3:6) and with the aid of social psychology for a better understanding of this historical context in which sectarian groups were flourishing, argues that the identity of the group of followers of Jesus in Galilee was closely linked to Pharisee observance. E. Miquel, making use of the sociology of ethics, studies Q and the independent sayings that do not belong to the redactional framework of Q to defend a Q group of sectarian tendency. The Q group would have belonged to the social stratum of "retainers," separated from the peasant world from whence came those who first sympathized with Jesus (and who were the original addressees of the sayings that do not belong to the redactional framework of Q). The paper by R. Aguirre tries to shed some light on the first generation of Christians from the study of the various Judeo-Christian traditions present in the Gospel of Matthew. The author suggests that these traditions, which came from different perspectives, were integrated in different forms by Matthew, who then modified some of them and developed others, as early as the second generation of Christians.

The papers by J. Núñez and C. Gil deal with continuity/discontinuity between Jesus and Paul. J. Núñez reviews the deeds and sayings of Jesus present in Paul's letters in an attempt to show that, in the continuity/discontinuity between the message of Jesus and Pauline theology, the resurrection, the constitution of the community, and the mission to the Gentiles played an intermediary role. The paper by Gil examines the adaptation of the message of Jesus in a new cultural environment with the aid of sociology of knowledge (Berger-Luckmann), social anthropology (M. Douglas), and history of religions. The author takes as a case study the sexual behaviors and family institutions in Corinth and argues that Paul makes use of the idea of the physical body, a symbol of the social and theological body, as the image of the *ekklesia* to counteract some threats to the community.

The next two papers have in common not only their language (Italian) but also their particular focus on the tensions between Jesus' relatives and other groups of his followers. C. Gianotto identifies some disputes between different groups claiming the right to be recognized as the legitimate heirs of Jesus (Peter and the group of disciples, on the one hand; relatives of Jesus, led by James, on the other) and claims that these clashes can also be seen in Mark's presentation of Jesus' relatives. E. Lupieri examines the various references to "brothers" present in the Gospel of Matthew to propose that they reveal some polemics between Matthean Christianity and other Christian groups, particularly between those who followed the "brothers of the Lord" (of an Ebionite or Judaizing type) and those represented by the Pauline-Lukan Christianity.

The paper by F. Rivas follows the sociologist Halbawachs to identify the prophets of the *Didache* as social frames of collective memory who are progressively substituted by the masters and, eventually, by the bishops. E. Norelli examines the process of normativity from the origins of Christianity, as a "normative time" when Jesus, his family, and his disciples were given a special status, down to Irenaeus of Lyons, when normativity was given by a connection between apostolic writings and apostolic succession.

Finally, J. Lieu tackles the question of the moment in which Jews and Christians parted ways. She argues for a better delineation of the geographical, social, conceptual, and textual contexts in order to establish more precisely the shared space and the contested space of both groups.

The fact that the main sources of our knowledge of Christian origins are those preserved by Christians who considered themselves genuine followers of Jesus might have motivated an emphasis on some aspects related to discontinuity between Jesus and his followers. We are to assume that to know more about what supposedly might have been lost in the process may offer us a better understanding of Christian origins. But to deal specifically with some elements of continuity may have also proved useful. It would be interesting, for example, to try to explain not only how some traditions prevailed over others (and to what extent they might have deviated from the original) but also to show how and why some traditions were recognized as authentic to Jesus' teaching and how and why Jesus' followers recognized only in certain writings the elements that confirmed their own continuity with the original message. This would give a more complete picture of the problem. Granted, this might be the topic of future congresses. All things considered, GERICO has left us an interesting volume that opens numerous paths of discussion and research, and we should be grateful for the effort.

Early Christian Mission, by Eckhard J. Schnabel. Downers Grove, Ill.: InterVarsity Press, 2004. 2 vols. Hardcover. $90.00. ISBN 0830827900.

Andreas J. Köstenberger, Southeastern Baptist Theological Seminary, Wake Forest, North Carolina

The publication of the present volume in English constitutes a major event in the missiological exploration of early Christianity (the work originally appeared in a one-volume German edition in 2002 and was translated by the author himself). A full century after Adolf von Harnack's *Die Mission und Ausbreitung des Christentums in den ersten drei Jahrhunderten,* Schnabel's work, over 1,900 pages in length, fills a major gap in the missiological literature by providing a treatment of the early Christian mission that not only considers the mission theology of the biblical material (as does P. T. O'Brien's and my *Salvation to the Ends of the Earth: A Biblical Theology of Missions,* also published by InterVarsity Press) but sets the early Christian mission in its full-orbed historical and geographical context. Overall, Schnabel's work is characterized by a magisterial command of the secondary literature. It truly represents an amazing achievement, especially in a day of specialization when it has become exceedingly difficult for any one person to master the vast amount of material that continues to be generated.

In the two-volume format, volume 1 is devoted to the missions of Jesus and the Twelve, while volume 2 is taken up with the missions of Paul and the early church. After an introduction covering methodological issues and laying out a basic chronology of events, Schnabel, who teaches New Testament at Trinity Evangelical Divinity School, commences his work by surveying the relevant teaching of the Old Testament and the Second Temple period (part 1: "Promise"). He concludes that (1) there was in Old Testament Israel no overt mission program with the aim of converting foreign nations or even individual polytheists; and (2) in the centuries prior and subsequent to Christ's birth there was no direct Jewish mission that pursued the aim of converting non-Jews to faith in Yahweh. After this Schnabel turns to a treatment of the mission of Jesus (part 2: "Fulfillment"; a presentation of the mission theology of each of the canonical Gospels is provided toward the end of the volume). He draws on information from all four Gospels, excelling particularly in providing extensive geographical information on the various locales in which Jesus ministered.

A chapter on the mission of the Twelve is followed by a discussion of Jesus' mission and non-Jews. Here Schnabel contends that Jesus neither explicitly sought nor avoided contact with non-Jews, healing them and responding to their pleas for him to heal their relatives or friends. At the same time, Jesus' contact with non-Jews was not a major part of his mission. While he focused his overt activity on Jews and did not engage in an active mission to Gentiles, Jesus' ministry did attract non-Jews, thus anticipating the post-Pentecost Gentile mission of the early church. The next section discusses the mission of the early church. Schnabel draws attention to the surprising nature of Jesus' mission command in light of the Old Testament expectation of the nations' eschatological pilgrimage to

Jerusalem (part 3: "Beginnings"). This command to engage in active missionizing, according to Schnabel, is grounded in the removal of the exclusive importance of the temple and of the Torah: non-Jews need no longer become Jews but can be integrated into the messianic people of God as representatives of the nations (part 4: "Exodus").

Volume 2 commences with an extensive treatment of the mission of the apostle Paul (part 5: "Pioneer Missionary Work"). According to Schnabel, Paul's mission is shown to follow a recurring pattern: (1) his arrival in a given city with several associates; (2) contact with Jews in the local synagogues, who can provide him with work and/or accommodations; (3) initial preaching and discussions in the synagogue in recognition of the Jews' salvation-historical preeminence; (4–5) after initial success and the making of converts, opposition mounts, which usually (though not always) leads to Paul's moving to different venues; and (6) the gathering of converts in house churches, which meet regularly for worship, biblical instruction, and mutual edification. Schnabel observes that Paul did not call his churches to "world mission"; this was primarily the role of the apostles and of other church-sent gospel messengers. Nevertheless, churches are to contribute actively to making the gospel attractive to both Jews and Gentiles.

After a treatment of the centers of early Christian mission activity (Jerusalem, Antioch, Rome) Schnabel summarizes the mission theologies of Matthew, Mark, Luke-Acts, John, and Peter (part 6: "Growth"; a discussion of Paul's writings was already included in the section on Paul). This is followed by a concluding summary of the self-understanding, practice, and message of the early Christian mission, as well as a discussion of the early Christian mission and mission in the twentieth and twenty-first centuries (part 7: "Results"). Here Schnabel is properly critical of using the term "incarnational" as conveying a missionary paradigm (contra John Stott and much of contemporary mission literature), favoring instead terms such as "contextualization" or "inculturation." The volume is rounded out by 42 maps and figures, a 167-page, virtually exhaustive bibliography, and well over 100 pages of indices of names, subjects, geographical locations, and references to biblical and extrabiblical literature. As Schnabel himself acknowledges in an interview with Dan Reid (IVP's *Academic Alert* 13/3 [fall 2004]: 5), it remains for patristics scholars to complement his work on the first-century church's mission with a study of mission in the second, third, and early fourth centuries (in keeping with the scope of Harnack's work).

In his major contentions, Schnabel represents a coalescing consensus in recent thought and literature on the subject: (1) the role of Old Testament Israel regarding mission (largely passive); (2) the missionary nature of Second Temple Judaism (largely nonexistent); (3) the question of whether or not Jesus engaged in an active Gentile mission (he did not, although he attracted numerous individual Gentiles); and (4) the question of whether or not the New Testament warrants speaking of an "incarnational paradigm" of mission (it does not). Schnabel's personal engagement in mission—a native German, he is a former missionary to the Philippines and has taught at Asian Theological Seminary in Manila, Philippines, and the Freie Theologische Akademie in Giessen, Germany—is both apparent and appealing. Clearly, for him mission is more than merely an academic field of inquiry. Schnabel's knowledge is encyclopedic, his discussions consistently thorough, and his judgments judicious and well-informed by all the available data and literature. *Early Christian Mission* is the new mint standard for works on mission in the early church and will remain so for a very long time to come.

JESUS

Jesus and His Death: Historiography, the Historical Jesus, and Atonement Theory, by Scot McKnight. Waco, Tex.: Baylor University Press, 2005. Pp. viii + 451. Hardcover. $59.95. ISBN 193792295.

Craig A. Evans, Acadia Divinity College, Wolfville, Nova Scotia, Canada

Scot McKnight, Karl A. Olsson Professor of Religious Studies at North Park University, has written a superb book. In fact, the book is so good that it actually lives up to the endorsements printed on the dust jacket. McKnight addresses the most critical questions concerned with the life and death of Jesus, and he does so with masterful control of the primary and secondary literatures. We have here a truly significant work by a veteran scholar.

McKnight arranges his stout tome under four major headings: (1) "The Debate"; (2) "The Reality of a Premature Death"; (3) "A Ransom for Many"; and (4) "Jesus and the Last Supper." The first two sections contain three chapters each, the third contains five, and the fourth contains six, though the last chapter sums up the conclusions reached in the book as a whole. It is followed by a brief excursus on Paul. The book concludes with a bibliography and three indexes (scripture, author, and subject).

McKnight's review of the scholarly debate very helpfully orients readers. I found the first chapter, which wrestles with the philosophical issues that attend historiography and the whole question of what history really is, to be quite masterful. The second chapter is also very insightful. It lays bare the most egregious errors and idiosyncratic tendencies of modern scholarship concerned with the many questions touching Jesus' death. McKnight rightly calls attention to scholars' frequent failure not to ask if Jesus anticipated a premature death and, if he did, how he interpreted it. It is within the context of this competent and well-informed discussion that the balance of the work should be considered. The foundational conclusion reached, on which further reflections and conclusions will be based, is that Jesus did indeed anticipate a premature death. McKnight states: "The logic is simple and unavoidable: if Jesus called his disciples to a willing martyrdom, for which there is plenty of evidence (Q 12:4–9; 14:27; 17:33), we can infer with the utmost probability that he, too, saw his own death approaching" (155). Quite so.

If Jesus anticipated a premature death, how did he understand it? McKnight concludes that Jesus interpreted his premature death as having atoning value. He rightly draws our attention to a host of texts, mostly antedating the time of Jesus, in which Israel, or at least the righteous, benefit from the death of a pious, faithful Jew (e.g., 2 Macc 7:37–38; 4 Macc 6:27–29; 17:22; 18:4; 1QS 5:6; 9:4–5; Pseudo-Philo, *Bib. Ant.* 18:5). "The notion of personal death as an atonement is credible within Judaism, even if exceptional" (170). Jesus believed that his premature death was in keeping with the violent fate suffered by many of Israel's prophets. Furthermore, Jesus believed that his death was part of God's redemptive plan for Israel. "Not only did Jesus see his death as the onset of the eschatological tribulation, he knew (as a Jew) that the tribulation was to lead into the kingdom. Thus, Jesus must have seen his death as the onset of the kingdom of God" (337).

How Jesus understood is death is found in careful study of the saying in Mark 10:45 and in the words of institution in Mark 14:24. McKnight concludes that Jesus probably did not see himself in terms of Isaiah's Suffering Servant. Accordingly, the clause in Mark 10:45, "to give his life as a ransom for many," is an interpretive gloss. So also the clause in Mark 14:24, "which is poured out for many." Rather, Jesus' thoughts of suffering and ordeal more likely derive from Dan 7. McKnight concludes that Jesus viewed his death in a representative sense, as the "first in a group" of those who will suffer. Hence Jesus' summons to his followers to take up their cross and come after him (Mark 8:34). Through suffering and death, Jesus and his followers will find eventual vindication.

In the Last Supper (i.e., the meal the day before Passover—here McKnight rightly follows Johannine chronology) Jesus interprets his death in terms of the slain lamb that protects God's people. Jesus' death will protect his followers from God's wrath, which will come upon the earth in the Day of the Lord. "As the avenging angel of the Passover in Egypt 'passed over' the first-born children whose fathers had smeared blood on the door, so the Father of Jesus would 'pass over' those followers who ingested Jesus' body and blood" (339). Ironically, McKnight's study may have provided a solid basis for understanding the Johannine Baptist's cry, "Behold, the lamb of God" (John 1:29), as deriving from Jesus himself (see also 1 Cor 5:7). Finally, McKnight suspects that reference to "(new) covenant" derives from the Pentecost community, not from Jesus himself. "Jesus believed that the kingdom was yet in the future and that his own death was what would guarantee participation for his followers" (339).

McKnight completes his discussion with insightful assessments of the theological contributions made by the early Christian community. These include pre-Pauline formulations, Paul himself, M, L, Mark, Matthew, Luke-Acts, Hebrews, the Petrine tradition, and the Johannine tradition. McKnight's study of the ways in which Jesus' death was interpreted constitutes an important contribution to biblical theology.

Some will wonder if McKnight's attempt to distinguish the Passover significance of Jesus' death from the idea of atonement for sin is successful. After all, McKnight marshals impressive evidence, cited above, for the idea that the death of the righteous Jew benefits—even atones for—Israel. For example, righteous Eleazar prays: "Be merciful to your people, let our punishment suffice for

them. Make my blood their purification, and take my life in exchange for theirs"
(4 Macc 6:28–29); or as the righteous of Qumran think: "They shall atone for
the guilt of transgression and the rebellion of sin..." (1QS 9:4–5). In the mind
of Jesus, the blood of the Passover lamb and the blood of sacrifices for sin may
well have merged. Indeed, as a "Scripture prophet," as McKnight designates Jesus,
would not Jer 31's promise of a "new covenant" have impressed itself on Jesus?
It was important to the men of Qumran. If the rule of God was indeed coming,
would not the promised "new covenant" come with it? And is not covenant, in
the Israelite-Jewish tradition, often sealed with the shedding of blood?

I raise these questions, not because I find fault with McKnight's research or
even with his conclusions. He has opened up new avenues and fresh, intriguing approaches to old questions and much-discussed Gospel passages. But some
questions linger. Nevertheless, McKnight's work has stimulated my thinking, and
for this I am very grateful. I suspect most readers will also appreciate this book.

*How on Earth Did Jesus Become a God? Historical Questions about Earliest Devo-
tion to Jesus,* by Larry W. Hurtado. Grand Rapids: Eerdmans, 2005. Pp. xii + 234.
Paper. $20.00. ISBN 0802828612.

Felix Just, S.J., Santa Clara University, Santa Clara, California

For over twenty years Larry Hurtado has reflected upon the question of how
Jesus came to be seen and worshiped as a divine figure by the earliest Christians,
who nonetheless staunchly maintained that they were monotheists. His masterful tome, *Lord Jesus Christ* (2003), is already considered essential reading on
this topic. The present shorter work consists of two closely related halves. Part 1
contains the lectures Hurtado gave in March 2004 at Ben Gurion University of
the Negev, inaugurating the Deichmann Annual Lecture Series. Written for an
academic audience but not specialists in New Testament studies, these lectures
present a condensed version of the main points of his approach. Part 2 of the
book contains slightly edited versions of four articles Hurtado had published previously (1998 to 2003) on related topics. Thus, part 2 considers exegetical issues
more closely, discusses Greek expressions more often, and engages more explicitly
with other scholars' works, while part 1 more strongly highlights the implications
of this topic for Jewish-Christian relations. This combination of materials from
separate origins leads to some duplication between the two halves of the book;
yet since the articles reprinted in part 2 are frequently referenced in the footnotes
of part 1, it is helpful having these writings together in a single easily accessible
volume.

The introduction highlights the double entendre of the book's title question and gives a foretaste of each chapter's main points. Chapter 1 surveys some
"Approaches to Jesus-Devotion in Earliest Christianity" proposed by other scholars before compactly summarizing Hurtado's own approach. In contrast to the
influential work of Wilhelm Bousset (*Kyrios Christos,* 1913), Hurtado maintains

that devotion to Jesus did not develop only gradually among Hellenistic Christians but must have started "more explosively" (25) among the very first circles of Judean Christians. Moreover, Jesus-devotion did not arise from new theological insights about Jesus but originated in some powerful revelatory experiences his followers had:

> I contend that devotion to Jesus as divine was such a novel and significant step, and appeared so early as well, that it can only be accounted for as a response to the strong conviction in early Christian circles that the one God of biblical tradition willed that Jesus be so reverenced.... As surprising as it may seem, the evidence indicates that Jesus was first given the sort of devotion that we associate with a deity *among the circles of devout Jews* who comprised the earliest adherents of the young Christian movement. Jesus was treated as worthy of divine honor initially because Christians were convinced that it was obedience to the one God to do so. (29–30, emphasis original)

In chapter 2 Hurtado considers the relationship between "Devotion to Jesus and Second-Temple Jewish Monotheistic Piety." As the New Testament evidence shows, attributing divine prerogatives to Jesus began in the earliest pre-Pauline circles of Judean Christianity, not just with Paul or later Gentile converts. Moreover, this development was not an "apotheosis" (Jesus becoming a second god) but rather what Hurtado calls "Binitarian Monotheism," in which the one God is worshiped in and through Jesus, his "principal agent." This differs from di-theism in that Jewish and Gentile Christians alike remained strongly opposed to any form of polytheistic worship.

Chapter 3, "To Live and Die for Jesus," considers the "Social and Political Consequences of Devotion to Jesus in Earliest Christianity" (subtitle) in both Jewish and Gentile contexts. From the start, Christians not only had strained relationships within families but also encountered conflicts in broader social and political contexts. While other Jews would have considered the worship of Jesus threatening to their religion and blasphemous to God, other Gentiles would have failed to understand why Christians stopped participating in the polytheistic cults that were pervasive in households and in public. Although violent persecutions were most frequently directed against the leaders of the new movement, even ordinary Christians sometimes faced serious difficulties, especially Christian wives or slaves of non-Christian husbands or masters.

To conclude part 1, Hurtado investigates the well-known pre-Pauline hymn of Phil 2:6–11 as "A 'Case Study' in Early Christian Devotion to Jesus" (ch. 4). While most scholars focus on the self-emptying of Jesus in the first half of the hymn (vv. 6–8), Hurtado emphasizes the exaltation of Jesus in the second half (vv. 9–11). He sees this as a "Christological Midrash" (92) of Isa 45:23 and other Old Testament texts, with the divine honors previously accorded to God now applied to Jesus. Moreover, he suggests that such interpretative moves were "particularly characteristic of *Jewish-Christian* circles, as they mined their traditional scriptures for insight into God's purposes in Jesus, and also sought to find scriptural justification for their convictions about his significance and status" (93, emphasis original).

Part 2 begins with a closer look at "First-Century Jewish Monotheism" (ch. 5). In response to some scholars' objections to one of his earlier books, *One God, One Lord* (1988), Hurtado emphasizes that one must not take a deductive approach (begin with a modern definition of "pure monotheism" and then find it lacking in some ancient Jewish texts) but rather use an inductive approach that takes seriously the variety of ancient Jewish beliefs and practices, allows for change and development over time, and pays attention to cultic and liturgical practices, not just theological concepts and doctrines. Thus, he shows how most first-century Jews were unquestionably monotheists, not only in their verbal professions but especially in their worship practices. Even if some Jews ascribed divine attributes to God's agents or other heavenly figures, no cultic worship was ever offered to such beings. Only two major Jewish groups, namely, Christians and gnostics, seem to have gone too far, which eventually "produced a hardening of rabbinic monotheism in the direction away from a more flexible and monarchial monotheism and toward a more stringently 'monistic' stance." Therefore, the willingness of Christians to offer prayer and worship to Jesus, not just to God, was "a major innovation in previous Jewish monotheistic religious practice" (132).

In chapter 6, "Homage to the Historical Jesus and Early Christian Devotion," Hurtado considers possible connections between the "post-Easter" worship of Jesus and the historical Jesus. By analyzing various Greek expressions in the Gospels for "kneeling," "falling down," and especially "worshiping," Hurtado concludes that these mostly reflect the culturally common gestures for expressing homage or respect toward superiors, especially if one sought favors or benefits from them. The descriptions of persons "worshiping" Jesus during his public ministry (esp. in Matthew) are explained as the Evangelist's attempt to make certain stories more accessible for his own audience. Thus, "the far more intense devotion to Jesus that characterized early Christian circles so amazingly early was not simply the continuation of the pattern of homage given to the historical Jesus, and it cannot be accounted for adequately by reference to Jesus' ministry" (149).

Since "Early Jewish Opposition to Jesus-Devotion" is well known from John's Gospel, Hurtado's focus in chapter 7 is on the evidence from the Synoptic Gospels and Paul's letters. From the earliest stages, Jewish opposition was not merely against the doctrinal claims made about Jesus (in christological titles) but more intensely against the devotional practices in which Christians called upon the name of Jesus and accorded him acts of reverence deemed appropriate only for God. Hurtado emphasizes that "Jewish opposition was varied in nature and in causes" in the earliest decades (177), ranging from outrage that Christians exalted Jesus above such great figures of the past as Moses and Abraham to charges of "blasphemy" at the divine status accorded to Jesus. Hurtado concludes, "it may be that Jewish religious opponents saw earlier and more clearly than the Jewish

Jesus-devotees themselves that their devotion was a significant 'mutation' in Jewish monotheistic practice" (178).

In chapter 8, "Religious Experience and Religious Innovation in the New Testament," Hurtado asserts that New Testament scholarship has largely ignored or devalued the role of religious experience, focusing instead on theological interests and doctrinal developments. In contrast, he summarizes several social-scientific studies that have shown how important "revelatory religious experiences" have been in the development of other innovative religious movements throughout history. Hurtado then looks closely at several key New Testament texts to highlight the influence of religious experiences, often described as visions and revelations: "[F]rom the earliest years of the Christian movement, individuals experienced what they took to be revelations sent by God that conveyed to them the sense that a right response and obedience to God demanded of them the cultic reverence of Jesus" (199).

The book concludes with a brief epilogue, detailed indices, and two appendices: "Opening Remark to the First Deichman Annual Lecture Series," by Horst-Heinz Deichmann (207–14); and "Are There Good Reasons for Studying Early Christian Literature at Ben-Gurion University?" by Roland Deines (215–17).

As in all his publications, Hurtado's writing is crystal clear, his arguments solidly supported, and his conclusions quite convincing. This book's minor flaws stem mostly from its origin as a combination of public lectures (chs. 1–4) with previously published articles (chs. 5–8), which leads not only to much repetition but also to some editorial inconsistencies. For example, Greek words are printed in Greek characters in some chapters but transliterated in others; canonical titles are usually written out but sometimes abbreviated ("Gospel of John" versus "GJohn"); what "cultic" means (8) and where "Galatia" lies (33) are explained, but not "*portmanteau*" (27, 135) or "Halakhic" (159–60).

One major omission in Hurtado's work is the role of the Holy Spirit. Only rarely and briefly does he mention the Spirit (28, 55, 86, 179–82), due to his concentration on devotion to Jesus. Yet was not the Spirit also crucial for the earliest Christians, not just in late texts such as John 14–16 or Matt 28 but already before Paul? Just as Hurtado forcefully argues that Jesus-devotions predate Paul's letters and that Jesus was the focus not just theologically but also liturgically, is not the same also true about the Spirit, albeit to a lesser degree? To cite just one example: "But you were washed, you were sanctified, you were justified in the name of the Lord Jesus Christ and in the Spirit of our God" (1 Cor 6:11; see also 1 Thess 1:5–6; 1 Cor 12–14; Mark 3:36; etc.). Further attention to the complex interrelationships between the Spirit, Jesus, and the Father would not threaten Hurtado's astute analysis of the predominantly "binitarian" character of early Christian monotheism but would lead to an even fuller picture of the development of Christian beliefs and devotional practices in its earliest stages.

The Last Days of Jesus, by François Bovon. Translated by Kristin Hennessy. Louisville: Westminster John Knox, 2006. Pp. x + 101. Paper. $17.95. ISBN 0664230075.

Kevin B. McCruden, Gonzaga University, Spokane, Washington

This volume provides an English translation of François Bovon's *Les derniers jours de Jésus: Textes et événements* (2nd ed.; Geneva: Labor et Fides, 2004), which is the second edition of Bovon's 1974 monograph of the same title. Animated by a deeper awareness of the fallacy of absolute historical objectivity since the appearance of the first edition, Bovon outlines the events of Jesus' passion with a frank awareness of the Gospels' principally theological impulse. With this in mind, Bovon carefully notes how the events of the passion are never conveyed to the reader unmediated but only as interpreted from the earliest stages of the primitive tradition. Interpretation is evident not only in the paraenetic and apologetic concerns integral to the canonical passion narratives, but even the pre-Pauline confessional statements are marked by what Bovon describes as a "metahistorical dimension" (3) motivated by faith affirmation. As a historian, however, Bovon is committed to the principle that the New Testament evidence allows for a meaningful interpretive consensus concerning the general historical outline of Jesus' last days. This interpretive task continues to be mandated by the enduring problem of anti-Semitism, the renewed appreciation of Jesus' Jewish environment, as well as emergent advancements in our understanding of Roman penal procedures.

Chapter 1 examines the relevant sources comprising early Christian reflection on the death and resurrection of Jesus. Bovon provides an excellent summary of the various types of traditional material relating to Jesus' passion, ranging from pre-Pauline confessional statements to the continuous passion narratives found in both the canonical Gospels and the noncanonical Gospel of Peter. It should be noted that throughout this study Bovon bestows sincere attention on the latter as a potentially fruitful resource for historical reconstruction. This marks a change from the first edition, in which the Gospel of Peter received less attention.

The strength of Bovon's analysis rests in the way he links discrete traditional materials to plausible life situations within primitive Christianity. For example, Bovon locates kerygmatic proclamation to Jews as the generative ground for the traditional passion material gleaned from the missionary speeches in Acts. According to Bovon, this material is characterized by a two-part structure envisioning rejection of Jesus on the part of the Jewish ruling elite followed by God's vindication of Jesus through the resurrection. In terms of the specific issue of historical reconstruction, the Acts material—which seems to lack the historical reminiscence either of a Sanhedrin trial or burial by Joseph of Arimathea—may in fact sketch something of the contours of the earliest stages of the memory of Jesus' passion.

Bovon turns next to the Synoptic passion predictions. Although likely earlier than the continuous passion narratives found in the Gospels, the passion predictions—like the pre-Pauline confessional statements—are more preoccupied with the theological significance of Jesus' death and vindication than with precise historical memory. In contrast to the material found in Acts, these predictions are distinguished by a fourfold schema in which Jesus is delivered to the Jewish authorities, handed over to the Gentiles, and finally executed and raised after three days. Bovon plausibly contends that this fourfold schema provided the matrix for the emergence of continuous passion narratives, which themselves likely grew from within the matrixes of diverse liturgical settings. The chapter concludes with a delineation of the familiar Jewish and pagan sources confirming the existence and death of Jesus and offers some interesting observations on the theological and historical value of the noncanonical Gospel of Peter.

Taking as its point of departure the unanimous references to Jesus' royal status in all four of the canonical passion narratives, chapter 2 succinctly establishes what Bovon describes as the "best established fact of Jesus life" (26): Jesus was crucified as a royal pretender by the prefect Pontius Pilate. This chapter functions essentially as an introductory thesis statement preparing for the historical reconstruction to follow in chapter 3.

Chapter 3, the lengthiest chapter in the book, deals largely with reconstructing the details of Jesus' arraignment before both the Sanhedrin and Pilate. Working from the dual observation that (1) neither Luke nor John mentions a formal capital condemnation against Jesus on the part of the Sanhedrin and that (2) all four Gospels envision some type of a double-tiered appearance of Jesus before the Jewish ruling elite, Bovon argues for the likelihood that Jesus underwent some sort of a double interrogation rather than a formal trial per se. This dual interrogation on the part of the Sanhedrin resulted either in an informal recommendation of death subsequently pronounced and exacted by Pilate or in an actual pronouncement of a capital offense, which was then merely ratified by the Roman prefect. Bovon leaves open the possibility of the latter but judges the former the more secure historically. While the precise details of the Sanhedrin proceedings are clouded under the exegetical influence of the scriptural figure of the righteous sufferer, some kind of threat against the temple together with an implicit political claim were likely integral components of the Jewish grievance against Jesus. Bovon correctly points out that the political and religious dimensions of this grievance would have been linked in first-century Palestine. Therefore, any contemporary proposal that argues that the Sanhedrin disingenuously concocted a political crime against Jesus should be eschewed. Given that the contemporary problem of anti-Semitism appeared in the book's preface as one of the specific warrants for this study, I was somewhat surprised that a more detailed discussion of the express topic of anti-Semitism was missing here and throughout this main chapter of the book.

Bovon interprets Jesus' interrogation by Pilate as an example of the *cognitio extra ordinem* whereby the prefect, in lieu of a formal tribunal and judge, exercised considerable freedom in the formal investigation and sentencing of the accused. Bovon judges the Herod episode as related by Luke (23:6–12) as likely a Lukan piece of redaction. However, the fact that the figure of Herod appears in the noncanonical Gospel of Peter intimates perhaps some type of involvement on the part of the tetrarch in the events of Jesus' last days. Here we see a particularly good example of the author's changed estimation of the historical value of the Gospel of Peter.

Bovon is willing to concede a historical nucleus to the Barabbas episode, but, unfortunately, he does not explain what that would entail. As an explanation for the Gospels' portrayal of Pilate's reluctance to condemn Jesus, Bovon offers the plausible suggestion that Pilate's hesitation may have been calculated to demonstrate his superiority to the Jewish elite. Hence, Bovon correctly suggests that Christian apologetics may not be the sole factor in the Gospels' portrayal of the Roman prefect. As for the crucifixion scene itself, and in particular Jesus' last words from the cross, Bovon notes the likely influence of Christian exegetical activity rather than authentic historical memory. Lastly, Bovon juxtaposes the textual evidence for a private burial of Jesus at the hands of Joseph of Arimathea with the provocative notice from Acts 13:27–29 that seems to envision a burial of Jesus at the hands of his enemies, perhaps in a common grave.

Chapter 4 might have been better included as part of the appendix. It briefly analyzes—at times too minutely—what are essentially unanswerable questions relating to the precise times and places that figure into the passion events. Indeed, one might reasonably wonder to what degree the choice between crucifixion at the third hour (Mark) or the sixth hour (Gospel of John, Gospel of Peter) truly impacts the historical task in any substantive manner. Given the theological motivations guiding both Mark's and John's divergent chronologies, Bovon recognizes the difficulty attaching to any secure reconstruction of the chronology of the passion. What amounts to perhaps the firmest historical conjecture is that Jesus likely died between 28 and 32 C.E.

Chapter 5 concludes the study with some thoughtful reflections on the events of Easter. Bovon prefaces this discussion by making the important methodological point that historical reconstruction of the resurrection is inappropriate, since this event belongs properly to the eschatological new age. He then examines some of the ways in which early Christians attempted to interpret and articulate their faith in the risen Christ. Foundational for this task of articulation and interpretation was, of course, the appropriation of Scripture, in particular such triumphant texts as Ps 110 and Dan 13. Bovon also provides a helpful analysis of the two types of resurrection accounts integral to the Easter proclamation: appearance stories and accounts of the empty tomb. While the appearance stories attest to the transformation of the risen Christ as well as to the paradoxical continuity of the risen Lord with the crucified Jesus of Nazareth, the accounts of the empty tomb give narrative expression to the kerygmatic claim concerning the divine vindication over death. Translations of both the Lukan passion narrative and the noncanonical Gospel of Peter comprise the appendixes, and an updated bibliography is provided. Taken as a whole, Bovon's study is a truly excellent scholarly introduction for an advanced undergraduate course. It would also be quite

useful at the graduate level as a thoughtful, critical introduction to some of the
more comprehensive works that treat the topic of the passion, such as Raymond
Brown's *Death of the Messiah*.

The UnGospel: The Life and Teachings of the Historical Jesus, by Stephen S. Carver.
Eugene, Ore.: Wipf & Stock, 2004. Pp. ix + 285. Paper. $29.00. ISBN 1592446809.

Pieter J. J. Botha, University of South Africa, Pretoria, South Africa

The UnGospel is a well-written presentation of the original Jesus that contrasts with the dark and imposing developments by Christians of this original
Jesus. The original Jesus is an attractive and deeply inspiring example of service,
empowerment, and pacifism; the developments afterwards, as depicted by Carver,
much less so. The book leaves one with very ambiguous feelings. Not that the
prose is muddled. Carver's depiction is clear and exciting, but as critical discourse
it often seems facile and superficial. Strong words, but necessary precisely because
the historical Jesus is such an important subject. Yes, these values as presented by
Carver's Jesus are worth fighting for, but no, this presentation cannot be responsible historical understanding.

This study of the historical Jesus is a compact volume consisting of five parts.
The first is an introduction in which Carver briefly discusses the sources for
studying the historical Jesus, the criteria he uses to identify historical material,
and the reorganization of the material—meaning what was done with the Gospel
material after weighing against his five criteria (essentially an explanation of his
reconstruction of the primary traditions into an account about the historical
Jesus). Then follows, in part 2, "Prologue to the UnGospel," in which the author
outlines his understanding of the historical context of Jesus.

The bulk of the book is in part 3, where Carver presents the life and teachings of the historical Jesus in fourteen chapters. The chapters cover themes such
as John the Baptist, the major aspects of Jesus' ministry, the main themes of Jesus'
teaching, the conflict in Jerusalem, and Jesus' final hours. The format of his reconstruction is in five categories of information. Printed in regular text (and divided
into verses à la Scripture) are the primary traditions, sorted *out of* the sources
and translated into English and reorganized into a reconstruction of the events
of Jesus' life. Interspersed are italicized texts, reflecting Carver's paraphrases of
events or sayings, and bold print, representing transitional or explanatory comments added by Carver to "smooth out the flow" of his account of Jesus' life.
Within the narrative boxed frames are included that contain explanations of
issues in the surrounding text. Information about sources and translation are
added in endnotes to each chapter.

Part 4 is an epilogue in which Carver first gives a depiction of Jesus' actual
ministry (155–64), then discusses the secondary traditions in the canonical Gospels that were added to the original stuff or used to cover up reports
(164–77). After providing a historical overview of the evolution of the Christian

Jesus (177–207), Carver concludes with a summary of this part of the book. Throughout this part diagrams are used to summarize and visualize the processes described by Carver.

In this epilogue Carver draws out the conclusions of his reconstruction of the authentic Jesus traditions (the UnGospel): the historical Jesus wanted to change his society by preaching an inclusive approach to God's kingdom, encouraging human empowerment, servant leadership, and a pacifist approach to conflict. However, the early church added "layers of ideas about Jesus" into the original, authentic Jesus material. Carver identifies three layers (which finally resulted in the canonical Gospels as we know them). The first layer is the development of the idea that Jesus was raised from the dead, the development from Jesus as Son of Man to the resurrected Jesus. The second layer is the conviction that made the resurrected Jesus into the heavenly Christ. In this layer we find the development of the second coming, Christian hierarchy, Jesus dying for sins, and the demonizing of the Jews. The third layer is the shift from the heavenly Christ to the eternal Son of God, the preexistent Word. After the canonical Gospels we find the further evolution of the "Christian Jesus": the eternal Son of God became the God of the persecuted, who became the God who persecutes, who became the God of war—all contra the intentions of the "authentic" or historical Jesus. The God of war resulted in the "divided Christ" (the Reformation), which became the prelude to the historical Jesus (Carver refers to the conventional four periods of scholarly investigation: the first/no/second/third quests) and the evangelical response. All this has made it necessary that people ask which Jesus to follow: the Son of God as defined by traditional Christianity or the Jewish teacher as defined by critical scholarship (208). Carver's book is a presentation of the contrast of these two views and an indication of some implications for choosing one over the other.

Although I have absolutely no hesitation about where anyone's choice should be (with critical scholarship, of course), the ease with which Carver dispenses with extremely complicated historical questions in this section is disturbing. We do need to present history in summary form, but this borders on irresponsible simplification.

The last part, the conclusion, briefly discusses the "UnGospel" versus the gospel. Three appendices and a bibliography follows. The term "UnGospel" designates a deliberate contrast to "the *gospel* message of traditional Christianity" (224). The views promoted by "traditional Christianity" are at odds with what is known about the historical Jesus. Early Christians redefined the title "Christ" and maintained that Jesus descended from heaven, died for the sins of humanity, and then sat at the right hand of God, waiting to return and set up his kingdom. This, according to Carver, is essentially the "gospel." In contrast, the historical Jesus

> did not regard himself as the way to salvation, but rather he pointed to the ethical standard of the Law and the need to operate in a caring and forgiving fashion toward other human beings. Instead of attempting to avoid responsibility for one's neighbors by means of formulas, Jesus promoted the need for

accountability for one's neighbors and love of one's enemies. ... For the historical Jesus, the measurement of one's spirituality was ... based on how people actually lived their lives. ... Jesus was a radical, a gentle troublemaker for the conservative political and religious elements within his society. (226)

With regard to method, Carver discusses the "standard" set of criteria used to determine authentic Jesus material (multiple attestation, dissimilarity, uniqueness, coherence), emphasizing the inadequacy of these criteria. He also discusses the nonsupernatural criterion, that is, scholars using "a rational approach" to indicate especially miracle stories as inauthentic. Although Carver admits that "this criterion can be helpful," it is "at odds with the culture of Jesus' day," hence this criterion is not used. Rather, Carver attempts to supply "an interpretive framework for how supernatural references can be understood today" (21–22). Carver's statements are fraught with difficulties. Why are the other criteria not considered "at odds with Jesus' culture"? They most assuredly are. Crucially, Jesus himself must have made sense of the world, in Carver's words, by means of the "supernatural," so that it is *most plausible* that he presented himself and his actions and his experiences "supernaturally," negating the depiction of divine enhancements as secondary and "later," which can be removed from the traditions.

As noted, Carver rejects certain established criteria but finds others helpful, which he adjusts so that he claims to be working with the following criteria: (1) traditions that are culturally relevant; (2) traditions that reflect Jesus' ethnicity (his Jewishness); (3) traditions that affirm Jesus' humanitarian and spiritual insight; (4) traditions *unsupportive* of later systems of thought (after all, we do know that Jesus' divinity is a secondary development); (5) consistency with other primary traditions (26–29). I find this explanation unsettling: the terms are without exception conceptually muddled. For instance, what does "Jewish" mean as a criterion for authenticity? How would we know authentic first-century Jewishness, and on whose authority? Even monotheism in early Judaisms is a highly contested and elusive concept. How would we know what humanitarian and spiritual in a first-century Galilean context to have been? And so on.

The interaction of early Christians with Judaisms and Greco-Roman traditions are far, far more complex and supportive than conventional presentations allow. Surely the term "Jewish Christianity"—deliberately invoking the difficulties of definition for the moment—must be a vivid reminder of the ambiguities and, from our point of view, the uncertainties that we face. From authors geographically and chronologically diverse—Justin Martyr and John Chrysostom, for example—we learn about Christian groups remaining loyal to Torah and synagogue. In the middle of the second century even Justin Martyr admits the close association with Jewish-Christians as "kinsmen and brothers"—despite his undeniable bias (*Dialogus cum Tryphone* 47).

As an overall response to Carver's study, I point to two problem areas. First, the fallacy of the authority of the original word, the "authentic" report. Carver relies on the Byzantine text for his New Testament text; in an appendix he ably explains the problems and oversights of the conventional "critical" New Testament edition. But, and this holds equally for the criteria of authenticity debate, the point of these problems and inadequacies is not that the original and authentic is to be found elsewhere. Rather, we need to rethink our understanding of the processes underlying our so-called methods. Given the orally determined nature of ancient communication, the very idea of an original or first reading is suspect if not completely irrelevant; but the more important and general challenge of the textual evidence is to grasp the necessity of shifting our aim: from construing the supposed "authentic" to *understanding* texts, events, and processes. In other words, meanings rather than originality. *Whose* authenticity have we been searching for anyway? Authenticity is not an acontextual metaphysical entity. The problems underlying our construction of current critical texts do not prove that the Byzantine text (or any other) is "original" but require of us to review and rethink our understanding of current New Testament textual criticism.

The time has come to give up on rephrasing or adjusting the usual criteria. Their inadequacy has been shown, many times convincingly so. Imagine the "plausible theory of development" (209 n. 33) of the traditions according to Carver: an ingenious falsification of narratives about a creative Jew by Jews making use of mainly Jewish and some non-Jewish concepts that they, despite their honesty, commitment, and resourcefulness completed quite unsuccessfully, so that we can reconfigure it all.

Second, our understanding of early Christianity did actually advance in the past few decades. It is no longer possible simply to read *some* early Christian literature in such a way that it fits into a narrative of relentless dishonesty and the self-deceptive creation of the "church's Christianity." Need one still be reminded of the mind-boggling diversity in early Christian literature and the absence of *the* story of traditional versus nontraditional (whatever that means)? It is time to read early Christian literature for what the authors were saying and carefully to understand their very serious intentions.

Dancing Girls, Loose Ladies, and Women of the Cloth: The Women in Jesus' Life, by F. Scott Spencer. New Testament Guides. New York: Continuum, 2004. Pp. xi + 196. Paper. $24.95. ISBN 0826416128.

Patrick E. Spencer, San Ramon, California

The book is a compilation of F. Scott Spencer's research on and exploration of women in the four Gospels and the book of Acts over the past decade. Four of the seven chapters are versions of previously published articles and essays—each expanded and revised—whereas three chapters are published for the first time.

Spencer establishes his methodological framework in chapter 1. He then addresses the portrayal of women in Matthew, Mark, John, Luke, and Acts in chapters 2–7, with the last two chapters on women in Acts. Like many other books from Continuum, the book uses endnotes versus footnotes, a cumbersome format for some readers, especially since Spencer includes useful—and interest-ing—dialogue and an extensive listing of bibliographical citations. In this vein, a bibliography is not included. The book has a subject index but does not contain reference or author indices, omissions that will disappoint some readers.

Spencer is best known for his use of narrative and social-science criticisms in the investigation of Acts. In chapter 1 Spencer explains that his investigation will employ feminist criticism, a "colorful, sprawling big top under which all voices and viewpoints can be heard" (1). He argues that feminist criticism is an eclectic methodological approach that draws upon a variety of different methodologies, including historical, narratological, sociological, intertextual, cultural, and literary criticisms. With feminist criticism established as his methodological foundation, Spencer then examines some of the more noteworthy investigations of women in the Gospels and Acts, focusing on Ben Witherington III and Richard Bauckham. In the case of Witherington, he suggests that his positive portrait of women in the Gospels and Acts is "purchased at the price of a legalistic, myopic, and marginal-ized bowdlerization of Judaism" (8). As regards to Bauckham, Spencer proposes that he does not adequately address issues that inevitably arise when dominant male authors and readers attempt to speak for and about women's experience, on the one hand, and does not heed appropriate attention to the silence and absence of women in the New Testament narratives, on the other.

Spencer then goes in search of some examples where the methodologi-cal miscues of Witherington and Bauckham are not made. Ironically, he finds models more cognizant of and aligned with feminist criticism in the arena of the Hebrew Bible. These approaches, per Spencer, are more effective on sev-eral grounds: (1) they recognize that biblical criticism is male-centered and that female readers are needed; (2) the lens of literary criticism provides a solid starting point for interpretation but needs to be supplemented with additional methodological approaches such as deconstruction and feminism; and (3) "the good of the biblical text must be unraveled from the bad, the redemptive from the deconstructive" (17).

Chapter 2 looks at the oft-examined Matthean genealogy, specifically the four women who are included: Tamar, Rahab, Ruth, and the wife of Uriah. Spen-cer contends the focus of recent investigations misses the comic element in each of their stories in the Hebrew Bible by concentrating on interests that are wrong-headed: (1) the women as sinners; (2) their categorization as non-Jews or strangers; and (3) the scandalous, provocative nature of each woman's story. Spencer examines each of the four women within the context of their Hebrew Bible narratives and concludes that each stands out due to her shrewd dealings with bungling male authorities. Further, despite passive assistance from God (who sits on the sideline in each case), they successfully implement God's will. He then moves to the Matthean narrative, suggesting Joseph and his actions in Matt 2 mirror the actions of the four women. In particular, Joseph embodies the virtue of becoming a "eunuch for the sake of the kingdom of heaven (19:11)" (39), which turns the traditional notion of masculinity on its head.

In chapter 3 Spencer concentrates his analysis of women in Mark on the episode involving Herodias and her dancing daughter. He argues that the intertextual examples of Judith, Jezebel, and Esther serve as a backdrop to the narrative. He also proposes that the two preceding sandwiched episodes of the hemorrhaging woman and Jairus and his daughter (Mark 5:21–43) provide an intratextual frame for the narrative. Specifically, the hemorrhaging woman, just like Herodias and her daughter, manipulates male power to secure what she wants. Spencer also suggests the episode of the Syrophoenician woman with the demonized daughter (7:24–30) falls in line with this same theme: she holds Jesus to his proclamation of loving service. In addition, her status as a foreigner, and her prodding of Jesus, foreshadows the second feeding miracle that takes place in the Gentile region of the Decapolis (8:1–10). This leads Spencer to the conclusion that Mark portrays Jesus as "a developing, maturing figure—open to women's leadership and guidance" (68), with the hemorrhaging woman and the Syrophoenician woman prodding him along in his maturation, development process.

Spencer addresses the various appearances of women in John in chapter 4 from the lens of conversation analysis as developed by Deborah Tannen. He stresses the importance of recognizing linguistic differences between males and females and, in particular, the use of rhetorical power in the discourse. Biblical literature, according to Spencer, is replete with numerous examples of males struggling to attain honor by dominating women and other males in the use of rhetorical discourse. He breaks his analysis into three areas: the influence of setting, status relations, and linguistic conventions. At the end of his analysis, Spencer finds evidence for both volatile masculine and feminine discourse from Jesus in John. He also suggests that Jesus is a more complex figure than the women in the Gospel, although "he is also more unstable, vacillating in each dialogue between asserting his authority and power and protecting his honor and independence, on the one hand, and reaching out in intimacy and empathy and preserving community and solidarity, on the other" (100).

Spencer deals with each of the episodes involving women in John. First, in the case of the wedding at Cana episode, Spencer argues that Jesus' mother is depicted as a model disciple; when Jesus balks at her request for his cooperation in preserving the dignity of a family wedding due to the shortage of wine, she negotiates a resolution between Jesus and the servants to preserve Jesus' quest for independence. Second, in line with a number of scholars, Spencer recognizes the betrothal scene (Gen 24:10–61; 29:1–14; Exod 2:15–22) as the intertextual interpretive frame for the episode involving the Samaritan woman. He pinpoints three major topics in the exchange between Jesus and the Samaritan woman: water, husbands, and worship. He subsequently argues that the Samaritan woman in each of these instances presses Jesus to maintain vital continuity with relatives, past and present, and with realms, material and spiritual. Third, Spencer turns his attention to Martha and Mary and the episode involving the raising of Lazarus. The sisters challenge Jesus' honor by faulting him for failing his obligations as both Lord and friend. Jesus responds to Martha in a dominant, male-oriented manner, whereas he responds to Mary with sympathetic emotion, action representative of the feminine sphere. Fourth, Spencer asserts that Jesus' encounter with Mary Magdalene in the garden recalls other "garden scenes" in the Hebrew Bible, specifically Adam and Eve (Gen 2:15–25) and the passionate lovers in the Song of Songs (4:12–5:1; 6:2–3; 8:13). The personal use of names, Jesus calling Mary by name and Mary designating Jesus as Rabbouni, creates an intratextual connection with the episode of the Good Shepherd (10:3–4). While Jesus spurns Mary's clinging, he does not reject her. Instead, he redirects her to nurture the community of the living, to which she is the first and prime witness.

In chapter 5 Spencer focuses on the episode of the "loose" woman at the house of Simon the Pharisee. He cites the need to pay special attention to surrounding intratextual connections as well as intertextual linkages with Jewish wisdom literature. The narrative itself positions the woman as a deviant, one who fails to observe proper barriers between the male–female space and who exhibits varying forms of female erotica. Spencer draws a direct connection to the wisdom of God reference in the preceding episode (7:35) and the "loose" woman (viz., the seductive women of Prov 7:10–22; Sir 9:3-9). At the same time, he notes parallels with the female partner in the Song of Songs and even Woman Wisdom in Prov 1–9. In the end, Spencer points out that Simon focuses on the literal meaning of the woman's actions, failing to comprehend the larger intratextual and intertextual nuances at the disposal of the reader. Spencer concurs with previous findings by Cathleen Corley and Barbara Reid that the emotions and actions of the "loose" woman have intratextual echoes—"loose connections"—in the Lukan passion narrative (chs. 22–24), which he breaks into the two categories of kissing and caressing, and weeping and wetting. As a result, the woman, "though unnamed, unvoiced, and unmentioned" (135), stands as a model disciple for Peter and the other apostles and, in particular, coincides with the characteristics of the Isaianic suffering servant (as is the case with Jesus in the passion narrative). Her actions also stand as "counter-patterns" for the treacherous Judas, cowardly Peter, and fearful followers in the passion narrative. In addition, a narrative trajectory extends from her actions to the anonymous women who follow Jesus from Galilee and reemerge at the cross and tomb, where they prepare spices and anointments for Jesus' body (23:49, 55–56), although their mission is aborted when there is no body to anoint and they get "shuffled to the background in favor of Cleopas, Simon, and the eleven apostles" (136–37).

Chapter 6 examines the portrayal of slave girls and prophetic daughters in Luke-Acts. Spencer argues women as prophets in Luke-Acts largely receive no voice and are repeatedly overshadowed by men. He aims to discover in this chapter if female slaves encounter the same treatment and discovers they receive comparable treatment to the female prophets. Spencer pinpoints three different episodes involving slave girls for investigation: the unnamed slave girl in the passion narrative (22:54–62); Rhoda, the slave girl of Mary (12:12–17); and the slave girl who is silenced by Paul (16:16–18). Nevertheless, he determines that each of the slave girls has her testimony "squelched or challenged" in some way, and shadows of doubt are even cast on the character and competence of each girl. The narrative is open-ended in the case of the third slave girl, with readers left to decide if she sincerely wants to honor Paul and his companions or maliciously sets out to expose Paul's monotheistic mission in hopes of stirring up anti-Judaic hostility. Nevertheless, Spencer proceeds to call out lack of concern on the part of the implied author for the slave girl; she may be freed of her oppressive employers, but whether or not she finds a home and fictive family is left to the reader. In the end, Spencer concludes that the citation from Joel in Acts 2 is a failed prophecy in Luke-Acts, as for all practical purposes the liberation of female slaves functions as little more than "window-dressing" in Luke-Acts (159).

The final chapter (7) considers the roles played by the different laboring women in Acts. Spencer identifies the portrait of the ideal wife in Prov 31 and Tobit as likely backdrops to the laboring women in Acts. He concludes that "Luke does not liberate women from domestic duty, but he does significantly ennoble household service" (174). Tabitha is subordinated to Peter, and her almsgiving is matched by the God-fearing Cornelius in the next episode and later by Paul (24:17). In contrast to some who envision Lydia as a prominent member of Philippian society, Spencer draws upon recent work on class distinctions and artisans in Greco-Roman antiquity and places her on the lower ledges of hierarchy, outside the city walls. Priscilla is seen by Spencer as the most liberated of the women in Acts, although her leadership role as an authoritative teacher is not before a public audience but rather as a private tutor.

Spencer presents a provocative and compelling study on women in the Gospels and Acts. The following are several aspects of his investigation that deserve special note. First, in several places Spencer references the passionate lovers in the Song of Songs as an intertextual backdrop to the narrative in the Gospels and Acts. The intertextual relevance of the Song of Songs—and the female lover—has largely not been acknowledged in past scholarly investigations of these narratives. As a result, Spencer identifies intertextuality that produces several interesting readings. Second, just as the female lover deconstructs traditional models of behavior, Spencer argues the female type and antitype in Jewish wisdom literature serves as an interpretive lens for the actions and speech of the different women characters in the Gospels and Acts. Third, while not all scholars will concur with Spencer's reading of the four women in the Matthean genealogy, they will acknowledge that he presents an intriguing counterproposal to the three interpretive stances that exist today. Fourth, Spencer provides an in-depth reading of the "loose" lady in Luke 7:36–50. In particular, the intersection of intertextual, intratextual, and extratextual referents he culls engenders a quite stimulating—perhaps even arousing—interpretation of the text. (However, on the extent of sensual, erotic connotations in Luke 7:36–50, cf. the recent article by Charles H. Cosgrove, "A Woman's Unbound Hair in the Greco-Roman World, with Special Reference to the Story of the 'Sinful Woman' in Luke 7:36-50," *JBL* 124 [2005]: 675–92.) Finally, Spencer presents a critical reading within the context of Greco-Roman—and Jewish—antiquity, exercising readings that "struggle" with the sociohistorical and literary nuances of the narrative. He uncovers instances, as a result, where the narrative conforms to patriarchal structures as well as places where the narrative subverts or runs counter to those same structures.

Despite being a valuable contribution on women in the Gospels and Acts and virtual required reading for scholars and lay people alike who are interested in the subject matter, the book does contain some deficiencies, that I hope the author and publisher will consider addressing if additional versions are released. First, the volume lacks a concluding chapter and ends very abruptly with the analysis of laboring women in chapter 7. A synopsis of the prior chapters and examination of potential trends or trajectories would be a useful addition. Second, on a similar note, the author sets forth "feminist criticism" as his methodological approach in chapter 1, and while feminist criticism is a large methodological umbrella, he assumes different methodological approaches in each of the chapters (although dominated by narrative and sociological approaches). This ad hoc methodological mixture, specifically the use of different terminology, proves somewhat confusing. (Part of this may be due to the fact that four of the seven chapters originated as essays in other publications, and the author apparently chose to make minor changes, if that, when importing them into the book.) For example, in the case of the women in John in chapter 4, Spencer elects to draw upon conversation analysis, whereas he opts to use discourse analysis—as disseminated into biblical studies by Joel B. Green—to examine the episode involving the "loose" woman in chapter 5. In all, the author would present a more cogent investigation by establishing a methodological foundation—and accompanying terminology—in chapter 1 and then using it as the basis for his ensuing analysis. Finally, while the book addresses most of the texts involving women in the Gospels and Acts, it does not cover all of them (e.g., the episode involving Mary and Martha in Luke 10:38–42; the women at the tomb and resurrection in Mark). These additions in a revised edition would prove quite useful and help the author present a more compelling, expansive picture of women in the Gospels and Acts.

The publisher and author are to be commended for their editing and proofing of the manuscript prior to publication. However, there are several errors that should be corrected if an additional edition is released, and I am sure there are some additional ones that I failed to notice. The reference to F. Gerald Downing's essay "The Woman from Syrophoenicia and her Doggedness: Mark 7:24-31 (Matthew 15:21-28)" (75 n. 84) is missing the publication date, and the scripture reference on page 147 should read "(12:13–15; 16:16–18)," not "(12:13–15; 16–18)."

In spite of these minor drawbacks, Spencer provides an interesting and stimulating analysis of women in the Gospels and Acts, and the work should be on the reading list for scholars, ministers, and even many lay people. For those who are interested in an integrated hermeneutic that seeks critically to understand the biblical narratives within a literary and social matrix, the book will be warmly welcomed. Written in an accessible style, thought provoking, and with an easy-to-digest format, the book appeals to both scholars and lay readers alike. While readers will likely not agree with all of his conclusions, they will find that Spencer provides a thorough overview of the different issues related to each issue in purview and presents some compelling—or at the very least intriguing—insights on oft-looked-at narratives and characters.

SYNOPTIC GOSPELS

Untypische Texte im Matthäusevangelium? Studien zu Charakter, Funktion und Bedeutung einer Textgruppe des matthäischen Sonderguts, by Dagmar J. Paul. Neutestamentliche Anhandlungen NS 50. Münster: Aschendorff, 2005. Pp. viii + 364. Paper. €49.00. ISBN 3402047985.

Boris Repschinski, Leopold Franzens Universität, Innsbruck, Austria A-6021

Even though studies about Matthew's Gospel abound, its special material has been given little study recently. In her 2004 dissertation at the Technische Universität Dresden, Paul sets out to remedy this situation at least with regard to some of the narrative material unique to the Gospel. Her guiding questions are how the special material is integrated into the Gospel's literary design, whether the special material has within this design a specific function, and whether there are theological consequences for the interpretation of the Gospel. With these questions in mind, Paul acknowledges that her work is indebted to the redaction-critical method. She presupposes the Two Source hypothesis and defines the special material as being transmitted only by Matthew and not by the other canonical Gospels.

The introduction contains the overall question of the study and the rationale for the selection of texts. The texts Paul selects are all narrative in character and share an element of legend or folklore that connects them with apocryphal literature (3–4). In the infancy narrative Paul selects the birth of Jesus (1:18–25), the story of the magi (2:1–12), the flight to and the return from Egypt (2:13–15, 19–23), and the slaughter of the children of Bethlehem (2:16–18). From the stories concerning Peter she selects Peter's walk on the water (14:28–31) and the temple tax pericope (17:24–27). From the passion narrative Paul selects the end of Judas (27:3–10), the dream of Pilate's wife (27:19), Pilate and the call of all the people (27:24–25), the signs at the death of Jesus (27:51b–53), and the story of the guards at the tomb (27:62–66, 28:2–4, 11–15). A brief survey of previous studies of the special Matthean material then precedes the general plan of her study.

The main work of the study is divided into three parts. The first of these offers an individual analysis of the selected pericopae. Each analysis offers first Paul's own translation of the text, followed by a synchronous interpretation and a section asking whether the text offers hints as to whether it was developed in a tradition or was a creation of the author. The final interpretation tries to draw the connections between the literary design and its theological implication. Each analysis is completed by a summary.

In general the analyses are sound, reflecting her position that Matthew sees the separation of Israel and his community as final. Occasionally some oddities stand out. Thus Paul states that the infancy narratives in general, and 1:18–25 in particular, exhibit numerous significant details that are characteristic of Matthew. She then goes on to say that this proves that the final redactor took this text from oral tradition, redesigned it, and put it into writing (26). This is a large hypothesis to be hung on the Matthean characteristics. Furthermore, sometimes her translation does not support her analysis. When translating the pericope of the cry of all the people, Paul makes no difference between *ochlos* in 27:24 and *laos* in 27:25 (88). However, in her interpretation of the passage she gives precisely this differentiation a good deal of weight (92–93). Occasionally her interpretations can be hazy. Again in the interpretation of the call of all the people, she quotes Koch (*VT* 12 [1962]: 400) without further explanation. So what precisely is a "schicksalswirkende Tatsphäre … eine dingliche, raumerfüllende Substanz," and how does it relate to those asking for the blood of Jesus?

In the second part Paul studies the motifs that guided her selection of texts in their contexts in antiquity and in apocryphal literature. First she traces dreams, magi, cosmic signs, persecution of a child, walking on water, miraculous finds of fish, death of the evildoer, washing of hands as proclamation of innocence, guarding of tombs, and theft of corpses in the literature of antiquity. Some motifs occur in Hellenistic literature, others are more plausibly explained by parallels from Jewish tradition, and again others reflect a Greco-Roman influence. All of them occur in the context of folk religion; particularly significant in this context are dreams and the belief in stars and supernatural signs. Furthermore, these motifs are usually connected with the beginning or the end of a person's life. Matthew's contribution to this field of traditional legends and folklore is the rather sober narration and their often unusual function within the narrative. For example, the temple tax pericope does not show the unchangeability of fate or the reward of a just person but serves as an unconventional solution to a rather common problem (178). Paul concludes that these elements, though soberly narrated in the Gospel, still serve the demand for popular entertainment as a side benefit.

Paul then moves on to look at how these popular motifs are taken up and developed in subsequent apocryphal Gospels. She looks at the infancy Gospels of James and others, at the traditions surrounding Peter, and at passion narratives in the Gospels of Peter and Nicodemus and in the literature connected with Pilate. While the Matthean infancy and passion motifs clearly influenced later literature, the Petrine narratives were not taken up to any significant amount. In another strand of argument Paul suggests that there are shared interests between Matthew and the apocryphal Gospels in their interest to fill gaps in the narrative, to flesh out minor characters in the narrative, and to amplify miraculous and legendary elements.

The third part moves on to place the results of the previous parts into the context of the whole Gospel. In terms of literary design, Paul shows how the special material integrates into the overall narrative of the Gospel. She pays particular attention to the groups with whom Jesus is portrayed as being in conflict but also to other groups that appear in the Gospel narrative. Her purpose here is to show how the story of Jesus is the story of God, marred by conflict and designed to be transparent to the actual reader. In terms of theological design, Paul offers comments on the fulfillment quotations, on Christology, on the people of God, and on discipleship. Obviously there is some repetition when Paul relates the literary analysis to theological themes. However, the emphasis shifts when Paul shows how the rejection of Israel by the Baptist and Jesus becomes narrative theology through the special material in the passion, to name but one example. In this part it becomes clear that for Paul the special material in Matthew needs to be seen against the background of a very specific situation of a community that has separated from Judaism and denounces the Jewish rejection of Jesus and a rejection of God.

Paul ends her volume with a conclusion that not only offers a summary but also some thoughts on further study, among them the hint that literary and theological studies alone are probably insufficient to place the material in a specific historic situation. She suggests that such observations could be augmented by sociological and historical studies. The volume concludes with a bibliography, a partial index of biblical and ancient quotations, but no index of authors. In the end, the question of the title is answered in the negative: the Matthean special material is not atypical of the Gospel but fits neatly within its overall design.

This book is valuable for several reasons. It is good to see a study of Matthew's special material, particularly one that places some of the material in the wider literary context of antiquity and early Christianity. Paul's selection of just the narrative material in Matthew is a good decision in terms of keeping the volume to a still readable length. Her conclusions are usually based on a close reading of the texts, even though her firm assertion of the rejection of Israel is a matter of controversy. Her knowledge of secondary literature, particularly in German, is commendable, even though her knowledge of English works has some significant gaps. The strength of the work lies in the first part and in the close examination of the individual texts.

Having said this, some quibbles remain. Paul fails to lay out her particular question and reason for writing this book in narrow enough terms. Her interests are in the narrative and theological design of Matthew, in the legendary character of some of the texts, in providing a background in ancient literature, and in tracing the development of the material in later Christian texts. It would have been a service to readers had she been able to focus properly on any one of these topics. Granted that they are interrelated, I still found part 2 standing beside rather than leading up to part 3. Paul readily jumps from her conclusions about literary and theological design toward the reconstruction of a community behind the Gospel with breathtaking speed. This is particularly unsatisfactory because here in particular her gaps in the reception of recent English works are apparent. For example, in her interpretation of the cry of all the people she should engage some of the literature of a different viewpoint.

This book will probably not be the last word on Matthew's special material, but one should be grateful to Paul for bringing these parts of Matthew back to scholarly discourse and for her suggestive readings of it in the context of the literature of antiquity.

Matthew 21–28, by Ulrich Luz. Hermeneia. Minneapolis: Fortress, 2005. Pp. xliv + 681. Hardcover. $90.00. ISBN 0800637704.

Edgar Krentz, Lutheran School of Theology at Chicago, Chicago, Illinois

This volume covering chapters 21–28 [the Jerusalem ministry and the passion and resurrection accounts] completes the English translation of Ulrich Luz's massive commentary on Matthew. Volume 2, *Matthew 8–20*, appeared in 2001 in the Hermeneia series, while volume 1, *Matthew 1–7* (translated by Wilhelm Linss; Minneapolis: Augsburg, 1989), will appear in a revised Hermeneia edition. This rich, detailed, comprehensive commentary far outreaches what this review can say. It is now the basic commentary that every interpreter of Matthew must consult.

What contribution does this work make to the interpretation of Matthew? It fulfills the series title, providing a critical and historical commentary on the text. Luz gives rich bibliographies for the entire work and for each section, although the concentration is on German-language publications. The outline for the interpretation of Matt 23:37–39 is typical: "Bibliography," "Original Translation" (reflecting the nuances of the German translation), "Structure," "Tradition History," "Origin and Original Meaning," "Interpretation," "Summary and History of Interpretation" (158–65); at time he also discusses the "Meaning for Today." This goes beyond what the Hermeneia series usually does, since the four-volume German original in the Evangelisch-Katholischer Kommentar zum Neuen Testament includes sections titled "Wirkungsgeschichte," "History of Interpretation" in this English translation. (I find the translation "History of Influence" in the Linss translation of volume 1 much better, more accurately reflecting what is actually done in these sections.) Lutz departs from the design of the German original, which asked contributors to stress the role these texts played in interconfessional controversy and dialogue, rarely noticed in this commentary.

Luz includes and comments on sixty-four illustrations of art as part of the history of interpretation, something not done in the earlier volumes (although there is no list of this anywhere in the volume). The end papers display Oxyrhynchus Papyri 2685 and 4405 (P^{77}, from the late second century, containing Matt 23:30–34 and 35–39, the earliest fragment of the Gospel).

What is the specific character of Luz's interpretation? He says in the preface (xv) that he found it difficult to identify with some parts of the text, such as Matt 23 ("I sometimes wished that this chapter was not in the Bible") and sections of Matt 24–25. On the contrary, he feels much more empathy with the passion and resurrection accounts. This is clearly an interpretation after the Holocaust, sensitive to possible evil implications for Jewish-Christian relations today (see 94). Luz is clearly troubled by the anti-Judean character of Matthew in these chapters. (I intentionally avoid the term anti-Semitic as anachronistic.) Luz recognizes the anti-Judaic *Tendenz* of the Gospel and presents it clearly in many places, while also expressing his unease with it.

Matthew wrote his Gospel after 70 C.E., when Jews and Jewish Christians diverged, each going through the process of self-definition. Luz recognizes this (176). Exclusion from Judaism led Matthew to stress that Jesus already rejected the Judeans and Jerusalem, that his community keeps its Jewish heritage, and that it differs from the Judeans in terms of leadership. Luz notes the omission of δίκαιος καὶ σώζων αὐτός in Matt 21:5 but does not correlate it with the cleansing of the temple or the enacted parable of the fig tree in Matt 21:18–22 or the series of three parables in 21:28–22:14. He stresses rather the word πραΰς in 21:5 and argues that Jesus enters Jerusalem as a peaceable messiah with an absence of force (no horse but a donkey). Jesus, as I read Matthew, enters Jerusalem and the temple as its judge, a motif that runs through these eight chapters. Matthew 23 follows up on the temple series and continues the motif of rejection, here clearly recognized and disliked by Luz (97–177). He calls it the "unloveliest chapter in the Gospel" (94); his struggle to come to terms with it will benefit every reader (168–75, where calls for "public theological criticism of its contents [Sachkritik]").

The commentary on the passion and resurrection is detailed. I have little to disagree with here, although I find that his interpretation of the actual death puzzles me. The words ἀφῆκεν τὸ πνεῦμα (Matt 27:50) introduce the events that follow, including the resurrection of the dead saints (Matt 27:52). Luz does not consider the possibility that Ezek 37 lies behind the sending out of the spirit or breath. Here he leans too heavily on Mark's language to interpret the phrase. Matthew 26–28 are the most heavily illustrated (nos. 3–64) section. I wish he had included some other illustrations here: mosaics of crucifixion and resurrection from Hosios Loukas or Daphne in Greece or the Isenheim Altarpiece of Matthias Gruenewald. But Luz makes marvelous use of the ones he does present.

Luz is a careful guide through the details of the text. His extensive notes, his presentation of alternative interpretations, and his clear presentation as to why he opts for his interpretation offer the careful reader the possibility of intelligently differing with specific items. See, for example, his discussion of the four words μετὰ τὴν ἔγερσιν αὐτοῦ in Matt 27:53 on pages 568–69. He regards them as extremely difficult, presents three possible ways to account for them, and makes clear why he opts for alteration: rather careless gloss. That is a mark of an outstanding commentary. His comments about the meaning for today will assist the preacher to come to terms with difficult passages and find a message for today. Finally, he gives a brief summary of "The Basic Message of Matthew's Story of Jesus" on pages 637–44. One should read this before consulting his comments on specific passages in the Gospel. This commentary makes a significant contribution to Matthean scholarship and beyond that to the use of this Gospel in the proclamation and life of the church.

Redefining Ancient Borders: The Jewish Scribal Framework of Matthew's Gospel,
by Aaron M. Gale. New York: T&T Clark, 2005. Pp. x + 197. Paper. $55.00. ISBN
0567025217.

David C. Sim, Australian Catholic University, Fitzroy, Victoria, Australia

The social setting of the Matthean community has dominated Matthean
studies in the past decade or more, and this book is a further contribution to the
current debate. The study is based upon a doctoral dissertation at Garrett-Evan-
gelical Theological Seminary under the supervision of Richard William Stegner
(until his untimely death in January 2003). Gale explores four related issues with
regard to the Matthean community: its location, its economic status, its scribal
nature, and its level of literacy.

In the introduction Gale sets out his goals, his presuppositions, and, perhaps
most importantly, his conviction that it is permissible to use later rabbinic materials to interpret the Gospel of Matthew. On this last issue he follows and defends
the previous work of Geza Vermes.

Chapter 1 involves a discussion of the Matthean community and formative
Judaism. With some fresh insights, Gale largely follows the previous work of J. A.
Overman and other scholars in claiming that the two groups came into conflict
in the power vacuum left by the Jewish War. The discussion includes a section
on the Jewishness of the Matthean community, especially as demonstrated by its
continued observance of Torah.

The following chapter discusses the location of the Matthean community. It
argues against the majority view of Antioch on the Orontes and opts for Sepphoris in Galilee. In support of his view, Gale first discusses the issue of language.
Matthew was written in Greek, but this need not point to Antioch, since Greek
was also widely spoken in Galilee. He then argues that the conflict between the
Matthean community and formative Judaism is more likely to have taken place in
Galilee, where formative Judaism was centered. Then, having dismissed the other
arguments for Antioch, Gale mounts a case for the specific location of Sepphoris.
This was the largest, wealthiest, and most influential city in Galilee. Its population
was largely Jewish, and after the Jewish War it became an important center of
traditional or conservative Judaism. For Gale, Sepphoris appears as a much more
likely candidate for the setting of Matthew's Gospel than Antioch.

Chapter 3 is a discussion of the wealth of Matthew's community. It begins
with a general survey of trade and commerce in Galilee and turns after this to
the topic of wealth in the Gospel. Gale analyzes Matthew's references to slaves,
coinage, wealth, and taxes and suggests that these imply a wealthy readership.
The fourth chapter is a study of the scribal tradition in Matthew. After an analysis of the diverse roles of the scribe in the first century, such as teacher, scholar,
interpreter, and copyist, Gale argues that scribes were the leaders of Matthew's
community and were responsible for the production of the Gospel.

The following chapter expands upon this conclusion and provides detailed
examples of scribal expertise in the Gospel itself. Here Gale highlights the

authors' creative use of various Old Testament sources and their employment of Jewish exegetical and rhetorical techniques. These bits of evidence lead Gale to the conclusion that the members of the Matthean community were themselves learned and well versed in both Hebrew and Greek.

Gale's study of the Matthean community is both welcome and timely, even if there is little in it that has not been said before. The location of the Matthean community in Galilee has been suggested by a number of scholars, although Gale does offer something new in his arguments for the specific location of Sepphoris. His discussion of the conflict between Matthew's community and formative Judaism owes much to the work of Overman and other scholars, while the point that this community was wealthy has been made by J. D. Kingsbury and others. The same is true of his work on the scribes in Matthew's community and their expertise in Jewish exegetical techniques. And it must be said that Gale always acknowledges his debt to earlier scholarship. But what is new in Gale's study is his attempt to take what have been up to now independent views about the Matthean community and to forge them into a single hypothesis. In doing so, Gale has made a very important contribution to the current debate on the setting of this community, and his work will doubtless initiate further discussion.

While reading Gale's book I often found myself agreeing with his conclusions. The Gospel does seem to be the product of a law-observant Christian Jewish community that was in conflict with formative Judaism and a community that was certainly learned and probably wealthy. I remain unconvinced that the Gospel should be located in Galilee in general and Sepphoris in particular. Despite the evidence that Greek was spoken and read in Galilee, though how widely is a matter of debate, it still seems improbable to me that a Christian community located there would have produced its definitive community document in Greek. Moreover, there is little substantial evidence for Christians in Galilee in the first century, either prior to or after the Jewish War. Whatever the inherent weaknesses of Antioch on the Orontes, it still appears to me to be the more likely location for this Gospel.

My major qualm about Gale's work is not so much what he does but what he does not do. The book is rather short for the wide range of topics it covers, and this results in it lacking detail at a number of points. For example, his contention that the Matthean community was Jewish as well as Christian and that it continued to observe the Torah is covered in the space of a few pages. Yet this is a debate that has dominated recent Matthean scholarship, and Gale's hypothesis needed to be established in detail. I happen to concur with Gale's position, but scholars who adopt a different view would be correct to call for a more substantial analysis of the complex evidence.

Gale's study also fails to mention many important books and articles by Matthean scholars. A glance at my own library of Matthean studies reveals a large number of recent texts that should have received some mention by Gale. Gale is well aware of this problem. He comments on page 1 that some fine books and articles have been omitted from his study, and he even apologizes for this on page

162, but he never really explains or justifies why this is so. While it may be the case that there were limits of space imposed by the original dissertation, these would not apply to the commercially published book. By not expanding the dissertation and thereby referring to the many important studies that one would expect to see referenced in such a wide-ranging book, Gale's work looks a little thin and not entirely up to date.

While these are serious omission in Gale's book, they do not outweigh its positive aspects. Gale has written a stimulating book with a number of fresh insights, and it deserves careful consideration by those who are interested in locating and understanding the Matthean community.

L'Evangile de Marc: Un original hebreu? by Jean-Marie Van Cangh and Alphonse Toumpsin. Langues et cultures anciennes 4. Brussels: Editions Safran, 2005. Pp. 456. Paper. €60.00. ISBN 2960046986.

Sylvie Raquel, Trinity International University, Deerfield, Illinois

The Greek language of the Gospel of Mark has always perplexed Greek scholars because of its awkwardness. Many deduce that Mark was the first Synoptic Gospel written and that Luke and Matthew corrected its bad grammar, even emended its historical and geographical blunders. Most scholars believe in an original Greek written text, although they discern a Semitic flavor in certain obvious Hebraisms (as Τί ἡμῖν καὶ σοί in Mark 1:24). Echoing Manolis Chakéis, Jean-Marie Van Cangh and Alphonse Toumpsin propose that "Greek Mark" was a translation full of errors partly due to the misreading of a Semitic source. They treat the Greek text as a filter and attempt to unearth what they deem a Semitic original text. They do not pretend to divulge the nature of this source, although they accept the usual view that Mark is a compilation of Peter's homilies. Using a comparative linguistics technique, they undertake an (admittedly purely academic) exercise to uncover the Hebraic substratum of Mark's Greek text. Their intent is to sensitize readers to the Semitic background of the Gospel and to teach them to read Mark in the light of its underlying text.

To accomplish their purpose, Van Cangh and Toumpsin work with four main hypotheses. Because the Synoptic Gospels are grounded in the same cultural and religious substratum as the Dead Sea Scrolls, they assume that the Semitic Markan source used the same biblical Hebrew language. Second, they speculate that Mark relied heavily on the LXX not only for Old Testament quotes but also for its lexicon, notably in the Siracide. Third, when the text follows the Greek order, Van Cangh and Toumpsin consider it as systematically altered (Mark 10:25). Finally, they take into consideration Mark's lexical particularities, such as Semitic transcriptions (Αββα), composites of LXX words (μονόφθαλμος), Greek loanwords brought into Semitic languages (λεγιών), and other lexical equivalences (ἀλεκτοροφωνίας). Keeping the textual configuration of the Greek uncial manuscripts, Van Cangh and Toumpsin's commentary nevertheless follows a verse-by-verse layout. Each page displays the Greek UBS text combined with the authors' Hebrew reconstitution and literal French translation of that hypothetical Semitic source. These versions, enriched by a meticulous grammatical, textual, and lexical commentary, makes *L'Évangile de Marc: un original hébreu?* an appealing reference book.

Although the authors aim for a purely theoretical exercise, certain puzzling passages of Mark find meaning when seen in the light of a Hebrew substratum. For example, some of their reconstitutions bring new semantic perspectives. The best example is found in their rendition of Mark 9:49. The UBS reads πᾶς γὰρ πυρὶ ἁλισθήσεται, which most translations render as "for everyone will be salted with fire." Van Cangh and Toumpsin found examples in the Dead Sea Scrolls of the Semitic root מלח, which means either "to salt" or "to volatilize, to reduce to pieces" (see Isa 51:6). Selecting the latter meaning, they translate the verse, "all will be reduced to pieces by the fire," thus clarifying an ambiguous verse. They suggest also that other enigmatic passages may be the result of a wrong reading of the original Semitic word. In Mark 14:54 they affirm that the Hebrew word translated "τὸ φῶς" was אור. If vocalized with וֹ, the word means "light," but if vocalized with וּ, the word means "fire." Accordingly, Van Cangh and Toumpsin's rendition "Peter ... who was warming up by the fire" improves on the traditional translation. Along the same vein, Mark 8:33 could also be due to an interchange between a *patach* and a *tsêrê*. The writers' reconstituted original sentence becomes, therefore, אַחֲרֵי הַשָּׂטָן לֵךְ לְךָ "then be Satan's disciple." With this translation, Jesus did not rebuke Peter by "calling" him Satan but asked him to choose between Satan in verse 33 and himself in verse 34. Here Van Cangh and Toumpsin show that the wrong vocalization of an original Hebrew may have had theological implications. Finally, their approach allows them to solve diverse textual problems. In Mark 5:2 the possessed man comes to Jesus (ὑπαντάω), while in verse 6 he sees Jesus from far away (ἀπὸ μακρόθεν), runs, and falls at his feet. If ὑπαντάω translates the verb קָרָא (see Sir 12:17), as the authors suggest, that same verb can also mean "scream"; this latter meaning fits the context of the passage.

Van Cangh and Toumpsin exploit their method to make textual decisions concerning the Greek text. At times their approach directs them to decide between two equivalent textual variants. In Mark 6:22 they choose the pronoun αὐτῆς over αὐτοῦ as the only possible solution because it corresponds to an Aramaism where a personal pronoun is used to anticipate or to emphasize the following noun. At other times Van Cangh and Toumpsin choose variants against the decision of the UBS committee. Instead of ἐπὶ Ἀβιαθὰρ ἀρχιερέως "Abiathar the high priest" in Mark 2:26, they consider the variant ἐπὶ Ἀβιαθὰρ τοῦ ἀρχιερέως, which would translate עַל אֶבְיָתָר אֲשֶׁר לַכֹּהֵן "Abiathar of the high priest's family." This reconstruction allows them to erase a seeming historical error. The writers also reassess some UBS ratings. For example in Mark 6:44 the question about the original τοὺς ἄρτους does not arise, since the term לֶחֶם can take the general sense of "food."

Despite some interesting new readings, Van Cangh and Toumpsin's methodology is inconsistent and leads them to make contradictory statements. They consider that Mark was at times approximate about his translation, while at other times they credit him with meticulous selections of Greek words (ἱματίζω over ἐνδύω or ἐνδιδύσκω in 5:15). While they confer on Mark primarily a Hebraic original, they posit occasionally an Aramaic original. For example, in Mark 9:18 Van Cangh and Toumpsin argue that a confusion between the hiphil forms of יָבֵשׁ "to dry up" and בּוֹשׁ "to be shameful" is at the origin of the Greek translation, a confusion impossible in Aramaic. However, in Mark 1:45; 3:4; and 9:22 they choose the Aramaic term over the Hebrew one without the benefit of explanation. Their hypothesis about Mark's use of the LXX also leads them to dead ends. For example, they cannot answer why "Greek Mark" used in 6:21 the expression τοῖς γενεσίοις, which is foreign to the LXX. Other inconsistencies include the fact that they think Mark 7:16 should be added but ignore its translation and that 16:8 marks the end of the original Gospel but continue the reconstitution beyond that point.

Besides the issue of the Hebrew and Greek texts, a disconcerting undertone transpires in the French translation. Why did Van Cangh and Toumpsin use "se déplaçant" instead of "marchant sur la mer" in Mark 6:48, rendering the translation "he came toward them moving (instead of walking) on the sea?" Jesus appears to hover as a ghostly figure, as if he were unable to defy the laws of nature in his humanity, as if he were obliged to step out of his humanness for a short while. In the same way, the authors never use the word "résurrection" and replace it by the word "relèvement," which simply means "raising" as "standing up" (Mark 12:18, 23). This translation removes the supernatural and miraculous aspect of the event, reducing it to the scale of a mere explainable fact. To what degree was the French translation really dictated by the Hebrew text?

Despite the various inconsistencies, Van Cangh and Toumpsin have achieved their goal to sensitize the readers to the Semitic color of the Gospel of Mark. Yet the present book raises one question on the issue of authorship. Based on Papias's statement, the writers affirm that Mark used Peter's Hebrew and Aramaic oral preaching and transposed them into Greek. The question is whether Mark wrote his Gospel from memory or translated his own handwritten notes. Van Cangh and Toumpsin seem indecisive and treat the Greek text sometimes as the translation of an oral source but most of the time of a written source. If the Gospel of Mark is the product of Peter's secretary, an original writer who did not have a good command of Greek, how could he make such mistakes as the authors suspect in 2:26; 5:1–6; 9:49; and 14:54? Certainly Mark would have known the original content of each homily and avoided such misreading. Or is Mark's Gospel the work of a translator who was not well acquainted with Hebrew but so concerned with his loyalty to the text that he rendered an extremely literal Greek translation? Van Cangh and Toumpsin's interpretation would suggest so.

Die Gleichnisse Jesu im Matthäusevangelium: Eine Studie zu ihrer Form und Funktion, by Christian Münch. Wissenschaftliche Monographien zum Alten und Neuen Testament 104. Neukirchen-Vluyn: Neukirchener, 2004. Pp. x + 331. Cloth. €54.00. ISBN 3788720352.

Ruben Zimmermann and Georg Gäbel, Universität Bielefeld, Bielefeld, Germany

Contemporary scholarship on the parables is characterized by a remarkable tension. On the one hand, the parables of Jesus have, since Jeremias, been regarded as the "bedrock" of the Jesus-tradition; on the other hand, since Via's study, parables have been considered to be "autonomous works of poetic art." Chr. Münch's Ph.D. dissertation, which was accepted at the University of Bochum, consciously aims at combining diachronic and synchronic questions. It consistently places the parables within the context of one Gospel, but in so doing, it pays attention especially to their literary form and to the narrative devices used in the telling of parables.

The aim of this study, then, is to describe the way Matthew received parables and shaped them according to his particular understanding of that genre (3–7), thus describing, in an exemplary fashion, the understanding of parables in one Synoptic Gospel. Münch's study of the parables is not a contribution to the ongoing quest for the historical Jesus. Münch's approach is a synchronic one, and his methodology is strongly influenced by narrative criticism. Although Münch does not in principle avoid diachronic questions, he firmly places them within the context of his investigation of Matthew's understanding of the parables. Here Münch follows recent research and attempts to complement it (56–57). In choosing the texts that serve as the material for his study, Münch therefore works with definitions of "parables" that are common in modern secondary sources (6–7).

The book is subdivided into three parts (A: 3–60; B: 61–290; C: 291–306). Part A gives a short overview of the relevant aspects of scholarship since Jülicher's *Die Gleichnisreden Jesu* and describes the aims, methods, and structure of Münch's own work. Part C is a short summary of the main results.

In Part B, Münch describes the specific shape of Matthew's understanding of the parables. This part is broken down into five chapters that deal with (1) the frames of the parables, (2) Matthew's use of the term παραβολή and his particular version of the parable theory, (3) the introductions of the parables, (4) the narrative devices used in the parables, and (5) the endings of the parables. Although Münch generally follows the methodology of *Erzähltextanalyse*, or narrative criticism, he includes analyses of tradition and Matthean redaction in the chapters on the introductions of the parables, the narrative devices, and the endings of the parables.

Without following the course of the investigation in detail, the most important results may be summarized in the following four points. (1) Matthew has a clear awareness of "parables" as a particular genre and of their formal features, and he makes specific use of the term παραβολή. He consciously cultivates this genre and has a tendency to increase its uniformity. His parables can be described with regard to their form (narrativity increasingly emerges as one typical, though not strictly necessary, feature), content (Matthean parables are generally concerned with the βασιλεία), and function (they mostly have to do, in one way or another, with the problem of understanding or lack thereof).

(2) Parables as a genre draw attention to the difficulties and preconditions of understanding the person, message, and ministry of Jesus Christ and the coming of the βασιλεία in him. Thus, understanding the parables as well as a failure to understand them mirrors those difficulties and conditions in an exemplary fashion, but it is not the parables themselves that cause these difficulties. As parables require interpretation and refer to Matthean and wider biblical contexts, they turn out to be a particularly suitable medium for discourse concerning the βασιλεία.

(3) Parables contain numerous contextual references created by means of their introductions, endings, and narrative devices. They refer to Jesus, to his proclamation, and to his story as told in the Gospel, to the history of Israel and of the church, and to the eschatological future. Using conventional metaphors, motives, and formulae, they locate themselves within the framework of biblical tradition. Yet the significance of parables goes beyond their literary contexts. Although narrative devices serve, as it were, to fade in a second level of meaning, indicating the intended interpretation, the narrative itself always remains indispensable for the constitution of meaning.

(4) Münch practices considerable moderation in his evaluations of diachronic analyses. He finds that in shaping the parables Matthew largely follows tradition. His redactional activity lies in the strengthening of individual traits, the sharpening of profiles, and the standardizing of the genre's formal features. Matthew creates compositions and references to the context, and he sharpens details that can serve to influence the interpretation.

Münch's study is characterized by a highly reflected methodology and intensive exegetical engagement with the texts. Furthermore, he presents his results in systematic overviews (in parts B and C). Still, this form of presentation does not always make it easy for readers to follow Münch's reasoning. It might have been more helpful had he elucidated his approach in a paradigmatic exegesis of one parable. His decision to concentrate on longer narrative texts is based on previous scholarship, not on Matthew's own terminology (cf., e.g., Matt 15:11 with 15:15–20). It is also hardly convincing that Münch deals only marginally (B.iv.4b) with longer compositions of parables (Matt 13; 21; 24), which are so important for the redaction process of the Gospel. And in some places readers might wish to be given more detailed information, as relevant insights are expressed with remarkable brevity (one thinks, e.g., of the functioning of the interplay between metaphors and parable narratives [B.iv.2a]). Given that Matthew expressly calls parables the form of speech addressed to the obdurate and to those who are hard of hearing (Matt 13:13–15), does it really suffice to say that parables need special interpretation (112–14)?

These critical remarks notwithstanding, attention should be drawn to the valuable insights resulting from Münch's study, of which three in particular could have far-reaching consequences. (1) Matthew's parables are not autonomous literary entities. Rather, they are firmly connected to their contexts in the Gospel. Therefore, efforts to understand Matthew's parables should be embedded in an appraisal of that Gospel as a literary and theological whole. (2) As he examines Matthew's devices of contextualization and reference, Münch provides an important impulse toward overcoming the dichotomy of diachronic and synchronic approaches. This could lead, as it were, to a form-critical approach in reverse order. Matthew's position could be described as one step in the history of the evolving genre of parables. It would be worthwhile to compare Matthew's concept of parables with other concepts in the early Christian stream of memory, tradition, and literature and to place it within their context. (3) Given Matthew's awareness of parables as a genre, we need to call into question Jülicher's classifications of parables. The distinction between *Gleichnis* and *Parabel,* still prevalent in German-speaking exegesis, is not justified here, nor is the exclusion of shorter units (which Münch, unfortunately, adopts); see Matt 15:11, 15.

Thus, Münch's study offers numerous impulses for further study. With its methodological reflections, meticulous exegesis, and balanced judgments, this book will doubtless find the attention it merits in scholarship both on Matthew and on the parables.

From Q to "Secret" Mark: A Composition History of the Earliest Narrative Theology, by Hugh M. Humphrey. London: T&T Clark, 2006. Pp. v + 170. Paper. $29.95. ISBN 0567025128.

Kari Syreeni, Uppsala University, Uppsala, Sweden

Hugh Humphrey is Professor of Religious Studies at Fairfield University, Connecticut, and author of *"He Is Risen!": A New Reading of Mark's Gospel* (New York: Paulist, 1992). In his new book he moves beyond narrative criticism toward the compositional stages of the earliest narrative Gospel. The subtitle combines literary and theological interests: "If 'theology' first of all is the process of bringing faith to expression, the composition history of Mark's Gospel illustrates that process" (7). Humphrey goes programmatically behind the text into its composition, theological interests, the communities for which Mark wrote, and even Mark's biography.

The main title, however, promises more than the book delivers. This is not a book about Q or the so-called "Secret" Mark; the focus is solely on the making of the canonical Mark. To summarize the thesis, the present Gospel of Mark came into being in three stages. The largest and oldest constituent was a narrative version of Q ("QN"), a text comprising most of Mark 1–13. To this was added the passion-resurrection story ("PN," most of Mark 14–16). As these were put together, some necessary and complementary editing was done, which produced the Gospel as we now have it. One and the same person was responsible for the whole composition process: "In my view, the Gospel of Mark results not from the editing of unattested documents by an unknown redactor for unspecified purpose(s), but from the ever-maturing theological reflection of the Christian tradition's first evangelist, Mark" (7). This Mark does not seem to be the John Mark of Jerusalem but rather an educated and affluent person from Alexandria (see 84 n. 30). He was at one time Peter's interpreter in Rome, then the founder of the Alexandrian church. The place of composition is of minor importance because the writing and editing may have taken place in different situations during "some fifteen to twenty years" (141). More specifically, Humphrey suggests that QN was written in Alexandria in the late 30s and PN was begun in Rome in the 40s (88, 140–41); the final Gospel was edited in Alexandria in the 50s.

Much of the possible appeal of this bold hypothesis rests on Humphrey's reading of the early church fathers. Chapter 1 ("Revisiting the Fathers" [9–38]) rehearses the patristic evidence but, unfortunately, stretches the data. Papias's testimony in Eusebius (*Hist. eccl.* 3.39) would refer not to the present Mark but to an earlier text without a passion story. This makes quite a lot of the fact that, according to Papias's Elder, the Markan document recorded "the things said and done by the Lord." Clement of Alexandria, again according to Eusebius, wrote as follows: "As Peter had preached the Word publicly at Rome, and declared the Gospel by the Spirit, many … requested that Mark … should write them out." Humphrey concludes that, if Clement is referring to something that happened as early as the 40s, "then it would be likely that the content of 'the Word' and of 'the Gospel' was simply the proclamation of the death and resurrection of Jesus" (16). This is hardly a compelling interpretation, but it provides Humphrey with a reference to the Markan passion-resurrection story (PN).

To find a reference to the (next-to-)final version of Mark's Gospel, Humphrey employs the controversial document found (if that is the word) by Morton Smith: Clement's letter to Theodore. Humphrey is aware of the "quite tentative value of this text" (33), but its authenticity would obviously suit his thesis, if only after another unexpected interpretation. Smith's "Clement" writes as follows: "But when Peter died a martyr, Mark came over to Alexandria, bringing both his own notes and those of Peter, from which he transferred to his former book the things suitable to whatever makes for progress towards knowledge. Thus he composed a more spiritual Gospel for the use of those who were being perfected." Humphrey takes the "former book" for his QN and the "more spiritual Gospel" for his PN. The latter text was "secret" because it "disclosed the 'secret' of God's plan for Jesus and for all humankind: the complete giving of self" (35). Humphrey further concludes that Smith's "Clement" would not yet refer to the final Mark but to a penultimate version kept in Alexandria that "apparently included materials now lost to us," such as the insertion between Mark 10:34 and 10:35. (35 n. 47) However, Smith's "Clement" is hardly saying that the "secret" Mark consists of the passion-resurrection story of Mark 14–16. One also wonders why the passion story that (according to Humphrey's reading of an undisputed Clementine excerpt) was preached by Peter publicly in Rome became a secret in Alexandria.

Chapter 2 ("A Narrative Version of 'Q'" [39–88]) deals with the assumed

Vorlage of Mark 1–13. The sample of thematic parallels with Q and Mark 1–13 is taken to prove that Mark compiled a narrativized version of Q. This rather original hypothesis is alleviated by Humphrey's contention that "Q" (with quotation marks) was a common tradition known to all the (Synoptic) Evangelists, rather than a written document used by Matthew and Luke (40). After a full reconstruction of the QN text (50–83), Humphrey discusses the community behind this document (84–88), concluding that it was an apocalyptically oriented Jewish Christian community open toward the Gentile world. Typical of QN is the designation of Jesus as the "Son" (of God, of Man) and the "Teacher." Also, the motifs of the Lord's Prayer would be implicit throughout the text. Humphrey does not mention Peter in this chapter. Later it is suggested that Mark "learned the traditions about Jesus' teachings (the Q material) from Peter" (141).

Chapter 3 ("The Passion Narrative in Mark" [89–116]) interprets the passion-resurrection story as a narrative dramatization of Pauline themes, especially those present in the Christ hymn of Phil 2. Apart from minor glosses, the end chapters of the final Mark reproduce the PN document (full reconstruction, 103–12). Lastly, there follows a discussion of the community reflected by the passion narrative (112–16). Having previously stressed the impact of Pauline theology, Humphrey now characterizes the community as Jewish Christian and nonapocalyptic. The relation of this material to Peter is not at issue. Elsewhere we learn that Mark was particularly influenced by Peter's passion-resurrection kerygma in Rome (36, 141).

Chapter 4 ("Assimilation and a Focus on Discipleship" [117–38]) describes how Mark edited his earlier texts to produce a coherent whole. At this late stage his interest moved from Jesus' life and teachings to paradigms of disciples for the period after Jesus. The secrecy theme belongs here: "the effect of the motif of Jesus' privately explaining the secrets of the kingdom of God to his disciples (4:10–20) and of his private disclosures to his disciples about his impending death and resurrection (8:31; 9:31; 10:33–34) create a sense of a secrecy" (117). The secrecy motif was vital for Mark and the community he led in Egypt, because they perceived themselves as pressured and persecuted by Jewish neighbors and Roman authorities.

Chapter 5 ("The Composition History of the Gospel of Mark" [139–47]) summarizes the study's results and fleshes out the emerging picture of Mark the author. Two appendices follow. The first (149–54) argues against the "Mark without Q" hypothesis (Goulder, Goodacre). The second (155–62) deals with the Proto-Mark hypotheses proposed by Burkett and Boismard. In both cases most readers would accept Humphrey's main criticisms. I doubt, however, that his own hypothesis will gain wider acceptance. My problems begin with the ambiguities and the diffuseness of the hypothesis. For instance, was Peter the source and representative of two quite distinct theologies (those reflected in Q/QN and PN)? Further difficulties arise from the credulous and harmonizing use of patristic witnesses. The extremely early date for Mark's initial composition (a narrative elaboration of Q material in the 30s!) is another oddity, and the list could be made longer. However, the idea that Mark combined two larger blocks of material, still to be discerned in Mark 1–13 and 14–16, is interesting and deserves further scrutiny.

Despite its obvious shortcomings, the present study might be a sign of the times. The decades since Rhoads and Michie's *Mark as Story* (1st ed. 1982) have been characterized by a growing interest in the narrative shape of the final Gospels (which I think is good) and a diminished or absent interest in the literary and real-life history behind them (which is a pity). Are redaction criticism, diachronic study, and historical survey coming up again? Or are the Gospel studies just becoming more diversified so as to allow any relevant method of inquiry, old or new? In either case, I would not regret it; what matters is the quality of the analysis.

The Empty Tomb Tradition of Mark: Text, History, and Theological Struggles, by Mark W. Waterman. Theology, History, and Biblical Studies Series 1. Los Angeles: Agathos, 2006. Pp. xiv + 255. Cloth. $150.00. ISBN 1933740000.

Michael R. Licona, University of Pretoria, Pretoria, South Africa

Waterman completed his Ph.D. program at Fuller Theological Seminary in 2005, where Colin Brown was his mentor. This monograph is his published dissertation. The goal of his research was "to clarify the theological role of the Markan empty tomb tradition, as compared with that of the appearance tradition" (2). Moreover, Waterman claims that "if this study is successful, we should be able to test the truth-claim and historicity of the empty tomb" (8). Waterman considered literature written on the subject since 1980 in English and German and claims that, while other scholars focus on the priority of the appearance traditions, his monograph is the first "book length effort in North America to set the empty tomb at center stage in resurrection studies," with the lone exception of a 1966 Harvard Th.D. dissertation (7).

In chapter 1 Waterman discusses (1) the nonrecognition element in the reports of the empty tomb and the resurrection appearances (appearances) and (2) the appearances in Matthew, Luke, and John. Although understanding that every historian brings his or her horizon to the text, Waterman approaches the text with "Cartesian methodical doubt," which pauses frequently to ask whether the assertion is actually known, but also with a methodical credulity that defaults to belief rather than skepticism (12–13). Waterman sets out to discover how the disciples came to know and believe that Jesus had been raised. He acknowledges that contemporary scholars almost universally reject the position that the empty tomb alone kindled the belief that Jesus had been raised (15). But are the appearances alone responsible? Waterman answers in the negative (19). The Gospels and especially the Synoptics speak of a certain ambiguity in the appearance reports. In Matthew, some "doubted" when they saw Jesus. In Luke, the Emmaus disciples did not recognize Jesus, and the group of disciples were "unbelieving" upon seeing him. In John, the disciples did not recognize Jesus, who called to them from the beach. Accordingly, he concludes that "the appearances on their own could not confirm the resurrection of Jesus" (35).

In chapter 2 Waterman discusses the textual variances of Mark's ending. He identifies three major endings: 16:1–8; 16:1–8 plus the "shorter ending"; and 16:1–20, often referred to as the "longer ending." He also notes two other forms: the Freer Logion, which is 16:1–20 plus some text inserted between verses 14 and 15 found only in W; and 16:1–8 plus the "shorter ending" plus 9–20. Waterman notes that Mark's longer ending has "enormous" manuscript support and that the earliest manuscript for the longer ending is very close in time to the earliest manuscript that ends with 16:1–8 (46). The longer ending likewise finds support in many of the ante-Nicene fathers in the second and third centuries. Notwithstanding, the vocabulary and style of 9–20 casts doubt on its authenticity (47). The authenticity of the fourth form (W) "has been rejected by almost all modern critics" (47). Waterman concludes with the majority of scholars that the first form, which ends with 16:1–8, "is the oldest, most authentic *extant* textual evidence at our disposal" (50). However, he brackets the question of whether this was Mark's intended ending until chapter 3, in which he concludes that it was (83).

In chapter 3 Waterman discusses scholarly positions on the empty tomb in consideration of Markan endings and possible pre-Markan tradition. He divides these positions into four categories: (1) 16:1–8 is Mark's intended ending/empty tomb is unhistorical; (2) 16:1–8 is Mark's intended ending/empty tomb is historical; (3) 16:1–8 is not Mark's intended ending/empty tomb is unhistorical; and (4) 16:1–8 is not Mark's intended ending/empty tomb is historical. Although advocates of 3 and 4 claim that the original ending was either lost, suppressed, or never completed, Waterman claims, "As far as I can tell, there is no serious concrete proposal of these options in the academic literature" (56). By this, I understand Waterman as claiming that there are none that include detailed positive arguments for how the ending was lost, rather than an absence of arguments that it was lost. Based on his research of the literature since 1980, Waterman states that the number of scholars supporting category 1 has been decreasing since 1980 (82). Category 2 enjoys a "significantly large" majority, and Waterman lists thirty-one scholars in support (67–68, 82, 83, 213–19). He found no one since 1980 who embraced category 3 (75, 83). Although category 4 consists of a minority, "the recent trend of scholarship is surely in the direction of this thesis" (83), and a number of those in this camp "are becoming very influential on this topic" (75). He then gives some space to arguments offered by Grant Osborne, Robert Gundry, Craig A. Evans, Ben Witherington III, N. T. Wright, and Richard Swinburne (75–82).

In chapter 4 Waterman discusses the Markan continuation theory, which sees continuity between Mark's passion and resurrection narratives, in contrast to Markan redaction theory and Markan creation theory. With Dunn, Waterman finds it difficult to draw the line between source and tradition (85). Answering Crossan's arguments against the historicity of the empty tomb, Waterman writes that Crossan only displays his convictions rather than providing arguments. Thus, his creation theory is "an unreasonable and wrongheaded discussion of the tradition *before* Mark" (96). He later adds that "Crossan's complicated reconstruction … of the Markan text, is untenable, or at least unarguable, because of its intangible basis and presuppositions" (209). Waterman asserts that there is "no consensus on the historicity of the 'Markan community'" (103), and agreement among scholars on the content of a pre-Markan tradition is rare (119). Accordingly, "it is practical to seek the tradition behind the text rather than to run after the imaginative 'original' text" (120). Waterman believes that Perkin's Markan continuation theory is "promising and plausible" because of its "logically consistent theological meaning owing to the continuous events of Jesus' death and resurrection" (209).

In chapter 5 Waterman attempts to identify the "historical nuclei of the Markan tradition" in the empty tomb narrative (121). He discusses three areas of interest. First, the archaeological and historical evidence affirms that the traditional site of the empty tomb is authentic. Second, the early tradition of Sunday worship is affirmed by the majority of scholars (135). Having discussed three major texts (1 Cor 16:2; Acts 20:7; Rev. 1:10), he concludes that, although a firm connection cannot be made, there is "no conclusive information to negate some connections between Sunday worship and Jesus' resurrection" (139). His third area of interest is the tradition of witnesses, namely, the women. Although there are no rules in the Torah that women must be excluded as witnesses, the first-century Mediterranean world was decisively androcentric. Moreover, Mark employs a term related to an eyewitness (*theorein*) and notes a sufficient number of witnesses (two or three; Deut 19:15) for the empty tomb. Granted, it is certainly possible that Mark employed these only to lend a ring of authenticity to his fictitious narrative. However, given the truth of the Markan creation theory, why not create male witnesses in order to get more mileage (143)? Mark listed the women only because "they were the sole eyewitnesses to the scene of the empty tomb" (144). Although Waterman admits the absence of any "crucial evidence" in support, he conjectures that a very young Mark witnessed Jesus' crucifixion and/or burial, but not the empty tomb, and that his age prohibited him from acting as a witness (144). He concludes that the three areas of interest just discussed—the site of the empty tomb, the early tradition of Sunday worship, and the women as witnesses to the empty tomb—provide historical credibility to Mark's empty tomb narrative, although they stop short of proving historicity (146).

In chapter 6 Waterman investigates the traditions pertaining to the tomb's location embedded in Mark's empty tomb narrative. It is historically plausible that Jesus was buried by Joseph. The description of the tomb in the resurrection narratives is that of a tomb owned by a person of wealth and/or prestige. Constantine's erection of the church of the Holy Sepulcher and a recent archaeological find indicate that Jesus' tomb was probably venerated by pilgrims.

In his seventh chapter, Waterman completes his comments pertaining to the theological challenges in Mark's empty tomb tradition. Contra Bultmann, "signs and wonders can be demonstrable and can be understood logically and intellectually, but the demonstration is, to be sure, not always accepted by everyone" (173). However, Waterman admits that it is an epistemological issue and provides no defense of his position in this volume. (Granted, he argues for the historicity of the empty tomb, but he does not argue for a supernatural cause for its emptiness.) However, he criticizes simple dismissals of the miraculous by Lüdemann as "a naïve reductionistic view" (178). In answer to Küng that *the conclusions of natural science have rendered [the empty tomb] suspect,*" he writes, "there is no scholarly conclusion of 'natural science' regarding the empty tomb; in my view, this is an irresponsible and nonsensical comment in the name of science" (193). Instead, "historical criticism" has generated a different conclusion that "not a few, but rather a majority, of contemporary scholars believe that there is some historical kernel in the empty tomb tradition" (192–93). He also maintains that the empty tomb tradition is more firm than the appearance traditions: "While the appearance tradition has a variety of details or sub-traditions in mostly unidentified timeframes and locations, the empty tomb tradition, at least within the four canonical Gospels, enjoys a consistent story line in the specific timeframe, 'early morning on the first day of the week,' and in the specific locality, the City of Jerusalem" (198). Finally, Waterman discusses Petrine tradition behind Mark. At present, the majority of recent scholarship is inclined to trust Papias's testimony about Mark, although it is "roughly plausible" and "still controversial" (201–2). One of the reasons for this confidence is that Sinaiticus and Vaticanus preserve Mark with the difficult ending at 16:8. Petrine tradition, which no one dared omit, explains well this preservation with the three other Gospels. He cites arguments by Dewey and Marcus to the contrary and comments that Marcus's in particular is "doubt for the sake of doubt—unlike the Cartesian methodical doubt" (201).

In the end, Waterman concludes that the resurrection faith of the earliest Christians "cannot be explained solely by the post-Easter appearance stories of the risen Jesus" and that "[i]n view of the Markan continuation tradition, there could be no appearance traditions (in either Galilee or Jerusalem) apart from the empty tomb" (211–12). An appendix provides abstracts on thirty-one scholars since 1980 who maintain that Mark ends with 16:8 and that the empty tomb tradition contains kernels of historical truth.

Waterman has contributed to the present discussion pertaining to the historicity of Jesus' resurrection. His goal of clarifying "the theological role of the Markan empty tomb tradition, as compared with that of the appearance tradition," was accomplished. Moreover, his broad knowledge of scholarly discussions on the empty tomb since 1980 and their positions is confirmed by the recent research of Gary R. Habermas, who arrived at similar conclusions pertaining to trends ("Resurrection Research from 1975 to the Present: What are Critical Scholars Saying?" *Journal for the Study of the Historical Jesus* 3 [2005]: 135–53, especially 140–41). Waterman provides welcomed friendly aids throughout, such as a statement of content at the beginning of every chapter and a brief conclusion chapter that summarizes his chapter-by-chapter findings as well as a summary of his conclusions.

The subtitle of this monologue is "Text, History, and Theological Struggles." While the "text" and "theological struggles" components are strong and helpful, the "history" component is somewhat weak. Waterman's historical method is rarely explained or defended. For example, although he is public with his approach of methodical credulity (12–13), he would have done better to have gone further and defend why credulity is preferable to the methodical skepticism he criticizes Lüdemann (178) and Marcus (201) for employing. Moreover, his treatment of alternative hypotheses is limited. Furthermore, his treatment of Paul's pertinent texts, while helpful, fell short and could have benefited from a more rigorous discussion on Paul's view of resurrection.

The Pre-existent Son: Recovering the Christologies of Matthew, Mark, and Luke, by Simon Gathercole. Grand Rapids: Eerdmans, 2006. Pp. xii + 344. Paper. $32.00. ISBN 0802829015.

James D. G. Dunn, Durham University, Durham, United Kingdom

In short order Simon Gathercole has produced another strongly argued thesis in close dialogue with a host of other scholars who have ventured into the field. His mastery of ancient sources and of languages ancient and modern is impressively displayed. And his thesis is argued with lucidity, tenacity, and a consistent desire to let the text speak for itself. His case is, briefly, that, in contrast to the dominant strain of English-language scholarship on the subject, there is substantial evidence for the view that the Synoptic Evangelists thought of Christ as preexistent: "the really controversial point to be made in this book is that *the pre-existence of Christ can be found in the Synoptic Gospels*" (1).

After a brief introductory review of previous research, the subject is introduced with two preliminary chapters. The first briefly restates the general consensus that preexistence Christology was already widespread in Christian communities well before 70 C.E., as attested by Paul and other New Testament texts (including a rather extensive treatment of Jude 5). The second reviews more extensively the evidence that Matthew, Mark, and Luke regard Jesus as already in his earthly, pre-Easter situation having a heavenly identity and as "also operating at the same time in the heavenly sphere" (47), with reference to the transfiguration narrative, texts such as Mark 13:32, Luke 10:18–20, and Matt 18:20, and episodes of Jesus forgiving sins, walking on water, and the like.

The main case is built, in part 2, on the "I have come" sayings of Jesus (chs. 3–6); these form the heart of the book (83–189). These suggest a coming from *somewhere* with *a prior intent*; that somewhere is heaven, while the prior intent is that of the preexistent Son. More detail will become clear in the critique that follows the summary overview.

Part 3 focuses on a critique of the Wisdom Christology hypothesis (ch. 8) and a detailed study of Matt 23:37 (ch. 9). The claim here is that "rumors of a full-blown Wisdom Christology in the Synoptics have in some cases been greatly exaggerated" (209), referring particularly to Matt 11:18–19, 27–30 and 23:34 (with Lukan parallels). Matthew 23:37, however, portrays Jesus "as a figure who transcends the particular generation of Israel into which he was born" (221).

Part 4 focuses on various christological titles in the Synoptics. The *anatolē* of Luke 1:78 cannot be reduced to "a merely human, Davidic Messiah" (242). Mark 1:2–3 could possibly be describing "a prehistorical scene which stands outside of the narrated time of his Gospel" (251). In Matthew's use of Ps 78:2 (Matt 13:35), the "I" "makes best logical sense as the pre-existent Son of Man" speaking (265). In Matt 11:27 the imagery of Jesus' presence in the heavenly council at the deliberation of the predestined divine purpose, and the talk of the Son being sent in Mark 12:6 may point in the same direction (ch. 13). A final chapter makes a few brief comments on a number of adjoining issues, including the relation of preexistence to virgin birth, Christ's humanity, and the cross, as well as on the concept of "ideal" pre-existence.

I have already communicated directly with Simon (Dr. Gathercole) to indicate various concerns about his thesis. In particular, on his major "I have come" thesis, it seems to me that he makes too much of a distinction between a once-only mission and a lifelong ministry. This allows him to discount the well-known parallel of Josephus' claim to speak with divine authority when prophesying Vespasian's accession to the imperial throne: "I have come (*hēkō*) to you as a messenger of greater things" (*War* 3.400). But the parallels he then draws on for his support—angels saying "I have come"—are for the most part of the same order (once-only missions). So the more appropriate inference to draw, I think, is that the "I have come" formula expresses a sense of or claim to divine commissioning, whether the commission is short- or long-term. I am also surprised that he does not consider other parallels, in particular:

♦ Ps40:7 (quoted on 174): "I have come (*hēkō*) to do your will" (as quoted by Heb 10:9); in Ps 40 the psalmist is speaking.
♦ John the Baptist as the "coming (*elthein*)" of Elijah (Mark 9:11–13), with allusion to Mal 3:1–2 and 4:5–6; the Baptist is clearly thought of as divinely commissioned, but does that imply that the Baptist is also preexistent?
♦ We also need to mention the Baptist's expectation of *ho erchomenos* (Matt 11:3). Can we be sure that the Baptist implied or was understood to imply a heavenly rather than a divinely commissioned figure? Justin Martyr reminds us that Messiah was widely understood to be a "man born of men" (*Dial.* 49).
♦ Likewise, the equivalence of "I have come" with "I was sent" suggests an equivalent sense of divine commissioning such as prophets expressed.

So again the question arises whether talk of "coming" is simply a way of speaking of someone's appearance as foretold or as divinely commissioned.

I am particularly surprised that Simon does not give consideration to the possibility, I would say likelihood, that Jesus himself at least occasionally used the form "I have come." I know Simon does not want to become caught up in historical Jesus issues, but the issue cannot be escaped. Because, if Jesus himself did use the key phrase, then that in itself could explain why the Synoptic Evangelists use it: Jesus himself, we could then say, was the source of the usage. Moreover, if Jesus did use it, should we not ask how he would have understood the phrase or, if that is too difficult a question to deal with, how his words would have been understood by Jesus' auditors? Here it should be noted that there is no indication in the Synoptic tradition of any of his hearers taking offense at the formulation, no one saying, "Who is this that claims to be an angelic emissary?" Such considerations cannot be ignored so completely if we are fully to investigate the implications of the Synoptic usage.

As a second large concern, I am sorry to say that I find a degree of naiveté in some of the basic conceptuality being employed. Simon declines to spell out what he means by "preexistence" but is happy to speak of Jesus preexisting "as a person," "having actual prior existence," "personal preexistence," "an actually preexistent person or being," "a transhistorical persona" (5–6, 8, 209, 218 n. 23). In the last few pages he acknowledges that "the concept of 'person' (raises) another set of questions of its own" (291 n. 31), but he does not follow them up. But this is a crucial issue. What constitutes a "person"? Was the person Jesus preexistent as Jesus? If that is what is claimed, Simon needs to be up front about it. In the penultimate section of the monograph, entitled "The Nature of Preexistence," the subject is barely touched in a mere twelve lines.

There are similar problems with the language of "identity," borrowed from Richard Bauckham. Simon speaks quite comfortably of the "heavenly and divine contours to Christ's identity," of "the inclusion of Jesus within the divine identity," of Jesus' "close identification with Yahweh in the OT," of the Synoptic Jesus claiming to share "the identity of God" (17, 41, 64, 76, 244). But "identity" is just as slippery a term as "person." How is "identity" defined: in mathematical terms, where "a *equals* b" means that for *some* values of a and of b, a is the same as b, and where "a is *identical* with b" means that for *every* value of a and b, a is the same as b? Or is it to be defined in genetic or ethnic terms—are we already into a concept of "eternal generation"? Or in terms of character or personality, the Logos as the soul, "the ghost in the machine"? Or in social terms—identity defined by the differing relations of the same individual being a son, a husband, a father, a teacher, a friend, and so forth? Would Evangelists who depict Jesus as praying to God really have considered Jesus to be "identified with Yahweh'? Would Paul, for that matter, who, for all that he uses Yahweh texts of Jesus, also makes a point of speaking of "the *God* and Father of our *Lord* Jesus Christ"?

I am rather saddened here for two reasons. One is Simon's failure to engage with a Jewish conceptuality of divine immanence that is sophisticated in its complexity and refusal to make simplistic equations. So we meet figures such as "the angel of the Lord" and the mysterious Melchizedek. In what sense is the one "identified" with Yahweh or the other preexistent? Above all we have Wisdom, whom Simon discounts as a factor, precisely because Wisdom was "not regarded in Judaism as a pre-existent entity distinct from or independent from God, ... a personification rather than a person" (209). So Jesus is to be regarded as "a pre-existent entity distinct from or independent from God," is he? Let's dispense with Jewish subtleties in how to conceive of the divine presence and activity in the world! Let's press for a crudely straightforward, "simple" conceptualization of Jesus as "an actually pre-existent person or being"! The convenience of this for Simon's thesis, of course, is that possible parallels to Jesus as incarnate, such as Simon ben Onias being depicted as the embodiment of Wisdom in Sir 50 or Sarah as representing Wisdom in Philo or the "identification" of Wisdom as Torah in ben Sirach and Baruch, can, once again, be discounted. Here I could mention also the unsatisfactoriness of Simon's dismissal of the concept of "ideal preexistence," yet one more attempt to reflect something of the subtlety of Jewish reflection on the purposes of God. It is hardly a sufficient reason to dismiss it because "*everything* is ideally pre-existent in the mind of God" (12, quoting Wayne Meeks). The difference, of course, is in who/what is in the mind of God and in the self-expressive energy God expends in bringing his purpose in Christ to expression within time.

The other misgiving I have is what might have to be described as a degree of irresponsibility in Simon's pushing this line so hard, both in the rawness of his conceptualities and in his eschewing the subtleties of both Jewish and patristic reflection on the subject. For what Simon promotes (claiming it to be the view of New Testament authors) seems to be basically a form of bi-theism. For if Jesus is preexistent as Jesus, then he preexists as the person who was encountered in Galilee in the late 20s C.E., and our conceptuality is caught into envisaging God and the preexistent Jesus as two such persons. This I believe is a far cry from the christological monotheism of the New Testament and from the subtleties of the Logos Christology that led up to the Nicene Creed. Or is it indeed the case that the sophisticated understanding of differentiation within the Godhead that it took another three centuries to conceptualize and formulate was already grasped by the Synoptic Evangelists? My fear is that Simon's too simplistic thesis will encourage the tritheistic polytheism that many Christians effectively believe to be orthodox Christian faith and will justify the criticisms of Jew and Muslim that Christianity is not monotheistic, that is, if, alternatively, the thesis does not promote the modalist heresy that Jesus was Yahweh.

As a third major concern, I confess to being very unhappy over what comes across as the rather wooden literalism of so much of the exegesis that Simon entertains or commends. This is illustrated by his readiness to entertain an appeal to what the passage in question "actually says" (as on 28) or to the "plain sense" (44). It is almost as though the distinction between "what it says" and "what it signifies/means" has been wholly forgotten. What about typology and symbol and metaphor? What about poetic speech? What about partial analogy? At one point Simon does recognize the possibility that "the author [of Hebrews] regards the OT as a kind of script for a drama" (45). But otherwise, regrettably, the exegesis often seems wiling to pander to an uninformed faith. For example:

♦ Matthew's description of Jesus as "Emmanuel," God with us, "should probably be understood as highlighting Jesus' identification with God in a *hard* sense" (75–76). Is that equivalent to the mathematical distinction between "equals" and "is identical with"—for all values of "Jesus" and "God" Jesus and God are one and the same? And what about the original prophecy of Isa 7:14: Was the expected child in the time of King Ahaz to be identified with God "in a *hard* sense"?

♦ Does "I have come" necessarily carry with it the implication that "I have come *from somewhere*"? We saw the danger of pressing an analogy too far in the metaphor of redemption. Does it require us to ask "To whom was the price paid?" That was a mistake made by medieval theology that we have learned to avoid.

♦ Does "the son of man came not to be served" (Mark 10:45) really carry with it the implication that the preexistent son of man had the right to be served (168)?

♦ Matt 23:37, "How often have I longed to gather you," referring to Jerusalem—Simon infers that Jesus is addressing a Jerusalem that spans generations throughout Israel's history, with the obvious corollary that the "how often" includes Jesus' preexistent anguish for Jerusalem or, alternatively, "some kind of identification of Jesus with the Lord of Israel in the OT" (214–18).

♦ In the same connection Simon mentions the possibility of attributing to Jesus a "hyperbolic manner of speaking," but then adds "This ... should of course remain a last resort" (219). Why "of course"? Was it not Jesus who is remembered as speaking of the necessity for the would-be disciple to "hate" his father and mother and wife and children (Luke 14:26) and of his coming to bring not peace but a sword, to set families against one another (Matt 10.34–36)? The thought of a rich man passing through the eye of a needle (Mark 10:23) isn't exactly literal speech.

♦ I would have hoped for a more robust dismissal of the suggestion that by quoting Ps 110:1 ('The Lord said to my Lord...") Mark (12:35–37) must have thought that God was addressing the preexistent Jesus when the words were first said. As well might we infer that Jesus was personally present with God when God said through Hosea, "Out of Egypt have I called my son" (Matt 2:15). Or that Rachel was weeping not for her own children or the generation destroyed by Nebuchadnezzar (Jer 31:15) but in reality for the infants slaughtered by Herod (Matt 2:18). Or when Ps 2:7 was pronounced at the coronation of a king such as Josiah ("You are my son, today I have begotten you") that king Josiah was really Jesus! But Simon is quite prepared to argue that Matthew's quotation of Ps 78:2 in reference to Jesus' parabolic teaching ("I will open my mouth in parables…") "makes best logical sense" if we infer that the "I" is the pre-existent son of man (265).

♦ In the same context Simon argues that "the kingdom (of God) is a preexisting reality in heaven" (263–64). But of course: where God rules is God's kingdom; it is "the kingdom of heaven" in Matthew's terminology. But to reify that as "a preexisting reality in heaven" is an odd line to take.

♦ Similarly with Luke and the words of the Benedictus, "the *Anatolē* will visit us from on high" (Luke 1:78) (238–42): Are they any less poetic than Virgil's representation of Augustus as Apollo come to earth (*Eclogues* 4.6–10) or Horace's representation of Augustus as Mercury descended in the guise of a man (*Odes* 1.2.41–52)? After all, in Zechariah, as Simon notes, *anatolē* is the translation of *semach,* "branch," a standard way of referring to the hoped-for son of David. Here at least Simon recognizes that "poetic statement" is involved, although only in the penultimate paragraph of the book (296)! But what is the "plain sense" of a poetic statement? And how does this acknowledgment square with Simon's earlier insistence that "attempts to reduce the sense to a merely human, Davidic Messiah fail particularly to explain away 'from on high' in Luke 1:78"? So a poetic understanding "reduces the sense"! A refresher course in hermeneutics seems to be called for here.

♦ Equally strange is the deduction that the talk of the Son of the Most High being given the throne of his father David, reigning for ever, and his kingdom having no end (Luke 1:32–33), implies the Son's "everlasting life" and "immortality" and again by further inference his preexistence (281–83). All this despite the obvious allusion to the promise to David in 2 Sam 7:12–14 that God would be a father to his son and that the throne of David's kingdom would be established "forever." So David's descendants are all "immortal"? And when the people cry, "Oh king, live for ever," they mean it literally?

To such examples of failure to allow for the richness of imagery, metaphor, and form I add a few examples of rather hasty or overstated exegesis:

♦ In 1 Cor 15.47's talk of "the man from heaven," he ignores the fact that the earthly precedes the heavenly and that the heavenly Adam is the resurrected Christ (26); to read "from heaven" as a reference to incarnation runs quite counter to Paul's argument.

♦ The discussion of the significance of Jesus' saying "Your sins are forgiven" (57–60) ignores the Qumran parallel in the Prayer of Nabonidus, where Nabonidus says "an exorcist forgave my sin" (4QprNab 242 4).

♦ The inference, suggested as a "strong possibility," from Jesus' encounter with the rich young ruler (Mark 10:17–22) I find, frankly, astonishing—that God alone is good and (Simon adds) able to give commandments, and therefore because Jesus commands (not in the text) the young man to sell everything, give it to the poor, and follow him, therefore Jesus is also "giving commandments" and therefore is also "good ... in the absolute, divine sense" (74). This is special pleading with a vengeance!

♦ Does Peter's reaction to Jesus, "Depart from me, for I am a sinful man, Lord" (Luke 5:8) really warrant the conclusion that it evidences "a fundamental distinction between Jesus and sinful humanity" (75)?

I should perhaps add that the robustness of my response follows the character of our regular exchanges for many years now, which continued at the SBL Annual Meeting in Washington (November 2006), when I was on the panel reviewing his *Pre-existence* book. It is because I admire Dr. Gathercole's scholarship and his ability to mount a weighty exegetical argument (from which I continue to learn), and because I believe it to be by such robust dialogue that discussion can progress most fruitfully (so I fully expect him to respond in the same manner), that I have offered this review.

Baptist Traditions and Q, by Clare K. Rothschild. Wissenschaftliche Untersuchungen zum Neuen Testament 190. Tübingen: Mohr Siebeck, 2005. Pp. xvii + 309. Cloth. €74.00. ISBN 3161487915.

John S. Kloppenborg, University of Toronto, Toronto, Ontario, Canada

The past two years have seen the publication of two monographs that endeavor to change the way we thing about Q in fundamental ways. Melanie Johnson-DeBaufre's *Jesus among Her Children: Q, Eschatology, and the Construction of Christian Origins* (HTS 55; Cambridge: Harvard University Press, 2006) argued that Christology is not nearly as important an interpretive category for Q as most critics have made out and contends that Q stresses exhortation and paraenesis over polemic, a communal and cooperative vision of the *basileia* over the language of judgment and separation, and the communal project of transformation over a stress on the incommensurability of the figure of Jesus. The thesis of Clare Rothschild's monograph is yet bolder: that Q originated not in the circles of Jesus but in those of John the Baptist; that sayings originally attributed to John have been placed on Jesus' lips by Matthew and Luke; that Mark christianized Baptist materials and used them in Mark 8–13; that the so-called "coming Son of Man sayings" belong to John's original proclamation, not Jesus'; and that many of the kingdom sayings come from John and have been adopted by the Jesus movement (closely associated with John) for their hero.

Rothschild begins by arguing that, contrary to the conclusions of "redaction criticism," John is not systematically subjugated to Jesus. On the contrary, despite some obvious efforts to co-opt John or to efface his distinctiveness—Matthew's assimilation of John's message in 3:2 to Jesus' in 4:17, for example—various elements of the Gospels' presentation of John use descriptions of John that one would think ought to be reserved to Jesus. For example, Luke 3:18 and 16:16 use εὐαγγελίζεσθαι to describe John's preaching activity, which, according to

Rothschild, the early church would hardly have done on its own accord, since it would have detracted from Jesus' preaching (59). Perhaps, but she does not consider the fact that the use of εὐαγγελίζεσθαι, which is overwhelmingly Lukan, appearing twenty-five times in Luke-Acts (once in Matthew, never in Mark), may be just as much Luke's way to co-opt John for the Jesus movement as Matthew's attribution of Jesus' preaching in Matt 4:17 to John in 3:2. In any event, redaction criticism as such is hardly responsible for an erroneous assessment of John's significance in the Jesus tradition. Rothschild might disagree with individual critics—she focuses on C. H. Scobie, John Meier, and Joan Taylor—but she never explains how the method *qua* method is defective.

The heart of the thesis is developed in chapter 3, which argues that significant portions of Q are in fact Baptist in provenance. The key argument here is that the "Jesus" of Q is at odds with the "Jesus" outside of Q and that Q's Jesus has strong affinities with the Baptist. In fact, "*sayings of John in Q are attributed to Jesus in Synoptic materials outside of Q*" (88, emphasis original). For example, while outside Q Jesus is said to have participated in feasts (Mark 2:15–17, 18–22; Luke 15:2; John 2:1–11), the Jesus of Q, like John, fasts and encourages others to fast. Rothschild points to Q 4:2 and, much more problematically, Q 6:21a; 11:3; 12:22b–24, 29, 45–46, and observes that Jesus' opponents in Q also eat and drink (Q 13:26–27; 17:26–27, 28–30). Of course, Rothschild recognizes that Q 11:3 and 12:22b–32 do not enjoin fasting at all, so she argues that "minimal subsistence is, however, one definition of fasting" (90), and in this sense Jesus is like John, who also has a marginal existence. Rothschild's reading of the text of Q is, however, selective or skewed. Q 13:26 has the "opponents" claim to have eaten and drunk *enōpion sou*, "in your presence," which imagines for Q's Jesus a convivial setting. Q 17:26–30 does not stress feasting but the utter normalcy of day-to-day life prior to the coming of the day of the Lord. This text neither encourages nor discourages feasting (or fasting); its point, rather, is that contrary to the apocalyptic scenarios that imagine messianic woes and a series of disasters presaging the end of the age, the end will come in the midst of the routine. Even less convincingly, Rothschild conjectures that Q 7:33–34, which contrasts John's ascetical behavior with Jesus' more convivial practices, might be an interpolation in Q, or perhaps that the "Son of Man" in 7:34 is not Jesus at all but John. The latter suggestion, however, creates an unbearable contradiction, since John can hardly simultaneously eat (7:34) and not eat (7:33).

With somewhat more plausibility Rothschild observes that outside of Q Jesus is represented as active in urban centers while the Jesus of Q, like John, is critical of urban centers. Care is needed here, however, since apart from the temptation story Q does not locate Jesus in the wilderness, even if Q links opposition and rejection to civic institutions and landmarks (the *agora, plateia*) and to Jerusalem and the towns of Chorazin, Bethsaida, and Capernaum. Family life is another *topos* where Rothschild claims that Q's Jesus aligns with John against the Jesus outside of Q. She asserts that John "exhorts others to [leave family connections]" in Mark 1:2–6 and parr. (94). This is not at clear. Moreover, outside Q we find

Mark 10:28–30, which belongs as much to antifamilial discourse as Q 9:59–60; 12:53; 14:26–27. On the other hand, Q's categorical prohibition of divorce (16:17) does seem closer to John's view (Mark 6:18) than Matthew's, which makes concessions to divorce and remarriage.

Rothschild also argues that Q's reticence regarding signs (Q 11:29) "contradicts the prevailing emphasis on Jesus' display of the miraculous outside of Q, but coincides with near absence of data on John's performance of signs" (94–95). This argument seems rather too quick: on the one hand, from the fact that John was not a signs-prophet one cannot infer that he was reticent concerning signs; on the other, Q seems to regard the events of 7:22—whether they are deeds of Jesus or not—as indications of the end times (but see below for Rothschild's interpretation of 7:22–23).

A much stronger argument for connections between Q and John is Rothschild's observation that the major themes in Q have affinities with traditions about John. Prominent among these is Q's emphasis on announcement of judgment and call for repentance, but also use of the Lot cycle, which is expressly invoked in Q 3:2; 10:12; 17:28–30 and implicitly in 3:7–9 and 17:34–35, since the framework of Q (3:2; 17:28–30, 34–35) and redaction at or near the stage of Q's final compilation (10:12) invoke the story of Lot and place *John* (not Jesus) in Lot's locale. While the present writer had supposed that Q's use of the Lot cycle to frame Q was a purely literary choice (*Excavating Q: The History and Setting of the Sayings Gospel* [Minneapolis; Fortress; Edinburgh: T&T Clark, 2000], 119–21), Rothschild reasons that Q's redactional choices reflect the original complexion of Q's material. She could well be right.

In order to bolster the thesis of the Baptist origin of Q, Rothschild argues that some *Sondergut* with Baptist affinities also comes from Q. In principle, the attribution of *Sondergut* to Q is defensible, since it is a priori likely that neither Matthew nor Luke took over the entirety of Q. In practice, however, rigorous criteria are needed in order to avoid the casual or whimsical expansion of Q. For example, one ought to show not only that the proposed candidates for Q-membership cohere with the style and conceptual array of the double tradition but that there are good redactional reasons for Luke, in the cases of Matthean *Sondergut,* to have omitted the material (*mutatis mutandis* for Lukan *Sondergut*). It is at this crucial point of method that Rothschild's case is weak. Suggesting that Matt 6:16–18, which presupposes that Jesus and his followers fast, is from Q, she does not address the issue of why Luke, who can also contrast ostentatious displays of piety with less visible ones (Luke 18:9–14), passed over this "Q" passage. Much stress is placed on Betz's suggestion that the original *Sitz im Leben* of Matt 5:3–12 was a baptismal liturgy (*The Sermon on the Mount: A Commentary on the Sermon on the Mount* [Hermeneia; Minneapolis: Fortress, 1995], 92–105), which then allows the conjecture that this material also comes from Baptist circles. But the initial suggestion, as Betz himself indicates (95), is far from certain. Hence, it seems unwise to base so much on a mere possibility. And Rothschild fails to address the issue of why Luke passed over such important Q material. Rothschild also proposes a few pieces of Lukan *Sondergut* for membership in Q: Luke 3:23–38 (Jesus' genealogy, which she suggests was originally John's); 1:68–79; 7:11–17; and 12:50. Again, reasons ought to be supplied for Matthew's neglect of such "Q" material.

One of the more adventuresome aspects of the book is Rothschild's argument that the transfiguration story ought to be seen not as an anticipation of Jesus' resurrection or as a misplaced appearance scene but rather as the resurrection of John. The "Elijah" who appears with Moses in Mark 9:4 is John, as he is later identified in 9:13. This leads to the observation that most of Mark's parallels with Q material either explicitly concern John (Mark 1:2 [Q 7:27]; 1:4 [Q 3:2]; 1:7–8 [Q 3:16–17]; 1:9–11 [Q 3:21–22]; 1:12–13 [Q 4:1–13]) or appear in the section of Mark following John's death (6:14–29) and "resurrection" (9:2–9). According to Rothschild, Mark knew the Baptist provenance of Q materials and deliberately placed these Baptist materials following John's "resurrection": "the risen John descends from heaven with Moses to sanction Jesus as successor, formally inaugurating Jesus' appropriation of John's well-known teachings for his own teaching ministry" (171).

The final two chapters argue that Jesus referred to John as the Son of Man (Mark 9:12) and that the characterization of the Son of Man coming in judgment (Q 12:8, 10, 40; 17:24, 26, 30) does not cohere with the Isaianic miracle worker of Q 7:22 but does agree with John's Coming One of Q 3:16–17. In fact, Rothschild argues that Jesus' answer to John's question in Q 7:18–23 ("Are you the Coming One?"), which most exegetes have taken to be an elliptical affirmation, should be regarded as a denial: "No, I am not the Coming One. But I merely work wonders." Jesus first connected John with the Son of Man (Mark 9:12), and his followers later multiplied coming Son of Man sayings, interpreting them as *Jesus'* return. Finally, Rothschild argues that the kingdom sayings are also Baptist sayings: Q 6:20b (because it is a macarism that allegedly belonged to John's baptismal liturgy); 7:28b (a self-deprecating saying of John); 10:9 (because it espouses a vagrant way of life); 11:2b (introduced by Luke in relation to John's prayers); 11:52 (a woe better associated with John than with Jesus); 12:31 (because of its rigorist tendency); 13:18–21; 13:28–29 (connected with John because of the mention of Abraham; cf. Q 3:7–9); 11:20; 17:20–21; and 16:16. Much of Rothschild's argument here depends on positing a binary opposition between John as prophet of judgment and speaker of woes and Jesus as a healer and banqueter. The parables of the mustard seed and leaven are ascribed to John only by interpreting them (implausibly) *via* Mark 4:26–29 and John 12:24, as sayings about risking all and personal jeopardy. It is hard to imagine how the metaphor of the leaven fits this reading. Rothschild's general strategy, distinguishing sharply between John and Jesus, only renders more improbable the hypothesis that the material that originated with the Baptist could have been transferred to Jesus.

Baptist Traditions and Q is ambitious, clever, and relentless in its efforts to "baptize" Q. The danger of so ambitious a thesis is that its very enthusiasm—

which unfortunately allows many weak arguments and mere conjectures to pass—becomes its own undoing. If most or all of Q is from the Baptist, if Mark knew this (and yet hid it), if Matthew and Luke knew it and effaced John's teaching by ascribing them to Jesus, and if both the Son of Man and the kingdom were central to John's preaching, then as historians we are faced with the puzzle of how the follower and disciple, Jesus, managed to eclipse his teacher so completely, especially if, as Rothschild must insist, John and Jesus were significantly different in crucial respects. The eclipse is complete in the case of Son of Man and kingdom sayings, since no hint remains in the literary record that either term passed John's lips. Rothschild's argument might have been more successful had its scope been more modest, for example, arguing that Q shows significant influence of Baptist thinking in its representation of Jesus as a repentance preacher (Q 10:13–15; 11:31–32) when, if E. P. Sanders is right, this was not the dominant character of Jesus' preaching (*Jesus and Judaism* [London: SCM, 1985]). Nonetheless, this is an important work and well worth considering and arguing with, precisely because it proposes so radical a rereading of Q.

Das Markus-Evangelium im Rahmen antiker Historiographie, by Eve-Marie Becker. Wissenschaftliche Untersuchungen zum Neuen Testament 194. Tübingen: Mohr Siebeck, 2006. Pp. xvii + 516. Cloth. €129.00. ISBN 3161489136.

Christine Gerber, Institut für Urchristentum und Antike, Humboldt-Universität, Berlin, Germany

‚Markus' ist zwar nicht der erste frühchristliche Historiograph, aber „das Markus-Evangelium lässt sich geschichtstheoretisch, historisch und literaturgeschichtlich im Kontext antiker Historiographie verorten" (51, dort hervorgehoben). Dies ist die zentrale These des vorzustellenden Buches, der Publikation der Erlanger Habilitationsschrift Beckers, die mittlerweile als Neutestamentlerin in Aarhus wirkt. Sie will mit dieser Fragestellung sowohl die Markusforschung vorantreiben, indem sie Deutungsalternativen überwindet, wie die Literaturgeschichtsschreibung, denn, so der Anspruch, es „wird die antike Geschichtsschreibung um eine weitere Quelle bereichert" (1). Zwar sei das Markusevangelium (=Mk) als ältestes Evangelium eine Gattung *sui generis*, doch seine Zugehörigkeit zur in verschiedenen Formen verwirklichten antiken Geschichtsschreibung zeige sich sowohl formal und methodisch, d.h. in der Einarbeitung von Quellen zu einem geschichtlich orientierten Werk, wie inhaltlich in der Verwandtschaft von Themen und Motiven. Im Blick auf die Markusauslegung repristiniert B. deshalb die produktionsorientierte redaktionsgeschichtliche Erforschung, die den Endtext wie dessen Entstehung berücksichtigt, da sich die Zugehörigkeit des ältesten Evangeliums zur Geschichtsschreibung gerade an der redaktionellen Arbeit erkennen lasse. Im Blick auf das Verständnis von Geschichtsschreibung rezipiert B. die jüngeren hermeneutischen Diskurse über das Verhältnis von Faktualität und Fiktionalität oder „Ereignis und Erzählung"

(47–49, 67–73). Diese seien gleichfalls konstitutiv, um die historiographische Leistung des Autors zu bestimmen (73).

Gegliedert ist die Untersuchung in vier Teile; zwischen einer Einleitung (I) und Ergebnissen (IV) sind zwei inhaltliche Hauptteile dem Markusevangeliums innerhalb der frühchristlichen Historiographie (II) und—am umfangreichsten— Textvergleichen des Evangeliums mit hellenistischen Geschichtswerken (III) gewidmet. In diesen Teilen finden sich in unterschiedlichen Zusammenhängen ausführliche diachron orientierte Auslegungen von Texten des Mk. Erschlossen wird die thematisch sehr breit angelegte Untersuchung durch Stellen-, Autoren- und Sachregister; zwei tabellarische Anhänge fassen Nebenaspekte der Untersuchung zusammen.

Mit einem weit ausholenden, chronologischen Abriss der Forschung zu Methodenfragen der Markusauslegung im 20. Jh. (I) verortet und pointiert B. ihre Frage im Anschluss an ältere historiographische Deutungen des Evangeliums. Deutlich wird, dass sie hier einen neuen Aspekt in die Diskussion bringt und sich von anderen Entwürfen abgrenzt. Dies tut sie einerseits zum Ansatz, Mk als Biographie zu lesen, in Hinsicht auf redaktionskritische Technik und Intention (vgl. 61–67). Es gehe Mk nicht um Leben, Person oder Ethos Jesu, sondern um den Bericht vom Evangelium, das mit Jesu Leben und Wirkung in Erscheinung tritt (298). Der Vergleich mit historiographischen Werken (bes. des Nikolaos von Damaskus, 297ff.) relativiert zugleich die Unterscheidung von Biographie und Historiographie, insofern er deren Verwandtschaft zeigt.

Andererseits ist B. die Differenz zur Deutung des Mk als Mythos wichtig. Sie ergibt sich aus der Interpretation von *arche tou euangeliou* (Mk 1,1) als Initium, das den „Beginn des Berichtszeitraums" benennt. Anders als die Lektüre vom Mythos her sieht B. das Ziel der Darstellung des Vergangenen nicht in der Gegenwartsdeutung, sondern in der Wahrnehmung und Deutung des Vergangenen als solchen (vgl. 56–61.111–16).

In Teil II werden die klassischen Einleitungsfragen im Blick auf das Thema der Arbeit beantwortet. B. datiert Mk ausgehend von Mk 13 in die Zeit nach 70 n.Chr. (77–102). Grund zur Entstehung des Evangeliums sei die Krise um 70 n.Chr. gewesen, die das Bedürfnis nach Sicherung der Tradition wachgerufen habe. Unter Annahme der Markus-Priorität stütze retrospektiv die Lukasrezeption den historiographischen Charakter des ältesten Evangeliums.

Für die Textvergleiche (Teil III) werden antike historiographische Schriften herangezogen, die verschiedene Zeiten, Literaturformen und ideologische Hintergründe präsentieren (133–43): Werke von Polybius, Artapanos, Sallust, Nikolaos, Josephus und Tacitus. Bereits die Aufzählung macht deutlich, dass es nicht um genetische Zusammenhänge geht, sondern um Parallelphänomene, an denen der historiographische Gestus des Mk-Evangeliums sichtbar werden soll. Gefragt wird nach Umgang mit Topoi und Motiven, gattungsspezifischen Aspekten, Deutungsprinzipien und Datierungsaspekten der Schriften im Vergleich mit Mk und insbesondere nach der jeweiligen Art der Quellenbenutzung. Ausführlich werden in diesem Zusammenhang markinische Texte im Blick auf ihren überlieferungs- und traditionsgeschichtlichen Ort analysiert (bes. 1,1–4 und 16,6–8; Passagen aus Kap.6–8 und 13,1–2 sowie der Passionserzählung, aber auch weitere). Beispielhaft für die Studien, deren Detailergebnisse hier nicht referiert werden können, sei der Vergleich mit Polybius vorgestellt (144ff.). Ausführungen über den hellenistischen Geschichtsschreiber der pragmatischen Richtung und seine Quellen-benutzung stellt B. eine Analyse von Mk 15,22–26 zur Seite, die nach den historischen Hintergründe des *titulus crucis* fragt und ergibt, dass der *titulus* verifizierbar ist und auf historisches Quellenmaterial verweist. Dann wird die polybianische Geschichtsdeutung, d.h. die Darlegung transhistorischer Ursachen (*aitiai*) der römischen Machtvielfalt als Wirken der *tyche*, verglichen mit Mk 8,31-33, weil sich auch dort „teleologische und metageschichtliche Aspekte wahrnehmen lassen" (168; im Orig. z.T. hervorgehoben). Mk benenne hier Ursachen (*aitiai*) für die Hinrichtung Jesu. Vorausgesetzt ist eine eingehende traditions- und redaktionskritische Analyse des Textes, die ergibt, dass u.a. das *dei* Mk 8,31 redaktionell sei, und die Beobachtung der kompositorischen Technik der Leidensankündigungen. B. stellt also geläufige Fragen und Antworten in einen ungewohnten Rahmen, indem sie sie als „historiographische Leistung" (175) würdigt.

Übergreifende Ergebnisse werden am Schluss (IV) im Blick auf die von Mk verarbeiteten Quellen (in der Passionserzählung) sowie Traditionen und deren redaktionelle Bearbeitung gezogen. „Markus ist weder nur Tradent, Sammler und Kompositeur von Tradition noch allein ‚Theologe' im Sinne einer theologischen Überformung und Deutung seiner Vorgaben. Markus betätigt sich vielmehr in dem Sinne als prähistoriographischer Autor, dass er Traditionen und Quellen aufnimmt und mindestens ansatzweise historiographisch konzipiert" (407). In seiner ereignisgeschichtlich orientierten Darstellung veränderte auch die aufgenommene Quelle der Passionsgeschichte ihr Profil, und mit der Präsentation von bereits geschehenen Ereignissen wie der Tempelzerstörung als Prophetie (13,1f) historisiere er prophetisch-apokalyptische Elemente (412). „‚Geschichte' und ‚Theologie'", so der Schluss, der beide personifiziert gegenüberstellt, „interagieren im Entwurf der Evangelienschrift ... und befördern sich gegenseitig" (418).

Die Untersuchung zeigt sich informiert in verschiedensten Diskursen und bietet sehr viele Informationen zur Forschungsliteratur. Definitionen der Begrifflichkeit, eine klare Untergliederung, viele Metabemerkungen und Zusammenfassungen erleichtern die Lektüre, allerdings auf Kosten des Leseflusses häufig im Stile eines Staccato. Wegen der chronologischen und topischen Ordnungsprinzipien der Stoffmenge wird zudem in Teil I und II inhaltlich Zusammengehörendes auseinandergerissen. Die Lesbarkeit leidet in diesen Partien auch unter dem Wunsch, das Feld möglicher Diskussionen im Zusammenhang der Fragestellung in seiner Breite abzustecken. Dieser führt zu einer Fülle von Distinktionen und Hinweisen auf Debatten und Sekundärliteratur, die den gelehrten und informativen Gehalt der Untersuchung ausmachen. Gelegentlich bleibt jedoch die Relevanz der Diskussion für die Argumentation der

Untersuchung unklar. Nicht erkennbar wurde mir z.B., was B. für ihren Ansatz aus der geschichtshermeneutischen Debatte folgert.

Das Grundanliegen, Mk als eine historische Erzählung zu lesen, wird durch die Darstellung als eine mögliche und plausible, wenn auch nicht notwendige Lektüre begründet. Diese Perspektive und damit der vergleichende Blick eröffnen in Teil III neue Sichtweisen auf Mk und auf einzelne Perikopen, insbesondere die Hinweise auf ähnliche Topoi und Motive. Wie viel der Vergleich einzelner Mk-Passagen mit den jeweiligen historiographischen Schriften im Blick auf die Frage der Quellenbearbeitung austrägt, bleibt zu fragen. Denn die Verf. rekonstruiert die Textentstehung und Traditionsverarbeitung des Mk-Texte mit den üblichen historisch-kritischen Argumenten unabhängig vom Vergleichstext. Wenn B. z.B. folgert : „die Beschäftigung mit Sallusts Bellum Iugurthinum hat gezeigt, dass Quellen-Benutzung oft vorausgesetzt, aber nicht immer präzise rekonstruiert werden kann" (247), so hätte diese Einsicht sicher auch auf kürzerem Wege erreicht werden können.

Die Vielfalt der angesprochenen Themen, Texte und Debatten macht das Buch bedeutsam für verschiedene literaturgeschichtliche Forschungsdiskurse. Die Untersuchung verdiente deshalb eine Würdigung und Diskussion ihrer Thesen aus verschiedenen Perspektiven, die hier nicht zu leisten ist. Ich nenne nur zwei Anfragen. Erstens: Da die Einordnung in die historiographische Literatur keine Gattungsbeschreibung im engeren Sinne sein will und da diese Zugehörigkeit nicht formal und pragmatisch, sondern inhaltlich und im Blick auf die Quellenverarbeitung bestimmt wird, bleiben mit der Gattungsbeschreibung verbundene Erkenntnisse über die Pragmatik blass. Zweitens scheint mir die Untersuchung ihren Anspruch nicht einzuholen, die Diastase von historischen und narratologischen Zugängen zu überwinden. Narratologische Lektüren des Mk übergehen diachrone Analysen nicht nur deshalb, da die Frage der Textentstehung zu hypothetisch bleibt (so 2), sondern auch aufgrund der hermeneutischen Prämisse, dass ein Text erst in der Lektüre seinen Sinn entfaltet. Überdies gibt der Text des Evangeliums selbst ja keinerlei Hinweise, dass er als Redaktion von Quellen und Traditionen oder als erste historische Darstellung des Evangeliums gelesen und gedeutet werden sollte. Und auch wenn man nicht rezeptionsorientiert ansetzen will, müsste die These, dass es Mk um die Darstellung des Vergangenen und die Sicherung der Tradition geht, am Gesamttext bewährt werden, der mehr ist als die Summe der Redaktionsarbeit. Doch hier bleiben für die Lektüre des Evangeliums als Geschichtsdeutung wichtige Texte unerklärt, wie z.B. das Ende des Evangeliums, das literarische in 16,8—warum schweigen die Frauen?—und das chronologische in Mk 13—wozu der Blick in die Zukunft auch jenseits der Zeitgeschichte des Evangelisten innerhalb des Evangeliums?

Dass die Untersuchung wenig austrägt für das Verständnis des theologischen Beitrags des Mk zur Deutung seiner Gegenwart, entspricht dem Ansatz bei der Geschichtsschreibung und der ihr unterstellten Pragmatik, stellt aber doch nicht zufrieden. So wird die Untersuchung selbst im Prozess ihrer Lektüre zu einer Wissenserweiterung, lässt aber genug Raum zum Weiterdenken.

JOHN

Voyages with John: Charting the Fourth Gospel, by Robert Kysar. Waco, Tex.: Baylor University Press, 2005. Pp. 339. Paper. $22.95. ISBN 1932792430.

Tom Thatcher, Cincinnati Christian University, Cincinnati, Ohio

Those who have followed Robert Kysar's storied career as a Johannine scholar are aware of his notable pilgrimage from historical criticism to postmodernity. *Voyages with John* traces the evolution of Kysar's thought by reprinting, in roughly chronological order, sixteen papers that represent major currents in his research. Kysar opens and closes the collection with autobiographical reviews of his own ideological development and organizes the essays into the major stages of his career (which has now spanned four decades). The book includes a number of Kysar's most recent papers that have not yet appeared in print elsewhere, along with a thorough bibliography and helpful indexes.

In the introductory essay—written in a conversational and, indeed, at times confessional tone—Kysar identifies four methodological phases in his own work: historical criticism; theological criticism; "the so-called new literary criticism"; and, finally, "what some call postmodernism" (1). These four phases serve as the outline for the remainder of the book, which includes six "historical" essays (including two of Kysar's valuable surveys of trends in Johannine studies), two essays reflecting Kysar's theological interests, four on literary criticism, and four advancing Kysar's current postmodern perspective. In a brief introduction to each section, Kysar outlines the issues he was attempting to address at each stage of his career. A brief review of these introductory sections will indicate the overall logic of the collection.

The essays in part 1 derive from the early phase of Kysar's career (ca. 1970–1985), an era when Johannine scholars were preoccupied with the historical-critical approach. In Kysar's view, historical criticism is grounded in the premise of authorial intention and insists that the Fourth Gospel is only meaningful when understood against its historical backdrop. This backdrop includes both "the original setting and meaning" of the text and also "the development of the document itself"—that is, the editorial history of the text (7–8). The two essays in part 2 reflect Kysar's ongoing interest in "theological criticism," which he defines as "the investigation of the biblical texts for constructing a statement of the text's views of faith and life for the sake of the church" (109). Theological criticism is thus concerned not only with major theological themes in the Fourth Gospel but also with the appropriation of these themes by modern religious communities, an emphasis that explicitly reflects Kysar's work as an ordained pastor (110). Over time, however, Kysar became aware of "a nearly unconscious dissatisfaction with historical studies," an unrest driven by a growing suspicion that Johannine scholars had become too speculative in their reconstructions of community history (145–46). Part 3 includes a number of essays reflecting Kysar's gradual shift toward the premises and conclusions of "narrative, reader-response, structural, [and] rhetorical" criticism (143). These methods counter historical criticism by locating the "meaning" of the Fourth Gospel in the text itself and/or in the experience of reading that text (145). The essays in part 4 reflect the final evolution of Kysar's thought, which is grounded on three premises: that "texts arise from the author's own assumptions and perspectives" and seek to "sustain social structures" and power relations; that "most historical reconstructions" of the Fourth Gospel's background history "are excessively speculative and beyond probability"; and that language is unstable, making every text "hopelessly multidimensional" (217–18). Three of the four short papers in part 4 are explicit commentary on commentary, as Kysar seeks to dismantle many of the foundational assumptions of his own previous research.

The evolution of Kysar's thought may be illustrated by comparing three essays in *Voyages* that focus on John 6—the story of Jesus' feeding of the five thousand and subsequent dialogue with the Jews about his identity as "the bread from Heaven." Like most scholars, Kysar is struck by the theological aporias in this passage, particularly its apparently self-contradictory soteriological and eschatological statements. On the former problem, it is clear that "some sections [of John 6] seem to presuppose an act of free will in accepting Christ, while others suggest that faith is a divine act" (45, 203–5); on the latter, Kysar notes the "commonly recognized polarity of realized and futuristic eschatology" in the chapter (48). These tensions may be resolved in a variety of ways, as evident from Kysar's various readings of the passage.

In his 1985 essay "Pursuing the Paradoxes of Johannine Thought" (ch. 4 of *Voyages*), Kysar proposes that the tensions in John 6 can be readily explained by distinguishing "between tradition and redaction" (43). In the traditions and sources behind the Fourth Gospel—including here Robert Fortna's reconstructed Signs Gospel—faith was portrayed as a free-will response to stories about Jesus' miraculous signs. But after their expulsion from the synagogue and failure to convert a significant number of fellow Jews, the Johannine Christians became more pessimistic and gradually concluded that faith must be a divine gift; this perspective was superimposed onto the earlier tradition, producing the problems evident in the current text (46–47). Similarly, the earlier Johannine tradition most likely espoused "a Jewish view" of eschatology, one with an essentially futuristic orientation. But as time and experience led the Johannine Christians to distinguish their beliefs from those of the synagogue, they began to long for "a more meaningful present," taking comfort in the belief that God's future blessings are immediately available (47–48). Viewed in historical-critical perspective, the tensions in John 6 may be explained as a natural byproduct of the Johannine community's attempt both to preserve and to revise their Jesus tradition in light of new experiences (50).

While this developmental reading offers a coherent explanation for the tensions in John 6, by 1997 Kysar could no longer affirm his earlier approach. His essay "Dismantling Decisional Faith" (ch. 12 in *Voyages*) rejects redactional and developmental models categorically in an attempt to highlight "the general function of the language of the passage [John 6:25–71] on and in readers" (199). Specifically, Kysar now wishes to achieve "a greater self-consciousness in the reading of the text"; in pursuit of this goal, he proceeds to offer an "intensely personal" reader-response analysis of ways that one reader (Kysar himself) experiences the tensions in John 6 (199–205). The narrative confuses the reader by selectively manipulating the reader's identification with various characters, all of whom are ultimately shown to possess a deficient perception of Jesus (204–5, 209–10). By subverting the reader's expectations, the text suggests that faith in Jesus, though prerequisite to eternal life, cannot be achieved by one's own volition. Hence, while John 6 may have functioned in its original context "to account for why it is some believe while others do not," Kysar can only say for certain that "the work of the text for this reader has undermined any confidence and certainty in the human will alone to believe" (214).

If the above reading reflects a remarkable shift in Kysar's methodology, his previously unpublished paper "The Sacraments and Johannine Ambiguity," delivered at the 2004 Annual Meeting of the Society of Biblical Literature, reveals that he is now completely disillusioned with historical-critical models (see ch. 16 in *Voyages*). Johannine scholars have long debated whether John 6:53–58 ("you must eat my flesh and drink my blood") should be viewed as an allusion to the Eucharist and, possibly, as a redactional addition to the text. Kysar opens his analysis of Raymond Brown's commentary on the passage by candidly noting that attempts to distinguish between tradition, source, and redaction "are now tiresome, exhausted, and largely irrelevant" (247). Indeed, "there can be no purely objective and scientific interpretation of Scripture" simply because the whole notion of "the author's intention" is a fiction, an "appeal to the *interpreter's intention for the passage*" (248; emphasis original). All this being the case, Kysar must now admit that his previous efforts were vain: John 6 is "hopelessly ambiguous and no amount of research or study will (or even should) finally resolve that ambiguity" (249).

The tone of the immediately preceding quote reveals the overall objective of Kysar's collection. The title of the book and the division of his career into four hermeneutical journeys is entirely appropriate, inasmuch as it is everywhere clear that *Voyages* is Kysar's appeal to Caesar on behalf of postmodernity. While some readers—particularly those who remain invested in historical issues and developmental models—will feel uncomfortable with this dimension of the volume, *Voyages* is in fact a microcosm of hermeneutical trends in Johannine Studies over the past thirty-five years. Robert Kysar has always been nothing if not current, and *Voyages* serves as an excellent introduction to recent research in the Johannine literature and, indeed, to the last quarter century of biblical studies. Veteran scholars will find the book to be a useful reference tool for citing Kysar's essays, which are essential to any history of recent research; students will find *Voyages* to be an accessible introduction to historical, literary, and postmodern approaches to the New Testament.

The Gospel of John: Text and Context, by Francis J. Moloney. Biblical Interpretation Series 72. Leiden: Brill, 2005. Pp. xv + 389. Hardcover. $155.00. ISBN 0391042467.

Paul Anderson, George Fox University, Newberg, Oregon

As one of the premier Johannine authorities of our day, Frank Moloney draws together fifteen first-rate thematic and exegetical essays representing what he calls his "mature reflection upon this fascinating Gospel text" (ix). Nearly all of these essays have been published within the last decade or so, and each advances a particular thesis or set of points that will be of interest to other Johannine interpreters. Whereas some collections suffer from unevenness or lack of coherence, this one does not. With the volume divided into two complementary parts, "History and Theology" and "Exegetical Studies," the reader is treated to what may be considered some of Moloney's most incisive and clearly argued exegetical work yet. Sounding a five-word aphorism at the outset, "text without context is pretext" (x), Moloney exemplifies that exegetical concern as thoughtful interpretations are advanced in the light of the literary and socioreligious contexts out of which particular Johannine texts emerged. He also declares his hermeneutical investments in laying out his questions but invariably sides with exegetical evidence in outlining his conclusions.

Moloney leads off part 1 with two essays dealing with subjects of prime interpretive importance. In "The Gospel of John and Evangelization" (3–19) Moloney advances the thesis of Raymond Brown that the purpose of the Johannine Gospel as declared in 20:30–31 is not concerned with leading people to initial faith commitments but rather "presupposes that those who are reading or listening to this story already believe that Jesus is the Christ, but demands that they *go further* in their commitment to what God has done for humankind in and through the life and teaching, death and resurrection of Jesus" (4). In arguing his thesis, Moloney surveys the ways major sections and leading characters feature the exhortation to keep on believing. Indeed, the Samaritan woman, the man born blind, Mary and Martha, and Mary Magdalene and Thomas might all exemplify abiding faith, but they all demonstrate pivotal crises involving coming to faith as well. While continuing in faith is indeed a clear rhetorical emphasis, one questions whether it can be inferred to the total exclusion of any emphasis upon initial decisions of faith. Perhaps a dialectical approach would be more consonant with the textual evidence. Interestingly, Moloney nuances the claims of his first essay with the thesis of his second, "'The Jews' in the Fourth Gospel: Another Perspective" (20–44). The Johannine negative presentation of the *Ioudaioi* should not be interpreted as anti-Semitism or as Christian exclusivism but should be understood in the light of an idealized "Israel" that embodies "a universal call: that Jew and Gentile might believe in Jesus as the unique and saving revelation of God (see 20:31)" (43). This is a worthy consideration, but it also sounds to me a bit like the "evangelism" Moloney eschews in his previous essay—despite the fact that the work of some televangelists would certainly be improved by its consideration. The point here is that a *both-and* approach is here preferable to *either-or* ones, as is the case in many other aspects of Fourth Evangelist's dialectical approach to many a weighty issue. The failure to appreciate fully the Johannine operational dialectic is a factor of many a flawed Johannine interpretation, and this may also apply to understanding adequately the purpose(s) of the Fourth Gospel.

In his next three essays Moloney advances important theses convincingly. In "The Fourth Gospel and the Jesus of History" (45–65) Moloney rightly challenges the prevalent inclination of modern scholars who diminish John's historicity without having seriously engaged the seminal works of Dodd, Robinson, Hoskyns, and others. Here Moloney argues that the first four chapters of John pose a "skeleton framework" for the early ministry of Jesus, including a dozen features surrounding the relation of Jesus to John the Baptist. While one questions whether Jesus' first visit to Jerusalem was necessarily occasioned by the death of John the Baptist, on many of these accounts the Johannine presentation may be considered preferable to Synoptic ones in terms of historical plausibility. Against the grain of prevalent interpretive trends, Moloney on this matter may well be right. In "The Johannine Son of Man Revisited" (66–92), Moloney engages the most significant of scholars' responses to his monograph of thirty years ago, *The Johannine Son of Man*. While reading the text more synchronically now, in contrast to earlier diachronic readings, Moloney still maintains his original thesis. The Son of Man is paradoxically lifted up on the cross, glorifying God and thereby receiving his own glorification through his faithful suffering and death. Moloney's next essay, "Telling God's Story: The Fourth Gospel" (93–111), presents a narrative analysis of the Fourth Gospel as a means of revealing the God represented by the Johannine Jesus, whose love for the world is disclosed in his laying down his life for his friends. Therein Johannine theology and narrative converge.

Moloney's next two essays review and analyze significant trends in Johannine studies. "The Gospel of John: The Legacy of Raymond E. Brown" (112–36) was first presented at the Life in Abundance Conference commemorating the contribution of Raymond Brown at St. Mary's Seminary in Baltimore in 2003, an event celebrating the publication of Brown's *A New Introduction to the Gospel of John*, so ably edited and introduced by Moloney himself. In this essay Moloney outlines Brown's profound contributions to Johannine studies, showing also Brown's role in the integration of first-rate Catholic biblical scholarship and historical-critical methodology, the latter of which need not be a challenge to faith where it is authentically verified. This being the case, the development of the Johannine tradition, John's composition history, and the history of Johannine Christianity all contribute to confessional Christianity if undertaken with truth-seeking integrity.

Then "Where Does One Look? Reflections on Some Recent Johannine Scholarship" (137–66) catches the reader up on some of the most interesting of recent Johannine studies. While many others could have been included, Moloney engages the contributions of Adeline Fehribach, Manfred Lang, and Michael Labahn as recent worthy ones. Fehribach's work elevates the place of women within many of the Johannine narratives; Labahn elucidates the relations between Johannine and Synoptic traditions as being factors of secondary orality; and Lang attempts (unsuccessfully, according to Moloney) to establish Johannine dependence on Markan and Lukan traditions with reference to the passion narrative. The result is a set of theories confirming Johannine familiarity with—but independence from—Synoptic traditions, bolstering Dodd's view of Johannine autonomy, developing in its own distinctive way. New issues emerging, however, include the importance of considering a broader understanding of the Gospel's religious background, a fresh consideration of the histories of Gospel forms and their functions, the rhetorical functions of characters within the narrative, and the ideological stance of readers over and against the text.

In part 2, "Exegetical Studies," Moloney gathers seven exegetical essays that also cohere in reinforcing ways. In "The Function of Prolepsis for the Interpretation of John 6" (169–92) Moloney connects several proleptic sayings of Jesus in John 6 (vv. 12–13, 27, 35, 51c, 53–54) with believers' assimilation of God's saving-revealing work in the bread-breaking, word-delivering, and cross-embracing work of Jesus. Rather than a formalistic ceremony, this eucharistic set of associations celebrates the memory of the cross for the Johannine community and its implications for faithful discipleship. That vein is indeed a worthy approach to John 6, which advocates centrally the importance of choosing the life-producing food that Jesus gives and is (vv. 27, 35) over its alternatives. The next essay, "Narrative and Discourse at the Feast of Tabernacles: John 7:1–8:59" (193–213), interprets John 7 and 8 as a unity read in the light of the Feast of Tabernacles. Connecting these chapters also with John 4 and 5 and with John 9 and 10, Moloney identifies many unifying themes despite disunitive features in these passages. With Tabernacles as the backdrop, the uneven reception of Jesus would have been existentially meaningful to Johannine Christians, who themselves had likewise been unevenly received by their Jewish contemporaries. "Can Everyone be Wrong? A Reading of John 11:1–12:8" (214–40) shows the corrective function of misunderstanding in John 11:1–12:8, where everyone gets it wrong except for one. Mary alone, in anointing the Lord (12:7), gets it right.

"The Gospel of John: A Story of Two Paracletes" (241–59) shows how community members caught in between the former ministry of Jesus and his present absence are ministered to by the second paraclete, nourished by the story about the first one. Moloney, in "The Function of John 13–17 within the Johannine Narrative" (260-83), interprets John 13–17 together as a unity, identifying a chiastic structure with 15:12–17 at the center, surrounded by 15:1–11/15:18–16:3; 14:1–31/16:4–33; and 13:1–38/17:1–26. Within this treatment Moloney chooses not to deal with the rough transition following 14:31 (which appears to have originally been followed by 18:1) as a clue to its composition history, and one wonders how seeing chapters 15–17 as later material added to an earlier edition might affect his inference of chiastic symmetry. Determining the beginning of one chiastic unit hinges, of course, upon determining where the previous one ended. Another problem with chiastic readings is that the main emphasis is often *a* and *a′* rather than the center. Nonetheless, whatever the literary history, these four chapters present themselves as a coherent unit within Moloney's interpretation, encouraging believers facing struggles in a hostile world with a reminder of the self-giving love of Jesus. The priestly prayer of Jesus, however, hangs together in its own special, unitive way, and one wonders whether it should be taken as completing the great discourse or the entire Gospel narrative. In "To Make God Known: A Reading of John 17:1–26" (284–312) Moloney highlights the progression of the prayer. Verses 1–8 feature Jesus' prayer for God to be made known, verses 9–19 feature Jesus' prayer that his followers will be kept and made holy, and verses 20–26 feature Jesus' prayer again to make God known. As participants in the narrative, hearers and readers are invited into relationship with Jesus, and therefore God, in the rendering of this prayer within the Johannine situation.

In "John 18:15–27: A Johannine View of the Church" (313–29) Moloney develops the ecclesial implications of the passage narrating the threefold denial of Peter and the faithfulness of the other disciple. While Peter's threefold confession in John 21 affirms his loyalty, this parallel passage displays his fearfulness while at the same time showing that the church will go on despite human failures of faith. Moloney concludes his book, then, with "The Gospel of John as Scripture," which serves as its "conclusion" (333–47). Here Moloney builds upon Moody Smith's 1999 SBL presidential address, inquiring as to the emergence of the Johannine text being regarded as "Scripture." As readers and hearers of the book are called to believe on behalf of the written story without ever having seen Jesus, they are blessed with a book of Scripture as an intermediary bridge. In that sense, the author probably *intended* to write his narrative as "Scripture" in order to further such a venture. Moloney expresses his surprise at his own conclusion, but from a literary-critical standpoint—despite appearing to bolster traditional authority—his judgment seems a sound one.

The overall impression of this collection is of a remarkably coherent and well-balanced set of essays that reinforce each other helpfully. Throughout the collection Moloney interprets his themes and texts under the following approaches: (1) first he operates synchronically, interpreting the text in its final form; (2) he interprets the Johannine text as an autonomous tradition connecting earlier and later phases of its development; (3) he interprets passages with special sensitivity to how texts would address the concerns of original audiences; and (4) he invariably brings interpretations to bear on present readers, connecting themes with meaningful readings for today. Perhaps engaging each of these features briefly might serve the interests of other Johannine scholars; it certainly is of interest to this reviewer.

On synchronicity, Moloney's commitment to interpreting the completed text as it stands is the final responsibility of every interpreter. Moloney's refusal to infer hypothetical sources such as a signs source or a sayings source is also well founded, as interpreters over the last decade or two have found such theories to be evidentiarily lacking. Still, even with a synchronicity of tradition there appears to have nonetheless been something of a diachronicity of composition. Some consideration of differences in situation between the audiences of John's earlier and later material (with supplementary material including at least the prologue and chapters 6, 15–17, and 21) would actually sharpen some of Moloney's good insights. For instance, most of the exhortations to abide with Jesus and his community appear primarily in the supplementary material (using Lindars's view of a two-edition theory). That being the case, the tension between Moloney's first two essays might be explained on the basis that the first edition of John was written to invite Jewish and Gentile members of the audience to believe in Jesus as the Jewish Messiah (involving evangelism [20:31]), whereas the supplementary material (following some of the divisions represented by the Johannine Epistles) contains most of the emphases to maintain solidarity within the community. It also could be that the Evangelist was operating dialectically on the evangelistic-pastoral continuum, but this tension also appears to reflect somewhat different literary purposes between the first and final editions of the Johannine evangel.

On Johannine autonomy and relation to the Synoptic traditions, Moloney wisely sides with Gardner-Smith but also allows for engagement between traditions in their oral stages. His citing of Labahn's work with secondary orality is also on the right track, in that Johannine familiarity with Markan traditions might explain some of the contacts without implying dependence. That being the case, one wonders whether Moloney's essay on historicity might imply a Johannine interest in augmenting Mark. Likewise, Moloney's essays on ecclesiology and the second paraclete might be understood to be in dialogue with Matthean presentations of Petrine leadership, posing a Johannine pneumatic alternative to more structural approaches to leadership. Given Raymond Brown's description of "cross-influence" between Johannine and Synoptic traditions, a larger theory of Gospel-tradition "interfluentiality" might pose a way forward, although such is beyond the scope of the present work. Of value for consideration, however, is what one makes of particular Johannine-Synoptic similarities and differences, given Johannine autonomy-and-yet-familiarity with other traditions—at least the Markan.

With regard to sensitivity to the concerns of Johannine audiences, Moloney shows special thoughtfulness on the sorts of issues they would have been facing, including a multiplicity of concerns instead of a singular one. Especially thoughtful is his essay on John 6, which shows evidence of addressing several sets of issues faced by Johannine audiences over time. The emphasis upon the gathering up of the broken fragments has an impressive resonance with the bread Jesus offers (6:51), which is his flesh given for the life of the world on the cross. Embracing the suffering of Jesus as the basis of eucharistic fellowship is at the heart of John's incarnational sacramentology rather than a formalistic requisite, and the comforting work of the Holy Spirit in the essays on John 13–17 bears special relevance for later audiences also enduring hardship. Likewise, his work with the Feast of Tabernacles and treatments of Johannine engagements of Jewish and Gentile audiences demonstrate judicious incorporations of latest scholarly approaches to the Johannine situation in ways that are also profitable for interpretation today.

Finally, Moloney's work has considerable implications for meaningful interpretation among contemporary readers. His outlining of Raymond Brown's major contributions to Johannine scholarship serves as a fitting overview of the most important work of arguably the most significant biblical scholar during the second half of the twentieth century. I would likewise consider Brown the most important American biblical scholar ever, so Moloney's contribution here is by no means insignificant. The rhetorical function of misunderstanding also has impressive implications for meaningful interpretation, and Moloney's treatment of the Gospel of John as Scripture poses an intriguing contribution to appreciating the authoritative function and impact of the Johannine text originally, as well as eventually. In sum, Frank Moloney here offers readers a book that is faithful to his own interpretive stance and context, while at the same time being faithful to the literary and socioreligious contexts of the Johannine text. Johannine interpreters are helped by this collection, and Patrick Alexander and Alan Culpepper are to be commended for including this fine book within the Biblical Interpretation Series.

Departure and Consolation: The Johannine Farewell Discourses in Light of Greco-Roman Literature, by George L. Parsenios. Supplements to Novum Testamentum 117. Leiden: Brill, 2005. Pp. x + 174. Hardcover. $99.00. ISBN 9004142789.

Jan G. van der Watt, University of Pretoria, Pretoria, South Africa

A large measure of consensus exists that the Gospel according to John was written mainly within a Jewish social ecology. This is the case since the tide turned against gnostic and Hellenistic interpretations during the latter part of the previous century. In *Departure and Consolation* arguments are presented to show that the Johannine Farewell Discourses in particular are modeled upon, and should be understood in the light of, *inter alia*, Greco-Roman literature and not only within a Jewish framework. Acknowledging this could help explaining certain difficulties interpreters have experienced with, for instance, John 14:31, where Jesus says that they (he and the disciples) should get up and leave and then continues with his speech up to the end of John 17 before departing.

In this argument the presence of a Jewish sociocultural and a Greco-Roman ecology are defended. In recent Johannine research there is indeed uneasiness with restrictively narrow categorizations of the sociohistorical framework. This stems from the recognized complexity of the intermingled nature of the thought patterns in the Gospel and the resultant variety within Judaism in its relation to Hellenism. This book again warns against being too exclusive when choosing the sociocultural ecology of the Gospel of John. It does so by arguing for the influence of a wider sociocultural circle on the Gospel that becomes evident in the use of different genres from different origins in John 13–17.

It is argued that, although the Farewell Discourse is usually seen as a testament that was common in the Jewish world, this should not be seen as the full story. There are also other genres present in John 13–17. Genre bending occurs to fit the larger interests of this Gospel: "the Gospel bends and twists the various raw materials that existed in ancient literature" (10) to fit its specific purpose. This process of genre bending has to do with the theme of the presence and absence of Jesus. To accommodate the reality of the abiding presence of Jesus with his disciples, the testament genre had to be bent in order to blend with the varying literary forms in the Gospel. In this way, the expectations of a testament are transcended.

The argument is presented in five chapters. The first chapter, entitled "The One and the Many," deals with the different genres present in the Farewell Discourse. Issues dealt with are the ancient testament form, exits in ancient dramas, ancient consolation, and symposia. He also gives attention to synchronic and diachronic approaches to the text. In chapter 2, "Arise, Let Us Go Forth," (delayed) exits to death in ancient literature are investigated. The author then moves on to chapter 3, where he deals with "The Thematics of Tokenness." Consolation and the presence of the Paraclete come into focus in this section. He illustrates that remarks of consolation in John 13–17 resemble ancient consolation literature, although they were not that common in testament literature. The purpose was, in essence, to combat grief. Under the title "And the *Flesh* Became *Words...*" (ch. 4), he points out that the Farewell Discourses resemble the literary symposium tradition. This means that certain of the Greco-Roman traditions are visible in the Farewell Discourses. Judas plays a central part in focusing on different themes related to table fellowship, such as love and friendship at the table. After Judas leaves, the discourse of Jesus with his disciples takes place in an atmosphere of loyalty and friendship; that is, the feast is a feast of words. This practice of concentrating upon speeches is known by Plutarch and has the function of allowing later generations to share in the feast of words. This is how the presence of Jesus is experienced now. A summary and conclusion follows in chapter 5; of importance here is the remark on page 151: "The Farewell Discourses are not merely one more example of the biblical testament. They also resonate with Greek tragedy, ancient consolation literature and the literary symposium." The author of John consciously moves from one genre to the next for the purpose of painting a particular portrait of Jesus and his work.

This remark is significant, since within certain communication theories it is argued that meaning is decisively determined by genre. For instance, if you do not recognize the genre of a text as a joke, you might understand the words but misunderstand their communicative intent or "meaning." The result could thus be that words intended to be a joke are misinterpreted as an insult. This confirms the supposition that the meanings of words are *inter alia* determined by correctly assessing their genre. This implies that if one misunderstands or misjudges the genre of a particular passage, effective communication might be jeopardized.

Genre bending plays a central role in the argument of this book. It is an interesting concept, but its functionality and usefulness for the interpretation of this Gospel should be explored further. This is said in light of the question of whether the insights gained from this approach add any interpretive value to the relevant texts. If, as is stated above, knowledge of genre plays an important role in creating meaning when reading a text, it follows that the idea of genre bending should have decisive influence on the understanding and meaning of a particular text. If genre is important for the semantic process, then bending the genre should have illustratable and decisive influences on understanding the text. To press the point further: if identifying the genre adds to the semantic process, and the genre (or different genres that are "bent" in these chapters) had not been recognized all these years, but are now identified, then a different or at least significantly enriched meaning and interpretation should emerge (i.e., if one does not realize something is a joke, one will not be able to interpret it fully; however, the moment one realizes that it is a joke, one will immediately understand it in a different light and a different set of semantics will result—perhaps the result would be laughter rather than irritation).

The crucial question is thus: Does this book offer a different, richer, or novel interpretation of the relevant passages that was not realized before or was overlooked when we did not realize that there is genre bending? To put it even simpler: Is there any interpretation of the Gospel text that is completely new and novel, where it is semantically richer than before? Although the author builds his arguments systematically and in a clear way, I am not convinced that there is significant semantic gain, in spite of the fact I would have loved to have been able to say that there was. The obvious question, then, is: If what this book is telling us with the theory of genre bending is already known, what is the significance of identifying these genres, and is the awareness of their bending really necessary to interpret the text? Stated differently, what does the knowledge of genre bending really contribute to the semantic enrichment of the text, since it is expected to make a definite contribution?

I have not found any semantic perspectives that are not already known in Johannine research. However, a novel and interesting application of this approach is shown in the way that the problem of 14:31 is solved. In this verse Jesus tells his disciples that they should go, yet he then continues to speak for several chapters. This approach explains the anomaly in the light of exits in ancient tragedy. However, this does not result in a semantic enrichment of the text and its message but only supplies another explanation (with the dozens of others) for how the textual break between John 14 and 15 could be understood.

It must be remembered that what we know as genres are literary constructions that are developed through analyses of similar texts. On the basis of these analyses, broad characteristics are identified and classified as "genre." The implication is, of course, that such constructions of genre, as well as their semantic effects and functionality, must have been know to the author as well as the receivers of a particular text to have any effect. In arguing for genre bending, the existence of these genres, as well as a thorough knowledge of them by the author/receivers, must be illustrated clearly. This is necessary, since two processes are suggested in this book: (1) the mixing of different genres from different sociocultural backgrounds; this means that the reader should be able to jump from one genre to the other with ease as she or he reads John 13–17 and to make the necessary sense of it; (2) the genres are bent (changed), which implies that the reader will be able to identify the divergence from the particular known characteristics of the commonly established genre, that the reader will be able to see that it is partly used in a new way (certain fixed characteristics are still there while others are not) and will be able to redefine the use of said genre and give this new creation its proper semantic significance.

In light of these two suggested processes, there are several problems that I feel should still be addressed, since the process of genre bending implies a complicated process of interpretation. Were the genre forms so fixed, well characterized, and so well known in those times by the author/receivers of the letter that they could move with ease while reading these chapters from one genre to another, identify, and making sense of all the changes suggested? For Parsenios's theory to work, this needs to be the case and should therefore be indisputably proven. Moreover, while the book does try to argue that such genres existed in sufficiently fixed forms and that these forms were known well enough by the original authors and readers to be used as argued above, this argument deserves more detailed attention. Apart from this, a plausible theoretical framework should be offered of how it was possible for all these different genres to form such an integrated part of the Johannine social ecology. What type of community in ancient times would have possessed all this detailed knowledge of genres from different social frameworks, and how did the Johannine community develop into such a community? I do not imply that these aspects could not be plausibly worked out, but it would have enhanced the quality of the book if these aspects were considered in greater depth.

A related point should also be noted. Parsenios suggests that the Farewell Discourses "are not a drama … not a treatise on consolation … nor … a symposium. But, each of these three literary forms bears close resemblance to aspect of the Farewell Discourses, and attending to these additional forms clarifies the unique shape of the testament of Jesus" (154). What is suggested is that these literary forms simultaneously overlap and pop up here and there in the Farewell Discourses. How this works concretely still remains a bit vague to my mind. A genre has different characteristics. What Parsenios seems to suggest is that all these literary forms are present in the Farwell Discourses, and as the discourses progress some characteristics of the one and then of the other come into focus to solve certain problems or contribute at certain points to the understanding of the text. We know that genres can be embedded (a poem can contain a brief letter while a letter can also contain a poem), but then such genres are much more clearly definable. But Parsenios does not seem to suggest this. As I understood it, he suggests that the genres are all potentially present and come forward and recede during the flow of the text. This needs to be explained further. How should the reader *formally* recognize this "coming and going" of the varied characteristics of each of the genres?

It should also be noted that it is often problematic to work with too strict a set of characteristics for a particular genre or to overemphasize some of these characteristics to the detriment of others. Parsenios, for instance, remarks that in the literary symposium guests commonly departed when their presence was no longer welcomed. This is then applied to Judas. While this is true, there is also evidence from ancient sources that movement in and out of a symposium was freer than what Parsenios would like to acknowledge. Thus, an interpretation based on the assumption that leaving a symposium indicates being unwelcome might not be as solid as one would like it to be. It might even sound a bit forced.

A worrying factor is the use of sources. There are extensive libraries of work on the Farewell Discourses written in German and French. I was disappointed to note how few of these sources were consulted in the writing of this book. New suggestions that seek to be taken seriously must be cognizant of prior research; of course, this also requires an awareness discussion from across the oceans. The rationale is simple: you should be able to show that your hypothesis is better and makes more sense than others.

Although I have made points of hopefully positive criticism, I think that what Parsenios has done is creative and opens the discussion about genre and John's Gospel in a novel way. I believe the book should and will be taken seriously in further discussions on John's Gospel.

Identity Matters: John, the Jews and Jewishness, by Raimo Hakola. Supplements to Novum Testamentum 118. Leiden: Brill, 2005. Pp. x + 294. Cloth. $145.00. ISBN 9004143246.

Mary L. Coloe, Australian Catholic University, Brisbane. Australia

Hakola's book is an essential read for anyone in the field of Johannine literature and first-century Jewish-Christian relationships. It is a revised form of his doctoral thesis for the University of Helsinki under the supervision of Ismo Dunderberg. The entire study deal with the issue of the way the Jews are presented in the Fourth Gospel.

Hakola introduces his theme by taking a very critical approach to the hypothesis presented by J. Louis Martyn, based on John 9, that the Gospel reflects a two-level drama addressing the problem of the Johannine Christians having been expelled from the synagogue. This expulsion was seen to be the result of an addition to the synagogue Morning Prayer service following the rabbinic council of Yavneh. While Martyn's study suggests this as a historical *hypothesis*, his historical reconstruction has been taken as an accepted fact until recent years, when it began to be called into question. Even so, the presentation of the Jews in John has continued to be interpreted as the result of some Jewish-Christian conflict experienced by the community, even if this conflict was localized. Hakola argues that this portrayal of the Jews as "other" was not initiated from within Judaism but had its origins within this Christian community as it came to recognize that its identity was no longer dependent on many of the major features that made one "Jewish," such as worship, Sabbath, temple, Torah, Abraham, and circumcision.

The long introductory chapter introduces Hakola's methodology, where he draws on a three-world model based on the work of Kari Syreeni. This model is based upon the distinctions between the *text world,* the *symbolic world,* and the *real world* behind the text, where in argumentative texts the text and symbolic worlds lie close to one another. One advantage of this model is that it acknowledges the ideological aspect of writing. Hakola would place the term *Ioudaioi* within this ideological aspect of the Gospel.

Following his introductory arguments and explanation of his methodology, Hakola's second chapter carefully examines the Birkat Haminim, giving particular attention to its Jewish context and establishing that there is no evidence that this was ever directed toward Christians in the first century or that it could have been used as an instrument of expulsion of groups from the synagogue. This second chapter provides valuable insights into the early significance (or lack thereof) of the rabbis and Pharisees in post-70 Judaism, and he critically evaluates the Jewish and Christian evidence for the persecution of Christians by Jews. His conclusion is that "the separation of the Johannine group from the synagogue was not due to the violent policy of the early rabbinic movement" (85). This leads to his proposal that the alienation from Judaism emerged from within the Christian community as a result of its high ambivalence to some matters that were essential to Jewish identity, not for their profession of faith in Jesus as Messiah. The following chapters (ch. 3, "Jesus, the Jews and the Worship of God"; ch. 4, "Jesus, the Sabbath and Circumcision"; ch. 5, "Jesus, the Jews and Moses"; ch. 6, "The Believing Jews, Abraham and the Devil") take up each of these Jewish identity markers and how they are presented in the Gospel. The final chapter provides a synthesis and briefly proposes some arguments for looking at the Johannine *Ioudaioi* as part of a symbolic universe created by the writer as a strategy to strengthen a developing, new self-identity other than Jewish. In this chapter Hakola raises the paradox present in the Gospel where there are both Jewish and anti-Jewish tendencies as well as continuity and discontinuity with its Jewish heritage.

In his third chapter Hakola examines the temple scene in John 2 and the discussion with the Samaritan woman in John 4 and describes Jesus' attitude to the Jerusalem temple as "ambivalent." This term is chosen to reflect the three-world model that Hakola explained in his methodology. "In their symbolic universe, the Johannine Christians pictured Jesus as a loyal cherisher of the best Jewish traditions." While this is probably how they saw themselves, in real life these two scenes suggest that the Johannine Christians have become alienated from their Jewish heritage: "they identify themselves neither with the Jews nor with the Samaritans but regard themselves as true worshippers who have been able to put behind earlier … untrue ways of worshipping God" (110).

In chapter 4 Hakola examines Jesus, the Sabbath, and circumcision and discusses John 5 and 7:19–24. As in his treatment of the temple and worship, Hakola concludes that "neither of these principal matters of Judaism was of practical importance" for the Johannine community (145). He pays particular attention to the way the Sabbath theme in John 5 is quickly lost sight of, in the discussion of Jesus' relationship with his Father. In other words, Christology is more important than Sabbath for this community.

The following chapter on Moses highlights the tension between continuity and discontinuity. On the one hand, Moses is appealed to as a witness to Jesus (5:39); on the other hand, there is a sharp contrast established between the manna and the true bread from heaven, where both the manna and bread are symbols for divine revelation. The manna of Moses is unable to bring life, whereas Jesus, the true revealer, is able to offer life. Here again Hakola speaks of the symbolic world of the Johannine Christians that allowed Moses and the law to bear witness to Jesus and of the real life of these believers who have already abandoned aspects of the law essential for Jewish identity.

The discussion of John 8:31–59 clearly brings out the matter of identity. Who is your Father: Abraham? God? or the Devil? This passage contains the harshest condemnation of the Jews in the New Testament, where they are named as children of the devil. Hakola argues again that the purpose of this harsh language is to convince the Johannine community that it is not possible to be a believer in Jesus and at the same time to practice traditional Judaism. Here he challenges Raymond Brown's theory of conflict with secret believers inside the synagogue. Hakola claims that the problem lies within the community, where some are struggling to leave behind Jewish practices. In this discussion he situates the dualisms of the passage, and of the Gospel as a whole, within an eschatological framework where on one level the Johannine Gospel reflects a cosmic struggle between the powers of good and evil. The harsh rhetoric is part of the Johannine symbolic universe, not necessarily a reflection of the community's social reality. In making this distinction between the symbolic world of the narrative and the real world, Hakola notes that that this has given a "strong impetus to the growth of anti-Jewish Christian tradition. John cannot be kept completely apart from the sad and far-reaching development, even though the evangelist and his community could in no way anticipate the coming horrors of history" (214).

While generally finding Hakola's arguments convincing and his overall thesis sound, I have some points of disagreement, particularly his reading of Jesus' temple act, as that of a pious Jew reacting to the trade of animals within the temple. I have argued (*God Dwells with Us: Temple Symbolism in the Fourth Gospel* [Liturgical Press, 2001]) that his action critiques and nullifies the entire temple sacrificial system, rather than being the action of a "keen reformer of the cult who is upset by the present corruption of the temple and wants to restore its sanctity" (92). My work would also strengthen Hakola's arguments in his treatment of John 4 and his discussion of Abraham in John 8. The discussion on worship may have also been enhanced through a discussion of John 1:1 and 20:28, where Jesus is given divine status. But these are minor points reflecting as much my bias as any weakness in Hakola's approach.

The strength of Hakola's work is his very careful and detailed arguments based on extensive use of primary Jewish sources. Scholars will find this particularly helpful for further research. In addition, Hakola does not back away from contentious contemporary issues in Jewish-Christian relations. He notes that in the discussion about Moses and the law there is already "a point of departure for a later Christian belief that saw the Hebrew bible exclusively in the light of Christology" (176). He also carefully nuances the naming of this group as "Christian," recognizing that, while the Gospel is well on its way to a distinctly non-Jewish identity, it may not yet be the historical marker for "the parting of the ways." He looks at the issue of the Gospel's anti-Jewishness and later anti-Semitism. On this point he makes a plea for Christians to search for new ways to define themselves that allow the legitimacy of other religious identities.

This is an excellent study adding significantly to our knowledge of the first-century religious world and the place of John's Gospel in this world. As is customary in Brill publications, the book concludes with an extensive bibliography, an index of authors cited, and an index of primary sources.

ACTS

Acts and Ethics, edited by Thomas E. Phillips. New Testament Monographs 9. Sheffield: Sheffield Phoenix Press, 2005. Pp. xi + 161. Hardcover. $85.00. ISBN 190504822x.

Gert J. Steyn, University of Pretoria, Pretoria, South Africa

There is an increasing interest in the field of New Testament ethics, and this collection of essays on *Acts and Ethics* under the editorship of Thomas E. Phillips is a valuable contribution in this regard. It consists of nine essays that were originally read during the Annual Meeting of the Society of Biblical Literature in San Antonio, Texas, during November 2004. It is important to note that the title is "Acts *and* Ethics," not "Ethics *in* Acts," although the editor used this formulation in his preface (xi). Although reference is made to a subtitle that was intended to refer to "a glimpse into some of the most important contemporary explorations and proposals for reflection on the ethical discourse within, and the implications of, Luke's second volume" (xi), such an intended subtitle obviously was omitted during the final editorial stages. The essays were written by "familiar voices within the chorus of Acts scholarship, while others are emerging voices within Lukan studies" (xi). They cover a wide range of issues and chapters in the Acts of the Apostles. The editor arranged the essays in a logical sequence.

The opening essay is one of a high scholarly standard and theoretical in nature, written by Stanley E. Porter on "The Genre of Acts and the Ethics of Discourse." The question raised is: "what were the ethical implications for the author, the audience and the nature of interpretation if Acts was written according to the canons of the various genres?" (1). Three proposals are examined: Acts as an ancient romance, a historical monograph, or an ancient biography. Regarding the first two, Porter states that "there is little evidence that any ancients read the work as a romance" (6) and that "historical writing was diverse in the ancient world" (9). His choice is with the third, which he wishes to pursue (9). "The ancient Greeks, and the Romans who followed them, thought of historical writing in different terms" (10). Five such categories are identified by the fifth century B.C.E.: "genealogy, ethnography, history (accounts of men's [and it usually was men's] deeds or acts), horography (local history), and chronography." It is especially the analysis of character that explains the events in a biography (11). Having explained how different literary techniques became part of the biographical approach, Porter mentions that "the definition of biography in terms of the ethical implications of a study of an individual's character (often from birth to death), supported by rhetorical elements such as speeches, its use of genealogies, the typological nature of the character, and especially the use of sources, certainly pushes us to see the Gospels as forms of ancient biography, but the book of Acts as well" (12–13). Porter's conclusion is that it is easy to see that the reader would have thought of Acts as biography in the light of the ethical issues presented and that the book itself is "definitely a study in ethical depiction of character" (14).

The second essay is written by Robert L. Brawley on "Social Identity and the Aim of Accomplished Life in Acts 2." His interest in "the characterization of God in Luke-Acts as the point of embarking on the quest for ethics" is enlarged here by his attention to the human characters (16). He first focuses on the source for ethics (identity and ethics), then pays attention to behavior itself (ethical implications). Brawley makes the observation that "an essential component of the new social identity that is unfolding in Acts is a relationship with God" (29). In the past, this relationship was with the prophets of Israel; in the present, God's relationship is seen in Jesus' resurrection, the outpouring of the Spirit, and the proclamation of God's deeds; in the future, God's relationship is seen in the coming of the Lord's day, Jesus' position at God's right hand, and God's promise for all who are far away. The conclusion is that "social identity theory helps to elucidate the development in Acts 2 of a new social group whose identity is in the making" (32). Brawley gave us a thorough contribution that focuses on the text of Acts 2.

The third essay is written by F. Scott Spencer on "Wise Up, Young Man: The Moral Vision of Saul and Other νεανίσκοι in Acts." Assuming a literal fulfillment in the rest of Acts, the author uses the "agenda" set in Acts 2:16–21 (the quotation from Joel 3:1–5 LXX) in order briefly to refer to the disappointing role of the "official" female prophets. We encounter, in a sense, a failure in Acts "to deliver the programmatic promise of female prophets," which spurs the author "to examine how other groups from Peter's Joel citation fare" (35). The focus in the rest of the contribution is, however, only on the young men. He first looks at typical young men from the Bible and Josephus's biography, stating that they "were prone to thoughtless, reckless behavior—a lack of vision and insight coupled with (and maybe caused by) a surplus of violence and ignorance, adrenaline and testosterone, clogging the pores of restraint and reason" (39). After having established the stereotype, Spencer looks briefly at the different sections in Acts where young men are encountered: the burial squad (5:1–11); the religious terrorist (7:58–8:3; 9:1–19); the "lucky" sleeper (20:7–12); and the timely informant (23:16–22). Some formulations would raise the eyebrows in scholarly circles and gets closer to sermon style. Spencer's conclusion is that vision in Acts "blends insight and character, theology and ethics" and is "a profoundly *moral vision* grounded in a praxis-focused biblical *model of wisdom*" (48).

The fourth essay is by the editor, Thomas E. Phillips, on "Paul as a Role Model in Acts: The 'We'-Passages in Acts 16 and Beyond." His purpose is "to ask a previously neglected narrative question: what is the literary effect of the 'we'-passages within the narrative of Acts?" (50). His first thesis is "that the presence of first person narrative places the narrator (and the implied author) of Acts in post-apostolic times with Paul"; the second, "that this temporal framework of Acts enables the reader to historicize many of the traditions about the apostles" (50). He expands on these theses and convincingly indicates that the "we"-passages, "regardless of their origin—provide the literary context for understanding the temporal framework of Acts" (61). An appendix on the problem of the textual history of Acts is added. Phillips presents us with an excellent article of a high scholarly standard, well researched and well thought through, with a good list of secondary literature in the footnotes that involves more than just English literature.

The fifth essay, by Richard P. Thompson, has as its title: "'What Do You Think You Are Doing, Paul?' Synagogues, Accusations, and Ethics in Paul's Ministry in Acts 16–21." The author points to the fact that "Although the term 'ethics' is often used ... to refer to persons' actions and behavior, one may rightly contend that within biblical narratives it also includes both the reader's and narrator's evaluative reflection about particular actions or practices" (64). Looking then particularly at Paul in this regard, it is clear that the other characters "had difficulties interpreting what Paul was doing (i.e. his actions)" (64–65). The accusations against Paul in Acts 21 should be understood in the light of Paul's ministry in Corinth and Ephesus, which in turn "raise potentially serious concerns and questions about Paul's ethics due to his ministry activities apart from the synagogue setting" (65). Thompson first examines the accusations against Paul in Acts 21, then assesses these in the light of Paul's ministry practices and ethics associated with the Jewish synagogue, and before finally suggesting some plausible implications. Regarding the latter, Thompson points out that the focus was more on the context of Paul's activity than on the content of his preaching; not only the actions, but also the evaluation of those actions ought to be considered; and the dynamic interplay between creative text and interpretive reader asks how such readings functioned for the Lukan audience. The function is "to tease the interpreters of Acts to reflect upon and evaluate the actions of Paul" (78). Thompson's contribution is systematic, logical, stimulating, and thought-provoking.

Matthew L. Skinner's "Unchained Ministry: Paul's Roman Custody (Acts 21–28) and the Sociopolitical Outlook of the Book of Acts" intends to focus "less on pronouncing judgments about the adequacy of specific definitions of Luke's 'apolo-getic' or 'legitimating' interests, and more on exploring features of the narrative world of Acts 21–28" (82). Three aspects of the narrative rhetoric of Acts 21–28 are highlighted: a "surprising lack of attention given to physical violence or suffering in Paul's detention"; Paul' abilities "to seize opportunities to evangelize new audiences as a prisoner"; and "Paul's assumption of roles that deify his status as an imperiled captive" (82). Skinner convincingly "demonstrates that it is incorrect to conclude from these observations that Acts depicts a church or gospel that is 'politically harmless, no threat to the state'" (94). Skinner's essay contributes to Lukan scholar-ship and is certainly meets a high scholarly standard with its consultation of a wide range of literature that includes German, French, and Spanish works.

In "Authority and Community: Lukan *Dominium* in Acts," C. Kavin Rowe seeks "to bring some clarity to the topic and so to stimulate our thinking about Acts and ethics" (96). Rowe moves through "crucially important conceptual house cleaning," finding "a point of entry into the ethical underpinnings of the emergent Christian community," through the issue of human equality and the apparent antithesis of equality to the nature of authority and community in Acts. The conclusion reached is that authority is not "top down," but rather "bottom-up." Authority in Lukan perspective is "to refuse essentially negative accounts of authority in which authority is basically injurious to human flourishing or, at best, a necessary evil" (108). Rowe makes important observations about authority and community that are in line with the Lukan theology.

The eighth essay is by Robert C. Tannehill on the very interesting question: "Do the Ethics of Acts Include the Ethical Teaching in Luke?" Tannehill opens his contribution with the remark that "there is little explicit ethical teaching in Acts, especially in comparison with Luke's Gospel" (109). His hypothesis is "that vari-ous characters in Acts provide models of behavior that illustrate how the teaching of Jesus may be applied in the life of the church." He tests it in the ethics of mis-sion, church leadership, love of enemies, and the ethics of possessions. It is quite visible that this work is that of a specialist with many years of research experi-ence in Luke-Acts. It is a logical and well-structured exposition, with numerous references to the primary text and discussion of terminology, constantly linking the information in Acts with the Gospel of Luke. Tannehill concludes "that there is a significant difference in emphasis between Luke and Acts on some points" and that it is only in the ethics of mission where there might be evidence of con-tinuity. He, nonetheless, believes "that reading in continuity is a hermeneutical *option*" (121).

The last essay, written by Pamela Hedrick on "The Good Samaritan, Corne-lius and the Just Use of Force," provides an interesting and thought-provoking perspective. Her purpose is "to resist relinquishing the gospel and New Testament tradition … too readily in the cause of a just use of force," and she suggests that "we can find a foundation for a use of force in defense of the victim" (124). Work-ing her way through the Gospel of Luke and the Good Samaritan, she introduces Cornelius in Acts. A key thought in her argumentation is that love is "mercy in action," that "force may be required to show mercy" (124), and that there is "a challenge to exercise mercy in any profession, even one that may involve the use of force to intervene, in love, for the helpless" (133). Hedrick's essay, and the book itself, ends with a real ethical case when referring to the Rwandan genocide. Acts and ethics meet each other, pondering the thought what the "outsider" Cornelius would have done in this situation.

The essays are generally of a high scholarly standard, testifying to in-depth research and using the primary text with references to the Greek. Footnotes contain helpful lists of literature that point to key sources in the relevant areas. Highly impressive is the fact that almost all the essays include literature from a range of languages such as German, French, Spanish, and so forth—a strange phenomenon these days in English-language scholarly literature! They all clearly state the research question or thesis, present a brief research history in the accompanying footnotes, indicate the manner in which their study will be discussed, and provide a conclusion that picks up the initial problem. It is clear that the essays deal with the relation between Acts and ethics, as the title rightly states and not in the first instance with ethics in Acts. Indices of biblical references, ancient writings, and modern authors are also provided. The collection is highly recommended to scholars in the fields of Acts and ethics.

Judas and the Choice of Matthias: A Study on Context and Concern of Acts 1:15–26, by Arie W. Zwiep. Wissenschaftliche Untersuchungen zum Neuen Testament 2/187. Tübingen: Mohr Siebeck, 2004. Pp. xxi + 270. Paper. €54.00. ISBN 3161484525.

Loveday Alexander, University of Sheffield, Sheffield, United Kingdom

Arie Zwiep must be kicking himself. When *Judas and the Choice of Matthias* was published in 2004, Codex Tcachos was still in the hands of the small team in the suburbs of Geneva who were engaged in the long and painstaking task of preserving and reassembling its "disheveled" fragments (Bart Ehrman's apt description in *The Lost Gospel of Judas Iscariot: A New Look at Betrayer and Betrayed* [Oxford: Oxford University Press, 2006], 8). At that time, the codex itself was a closely guarded secret: nobody, apart from its owners and a tiny team of experts, knew that this long-lost Coptic codex would contain, alongside other already-known gnostic texts, a text describing itself as the "Gospel of Judas." Nobody could have predicted the explosion of Judas studies that would hit the airport bookstalls in the wake of the National Geographic launch of *The Gospel of Judas* in April 2006 (Rodolphe Kasser, Marvin Meyer, Gergor Wurst, eds., *The Gospel of Judas* (National Geographic, 2006). When Zwiep's study was published, all of this was still in the future.

Zwiep's main concern is the narrative of Judas's death and the election of Matthias as his replacement in Acts 1. It therefore follows on from his Durham doctoral dissertation on *The Ascension of the Messiah in Lukan Christology*

(NovTSup 87; Leiden: Brill, 1997) and takes the narrative-theological analysis developed there further into the first chapter of Acts, a chapter that Zwiep confesses to regarding originally as "one of the most tedious stories in the entire New Testament, an unhappy digression from the more spectacular events of Ascension and Pentecost" (vii). On analysis, however, he finds that this apparently "dull election of a church official" plays an important role in the narrative world of Acts and offers insights into Lukan eschatology and ecclesiology. Far from being a "flat character," Judas "plays the role of an absentee antagonist who tries to determine the plot even if he is not on stage" (176–77). His defection raises pressing theological problems about the role of the apostles and the efficacy of the divine calling, problems that resonate through the Judas-tradition to this day.

Zwiep follows a classic redaction-critical approach, building his exegesis on a thoroughgoing analysis of previous research and of the ancient sources. His first chapter on the *status quaestionis* offers an illuminating account of the "dominant themes and questions of critical Judas-*Forschung*" (5); for English speakers, this is particularly useful in drawing on the extensive scholarly literature published in German in the past century. Zwiep draws on Klauck's 1987 *Herderbuch* (*Judas: Ein Jünger des Herrn* [QD 111; Freiburg: Herder, 1987]) to analyze the *Wirkungsgeschichte* of Judas over the centuries in terms of seven "interpretative types" (10–12). In the pre-Enlightenment period, the dominant type in Christian tradition sees Judas as the embodiment of evil; gnostic tradition sees him as a symbol of subversion; while the medieval Jewish *Toledoth Jeshu* tradition sees him as a hero who rids the world of a false messiah. In post-Enlightenment interpretation we may add: the innocent victim of a tragic concurrence of circumstances (Reimarus); the result of historicizing a timeless Christ-myth (David Friedrich Strauss); the scapegoat who absorbs all the dark aspects of divinity (Dieckmann); and the stage villain who plays an essential role in precipitating the salvific action of the hero (Marin). These traditional types in their turn have inspired an array of historical revisionist rewritings of the role of Judas from scholars such as Klassen and Maccoby, highlighting the malign role played by these typologies in the scapegoating of Jews in European history.

Zwiep then moves on to a careful analysis of the New Testament Judas traditions, noting that Mark's account leaves the reader with a number of unanswered questions—questions that are "clearly addressed *and* answered" (although in different ways) in Matthew and Luke (39). In John's Gospel, which presents the most metaphysically developed treatment of the story, "The Judas event was not an unhappy coincidence of circumstances but a planned part in a cosmic battle between God and Satan. In this spiritual combat Judas is not an innocent victim but fully responsible for what he did, even though satanic forces are at work" (45). The silence of other New Testament authors on the subject of Judas, Zwiep suggests, may be tentatively explained in terms of a Freudian theory of collective repression: the story of the disciple who betrayed his master was simply too embarrassing and painful for early Christian collective memory to cope with (47), an embarrassment still evident to Celsus at the end of the second century

(53). Both Matthew and Luke, on this hypothesis, represent divergent (and mutually contradictory) attempts to deal with this sense of embarrassment, which is
dramatically highlighted by the promise that in the eschaton the apostles would
sit on thrones judging the twelve tribes of Israel (Luke 22:28–30 // Matt 19:28).
However we interpret Luke's omission (or Matthew's addition) of the number
"twelve," the saying cries out for an explanation in the post-Easter period: "An
empty seat would be a disgrace to the Messiah! In the light of what had happened
to Judas, the integrity of Jesus as a divinely-sent prophet and hence the *asphaleia*
of the gospel (Lk 1:4) were at stake" (52).

The Judas-Matthias pericope in Acts 1 provides answers to at least some of
these issues (54). Zwiep helpfully sets his analysis of the structure and form of
this pericope (ch. 3) within the context of ancient Greek and Jewish accounts
of the horrible deaths of persecutors and *theomachoi*, a tradition whose impact
can also be seen on the second-century treatments of Judas's death in Papias and
others (ch. 5). Luke's use of scriptural quotations at Acts 1:16–20 represents a
parallel apologetic strategy for dealing with the theological problems posed by
Judas's defection (ch. 4). Detailed analysis of the parallel traditions in Matthew
reveals minimal agreement between the two New Testament accounts of Judas's
death and a concerted movement to harmonize the two traditions in patristic
exegesis (ch. 5). All of this suggests that in early Christian tradition "Judas and his
deed were widely regarded as a 'stumbling block', an enigma that could only be
resolved by the highest authority thinkable, that is by God himself. Historically,
Judas could not be erased from history: he was a firm part of the Christian tradition that had to be dealt with rather than ignored or eliminated" (124). Luke had
no ready-made traditions about the death of Judas (apart from the local Jerusalem
oral tradition that surfaces also in Matt 27:8) or about the reconstitution of the
twelve by the Risen Lord (124): if he had, he would have used them. Paradoxically,
the contradictions and redactional artistry of the Matthean and Lukan narratives
testify indirectly to the irreducible historicity of the embarrassing event they were
designed to explain. Finally, Zwiep provides a detailed textual and philological
exegesis of the Acts narrative (ch. 6), dealing with linguistic and historical problems (including the background to the casting of lots [168–72]) and highlighting
the eschatological concerns that drive the Lukan narrative (180–82).

Would the discovery of the Gospel of Judas have made any difference to
Zwiep's book? It would make an interesting appendix someday, if he ever feels like
issuing a second edition. It would certainly prompt some sharp reflections on the
vagaries of the academic publishing industry and its less academic spin-offs, and
adds force to Zwiep's assertion that "The very dramatic and painful *Wirkungsgeschichte* of Judas Iscariot, especially the ever-increasing demonizing of his person
and the unfortunate identification with the Jewish people, should make every one
of us acutely aware that neither the modern interpreters nor the biblical authors
are doing exegesis in an ideological and historical vacuum" (3). But none of the
subsequent furor detracts from this meticulous and scholarly study of the figure
of Judas in the New Testament and Christian tradition: if anything, it increases

its value as a dispassionate and independent account of what there was to know about Judas before the *Gospel of Judas* came to light.

PAUL AND THE PAULINE EPISTLES

Marks of an Apostle: Deconstruction, Philippians, and Problematizing Pauline Theology, by James A. Smith. Semeia Studies 53. Atlanta: Society of Biblical Literature; Leiden: Brill, 2005. Pp. xiii + 185. Paper/cloth. $26.95/$107.00. ISBN 1589831721/9004137726.

Joseph A. Marchal, Austin College, Sherman, Texas

In an occasionally intriguing fashion James A. Smith has attempted to answer the perhaps impertinent question: Why doesn't Paul care whether a message is proclaimed in pretext or truth (Phil 1:18a)? This study goes some distance to answer this query, curving through ancient moral philosophers, Paul's imprisonment, J. L. Austin, and, most particularly, Jacques Derrida, a curious partner for Paul (at least to most Pauline scholars). In what appears to be a revision of his Sheffield dissertation (although there are no explicit acknowledgments of this within the work itself), Smith focuses on this crisis between word and deed, motive and outcome, seeking to wedge open Pauline theology for a radical, deconstructing, proclamatory Paul.

After a brief introduction, the work begins in earnest with its first and quite possibly most promising chapter ("The Marks of an Apostle: Writing about Paul" [3–35]). Here Smith profitably problematizes some of the predominant procedures of Pauline theologians, especially the focus on the so-called *Hauptbriefe* for ascertaining the "center" of Paul's thinking. This move clears the deck for beginning with the apparently minor letter of Philippians, while questioning the micro-politics of commentary writing as an act of paternal displacement. A neglect of the occasional nature and rhetorical function of these letters stresses that analysis should begin with what the text *does* before claiming what it *means* (21). Noting the performative function of a letter, then, leads smoothly into Austin's deconstruction of the apparent constative/performative opposition, which, in turn, is deconstructively mimicked by Derrida as premised upon a serious/nonserious binary. Thus, the iterability of the sign, crucial to the argument operative in Phil 1:12–18, deconstructs the opposition of serious/original/present to nonserious/citation/absent. An analysis of Philippians, then, means a fuller engagement with precisely these dynamics.

In treating the requisite matters of historical background, the second chapter ("Historical Context of Paul, the Philippians, and the Letter" [37–70]) reads as strikingly digressive, seeming to add little to the main argument. Such a chapter is all the more curious in a work meant to engage the deconstructive philosophical or theological significance of a slender bit of Pauline reasoning, while mourning the view of "Pauline studies as one of the few real strongholds of the historical critics into which critical theorists seldom dare to go" (1). To this reviewer's sore eyes, we biblical scholars would do well to rethink this persistent feature of monographs, resilient to the changes in our field(s), no matter which particular methods seem to be the main avenue into our inquiries. Nevertheless, Smith perfunctorily treats issues of provenance, integrity, imprisonment, and conflict. In this study the intimacy and suffering on display in the letter indicates its larger purpose: reassurance, in order that the audience might take up Paul's view of a Christic *phronēsis*.

The third chapter ("The Socio-philosophical Context of Paul and His Writing" [71–100]) presents a context for Paul's writing: Greco-Roman psychagogy. As a rhetorical model for Paul, this particular feature of ancient moral philosophy precedes him and, thus, constrains the argumentative possibilities for clarifying any potential negative views about Paul's imprisonment. The language of friendly frank speech versus flattery is prominent among these thinkers and recurs in 1:12–18. Thus, Smith asserts that this section of the letter should not be overlooked as a minor historical side-note; rather, it is the main reason for writing (78).

Turning to the argument of the letter, the fourth chapter, "(Dis)Closure: Closely Following Philippians 1:1–18" (101–37), posits that 1:12–18 develops a particular "reading strategy" that Paul wishes his audience would adopt. If it were effective, this perspective would reframe the meaning of both proclamation and imprisonment. On Smith's reading, Paul cannily comprehends the iterable nature of language, so that it soon escapes the control of its producer (108). This, in the end, is the reason why the letter allows for the two modes of proclamation (truth or pretense in 1:18a), despite Paul's penchant for condemnatory oppositions (1:15–17) and the years of puzzled commentary that have followed this tendency.

The fifth chapter, "Failing to Close: (Re)Citation, (Re)Iteration, Comment" (139–58), details how the Paul of Philippians has much in common with Derrida, since neither accept the difference between serious and nonserious speech. On surveying most commentary, though, Smith finds that the crisis invoked by such a stance in the face of negatively characterized preachers is typically smoothed over by prioritizing a magnanimous or "mellow" Paul who preserves the metaphysical over the earthly. Ironically, through the act of writing such s(m)oothing explanations, "commentary participates in the very thing that is shocking about Phil 1:18 by becoming the very thing it seeks to displace" (152).

The potential for a study of this sort seems immense. Philippians is, indeed, a criminally underexamined letter. Critical theories of interpretation have already proved to be engaging, incisive modes for reflection and assessment. Finally, "biblical theology" is well overdue for a thorough rethinking. In this regard, Smith's work opens a vista for examining each of these issues.

However, for all of its potential (especially evident in the first full chapter), the bulk of the analysis, most particularly the textual argument, is remarkably toothless. Despite the author's repeated claims as to the radical, dangerous, or subversive import of his work, this reader fails to see the overarching import of the study. The deconstructive wedge Smith has found in this argumentative moment in Philippians serves only to (re)prioritize proclamation, which again strikes this reader as hardly innovative or subversive and might just be functioning as a veiled apology for evangelism in the first and twenty-first centuries.

For all the care and the occasional suspicion Smith uses to develop this analysis, his examination of the letter frequently lapses into an unexpected and unexplained hermeneutic of trust. The argument vacillates between accepting Paul's letter as an accurate description of key elements such as intimacy or suffering ("there is no reason to contest his sincerity" [103]) and recognizing the rhetorical nature of the letter as Paul's very particular perspective. Instead of turning to Acts or other Pauline (and Pastoral!) letters to shore up such claims, the study would have been better served to engage the argumentative flow of the whole letter, particularly in light of the claims that 1:12–18 constitutes the main point of the letter.

If the author had taken up this task, it seems far more likely that he would have found the time to engage some of the more recent rhetorical analyses of Philippians (Bloomquist 1993; Kittredge 1996, 1998; D. Williams 1997, 2002) or some of the sophisticated rhetorical hermeneutical work of Wilhelm Wuellner, who also engaged many of the same theorists treated in this book's opening. (Bloomquist would have proved particularly relevant if Smith's analysis had kept its apparent focus on suffering.) For his marked interest in friendship rhetorics, Smith also seems unaware of John T. Fitzgerald's key work on this topic, even on Philippians (1996). Given the declared interest in both ancient and contemporary philosophical approaches to ambiguity in word and text, the study might also have benefited from an acquaintance with Mark Given's work (1997, 2001) or a whole host of European thinkers turning to Paul's letters (Taubes 1993, 2004; Badiou 1997, 2003; Agamben 2000, 2005; Žižek 2000, 2003). (In all fairness and suspicion of this specific speech-act, though, the insightful reader might wonder what *ethos* the reviewer performs by [re]citing these references.)

Most recently, Theodore Jennings has engaged this last group of thinkers en route to his own interwoven meditation on Derrida and Paul. Indeed, one might imagine a conversation between Smith, Jennings, and some of the aforementioned scholars to be vigorous, intriguing, and still rather fruitful. A work such as Smith's could and should provoke this and many other conversations, especially among Pauline scholars, those who describe themselves as "biblical" theologians, and anyone interested in engaging critical theory. This study presents us with some of the elements to have this conversation but ultimately does not provide as substantial a contribution as it could have.

The Second Epistle to the Corinthians, by Murray J. Harris. The New International Greek Testament Commentary. Grand Rapids: Eerdmans/PaterNoster, 2005. Pp. cxxviii + 989. Hardcover. $75.00. ISBN 0802823933.

H. H. Drake Williams III, Tyndale Theological Seminary, Badhoevedorp, The Netherlands

The New International Greek Testament Commentary series was initiated to cater particularly to the needs of students of the Greek text. Volumes in this series also aim to provide a theological understanding of the text, following a historical-critical-linguistic exegesis. While volumes in this series do collect the results of modern scholarship and make these findings accessible, they are less technical than full-scale critical commentaries.

Within these parameters, Murray Harris, Professor Emeritus of New Testament Exegesis and Theology at Trinity Evangelical Divinity School, Deerfield, Illinois, provides a substantial commentary on 2 Corinthians. Much of his commentary focuses on the close attention to the Greek text, providing lengthy discussions on issues of grammar, syntax, and textual detail. Instead of bypassing past grammatical or syntactical questions and getting to issues of history or theology, Harris takes time to analyze in detail competing exegetical options.

This leads him, for example, to analyze a text such as 2 Cor 5:1 and to spend a great amount of space analyzing the grammar and syntax before discussing competing theological options. Harris translates the verse in the following manner, "For we know that if our earthly tent-house is destroyed, we have a building from God, a permanent heavenly house not built by human hands." The question that has the greatest theological value in 2 Cor 5:1 is what the Christian believer has in possession. Harris, rightly, isolates the five options for the possession of the building as follows: Is it a present possession of the spiritual body in heaven? Is it a present possession of the spiritual body on earth, in embryonic form? Could it be a future acquisition of the spiritual body at death, in reality? Is it a future acquisition of the spiritual body at death as an ideal possession actualized at the parousia? Or is it a future acquisition of the spiritual body at the parousia? (375–80).

Before arriving at his conclusion, however, he spends nearly seven full pages discussing the grammar and syntax of the verse (369–75). This discussion involves comments on the following: understanding of the conditional clause (*ean* rather than *ei*); justification for the translation of "earthly tent-house" (from *hē epigeios hēmōn oikia tou skēnous*); contextual analysis of the meaning of building (from *oikodomē* in parallel with 2 Cor 4:16 and *oikian*); grammatical analysis of two prepositional phrases, "from God" (from *ek theou* belonging with *oikodomē* rather than *echomen*) and "in heaven" (as qualitative rather than locative); and the meaning of *echomen* as a present active indicative verb. Following this lengthy grammatical analysis, Harris concludes that Christians can expect to acquire a spiritual body at death as an idealized possession actualized at the parousia. Most other commentators do not spend the same amount of space on these grammatical issues before drawing theological conclusions. This, however, is Harris's custom, namely, to analyze as much grammar and syntax from the Greek text as possible before moving on to theological issues.

The same detailed attention to the written text can be seen in the way that Harris considers textual criticism. His commentary pays a great amount of attention to these issues found within the Nestle-Aland[27] Greek text. His translation of 2 Corinthians contains many notes referring to manuscripts that favor or challenge his own translation. Some of these comments are quite extensive, such as his discussion of the textual variants in 2 Cor 1:10 and 7:8 (151–52, 532–33). Sometimes his comments on textual notes on a particular section in 2 Corinthians fill two pages (see 2 Cor 12:1–10 [828–30]). While I did not check to see if Harris commented on every textual reference, it appears that nearly all, if not all, have at least some comment.

Two passages upon which Harris spends a greater amount of attention are 2 Cor 1:8–11 and 5:1–10. In his exegesis of 1:8–11 he argues that the *thlipsis*, or "affliction," that led to Paul's despairing of life was a severe physical illness rather than a "fighting with beasts in Ephesus," opposition at Ephesus, imprisonment in Asia, or the Demetrius riot. He also identifies this affliction as the *skolops*, or "thorn in the flesh," of 2 Cor 12:7, in agreement with a viewpoint promoted by W. M. Alexander in 1904. According to Harris, the three times that Paul prayed for relief from the thorn in the flesh in 2 Cor 12:8 were once in Cilicia in A.D. 43, once in Perga in A.D. 47, and once in Troas in A.D. 56 (see 172). This great affliction forced Paul to lessen his self-reliance and to surrender his expectation, but not his hope, of being alive at the parousia. From this experience Paul then formulated his words of the significance of physical death of the believer in 2 Cor 5:1–10. While it will remain to be seen whether Harris's viewpoint on Paul's affliction will gain widespread support, his reasoning has credibility. It also fits well within the picture of Paul that is found in 2 Corinthians, where his suffering is on display as a prominent feature in his apostolic ministry.

Harris provides insight on many individual passages within 2 Corinthians, and he also makes a few contributions to the overall understanding of the book. He promotes a new idea for Paul's opponents. He suggests that Paul faced two groups that banded together to counter him: "proto-Gnostics" who were present in Corinth throughout Paul's ministry and "Palestinian Judaizers" who crept into the church before 2 Corinthians as Paul's opposition (67–86). Both groups found common ground in their opposition to Paul. The idea is a plausible one, but Harris leaves unanswered how such an alliance would have formed.

He also supports a unified rather than fragmented view of the epistle. After surveying and evaluating integrity issues for over forty pages (8–50), he supports the traditional view that 2 Corinthians is to be considered a unity. Following four arguments, two of which appeal directly to the Greek text, he argues for a unity of the letter, stating that "though sent as a single letter, 2 Corinthians was composed in stages, not a single setting" (51). His argument on this matter is substantive. His stance has shifted slightly from his commentary on 2 Corinthians in the Expositor's Bible Commentary in 1976, where he concluded that Paul wrote the epistle entirely at one time.

A further uniqueness of Harris's commentary is his presentation of the relationships between Paul, Timothy, and Titus with the Corinthian church. These relationships provide significant background to the entirety of the Corinthian correspondence and are oftentimes difficult for students to follow. Harris has helpfully placed this information on four pages in a helpful column format (102–5). The table sets the many events in relation to biblical references and dates. Underneath the table are footnotes where abbreviated defenses for Harris's reconstruction can be found. By providing this data in table format, readers can see the commentators' position at a glance rather than needing to find that position by reading through many pages.

Some may find Harris's attention to some historical issues more frustrating. For example, he spends much less space surveying the multiple viewpoints for Paul's thorn in the flesh than others do. Commentaries by Thrall and Plummer spend nine pages on the matter, while Hughes takes six pages and Martin four. Harris, however, is content to summarize their discussions in one page and to refer the reader to the arguments of other commentators. He is content to state his belief that the thorn is some kind of physical ailment, but he does not go into an exhaustive discussion summarizing all of the options.

Some who are looking for a commentary that is in touch with the concerns of church attendees will find this commentary too technical. While the themes and the theology of 2 Corinthians are displayed in accessible and warm-hearted ways, pastors whose Greek is not fresh may find this commentary too detailed. Also, there are fewer connections with modern readers of the text than some commentaries make. Those who are looking for a detailed examination of the Greek text will find this volume satisfying. It should be a standard reference work for those who value preaching or teaching from the Greek text as well as those who want to teach from 2 Corinthians, one of the most intimate of Paul's letters.

Colossians Remixed: Subverting the Empire, by Brian J. Walsh and Sylvia C. Keesmaat. Downers Grove, Ill.: InterVarsity Press, 2004. Pp. 256. Paper. $22.00. ISBN 0830827382.

Angela Standhartinger, Philipps-Universität Marburg, Marburg, Germany

„The epistle to the Colossians … was an explosive and subversive tract in the context of the Roman empire, and it can and ought to function in an analogous way in the imperial realities of our time" (7). Diese Grundthese leitet Brian J. Walsh und Sylvia C. Keesmaat in *Colossians Remixed*. Ihr Buch versteht sich selbst als ein Anti-Kommentar (7), dessen implizite (und eingeschriebene) Leser nicht der Wissenschaftsdiskurs der Moderne, sondern die Bibelleser der Postmoderne ist. Die Auslegung des Kolosserbriefs wird hier ganz bewusst mit einer kritischen Gegenwartsanalyse ‚vermischt' und gerade deshalb explizit nach der Bedeutung des Textes heute gefragt. Teil 1 *Context Remixed* gibt Auskunft über die zu Grunde gelegte Gegenwartsanalyse und die historisch-soziale Verortung des Kolosserbriefs. Postmoderne, so Kapitel 1 *Placing Ourselves,* stelle die Hermeneutik des Verdachts gegen alle überkommenen Werte und Wahrheiten ins Zentrum oder anders gesagt sei die Skepsis gegen alle Metaerzählungen (Lyotard). Der in der Postmoderne gefeierten Vielfalt und Heterogenität stehe jedoch die alles vereinheitlichende Globalisierung mit ihrem quasireligiösen Mythos des unbeschränkten ökonomischen Wachstums gegenüber. In der imperialistischen Strategie der weltweiten Globalisierung wirke die postmoderne These von der Verschiedenheit und Möglichkeit der eigenen Wahl als Deckmantel, der die homogenisierende Kraft der Globalisierung verdecke. Im 2. Kapitel *Colossians and the Disquieted Globalization* werden anhand einer aktualisierende Neuerzählung von Kol 1,1–14 die evozierten biblischer Bilder und Traditionen herausgearbeitet. Eine imaginative Erzählung der Nympha (vgl. Kol 4,15) leitet auch das 3. Kapitel *Placing Colossians* ein, das den antiken imperialen Kontext des Kolosserbriefs mit seiner systematischen Zentralisation der Macht, der sozioökonomischen und militärischen Kontrolle, seinen machtvollen Mythen in Gestalt der Pax Romana und ihrer bildlichen Repräsentation (mit der modernen Logo-Kultur gleichgesetzt) beschreibt. Hier sei allerdings schon kritisch angemerkt, dass die VerfasserInnen nur eine grobe Zusammenfassung wichtiger Beiträge aus dem althistorischen Diskurs bringen (6 Seiten), die zudem global dem Kolossertext gegenübergestellt wird. In Kapitel 4 *Contested Fruitfulness in the Shadow of Empire* (vgl. auch Kapitel 2) wird als Gegenstrategie gegen den imperialen Diskurs Israels Geschichte und Mythen benannt. Beispiel ist zunächst die Metapher ‚Frucht tragen‘ (Kol 1,6.10): „Just as Israel was called to be a fruit-bearing community in the shadow of various empires making arrogant claims to provide fertility and abundance to their people, so also does this small Christian community in Colossae struggle to bear the fruit of a gospel that is counter to the dominant ideology all around them" (75).

Im zweite Teil *Truth Remixed* wird die Wahrheitsfrage im Kontext imperialer Ideologien und postmoderner Diskurse diskutiert. Kapitel 5 *Subversive Poetry and Contested Imagination* liest den Kolosserhymnus (Kol 1,15–20) als eine subversive Poesie, die die okkupierte Imagination und Vorstellungskraft freisetzen könne, die in imperialen Systemen gefangen genommen wurde. Dazu werden Begriffe wie εἰκὼν θεοῦ oder πρωτότοκος mit ἐν πᾶσιν αὐτὸς πρωτεύων mit den Aussagen der berühmten Evangeliumsinschrift aus Priene (OGIS II.405) gleichgesetzt (wo sie freilich alle nicht zu finden sind). Paulus stelle in Kol 1,15–20 die kulturellen Mythen auf den Kopf und ersetze die falschen Autoritäten, Zeus, Caesar, Rom, mit Christus und das römische Imperium mit der Kirche (89–90). Kapitel 6 *Regimes of Truth and the Word of Truth* setzt sich anhand Kol 2,8–23 mit Foucaults Infragestellung universaler Wahrheitsbehauptungen auseinander. Gefragt wird, ob und wenn ja inwiefern sich die Wahrheitsbehauptung des Kolosserbriefs von anderen autoritären Wahrheitsregimen unterscheide. Die Antwort von Walsh und Keesmaat ist ein Verweis auf die Früchte der im Kolosserbrief behaupteten Wahrheit einer ethische Praxis der weltweiten Versöhnung. Kapitel 7 greift die Frage *What Is Truth?* erneut in einem fiktiven Dialog auf und bestimmt die christliche Wahrheit in der positiven Existenz der Gemeinde: die als hörende Gemeinde die Schreie der Armen wahrnimmt und damit imperialistische Wahrheitsbehauptungen destruiert. Kapitel 8 *Faithful Improvisation and Idolatrous Lies* greift erneut Kol 2,8–3,4 in einer aktualisierenden Neuerzählung auf. Solche auslegenden Neuschreibungen des Textes seien, so Walsh und Keesmaat, notwendig, weil Paulus hier in biblischer Tradition götzendienerisches Leben demaskiere und die Auslegung damit aufgefordert ist, dieses für heute zu benennen.

Im 3. Teil *Praxis Remixed* wird schließlich die subversive Ethik des Kolosserbriefs vorgestellt. Kapitel 9 *An Ethic of Secession* findet in Kol 3,1–8 den Aufruf, sich von der Kultur ökonomischer Brutalität, die (nicht nur) die (US-amerikanische) Gesellschaft bis in die intimsten Sphären prägt, zu befreien. Kapitel 10 *An Ethic of Community* versteht Kol 3,9–17 als Poetik einer alternativen Gemeinschaft und ihrer politischen und ökologischen Visionen. Kapitel 11 *An Ethic of Liberation* nimmt die Haustafel (Kol 3,18–4,1) in den Blick. In einem fiktiven Brief des Onesimus, der eine Gemeindediskussion erzählt, wird die Haustafel zum Befreiungstext, denn Paulus habe nicht nur die Strukturen des Imperiums, sondern auch der ihm zu Grunde liegenden Vaterherrschaft demaskiert und in seiner Gemeinde die Herrschaft beschränkt. In der Übertragung auf die Gegenwart wird allerdings auch die Autorität der Eltern (vgl. Kol 3,20–21) herausgefordert, ihre Kinder vor den dämonischen Einflüssen einer MacDonald-Kultur zu bewahren und sie statt dessen möglichst allein von der christlichen Gemeinde erziehen zu lassen. Das letzte 12. Kapitel *A Suffering Ethic* hebt anhand von Kol 4,18 noch einmal die Ernsthaftigkeit des paulinischen Rufes zu Christus hervor.

Das Thema ‚Empire‘ gehört seit einigen Jahren zu den zugkräftigen Themen der Society of Biblical Literature. Der Versuch von Walsh und Keesmaat, nun den Kolosserbrief auf dem Hintergrund des römischen Imperiums zu lesen, enthält sicher einige gute Ansätze. Besonders hervorheben möchte ich das hermeneutische Bemühen um eine aktuelle Gegenwartsdeutung. Jedoch, obgleich die Kritik an postmodernen Bestreitungen jeder Wahrheitsbehauptung nicht unberechtigt erscheint, soweit sie sich tatsächlich als machtlos gegen scheinbar faktisch reproduzierende Wahrheits- und Realitätsbehauptungen in der globalisierten Welt erweist, so erweist sich die mit Kol 2,3 gemachte Gegenbehauptung „in Christus sind alle Schätze der Weisheit und Erkenntnis verborgen" machtlos gegen jede fundamentalistische Wahrheitsbehauptung (vgl. insbesondere Kap. 7, 130, sowie Kap. 10). Walsh und Keesmaat suchen dieser fundamentalistischen ‚Gefahr‘ durch die starke Betonung der in der biblischen Tradition verwurzelten Praxis der sozialen und universalen Versöhnung aller Menschen zu begegnen. Jedoch nimmt ihre vielfach kreative Auslegung des Kolosserbriefs den Text und seine tatsächlichen antiimperialistischen Implikationen m.E. viel zu wenig ernst. Irritierend ist zum einen, dass die Verfasser die Frage nach den Verfasserinnen und Verfassern ablehnen und anscheinend Paulus selbst für den Verfasser halten. Dies übersieht nicht nur den sich eklatant von den Paulusbriefen unterscheudenden Stil, sondern vor allem, dass der Kolosserbrief eindeutig den Tod des Paulus reflektiert (vgl. Kol 1,24–25; 2,1–2; 4,3–4). Die tatsächliche Gemeindesituation des Kolosserbriefs kommt so überhaupt nicht in den Blick. Zudem unterscheiden sich Theologie, Christologie und Ekklesiologie des Kolosserbriefs ganz erheblich von den genuinen Paulusbriefen. Die im Kolosserbrief vorgetragene mystisch-spekulative Weisheitchristologie reagiert auf eine Gemeinde, die sich—nicht unähnlich vieler heutiger Gemeinden—in Auflösung und Depression befindet, und sucht gerade deshalb den Blick auf eine himmlische Perspektive zu richten. Eine Analyse der Entstehungssituation des Briefes hätte auf die Frage verwiesen, warum und wo Paulus eigentlich zu Tode gekommen ist und damit einen weiteren imperialen Kontext der Interpretation geliefert.

Dies alles gerät Walsh und Keesmaat auch deshalb aus dem Blick, weil sie, anstatt den Text und seinen historischen Kontext im Detail zu diskutieren, ihn in interpretierenden Neuerzählungen präsentieren. Gegen solche ist durchaus nicht grundsätzlich etwas einzuwenden, obgleich ich sie aus Achtung vor der jüdischen Tradition und den tatsächlichen Midraschim und Targumim keinesfalls mit diesen Namen belegen möchte. Aber solche aktualisierenden Auslegungen könnten nicht der Beginn der Befragung des Textes sein, sondern nur ihr Ergebnis. Was Walsh und Keesmaat an tatsächlichen Anspielungen auf das römische Imperium im Text finden, bleibt oberflächlich und global. Hier wäre viel mehr zu entdecken gewesen. Dazu hätte man allerdings auch kritische Fragen an den Text stellen müssen, z.B. warum der Verf. in der Haustafel den Hofphilosophen des Augustus (Areios Didymos) zitiert oder ob die hierarchische Transformation des Leibbildes in Kol 2,18–19 (vgl. 1 Kor 12, Röm 12) nicht doch mehr imperiale Ideologie wiederholt als sie kritisiert. Die Gegenüberstellung bzw. Ersetzung des römischen Imperiums alias US-Imperialismus mit einem Christusimperium rettet aus den zu Recht kritisierten Strukturen jedenfalls nicht. Die in den letzten Jahren verstärkt diskutierte Wiederentdeckung des römisch-imperialen und lateinischen Kontextes neutestamentlicher Texte halte ich für einen Gewinn. Aber, und das zeigt der Ansatz von Walsh und Keesmaat leider auch, ohne eine gründliche Analyse sowohl der Aufnahme als auch der Kritik der im und durch das römische Prinzipat verfolgten Utopien im Text selbst, führt dies allzu leicht zu einer Neukonstruktion frühchristlicher Theologie und Wirklichkeit, die als abstrakte Negation der von ihr kritisierten imperialen Ideologie den kritisierten Fundamentalismus letztlich einfach (und vermutlich fataler) wiederholt.

Apostle Paul: His Life and Theology, by Udo Schnelle. Translated by M. Eugene Boring. Grand Rapids: Baker, 2005. Pp. 695. Hardcover. $49.99. ISBN 0801027969.

Kenneth Atkinson, University of Northern Iowa, Cedar Falls, Iowa

Apostle Paul: His Life and Theology is an English translation of the German original, *Paulus: Leben und Denken* (Berlin: de Gruyter, 2003), written by the distinguished New Testament scholar Udo Schnelle of the University of Halle. Its translator, M. Eugene Boring, was the I. Wylie and Elizabeth M. Briscoe Professor of New Testament at Brite Divinity School and is also an eminent New Testament scholar. The translator, moreover, has greatly enriched the book with an expanded bibliography that includes additional English monographs and articles that supplement Schnelle's extensive list of German publications. In addition, at the request of the author and the publisher, Boring has also included occasional notes on the German text that explain difficult theological vocabulary, translation problems, and European debates that are likely unfamiliar to many American readers. Boring's notes greatly enhance the usefulness of this volume and contain a wealth of information. Schnelle in turn has read Boring's translation to check its accuracy, thereby guaranteeing to the reader that the present English work is an accurate rendition of his original German publication. The result of their combined efforts is a magisterial work that will become an essential reference volume for students and scholars alike desiring a convenient book that examines all important primary texts and scholarly positions in Pauline research, particularly in English and German.

Schnelle's book explores virtually every conceivable topic related to Paul's life and theology. Each chapter is designed to be read as an independent unit. There are surprisingly few repetitions in this massive study, so each section does stand on its own as the author intended. The book is divided into two parts that explore Paul's life and theology. The first, "The Course of Paul's Life and the Development of His Thought," explores Paul's life and writings in light of their historical context. In part 2, "The Basic Structures of Pauline Thought," Schnelle explores a wide variety of themes, such as Paul's understanding of God, Christology, the body, and the church. Perhaps the most valuable contribution of Schnelle's study is his extensive use of primary sources from the Hellenistic world. Throughout the entire work Schnelle seeks to summarize all major positions and relevant texts before offering his own interpretation. In many instances, lengthy passages, often from lesser-known Greek authors, are quoted in full. The result is a study that is quite balanced and thorough in its treatment of all major issues pertaining to Paul's thought.

Schnelle begins his study with an insightful prologue that not only examines the problems inherent in studying Paul but also defines his approach. Of particular interest is Schnelle's discussion of historiography. Schnelle emphasizes that within the realm of historical constructions there are no "facts" in the "objective" sense but that interpretations are built on interpretations (29). The problem, as he aptly highlights, is that historians wishing to understand Paul's life, and the influence of his career upon his theology, must explore both how and when his letters have been transmitted. Schnelle comments that a chronological outline makes it necessary to determine not only the number of authentic Pauline letters but their dates of composition as well. He begins by offering the reader a detailed chronology of Paul's life that is based on the authentically Pauline corpus (1 Thessalonians, 1–2 Corinthians, Galatians, Romans, Philippians, Philemon) and the book of Acts. Throughout the book Schnelle emphasizes the importance of chronology for understanding Paul's theology, a topic that he discusses in some fashion in nearly every chapter. For example, he comments that it is of considerable significance for understanding the place of the doctrine of justification in Paul's thought whether one dates Galatians after 1 Thessalonians but before the Corinthian correspondence, or prior to Romans. The result of such a chronological approach—in contrast to a purely thematic outline of Pauline theology—is a book that takes seriously the fact that each of Paul's letters was embedded in, and affected by, its own situation.

Many readers will undoubtedly find Schnelle's discussions of the discrepancies between Paul's letters and Acts to be the most insightful sections of his book. Schnelle recognizes that both Paul and the author of Acts incorporate fictional elements and that all historical reconstruction is to a great degree uncertain. To assist in distinguishing novelistic elements from historical truth in these writings, Schnelle considers each document's theological emphasis, giving primacy to Paul's own accounts of events whenever possible. He devotes much attention to what is perhaps the central problem in understanding Paul's theology and life, namely, the exact sequence of events following his conversion. Regarding the testimony of Acts that Paul visited Jerusalem immediately after his conversion (Acts 9:26), in contrast to Paul's statement that he did not (Gal 1:17), Schnelle favors Paul's own account. Schnelle notes that the author of Acts sought to emphasize the continuity of salvation history and church unity and therefore placed Paul's contact with the Jerusalem apostles immediately after his conversion. Although Schnelle recognizes that it is often difficult, perhaps impossible, to separate truth from fiction in Paul's writings and Acts, he generally prefers Paul's testimony, since Acts often presents a later theological interpretation of Paul's thought in light of his life. Schnelle's examination of fictional elements and rhetoric in Acts, in relation to Paul's mission and writings, complements the seminal work of Richard Pevro (*Profit with Delight: The Literary Genre of the Acts of the Apostles* [Philadelphia: Fortress, 1987]), which explores Acts' fictional qualities in light of Jewish, Christian, and pagan novels.

Schnelle adopts a chronological, rather than a thematic, approach throughout this volume to stress Paul's changing theology over the course of his life. He emphasizes that Paul's letters should be read as individual documents, constantly stressing that none presents a complete compendium of mature thought in light of the Damascus event. Although Schnelle recognizes that Paul's conversion experience contributed to his theology of justification and faith as developed in Galatians and Romans and that he undoubtedly thought about these topics prior to his conversion experience, we cannot assume that he had always thought about them in the categories found in Galatians and Romans. Schnelle comments, "The *subject matter* of justification and law had always been of concern to Paul since his conversion, but not the *doctrine* of justification and law as found in Galatians and Romans" (100). Concerning Romans, which many tend to read as *the* Pauline theology, Schnelle, in keeping with his attention to chronology, states that it should be understood as Pauline theology in the year 56 C.E. as set forth for the Roman church (42). The result of this approach is a book that portrays Paul as a man whose theology grew, changed, and adapted over time in light of his expanding understanding of the Torah and Gentile mission and in reaction to the incidents that took place during his own mission.

Among the many notable discussions of Paul's life and thought in this book is Schnelle's examination of early Christianity and Paul's persecution of Christians. Regarding the debate over the influence of Hellenism on Judaism, Schnelle seeks a middle course and believes that Paul, and the early Christians as well, participated in debates that were carried on both within Judaism and the Greco-Roman world. For this reason, Schnelle seeks to highlight the contributions of pagan Greco-Roman literature and Jewish texts for understanding Paul's life and thought. However, whereas the authors of pagan Greco-Roman material were certainly not Jewish or Christian, since these writings reflect a polytheistic culture, Schnelle, as with many New Testament scholars, uncritically accepts a Jewish authorship for many noncanonical texts. For example, Schnelle uses *Joseph and Asenath* to explore possible Jewish antecedents to the later Christian mission to the Gentiles without any mention of the dating controversy of this book, which several scholars view as a product of late antiquity and not Jewish. The pioneering work of James R. Davila (*The Provenance of the Pseudepigrapha: Jewish, Christian, or Other?* [JSJSup 105; Leiden: Brill, 2005]), as well as the new edition of George W. E. Nickelsberg's classic text on Second Temple Jewish Literature (*Jewish Literature between the Bible and the Mishnah* [2nd ed.; Minneapolis: Fortress, 2005]) should force New Testament scholars to exercise caution when using the pseudepigrapha for reconstructing early Jewish thought, since it cannot be excluded that some of these works could have been written by Christians. Nevertheless, Schnelle's use of Jewish and Greco-Roman texts in particular makes this an essential reference book, since many lengthy passages of lesser-known works are quoted in full.

Schnelle's use of the Qumran texts for understanding Paul's thoughts, and his attention to Hellenistic Jewish literature and culture, is quite welcome and often lacking in many works on Pauline theology. His discussion of Jewish literature and Paul's theology is among the more insightful contributions of his volume. Schnelle highlight's Paul's background as an observant Pharisee raised in the Greco-Roman world who was comfortable in two cultural spheres. He emphasizes that Paul was a Torah-observant Jew who persecuted the nascent Christian sect because of its proclamation of the crucified Jesus as the Messiah, its critical view of the temple, and the growing independence of its organizational structure and missionary practice. Schnelle's comments on Paul's thought and background could have been strengthened by a more extensive treatment of Pharisaic religion, as well as the problems inherent in reconstructing the beliefs and practices of this religious sect. Although Schnelle cautiously weighs the evidence, and considers the apologetic character of Paul's writings and Acts, he often accepts the testimony of Josephus at face value. Rather than accepting Josephus's statements regarding the Pharisees as factual and then using this information to reconstruct

Paul's background, Schnelle fails to recognize that Josephus's writings are also apologetic historiography. Josephus often obscures or distorts historical facts in light of the post-70 C.E. destruction of the temple and his situation in Rome, to buttress his own agenda in the same manner as Paul and Acts. (For an examination of this important issue, see now the collection of essays on the topic edited by Zuleika Rodgers, *Making History: Josephus and Historical Method* [JSJSup 110; Leiden: Brill, 2006].) A reference to Steve Mason's classic study on this issue (*Flavius Josephus on the Pharisees: A Composition-Critical Study* [Leiden: Brill, 1991]) could have helped this section, as well as a reference to more recent literature on the *Psalms of Solomon,* which has challenged its Pharisaic authorship.

Schnelle builds upon his discussion of Paul's Pharisaic background to discuss the apostolic council as recounted in Acts with Galatians. The basic issue dealt with at this council, according to Schnelle, was how to account for Gentiles in the movement, whose presence alongside Jews outside the land of Israel was not sufficiently dealt with in the Torah. Schnelle believes that the apostolic council did not unite Paul's Gentile mission and the mission to the Jews into a single view. Rather, it regarded each as a legitimate expression of the Christian faith: "It was the equal status, not the identity, for each version of the gospel that was confirmed at the apostolic council" (129). Paul's innovation at this council was in separating circumcision and Torah observance from membership in the church for Gentile Christians. For this reason, Schnelle argues that it is erroneous to connect the origin of the Pauline doctrine of justification in the exclusive sense with this council or with the Antioch incident. At this time Paul both defended his view that Gentiles were free from the requirement of circumcision and acknowledged that Jewish Christians were obligated to follow the Torah. However, by the time he wrote Galatians, Paul believed that there was only one gospel that was valid for Jews and Gentiles and that the Torah no longer had constitutive significance for Jew (Jewish Christians) or Gentile (Gentile Christians).

There are too many issues raised in Schnelle's book to discuss in this review. Readers will find a wealth of material in this book, as well as several provocative theses. Schnelle believes that Christianity's early success, and the eventual parting of the ways between Christianity and Judaism, were to a great extent the consequence of Christianity's unique universal plan of messianic redemption that included people of all nations and cultures. He proposes that the success of the Christian mission among Gentile sympathizers of the synagogue in Rome led to a defensive reaction within Judaism, which was acerbated in the aftermath of Claudius's edict. In his discussion of the early Christian movement, Schnelle highlights the important role of house churches, which, like Hellenistic Jewish synagogue congregations, appeared to outsiders as clubs or associations. (For this issue, see further the insightful study of Philip A. Harland, *Associations, Synagogues, and Congregations: Claiming a Place in Ancient Mediterranean Society* [Minneapolis: Fortress, 2003].) He also highlights the growing skepticism among many pagans regarding the multiplicity of gods and the rise of pagan monotheism as a factor that greatly helped the early Christian mission. (For this important observation, see further the essays in Polymnia Athanassiadi and Michael Frede, eds., *Pagan Monotheism in Late Antiquity* [Oxford: Oxford University Press, 1999].)

Schnelle's book, although quite lengthy, is written and translated quite well: it is a pleasure to read. The author and translator have worked well together to produce a work that surpasses the German original: it should be regarded as an entirely new study! Schnelle's book will undoubtedly become a classic in the field. For the size and scope of this volume, its price is quite reasonable. It is an ideal work for both seasoned scholar and novice alike: both will discover plenty to ponder in this massive work. For those interested in the New Testament and early Christian history, Schnelle's book is essential reading.

Die Briefe des Paulus an die Philipper und an Philemon: Ein Kommentar, by Wilfried Eckey. Neukirchen-Vluyn: Neukirchener, 2006. Pp. xiv + 241. Paper. €19.90. ISBN 3788721456.

Stephan Witetschek, Katholieke Universiteit Leuven, Leuven, Belgium

This commentary on Paul's letters to the Philippians and to Philemon is one volume in a series of commentaries on diverse books of the New Testament that Wilfried Eckey has been publishing for some years now (the commentaries on Mark, Acts, and Luke are already published). One may regard these commentaries as the *summa* of his scholarship and the fruit of several decades of teaching at the Bergische Universität Wuppertal.

The volume contains two commentaries, on Philippians (1–144) and on Philemon (145–221), followed by a structured bibliography (222–41). This arrangement already reveals that Eckey—justifiably—considers Philippians and Philemon as more closely related than Colossians and Philemon, which are treated in a single volume in quite a number of commentary series (e.g., HNT, KEK, NIGTC, ÖTBK, WBC).

The commentary on Philippians begins with a relatively extensive introduction (1–39). First, Eckey gives a short but well-informed historical survey about the ancient city and Roman colony of Philippi (3–8). After a brief sketch of the letter's line of thought (9–10), he comes to the most hotly debated introductory questions concerning Philippians: the literary integrity (10–20) and the place from which Paul wrote the letter(s) (20–31). Then follow some remarks on what can be known about the Christian community in Philippi in the first and early second centuries C.E. (31–39).

As to the question of literary integrity, Eckey favors the theory that Philippians consists of three originally independent letters: A (4:10–20); B (1:1–3:1; 4:4–7, 21–23); and C (3:2–4:3, 8–9). He begins his treatment of this topic by imposing the burden of proof upon those who vote for literary integrity. For his basic decision—Philippians as a compilation of three originally independent documents that are now so complexly intertwined with each other—Eckey refers to a number of other scholars who also hold this view; he gives his own argumenta-

428   Review of Biblical Literature

tion on some debated details, such as the status of Phil 4:21–23. Although this reviewer remains skeptical about such complicated partition theories, this rather small commentary is certainly not the place to develop at length the arguments for and against the literary integrity of Philippians.

As to localization (and date), Philippians (rather: Philippians A and B) and Philemon are treated together, since both letters were written in the same situation of captivity. So the search for a place of composition is at the same time the search for a place where Paul spent some extended time in prison. Eckey discusses all the relevant arguments for and against Rome, Caesarea, and Ephesos as places where the prisoner Paul might have composed Philippians and Philemon. In the end, he opts for Ephesos, since this solution best fits the situation presupposed in the two (or three) letters, and the only serious objection, Luke's silence about an imprisonment in Ephesos, does not positively exclude the imprisonment (30: "Lukas wußte vermutlich mehr, als er aufgeschrieben hat").

After these controversies, Eckey sketches the history of the Christian community in Philippi, for which he relies on Philippians, on Acts, and on what is known from the excavations in Philippi. The letter Philippians C finds a place in this history: Paul wrote it after the second visit to Philippi, while he was in Corinth; hence Philippians C is almost contemporaneous with Romans. The introduction is concluded by a few words about the Christian community in Philippi in the early second century, for which, however, only Polycarp's letters are available as sources.

In the exposition proper, Eckey draws the logical consequence from his literary-critical decision and comments on each of the supposed three letters separately: Philippians B (40–103), A (104–12), and C (113–44). He consistently understands them as addressed to a community in a given historical situation, that is, to Christians in a Roman colony in the Greek-speaking East—in the Macedonian "little Rome," as he puts it. However, one may question whether Phil 1:27–30 really betrays a situation of pressure amounting to persecution (69–73); the passage could also be understood as referring to Christian adversaries, a reading that would give some thematic coherence to Philippians as a whole (i.e., Phil 1:1–4:23). Not only the exposition itself but also numerous excursuses shed light on the Roman, Hellenistic, or early Jewish background of certain motifs and topics, such as the office of ἐπίσκοποι (45–46) or the use of metaphors from the field of sports (128–29).

The commentary on the letter to Philemon likewise begins with an introduction (147–55). Since the place and date of composition have been discussed in connection with Philippians (see above), Eckey here deals only with the destination, which he, like most other exegetes, identifies with Kolossai (153–55). The larger part of the introduction, however, is concerned with the background of the letter, with the question whether Onesimus was to be considered a *fugitivus* in terms of Roman law and with the question why he left his master and met Paul in prison. With regard to the latter, Eckey openly and soberly reveals how much we do *not* know and can only presume.

The exposition (156–79) again considers the cultural, geographical, and legal contexts; the letter to Philemon is interpreted as one piece in a larger communication. As seems to become usual in commentaries on Philemon, Eckey adds a number of additional reflections. First, there is a chapter "Skopus und Stellungnahme" (179–91), where he gives a guess as to how the story could have continued (180–82); then follow two substantial excursuses on similar cases of intercession for slaves or freed-persons (182–83) and on attitudes toward slavery in antiquity (183–91). Second, Eckey tries to elaborate Paul's view on slavery by comparing the letter to Philemon with 1 Cor 7:21–24 (191–98). Paul's attitude appears pragmatic and flexible. While he neither advocates nor denounces slavery in itself and gives to Christian slaves the general rule to remain in their state (1 Cor 7:21a, 24), he encourages them to use the new opportunity in case they should be set free (1 Cor 7:21b: ἀλλὰ … μᾶλλον χρῆσαι), and he seems to expect Philemon to set Onesimus free (esp. Phlm 21). Third, there is an appendix (199–221) with a number of early Christian texts dealing with Christian slaves and their masters—Col 3:22–4:1; Eph 6:5–9; 1 Tim 6:1–2; Tit 2:9–10; 1 Pet 2:18–25; *1 Clem.* 55:2; Ignatius, *Pol.* 4:3; *Did.* 4:10-11; *Barn.* 19:7; the account of the martyrs of Lyons and Vienne (Eusebius, *Hist. eccl.* 5.1.1–63)—and a glance at slaves as holders of church offices. Thus, this part of the volume is not only a commentary on the letter to Philemon but also a short repertory of source texts about slavery and slaves in early Christianity.

As to the commentary as a whole, the reader can clearly perceive that this book is written by someone who has been professionally concerned with the formation of teachers of religious education. Eckey avoids unnecessarily technical language and explains the technical terms he uses. At times his language even becomes colloquial, such as when he translates Ἐχάρην δὲ ἐν κυρίῳ μεγάλως (Phil 4:10)—not incorrectly—with: "Ich habe mich im Herrn riesig gefreut." On the other hand, however, his sentences are sometimes rather lengthy. He often draws mostly instructive parallels to modern social conventions or figures of speech. Greek words and phrases always appear together with a translation, sometimes with a transcription as well. Consequently, the commentary is a helpful tool also for readers who are not so fluent in Greek or never learned it at all—and for those who, in school or pastoral service, have become somewhat out of touch with "hard" scholarly exegesis. All in all, with this commentary a retired academic teacher has met the needs of his former students who might look for some concise exegetical treatment of and background information on a biblical text to be dealt with in the classroom. Let me warmly recommend this book to their critical, perceptive, and open-minded reading.

Solidarity and Difference: A Contemporary Reading of Paul's Ethics, by David G. Horrell. London: T&T Clark, 2005. Pp. xvi + 339. Paper. $49.95. ISBN 0567043223.

Victor Paul Furnish, Southern Methodist University, Dallas, Texas

This isn't just another good book on Pauline ethics. True, David Horrell (Senior Lecturer in New Testament Studies, University of Exeter, UK) addresses many of the usual questions and offers interpretations of some of the usual passages. But his approach is unusual, in that he seeks to engage Paul's letters in the light of certain present-day ethical theories. And his fresh interpretation of the apostle's moral argumentation significantly advances the discussion of his ethics.

In the opening chapter Horrell identifies various topics in Pauline ethics that emerged "from Bultmann to Boyarin." These include the integration of indicatives and imperatives; Paul's moral heritage; the social context of Pauline ethics; and how the apostle's ethics might be appropriated today. While he espouses a social-scientific approach to Paul's letters, he believes that more attention must be given to the moral "arguments" and "framework" of the apostle's thought than he finds, for example, in the work of Wayne Meeks. And he identifies his own primary aim as engaging Paul's "community-forming discourse" with "contemporary ethical theory" (45, 46).

Chapter 2 is devoted to expositions of "liberal" ethical theory, exemplified especially by Jürgen Habermas, and "communitarian" theory, exemplified especially by Stanley Hauerwas. Habermas's "discourse ethics" are characterized as deontological and committed to a "rational and universalistic basis for public morality" (51), while Hauerwas's "ecclesial ethics" are described as summoning the church to "be the Church and not the world," remaining faithful to "its own particular, true story" (64). Although Horrell notes ways in which each of these positions must be criticized, he nonetheless maintains that the debate suggests some questions worth raising with respect to Paul's ethics, including: What are Paul's most fundamental norms? What, for him, gives the Christian community its distinctive identity? And does he allow for any "differences" within the community or for any sort of "universal rationality" that would involve a broad sharing of ethical values?

Horrell keeps these questions and the liberal-communitarian debate in view as he examines the apostle's ethical thinking (his sources are the seven certainly-Pauline letters). In chapter 3, invoking social-scientific categories (e.g., symbolic universe, story, ritual, ethos), he offers preliminary remarks about the "conceptual framework" of Paul's ethics. While he maintains that the apostle's letters contain "explicit and self-conscious" moral argumentation, he also holds that "at least in a general sense, everything in [them] is potentially relevant to a consideration of his 'ethics'" (98). The aim in chapter 4 is to show that, for Paul, "corporate solidarity" is a "metanorm" (the "key moral norm" [101]), in that it "determines the moral framework within which other norms, values and customs can be articulated and practised" (99 n. 2). Noting that Paul regards Christ's death and resurrection as the "central events in a cosmic story," he argues convincingly that, for the apostle, this story provides the "fundamental hermeneutical orientation by which [the world] is to be understood" (110), that "incorporation into Christ" establishes the community's "solidarity" (131), and that this "solidarity in Christ" is the "central theme of the Christian ethos" (110).

In chapter 5 the author shows that Paul's emphasis on the solidarity of the Christian community involves "a sense of [its] distinction and separation from the world" (133) and a concern for the maintenance of appropriate boundaries. He points out that Paul's "language of distinction" functions to "reinforce a strong sense of positive group identity," that he conceives of the group's boundaries as encompassing "all who are in Christ, both Jews and Gentiles" (138–39), and that he seeks to protect the "purity" of this community from unions (with the world, etc.) that endanger its union with Christ (152). But Horrell also takes note of the apostle's recognition that believers cannot exist in sectarian isolation from society, and he makes the important point that "Paul's claim [is] *not* so much that Christians live by *distinctive* ethical standards but rather that they live up to, and beyond, the ethical standards that others share but do not follow" (162, emphasis original).

The argument of chapter 6 is that "Christ-like other-regard," like solidarity in Christ, functions as a metanorm for Paul and that these two, taken together, form the conceptual framework for his ethic. In 1 Cor 8–10 and Rom 14–15, Horrell sees Paul writing as a moral philosopher, engaging in "reflection and argument on issues of ethics and morality" (167). In both passages Paul is responding to conflicting views that threaten to subvert the community's solidarity in Christ. Yet in neither case, as Horrell sagely observes, is it Paul's aim to *resolve* the differences or to educate one side or both to his own point of view. Rather, he aims to create "a pattern of relating within which these differences of conviction can remain, even though the practices that reflect these convictions must often be restricted out of concern for others" (198). Horrell rightly notes that Paul had confronted a different sort of situation in Antioch (Gal 2:11–14). In that case he perceived the exclusion of Gentile believers from table fellowship as violating the metanorms themselves and hence insisted that the "culturally-specific norms" followed by those who withdrew from the table had to be set aside (201–2).

The christological grounding of Paul's ethic that is reflected in its two metanorms is explored further in chapter 7. Here special attention is given to Phil 2:5–11; 1 Cor 9:14ff.; the apostle's reference to a "law of Christ"; and his appeal in 2 Cor 8:9–15 on behalf of the collection for Jerusalem. Horrell concludes that the metanorm of other-regard is not promoted as an abstract moral principle (e.g., like the Golden Rule) "but rather as a pattern of behaviour which constitutes a conformity to the pattern of Christ's self-giving" (241). Thus "other-regard" is to be seen as a concise and concrete definition of what Paul understands love to imply (242).

The question posed in chapter 8 is whether Paul has "any sense that all

people can, should, or do have the scope to recognize common, universal, ethical norms" (247). Especially in Rom 1–2 and 13:1–7, Horrell finds evidence that
Paul does indeed believe that "Torah-defined good and evil" is recognized even
by those who do not know the law of God (250) and that the apostle would identify the worship of God and love of neighbor as "universal moral imperatives"
(252). Moreover, underlying Paul's injunctions to practice good toward outsiders
(e.g., 1 Thess 3:12; 5:15; Gal 6:10), he rightly discerns the presupposition that, to
a significant extent, Christians share with all people a common understanding of
what constitutes "good" conduct.

The concluding chapter of the book opens with a series of seven theses that
draw together the author's conclusions about Paul's ethics. These highlight the
metanorms of corporate solidarity and other-regard; how the latter enables differences to remain even as it relativizes them; the substantive, not just motivational
importance of Christology for Paul's ethic; the "considerable extent" to which the
church and the world share the same ethical values; and that some of Paul's "specific ethical convictions" were derived from "his contemporary world, especially
Judaism" (279). In a second section, Horrell compares Paul's ethic to liberal and
communitarian views. On the one hand, he believes that there is a "fundamental congruence" between Paul's ethic and the ecclesial ethic of Hauerwas (280)
and important differences between the apostle's views and those of liberals like
Habermas. Yet he also acknowledges "notable and significant structural and substantive similarities" between the liberal ethic and Paul's (282). The chapter closes
with brief descriptions of three different models for appropriating Paul's ethical thought today. The first ("Paul's ethics for the 'politics called church'") is not
unlike the ecclesial ethics of Hauerwas; the second ("Paul's ethics for the church
and the world") shares the liberal goal of achieving a broad consensus of ethical
values; and the third ("Paul's ethics for a plural society") would develop "new
stories, new myths about human solidarity and difference which avoid the notion
that only Christ can provide their basis, and in so doing go not only beyond but
against Paul" (290).

Probably the most innovative aspect of this book is Horrell's examination
of Paul's ethics in the light of modern ethical theories. He shows, in particular, that Paul can be fruitfully queried with reference to certain issues that have
emerged from the communitarian-liberal debate. To his credit, he accomplishes
this without allowing modern questions to control his exegesis; nor does he,
anachronistically, force the apostle to pledge allegiance either to liberalism or
communitarianism. Beyond this, three particular contributions of his study may
be singled out as especially noteworthy.

First, Horrell's work demonstrates that a social-scientific approach need
not rule out considering the role played by theological convictions in shaping
the ethos and worldview of the early Christian communities. He is attentive to
religious beliefs and contexts as well as to social forces and contexts. Similarly,
while he appreciates the need to take account of the particularities of the individual Pauline letters, he also recognizes that important elements of the apostle's

thought and certain ethical imperatives and forms of argumentation appear with some consistency throughout them.

Second, Horrell rightly emphasizes the importance of distinguishing between the "metanorms" that provide the conceptual framework of Paul's ethic and the apostle's specific moral directives. He shows that the latter (which are not, however, his focus in this study) are usually oriented to particular situations and culturally derived, while the metanorms are rooted in Paul's gospel (especially his Christology). Horrell makes a strong case for identifying these metanorms as "solidarity in Christ" and "Christ-like other-regard" and for regarding them as the essence of the love that Paul urges believers to pursue.

Third, Horrell takes Paul seriously as a "moral philosopher." He shows, for example, that Paul's Hellenistic moral heritage (especially but not only Jewish) plays a role in both his thought and his argumentation and further that numerous passages in his letters disclose the apostle consciously reflecting on moral issues. This, of course, does not mean that Paul's ethical thought is perfectly consistent; Horrell does not hesitate to point out the ambiguities as well as complexities of some of his moral judgments and does not try to explain them away.

Many readers, like this reviewer, will be concerned that Horrell's exposition of Paul's ethics includes no discussion of the apostle's eschatological outlook or the apocalyptic character of his thought. He explains, but not until the last chapter, that this is because "eschatology, the Spirit, and so on," although "motivating bases for ethical exhortation," do not show "what *constitutes* ethical action" (278, emphasis original) and also because he has tried to expound Paul's ethical exhortations "in terms that are meaningful outside the bounds of theological discourse" (279). It could be argued, however, that the second of these reasons applies no less to the apostle's Christology, which Horrell rightly identifies as the ground of his ethics. Moreover, is it not the case that Paul's Christology must itself be understood within the framework of an apocalyptic eschatology? Does he not proclaim Christ's death and resurrection as the revealing (ἀποκάλυψις) of a reality that places all human constructions of reality under judgment and therefore has consequences for all human aims, values, and institutions? In short, does not this apocalyptic-eschatological dimension of Christ's "self-lowering" give to the metanorms of "solidarity" and "other-regard" a character that they would not otherwise have? One wishes that Horrell had addressed the question of Pauline eschatology earlier and more extensively, if for no other reason than to justify his claim that it does not, in fact, contribute to the substance of Paul's ethic.

A second question is prompted by Horrell's comment that, given the metanorm of "other-regard," Paul directs that the practice of the "strong" in Corinth be "compromised insofar as it endangers the weak" (182) and his similar comment (192–93) concerning the apostle's own practice of accommodation to the situations of others (1 Cor 9:19–23). But is it *compromise,* or—as Horrell also says—the "*abandoning*" of "legitimate rights ... and freedom" (181, emphasis added) that Paul is asking of the strong and exemplifying when he becomes "weak" for the sake of the weak? Horrell rightly observes that Paul does not regard freedom as an "absolute value" (192). Is it not also true that Paul values freedom, not as an end in itself, but because it allows the unrestricted giving of oneself to God in obedience (Rom 6:12–23) and to others in love (Gal 5:13)? Arguably, the participle in 1 Cor 9:19 (ὤν) is best read, not as concessive (NRSV: "For though I am free with respect to all…"), but as causal: "*Because* I am free with respect to all, I have made myself a slave to all, so that I might win more of them" (see W. Schrage, *Der erste Brief an die Korinther* [1995], 2:338–39). Similarly, one may say that the strong are not directed to *compromise* or *restrict* their freedom but to *employ* it in order to build up the weak. The issue here is not just semantic. The question is where freedom is to be situated within the conceptual framework of Paul's ethic as Horrell has portrayed that. Although the apostle does not value freedom absolutely, neither does he count it among the culturally specific norms that can be "given up," for he understands it to be a gift of God and integral to one's calling in Christ.

There are various additional points where attention to related Pauline themes would enrich the exposition or where more detail would bolster the author's case (an example of the latter: his sketchy presentation of possible models for appropriating Paul's ethics). Yet there is far more to praise than to query about this book. It is an engaging and important contribution to Pauline studies.

1 and 2 Thessalonians: A Socio-Rhetorical Commentary, by Ben Witherington III. Grand Rapids: Eerdmans, 2006. Pp. xxxi + 286. Paper. $30.00. ISBN 0802828361.

Craig L. Blomberg, Denver Seminary, Littleton, Colorado

This illustrious New Testament professor at Asbury Seminary is closing in on his goal of having written commentaries, most of them sociorhetorical, on every book (or small groups of books) in the New Testament. His offering on the two Thessalonian letters is more substantial than most of his efforts, devoting almost as much attention to their eight chapters as he does, say, to Mark's sixteen or 1–2 Corinthians' twenty-nine.

His introductory conclusions largely match traditional evangelical commentary. Paul is writing around 50–51 from Corinth, with his co-workers, in light of a comparatively brief time spent in Thessalonica planting the church there. That time ended in fierce Jewish opposition and has spawned persecution from Jew and Gentile of the fledgling Christian church in town ever since. Second Thessalonians should not be viewed as pseudonymous; epistles were the one main genre of the day for which we have by far the smallest amount of evidence of Jewish or Greco-Roman acceptance of pseudonymity, and none whatever in Christian circles. The arguments against Pauline authorship, like those for reversing the chronological order of what we have come to call 1 and 2 Thessalonians, are comparatively weak.

With respect to sociological backgrounds, Witherington follows the recent, persuasive consensus that sees the abuse of patron-client relationships, of which

Paul wants to wean Greco-Romans off when they become believers, as behind the problem of the idle, hinted at in the first letter and addressed head on in the second. There is, to be sure, the false belief among some that they had missed the (entirely spiritual) resurrection (2 Thess 2:2), but this belief does not account for their idleness, not least because it is *not* the same as believing that the resurrection was still imminent on the horizon.

It is with his rhetorical analysis that Witherington makes his most distinctive contributions, and, thus, it is here where he will be alternately hailed or questioned the most. Positing a sharp distinction between epistolary and rhetorical forms, he opts unequivocally for the latter, dividing 1 Thessalonians into an epistolary prescript and *exordium* (1:1–3), a large *narratio* (1:4–3:10), a *transitus* (3:11–12), *exhortatio* (4:1–15), *peroratio* (5:16–22), and an invocation and epistolary closing (5:23–28). Because he sees the letter as largely epideictic (praising and blaming) rhetoric, there is no need for a *propositio*, while the narration of what is praised and blamed can be extensive.

Second Thessalonians, however, utilizes mostly deliberative rhetoric and subdivides into a prescript and *exordium* (1:3–10), a *propositio* (1:11–12), a *refutatio* (2:1–12), a section on prayer (2:13–3:5) and another on work (3:6–12), a *peroratio* (3:13–15), and closing (3:16–18). The unusual placement of a refutation immediately after the proposition is not unprecedented and shows the urgency of the problem.

All these concepts get unpacked, explained, and illustrated both in the introduction and at the relevant places in the commentary. Some dovetail nicely with more conventional outlines that follow the typical structure of the Hellenistic letter. For example, exhortational material typically forms the last main section of the letter body, while opening greetings and prayers/thanksgivings, like their counterparts at the *ends* of epistles, mesh reasonably well with the more rhetorical outlines Witherington utilizes. It is not as clear, however, that 1 Thess 1:4–3:10 all belongs together (rather than keeping 1:5–10 with the opening prayer or word of thanksgiving), nor that 2:1–12 is not more comprehensively explained as simply the information-providing main section of a letter body, nor that the three segments Witherington identifies in 2:13–3:12 fit rhetorical categories, especially when two of them he does not even try to fit into such a structure, nor that the last two verses of a prayer (2 Thess 1:11–12) form a thesis sentence for the letter (especially when 2:2 fits much better into this role). But if we recognize, with Janet Fairweather and others, that the lines are not so hard and fast between oral rhetoric and written epistles, not least because letters such as these were meant to be read aloud publicly to the congregations they addressed, then we do not have to feel forced either to analyze them entirely via classical rhetorical categories or to reject such categorizations altogether.

When one turns to Witherington's passage-by-passage exposition, as is typically true of his commentaries, the vast majority of his insights prove reliable, helpful, and incisive. Whenever he gets a chance to put in a plug for his Wesleyan-Arminianism, he does so, including some very helpful and balanced comments and contemporary applications of the juxtaposition of commands concerning prayer and work at the end of the second epistle. As elsewhere, too, and even more convincingly than in his promotion of corporate election, he has no time for classic dispensationalism; 1 Thess 4:17 makes no sense as the description of a pretribulational rapture. The meeting (Greek *apantēsis*) often referred to the arrival of a triumphant general or visiting dignitary who would be welcomed by townspeople outside the city gates and escorted back into the city with honor. Given all the other language that so often was co-opted by Caesar to refer to what he thought he could offer (good news, peace, safety, epiphanies, salvation, etc.), it is hard to imagine the language here not similarly implying that Jesus is the only one who can really do what the emperor requires acclamation for being able to do. Jesus will return to earth, and believers will be caught up to greet him in the air and escort him back to earth in triumph at the Parousia.

The additional eschatological debates surrounding 2 Thess 2 find Witherington, a bit more curiously, accepting the "temple of God" as the literal edifice in Jerusalem (even though every other use of "temple" in Paul refers to the church), because he believes that if Paul had lived to see the Roman general Titus over-run the temple precincts in A.D. 70 he would have seen plenty of foreshadowings of the ultimate end of the age. For the same reason he does not want to iden-tify the restrainer with the emperors or any comparable system of government (that would be too positive a role for them), but more likely with the man of law-lessness. With Colin Nicholl, Witherington suggests that the archangel Michael should be understood to be the restrainer.

More satisfying are Witherington's detailed and nuanced remarks showing how even as strong a passage as 1 Thess 2:14–16 is not anti-Semitic. So, too, fol-lowing Malherbe, is his repeated insistence that Paul is contrasting his behavior with the huckster Greco-Roman philosophers of his day and reminding his audi-ence about his exemplary behavior among them, even as he commends them for the good reports he has heard about them from others. Imitation of older and/or more mature Christians in every walk of life remains crucial for growth in Chris-tian living and a particular challenge for those of us who have so professionalized ministry that our charges seldom if ever have a chance to see how we live away from the office (or pulpit), as it were. Bucking current trends a little is Witherington's return to an older view that saw the vessels of 1 Thess 4:4 that men were to acquire or maintain in honor referring to wives rather than to their own bodies. But this approach may well make better sense of the warning not to defraud other believers in the process (despite what I just wrote in my newly released *From Pentecost to Patmos: An Introduction to Acts through Revelation* [Broadman & Holman] under this passage!).

As in many of Witherington's commentaries, when it comes to Greek transliteration or lexical forms, one has to check every one of the words very carefully, and it seems there are almost always far too many errors. On page xxxi, in the reference to Witherington's own previous journal article, the Greek word should read *Eidōlothuton,* not *Eidolathuton*; on page 50 the word is *sunagōgē,* not *sunagōgos*; on page 57 *adialeptos* requires a long *o*; on page 58 *proseuchon* should be *proseuchē*; on page 72 *thilipsis* should be *thlipsis*; on page 87 *symphyletos* needs to read *symphyletēs*; on page 92 note 133, *synergos* should read *synergon,* and so on, throughout the book. But these annoying errors notwithstanding, the volume contains a wealth of helpful information at a medium-level and length that every serious theological student or graduate should be able to handle and find exceedingly useful. From the sociorhetorical portions, scholars, too, will learn new options, even if they may evaluate their relative merits variously.

Hierarchy, Unity, and Imitation: A Feminist Rhetorical Analysis of Power Dynamics in Paul's Letter to the Philippians, by Joseph A. Marchal. Society of Biblical Literature Academia Biblica 24. Atlanta: Society of Biblical Literature; Leiden: Brill, 2006. Pp. viii + 261. Paper/cloth. $39.95/$122.00. ISBN 1589832434/900415115X.

Jennifer Bird, Vanderbilt University, Nashville, Tennessee

This rhetorical analysis of Philippians is an engaging and forward-looking dissertation. In addition to the expected history of scholarship on the relevant aspects of the letter and the "one thing new" that a dissertation is "allowed" to do, Marchal dives into the implications or usefulness of Paul's rhetorical savvy and highlights some of the sociopolitical dynamics often overlooked in discussions on friendship and military imagery in this letter. In addition to those who are normally interested in feminist analyses of biblical texts, those who would benefit most from this book, in my estimation, would be anyone interested in rhetorical studies in biblical scholarship (ch. 4 in particular) or in Pauline studies in general.

Marchal's brief introduction, setting the context, purpose, and procedure of the monograph, summarizes various rhetorical approaches applied to biblical studies; explains his feminist rhetorical approach, which includes the seven steps of Schüssler Fiorenza's "dance of interpretation"; and of course touches on some of the major issues related to working with Philippians. Marchal draws upon the rhetorical analytical work of Antoinette Wire, Elizabeth Castelli, and Elisabeth Schüssler Fiorenza. In concert with their approaches, one of the primary assumptions behind Marchal's rhetorical analyses is the claim that "the letter as argumentation makes the most sense in a context where authority is still a contested issue and the issues discussed are not settled dogma but living concerns" (13). Thus, the reader who posits Paul's authority for the Philippian communities and the early church in general as "a given" may take issue with Marchal, but if she or he pushes through, I think the reader will find many helpful insights can be culled from this book. It is divided into two parts, "Setting the Stage" and "How Philippians Implements These Rhetorics," with two and three chapters, respectively.

In chapter 2, "Critical Overview of Scholarship on Prominent Images,"

Marchal begins with an initial survey of the scholarship on friendship and military imagery, the two sets of images scholars address most often. It is in his "feminist reassessment" that Marchal highlights the political, gendered, and class dynamics and hierarchical/kyriarchal social structure of friendships at the time, noting the connection with patronage systems. A critical engagement with some of the dynamics under the surface of military imagery, including issues of settlement and occupation of various colonies, produces a similar reconfiguring for baseline assumptions about the use of military language and the effects it may have had on the initial audiences. These two aspects of society, friendships and the military, were part and parcel of the kyriarchal social structures. As such, scholarship that deals with these realms, Marchal suggests, would benefit from considering the exploitation and domination that such language engenders and at times prescribes. Two "cues" from this critical engagement direct the remainder of the book: scholars are charged to pay attention to the "potentially oppressive power relations reflected in the letter" (71) and to recognize that, even if one can delineate multiple rhetorical strategies at work, they may be "interrelated and mutually supporting in the argumentation" (72) in oppressive or possibly liberating ways.

The third chapter, "Situating the Rhetorics of Philippians," is relevant to the overall purpose but, ironically, is not situated well within the flow of the book. Given the previous chapter's dual foci of friendship and military imagery, I was somewhat blindsided by a discussion of women in cultic life and in the early Jesus movement in Philippi. Those topics plus his succinct appraisal of unity rhetorics in ancient civic speeches and the colonial status and military situation at Philippi do indeed demonstrate the need for a "multi-factored analysis and an analytic of domination" (112) of not just the situation in Philippi but of the content of the letter and of the scholarship on it.

In part 2 of the book, "How Philippians Implements these Rhetorics," chapter 4, "Evolving Rhetoric: The Interaction of Arguments as They Develop," provides a section-by-section analysis of the developing or evolving rhetoric of the letter, and chapter 5, "Prevailing Rhetoric: The Major Arguments," analyzes the way the rhetorical devices function in the overall effect of the letter using Olbrechts-Tyteca and Perelman's rhetorical categories (arguments of dissociation, quasi-logical arguments, arguments based on the structure of reality, arguments establishing the structure of reality).

I found chapter 4 more helpful than the next in giving an analysis of the rhetoric of the letter, with a nod toward the implications of such language. In both of these rhetorical analyses, Marchal makes much of Olbrechts-Tyteca and Perelman's unique contribution to rhetorical studies: the "interaction of arguments" that their "flexible and interdependent conceptualization of argumentation" (118) allows. While thoroughly versed in the rhetorical scholarship related to New/Second Testament studies, Marchal has gone beyond simply noting the rhetorical moves to suggesting the implications of them from a position that does not need to produce a positivistic interpretation.

The conclusions Marchal can and does draw from this project have significant implications in light of previous scholarship, specifically within the realm of analyzing potentially oppressive aspects of the text through the rhetorics of both the letter and its interpretation. He has provided an entrée into several other avenues for feminist and liberationist interpretations of this text, starting with a fuller evaluation of the charge to Euodia and Syntyche to "think the same" as Paul. The sameness rhetoric when paired with authority, divine or otherwise, taps into numerous other realms of discourse, such as issues of identity and experience, colonization and neocolonialism, class and gender concerns, and so forth. Ultimately, Marchal would have us take into account the interconnectedness of all of these possible approaches to Philippians.

The book also has an appendix of Marchal's outline of the argumentative techniques used in Philippians, a thirty-page bibliography, and indexes of ancient sources and modern authors.

The work as a whole left me wanting more in the following four ways. (1) The work on friendship and military language could have been threaded into the rhetorical analysis in some way, especially given the power dynamics of such imagery and its role in constructing social relations/reality, as Marchal notes in chapter 2. (2) For those who are not completely familiar with Olbrechts-Tyteca and Perelman's four categories, a more thorough explanation or discussion of dissociative rhetoric would benefit the reader, as this is a distinctive aspect of their work and is pivotal to Marchal's evaluation of the rhetoric in Philippians. (3) A smoother transition into and out of chapter three would be helpful, in particular as he discusses "unity rhetorics" and the military situation of Philippi. The thesis could have been strengthened by making clear the connection between these issues and the systematic analyses of Paul's rhetoric. (4) On a more personal note, I did miss the flair that I know Marchal to have in other scholarly settings, but that, I suppose, will have to wait for his next book.

1. *Korinther*, by Peter Arzt-Grabner, Ruth Elisabeth Kritzer, Amfilochios Papathomas, and Franz Winter. Papyrologische Kommentare zum Neuen Testament 2. Göttingen: Vandenhoeck & Ruprecht, 2006. Pp. 576. Cloth. €99.00. ISBN 3525510012.

Joseph Verheyden, University of Leuven, Leuven, Belgium

This is the second volume in an ambitious project to write a series of commentaries on all the books of the New Testament that has as its major focus the evidence from the documentary papyri. The first volume, on Philemon, appeared in 2003 and was from the pen of Peter Arzt-Grabner, who is one of the three co-editors of the Papyrologische Kommentare (the other two are Amphilochios Papathomas and Mauro Pesce) and the driving force behind the whole project. To a far larger degree than this first volume, the one on 1 Corinthians is the result of teamwork. The team consisted mainly of Peter Artz-Grabner, Ruth Elisabeth

Kritzer, Amphilochios Papathomas, and Franz Winter, but also included are two contributions by Michael Ernst, the long-time fellow traveler of Artz-Grabner in this project. The contributions of each member of the team are duly indicated. The volume has been prepared in three dissertations. Papathomas studied the juridical terminology in 1 Corinthians. His work is now being published as a monograph in the series of NTOA (*Juristische Begriffe im ersten Korintherbrief*). The reader is referred to it as an absolutely indispensable supplement to the commentary (5: "unbedingt empfohlen"). Winter (2000) and Kritzer (2004) submitted dissertations on, respectively, 1 Cor 1–4 and 5–6 that have been largely included in this volume ("die hiermit veröffentlicht werden, teilweise gekürzt"). Artz-Grabner was responsible for the final redaction and has himself contributed numerous sections, some of them in collaboration with Winter or Kritzer. The German translation of the letter was prepared by Kritzer and Artz-Grabner.

Those familiar with the volume on Philemon will notice the similarities in the approach, but probably also the differences. *Philemon* was introduced by a very long chapter surveying the papyrological (and some other) evidence for slavery in antiquity. By contrast, the introduction to this second volume is very short (27–34) and basically limited to the question of the epistolary genre. On the other hand, *1 Corinthians* contains thirteen excursus, most of them on functions (scribes, teachers), on the status of certain categories of people (widows, virgins), or on certain social and legal practices (divorce, manumission of slaves).

Paul's letter to the Corinthians offers ample opportunities for citing papyri, and the authors do not seem to have missed one to do so. The list of papyri or ostraca cited or referred to contains about 3,800 documents! As one might expect, by far the larger part of the evidence that can be gained from the papyri informs us about socioeconomic realities rather than about religious or, for that matter, theological issues. Due place is given to papyri illustrating marriage and divorce procedures, invitations to (cultic) meals, or realia of various sorts. One will understand that not all of these references bear equal weight. But even comments or illustrations of a more "mundane" nature can be of some interest for clarifying the text, if only to show that some words one would consider to be part of the common vocabulary are only rarely or not attested at all in the papyri. Thus, in the "daily-life" image in 5:6 of "the leaven leavening the whole lump," φύραμα is found only once in the whole corpus of papyri that are studied, and no illustration can be cited for the verb ζυμόω (210). Likewise, a word such as μάκελλος in 10:25 is not so well attested as one would assume, and then only from the third century c.e. on (see 374).

In other cases the evidence of the papyri, while quite substantial in documenting a particular praxis, offers no help for deciding on the interpretation of the letter. The elliptic μᾶλλον χρῆσαι in 7:21, for example, has been interpreted as "avail of the opportunity to get one's freedom" or, on the contrary, "to remain in slavery" or even "of the opportunity of being a Christian." Different procedures of manumission are mentioned in the papyri, but so far they have not produced an instance that would support the second possibility. It has been argued on this basis that one simply could not refuse the offer to be freed, but Artz-Grabner notes that it would be hard to find such evidence proving that one decided to remain in slavery, as this kind of decision was probably not put in writing (281: "der Nachweis für einen solchen Fall [kann] zumindest aus dokumentarischen Quellen gar nicht erwartet werden, da die von Paulus beschriebene Situation offensichtlich noch im Vorfeld eines rechtlichen und somit schriftlich erfassten Aktes liegt").

In yet other instances the negative evidence of the papyri may help to realize the exceptional character of Paul's thought. The papyri apparently offer only one late (sixth–seventh century) and somewhat ambivalent instance of the expression ἄνδρα ἔχειν (7:2). Kritzer comments: "Dieser Befund macht deutlich, wie lange eheähnliche Verbindungen im griechisch-römischen Kulturkreis ... in grossem Ausmass vom Mann bestimmt waren" (255). Paul, on the contrary, takes care to describe the situation from the perspective of both parties, and he goes on to do so in verses 3–4 as well. In this respect, it is worth noticing that the papyri describe instances of (financial) debts between partners, but not the kind of "obligations" ("marital duties") Paul is speaking about in 7:3 (256: "Eine direkte Parallele dazu ist in den Papyri bisher nicht zu finden"). Similarly, if the evidence of the papyri obviously does not help to decide on the authenticity of 14:34–35, it offers a rare example of the passive use of ἐπιτρέπω with a positive meaning (BGU I 347, col. ii), the subject subsequently being identified as the archpriest (466).

These few examples, selected at random, may illustrate that, even though for many a word papyrological evidence can be cited, it is not always easy to find a real "match." On the other hand, the papyrological material as often helps to clarify the background against which a particular word or expression may have been understood by Paul's readers. But the major asset of this project is the help it provides in opening up and sifting through a corpus of texts that still largely remains a sealed book for many biblical scholars, Deissmann or Moulton-Milligan notwithstanding. To wit, Berger-Colpe-Boring's *Hellenistic Commentary* contains only three references to papyri for the whole of 1 Corinthians: 5:1–13 (PGM I 4.1227–1264); and 8:10 (P.Oxy. I 110 and III 523). The famous PGM I 4 is now cited no less than seven times: at 5:4 (206 n. 53); 5:5 (208 n. 67); 10:1 (363); 14:7 (447); 14:23 (459 n.942); 15 (474); and 16:13 (517 n. 60). One should realize, however, that the same evidence can be used in somewhat different ways. The Papyrological Commentary duly refers to PGM I 4.1238 for the word "Satan" at 1 Cor 5:5. Boring (398) rather draws attention to the curse formula by which one is delivered to perdition, thus apparently taking Paul's παρὼν δὲ τῷ πνεύματι in this sense. The Papyrological Commentary does not comment on this interpretation and understands the expression in a neutral or even a positive way (202: "diese sorgende 'geistige Anwesenheit'"), citing UPZ I 69.2–3 and BGU IV 1080.6–8. One should further realize that sometimes an element of subjectivity may have played in deciding which text can or should be cited in a particular instance. The *Neuer Wettstein* cites only one papyrus for 1 Cor (P.Oxy. I 110, at 10:27). Boring cites the same text at 8:10. The Papyrological Commentary mentions it twice in the introduction to 1 Cor 8 when dealing with invitations to meals (321–27) but does not quote the text and instead prefers to cite P.Oslo III 157, P.Köln VI 280, and P.Oxy. XXXI 2592 and LII 3964,3–4.

One hopes the editors and collaborators of this giant project will find the courage and means to continue their research. The project certainly has the support of several prominent papyrologists, as indicated in the preface (6).

The Letters to Timothy and Titus, by Phillip Towner. New International Commentary on the New Testament. Grand Rapids: Eerdmans, 2006. Pp. xlviii + 885. Hardcover. $52.00. ISBN 0802825133.

Raymond F. Collins, The Catholic University of America, Washington, D.C.

Towner's commentary on the Pastoral Epistles, a title that he eschews, is certainly one of the largest, if not the largest, commentary to appear in English on these letters in recent years. Towner was well suited for the task. A revised version of his doctoral thesis, *The Goal of Our Instruction,* appeared under the Sheffield imprint almost twenty years ago. Since then he has not only published a number of articles on the Pastoral Epistles, but he has also worked with I. Howard Marshall in the preparation of the latter's ICC volume on the Pastorals.

Towner's disavowal of the "Pastoral Epistles" nomenclature forms a ring construction around his 89-page introduction (2, 88–89). At bottom he is less concerned with Pastoral Epistles language than he is with the idea that the use of such language promotes the idea that the three letters should be read as a single corpus. Towner prefers that they be read as individual compositions, with each individual letter serving as the primary context for the interpretation of any of its parts. At best, following an opinion promoted by Luke Timothy Johnson, Towner would allow that the three letters be identified as a cluster, similar to the Romans-Galatians, 1–2 Corinthians, and Ephesians-Colossians clusters of the Pauline epistles. From Johnson Towner has also taken the idea that the *mandata principis* provide an adequate paradigm for understanding the alternation of second-person and third-person passages within the letters.

Likewise contributing to Towner's dislike of the corpus notion as a useful tool in understanding these letters is his conviction that the letters are best read as genuine Pauline compositions. Towner considers the hypothesis of their pseudepigraphic nature as an assumption and takes issue with some, although not all, of the arguments advanced in favor of their late and pseudepigraphic nature. On the whole his arguments are consistent with those of Johnson, to whom he liberally refers, but Towner's rebuttal of the contemporary consensus with respect to authorship seems to this author to be rather weak. Towner's preference for Pauline authorship seems to be as much an assumption as the position with which he takes odds.

In addition to opting for the individuality and Pauline origin of each of the letters, Towner's exegesis supposes two other methodological principles: Paul's engagement with biblical (Old Testament) texts; and the importance of the location of the named addressees. Each of these principles is important, but they seem not to have consistent application throughout the millenary pages of the commentary. Towner makes good use of material pertaining to Crete and offers a valuable compendium of the ancient sources containing documentation pertinent to Crete (659–62). However, he uses material pertaining to Ephesus less often and less successfully. As far as the biblical material is concerned, many of the cited references are valuable, providing some good insights, but some of the referenced material seems to this reader to have been stretched a bit too far.

Three additional features of this commentary should likewise be noted in advance. First, rather than giving Towner's own translation of the Greek text, the commentary offers the English text of the TNIV. Towner sometimes distances himself from the interpretation of that version, but for the most part he lets it stand. Second, the commentary is heavily footnoted. Most of these notes are lexical in nature or provide secondary references. Third, the commentary contains six relatively short excursus ("Conscience in the Letters to Timothy and Titus"; "The 'Trustworthy Saying' Formula"; Godliness and Respectability"; "Self-Control"; Good Deeds"; and "The Epiphany Concept"), all of which are embedded in the commentary on 1 Timothy. For the most part the material contained in the excurses is lexical. They contain occasional useful reference to contemporary Hellenistic literature and sometimes compare the differences of usage among the three letters.

A work as massive as this one contains a valuable amount of interesting and useful commentary, but it suffers from occasional repetition prompting an "I have read that before" reaction from the reader. On the other hand, the commentary profits from the author's analysis of similarities between these three letters and the Pauline *homologoumena*.

It is obviously impossible to comment on Towner's analysis of each of the individual passages in this voluminous work. One particular feature, however, stands out. That is the influence of Bruce Winter's reconstruction of the "new Roman woman," a sort of sexual revolution before the sexual revolution of the 1960s, on Towner's interpretation of the passages dealing with women, notably, 1 Tim 2:9–16, a passage that Towner urges should be read in close connection with 2:8. Towner cites the new woman paradigm as well as realized eschatology and the teaching of the heretics as coalescing to produce the image of the woman susceptible to error/heresy that occasionally appears in these letters.

With regard to leadership positions within the church, Towner opines that the women of 1 Tim 3:11 are female deacons, albeit with lesser responsibilities than those of male deacons. His position on the individuality of each of the letters allows him to opine that the "overseers" and "elders" are separate entities in 1 Timothy, whereas both terms come together to describe one individual in Titus 1:5–7.

On reading the author's commentary on its various pericopes, I found myself sometimes saying "I agree," "I wish that I had said that," "I disagree," or "That's a stretch." That is probably a good thing, since it reminds me that this commentary contains a wealth of material and that its author is a good partner for dialogue about the significance of the letters to Timothy and Titus.

GENERAL EPISTLES AND HEBREWS

"Weist nicht ab den Sprechenden!": Wort Gottes und Paraklese im Hebraerbrief, by Tomasz Lewicki. Paderborner Theologische Studien 41. Paderborn: Schöningh, 2004. Pp. 159. Paperback. €26.00. ISBN 3506713264.

Harold W. Attridge, Yale Divinity School, New Haven, Connecticut

Lewicki's monograph, his dissertation at Paderborn under the direction of Professor Knut Backhaus, offers a sensitive and nuanced study of the motif of God's speech in the Epistle to the Hebrews. The work is carefully argued and well researched, in constructive dialogue with contemporary European and North American scholarship on Hebrews. The result is a serious, exegetically informed monograph on the theology of Hebrews.

The analysis begins with the obvious importance of the motif of God's scriptural voice in Hebrews. Key features of the motif are the sustained dialogue between God and Jesus that runs through the text and the direct address by the Spirit to hearers in the present. All of this speech is, of course, scriptural, and the anonymous discourse that is Hebrews channels and gives new life to the written word.

The conceit of making God's voice come alive through the medium of this "word of exhortation" serves a pastoral purpose, revivifying the faith of a community oppressed by external forces and tempted to abandon their commitment to a Christ whose ignominious death hardly helps their social standing. Lewicki's analysis of the situation of the addressees is fairly conventional and keeps open various social and theological explanations for the situation apparently addressed by the text. He has no doubt that the situation of the addressees is serious.

Lewicki's emphasis on the revitalized word of God as the solution to the pastoral problem does not ignore the conceptual moves that Hebrews makes. Lewicki believes that Hebrews is operating at least in part within a context where middle Platonic conceptual schemes are operative. Part of the response addresses that conceptual world, which posits a significant gulf between God and humankind; Jesus, the heavenly high priest, bridges that gap. Yet other issues also confront the community addressed, including the reality of sin, and the author emphasizes the definitive way in which the atoning death of Jesus deals with that problem. Jesus, in any case, is the definitive solution to the problems of access to God, as the Son through whom God speaks his final and definitive word and as the one who models for all his followers the kind of faithful response that God requires. Lewicki thus holds together several of the important theological strands of Hebrews and is particularly helpful in showing the close relationship between the innovative Christology of the text and its parenetic aims.

One observation and one question arise from reading this careful dissertation. Lewicki is certainly correct to catalogue the ways in which Hebrews calls for a community to respond to the vital word of God that it channels. The insistence on patient endurance, faith that is conceptual and active, and bold speech (*parrhesia*) that issues in a public confession (*homologia*) all are part of the behavior that Hebrews tries to inspire. To this mix might be added one further point. Hebrews does indeed construct a dialogue between God and the Son. God addresses his Son in words of the Psalms (Heb 1:5–13; 5:5–6; 6:21). The Son replies, also using the words of the Psalms (Heb 2:12–13; 10:5–7). It is noteworthy that God continues to speak in the text (Heb 10:30; 12:26; 13:5), explicitly "to us" (Heb 12:4–6). The Son has fallen silent, but at the end "we" respond, as did he, using the words of a psalm (Heb 13:6), words that express the bold and confident faith for which Hebrews calls. Hebrews thus hints that the dialogue between God and God's children continues, perhaps in the liturgical life of the *episynagoge* that some are in danger of abandoning. The motif to which Lewicki calls attention is indeed a pervasive and fundamental one for Hebrews.

The significance of the motif calls out for further comparative analysis, and hence my question. What cultural conventions or conceptual models might have inspired Hebrews to develop such an elaborate practical theology of the word of God? Was the author inspired by conventions of rhetoric? of the theater? of scholastic diatribe? Is there lurking behind Hebrews a philosophical analysis of the effects of speech, intoned and embodied, and its educational use? It may be that our author was a thoroughly original genius, but I suspect that he had some models that inspired this marvelously intricate and subtly sophisticated reflection on the significance of the Great High Priest. Lewicki's dissertation makes a good contribution to the analysis of the theology of Hebrews, but many more interesting dissertations remain to be written on this fascinating text.

1 Peter, by Karen H. Jobes. Baker Exegetical Commentary on the New Testament. Grand Rapids: Baker, 2005. Pp. xvii + 364. Hardcover. $39.99. ISBN 0801026741.

John H. Elliott, University of San Francisco, San Francisco, California

The author, professor of New Testament at Wheaton College, offers a concise commentary on 1 Peter that is eminently suited for the series in which it appears. The series' aim is to provide readers with "the latest scholarly research … in the context of a conservative theological tradition" and targets an audience of both scholars and general readers, especially those "involved in the preaching and exposition of the Scriptures" (ix). As a competent guide to the content and message of 1 Peter, the commentary is sure to win a wide circle of readers.

Jobes, who has published only one article on 1 Peter prior to this commentary, relies extensively on the secondary (especially English-language) literature, reporting agreements and disagreements fairly and accurately and ably evaluating the strengths of alternate interpretations. At the same time, she sees her work making three distinctive contributions to 1 Peter scholarship (xi). These include (1) a new suggestion concerning the identity of the addressees (more on this below); (2) attention to the role that *context* plays in passages of the LXX selected for citation—in actuality more a development of observations made by others than an innovation; and (3) a new means for assessing the quality of the Greek of 1 Peter. Examining the syntax of 1 Peter in the light of fourteen criteria for measuring "bilingual interferences," specifically Semitic influence on Greek composition (appendix [325–38]), Jobes shows with statistical evidence that "the extent of Semitic interference in the Greek of 1 Peter indicates an author whose first language was not Greek" (337). She uses this conclusion to bolster the case of possible authorship by the apostle Peter. Not all will concur with this move, but her providing this objective means of assessing key aspects of the letter's literary quality is certainly to be welcomed.

The volume's opening introduction (1–57) covers the standard isagogical issues: the letter's significance, date, authorship, destination and addressees, major themes and theology, literary genre and unity, and outline. Joining the current consensus, Jobes sees 1 Peter as a genuine, integral letter (not a composite writing or baptismal homily or liturgy or group of hymns set into an epistolary framework. It consists of three major sections (1:3–2:10; 2:11–4:11; 4:12–5:11) framed by a prescript (1:1–12) and postscript (5:12–14). She recognizes that *parepidêmoi* and *paroikoi* (1:1, 2:11; cf. 17) identify the addressees as actual "foreigners" and "resident aliens." Her speculation, however, that they may also have been adherents of the Judean messianic movement in Rome who were then among those expelled from Rome by emperor Claudius (41–54 C.E.) in the 40s and deported to Asia Minor as colonists (23–41, 61, 85, 267) is an interesting conjecture but devoid of confirming evidence. Neither of the terms, moreover, means "exiles" or "deportees," and exiles are a quite different kettle of political fish from colonists. She further supposes that the apostle Peter could also have been in Rome in the 40s (34–35) and, having known the deportees, wrote them this letter in the early 50s when he learned of the hostility they were experiencing. Dismissing the body of evidence pointing to a date of composition after the apostle's death (ca. 65–67 C.E.) and concluding from an analysis of the letter's syntax that its literary quality is "consistent with a Semitic speaking author for whom Greek was a second language" (xi, 325–38), she allows for a date of the letter in the early 50s and a direct composition by the apostle himself. Here Jobes weaves a web spun of threads of conjecture and supposition with little if any historical evidence connecting the dots. By contrast, the work shifts to solid ground when it lays out the purpose of the letter—encouragement of believers, who are suffering unjustly from verbal abuse and slanderous reproach as evildoers, to resist evil and stand fast in God's true grace (5:12)—and when it sketches the letter's theology and seven major themes (42–44, 44–53, respectively). Although Jobes sees 1 Peter portraying the believing community on the whole as an "alternate society" (214 and *passim*) called to holiness and resistance, she also is lured to the contrary theory that takes portions of the letter (especially 2:18–3:7) as urging accommodation to the values of the macrosociety (see esp. 180–209). This hernial stance is bound to present confusion for the readers.

The commentary proper has an unusually attractive, reader-friendly format: an introduction to each major section is followed by an introduction to each subsection, the author's translation, and then a verse-by-verse analysis of individual units, most concluding with a final summary. Headings at the top of each page keep the reader oriented as to literary location and theme of the unit. Jobes writes clearly and concisely. She is especially deft at reporting and evaluating scholarly opinion. Among those she cites repeatedly and approvingly are Calvin, Hort, Selwyn, Michaels, Grudem, Goppelt, Achtemeier, Thurén, and Elliott. Minimal attention is given to tradition and redaction, form-critical, or rhetorical issues. When commenting on the use of tradition in 1 Peter, she follows R. Gundry in suspecting that much of it originates in the teaching of Jesus (86, 93, 146, etc.). On the other hand, grammatical and syntactical problems—so abundant in 1 Peter—are ably unpacked and solutions competently weighed. Touching on historical and social issues only occasionally in the commentary proper, she gives most attention to the letter's flow of thought and its theological message.

Her translation adheres closely to the original Greek, although there are a few rather infelicitous renditions. Some are anachronistic for the ancient world: "race" (2:9, where "stock" for *genos* is preferable); "nation" (2:9, where "people" for *ethnos* is preferable); "institution" (2:13, where "creature" for *ktisis* is preferable). Other terms have different problems. *Hierateuma* (2:5, 9) is not an abstract concept of "priesthood" but a concrete and collective "priestly community." The rendition "royal priesthood" (2:9) disregards the convincing evidence favoring taking *basileion* and *hierateuma* as separate substantives: "royal house," " priestly community. "Amaranth" (5:4) as the modifier of "crown of glory" will say little to nonbotanists and modern readers; why not "unfading"? *Agathopoieô* has the same meaning in 2:15 that it does elsewhere in the letter (2:20; 3:6, 17), namely "do what is right," not "undertake good works" as benefactors (175), and so says nothing about the economic level of the audience (*pace* Winters, whom Jobes cites here). "Submit" for *hypotassô* (2:13, 18; 3:1, 5, 22) is less capable of communicating the concern for social order (*taxis*) behind this Greek verb than the preferable "subordinate." *Syneidêsis* is aptly rendered "consciousness" (of God) at 2:19 but less felicitously, "conscience" at 3:16 and 3:21.

I welcome especially her exposition of the complex passage 3:18–22, which follows Elliott 2000, 637–710 quite closely. This includes seeing the influence of the Enoch-Noah-flood tradition on these verses, the "disobedient spirits" as the rebellious spirits of primordial time to whom Christ upon his ascension into heaven announced their continued condemnation, rejection of the *descensus* theory, a comparison of the *saving* of Noah and family with the *saving* effected by baptism, and a distinction of the terms and focuses of 3:19 and 4:6. Her demonstration of the echoes of Ps 33/34 throughout the letter (220–23) illustrates the quality of her helpful comments on the letter's use of the LXX in general.

Of the issues or comments calling for more discussion I mention only the following. At 2:5 and 4:17 Jobes translates *oikos* as "house" but understands this as "temple" and so overlooks the central role *oikos* plays in 1 Peter as a contrast to *paroikoi* and as core symbol of the believing community as "household/family of God." In her exposition of 2:4–10 she overlooked the most extensive analysis of this text to date, namely, J. H. Elliott, *The Elect and the Holy* (1966). Although she notes the role of doxology in 1:3–12, she fails to stress, say, at 2:12 or 4:16, how glorification of God is presented in 1 Peter as the ultimate goal of Christian living. In her sensitive comments on 3:1–7 she fails to direct attention to what has been called the "evangelical breakthrough" represented by the unique designation of believing husbands and wives as "co-heirs of the grace of life." The notion that unbelieving women may be meant here in 3:7 (207–8) is hardly likely. Given the importance of, and heated debates over, 4:12–19 and the abundant information it provides on both the social situation and rhetorical strategy of the letter, its treatment (285–97) speaks too much of judgment (290–95) to allow adequate comment on other issues. Given how rare and yet telling the term *Christianos* (4:16) is as a pejorative label for the followers of Jesus Christ in the New Testament, it is remarkable that Jobes says so little about it. The term *adelphotês* also gets short shrift, though its double appearance in 1 Peter (2:17; 5:9) is unique in the New Testament and though it forms a key communal designation related to the core symbol of household/family of God. The commentary of C. Bigg on 1 Peter was published in 1902 and only *reprinted* in "1956" (340)

Finally, as a commentary in the best evangelical tradition, the volume falls a bit short in clarifying the Petrine good news and the evangelical thrust of such passages as 1:12 (addressees as privileged targets of the good news by which they were brought to faith) or allusions to this oral evangelical proclamation in 1:23–25; 2:3 and its "for-you-ness" character (1:12, 20; 3:18, etc.). A comprehensive statement on 1 Peter's good news as it addresses his readers' precarious situation would have been welcome, as would a summarizing statement about the recommended response to unjust suffering, issues surely of relevance to modern readers as well. But perhaps this is asking for another volume. What is presented is more than enough to entice readers into a sustained wrestling with this text and its evangelical spirit.

With many references to today's believers: (89, 165, 262, 267, 279, 286, 295–95; esp. 209–12 on 3:1–7, etc.), Jobes compares and contrasts our modern situation to that of ancient time and reflects on the continuing relevance of 1 Peter. She does not dodge or sugarcoat the tough theological issues present here but seeks their resolution in a manner that is faithful to the intent and thrust of the letter. I do not agree with all her conclusions, but as an evangelical catholic of the Lutheran persuasion I welcome her holding up 1 Peter, its content and evangelical agenda rather than conservative tradition or ecclesiastical dogma, as the ultimate arbiter of meaning. Students, pastors, general readers and scholars will all be well-served by this learned guide to the letter's treasures.

Hebrews, edited by Erik M. Heen and Philip D. W. Krey. Ancient Christian Commentary on Scripture 10. Downers Grove, Ill.: InterVarsity Press, 2005. Pp. xxvi + 292. Hardcover. $40.00. ISBN 0830814957.

George H. Guthrie, Union University, Jackson, Tennessee

The past two decades have witnessed a welcomed, steady stream of new commentaries on the New Testament book of Hebrews. A number of these commentaries have been thorough, aware of the latest Hebrews research, insightful in their reflection on the Greek text, and demonstrative of the fruit of a variety of critical methodologies. Yet commentaries and commentators of any era are given to certain patterns (and dare we say ruts) both of style and interpretation. As C. S. Lewis noted in his essay "On the Reading of Old Books," "Every age ... is specially good at seeing certain truths and specially liable to make certain mistakes." Thus we need "to keep the clean sea breeze of the centuries blowing through our minds." Enter the *Hebrews* volume in the Ancient Christian Commentary on Scripture (ACCS) series from InterVarsity Press, an attractively produced, contemporary book of ancient readings edited by Erik M. Heen and Philip D. W. Krey, both of Lutheran Theological Seminary in Philadelphia.

This commentary presents collected reflections on Hebrews from fifty early church fathers whose lives and ministries spanned nine centuries, drawing from 129 of their works. Curiously, the general introduction to the series suggests that these works extend to the mid-eighth century, the time of John of Damascus (650–750), but Photius (820–891), Photius's disciple Arethas of Caesarea (860–940), and Symeon the New Theologian (949–1022), all of whom postdate the eighth century, are quoted in the commentary, Photius and Symeon extensively. The fathers quoted in the commentary, some well-known and others little-known to those who are not patristic specialists, are diverse both linguistically (Greek, Latin, Syriac, Armenian, and Coptic) and geographically, hailing from every corner of Christendom, from the British Isles to Northern Africa to Mesopotamia. This temporal, linguistic, and geographical diversity gives the commentary the rich flavor of a fascinating community of varied voices. Their long-developed interpretive dialogue at times evinces great harmony and striking insights but is not without its theologically and hermeneutically discordant discussants. These voices have been largely lost to the contemporary scholar and layperson alike, and the redressing of this deficiency stands as a primary goal of the ACCS series. This revival of the *glossa ordinaria* and catena traditions, therefore, constitutes an important endeavor, and the *Hebrews* volume accordingly makes a worthy contribution to contemporary literature on Hebrews, both in terms of exposure to long-buried reflections and stimulation for the modern interpreter.

Heen and Krey, however, note that the great diversity represented in the works of these fathers also presented certain challenges in the presentation of the commentary (xvii). The variety of interpretive genres, translation issues, ways of referencing verses, the juxtaposition of at times temporally and contextually disparate readings all present challenges to the reader. Thus, to provide a sense of the broad interpretive context of those early centuries, the editors begin the commentary with a brief reception history of Hebrews, culminating in an explanation of the Antiochene and Alexandrian hermeneutical traditions (xvii–xx). For a variety of reasons, including a desire that the commentary have a sense of continuity, the editors ground their work in John Chrysostom's *On the Epistle to the Hebrews* (*In epistulam ad Hebraeos*). Chrysostom (344/54–407), preacher and bishop of Constantinople, eloquently crafted this collection of homilies, which is the earliest comprehensive commentary on the book still extant. This work profoundly influenced subsequent interpreters of both East and West and, therefore, had a vitally important role in Hebrews interpretation of the first Christian millennium. Consequently, the strategy to use Chrysostom as an anchor for the commentary works quite well, providing a sense of cohesiveness to the whole.

As to format, the editors divide Hebrews into thirty main units, providing a heading for each unit, which includes chapter and verse divisions and a title in all capital letters (e.g., 1:1–4 THE PROLOGUE). The RSV translation of the passage follows, and the editors then provide a summary overview of the fathers' thoughts on the passage. The real substance of the commentary, however, comes in the form of the fathers' comments on the text of Hebrews. As the fathers' reflections are presented, the editors break each unit down further so the reader can discern which verse(s) is currently under consideration, and these verse divisions too receive a title in bold. Thus the first verse of the book reads, "**1:1** *God Spoke to the People of Old.*" As the editors present the patristic comments, each quotation has a title descriptive of the selection, followed by the name of the person being quoted, then the quotation itself, and, finally, the name of the document from which the quotation was taken. Although Heen and Krey's *Hebrews* evidences little understanding of Hebrews' structure and development—indeed the unit divisions seem somewhat arbitrary at points—the format works to keep the reader oriented to which unit, verse, or reading from a church father is in view.

As the editors note (xxvi), the exact connection between the quotation from a church father and the portion of Hebrews under consideration might not always seem readily apparent. For instance, Chrysostom's condemnation of too much levity in church services seems barely connected to the cries and tears of Christ in Heb. 5:7–10 (72). In another instance, at Heb 10:1–2, one must wade through Origen's explanation of the threefold sense of Scripture to find a brief allusion to "a shadow of good things to come" from Heb 10:1 (149). There are also a few points at which the editors miss the canonical order of phrases in Hebrews. At Heb 6:13–20, for instance, the heavenly curtain of 6:19 (92) precedes consideration of the "two unchangeable things" of 6:18 (93). These minor criticisms aside, the general layout and presentation of the commentary accomplishes its goal of walking the reader through the rich resources found in the fathers' comments on the text of Hebrews.

The back matter at the end of the book constitutes one of the truly wonderful features of this commentary series, offering a mini-course on the patristic authors and their works. The back matter first presents a list of the "Early Christian Writers and the Documents Cited" in this volume, complete with the authors in alphabetical order, the English title of the work with the Latin designation in parentheses, and, finally, if available, the Thesaurus Linguae Graecae digital references or the Cetedoc Clavis numbers. Next comes a section of "Biographical Sketches and Short Descriptions of Select Anonymous Works," which provides usually no more than one or two sentences on each writer cited in the ACCS series to date. Third is a six-page timeline of the writers of the patristic era, with the centuries marked down the left side of the pages and geographical regions across the top. At the appropriate point on the timeline, the name of the father or anonymous work and location are followed by the date and language used. Two bibliographies are provided: the first of the patristic works in their original languages, and the second in the standard English translations. The volume concludes with a series of indices: an authors/writings index, a subject index, and a Scripture index.

Because the substance of this commentary is so refreshingly out of sync with our contemporary context, the reader will note a number of prominent characteristics that mark this volume as distinct among current commentaries on Hebrews. First, the constant reference to Paul as author of the book seems conspicuous in an era in which almost all commentators, no matter their theological orientation, have abandoned Pauline authorship as a viable option. Second, unlike much of modern biblical scholarship, in which many deem distance from the faith as offering necessary critical objectivity, these comments on Hebrews were offered by churchmen as an act of ministry and devotion for the church. Moreover, their comments on Hebrews integrate a number of genres, including historical and grammatical arguments, theological reflection, liturgical instruction, exhortation, spiritualizing, and devotional writing. As to theological reflection, the selections are permeated with the theological concerns of the day, especially the great christological discussions of the era. Gregory of Nyssa, for example, utilizes Heb 1:3 to speak against the Arians concerning the two natures of Christ (12); Cyril of Alexandria, commenting on 2:14, speaks of the nature of the incarnation, noting that Christ became truly human (44); and Theodore of Mopsuestia writes against the teachings of Apollinaris by pointing to Jesus' "fear" noted in Heb 5:7–10. Third, due to the dominant theological concerns of the day and the fact that the editors were limited to the documents from the patristic era still available, some passages in Hebrews are given great attention, while others are given comparatively little, and this necessitates a certain degree of imbalance in the commentary. For example, the first four verses of Hebrews, perhaps the most dense and rich christological text in the New Testament, are given eighteen pages, more than all the hortatory material from 3:1 to 4:13 combined.

Given its unique form and intention, the *Hebrews* volume of the ACCS should be judged on its own terms and not by the standards of contemporary commentary writing. By modern standards, the treatment of Hebrews here is neither balanced nor comprehensive. For instance, these fathers often entirely missed important aspects of Old Testament background and rabbinic techniques of exegesis woven throughout the book. Moreover, their comments at times contradict one another, and some reflections seem obviously skewed by the philosophical and theological currents of the day (as is certainly true of us, in our day, as well!). Some soar with notable insights, while others demand a great deal of imagination to draw any true connection to the text of Hebrews at hand. As in any age, discernment in the use of this commentary is needed as one seeks to study and reflect on the message and implications of Hebrews and weighs the comments of each father against the text of Hebrews itself.

On its own terms, however, what this commentary offers is an extraordinary treasure, a rich, ancient repository of insight born of deep reflection on the text of Hebrews. The fathers of the patristic era are to be warmly welcomed as reflection partners, being sufficiently removed from the prejudices of our own age as to be genuinely stimulating. We can learn much from their exegetical insights, their theological ardor, and their devotion to Christ and the church.

Zion Symbolism in Hebrews: Hebrews 12:18–24 as a Hermeneutical Key to the Epistle, by Kiwoong Son. Paternoster Biblical Monographs. Waynesboro, Ga.: Paternoster, 2006. Pp. xviii + 248. Paper. $33.99. ISBN 184227368X.

Martin Karrer, Kirchliche Hochschule Wuppertal/Barmen School of Theology, Wuppertal, Germany

I

Der Hebr ist nicht nur sprachlich das ausgefeilteste Schreiben im Neuen Testament. Er sticht auch durch seine überaus umfangreiche Benützung der Schriften Israels hervor. Das reicht von der Schriftcatene in Kap. 1 (die vor kurzem durch M. C. Albl, And Scripture Cannot be Broken, Leiden 1999 untersucht wurde, den Son [5 u.ö.] nicht mehr benützt) über das längste neutestamentliche Schriftzitat (aus LXX Jer 38) in Kap. 8 bis hin zu Sachreferaten wie dem der Epiphanie am Sinai in 12,18–21 (nach Ex 19,12–13.16–19 und Dtn 4,11–12; 9,19). Demnach kennzeichnet den Hebr eine spezifische Stilistik und Rhetorik der Schriftdarlegung. Sein Sprachgestus ist nicht allein und nicht primär an der griechischen Rhetorik zu bemessen (so gewiss auch diese Beachtung verdient, 19–21). Er ist im Sinne eines eigenen theologischen oder besser, wie Son sagen würde, hermeneutischen Ansatzes zu begreifen.

Diesen hermeneutischen Ansatz entnimmt Son Hebr 12,18–24 (wie der Untertitel sachgemäß vermerkt): Der Zion überbiete den Sinai. So ergebe sich eine Kategorie der Überlegenheit („superiority"; zusammenfassend 199[–202]), die sich an den entscheidenden Briefthemen bewähre, angefangen bei der Überlegenheit Christi (analog zum Zion) über die Engel (analog zum Sinai) in Kap. 1 (199 nach 105–24). Forschungsgeschichtlich ist das bis ins 13. Jh. zurück verankert (Son [14] nennt Thomas von Aquin, allerdings ohne dessen bedeutenden

Kommentar [In omnes Pauli epistolas commentarius II 281–452, Turin 1902] selbst einzusehen). Trotzdem stellen sich zwei schwierige Fragen.

Zum einen verwendet der Hebr das Stichwort „Zion" nie vor und außer 12,22 sowie „Sinai" überhaupt nicht. Das fällt umso mehr auf, als Ps 110/LXX 109, der Schlüsselpsalm für die Melchisedek-Christologie in Hebr 5–10, ausdrücklich vom Zion spricht (in Vers 2), der Hebr aber nur die umgebenden Verse (LXX 109,1.4), nicht diesen Zionsvers zitiert. „Zion" in 12,22 ist, wenn wir das berücksichtigen, eher Ziel der Argumentation als Leseanweisung für alle Kapitel des Hebr (eine solche Leseanweisung würde ich in Kap. 1 erwarten), und „Sinai" bietet eine sinnvoll summierende Kategorie des Auslegers für all die Sinaitexte des Hebr (Hebr 3,7–11 nach LXX Ps 94,7–11 usw.), indes nicht die Sprache des Hebr (ihm genügt z.B. in 3,8.17 „Wüste"). Anders gesagt, werden „Sinai and Zion" entscheidend erst durch den Ausleger zu „theological symbols embracing all the theological subjects discussed in the epistle" (200). Der Ansatz Sons kann und darf Alternativen nicht ausschließen. Als jüngste sei S. Fuhrmann genannt, der (seinerseits nicht minder einseitig) Hebr 8 und Jer 31/LXX 38 zum Schlüssel des Hebr erklärt (Vergeben und Vergessen. Christologie und neuer Bund im Hebräerbrief, Diss. theol. HU Berlin, 2006, noch unveröffentlicht). Verallgemeinern wir, dann profitiert die Forschung gewichtig von solchen Durchdringungen des Hebr, weil sie ein Ganzes wagen, wird sie wie bisher verschiedene Zugänge prüfen müssen.

Zum zweiten stellt sich ein Übersetzungsproblem, das im Deutschen schwieriger als im Englischen zu handhaben ist. „Superior" gibt in etwa das berühmte κρείττων des Hebr wieder, das—wie Son herausarbeitet—in räumlichen Kategorien auf Höheres verweist (höher ist der Himmel als die Erde etc.), in einer Rhetorik der Kraft auf Machtvolleres/ Gewaltigeres (202 nach 125–28 u.ö.). Beides bedarf keiner Polemik, und tatsächlich wird Mose im Hebr nie abgewertet (127 u.ö.). Durch die Auslegungsgeschichte aber gewann eine Rede von Überlegenheit die Konnotation, das Unterlegene sei von minderem Wert und polemisch abweisbar. Angesichts dessen fragt sich, ob Sons Vorliebe für die Kategorie der „superiority" nicht zu Missverständnissen einlädt.

Verdeutlichen wir das Problem am für Son zentralen Text, Hebr 12,18–24. Der Hebr skizziert dort die Theophanie vom Sinai als so gewaltig, dass selbst Mose Angst befällt, zumal er um die Schuld des Volkes weiß (s. den Kontext von Dtn 9,19, der in 12,21 mit anklingt). Seine Erzählung mindert nicht die Theophanie, sondern unterstreicht sie und erinnert an das paradoxe Handeln des Volkes, das die unmittelbare Begegnung mit Gott und seinem Wort scheut (12,19). Was am Zion neu ist, ist nicht eine Abwertung des Sinai, sondern die Überwindung der einstigen Schwäche des Volkes. Vom Sinai zum Zion verläuft, wenn man so will, eine Steigerung (der Berg gelangt v. 22 in die Höhe des Himmels), im Verhalten des Volkes eine Korrektur. Vielleicht verhinderte diese Differenzierung, dass der Autor des Hebr den Namen Sinai in den Mund nimmt. Son versucht, dem gerecht zu werden (zur Passage 77–103, 199, 200) und neigt doch dazu, Offenbarungsorte etwas stärker als vom Text gefordert gegeneinander auszuspielen, kurz von einer „antithesis of Sinai and Zion" zu sprechen (77, 103 u.ö.).

II

Diese Einwände dürfen das Verdienst Sons nicht schmälern. Vielmehr zeigen sie, wie stark er die Diskussion anregt. Seine These, die Strategie des Hebr sei einer Perspektive Zion versus Sinai zuzuordnen, verdient Beachtung. Nennen wir einige ihrer Details.

1. Son baut seine Studie klar auf. Er erörtert nach der Einleitung (Kap. 1; Forschungsgeschichte u.ä.) zunächst religionsgeschichtliche Hintergründe (Kap. 2 [29–74]) und die Leitpassage Hebr 12,18–24 (Kap. 3 [77–103]), dann als weitere Schlüsseltexte Hebr 1; Hebr 3,1–4,13 und 4,14–7,28 (Kap. 4–6 [105–67]), schließlich die Tempelsymbolik (Kap. 7 [169–97]). Auf p. 199–203 fasst er die Ergebnisse zusammen.

2. Als religionsgeschichtlichen Hintergrund verfolgt Son (29–74) die Entwicklung der Zionssymbolik mitsamt ihrem Umbruch vom irdischen Ort (Zion in Jerusalem) zur eschatologischen Erwartung. Ziel ist für ihn die Apokalyptisierung und Erwartung einer Zionsoffenbarung, an die dann der Hebr anknüpft. Gewiss ließe sich manches verbreitern (z.B. ist die deutsche Diskussion um eine Zionstora nicht berücksichtigt) und kultische Strukturen vertieft bedenken (das Material zuletzt bei Georg Gäbel, Die Kulttheologie des Hebräerbriefes, WUNT II 212, Tübingen 2006). Aber im Ganzen fügt sich Sons These, der räumlich-theologische Dualismus des Hebr leite sich von der Apokalyptisierung der Hoffnungen Israels ab (103 u.ö.), gut in eine Forschungsentwicklung ein, die seit Hofius in großer Breite von der einstigen Fixierung auf gnostische Bezüge zugunsten jüdisch-apokalyptischen und -mystischen Denkens Abschied nimmt (zu Hofius und Käsemann 11 u.ö.; Erich Gräßers großen Kommentar mit seinen Differenzierungen benützt Son nicht).

3. Was die Exegesen angeht, stellt Son sich dem angesprochenen Problem, dass der Hebr die für seine These zentrale Zionshoffnung erst in 12,18–24, also lange nach einer erwartbaren Leseanweisung, expliziert. Zur Lösung erhebt er strukturelle Querlinien (Korrespondenzen zu 1,1–4; 2,1–4 usw. [85–86]). Außerdem bemüht er sich um ein abgewogenes Verhältnis zu Israel und fügt in seine Antithetik eine Doppelpoligkeit von Korrespondenz und Kontrast (78–79) sowie eine Erfüllung mosaischer Vorstellungen ein. Damit sichert er, dass sein Verständnis der Überbietung (superiority) von der Christologie bis zum Gesetzesdenken wesentliche Momente der Kontinuität wahrt (82 u.ö.).

4. Theologisch verfolgt Son vor allem das christologische Gefälle. Dabei konzentriert er sich in seinen Kap. 3 und 4 zunächst auf die Mitteilung von Offenbarung. Gerade hier ergibt sich für ihn die überlegene Stärke des Zions-Christus im Vergleich mit Mose (94–100) und den Engeln (105–11 u.ö.). Freilich wirkt die dazu nötige Systematisierung der Zitate in Hebr 1 manchmal etwas gezwungen; die christologischen Zitate (bes. 2 Sam 7,14; Ps 2; Ps 110 und Ps 45,6–7) betreffen laut Son durchweg den Zion, während die Anwendungen auf Engel Texten entstammen, die ursprünglich der Sinai-Offenbarung gelten (Dtn 32,43 LXX; Ps 104,4 [112–23]).

In Hebr 3,1–4,11 hebt Son sodann auf die überlegene Verlässlichkeit ab, mit der Christus als der Sohn in die eschatologische (Zions-)Ruhe geleitet (125–45). An Hebr 7,1–3 erarbeitet er den himmlischen Charakter von Christi Melsisedek-Priestertum. Das himmlische Geschehen schließt laut ihm an Zionsgedanken an (dank Gen 14,18–20 und Ps 110; zur Problematik s.o.), während alles Irdische samt dem Kult Levis vergeht (147–67; 199–200).

Alles in allem wird Christus in Sons Auslegung zum Priesterkönig des himmlischen Zion („king-priest of the heavenly Zion" [169]). Der Zion gibt allem Irdischen nicht nur das Bild vor (zu ὑπόδειγμα, Ez 42,15 LXX [diff. MT] usw. 177–81), sondern mehr noch die Richtung auf eschatologische Vollendung. Der Zion ist dem Sinai deshalb bis hin zu der Kraft überlegen, die das Herz reinigen kann; Son liest selbst Jer 31,31–34 in Hebr 8 auf die Zions-Vollendung hin (vgl. 202).

Ausgeschlossen ist, alle Details zu nennen, an denen Son darüber hinaus einzelexegetische Impulse setzt. Gehör verdient etwa sein Hinweis, in 12,28 spreche nicht das Blut Abels (wie die Übersetzungen praktisch durchwegs lesen), sondern Abel selbst. Damit würde 12,28 unmittelbar die Erwähnung Abels in 11,4 fortführen (100). Freilich kehrt 101 zur herkömmlichen Interpretation und damit zum Vergleich zwischen dem Blut Abels und Christi zurück.

III

Überschauen wir die Beobachtungen, ist der Dynamik schwerlich zuzustimmen, mit der Son überall im Hebr Ziellinien zum Zion und zu Zinstraditionen findet. Trotzdem regt seine Studie die Diskussion um den religionsgeschichtlichen Ort, das zentrale Thema und die Christologie des Hebr gewichtig und wertvoll an.

Hebrews: A Commentary, by Luke Timothy Johnson. New Testament Library. Louisville: Westminster John Knox, 2006. Pp. xxviii + 402. Cloth. $40.00. ISBN 0664221181.

Craig R. Koester, Luther Seminary, St. Paul, Minnesota

This commentary is a welcome contribution to recent literature on Hebrews. Substantial in content and readable in form, it will help a wide range of readers appreciate the message and artistry of this challenging New Testament book. The opening lines of Johnson's introduction strike an important tone, pointing out that the unnamed author of Hebrews summons people to a vision of reality and a committed faith that is at once distinctive, attractive, and disturbing. In the pages of Hebrews, modern readers find a world that is very different from the one that is familiar to them. It is a world in which the unseen is more real and attractive than that which can be seen and touched. "In a word, Hebrews proposes as real a world that most of us consider imaginary" (2). Moreover, Hebrews stretches readers' perspectives with a Christology that is replete with tensions between

Jesus' humanity and divinity, his crucifixion and exaltation. In the portrayal of Christ as high priest, the author invokes notions of sacrifice that will seem alien to many people today. To follow the Christ depicted in Hebrews means embarking on a course that requires endurance and a willingness to suffer for the sake of the faith. Entering into full maturity as God's children means being transformed by the suffering that comes from obedience, following the path of Jesus.

After sketching a helpful survey of Hebrews' place in the Christian tradition, Johnson turns to the literary shape of the book. He notes the high quality of the book's Greek and its pervasive use of metaphor. The center around which many of the leading metaphors revolve is the idea that life is a journey toward a destination, that is, a pilgrimage. This central idea is reflected in the many expressions for calling readers to move forward, to avoid falling away, to draw near the throne of grace, to run the race with perseverance, and to approach Mount Zion. Johnson rightly notes that Hebrews is a written text that has an oral character, so that interpreters do well to think of its audience as listeners more than readers.

On the disputed question of Hebrews' structure, Johnson notes several different approaches, some working mainly with subject matter, others with aspects of the form, and others with rhetorical arrangement. Rather than making a particular understanding of structure a major element, the body of the commentary traces the general flow of the book, exploring how one section leads into the next. The advantage of this approach is that, given the lack of consensus on Hebrews' structure, it may be prudent not to tie interpretation too closely to any one outline. The drawback is that this makes it more difficult to see how the parts relate to the whole or to distinguish the main points of the book's argument from its subpoints. Johnson gives greater attention to the internal mode of argumentation. For him, the pattern of comparison (*synkrisis*) establishes the basic shape of Hebrews. Comparing Christ to the angels, Moses, Aaron, and other figures from Israel's history points to the consummate quality of what the gospel offers.

In terms of historical setting, Johnson recognizes that the identity of Hebrews' author remains unknown. Although positing a relatively early date of composition (A.D. 50–70), he understands that those addressed by the book have been Christians for some time, have experienced suffering because of their faith, and are showing signs of disaffection. Although many interpreters have suggested that the addressees were being drawn away from Christianity to Judaism, Johnson rightly points out that this seems unlikely. Their disaffection seems to emerge from their negative experience as Christians rather than from a positive attraction to the synagogue. Recognizing this means that Hebrews can best be read as an argument for renewed Christian commitment rather than an argument against Judaism.

In an excursus Johnson takes up the sensitive question of supersessionism more directly. Hebrews is sometimes understood to argue for the superiority of Christianity to Judaism with the implication that Christians have now taken the place of Jews as the people of God. Johnson argues that this is not the case.

Despite the argument that aspects of the Mosaic covenant have been set aside, Hebrews affirms the ongoing place of the promises God made to Abraham. Hebrews speaks about the way God's will is carried out in and through Jesus, but the author does not disparage the Jewish community of his own time.

The commentary helpfully draws on a range of ancient sources to help elucidate the text. Since Hebrews' language and imagery reflect Greco-Roman culture, Jewish tradition, and early Christian teaching, elucidating the text requires attention to a wide range of sources. A long-disputed point in the interpretation of Hebrews concerns the extent to which it reflects the Platonic distinction between the noumenal world above and the phenomenal world below, with earthly realities serving as shadows and copies of the heavenly archetypes. Scholars who associate Hebrews with Platonism have usually assumed that the unnamed author presents the gospel message in the philosophical thought forms appropriate to his Greco-Roman context. Those who distance Hebrews from Platonism have often argued that such an appropriation of philosophical categories might signal a departure from the earlier Christian tradition. Johnson finds it helpful to read Hebrews in connection with the philosophical tradition, noting that Jewish authors such as Philo also used philosophical categories when interpreting Israel's tradition.

Theologically, Johnson gives special attention to several themes when commenting on the text. The first is the centrality of the living God who speaks a living word. Although God is identified as the principal speaker in Hebrews' memorable opening lines, interpreters have often overlooked the role of God in Hebrews' argument, generally focusing on Christology instead. Giving due attention to God, however, enriches our understanding of the text. Noting recent work on Hebrews' use of the Old Testament, Johnson also points out the ways in which Scripture addresses readers directly as a living word, rather than serving only as a repository of words from the past. Second, his comments recognize the book's multifaceted portrait of Christ. Although Hebrews is best known for its presentation of Christ as high priest, it also depicts him as the Son of God, heir, pioneer, perfector, and sanctifier, among other things, offering readers a rich and complex sense of his identity and role. Third, the book calls readers to a path of discipleship that is characterized by perseverance through suffering. A remarkable collection of images is used to depict the Christian life, including those drawn from athletics, education, and the heroes and heroines of Israel's past.

The greatest barrier that many modern readers of Hebrews face is the strangeness of the book. Johnson consistently keeps the modern reader in mind, sometimes explaining some of the book's peculiarities and sometimes allowing them to challenge readers to go beyond their ordinary modes of perception. This highly useable commentary will find an appreciative audience among scholars, pastors, and students.

REVELATION

The War between the Two Beasts and the Two Witnessess: A Chiastic Reading of Revelation 11.1–14.5, by Antonius King Wai Siew. Library of New Testament Studies 283. London: T&T Clark, 2005. Pp. xiv + 331. Hardcover. $140.00. ISBN 0567030210.

Pieter G. R. de Villiers, University of the Free State, Bloemfontein, South Africa

Despite extensive research on the book of Revelation in recent times, some major and vexing problems remain unsolved. The composition of the book is one such issue. Significant research by established scholars such as Yarbro Collins, Schüssler Fiorenza, Bauckham, Vanni, Lambrecht, and several others yielded valuable insights but failed to produce anything close to a consensus. This publication, a slightly revised edition of the author's doctoral thesis submitted at the University of Otago in New Zealand with Paul Trebilco and Tim Meadowcroft as supervisors, therefore investigates a relevant area of research, taking seriously the apt observation of Richard Bauckham that the major literary study that will do justice to Revelation as a composition has yet to be written (7).

This publication furthermore focuses on what is indeed one of the more problematic sections in Revelation as far as composition is concerned: Rev 11:1–14:5. These chapters are also noteworthy because they contain some of the best known and most discussed motifs and characters in Revelation. They seem to link the varying descriptions of the measuring of the temple, the two witnesses, the woman and the dragon, the war in heaven, and the two beasts rather loosely. They stand out in a book that is otherwise neatly patterned in terms of carefully designed and connected septets (seven letters, seals, trumpets, bowls). What makes it so much more difficult is that these chapters are located in the middle of Revelation, often regarded as providing a decisive hermeneutical key to the meaning of the book as a whole. The time is indeed ripe for an exact appraisal of the composition of this major passage.

The publication investigates the literary structure of Rev 11:1–14:5 in terms of its form and content and argues that these chapters form a chiasm. Moving from a methodological discussion in the first chapter in which chiasm is understood in terms of Hebrew literary conventions and in which recent research on it is discussed, it then (ch. 2) argues in a more comprehensive manner how shared key words and motifs form 11:1–14:5 into a coherent whole. A more specific study of the subunits in Rev 11 is made in chapter 3, followed by a close analysis of 12:1–14:5 in chapter 4. These chapters are then once again discussed together in chapter 5 in terms of the mutual relationships between them, before the sixth chapter investigates the identity of the two witnesses and the two beasts. In general, then, these chapters are regarded as presenting a chiastic pattern in which the two witnesses in Rev 11 are linked with the two beasts in Rev 13. In them events in the penultimate war on earth between good and evil are described. This earthly combat frames and mirrors the heavenly conflict between Michael and the dragon in heaven and between the dragon and the woman described in Rev 12.

One of the problems with the study of the literary composition of Revelation up to this time is that scholars mostly, and understandably so, analyze the book as a whole and on a higher hierarchical level, without always being able to provide a close, detailed reading of individual passages. This publication addresses this problem by focusing in depth and on a microlevel on a specific part of the text. From a certain perspective, this is the more adequate method for a discussion of composition, since it investigates the text on its most concrete level and helps to avoid regressive argumentation. The more abstract macroanalysis of Revelation thus can be substantiated by particular readings of its constitutive parts and specific textual references. Because it can be expected that an author of such a carefully composed text would be consistent, a reading on this level will yield clues and models for the composition of the book on meso- and macrolevels.

It remains challenging, however, to concentrate thus intensely on a minute analysis, since the meaning of parts of a text is sometimes decisively determined by the nature and composition as a whole. Minute and detailed analyses nevertheless have become a pressing need. There is little choice: in this chicken or egg situation, the state of research with its often conflicting analyses of the book as a whole directs us at this point in time to such a close study of the text. It is exactly because of its focused analysis on the composition of these few chapters that this publication reveals inadequacies in past analyses but also offers some refreshing insights into the text.

Of special relevance is the literary technique that Siew develops in his exegetical approach. His method (building on significant work done in the field in recent times and correctly assuming the striking literary integrity of Revelation), explained in his first chapter, develops the literary convention of chiasm as key to understanding the composition of 11:1–14:5. The chiastic nature of these chapters, similar to the style of prophetic books in Hebrew Scriptures, not only reveals how carefully the material had been composed in a well-balanced structure but also sheds new light on its meaning—as he spells out in his following chapters.

It will be unfortunate if readers of this publication judge it in terms of the use of the designation "chiasm," which is obviously a controversial term—especially because it is as a term of late origin and is thus linked anachronistically to a first-century text. It is sometimes understood exclusively in a technical sense as a much more limited literary figure of style (ABB'A'). The point that is made in this publication and that should not be blurred by the use of potentially controversial terminology is that the author of Revelation presents his material in a strictly ordered manner by creating a pattern of elements that he introduces one by one and that he then continues to discuss in reverse order. In order to avoid having this valuable compositional patterning questioned because of a potentially controversial term such as chiasm, more terminological precision and discussion of reservations about chiastic readings in this introductory chapter to the publication would have been helpful, or perhaps a more useful term such as ring composition could have been considered. But despite this, the fact remains that the material insights generated by the application of this figure of style are impressive. There can be little doubt that this publication significantly consolidates the important trend in recent research to read Revelation from the perspective of a chiasm or ring composition (see, e.g., the groundbreaking work of Nils Lund and the commentary of Giblin on Revelation).

Whatever one calls this patterning approach, it is there, and it is decisive for the interpretation of the book to understand the elements of this carefully designed pattern in their mutual relationships. In addition, the hermeneutical gains generated by this approach are huge. Such a chiastic-like approach serves to defamiliarize ancient texts such as Revelation by making us aware how they are composed in a manner that is not so common in our modern ways of text production, which is determined by other, contemporary ideals and norms for coherence and logic. It thus promotes a more precise historical study of the text as it opens our Western eyes to different ways of conceptualizing and producing texts. It is a patterning that also makes sense within an oral culture and within the oral setting of Revelation that promotes clarity through repetition. Such pattern- ing also fits the educational and literary situation within the social context of the author.

The importance of a comparison of mutually related elements because of and within a chiasm is clearly illustrated by Siew in chapters 2–4, where he applies his method and his theoretical insights to his passage and develops the themes of war and worship, expressed in key words and motifs. He shows how they draw a double portrait that binds the contents of these chapters quite artfully: the heav- enly war between the dragon and Michael in 12:7–12 (as the pivot of the chiasm) is paralleled by the double earthly combat between the two witnesses (Rev 11) and the two beasts (Rev 13) that frames it. The fifth chapter of this publication with the discussions of the different pairs in the chiasm that the author finds in 11:1–14:5 further offers illuminating perspectives. The many smaller sections in these chapters, causing interpretive headaches because of their perceived incoher- ence, are in fact chiastically linked and represent the development of important themes in a concentric and symmetrical manner.

There are quite a few challenging positions in this book—such as the literal reading of 11:1–2 and the attempt to reflect on the literal and symbolic use of characters and events in Revelation (22–28). One could pose the same question about consistency that Siew quotes elsewhere in reaction against a literal reading of the character of the male child in 12:5 to his own literal reading of 11:1–2. This is even more so when he regards the temple and city in 11:1–2 as literal but its measuring as symbolic. But these are specific issues that together with quite a few other questions about contents should not take the focus off the central thrust of this publication, namely, to describe the composition of 11:1–14:5. It is not that Siew's compositional analysis is without problems in its detail—something that he himself acknowledges as a possibility (284). It is not always convincing, or it could be made more convincing if other parts of the text and certain other formal textual evidence could have been taken into account. Revelation 11:1–14:5 is, for example, embedded in the septet of trumpets, as is pointed out in many ways in Siew's publication. But it is a question how Rev 10 about the little scroll (and not only 10:11) relates to the chapters under investigation and affects the chiastic pattern found in 11:1–14:5. Even more important, the explicit integration of 10:1–14:5 in the septet of seven trumpets creates a larger coherence that has clear implications for understanding this passage: in the septet of trumpets, for example, the sixth (!) trumpet focuses quite intensely and, significantly, also climactically on the motif of repentance (9:20–21), confirming how uppermost this motif was in the mind of John, especially in terms of the times before the end. After mooting this motif, the author of Revelation then moves on with new material, inserting the narrative about the two witnesses, thereby setting up a framework within which they should be understood. Siew, following Satake, rejects the theory that the two witnesses proclaim repentance to the nations, stressing that they "herald God's war on the world" and are thus executors of judgment (247). This view is problematic in the light of the statement that the nations glorified God after the ascension of the witnesses (11:13). Given John's preference for contrasting motifs and symbols, the giving of glory to God as an act of repentance mentioned as the climax of the narrative about the two witnesses must be related to and thus understood in terms of his previous references to the lack of repentance following the judgments in the sixth trumpet. In other words, the wider context of the septet of trumpets by necessity need to be taken into account in order to appreciate the meaning of its constitutive parts—which includes 11:1–14:5. This supports the view of many scholars who more convincingly regard the two witnesses as proclaimers of repentance—an issue that is of special significance for interpreting Revelation. Given the focus of this publication on a particular section, it is understandable that the wider context cannot always be mooted—which illustrates the above-mentioned restrictions that is typical of an analysis on the microlevel. But this example of Siew's unconvincing portrayal of the two witnesses illustrates why the careful microanalysis in this publication now awaits to be tested against information in the immediate context of the passage and the book as a whole. The important, original, and fresh contribution of this publication to the issue of composition, made possible by the detailed approach, is, therefore, but a first step toward further work that will inevitably require revision of some of its insights.

For the rest, I also enjoyed this work because it addresses the key issue about the future element in Revelation. Siew focuses on Rev 11 in his chapter 3, which, with its four subunits and its temporal/spatial indicators denoting three and a half years and the physical Jerusalem, would describe to the readers events (the trampling of the city and the ministry of the two witnesses) that will take place in the future before the final coming of the kingdom on earth. His reading in this regard will surprise some, but it certainly has special merit. The future element in Revelation is an issue that already Bousset, who otherwise decisively promoted the historical reading of the book in terms of a Greco-Roman context, pointed out as of key importance for understanding the book. It is an issue that does not always receive the attention it deserves, so that this publication is to be welcomed for once again drawing attention to it. In tandem with this, I found the criticism of the conventional identifications of characters in Rev 12–13 with Roman rulers and institutions equally valuable (in his ch. 6, in which he discusses the identity of the characters in this passage).

This work impresses with its extensive discussion of secondary mainstream research but also of scholarship from outside traditional centers and countries of learning. More important, it engages thoroughly with the primary text. Its major contribution, however, is to be found in its contribution toward consolidating the trend in scholarship that researches the so-called chiastic readings of New Testament texts and that develops its great potential for biblical interpretation.

"Those Who Call Themselves Jews": The Church and Judaism in the Apocalypse of John, by Philip L. Mayo. Princeton Theological Monograph Series. Eugene, Ore.: Wipf & Stock, 2006. Pp. x + 212. Paper. $24.00. ISBN 1597525588.

David L. Barr, Wright State University, Dayton, Ohio

This work began life as a Ph.D. dissertation under the guidance of David Scholer at Fuller Theological Seminary and retains the meticulous attention to detail and careful noting that are typical of the genre, without any of the sonorousness or timidity that often mars such works. Well-written and clearly argued, it addresses an important and complicated topic with some attempt at nuance.

After a short discussion of the date of the Apocalypse (favoring a late date), Mayo begins with a competent survey of recent scholarship that addresses John's attitude toward Jews and Judaism (Christopher Rowland, Adela Yarbro Collins, Peder Borgen, Michael Wojciechowski, Eduard Lohse, Alan J. Beagley, John W. Marshall, and Peter Hirschberg). His own conclusion is closest to Hirschberg, "that John does not promote a supersessionist view but that he sees the church as the fulfillment of Judaism accomplished through the redemptive work of the Lamb" (23). This is a difficult argument to make, and it strikes me as a distinction without a difference. If the church is "God's new spiritual Israel" (199), what can be the status of traditional Israel? The argument develops in three phases, before drawing back a bit.

First, Mayo traces the trajectory of Jewish Christian relations from 70 to 150, from the time when nearly all Christians were Jewish to the time of Gentile dominance when Justin Martyr and others like him could question whether Christians could also be Jews. Part of Mayo's goal is to set the Apocalypse within this trajectory and to make some small contribution to understanding the eventual split (2–3, 49). He interrogates the usual suspects—Acts, *Barnabas,* Ignatius, Melito, Justin, Polycarp, Josephus, and the Birkat Haminim—finding a consistent trajectory. He is aware of the critical difficulties of using these sources but tends to take them at face value. He finds two consistent themes: the appropriation of the Jewish scriptures; and a replacement theology, first fully articulated by Justin Martyr (49).

Second, Mayo does a careful analysis and interpretation of two crucial texts that refer to "those who call themselves Jews and are not, but are a synagogue of Satan" (2:9; 3:9). To whom does John mean to refer by this expression? Mayo carefully reviews the alternative meanings suggested by various scholars, with more nuance than I can suggest here: the majority of scholars think he is referring to ethnic Jews and that John is contesting their right to this title; some think he is referring to Gentiles who are claiming to be Jews; a few scholars think he is referring to some subgroup of the Jewish community, namely, those who have compromised with pagan society. After evaluating strengths and weaknesses, Mayo opts to go with the majority: it refers to ethnic Jews who are hostile to the Christian community and have in some way participated in their persecution (61).

Mayo traces the meager evidence available to suggest a strong Jewish community in Smyrna and Philadelphia, then argues that they would have had some protection as a legally sanctioned community and that they may have withdrawn this protection to the Christians among them so that the Christians' separate gathering would have been of questionable legality (64–66). Thus the Jews could have been indirectly responsible for the trials and punishment of Christians. Mayo shores up this argument by examining the language of suffering and slander in the Smyrna message (although lacking in the Philadelphia message). He struggles to assert that we should not see this as anti-Semitic, that John never uses "Jew" in a pejorative sense, that he "is not condemning the Jews as a race of people or even as a religion," and that John himself is a Jew (72). Nevertheless, the only true Jews are "those who acknowledge Jesus as the Messiah" (71), and the Jews "have lost their place as the heir to God's prophetic promise" (74). His final point here is that John is on common ground with later Christian writers who see the church as the new Israel.

The third phase of his argument is to examine other ways John redefines Jewishness in his Apocalypse, focusing especially on the 144,000 (ch. 3); the temple, the two witnesses, and the heavenly woman (ch. 4); and the New Jerusalem (ch. 5). In each case John is said to have chosen a thoroughly Jewish symbol, wrested it from the hands of ethnic Jews, and claimed the new Christian community as its true owner, thus claiming continuity with ancient Jewish tradition and rejection of the contemporary (unbelieving) Jewish community. While John's community is the New Jerusalem, historical Jerusalem is associated with Sodom and the crucifixion of Jesus. "This rejection of God's Messiah places them in league, wittingly or unwittingly, with Satan" (162–63).

While Mayo repeatedly asserts John's commonality with later Christian writers (49, 75, 162, 202), he seeks to draw back from the supersessionism and anti-Semitism that have characterized much of church history. He tries to distinguish John's position from that of Justin Martyr, for "John does not see Israel replaced by the church nor does he ever imply the Jewish people are abandoned by God" (204). This is a worthwhile impulse but quite at odds with the whole argument of the book. If, as he says on the same page, "Being a Jew is, therefore, not an automatic guarantee of membership in the covenant community. God's 'Israel' is defined through spiritual faithfulness not ethnicity," then John cannot be so easily rescued from these charges.

The book seems of two minds in other ways. Mayo recognizes the anachronism of talking about Christianity and Judaism in this period but does so anyway (1 n. 1). He recognizes the tremendous diversity of positions throughout this period but most often speaks as if there were a unified trajectory from Paul to Justin Martyr (2). He recognizes that there is scant evidence of persecution (from Rome, let alone from the Jewish community), yet he uses such persecution to justify John's radical statements (35).

The book itself is well produced and free of typographical errors but suffers from the lack of an index. In the end, this is a very important book that lays out the case for one way of reading John as clearly as I can imagine. It includes all but the most recent published scholarship—and some not yet published—and is able to offer a competent summary and insightful critique of the arguments thus far advanced. Finally, it forces all of us who attempt to make sense of John's Apocalypse to address explicitly the issue of Christian attitudes toward Judaism.

Das Ezechielbuch in der Johannesoffenbarung, edited by Dieter Sänger. Biblisch-theologische Studien 76. Neukirchen-Vluyn: Neukirchener, 2006. Pp. x + 126. Paper. €19.90. ISBN 378872143X.

John M. Court, University of Kent, Canterbury, Kent, United Kingdom

Few can fail to notice the Old Testament echoes that resonate through the chapters of the Christian Apocalypse, the book of Revelation. But precisely from where those echoes originate is by no means universally agreed; sources that have been identified (usually unilaterally, not multilaterally) include the prophecies of Isaiah, Ezekiel, Joel, Zechariah, and the book of Daniel. For instance, during my earliest researches in Revelation, some forty years ago, a postgraduate from the United States came to Durham to work on the use of Ezekiel's prophecies in Revelation; I read some of his thesis then, but I do not think it was ever published. On reflection, there is an irony, as well as substantial supporting evidence, in such a linkage between two texts, which have often caused problems for readers, one from the Old, the other from the New Testament.

As well as the chariot vision of chapter 1 (which became the foundation of *merkabah* mysticism) Ezekiel's book records other highly charged dramatic scenes. These visions include the army of dry bones (Ezek 37); the great battle of chapters 38–39 (which invites comparison with Armageddon in Rev 16:16); the rebuilding of the temple (Ezek 40); and the millennial capital of Israel in chapters 45 and 48, which resembles the holy city of Rev 21.

Professor Dieter Sänger of the University of Kiel has provided a foreword to this collection of four papers from a conference held in March 2005. The contributions focus on different aspects, examples, and critical methods, within what is consciously a study of the relationship of Old and New Testaments, appropriately dedicated to Hans Huebner on his seventy-fifth birthday. The central themes of prophetic commissioning and the visions of God, judgment, temple, and New Jerusalem are covered, together with questions on the form of the text. Given the diversity of the papers, it is a pity that the editor did not develop a fuller assessment to draw them together, but perhaps lack of space prevented this.

Thomas Hieke writes about John the Seer as a new Ezekiel. Hieke favors the methodology of reader-response and speaks of a sense of *déjà vu* when reading Revelation after Ezekiel. He quotes from the major work by J.-P. Ruiz (1989, 177), "it is agreed that the order in which the references appear in Revelation corresponds in broad terms to the order in which the texts appear in Ezekiel" (5), then adds from the 1985 Harvard thesis of J. M. Vogelgesang (p. 69): "this is conclusive proof that John used Ezekiel directly. ... he modeled his book on that of Ezekiel" (6). The overall structure invites the reader to see the Apocalypse and Ezekiel in parallel, as indicated by a table on page 6. However, the meaning of Revelation should not be seen as identical with Ezekiel, but rather developed from a national to a global perspective; the all-present God no longer needs a chariot.

In the second paper Beate Ego describes the intertextuality of the chariot/throne vision from Ezekiel within Judaism. She offers three kinds of examples: (1) the replication of the living creatures from Ezek 1:10; 10:14 (as in 4Q385, frag. 4, the Pseudo-Ezekiel text); (2) the use of key words rather than explicit references (as in 4QSongs of Sabbath Sacrifice); and (3) the reworking of Dan 7 under the influence of Ezekiel in *1 En.* 14–16. The range of examples is offered presumably for the purpose of comparison of methodologies, but unfortunately this is not identified or made explicit. Finally, there are interesting examples of midrashic intertextuality, up to and including the *hekhalot*. These show an allegorical use of the four creatures as symbols of dominance: the chariot vision linked to the Sinai revelation and producing an amazing multiplication of chariots; and the calf in Ezek 1:7 linked to the golden calf of Exod 32:1-6. Sadly, but explicably, there is only one cross-reference to Revelation in this paper.

The third paper is from Michael Bachmann, who concentrates on the topic of the measuring of temple and holy city in Rev 11:1–2 and 21:15ff. against the background of Ezekiel. This is related to an article he wrote for *New Testament Studies* 40 (1994): 474–80 and partly responds to feedback from that. The main issues are whether "measuring" means destruction or protection, and whether the primary reference in Ezekiel is to chapters 40–48 or the earlier temple vision of 8–11. Bachmann concludes, against Jauhiainen (*Bib* 83 [2002]) and Kowalski (2004), that "measuring" in Rev 11:1 means protection, seen against the background of Ezek 8–11; he quotes from A. Y. Collins (1984, 68): "the temple itself, with the altar and the worshippers, would represent the heavenly temple which the Gentiles cannot control, profane, or destroy" (72). In Rev 21:15, reference to Ezek 8–11 is still possible; this allows a universalizing of the restrictive and xenophobic aspects of Ezek 40–48. The Jewish image is remodeled in the light of the Christ event. There is, therefore, a continuity with Ezekiel in a double respect; however, to talk of intertextuality might be misleading, for what matters to the readers/recipients is the Christ event.

Finally, Martin Karrer writes about the Ezekiel texts of the Apocalypse. Given that there is no single Old Testament text of Ezekiel up to the Christian era (as the diversity of readings at Qumran and in *p967* testify), which text did the author use? Josephus saw Ezekiel as a prophet of doom; for whatever reasons of his own, Josephus was not interested in either the *merkabah* vision or chapters 40–48. Hebrews 11:37 suggests that the early Christian focus was on the prophet's violent death. In such a context, one must reckon that the book of Ezekiel was in no way widely known or regarded as authoritative. The author of Revelation used the book substantially but could not assume his readers' familiarity with it. Karrer concludes that the author knew the text in Greek, supplemented by an oral familiarity with the Hebrew. His text differed from our critical editions, particularly in the order and contents of Ezekiel 36–40. The author devoured the scroll (cf. Rev10:9; Ezek 2:8; 3:1–3) but conducted no real dialogue with Ezekiel, since he did not integrate the references with his own contemporary prophecies.

Like Hieke, Karrer asserts a correlation between the structure of the Apocalypse and the order of the texts referred to as they occur in Ezekiel. But the differences between Karrer's tabulation of the evidence on page 91 and that of Hieke on pages 6 and 26 are noticeable: Karrer, unlike Hieke, does not include the references to the whore (Ezek 16; 23; Rev 17). And in contrast to Bachmann's argument, Karrer relates Rev 11 exclusively to Ezek 37–38. Such differences are hardly surprising, and the readers of this volume can assess the reasons for themselves. But it would have been a bonus if we could have listened into the ongoing debate at the original conference.

NEW TESTAMENT AND BIBLICAL THEOLOGY

The City in the Valley: Biblical Interpretation and Urban Theology, by Dieter Georgi. Society of Biblical Literature Studies in Biblical Literature 7. Atlanta: Society of Biblical Literature; Leiden: Brill, 2005. Pp. xxviii + 370. Paper/cloth. $34.95/$170.00. ISBN 1589830997/ 9004130659.

Randy G. Haney, Monterey, California

Run-down inner-city areas are not usually seen as places for spiritual renewal, encounters with God, and theologizing about the mission of the church. Rather, they are viewed as places where people are to be found whom the rest of society might wish to avoid. Confronting questions of biblical interpretation and urban theology is this collection of twenty essays by the late German New Testament scholar, Dieter Georgi. The overall impact of the collection ends up as a satisfactory contribution to the ongoing theological discussions regarding biblical interpretation and urban theology. While many of the essays were written previously and have been published in the past, they are still relevant in acquiring a better understanding of the challenges in the life and mission of the church concerning a theologically based urban ministry. Among the topics are socio-economic reasons for the "Divine Man" as propagandistic patterns, the urban adventure of the early church, why Paul was killed, whether Augustine should have the last word on urban theology, the religious dimensions of the world market in the wake of the Middle Ages, praxis and theory in theological education, and whether theology can help understand urban society.

Judging by the subtitle of the book ("Biblical Interpretation *and* Urban Theology") and several of the essays, one gets the impression that the overall discussion will involve the reader in one of those interminable "dry-as-dust" theology debates that fail to address in any substantive and practical fashion a real societal issue confronting the church. This is not the case, per se, with Georgi's contribution (though it does border on it) specifically disclosed by his dual statements, one at the beginning of his book and the other at the end—"urban theology demands concreteness" (1); "urban theology is not the business of an ivory tower" (309)—and ultimately confirmed in the presentation of his arguments throughout the book, especially in chapter 19 (343–66), which serves as a sort of synthesizing section. One could only have hoped that the subtitle of the book could have used the preposition "in" (i.e., "Biblical Interpretation *in* Urban Theology") bespeaking a sort of announcement that would effectively have served to bypass many of the definitional problems associated with both terms being connected with "and."

Claiming that the primary challenge for urban theology is theological and praxis-oriented (309, 337–42, 343–66), Georgi hopes to lay a foundation in his analyses of various texts from the periods of early Judaism and Christianity as well as the early church in the six-hundred-year period from Alexander to Constantine. His is not a literalist biblical hermeneutic; instead, Georgi models theological reflection, bringing to the text questions raised by his own unique traditions and social context (xi–9) within the parameters of a theologically liberal bent.

His thoughtful, if somewhat turgid and heavy, book is an attempt to work out the framework of Christian sociopolitical praxis via biblical interpretation (in the New Testament primarily) in lieu of formulating an "urban theology." There is even an appended synthesis termed "En Route to an Urban Theology," coming *at the end* of the book. One wonders why Georgi waits until after some 340 pages of research and biblical interpretation to deal head-on with the subject of "urban theology." There is a possible clue in the subtitle of the book resident in the use of the conjunction "and." This use of the conjunction adumbrates in a definitional sense that "biblical interpretation" and "urban theology" are already "out there" in the world around us, even perhaps in juxtaposition to each other, and that we are already well-acquainted with them. Yet at this point is where the problems enter, as somehow we feel them slipping away from us, that we need to "define" them, and to compensate we argue that we have to study them more, to do more research, and to devise "new" concepts, new explanatory theories "to explain" what we think they are. After 340 exhausting (and stimulating!) pages of research results piled upon research results and biblical interpretation piled upon biblical interpretation, we are at last treated to a mere twenty-four pages of synthesis in which Georgi attempts to argue, as a sort of finale, for the truth of his concepts or theories in lieu of an "urban theology." Somehow we are now in a position, so to speak, to feel justified in applying Georgi's concepts and theories in practice after all of that "explanation" and "biblical interpretation." I think part of the reason for this "procedure" is that the dominant discourse in our Western academic cultures leads us to talk about our world as if we are mentally seeing everything in it through a certain kind of "image" in which we construe our knowledge as representational in nature and foundational in structure. Nevertheless, the two words in the subtitle do stand for things we can ostensibly observe and talk about. Just to mention both words in relation to each other immediately suggests some directions that academic conversations could take. Yet these two terms are defined very differently in current academic discourse. The concepts traditionally employed to define and/or characterize them have not taken seriously (Georgi is no exception) the plurality of voices in modern societies that now sustain multiple cultures along with their resulting contextualized methods of interpretations. To be quite frank about it, we are now forced to concede that terminology such as "urban theology" stands for a human construct, an "image" that is, at best, vaguely conceptualized, hardly defined, and barely describable.

Georgi's discussion is wide-ranging, and it is obvious that he has read widely, but at times the result of this is a narrative that is overloaded with material, some that is difficult to correlate with the topic at hand (e.g., engaging comparisons between Royce and Bultmann but hardly related to urban theology) and that at times loses its sense of direction with respect to the intended topic of urban theology. Insofar as the research context is an urban one largely, though not entirely, abandoned by much of the evangelical community (see the list of other writers below), Georgi renders a worthwhile service. In Georgi's system, the doctrine of God forms the proper foundation and starting point for an urban theology: God lives in community and works in partnership for both the creation and the redemption of the world.

Taking his cue at the outset of his discussion from the research tradition of studying ancient history in terms of "great men," Georgi nonetheless takes exception to it, advocating that such a perspective "does injustice to the ancient reality" (11). Instead, Georgi's starting point is the "city," conceived metonymically to speak of the material and temporal realities that humans live in. For most Christians, the "city" is the context within which they live, experience, and exercise their dealings with contemporary culture, the state, and the world. Thus, Christians are not simply supposed to interpret or comment about it from some lofty and comfortable distance (e.g., in the suburbs) but to indwell and transform the "city" wherever they happen to live. Too often, Christians have the mindset that the city is inherently dangerous and evil, while suburban and rural settings are inherently good. Georgi even argues at one point that, later on in its history,

"Christianity turned [from an urban religion] into a rural and small-town religion and has remained so until today. There is no consciousness in the contemporary church of really belonging to the city as to a universal phenomenon" (67). Indeed, a part of the positive contribution of Georgi's efforts is to unmask the myth of the dangerous and evil city and to remind us of God's fundamental love and concern for the city. Furthermore, to raise the question of the importance of the "city" for Christian theology no doubt involves one in a quite broad array of interdisciplinary discussions with the social, the religious, the anthropological, the political, and the economic at all levels. It is to his credit that Georgi is aware of this as evidenced in his research.

Any book with this broad of a scope will have by the nature of its shortness some potential shortcomings, some no doubt due to the need for more detail for a fuller understanding of a given topic. Such a need could be satisfied by including some mention of differing perspectives of other scholarly folk who come from other traditions and contexts that are not the same as that of Georgi but who are, nonetheless, dealing with the same issues and questions that he deals with. I was especially surprised at the exclusion of any discussion or mention of the work of Ray Bakke (specifically his *A Theology as Big as the City*) as well as the work of Harvey Conn and Manuel Ortiz (especially *Urban Ministry: The Kingdom, the City, and the People of God*). Furthermore, there is no mention of the scholarship of Robert Linthicum, Paul Fitzgerald, Jim Perkinson, or Lewis Mumford on the subject. Even more telling is the lack of any mention of the work of the evangelical organization known as "Word Made Flesh," whose members choose to live in the world's most destitute urban slums among the poorest of the poor.

In terms of a more detailed presentation as well as serving to set the tone and background for a Christian urban theology, ample reference to and exegesis of pertinent parts of the Old Testament, especially the Hebrew prophets and their living critique of the injustice structurally embodied in the city, would have helped, but unfortunately, it is scant (see 56–58 and scattered references to Isaiah and Ezekiel in ch. 4). Surprisingly, Georgi even mentions (263) that he is a biblical scholar who does not limit himself only to the New Testament but is also interested in the history of interpretation of the Old Testament. Notwithstanding Georgi's comment, a consciously focused section (and not just sparse comments) on the contributions of the Old Testament to the topic of an "urban theology" is sorely needed in my judgment.

Also, some idea or clue about how to respond to some key substantive questions in urban theology are noticeably lacking in Georgi's essays. A prime example is how churches can minister to people in cities where there is a great diversity of cultures, lifestyles, and beliefs. Mere theologizing on the part of Georgi about an urban theology of tomorrow regaining the "curious blend of Utopia and pragmatism" (see 219) found in the New Testament Pauline literature and John's Apocalypse does nothing in terms of practical instruction. Georgi (219) also wants to dispense with what he calls the "theological nonsense" of "limiting the figure of God's incarnation and humanization to the history of Jesus of Nazareth" and extending it and localizing it in the "body of Christ," the church. Even if one were to grant Georgi's initial premise regarding the dismissal of the history of Jesus of Nazareth for any aspect of a modern urban theology, it is not clear how Georgi thinks that the "body of Christ" can in fact act in a public way regarding the thorny issues inherent in a modern urban theology. Indeed, no one is gainsaying Georgi's central focus here that an important part of theological education involves a passion for the truth of God that can and must be imparted. Living human communities found in "the body of Christ" can do this, as Georgi points out, but it must first be modeled. The urban poor are not the subject of research in the classical sense of controlled experiments, single-system frames of analysis (as in traditional "biblical interpretation"), and objective observation. The point needs to be highlighted: the value of contextualized and hermeneutically self-conscious and community-conscious research and writing must be recognized and implemented in this modeling process.

Yet another question in the same "body of Christ" discussion context provoked by Georgi's analysis, but unfortunately left unanswered, has to do with the means by which "social relations" get transformed into "christological relations." Also, from the standpoint of the information age and its concomitant information overload, how does one who is interested in "doing" urban theology, à la Georgi's approach, gain a perspective on the real effects of governmental policies and institutions in lieu of intervention and confrontation? In short, one wonders how Georgi's "urban theologian," who ostensibly takes an active interest in democratic structures and procedures, would act so as to bring about true redress for imposed forms of suffering in urban communities (see 143–45, 364).

One of the final inadequacies and severe limitations of the book, besides the fact that it consists primarily of collected lectures and papers and thus suffers from the problem of being out-of-date with regards to recent bibliography, is the lack of any subject, author, or scripture indices. This major deficiency makes the book extremely difficult to use, especially when time is a factor and one needs to look up references.

In spite of the above-mentioned issues for consideration, I found the book lucid and somewhat helpful as a contemporary "prolegomena" to an urban theology with limited usefulness in the area of praxis. I would recommend it as supplementary, optional reading for an "urban theology" advanced undergraduate class on urban theology.

The City in the Valley: Biblical Interpretation and Urban Theology, by Dieter Georgi. Society of Biblical Literature Studies in Biblical Literature 7. Atlanta: Society of Biblical Literature; Leiden: Brill, 2005. Pp. xxviii + 370. Paper/cloth. $34.95/$170.00. ISBN 1589830997/ 9004130659.

Timothy A. Friedrichsen, The Catholic University of America, Washington, District of Columbia

Readers who are familiar with Dr. Dieter Georgi's works, such as *The Oppo-*
nents of Paul in 2 Corinthians (Fortress, 1986; German orig., Neukirchener, 1964)
and *Remembering the Poor: The History of Paul's Collection for Jerusalem* (Abingdon, 1992), will find in this new volume a collection of twenty papers, addresses,
and articles by Georgi that have been adapted into chapters for this book. When
dates for delivery and/or publication—not all have been previously published—
are clearly given, one sees that the adapted works range from 1967 to 1997. After
the adaptation of these pieces and the preparation of the preface (xi–xxviii, while
at Union Theological Seminary, Dasmariñas, Cavite, Philippines), but before
its publication, Dr. Georgi met "his untimely death" due to "increasing health
problems," according to Helmut Koester of Harvard University (foreword, vii–x,
esp. x). Koester also notes that this prevented further endeavors that Georgi had
undertaken, namely, the "writing of his commentaries on the Wisdom of Solomon and the Second Letter of Paul to the Corinthians" (x).

Georgi, who at the time of his passing was Professor Emeritus for New Testament Studies at the Department of Protestant Theology at the Johann Wolfgang
Goethe-Universität, Frankfurt am Main, Germany (back cover), notes that his
interest in urban theology and these twenty chapters "were drawn up in conscious awareness of urban and metropolitan situation around the Boston and
San Francisco Bays and on the islands and peninsulas of New York," as well as
Los Angeles, Ann Arbor, and Frankfurt on Main, which is "nicknamed Bankfurt
and Mainhattan with good reason" (xv). In addition, readers who are familiar
with Georgi's work will find in this volume his interest in relating biblical texts to
"social-historical inquires into the interplay of Judaism and the early church with
their pagan environment" (284). For the purposes of this investigation of biblical literature and urban theology, he focuses primarily on Pauline texts and the
book of Revelation, but not to the exclusion of prophetic literature and other New
Testament texts. In order to orient the reader—whether familiar with his previous
work or not—to this volume, Georgi begins with a chapter about his own diverse
theological experiences ("Personal Reflections on an American Theological Perspective," 1–9), in which he offers both his positive and critical observations on
those experiences with respect to a "vision of authentic community" in which
"we allow our loyalties to the human family at large to be as powerful as those
to our immediate neighbors and friends" (7). With that background, Georgi sets
forth the remaining chapters with a view toward urban theology. The aim of this
review is first to give an overview of the scope of the material contained in this
volume (limits prohibit including all chapter titles, not to mention indicating
each chapter's genesis and/or publication) and then to conclude with some general critical remarks.

To set the biblical texts to be considered in their first-century context and to
show their applicability to urban theology, Georgi treats (11–23) the social and
cultural interest in "great men" (11) of history, as well as the worship of them
in the Hellenistic world, most especially its urban centers (see 17), in which the
market of the Mediterranean world was most concentrated. While the poet and

prophet of Caesar and his religion, Horace, fails to show himself as a true prophet, John of Revelation does not (25–51), because John "saw the deterioration of Rome ahead of time, particularly the decline of its previously dominant role in world trade" (51). John's prophecy of the late first century nevertheless comes from within a church that, although rooted in the itinerant ministry of Jesus and his disciples of largely rural areas and small towns and villages, very soon spread to and found its major growth and life in urban centers. This is especially visible in the missionary preaching of the urbanite Paul (53–68), who understood the city and its place in the larger world. It is not surprising, then, that Paul found amenable for his communities of faith the urban, secular term, *ekklēsia*, which "means the assembly of the free citizens of a city" and the "basis of the self-governance of such places" (61).

Having introduced the two major biblical authors with whom he will deal—both of whom envisage a new society rooted in faith in Christ Jesus while engaging in a critical dialogue with Roman society and its religiosity—Georgi can move on to discuss issues of the city and its manipulation of time and space (69–92) and the challenge for Paul to espouse an anthropology that would ground and support his urban-situated communities (93–101) and that also criticizes the "dehumanizing tendencies that were essentially linked with the individualized concept of humans" (93).

Throughout this work Georgi strongly reclaims Paul's understanding of the cooperate nature of Christ and the communal nature of the believer. Even Paul's important tenet of justification is tied to cultural, economic, monetary, and political aspects of the city and of the Roman empire, as well as the place of Judaism and his early church communities within the empire (103–34; see below). In addition, Paul's ethics shows signs of being worked out from within the urban setting of his background and the communities he founded (135–45). In the end Georgi shows that Paul's willingness to be critical of the Roman Empire, most especially in the coded and subversive message of Rom 13:1–7, which does not encourage unquestioning subservience to the government officials but rather is Paul's call for a critical engagement with those authorities, makes sense of Paul's execution after being tried in the court of Caesar (147–60).

In this sort of critique of the Roman Empire, John of Patmos is a kindred spirit, for he, too, directed irony at the Roman Empire and the Caesar religion, while encouraging transformation of the urban ideals of the Greco-Roman world, which go back to Alexander's encounter with Babylon (161–86). This can be seen in John's vision that "conceived of the new Jerusalem, the city in the valley, not as the Jerusalem known but rather as ancient Babylon brought to life again" (xxv). In addition, John's vision of Rev 12, wherein the dragon endangers the heavenly woman and her child, prepares for the vision of Rev 13, where Caesar and his religion have their authority from the dragon of Rev 12—who is Satan or the devil (12:9)—so that these visions critique nationalism and the urban bourgeoisie (187–93).

Having engaged the reader in the above considerations, Dr. Georgi—from this reader's point of view—now turns more specifically toward discussion of urban theology. After the early church's move to urban centers, there is a turn back toward the rural, which is seen in Augustine's distancing of himself and his theology from the city. This in turn influenced Augustine's (mis)reading of Paul, which has had a lasting effect. Augustine should not, therefore, have the final word on the city and urban theology (195–220). Georgi is also critical of the resurgence of scholarly interest in the life of Jesus that is enamored, as was the Hellenistic world and the Middle Ages, with the heroic person (221–54). Although this interest is supported by urban and bourgeoisie interests, it does not show an interest in a true urban theology. Such a theology needs to engage the understanding of the world market, which, according to Georgi's thesis, is still rooted in the Middle Ages and lacks the challenge that Paul's concern for the collection for the "poor" of Jerusalem represents (255–82). The urbanite Paul himself had an intimate understanding of the world, its markets, and its urban centers. Paul consciously uses this understanding in his treatment of money and the language he chooses for his theological tenet of justification (283–307; see above). Thus, Paul can help in the development of a true urban theology.

The development of a true, relevant urban theology requires thinkers who are willing to be "very conscious trespassers" (309) into fields not of their own specialty as they work out their own understanding of the possibility of community in urban centers that are engaged in global interaction. Such a community would stand as a visible critique of the tendency toward individualism, isolationism, nationalism, and socially irresponsible capitalism. Georgi provides homage to two such "trespassers": Josiah Royce (309–22) and Paul Tillich—especially the "Frankfurt Tillich" (323–36). Urban theology "demands concreteness ... [of] personal, local, and regional specifics" (1) and thus "is not the business of an ivory tower, even less of professional specialization. It is first of all a matter of praxis, the praxis of everyone concerned" (309). As such, a true urban theology, Georgi believes, will be an important element in universities and churches, especially those in urban settings (337–42). He provides a vision of that education from his own experience (343–66) and shows that his view can be easily adapted for each of the urban centers in which he has taught (see above). As "a final upbeat" (xxvii), he concludes his volume with "On Sojourning" (367–70), an abbreviated version of his 1977 baccalaureate address for Harvard Divinity School, wherein he encouraged the graduates, scholars, and all "the people of God" to be "a community of sojourners, constantly on the road" (368), that is, on "the road to the city of God" (369).

In the interest of full disclosure, this reader—raised on a Midwest dairy farm and concentrating his own research and teaching in the area of the Synoptic Gospels—took on this volume in "fear and trembling" (Phil 2:12). Georgi himself gave me hope, however, for besides the broadening experience of overseas studies, I now teach in an urban area. Given that, in this reader's opinion, Georgi's treatments of Paul and Revelation and his willingness to address critical issues facing nations, cities, and markets—and the challenge they pose to Christian churches of various denominations—made for rich and engaging reading, which can be gladly recommended. Not only does Georgi offer stimulating interpretations of the biblical texts he treats, but he is also willing to critique scholarship that has "surrendered to a hypertrophic concern for methodology, something like a methodological messianism, with little relevance for anyone in other theological disciplines" (104). Georgi's approach can be seen as a two-front challenge or encouragement to any biblical interpreter: be intent on solid historical critical work in all its aspects, but also dare to trespass into other fields so as to bring biblical interpretation to the life of the church. Georgi's breadth of reading, critical thinking, and theological engagements are impressive. The breadth of his scholarship thus extends a challenge to professors of all stripes, especially those who "have taken the entrepreneur as the role model to follow." Instead, Georgi notes: "I am for professors who profess. Professing can be dangerous, but it has the promise to gain life—for all of us" (336).

With all its richness and strengths, in the end, this volume does not—at least for this reader—quite come together; it seems there is much to be done to excavate this volume's implied urban theology and the role biblical interpretation plays and the diverse methods and fields to be used in the development of a true urban theology. At times there is unevenness in the reading experience, for rather scholarly and heavily footnoted papers are followed by more meditative or informal presentations. For interested persons who would like to consult this volume for particular texts or topics, the volume could be much more user-friendly if good indices were provided (e.g., of biblical and other texts, of persons/authors, and of topics/themes). Finally, although any reader will find minor points with which to disagree (e.g., for this reader, some of the accepted partition theories of Paul's letters), they neither lessen the thought-provoking and more important purposes of the works of Georgi nor the overall quality of the volume.

Salvation in the New Testament: Perspectives on Soteriology, by Jan G. van der Watt. Supplements to Novum Testamentum 121. Leiden: Brill, 2005. Pp. xiii + 529. Hardcover. $172.00. ISBN 9004142975.

Frank J. Matera, The Catholic University of America, Washington, District of Columbia

The remarkable growth of early Christianity was due in no small measure to the salvation it promised and to the experience of salvation its original adherents enjoyed. It is not surprising, then, that salvation plays such a central role in the writings of the New Testament. What is surprising is how little attention New Testament scholarship has devoted to this topic. The appearance of this collection of essays on the theme of salvation in the New Testament, then, is a welcome contribution that responds to an important need.

With the exception of Craig Koester, all seventeen contributors to this volume are South African. All agreed to focus on the imagery and metaphors that the New Testament writers employed to express their understanding of salvation. These essays then became the basis for a conference on New Testament soteriology held at the University of Pretoria. Although the names of many of the contributors may be unfamiliar to some, these essays are uniformly good, and all of their authors are conversant with, and are careful to engage, current American, British, and European scholarship.

Divided into three parts, this volume follows the canonical order of the New Testament. Part 1 provides essays that deal with salvation in each of the Four Gospels and the Acts of the Apostles. Part 2 considers various Pauline metaphors for salvation and then focuses on Colossians, Ephesians, 1 Thessalonians, and the Pastoral Epistles. Part 3 discusses the concept of salvation in James, 1 Peter, the Johannine Epistles, and the Apocalypse of John. The volume concludes with Jan G. van der Watt's helpful synthesis of the soteriology in the New Testament, written in light of these essays. Although the arrangement of the material is not imaginative, readers will find it serviceable.

After discussing key soteriological terms, the essays in part 1 study the soteriology of the Gospels and Acts in light of their narratives. Andries G. van Aarde reads Matthew "as a story that re-tells the 'history' of how God sent Joshua from Egypt as Moses' successor to save Israel" (7). This story narrates how God heals Israel through Jesus, Israel's Davidic Messiah, by releasing Israel from political stress. H. J. Bernard Combrink shows how the narrative of Mark's Gospel communicates God's salvific intervention through Jesus. Salvation in Mark is healing, liberation from sickness and sin, and, ultimately, the protection of life from death.

The Gospel of Luke and the Acts of the Apostles are treated separately, with an essay on Johannine soteriology between them. Gert J. Steyn argues that the Lukan Gospel portrays Jesus as the prophet who announces salvation, which is portrayed as liberation. He then notes that Jesus' salvific work operates in two ways: the restoration of physical and mental health, and spiritual restoration through the forgiveness of sins. Thus the notion of salvation is holistic. In his essay on the soteriology of Acts, Hermie C. van Zyl deals with the Savior of salvation and with the salvation of the Savior. Zyl notes that, whereas in the Gospel Jesus' healing ministry is in the foreground, in Acts the religious dimension of salvation is in the foreground. Salvation is ultimately deliverance from sin. Thus, he concludes that Luke's anthropology is similar to what is found in the rest of the New Testament: "people need to be saved because of their alienation from God" (153).

Jan G. van der Watt notes that relatively little been written about soteriology as an independent theme in the Gospel of John. He then presents Johannine soteriology as resocialization. The moment of salvation is described "in terms of *being born into a spiritual family* and thus receiving eternal life" (124). This is accomplished by accepting Jesus as the revelation of God and becoming part of the family of God by being born from above.

Part 2 is the most interesting section of this volume, in large measure because

Paul offers the most sophisticated analysis of salvation in the New Testament. Cilliers Breytenbach provides two insightful essays: one on the "for us" phases in Pauline soteriology, and another on the Pauline metaphor of reconciliation. He notes that Paul inherited the tradition that Christ "died for our sins" and then developed his interpretation of Christ's death in four ways: by personalizing it; by universalizing it; by making it an expression of God' love; and by highlighting that this death resulted in salvation. Stephan J. Joubert approaches the notion of salvation from Paul's use of the metaphor of *charis*. God is the divine benefactor who manifests his favor by sacrificing his son, even for God's enemies. Consequently, this *charis* is a present reality that calls for a gracious response.

Andrei B. du Toit examines the forensic metaphors in Romans and concludes that they were eminently suited to highlight God's sovereign activity and the radical nature of God's favor. He writes: "*Ironical as it may seem, exactly by using forensic imagery, Paul completely delegalized the Christian message. In God's gospel court room grace reigns*" (243). In his study of redemption, D. Fancois Tolmie argues that Paul employed this metaphor to highlight the radical status reversal that Christ's death has effected for humankind and the new obligations this entails.

The remaining essays of part 2 deal with specific letters. Petrus J. Gräbe analyzes salvation in Colossians and Ephesians in terms of the alienation people experienced living in a hostile world ruled by cosmic powers. G. R. de Villiers describes the soteriology of 1 Thessalonians as belonging to a new community, the family of God. Abraham J. Malherbe draws upon his vast knowledge of Hellenistic philosophy to explain the soteriology of the Pastorals as divine education. Thus soteriology is related to the human condition from which people need to be saved. It is a process of learning to live godly lives, a process made possible "because God's saving grace appeared in order to educate people how to live" (356).

The final part of this work deals with several writings often overlooked in discussions of New Testament soteriology. For Craig R. Koester, salvation in Hebrews holds out the promise of entering into God's Sabbath rest, the holy of holies, into which Jesus, the great high priest, has already entered. Hebrews assures believers that they have inherited salvation in the world to come. In his study of James, J. Eugene Botha draws a connection between salvation and achieving perfection. Since ultimate salvation is imminent, "only those who have perfected their faith through deeds will be part of that glorious dispensation" (405) of which the members of the Jacobean community are the firstfruits. The soteriology of 1 Peter has been neglected, according to Fika J. Janse van Rensburg, who identifies three metaphors for salvation in 1 Peter: (1) the saved as a family with God as father; (2) the saved as a flock that has been returned to Christ the chief shepherd; (3) the saved as having been healed by Christ's wound. Dirk G. van der Merwe describes salvation in the Johannine Epistles as a change in status. Believers become children of God and form a community of faith in accordance with their confession that God is light, righteousness, and love. Finally, after discussing the narrative of the Apocalypse, Jan A. du Rand identifies "the Lamb-event" (the crucifixion of Jesus) as the central motif of the book's soteriology. This soteriology finds its climax in the marriage of the Lamb and the new Jerusalem. The eschatological destiny of the redeemed is the new heaven and the new earth, the restoration of perfect life with God.

After so many metaphors of salvation, readers may wonder if it is possible to speak in a meaningful way about *the* soteriology of the New Testament. Jan G. van der Watt acknowledges that this "complex landscape does not lend itself to being diminished into précis form" (505). But in a concluding essay, which brings some order to these many metaphors and images, he argues that the diverse writings of the New Testament should be seen as integrating the message of salvation into the particular situations of their original listeners. Because the New Testament writings address diverse situations, they express their understanding of salvation differently. Thus, to use van der Watt's image, as readers move from one writing to another they realize that they are in different rooms, but they also sense that they are still in the same house.

Given the challenge of bringing together so many essays, the editor of this volume is to be congratulated for assembling a collection that maintains its focus. While one might have hoped for more systematizing along the lines of van der Watt's final essay, this volume is a fine contribution to the theology of the New Testament.

He Came Down from Heaven: The Preexistence of Christ and the Christian Faith, by Douglas McCready. Downers Grove, Ill.: InterVarsity Press, 2005. Pp. 349. Paper. $26.00. ISBN 0830827749.

Martin Karrer, Kirchliche Hochschule Wuppertal/Barmen School of Theology, Wuppertal, Germany

Wer war Jesus Christus? Douglas McCready stellt diese Frage aus der Perspektive der christologischen Bekenntnisbildung. Den historischen Jesus heißt es in dieser Perspektive ernst zu nehmen. Aber den Einsatz der Christologie bildet— so McCready—nicht das irdische Wirken und Reden Jesu, sondern die in der Menschwerdung vorausgesetzte Präexistenz. Deren Rang und neutestamentliche Basis sind in jüngerer Zeit umstritten. So sieht McCready sich dazu herausgefordert, das klassische theologische Verständnis einer real-personalen Präexistenz Christi zu verteidigen oder—in seinem Sinne formuliert—als basiert im Neuen Testament darzustellen. Systematische und exegetische Reflexion soll das ineinander verzahnen und eine Brücke über den Graben schlagen, den modernes Denken zwischen dem Glauben und der theologischen Reflexion aufriss (8–19 u.ö.). Diese Aufgabe ist hoch respektabel, und wer würde sich nicht freuen, wenn sie gelänge! McCready allerdings zeigt dem kritischen Blick weniger ihre Lösung als ihre Haken und Ösen.

McCready´s Ausgangspunkt bildet der Konflikt der klassischen theologischen

Begriffe mit neuzeitlichem Denken (Kap. 1, „Setting" [11–39]). Doch McCready spitzt die Frage schärfer zu als er wahrhaben will. Denn die Präexistenz formte in der Alten Kirche nach Vorläufern in der philosophischen Ontologie ein Diskussionsfeld (προϋπάρχειν/ προϋπαρξις κτλ.; Gregor v. Nyssa, Adv. Apollinarem, PG 45, 1145D = op. 3,1 147) usw.), das begrifflich nicht unmittelbar in die Bekenntnissätze einging. Deshalb könnte die Diskussion größeren Spielraum erhalten. McCready nützt dies nicht.

Er definiert Typen der Präexistenzreflexion gemäß der neuzeitlichen Metareflexion (bes. 15–19). Dabei unterscheidet er die von ihm vertretene Sicht, nach der Christus real-personal, wenn auch ohne menschliche Leiblichkeit präexistierte und das alleine einer voll entwickelten Christologie entspreche, von zwei anderen Typen: Eine ideale Präexistenz führe die Idee ewiger Sohnschaft vor alle Zeit zurück, ohne die Personalität des Präexistenten zu sichern, und eine metaphorische oder eschatologische Präexistenz verliere tendenziell deren Realität. Eine solche Typenbildung ist gedanklich hilfreich. Andererseits verlockt sie dazu, jeden Typ am behaupteten klassischen Maßstab messen. Schleiermachers Urbild-Christologie (257ff.) genügt dann ebenso wenig wie das Nachdenken K.-J. Kuschels, der die Präexistenz im „Blick von Ostern her" entwickelt (Geboren vor aller Zeit? Der Streit um Christi Ursprung, München 1990, 639 u.ö.) und nach McCready unter den eschatologischen Typ fällt (9,18–19).

Die angestrebte Versöhnung zwischen Glauben und neuzeitlichem Denken nimmt damit die Gestalt einer Apologie an, die Präexistenz-, Gottessohn- und Gottheitschristologie miteinander verknüpft. Zum Schlüssel wird das Neue Testament, weil es in der kontroversen systematischen Diskussion, zu der Kap. 8 und 9 (234–307) zurückkehren, einen Anker zu bieten scheint. Ihn entfaltet McCready in der Mitte der Studie (Kap. 2 bis 5).

Freilich ist das Neue Testament nicht minder umstritten. Kap. 2 (40–69) skizziert daraufhin wichtige Forschungspositionen (selbstredend mit mehr Sympathie für die traditionelle Sicht als für die—durchaus ernst genommene—Studie J.D.G. Dunn´s, Christology in the Making, 1980) und den Streit um die Einschätzung der christologischen Titel und Sendungsformeln. Er nimmt Literatur hier und in der ganzen Studie in großer Breite wahr, wenn auch immer wieder vertiefungsbedürftig (Hurtado 56–57, 70 usw.). Vor allem aber trifft McCready eine grundlegende methodische Entscheidung: Die Gegenwart des göttlichen Autors („divine Author") hinter der Vielfalt neutestamentlicher Schriften erlaube, aus deren Vielstimmigkeit eine konsistente Synthese herzustellen (43).

Die Vielfalt des Neuen Testaments tritt damit bereits als Prämisse („premise" ebd.) in den Dienst einer theologischen Einheit. Neutestamentler und Historiker müssen das als problematische Vorgabe erachten. Ebenso problematisch geraten im Fortgang manche Entscheidungen der Einleitungsfragen. Jak gilt S. 70 als ältestes neutestamentliches Schreiben neben Paulus, was nur deswegen nicht wirksam wird, weil McCready dem Jak eine Christologie abspricht (was heute angefochten wird). Die umstrittenen und Deuteropaulinen werden nahtlos ins Pauluskapitel eingefügt (Kol 1,15–20 [81–86]; 1 Tim 1,15; 3,16 [97–98]) u.ä.

Differenzierungen fallen auf diese Weise schwer. Hüten wir uns davor, die Kritik zu überziehen. Viele Entscheidungen werden im Einzelfall überzeugen (z.B. wird die Mehrheit der Leserinnen und Leser unbeschadet der Beobachtungen von Dunn u.a. in Phil 2,5–11 mit McCready 73–80 eine Präexistenz- und keine Adamchristologie ausmachen). McCready verschweigt nicht, wie oft es neben der hoheitschristologischen und Präexistenzdeutung Alternativen gibt (z.B. Röm 1,3–4 und 9,5 [87–90, 91–92]). Aber für detaillierte Einzeluntersuchungen fehlt angesichts der Fülle der anzusprechenden Stellen zu oft der Platz. Die Tendenz ist unverkennbar:

Dank Paulus und (Deutero-)Paulinen wissen wir, dass die Präexistenz bis in älteste Zeit zurückreicht und ein breites christologisches Fundament besitzt (Kap. 3 aufgrund der erähnten Stellen [70–104]). Die synoptischen Evangelien (bes. Mt 11,27–30 und die „ich bin gekommen"-Formeln) lassen sich zur Präexistenz hin öffnen; der 1 Petr bezeugt sie unmittelbar (zur Schlüsselstelle 1 Petr 1,20 [122–23]), und der Hebr spielt mehrfach (1,1–8 usw.) auf sie an (Kap. 4 [105–34]). Die joh Schriften, namentlich Joh und 1 / 2 Joh (nach S. 136 vom gleichen Autor, dem Zebedaiden Johannes verfasst) vollenden das vorhandene Präexistenzdenken und entwickeln es nicht erst spätneutestamentlich, wie Kritiker meinen (Kap. 5 [135–62]); das zeigen neben dem Logos-Prolog (wo der λόγος als „preexistent deity" [161] gezeichnet sei) bes. Joh 8,57–58; 10,29–30; 12,41; 17,4–5; 1 Joh 1,1–4; 2,13a; 5,20; 2 Joh 7–9 (ohne Wahrnehmung des Streits um eine mögliche futurische Deutung des dortigen ἐρχόμενος) und Sendungsformeln. Alles in allem bietet das Neue Testament auf diese Weise „a consistent witness to Christ´s deity and preexistence" (161).

Seinen Intentionen entsprechend stellt McCready sein Kapitel zur Religionsgeschichte (Kap. 6 „Jewish and Hellenistic Background" [163–99]) hinter die neutestamentlichen Hauptentscheidungen. Denn so scheint ihm am Besten gesichert, was systematisch zu fordern sei: Jesus selbst ist die Schlüsselquelle des christlichen Glaubens von Präexistenz und Gottheitschristologie; Traditionen der Umwelt helfen lediglich, das zu formulieren und sind nicht überzubewerten (gegen jede „parallelomania" [163–64]). Wieder wird der kritische Leser vielen Einzelhinweisen um Messianismus, Menschensohn- und Weisheitstradition folgen und zustimmen, dass speziell die personale Präexistenz Christi nicht aus Vorläufern ableitbar ist (185). Doch bleibt und wächst sein Unbehagen. Denn methodisch zu verräterisch ist es, Denktraditionen von vornherein erst nachrangig zu prüfen.

Kap. 8 („Postapostolic Development of the Doctrine" [200–233]) rundet den Beweisgang ab: Alle bedeutsamen Quellen ab den apostolischen Vätern akzeptieren die Präexistenz, so gewiss sie Jahrhunderte benötigen, um die Implikationen dessen herauszuarbeiten. Ihre Begrifflichkeit besitzt dabei einen beträchtlichen Spielraum. Das wird bei McCready nicht unmittelbar sichtbar, da er ausschließlich englisch zitiert (und manchmal, wie bei einem Teil der Ignatius-Belege, mit fehlenden bzw. ungenauen Stellenangaben). Er schreitet insofern das Sprachfeld um „ungezeugt"/„vor aller Zeit" usw. sinnvoll aus, während er die Quellen speziell zum Leitbegriff (προϋπάρχειν/προϋπαρξις κτλ.; praeexistentia) nur am Rande streift (241 u.ö.).

Seine Unterscheidung von Ansatz und Entfaltung der Implikationen gäbe McCready nochmals die Möglichkeit, den neutestamentlichen Befund als Ansatz der Gedanken zu differenzieren. Doch widmet er seine Schlusskapitel nicht dem, sondern der systematischen Abrundung: Weil das Neue Testament zur real-personalen Präexistenz und von ihr weiter zur Gottheitschristologie geleite, seien die systematischen Ansätze der Moderne aus dieser Perspektive zu prüfen und der Glaube in der kritischen Auseinandersetzung mit ihnen zu sichern (Kap. 8–10 [234–317]). Viel Raum gewährt Kap. 8 der Kritik des Adoptianismus, der keines der Probleme löse, die er der Präexistenztheologie vorhalte (Ergebnis 256). Kap. 9 weist Alternativen und Einwände gegen die Präexistenz von Schleiermacher bis zur Geistchristologie (gegen Piet Schoonenberg 269ff.) sowie von Neutestamentlern (J.D.G. Dunn 272–77) bis zur Religionstheologie ab (John Hick 282–286, Hans Küng und Karl-Josef Kuschel 286–94). Eine Fülle theologischer Entwürfe tritt in großem Bogen vor Augen, gelesen zum Ziel hin, alle Alternativen zur real-personalen Präexistenz Christi seien „uniformly unsatisfactory" (309).

Zitieren wir das Gesamtergebnis: „A christology that seeks to do justice to the breadth and depth of the New Testament evidence will always attempt to express two things at the same time: Jesus' origin in time and his origin in the eternity of God himself; Jesus' birth from a woman and at the same time his origin 'from the father'; Jesus' concrete historical existence and at the same time his transhistorical preexistence. Only the traditional doctrine of Christ's real preexistent deity does this adequately" (311).

Eine Beurteilung fällt nicht leicht. Denn McCready ist, wie angedeutet, sehr belesen, sein Anliegen hochrespektabel, und viele Details, die er referiert, überzeugen oder sind Forschungskonsens. Aber die methodische Problematik der Studie überdeckt das. Ihr apologetisches Interesse überwiegt so sehr, dass ein unübersehbarer Zirkel der Argumentation erwächst. Wer McCready´s Überzeugung von Anfang an teilt, wird sich durch diesen Zirkel bestätigt fühlen. Ansonsten jedoch wachsen die Bedenken von Kapitel zu Kapitel. Selbst wenn ein Rezensent wie viele andere von McCready zitierte Autoren die Überzeugung vertritt, Hoheitschristologie und Wurzeln der Präexistenzvorstellung seien sehr alt, legt er die Studie zwiespältig aus der Hand. Sie bietet ein hochinteressantes Beispiel für moderne Apologetik, indes keine Weiterführung der neutestamentlichen Forschung.

Spirit and Kingdom in the Writings of Luke and Paul: An Attempt to Reconcile These Concepts, by Youngmo Cho. Paternoster Biblical Monograph. Waynesboro, Ga.: Paternoster, 2005. Pp. xviii + 227. Paper. $36.99. ISBN 1842273167.

John T. Squires, United Theological College, North Parramatta, Australia

For the past decade Paternoster Press has been publishing theses and monographs that stand within the broad evangelical tradition of Christianity in the

Paternoster Biblical Monographs series. Youngmo Cho's consideration of *Spirit and Kingdom in the Writings of Luke and Paul* is a fine example of the works included in this series: careful, detailed, cautious, and loyal to the tenets of what the series editors describe as "the historic faith." Exegetical insight, lexicographical analysis, hermeneutical scrutiny, and theological argumentation are combined with equal weight to produce a volume that proposes a thesis that privileges Paul over Luke as the more faithful interpreter of the views of Jesus regarding the kingdom of God.

Cho's thesis takes issue with what has come to be the accepted scholarly view regarding the similarity of pneumatology in Paul's writings and in Luke-Acts. He starts by reviewing the positions articulated by biblical scholars J. D. G. Dunn and Max Turner before noting the critique offered by Robert Menzies, and the reader finds these names returning often throughout the sustained exegetical considerations of the book. Cho accepts one element of the established scholarly view, namely, that early Christianity provided a clear development in understanding the role of the Spirit, moving on from the perspective that was dominant in intertestamental Judaism. This development takes as its point of departure the view that the Spirit was a charismatic entity that inspires prophecy or, in Cho's words, provides "extraordinary wisdom." He demonstrates his agreement with this element through the careful exegetical treatment of a wide range of intertestamental and rabbinic works.

The dominant scholarly view also proposes that early Christianity moved beyond this by developing an understanding of the Spirit as a soteriological agent that was "life-giving." Cho accepts this proposal but argues that the implementation of this change was not consistent throughout the early church. He considers that there are a number of texts within Luke-Acts that demonstrate that Luke, for one, had not adopted this change. In the Lukan writings the Spirit continues to function in the more limited, traditional sense as the force that inspires the message; there is, Cho maintains, no evidence in Luke-Acts that the Spirit was conceptualized as a soteriological agent.

This argument, once established, allows Cho then to propose that it was Paul, no less, who was responsible for this movement from the traditional Jewish understanding (the charismatic role of the Spirit) to the early Christian insight (the soteriological quality of the Spirit). A number of passages are canvassed to establish this claim. Further, Cho then proposes that Paul developed a theological position that was, in fact, faithful to the position adopted by Jesus, for whom the Spirit was more than a spirit of prophecy. For Jesus, he claims, the Spirit was seen and known through the kingdom of God; thus, all of the Synoptic sayings that report words of Jesus concerning the kingdom can be examined and correlated with Paul's many references to the Spirit.

This claim attempts to overcome a fundamental difficulty in the thesis as conceived: Paul wrote often about the Spirit but rarely referred to the kingdom of God. Jesus, conversely, had much to say about the kingdom but very little concerning the Spirit. Cho deals with this difficulty by arguing that what Paul said of the Spirit correlates closely with what Jesus said about the kingdom. Thus, the two concepts are, indeed, very closely related—if not, in fact, the same. He argues the case in two ways. First, Cho proposes that there is an innate similarity between the Spirit and the kingdom, namely, the present/future tension inherent within each of these concepts. Second, Cho considers four areas of "conceptual overlap" where both Spirit and kingdom appear related to the same set of ideas: sonship, resurrection, righteousness, and ethics. Paul sees these four concepts relating to the Spirit in a manner akin to the way that Jesus understood they related to the kingdom. Thus, Cho concludes, "the Spirit embodies the essence of the Kingdom" (108).

The consequence of this thesis is a paradox: Luke, the reporter of the deeds and words of the earthly Jesus, has failed to grasp the essence of Jesus' message; while Paul, who rarely seems concerned with the earthly Jesus and scarcely quotes his teachings, knows the essence and heart of what Jesus had grasped. At first glance, the claim appears counterintuitive. As the argument advances, elements of persuasive force are noted. Can it be that this was the reality of the developments that took place in the first century, that Paul was really more attuned to the essence of Jesus' message than was Luke? Not far below the surface lies the problem of distinguishing the "historical Jesus" from the Jesus who is presented in the Gospel accounts. It is an issue that Cho never addresses.

Cho writes clearly and argues carefully. There are some points in the thesis where he appears to have stretched the evidence beyond what it can bear. The similarities between kingdom and Spirit are sometimes heightened beyond what the evidence warrants; a zeal to demonstrate their coherence and interrelationship robs each of its distinctive qualities. Cho's discussion of ethics in the Synoptics is collapsed wholly into the love command; he ignores other elements such as teachings on poverty and the stewardship of resources, which is a major element in Lukan writings. Overall, his reduction of the Lukan view of the Spirit to the cause of the proclamation alone fails to convince. Evidence supporting his claim that Luke 11:2 was originally a prayer for the Spirit, rather than for the kingdom, is weak. The tracing of the Spirit through Acts (in ch. 5) limits the Spirit to the initiating cause for the proclamation of the kingdom; this fails to consider the Spirit within a wider network of factors that together provide a complex exposition for the implementing of the divine will through the events narrated: the Spirit works in conjunction with epiphanies, scripture citations, and contemporary prophecies that come to fulfillment in the narrative and direct interventions of God, who guides the story as it unfolds.

The book includes a thirteen-page bibliography and indices of references and authors, indicating that it has been carefully researched and integrally related to ongoing scholarship. There are some unfortunate errors in spelling, most prominently in some headings. "Synoptics" is missing its "p" in the heading on page 103, and so, too, is "Proclaim" in the heading on page 178; also in this heading "disciples" is misspelled as "dicsiples." More troubling is the fact that "Extraordinary Wisdom" in the heading for section 2.3.2 on page 23 should, in fact, be

"Life-Giving Wisdom," as the argument in the section following makes clear. It is a pity that the close attention paid to the exegesis of ancient texts throughout the body of this work is marred by these infelicities, which are readily detectable through the use of that modern invention, a spell-check program.

The Scriptures and the Lord: Formation and Significance of the Christian Biblical Canon; A Study in Text, Ritual and Interpretation, by Tomas Bokedal. Lund: Lund University, 2005. Pp. 374. Paper. ISBN 9162866079.

Tobias Nicklas, Radboud University of Nijmegen, Nijmegen, The Netherlands

In seiner an der Universität Lund erstellten Dissertation untersucht Tomas Bokedal Entstehung und Bedeutung des biblischen Kanons in der frühen wie auch der heutigen Kirche. Seine zentrale These stellt er bereits am Anfang des Buches vor:

> Integral to the life of the church, in particular the ecclesial practice of procla-mation and prayer, the formation and continuous usage of the Christian biblical canon is an act of literary preservation and actualization of the church's apostolic normative tradition, "the Scriptures and the Lord", by which the church is and remains church, appealing to a variety of textual, ritual and doctrinal materials. (31; vgl. auch 347–48).

Dabei betont der Autor einerseits die Notwendigkeit der Kontextualisierung des Kanons im Leben der christlichen Kirche sowie andererseits die Bedeutung des Ereignisses der Kanonisierung, worunter er den Prozess der Kanonwerdung, aber auch den der dauernden kirchlichen Verwendung bzw. Vergegenwärtigung des Kanons versteht. Bokedal interpretiert den Kanon also als eine Größe, die bewahrt und gleichzeitig dauernd aktualisiert werden muss—ein Prozess, den er für die Kirche, will sie in sich verändernden Situationen Kirche bleiben, als ent-scheidend ansieht.

Die komplexe Arbeit des Autors verbindet historische mit literaturwissen-schaftlichen Fragen, Probleme der Fundamentaltheologie und Dogmatik mit solchen der neutesta-mentlichen Wissenschaften. Berührt werden liturgiewissen-schaftliche, philosophische und hermeneutische Fragestellungen. Ich konzentriere mich in meiner Kritik vor allem auf die Punkte, in Bezug auf die ich mich als Neutestamentler kompetent fühle.

Anknüpfend an Gedanken des Origenes beschreibt Bokedal die christliche Bibel aus Altem und Neuem Testament als ein weitgehend selbstreferentielles, sich selbst interpretierendes Korpus an Texten. Bokedal spricht in diesem Zusammen-hang von kanonischen Schriften als einer theologisch definierten literarischen Einheit, deren Fokus er in der Formel „the Scriptures and the Lord" sieht. Damit trifft er sich zumindest teilweise mit wichtigen Anliegen auch deutschsprachiger Vertreter einer an Endgestalten des Kanons orientierten Exegese wie N. Lohfink,

G. Steins, Th. Hieke oder C. Dohmen, die er leider aber nur zum Teil kennt und rezipiert.

Im Folgenden werden verschiedene Dimensionen des Begriffs wie des Konzepts „Kanon" vorgestellt. Ausführlich werden verschiedenste Aspekte der Entstehung des christlichen Kanons diskutiert: Zumindest teilweise problematisch erscheinen mir Bokedals Aussagen zur Bedeutung der *Nomina Sacra* im Zusammenhang mit der Entstehung des Kanons: Bokedal spricht hier von „trinitarian textual markers" (97), die einen „Kanon im Kanon", eine „Mitte der Schrift" (97) markierten. Er geht davon aus, dass die Begriffe für „Herr", „Gott", „Jesus", „Christus", „Vater", „Sohn" und „Geist" die zentralen *Nomina Sacra* ausmachten und fordert, dass diese auch in modernen Bibelausgaben wieder markiert würden. Im Anschluss an L. Hurtado nimmt Bokedal an, dass das früheste Christentum zunächst die Abkürzung des Wortes „Jesus" als frühestes *Nomen Sacrum* akzeptierte. Der nächste Schritt habe dann in der Einführung der *Nomina Sacra* für „Herr" und „Gott" bestanden. Dies mag durchaus plausibel sein, findet aber nur sehr begrenzten Anhalt an den frühesten erhaltenen Manuskripten—die Gefahr, die konkret aus den Handschriften zu erhebenden Daten etwas vorschnell im Hinblick auf ein theologisches Ziel zu missbrauchen, scheint mir zumindest dann gegeben, wenn man von „trinitarian textual markers" spricht. Problematisch ist auch die Forderung, in heutigen Bibelausgaben ein zentrales Set von *Nomina Sacra* als „Mitte der Schrift" zu markieren: Tatsächlich zeigen die frühchristlichen Handschriften, an denen der Autor sich orientieren möchte, ein überraschend hohes Maß an Standardisierung, aber sicherlich keines, das von (nahezu) allen Schreibern so konsequent angewandt worden wäre, wie Bokedal es annimmt. Hier wischt der Autor die von C. M. Tuckett geäußerten Kritikpunkte allzu schnell vom Tisch. Was soll also markiert werden? Nur die angeblich frühesten *Nomina Sacra*, wie Traube sie voraussetzt, die von Bokedal aufgelisteten *Nomina*, oder auch weitere immer wieder in den Handschriften zu findenden Abkürzungen wie „Jerusalem", „Jesaja" oder „Petrus"? Ich würde zudem sehr daran zweifeln, dass die *Nomina Sacra* von Beginn an als „trinitarian textual markers" verstanden wurden. Natürlich könnte man fordern, Markierungen einzuführen, die sich *aus heutiger Sicht* so verstehen ließen, wie Bokedal es voraussetzt. Dann aber würde man sich das weitere Problem einhandeln, etwa mit „Jesus" eine „Mitte der Schrift" anzugeben, die in deren erstem Teil nicht begegnet.

In seinen Ausführungen zur Rolle des Codex für die Entwicklung des christlichen Kanons lehnt sich Bokedal in entscheidenden Punkten an die These D. Trobischs an, die Entstehung des Neuen Testaments sei als die Geschichte der Entstehung eines Buches anzusehen. Zu stark aber konzentriert sich Bokedals Argumentation m.E. auf Texte, die *heute* als kanonisch angesehen werden: Einerseits stellt er nie die Frage, ob das, was er als biblisches Manuskript begreift, im 2. oder 3. Jahrhundert wirklich als „biblisch" angesehen wurde; andererseits tauchen in seiner Darstellung kaum einmal christliche Apokryphen auf: Handschriften „apokryph gewordener Texte" (D. Lührmann) aus den ersten frühchristlichen Jahrhunderten sind in ähnlicher Zahl wie solche kanonisch gewordener Texte überliefert. Warum spielen sie in Bokedals Argumentation keinerlei Rolle? Zurückhaltend wäre ich auch mit Frühdatierungen eines (weitgehend anerkannten) Vierevangelienkanons. Typisch für die Argumentation Bokedals ist z.B. auch die Aussage, dass der kanonische Status der Apokalypse vor 220 „undisputed" war (151): Einerseits haben wir aus dem 2. Jahrhundert nur sehr begrenzte Evidenz für die Rezeption der Apokalypse, andererseits geht Bokedal auch darüber hinweg, dass aus dem 2. Jahrhundert kaum eine Aussage vorliegt, die die Apokalypse explizit als „kanonisch" bezeichnet oder voraussetzt—das *muratorische Fragment* sollte in diesem Zusammenhang nur mit großer Vorsicht herangezogen werden.

In einem weiteren Abschnitt stellt Bokedal die Frage nach dem Zueinander von mündlicher und schriftlicher Überlieferung kanonischer Texte. Der Autor zeichnet hier die Entwicklung von Papias über Justin, Irenäus und Tertullian nach; er unterstützt die These, dass der Anteil Markions an der Entstehung des Neuen Testaments eher gering zu veranschlagen sei. Die Kirche habe weder den Weg des Papias, noch den Markions angenommen: „[T]he church were to follow its mother religion [= Judaism; TN], becoming all the more a religion of the sacred text. Still it did not dismiss the oral dimensions (and phrases) of the gospel transmission" (188–89).

Interessant sind Bokedals Gedanken zur Frage der Textualität des Kanons: Der Autor geht davon aus, dass die in der Bibel zusammengefasste Sammlung von Texten durch Verbindungen auf verschiedensten Ebenen als „ein Text" angesehen werden kann. „In its capacity as classical and canonical writing, the biblical text can stand on its own. That is to say, it does not primarily refer back to the original speech or speech situation, but makes up a meaningful whole precisely as text" (224). Ich würde diese Aussage grundsätzlich unterstützen, dabei aber einige Einschränkungen formulieren: Der Text der Bibel ist nur in höchst komplexer Weise als *ein Text* zu verstehen; dabei interpretieren sich die Teile sicherlich gegenseitig, z.T. aber muss dieser Text auch enorme Spannungen aushalten. Auch steht ein Text nie völlig „in sich selbst", sondern ist auch nach außen auf kontextuelle bzw. intertextuelle Verankerungen angewiesen. Deren Veränderungen machen m.E. einen entscheidenden Teil der ja auch von Bokedal postulierten Dynamik des Textbegriffes aus. Anders als Bokedal würde ich die Interpretation des komplexen Textes Bibel als *eines* Textes nicht als Harmonisierung (225) um eine „Mitte der Schrift" bezeichnen: Die vier Evangelien auszulegen ist etwas anderes als eine Evangelienharmonie zu interpretieren. Es geht m.E. viel mehr darum, die verschiedenen Stimmen, die innerhalb der Bibel zu Wort kommen, miteinander ins Spiel, ins Gespräch zu bringen, sie gegeneinander abzuwägen, dabei aber ihre Komplexität nicht zu unterschlagen.

Die dauernde Rezeption des Textes mache die Tradition zu einem Bestandteil nicht nur der Vergangenheit, sondern lasse sie in die Sphäre der Gegenwart reichen. Die Interpretation des Kanons verbindet Bokedal immer wieder mit der Kirche—damit hat er sicherlich Recht. Unklar dabei aber ist, welches Bild von Kirche Bokedal voraussetzt, und welche Implikationen seine Aussagen für den konkreten Prozess der Interpretation bedeuten: Setzt man etwa die Idee von der Kirche als (einer) Gemeinschaft der Glaubenden—dem „Leib Christi" im Sinne des Paulus—voraus, so ergibt sich natürlich das schöne Bild, dass der durch die Zeit gehende „Leib Christi" in der Zeit den Text der Bibel aktualisiert und kontextualisiert. Wer aber entscheidet in einer Welt, in der konkret verschiedene Gemeinschaften als Kirchen Christus nachzufolgen suchen, dass eine konkrete Auslegung *de facto* „kirchlich" im gesagten Sinne ist? Und welche Rolle spielt dabei der Text? Kann der Text sich noch gegen bestimmte Auslegungen wehren und auf welche Weise geschieht dies?

Weitere Kapitel diskutieren Kriterien der Kanonisierung, hermeneutische Probleme des kanonischen Prozesses oder die Rolle der liturgischen bzw. rituellen Kontextalisierung für das Verstehen des Kanons—der Autor bezeichnet in diesem Zusammenhang den Gottesdienst der christlichen Gemeinde als „Heimat" (268. 351) der christlichen Schrift. Der Band schließt mit Gedanken zum Kanon als einem integralen Ganzen, dem textlichen Fundament der „einen" Kirche.

Der begrenzte Rahmen einer Rezension ermöglicht es leider nicht, all die vielfältigen Aspekte der Arbeit Bokedals vorzustellen und im Detail zu diskutieren. Als Fazit bleibt: In einer Reihe von Punkten stellt Bokedals Band sicherlich eine exegetische wie auch theologische Herausforderung dar. Seine zentrale These ist sicherlich auch dann der Diskussion wert, wenn man nicht mit allen Vorstellungen des Autors zur Entstehung des Kanons übereinstimmt. Der Autor hat sich ein für den Rahmen einer Dissertation sehr großes, vielleicht zu umfangreiches Thema vorgenommen; er zeigt sicherlich eine bemerkenswerte Kenntnis der jeweiligen Literatur und Problematik—manche seiner Lösungen aber werfen neue Probleme auf, die noch keineswegs gelöst sind.

The Nature of New Testament Theology: Essays in Honor of Robert Morgan, edited by Christopher Rowland and Christopher Tuckett. Malden, Mass.: Blackwell, 2006. Pp. xix + 314. Paper. $34.95. ISBN 1405111747.

Craig L. Blomberg, Denver Seminary, Littleton, Colorado

This particularly rich collection of essays forms a very appropriate Festschrift for Robert Morgan on the occasion of his early retirement from Oxford University. Questions addressed range from the definition, purposes, and scope of New Testament theology to the contributions of individual authors or corpora to issues of the role of the historical Jesus, Christian faith, and relevance for the life of the church in the enterprise.

After an introduction by the Archbishop of Canterbury, Rowan Williams, John Ashton authors the first of the seventeen chapters. In it he follows closely in the footsteps of Gabler's pioneering work in biblical theology in the late 1700s and William Wrede's at the turn of the twentieth century to argue for a sharp delineation between the work of the historian, who determines what the text meant, and the theologian who determines what it means for the church today. John Barton then complements Ashton by arguing for the same distinction but stressing that, for the most part, at least Old Testament scholars have until quite recently usually engaged even in historical work out of a desire to serve the church. Barton recognizes this is not the only possible motive for exegesis but applauds it as perhaps the best and most important one.

Adela Yarbro Collins turns to apocalypticism and New Testament theology. Again beginning with Gabler, she traces major approaches to her topic over time and then crafts a spectrum of contemporary perspectives with Hal Lindsey's fundamentalism at one extreme and Tina Pippin's harsh attacks at the other. In between are various approaches, including conservative and liberal principlizing and Walter Wink's and Elisabeth Schüssler Fiorenza's use of Revelation for social protest. Yarbro Collins concludes that what the text meant and what it means should *not* be as strongly separated as Ashton and Barton insisted, not least lest application be viewed as an optional second step in exegesis.

Philip Esler, as has become his custom, next discusses the social-scientific side of the topic at hand, in this case, "New Testament Interpretation as Interpersonal Communion." Appealing to such "old-fashioned" ideas as authorial intent and the communion of the saints, Esler maintains that we must read texts for their theological meaning in dialogue with the past. Morna Hooker follows this by demonstrating, with Christology as a test case, the unity as well as diversity of theological reflection on core Christian issues across the canon.

Luke Johnson explores the question of unity in diversity as well with his mandate to address the question, "Does a Theology of the Canonical Gospels Make Sense?" Recalling the standard fears of how an affirmative answer could blur all the proper distinctives and emphases of the four individual texts, he nevertheless observes ten points of commonality across all four, *none* of which apply to the apocryphal and gnostic Gospels, thus making canonical choices less arbitrary than some would claim. These commonalities involve (1) realistic narratives, (2) with specific historical roots in first-century Palestine, (3) connecting the story of Jesus to that of Israel using texts and symbols of Torah, (4) emphasizing the ways humans respond to Jesus, (5) highlighting his passion, (6) sharing an understanding of his resurrection that was continuous with his human experience, (7) agreeing that he was a representative agent and spokesperson sent on behalf of God for the sake of other humans even as he radically obeyed God, (8) driving no wedge between the God of Jesus and the God of creation, (9) with God's triumph still in the future, and (10) with discipleship as following in his footsteps in the path of selfless service to others. All ten points likewise demonstrate far more continuity with the later orthodox creeds than with the heterodox literature some would trumpet as better reflecting the earliest stages of belief in Jesus.

Leander Keck follows Johnson by tackling the logic of the major categories of Pauline theology. He plausibly opts for a sequence that reasoned from Paul's experience of the resurrection of Jesus to inaugurated eschatology and revised Christology, to a changed basis for soteriology and definition of ecclesiology, and finally (from solution to plight) to a revised anthropology.

Thus far one could almost imagine that there was a thematic rationale for the sequence of chapters—from more general methodological essays to those that treated a more delimited New Testament corpus or doctrine. Looking ahead to the remaining chapters quashes this idea, and one suddenly recognizes that the entire volume is arranged solely by the alphabetical sequence of the contributors' surnames! Thus Ulrich Luz next treats a topic we might have expected at the end of the book: the contribution of reception history to New Testament theology. In post-Christian Western Europe, reception history holds promise not only for awakening interest among nonpractitioners of the faith but also to bring together diverse Christian traditions, to avoid the arrogance of thinking what is most recent is necessarily best, to bring the scholarly and untutored in communication with each other, and to learn from prayers, liturgy, and hymnody, not just theological treatises, and indeed from other art forms, including painting, dance, and poetry, and other uses of Scripture altogether—in ethical decision making, politics, war, persecution, and even martyrdom.

Margaret Macdonald proceeds to isolate four central challenges for New Testament theologians that emerge from scholarship on early Christian women and then illustrates them from Eph 5:22–33: the contributions of Jewish feminists; the call to engage with modern issues rather than feigning value neutrality; recovering marginalized female voices from the past; and considering how the representation of women and gender issues is influenced by authors' distinctive styles, genres, and other literary conventions. John Muddiman returns to the issues raised in his Black's Ephesians commentary, defending on the one hand the pseudonymity of Ephesians and the Pastorals but denying, on the other, their *Frühkatholisizmus*. Heikki Räisänen pursues his antitheological agenda by sketching what a chapter (on individual eschatology) could look like from a book that merely describes ancient Christian beliefs on various central doctrines, comparing and contrasting them with other significant religious antecedents and heirs.

Quite differently, Christopher Rowland and Zoë Bennett argue that New Testament theology must issue in practical theology, with an illustration from the Center for Faith in the Workplace, based in San Antonio, Texas. Gerd Theissen returns to many of the issues raised by Räisänen, plotting four major approaches to the less prescriptive and more descriptive role of religious studies (as over against theology), only one of which even presupposes a Christian framework. The one he finds holding out the most promise subsumes its task under the broader project of charting the history of human cultures. Christopher Tuckett considers all the classic reasons why Jesus, who wrote nothing of which we know, and those reconstructions of his life carried out under the rubric of historical Jesus research, should not be the object of New Testament theology per se and eventually rejects them all.

Frances Watson creatively explores two quite different approaches to John's Gospel, one based on each of the two "endings" in 20:31 and 21:24–25. The former remains more enigmatic, labeling the entire Gospel as filled with "signs," thus referring not just to the overt miracle narratives. The latter eventually supersedes the former, viewing the narrative as compelling testimony. Given that both approaches find ample supporting evidence in numerous parts of the Fourth Gospel, one can understand why Käsemann labeled it naively docetic while many others have found it profoundly antidocetic. Michael Wolter posits the cross as the center of New Testament theology from which all *Sachkritik* may and must be performed legitimately. Finally, Frances Young briefly explores patristic Trinitarian theologizing, arguing that it faithfully reflects, albeit in appropriately contextualized forms, the New Testament's consistent teaching that the activity of Christ and the Spirit form the work of the one true God of Israel.

The largely "all-star cast" of authors of this book's essays alone ensures a sumptuous and diverse fare for hungry readers. Because of the mutually contradictory positions championed in a number of the chapters, no reader can expect to relish fully more than one main course in the methodological meal offered. But each course offers tantalizing tastes, some quite new and others not enjoyed much in recent days. If Festschriften could regularly achieve the consistent quality of contributions that the editors of this one have amassed, publishers might stop being so fearful that the genre would only produce money-losers!

EARLY CHRISTIANITY AND EARLY CHRISTIAN LITERATURE

Introducing Early Christianity: A Topical Survey of Its Life, Beliefs and Practices, by Laurence D. Guy. Downers Grove, Ill.: InterVarsity Press, 2004. Pp. 310. Hardcover. $25.00. ISBN 083082698X.

Peter J. Judge, Winthrop University, Rock Hill, South Carolina

This is a well-conceived and written introduction that familiarizes the reader with the development of Christianity from the New Testament period to the time of the Council of Chalcedon (A.D. 451; the B.C./A.D. system is used throughout to designate the era). Professor Guy (lecturer at both Carey Baptist College and the School of Theology at the University of Auckland, New Zealand) has deliberately set that *terminus ad quem* because it is at this point that, as he says, "most of the early church's evolution had occurred and much of the church's great debates over the nature of the Trinity and of Christ had been largely resolved," and it stops short of the tumultuous period of the collapse of the Western Roman Empire. The study is also confined within the boundaries of the empire ("to foster coherence"), although the author acknowledges the "spillage" of the faith across those boundaries, particularly in the fourth and fifth centuries.

The topical approach announced in the title provides an inviting rubric and produces a satisfying presentation of the myriad details and complex issues that comprise early Christian history. This will be a very useful classroom textbook for undergraduate courses or a quite readable guide for the layperson who has some background. The author, in fact, indicates these as his target audiences in the very first sentence of his preface, and he has done a good job of remaining consistent with this goal of bringing scholarship to "a more general audience." He does not take too much for granted, but he also does not insult his reader's intelligence; he provides plenty of detail but does not sink into a morass of intricacy that can frustrate one who wants intelligently to grasp the big picture. Hence, the material is organized thematically rather than purely historically, as is often the case with church history manuals. With the exception of chapters 2 (on the second Christian generation), 5 (on Constantine), and 11 (on the fourth- and fifth-century definitions of orthodoxy), one begins each chapter anew with the New Testament evidence and follows through to the mid-fifth century for each of the topics examined. This is a satisfying approach, as mentioned, because it allows the student to trace the origin, development, and significance of the issue at hand and because it gives the reader an ever-expanding familiarity with the material and, I think, greater and greater confidence in controlling the vastness of it all. Such an "introduction" succeeds when the user can say, "I know how to explore further!"

That brings us to a second self-conscious feature of the volume: it acquaints the reader with primary sources and the importance of using them. Each chapter is filled with citations and quotations (sometimes lengthy and set off in shaded boxes) from early Christian writers. Guy demonstrates his own command of the material in his comments and analysis along with that of other scholars, as he appropriately draws on the secondary literature as well. This, again, is a rewarding way to be introduced to these materials, a way that inspires confidence in the student who wishes to go further. The citations are provided in real footnotes at the bottom of the page, so that the reader has them right there, a feature I welcome in a day when endnotes (or no notes at all) seem to be more prevalent in books for a general audience. Secondary literature is also listed at the end of each chapter "for further reading" on the particular topic.

Chapter 1 ("If Paul Could See Us Now") prepares the reader for what is to come with a wide-angle glimpse of the development of Christianity from the small band of Jesus' followers to its status as the empire's religion in the fifth century. The issues surveyed are: the progressive growth of the number of Christians, the identity of Christians vis-à-vis Jews and the wider pagan population; the interaction between the growing Christian community with society at large and political authorities; the increasing institutionalization of the church; the changing physical settings for being church, from house gatherings to grand public buildings; and, finally, the development of Christian worship. One could argue here with Guy's use and understanding of the "curse on the *minim*" with regard to Christian self-identity; there is more recent comment to rely on than what he uses.

Chapter 2, as already indicated, discusses the period of the apostolic fathers, Christianity's second generation. It studies the church's self-consciousness as an institution and the tension between charismatic leadership and governance by order and hierarchy as well as the steady institutionalization of liturgical practices. Guy does this with an examination of the similarities and differences in four key documents: the *Didache, 1 Clement,* the letters of Ignatius of Antioch, and the *Shepherd of Hermas.*

Chapter 3, "Suffering and Dying for God," begins by dispelling some of the popular myths about the persecution of Christians and examines the motivations for both inflicting and enduring suffering and martyrdom. The prizing of the martyr-witness is rooted in the Hebrew Bible stories like that of the Maccabees and, of course, in the foundational event of Jesus' own death. Even after persecution had ended, the ethos of martyrdom left its mark on the church in the ideal of self-sacrificing commitment and the imitation of Christ.

Chapter 4 traces the development of the organization and structure of the church and ministry within it, continuing the theme of tension between charismatic leadership and the eventually dominant model of a special place and role for clergy and a hierarchical, monarchical form of governance. Some will disagree (here and in other chapters) with Guy's fairly conservative attribution of the Pastorals to Paul himself. Nevertheless, the subsequent discussion is a good presentation of the gradual unfolding and articulation of the concept of authority in the church and the needs and means for preserving unity and dealing with disagreement or waywardness.

Chapter 5 looks at Emperor Constantine's embrace of Christianity and the unfolding new relationship with the state gained by the church as well as the new set of challenges that came with this new position and perspective.

Chapter 6 initiates the reader into the multifaceted phenomenon of Christian asceticism and particularly monasticism. Again, the author guides his students in picking through some of the myths and taking care to be discerning about idealizations, even that of Athanasius in his *Life of Antony.* The variety of ascetic forms and practices is carefully examined, and the chapter concludes with a series of focused sections on the significance of number of very different individuals for monasticism: Pachomias, Basil of Caesarea, Augustine, John Cassian, and Simeon Stylites. Early Christian asceticism and monasticism was not only about the bizarre but more importantly about routine and everyday "radical discipleship."

Chapter 7, on "Women in the Early Church," begins with a warning against the danger of reading history through the lenses of twenty-first-century agendas and the temptation to "quarry for the material that one hopes to find, ignoring other data" (165). It is perhaps unfortunate for Guy to make this comment here instead of making it a more general rubric in his introduction to the whole book. In this spot it insinuates a negative attitude specifically about feminist concerns and starts a good chapter off on a possibly sour note. He examines the material well for the scope of the book, discussing the position of women in Greco-Roman society at large, in Judaism, and in the New Testament, pointing out the positive attitude toward women in the Gospels (and, apparently, in the life of Jesus) and making an effort to work through some of the thorny Pauline passages. He finds in the New Testament evidence a harbinger of the ensuing centuries: growing institutionalization and increasing activity in the public sphere served to marginalize the role of women in ministry. Whereas gospel and society are often in tension, on this issue, he laments, "the early church lost the tension" (191).

Chapter 8 concentrates on the emergence of Christian worship in the first four and a half centuries, with special attention to the form and meaning of the Eucharist, along with the associated practices of reading scripture and preaching, singing and chanting, taking up an offering, and discussion of the extent to which prayer should be formulized. Several pages are then devoted to the demarcation of sacred time on a daily and weekly basis as well as the great and small festivals of the Christian year.

Chapter 9, cleverly titled "Getting In and Staying In," examines the theological and ritual evolution of baptism and penance. There is a detailed discussion of the data and of the roots, meaning, and symbolism of these rituals along with the issues involved with initiation and reconciliation as the centuries progressed.

Finally, chapters 10 and 11 are devoted to the emergence of Christian theology, the development of doctrine, and the disputes over orthodoxy. The major issues and players are discussed succinctly and fairly evenly, and one has the distinct sense that these are real issues being hotly debated by real people of sincere faith, even when violently passionate and influenced, as is ever the case, by circumstances of society and political life. The reader being introduced to these issues that led up to the pronouncements of Nicaea and Chalcedon can come away with a nuanced sense of the context and a fairly decent appreciation for the theological intricacies. Professor Guy's background in the legal profession shows through here in his setting out of the points involved, the arguments put forward, and the struggles for resolution.

I mentioned above the virtue of this book in directing readers to primary sources, chiefly the writings of the early church fathers. For this, Guy uses the series the Ante-Nicene Fathers (ANF) and the Nicene and Post-Nicene Fathers (NPNF), the large translation project directed by Philip Schaff at the end of the nineteenth century. These volumes are not only in many libraries but are also in the public domain and so can be found on a number of websites; www.ccel.org/fathers2/ is his first recommendation, and a good one. The other recommended site, however, is rather strongly evangelical, even proselytizing in style, and is rather difficult to navigate for the referenced text; it may be irritating for academic work. The same texts are available at www.newadvent.org/fathers/, also a denominationally oriented site but easier to navigate, as it presents each ancient author by name alphabetically. The site /www.earlychristianwritings.com is also well presented and more neutral and academic in tone. And, of course, there are others. Another issue, though, is that these translations are rather dated; newer translations and collections, even if not complete, are available in print. For students in a course on early Christianity, the recent volumes assembled by Bart Ehrman, using a variety of previously published works, would be excellent resources.

Some suggested bibliographical additions: in chapter 2 the volumes by Niederwimmer (*Didache*) and Schoedel (*Ignatius of Antioch*) in the Hermeneia series are listed in the bibliography; that by Osiek (*Shepherd of Hermas*) should also be there. In chapter 8, on the Eucharist, the great liturgist Josef Jungmann is cited in the notes; his work should also be in the list for further reading. In the list for chapter 11, the works of Jaroslav Pelikan should perhaps be noted, especially *Credo: Historical and Theological Guide to Creeds and Confessions of Faith in the Christian Tradition* (2003).

This is a very readable book and thus rather useful for classroom or private use. While there are issues and points of interpretation that can surely be argued with, the book accomplishes its purpose of introducing the beginner to the important topics of belief and practice in the life of Christians in the first four and a half centuries.

Whose Acts of Peter? *Text and Historical Context of the* Actus Vercellenses, by Matthew C. Baldwin. Wissenschaftliche Untersuchungen zum Neuen Testament 2/196. Tübingen: Mohr Siebeck, 2005. Pp. xvi + 339. Paper. €64.00. ISBN 3161484088.

Thomas J. Kraus, Hilpoltstein, Federal Republic of Germany

This is a "modestly revised version" (vii) of Matthew C. Baldwin's dissertation written under the supervision of Adela Yarbro Collins (and the original readers Margaret M. Mitchell and Michael I. Allen) and submitted at the University of Chicago in 2002. Baldwin focuses on the *Actus Vercellenses,* part of Codex Vercelli Bib. Cap. 158, a Latin manuscript of the seventh century in the Chapter Library (Biblioteca Capitolare) in Vercelli, Italy. Among scholars this *Actus Vercellenses* is often referred to as the apocryphal *Acts of Peter,* which is regarded as having derived from a lost Greek text (πράξεις Πέτρου) written in the second century in Asia Minor and translated into Latin (*Actus Vercellenses*) sometime in the fourth century. Today the majority of scholars are convinced that the *Actus Vercellenses* preserves a short version of the original *Acts of Peter,* truncated before or during the process of translation. Baldwin now ventures to examine the *Actus Vercellenses* as what it is at first glance: a manuscript and a work in its own right. This appears to be a bold undertaking, since such an investigation might end with results opposed to the mainstream views of the *Acts of Peter* and of this significant witness to them. Nevertheless, in the eyes of someone who works on manuscripts, this is the only methodologically sound way of doing research into a manuscript and its extant text. Only then can implications and conclusions help to modify, verify, or even falsify long-established hypotheses. Baldwin disputes such hypotheses and succeeds in attracting attention to the manuscript itself and its texts.

Manuscripts that preserve any part of texts that did not make it into a canon and/or that are called New Testament apocrypha are of outstanding value, due to their rarity (in comparison with manuscript witnesses to the canonical writings of the New Testament) and the information they provide. In this respect, the genre of Acts is really extraordinary, as it reflects the interests of the early Christians in the destiny of the apostles. If only a few manuscript witnesses are available, as is the case with the *Acts of Peter*, the text has to be reconstructed and/or a manuscript must be accepted as the main witness, which then receives most (and sometimes sole) attention. What happened with the *Actus Vercellenses* is that it was integrated into a hypothetical conception about the origin of the *Acts of Peter*. The manuscript itself has never been investigated as a work and an artifact in its own right. That is why Baldwin dedicates six chapters to the text and the historical context of the *Actus Vercellenses*, as the title of his monograph tells.

In his introductory chapter (1–25) Baldwin defines the most significant terms and how he uses them throughout the book. He also lays the methodological foundation for his approach by pointing out problems in the study of the *Acts of Peter*: the presumed date of composition, the identification of the *Actus Vercellenses* as *Acts of Peter*, and some terminological confusions. Moreover, he clarifies his understanding of "text" and "book" and makes a programmatic statement that interpreters of ancient texts should always be aware of and accept for their work with manuscript witnesses: "Whatever we may have to say about the current condition of the text, this [the *Actus Vercellenses*] is no autograph, and the text was not composed of whole cloth from the imagination of a creative writer and shaped into its current manuscript form" (25).

Chapter 2 basically consists of a full-scale *Forschungsbericht* (26–62). Although this is very informative, sound in its summaries, and written in an attractive narrative, the specialist will find nothing new. The conclusions Baldwin draws from his history of scholarship are more or less descriptions of the following chapters and how they are the results from the shortcomings of research, or, in other words, how he himself attempts at solving the problems unsolved so far.

In chapter 3 Baldwin examines the external evidence for the *Acts of Peter* (63–133). Here he performs "a more thorough review of the evidence" (63), what he regards as a major deficiency of scholarly work. Then he deals with the issue of Petrine *Fabulae* and book titles between 190 and 326 C.E., starting with Clement of Alexandria and ending with Eusebius (and, of course, his classic categorization of Christian books into four groups in *Hist. eccl.* 3.25), before he addresses the Petrine materials to 858 C.E. The depiction of sources is sound, their treatment precise, and their discussion plausible, so that an attentive reader really profits from the information provided. In sum, "there is very little evidence for the early existence of a written *Acts of Peter*, and the data about the contents of early Petrine traditions are ambiguous." For some readers it may be an unlucky decision to mention this conclusion on page 61, that is, prior to the investigation into the external evidence. Be that as it may, the existence of a written *Acts of Peter* in the first quarter of the fourth century is proved by Eusebius, but we know nothing else about the book other than its name. Baldwin convincingly shows that Nicephorus cannot serve as a witness to the assumption that we are missing a third of the original (source behind) *Actus Vercellenses*, because his reference to the Περίοδοι Πέτρου is so vague that it may point to another Greek text. Further, different versions of the *Acts of Peter* seem to have circulated among Christians, above all in late antiquity. Interestingly, "Photius' *Bibl.* codd. 112–113 associates an *Acts of the Apostle Peter* with the ps.-Clementine *Recognitions*" (133), and *Codex Vercellenses* 158 also preserves exactly these *Recognitions* together with the *Actus Vercellenses*.

Chapter 4 is dedicated to the "Paleography and Latinity of the *Actus Vercellenses*" (134–93). Again Baldwin's approach is meticulous and his conclusions cautious. The details provided help to illustrate what kind of manuscript Cod. Vercelli Bib. Cap. 158 actually is, though some of his statements need further reflection. In note 32 on page 143, for instance, he argues that "long lines" are a clue hinting at "individual reading" and not at "liturgical use." But he neither defines what "long lines" are nor takes into account the size of letters, the number of letters per lines, and the space between lines, details that *are* important to discuss liturgical and private usage. Therefore, the facts he gathers about abbreviations and marginalia (153–54) could be of interest in that respect. Moreover, Baldwin did not see the original manuscript in Vercelli, Italy. Thus, he depends on "two different microfilms" and on "the published sources" (142–43 n. 30). Nonetheless, his selection of appropriate information is mainly correct and his judgments precise. The second part of chapter 4 deals with the Latinity of the *Actus Vercellenses*. Baldwin primarily focuses on orthography, syntax, and Latinity and comes to the conclusion that the text of this part of the manuscript "emerged in Spain in the late seventh century" and that the manuscript "preserves a writing which was translated form the Greek no earlier than the late fourth century, quite possibly even later" (193). In the future this will be a matter of general discussion, if philological investigations can really produce the decisive facts to determine the date of a manuscript. A philological investigation by another scholar might lead to a different result.

Consequently, in chapter 5 Baldwin draws attention to probable Greek predecessors from which the *Actus Vercellenses* was translated (194–301). Here he tackles the *Vita Abercii* (197–242, offering very helpful synopses), P.Oxy. VI 849 (242–51, with an odd note about Grenfell's and Hunt's usage of the terms *recto* and *verso* [242 n. 158]), and the *Martyrium Petri* (251–99, again with synopses). Apart from a few words and phrases, the parallels are not very close. If any parallelism is to be stated at all, it is "a 'source' parallelism" (300) between the *Actus Vercellenses* and the *Martyrium Petri*. Thus, Baldwin convincingly shows that the *Actus Vercellenses* is not a literal translation of any of its predecessors. Moreover, he is skeptical about finding the Greek source of a text by means of its Latin version at all (301).

The final chapter (302–14) is a kind of summary leading to the conclusion that the *Actus Vercellenses* must be treated as a work in its own right and that it is important to learn more about "the world of the Latin *scriptor* who composed it" (303). Baldwin's reflections are tentative and compelling, even if they are rather hypothetical. However, this is the only chance of getting closer to the scribe and his world, and Baldwin wisely titles this section "imaginations" (303–8).

In addition to a preface (vii–viii) and a list of abbreviations (xv–xvi), the book includes a fine appendix ("Codicological Notes on Vercelli, Bib. Cap. 158" [315–21], with a table of contents by gathering), a cumulative bibliography (322–29), and indices of modern authors, ancient sources, and subjects (330–39).

Baldwin's meticulous work challenges traditional notions of the *Acts of Peter* and the *Actus Vercellenses* as its potential main manuscript witness. His thesis will have to be considered by everyone participating in the debate. Of course, his conclusions will be challenged, and only then will we learn if they have the stamina to survive. However, anyone challenging this brilliant work will need a good deal of plausible argumentation and sound evidence to stand up against Baldwin's results. The author of this fine monograph is to be thanked for having shed new light on the manuscript and for starting the discussion of the *Acts of Peter* (and even of all the other Petrine traditions) anew.

The Spread of Christianity in the First Four Centuries: Essays in Explanation, edited by W. V. Harris. Columbia Studies in the Classical Tradition 27. Leiden: Brill, 2005. Pp. xiv + 176. Hardcover. $129.00. ISBN 9004147179.

Hennie Stander, University of Pretoria, Pretoria, South Africa

This book is the twenty-seventh volume in the series Columbia Studies in the Classical Tradition. It consists of seven papers that were read in 2003 at a symposium on behalf of the Center for the Ancient Mediterranean at Columbia University. The eighth contribution was added after the symposium and consists of reactions to the other papers. Edward Gibbon's magisterial work (*The History of the Decline and Fall of the Roman Empire*) has for a long time been regarded as the greatest work of history in the English language. It is therefore not surprising that this classic work forms the starting-place of many of the articles in *The Spread of Christianity in the First Four Centuries*.

Gibbon gave one primary reason for the victory of the Christian faith over the established religions of the world, namely, "the convincing evidence of the doctrine itself, and the ruling providence of its great Author." He then also gave five secondary reasons: (1) the inflexible and intolerant zeal of the Christians; (2) the doctrine of a future life; (3) the miraculous powers ascribed to the primitive Church; (4) the pure and austere morals of the Christians; and (5) the union and discipline of the Christian republic.

In later years other scholars proposed many other reasons why Christianity was a success story. Dimitris Kyrtatas discusses each of these "causes" in his article entitled "The Significance of Leadership and Organisation in the Spread of Christianity." He then gives very good reasons why these so-called causes do not pass the test. He shows, for example, that the doctrine of a future life was not a novelty of the New Testament. Neither were the early Christians the only people who valued pure morals. After noting that Gibbon's fifth cause ("the union and discipline of the Christian people") has up to now attracted less attention among scholars, Kyrtatas argues that this last aspect is not appreciated enough as a reason why this new religion was so successful. Kyrtatas says that the early Christians were led by outstanding personalities. He concludes that "it was through its sophisticated organisation and its able leaders that Christianity managed to become something more than an ephemeral phenomenon."

In "Models of Christian Expansion," Harold A. Drake also focuses on the fifth cause suggested by Gibbon (namely, the Christian organization). But Drake looks at this cause from a social-scientific angle. Gibbon was interested in questions of leadership and control, but Drake thinks more in terms of a more recent concept: the mass movement. According to the "mass movement" approach advocated by Drake, one should not ask *why* coercion occurs but rather *how* the coercive elements that can be found in any system come to prevail. Drake concludes that when scholars open themselves to the reformulations of traditional questions that modeling encourages, it will result in powerful new understandings of the spread of early Christianity.

In the next essay ("Christian Expansion and Christian Ideology") James B. Rives emphasizes that if one wants to understand the expansion of Christianity, one must also understand the processes whereby the number of Christians increased. He points out that the expansion of Christianity is much more than a new deity acquiring increasing numbers of adherents. Rives says that "it represents the growth of a new social and conceptual system, a new ideology of religion." He believes that this new ideology had three key elements: (1) exclusivity (i.e., exclusive devotion to one deity); (2) homogeneity (i.e., the belief that the adherence to the Christian God could take one form only); and (3) totalization (i.e., a coherent system of beliefs and practices grounded in a comprehensive view of the cosmos). Rives concludes his essay by saying that Christianity represented something genuinely novel.

In "Thinking with Women: The Uses of the Appeal to 'Woman' in Pre-Nicene Christian Propaganda Literature," Elizabeth Clark shows how apologists and other Christian writers employed the category of "woman" as a tool in their literature. Various ancient theologians emphasized that Christianity's openness to women, slaves, and the uneducated proved that its message was universally applicable.

The next essay, Stamenka E. Antonova's "Barbarians and the Empire-Wide Spread of Christianity," addresses the connection between barbarism and Christianity. The Christians were frequently referred to as "barbarians," and numerous church fathers accepted the association with "barbarians." The Christians were, of course, regarded as "barbarous" because of their antithetical position with respect to the Roman society. The term *barbarian* could also refer to people from a lower social class and to people with insufficient education. But Antonova says that the charge of barbarism was also true in the sense that many Christians were indeed of barbarian origin. Justin, for example, was a native of Samaria, while Tatian came from Syria. Antonova then concludes that the presence of "barbarians" within the Christian movement could have contributed to the growth of the following of this religious movement.

The next essay, "Outlawing 'Magic' or Outlawing 'Religion'? Libanius and the Theodosian Code as Evidence for Legislation against 'Pagan' Practices," by Isabella Sandwell, focuses on the role that the legislation of Christian emperors played in the suppression of pagan religious practices. She gives two reasons why she thinks scholars in the past have erred in their judgment on this issue. First, they often focused to such an extent on legislation against sacrifice that they ignored the other references to divination and other rituals in the laws. Second, scholars often referred to the Theodosian Code as proof of the legislation of the fourth century without asking how and why this code was constructed. Sandwell argues, *inter alia*, that the situation was much more complex than a mere persecution of pagan belief. One should rather look at the outlawing of specific practices. When emperors outlawed the use of rituals such as divination, astrology, and sacrifices, it concerned both Christians and pagans.

J. A. North's "Pagans, Polytheists and the Pendulum" gives a general reflection on the current study of the religious history of the Greeks and Romans. It focuses especially on the state of the religion in the latter half of the third century C.E. In "Roman Historians and the Rise of Christianity: The School of Edward Gibbon," Seth Schwartz comments on all the essays in this book. He says that all the authors have tried to modernize Gibbon's explanations for the spread of Christianity but have not surpassed them. He points out that all the religious groups in the ancient world had some interest in expansion, but the Christians were the only group who really tried to gain a religious monopoly.

This volume is not meant to give a comprehensive overview of the spread of Christianity in the first four centuries. There are far too many issues that are not addressed. As the subtitle ("essays in explanation") indicates, these essays merely shed more light on some aspects of this issue. To a large extent many of the essays are a mere revisitation of Edward Gibbon's theories on why the Christians managed to gain victory. Nevertheless, this book is valuable because it does challenge some of our traditional viewpoints on why the Christians eventually managed to gain victory.

Theodoret of Cyrus: Commentary on Daniel, by Robert C. Hill. Society of Biblical Literature Writings from the Greco-Roman World 7. Atlanta: Society of Biblical Literature; Leiden: Brill, 2006. Pp. xxxiv + 329. Paper/cloth. $39.95/$155.00. ISBN 1589831047/9004130519.

Randall L. McKinion, Shepherds Theological Seminary, Cary, North Carolina

In the volume at hand, Robert C. Hill has produced an invaluable contribution for the study of Old Testament interpretation in the early church. Theodoret (ca. 393–ca. 460), the bishop of Cyrus, wrote copiously on the Old Testament, so his works provide excellent examples of biblical interpretation in Antioch. Moreover, since his commentary on Daniel is the only surviving instance of an interpretation of the book by an Antiochene father, Hill's work is of particular importance.

The format of this volume is especially helpful, above all for those interested in dealing with the Greek text. Hill's readable translation is placed facing Theodoret's Greek text, which is that of J. P. Migne's *Patrologia graeca*. As of yet, there is no modern critical edition of Theodoret's *Commentary on Daniel*. In addition to the benefit of having the Greek text at hand and numbered consistently in both the Greek and English texts, Hill's footnotes within the translation provide both reference information (e.g., scriptural references) as well as explanations of and challenges to Theodoret's commentary. These notes, which Goldingay fittingly describes as "acerbic and droll" in a back-cover endorsement, are most useful to the reader.

The most valuable aspect of the book for those who are unfamiliar either with Theodoret or Antiochene interpretation is Hill's critical introduction (xi–xxxiv). Hill begins with a rather short summary of Theodoret's life and works, which serves merely as an introduction and would need to be augmented for a reader unfamiliar with Theodoret and the Antiochene fathers. Hill recognizes this fact and refers the reader to other, more comprehensive works. For his purposes in setting the circumstances that prompted Theodoret's commentary, particularly in regard to his apologetic *skopos*, the brief biographical introduction suffices. Thus, Hill's attention is given primarily to an evaluation of the commentary and to an explanation of Theodoret's (faulty) interpretations. These observations and critiques, although not treated comprehensively here, fall along the following major lines of thought.

First, Hill concludes that Theodoret was ill-equipped for the task of interpreting Daniel because he did not appreciate the apocalyptic genre of the text and consequently read the book through the eyes of misinterpreted New Testament texts. That is to say, Theodoret misread Daniel because he misread portions of New Testament apocalyptic, such as Matt 24. With his failure to recognize the true character of the book, which Hill believes is "symptomatic of flaws in their [i.e., Theodoret and his peers] exegetical formation," Theodoret's only recourse was to a historical, literalist interpretation. According to Hill, this historical reading of Daniel had both positive and negative effects upon the *Commentary*. Whereas negatively Theodoret was ill-equipped to read Daniel in light of its genre, Hill acknowledges positively that Theodoret excelled "in his readiness … to provide the background of his text for the benefit of the readers" (xxx).

Second, Hill believes that Theodoret's inability to read Daniel correctly provided the foundation for Theodoret's *skopos*, which was to accredit Daniel as a prophet. This purpose grew out of the contemporary milieu in which Theodoret wrote, namely, during a time when Jewish interpreters insisted on placing Daniel in the Writings and not among the other major prophets. Theodoret thus felt that such an understanding was a complete disavowal of the book's prophetic character. Since Theodoret's introduction makes this clear in no uncertain terms, Hill rightly spends much time analyzing this aspect of the commentary, and he critiques Theodoret for not thinking of the text as anything more than "prospective prophecy" (xxiii). Accordingly, it is this literalist, historical mode that prevents

Theodoret from appreciating the haggadic and apocalyptic material and from understanding the author's purpose.

Third, Theodoret's exegetical deficiencies were compounded, according to Hill, by his ignorance of the Hebrew language. Being bound to a Greek version of the book, at times Theodoret follows an improper understanding of the text that would have been easily corrected with a cursory knowledge of the Hebrew term in question. Such issues are explained appropriately in Hill's notes (e.g., 151 n. 130).

Fourth, Hill observes that Theodoret, who is so vehement in his preface that Daniel was a prophetic book, does not generally go directly to a christological interpretation as might be expected. Hill points out those passages that Theodoret does interpret in reference to Christ, but he also acknowledges that these interpretations are primarily in response to Jewish exegesis to the contrary (xxxi). This is an interesting characteristic of Theodoret's writing that deserves more explanation than Hill could make in this volume.

Finally, Hill discusses briefly the significance of Theodoret's *Commentary*. On the one hand, the *Commentary* is valuable because it is the lone representative of an Antiochene study of Daniel, and as such it has "particular significance in the history of exegesis" (xxxiii). On the other hand, since Theodoret spends an inordinate amount of time defending the prophetic character of Daniel, his *Commentary* provides a unique example of the Antiochene understanding of the nature and role of biblical prophecy.

In light of this summary, I hesitantly and humbly offer the following questions, which serve less as a criticism of Hill's evaluation of Theodoret's commentary than as some issues that I believe were not treated comprehensively due to the brevity of the critical introduction. Hill believes that Theodoret, being exegetically challenged in handling apocalyptic literature, completely missed the overall purpose for the book of Daniel, which was "to encourage Jews suffering persecution under Antiochus IV Epiphanes in the mid-second century" (xxiii). However, since Daniel is apocalyptic literature, should its purpose be limited to a single historical time period, or would it be applicable in more than one historical setting? If apocalyptic is not limited by its time or setting, then Daniel would give encouragement to any reader regardless of the reader's setting. Thus, Hill, who cries foul when Theodoret interprets the book in light of his own historical situation, seems to be limiting the author's purpose to a single historical occasion. This is not to say that Hill's criticisms of Theodoret are wrong, only that some treatment of this issue seems to be warranted.

Furthermore, Hill does not comment on the manner in which Theodoret was reading Daniel within the community of faith. He approaches this in speaking of some portions of the commentary that most likely originated in homilies. Hill also believes that Theodoret's misreading of the New Testament caused him mistakenly to read Daniel as prophecy and that Theodoret's commentary was intended as an apologetic against Jewish treatment of the book. However, he does not comment (sufficiently, in my opinion) on how Theodoret's presuppositions about Christ, specifically about Christ "according to the Scriptures," influenced the way he read the book of Daniel. Within his commentary on the text of Daniel, he seems to deal less with an apologetic for the prophetic character of the book and more with simply explaining the text as he understands it in light of the Christ-event. There is no doubt that Theodoret read Daniel neither as apocalyptic literature nor as set within an intertestamental historical setting, but a more thorough examination of the influence of the community of faith on his interpretation would be an added bonus to an already excellent work.

With his insightful introduction, readable translation, and fitting notes, Hill has provided a valuable tool both for the study of the Old Testament as well as for the study of early Christian (specifically Antiochene) interpretation. Thus, Hill's purpose of contributing "to a greater appreciation of the way the Old Testament was read in Antioch" (see his acknowledgements) is definitely fulfilled.

Theodore of Mopsuestia: Commentary on Psalms 1–81, by Robert C. Hill. Society of Biblical Literature Writings from the Greco-Roman World 5. Atlanta: Society of Biblical Literature; Leiden: Brill, 2006. Pp. xxxviii + 1137. Paper/cloth. $89.95/$279.00. ISBN 1589830601/9004127224.

Claudio Zamagni, Université de Genève, Geneva, Switzerland

Theodore of Mopsuestia is one of the masters of the ancient "Antiochene exegesis," the interpretation of the biblical text that supplanted the "Alexandrian exegesis" during the second half of the fourth century. While "Alexandrian exegesis" excelled in interpreting the allegory of the biblical books (especially the Old Testament), the "Antiochene" reacted to such penchant (well established since the time of Origen and of his *didaskaleion*), proposing a new kind of reading, very close to the literal meaning of the texts themselves. Theodore, bishop of Mopsuestia, was born in Antioch around the middle of the fourth century and died in 428. This commentary on Psalms is one of his first books, written in the second half of the fourth century and considered one of the masterpieces of his entire production. Unfortunately, like many of his other works, it does not survive in its original form, because Theodore (like Origen) was stated to be a heretic more than a century after his death, and this obviously caused the loss of the larger part of his work; he was in fact accused of holding erroneous christological convictions that are considered to be the forerunners of Nestorius's views.

This volume by Robert C. Hill reproduces the text of the only critical edition that has tried to reconstruct the *Commentary on Psalms* by Theodore, the text published by Robert Devreesse in the excellent collection Studi e testi of the Vatican Library (Robert Devreesse, *Le commentaire de Théodore de Mopsueste sur les Psaumes [I–LXXX]* [ST 93; Vatican City: Biblioteca Apostolica Vaticana, 1939). The text and the critical apparatus of that edition are reproduced in a size a bit smaller than the original volume, but the original page numbering is not preserved. The introduction and the indexes of Devreesse are here discarded, but the new volume still reproduces the larger part of the original edition, consisting of 561 pages of Greek fragments and Latin versions of Theodore's commentary. This means that, unfortunately, all the information provided by Devreesse in the introduction and in the indexes is not available here in any way. The introduction (Devreesse, ix–xxxiii) mainly concerned the textual tradition, which is very complicated, since the text is extant only in translations or in exegetical chains. Devreesse described the manuscripts, discussed his way of building his critical text, and explained his choice to discard the Syriac traditions. More important, that part also contained the keys for the identification of the manuscripts used in the critical apparatus (xxxiii) and a list of some forty-one corrigenda (xxxiii and 572), which are also lost in new Hill's reproduction. So, even if the critical apparatus is reproduced along with the Greek and Latin text fixed by Devreesse, this edition lacks some very important parts of the original 1939 volume.

This can seem of little interest, but it tends to leave the reader with the impression that the text is certain and fixed in stone, for what is possible (see Hill, xvii), but this is not really the case. In fact, the text as stated by Devreesse was only an attempt—necessarily partial—to reconstruct a commentary that is lost in its original form, and, even if Hill mentions the textual problems involved (xix), his presentation does not take into account all the aspects of the making of this particular critical text that a reader needs to know. First of all, Devreesse considers spurious a large part of the Greek fragments that are ascribed to this commentary by the exegetical chain and edited in Migne's *Patrologia graeca* (66:648C–696D). Devreesse is surely right in calling attention to the fact that not all those fragments can be ascribed with certainty to Theodore, but, nevertheless, one should be aware that—as always with Devreesse, such as with Origen's commentaries on Psalms—his assumptions are based on his personal taste and sensibility: this does not mean he is not right, only that his text is a result of personal attributions. A second order of questions concerns the traditions that are used or disposed by Devreesse. For his text, he uses mainly the Latin commentary of Julian of Aeclanus for Pss 1–32 (especially using MS Ambrosianus C.301. inf. and Taurinensis F.IV.I—and discarding the rest of the work of Julianus) and the Greek testimonies for the rest (the chains for the whole second section and MS Coislinianus 12 especially for Pss 33–41). The text of Julian has since 1939 been newly edited in its integrity in a volume that is not mentioned by Hill but that can be of some interest to the reader (because of the new critical text): *Theodori Mopsuesteni Expositionis in Psalmos Iuliano Aeclanensi interprete in latinum versae quae supersunt* (aux. M. J. D'Hont; ed. L. De Coninck; CCSL 88A; Turnholt: Brepols, 1977). The text of Julian covers the totality of the Psalter, but only the first part (the one used by Devreesse) is really interesting for Theodore's exegesis. Much more worth mentioning appears to be the Syriac translation, which is the best extant testimony of a famous section of the *Commentary on Psalms*, the prologue to the explanation of Ps 118, which is a methodological exposition of the manner of explaining the biblical texts according to Theodore (this part was distributed also individually in a form of a small treatise entitled *Against*

Allegorists). This important section of the commentary of Theodore, as well as other parts, cannot be read in Hill's translation, nor there is reference to the critical edition available: *Théodore de Mopsueste, Fragments syriaques du Commentaire des Psaumes (Psaume 118 et Psaumes 138–148)* (ed. L. van Rompay; 2 vols.; CSCO 435–436 = Scriptores Syri 189-190; Leuven: Peeters, 1982).

Hill has nevertheless done a magnificent job, and it is a true pleasure to read this celebrated commentary in an English translation along with the critical edition by Robert Devreesse (which is still the most complete available). Moreover, Hill's introduction is very interesting because it defies some commonplaces about this commentary. Although his notes on the structure of the work cannot really explain, in my opinion, the way Theodore conceived his commentary (see xxvi–xxix), it is important to remark with Hill that Theodore's knowledge of Hebrew, Syriac, and the different Greek versions of the Psalms are to be considered primarily secondhand, because he did not really control all such domains, being very young writing this text (xviii–xxi). Another interesting remark concerns the interpretation of the Psalms in their context by Theodore; in fact, although Theodore is famous for such recontextualization of the Old Testament books, this does not appear to be true in all cases. This does not mean that Theodore was more an allegorist than he is commonly considered but rather that his "historico-critical" exegesis is not methodologically comparable with ours. And, obviously, even Theodore of Mopsuestia had to recognize the messianic intent of key psalms (xxxi–xxxv). This was the case, for example, with Ps 2. At any rate, even in such cases Theodore can be easily distinguished from Alexandrian exegetes; Origen, for example, read Ps 2 using the rhetorical figure of the *prosopopoeia,* which consists in attributing the different verses of the psalms to different speakers (see Origen, *Selecta in Psalmos* 2).

This could not be Theodore's approach, even when he—very rarely—showed a conviction of a messianic meaning. Theodore's typical exegetical scheme is here clearly recognizable, and it consists in settling first of all the historical context of a chosen section, then in a literal interpretation, almost a simple paraphrase, that explains the main details involved in the text (about history, geography, and so on). This new erudite interpretation succeeded, first of all, because it arrived at the right moment in the history of Christian exegesis. The Alexandrian interpreters had shown that the biblical books supported an allegorical meaning, and this signified that they were major texts (like Homer, which was also considered an allegorical text at the moment), and this helped in developing the first Christian theology on a shared intellectual basis. Second, it is also because of the new political situation and the new context of a Christian empire that exegesis could now consider a literal interpretation of biblical books (especially Old Testament ones) without any fear (of Gnosticism, for example). This commentary is one of the most famous works by one of the most important "Antiochene" exegetes. It is even one of the main and largest commentaries on Psalms from antiquity. This is a genuinely great book that any exegete of Psalms will need to check. In conclusion, this is a major new edition that does not make changes in the critical text but offers for the first time in an usable volume an annotated translation that allows one , for the very first time, easily to approach the more than five hundred pages of the original edition of Devreesse, a vital starting point for any new research on Theodore.

The Cambridge History of Christianity, Volume 1: Origins to Constantine, edited by Margaret M. Mitchell and Frances M. Young. Cambridge: Cambridge University Press, 2006. Pp. xlv + 740. Hardcover. $180.00. ISBN 0521812399.

Everett Ferguson, Abilene, Texas

This is volume 1 of a projected nine-volume history of Christianity in all its aspects from its beginnings to the present day. The editors state their perspective as follows: "We have endeavoured to capture the complexity of early Christianity and its social-cultural setting, whilst also indicating some of the elements that make it possible to trace a certain coherence, a recognisable identity, maintained over time and defended resolutely despite cultural pressure that could have produced something other" (xiii). The volume represents the current replacement of an older consensus of a fairly uniform development of early Christianity with the current "critical orthodoxy" on the New Testament and the recognition of many more ambiguities than previously and popularly thought in the history of early Christianity. The authors make a dutiful acknowledgment of diversity while recognizing that some things made the Christian movement(s) distinctive. They aim at a balance between affirming diversity and noting common elements. To take an instance, despite the regional differences the churches had a "sense of being part of a worldwide phenomenon" (265).

Including the editors, twenty-eight authors—thirteen from the U.S., ten from the U.K., one from Ireland, and four from Germany (two of whom are teaching elsewhere)—write the prelude and thirty-two chapters. The authors are often *the* choice for a topic, and all are among the expected choices. Thirteen black-and-white illustrations, six maps, and a chronological chart of Roman emperors and bishops of Rome and Alexandria support the text. A particularly strong point of the volume is the bibliographies (590–682) classified by primary sources, secondary sources, and specialized bibliographies on each chapter.

Frances Young writes the prelude: "Jesus Christ, Foundation of Christianity." Her judicious remarks prompt the observation that, unlike the view that doctrine created the picture of Jesus, it is rather that doctrine arose from the effort to explain what was known and experienced about Jesus, even if accounting for the data produced paradoxes. Part 1 then sketches "The Political, Social, and Religious Setting," comprising articles on "Galilee and Judaea in the First Century" (Sean Freyne), "The Jewish Diaspora" (Tessa Rajak), and "The Roman Empire" (Hans-Josef Klauck).

Part 2 characterizes "The Jesus Movements" with contributions on "Jewish Christianity" (Joel Marcus), "Gentile Christianity" (Margaret Mitchell), "Johannine Christianity" (Harold Attridge), and "Social and Ecclesial Life of the Earliest Christians" (Wayne Meeks). The authors offer some original approaches to critical issues in New Testament scholarship. There are useful listings of sources for Jewish Christianity (90 n. 13) and of the inscriptional evidence for Jewish elders (149 n. 11). The often repeated mistake that early Christian art depicts baptism by pouring (161) should be corrected, for in the representations the hand of the administrator uniformly rests on the head of the baptizand. The next paragraph is right in stating that for the early Christians, unlike in the mystery religions, "baptism was not a preparation for initiation; it *was* the initiation" (161). The statement that the baptistery at Dura Europos "contained a baptismal basin too shallow for immersion" (161) is contradicted in a later article, which cites the baptismal room at Dura as an example of "a special room equipped with a font deep enough for immersion" (584).

Part 3, "Community Traditions and Self-Definition," includes the following articles: "The Emergence of the Written Record" (Margaret Mitchell), "Marcion and the 'Canon'" (Harry Gamble), "Self-Definition vis-à-vis the Jewish Matrix" (Judith Lieu), "Self-Definition vis-à-vis the Graeco-Roman World" (A. J. Droge), "Self-Differentiation among Christian Groups: The Gnostics and Their Opponents" (David Brakke), "Truth and Tradition: Irenaeus" (Denis Minns), and "The Self-Defining Praxis of the Developing *Ecclēsia*" (Carolyn Osiek). Mitchell appropriately emphasizes the importance of writing in early Christianity. A slip reverses the order of Romans and Hebrews in Papyrus 46 (184 n. 50). Brakke identifies the "Gnostic school of thought" with those some modern scholars call "Sethian Gnostics." The Valentinian school adapted the gnostic myth and were closer to the orthodox church. Minns corrects the distortion of Irenaeus that assigns him the chief role in establishing an episcopally governed orthodox church.

Part 4 discusses "Regional Varieties of Christianity in the First Three Centuries." After two general articles—"From Jerusalem to the Ends of the Earth" (Margaret Mitchell) and "Overview: The Geographical Spread of Christianity" (Frank Trombley)—the section continues with articles on specific regions: "Asia Minor and Achaea" (Christine Trevett), "Egypt" (Birger Pearson), "Syria and Mesopotamia" (Susan Ashbrook Harvey), "Gaul" (John Behr), "North Africa" (Maureen Tilley), and "Rome" (Markus Vinzent). Each discusses the sources available for study of Christianity in the region and major developments affecting the region. In Egypt, for instance, this means considering the origins of Christianity in Egypt, social groupings, the "catechetical school" (originally private before becoming church governed) in Alexandria, Gnosticism and Manichaeism in Egypt, Christian expansion into rural areas, and the origins of monasticism.

Part 5, "The Shaping of Christian Theology," includes studies of "Institutions in the Pre-Constantinian *Ecclēsia*" (Stuart Hall), "Monotheism and Creation" (Gerhard May), "Monotheism and Christology" (Frances Young), "Ecclesiology Forged in the Wake of Persecution" (Stuart Hall), and "Towards a Christian *Paideia*" (Frances Young). May removes Hermogenes from the ranks of the gnostics, where Tertullian put him, and classifies him as a Platonist; he finds Theophilus of Antioch and Irenaeus to be the first thinkers to make creation out of nothing fundamental to "expressing the absolute freedom and boundless power of God" (451). Young concludes that the Logos doctrine was articulated primarily in the context of cosmological debate, not primarily in response to the christological question. She suggests that a better image than the development of doctrine is a dialectical process of argument and counterargument. Ironically, the desire for unity resulted in the demand that deviant teachings be excluded. Young's treatment of Christian *paideia*—teaching and learning—covers an aspect not usually discussed in the histories but of great importance for the nature of Christianity and its progress in the ancient world. Christian meetings focused on reading and interpreting texts, and outside these assemblies semi-independent teachers set up schools and developed an educational curriculum based on the Bible rather than on the classical texts of paganism. These activities were significant for what the editors note in their conclusion: "The Christian 'gospel' by the time of Constantine ... had put in place elements of a cultural system that would transform, even as it assimilated, the cultural resources of the Graeco-Roman world" (587).

The last part (6), "'Aliens' Become Citizens: Towards Imperial Patronage," contains these articles: "Persecutions: Genesis and Legacy" (W. H. C. Frend), "Church and State up to c. 300 CE" (Adolf Martin Ritter), "Constantine and the 'Peace of the Church'" (Averil Cameron), "The First Council of Nicaea" (Mark Edwards), and "Towards a Christian Material Culture" (Robin Jensen). Ritter finds no fundamental difference between West and East on the subject of "church and state." Mark Edwards offers some fresh perspectives, cryptically expressed, on the Council of Nicaea and notes that there is no evidence of its creed being recited at baptisms nor of its use (unlike the creed of 381) in the liturgy.

The result of the format of the book is that there is no continuous narrative. The interlocking topics create unavoidable repetitions. Although the volume conveys some basic information on each topic, it assumes an understanding of the broader outline of church history in the first three centuries and in some cases requires a rather advanced knowledge. For an instance of the latter, there is assumed a knowledge of the definition of Gnosticism associated with the colloquium at Messina in 1966, which is not quoted (248 n. 11). Even specialists will find new details and new perspectives in the articles. I will keep the volume handy for reference on the matters discussed.

From the Lost Teaching of Polycarp: Identifying Irenaeus' Apostolic Presbyter and the Author of Ad Diognetum, by Charles E. Hill. Wissenschaftliche Untersuchungen zum Neuen Testament 186. Tübingen: Mohr Siebeck, 2006. Pp. ix + 207. Cloth. €49.00. ISBN 3161486994.

Mark Weedman, Crossroads College, Rochester, Minnesota

It seems as though I have encountered a number of reports recently that declare a crisis in academic publishing. The source of the problem, and the chief victim of it, is often thought to be the academic monograph. Academic publishers are finding it increasingly difficult to subsidize the publication of tightly focused books on single subjects that are of interest only to specialists within a narrow field. I do not doubt the veracity of these reports, and so it is with some relief, and a great deal of pleasure, that I find Charles Hill's *From the Lost Teaching of Polycarp*. This book is an academic monograph in the strictest sense of the term. Hill is not attempting to make sweeping claims about the development of second-century theology. Instead, he is investigating a very specific question—Can we find Polycarp of Smyrna in two second-century texts?—by means of a careful analysis of the relevant texts. The result is a fine example of a traditional academic monograph, one that could be of interest to a number of different kinds of scholars despite its narrow focus.

The book is divided into two parts, and since, as the author admits, the arguments in each section function independently of the other, I will treat them separately. The first section attempts to identify Polycarp as the "Presbyter" in Irenaeus's *Against Heresies* 4.27–32. Hill walks through the arguments for this identification very carefully, beginning in chapter 1 with an examination of the passage's textual history. The text of *Against Heresies* is confused in any case, since we do not have reliable access to the original Greek, but Hill uses a literal Armenian translation to ascertain that in 4.27–32 Irenaeus is reporting on the teaching of a single presbyter with apostolic connections, not presbyters, plural, as the Latin seems to indicate. The question, then, is: Who is this apostolic presbyter? The obvious answer is Polycarp, since this is how Irenaeus talks about Polycarp in other places, and this is the answer Hill wants to pursue as well.

The evidence for Polycarp, which Hill unfolds over the next two chapters, rests largely on correspondences between the teaching of the Presbyter in *Against Heresies* 4 and other confirmed teachings of Polycarp. Some of this evidence is circumstantial but suggestive. For example, Irenaeus appears to have a personal connection with the Presbyter that is similar to the relationship he has with Polycarp. Also, the Presbyter's teaching in this section concerns Marcion, and in another place Irenaeus reports that Polycarp had a personal encounter with Marcion. It is, in fact, this Marcion connection that yields what may be the strongest piece of evidence in favor of Polycarp as the Presbyter. In his *Letter to Florinus*, Irenaeus addresses a problem that corresponds closely to the one he addresses in the *Against Heresies* section. This correspondence is significant because the Letter to Florinus also contains Irenaeus's most well-known description of Polycarp, including Irenaeus's claim that he could remember many of Polycarp's actual words. The fact that in *Against Heresies* 4. 27–32 Irenaeus reproduces a respected teacher's teaching about Marcion in ways that are virtually identical to what he says about both Marcion and Polycarp in the *Letter to Florinus* would seem to confirm the identity of Polycarp as the Presbyter.

Hill follows his discussion of the evidence for Polycarp with a chapter that examines the specific teaching of the Presbyter. This involves identifying and commenting on all of the fragments in *Against Heresies* 4.27–32 where Irenaeus

appears to reproduce the teachings of his Presbyter. This chapter does not contribute much to Hill's argument, but it will become more important as Hill's thesis
gains acceptance, since it provides, in one place, the Latin, Greek retroversion, and
English translation of (and commentary on) Polycarp's actual teaching. Chapter
3, then, concludes the first part of this book by drawing some implications of this
identification for our understanding of second-century Christian thought and history. Hill believes that we do learn some things about Irenaeus and Marcion when
we identify the Presbyter as Polycarp, but the most important implications concern
our knowledge of Polycarp himself. Hill is fairly expansive in the range of conclusions he draws on the basis of limited evidence, but I found his conclusions largely
compelling. Of special interest is what this might say about the development of
Christian exegesis. As Hill points out, Irenaeus is often identified as the first true
Christian exegete, but as these fragments indicate, Polycarp may have played an
important role in training Irenaeus in exegetical method.

I am willing to regard as settled the identification of the Presbyter in *Against
Heresies* 4.27–32 as Polycarp. The connection with the *Letter to Florinus* seems
especially strong, and as a whole Hill's argument is so amply documented and
closely reasoned that the case is very strong. Less certain, by Hill's own admis-
sion, is the argument of the book's second part, the identification of Polycarp as
the author of a second-century document known as the *Epistle to Diognetus*.

As with the first part, Hill's case relies heavily on correspondences between
the *Epistle* and known works by Polycarp. Before turning to this evidence, however, Hill has first to make several points about the character of the *Epistle* itself.
The first point is that what we call an epistle actually has the form and character
of an oral address. The second is that the work as we have it is a unity, which
means that chapters 11–12, which some scholars regard as later additions, belong
to the same author and overall purpose of the entire letter.

These arguments about the form and structure of the letter become important when Hill turns, in chapter 5, to the evidence that Polycarp might have
written the *Epistle to Diognetus*. That the "epistle" is actually an oral discourse is
significant because there is evidence from the *Martyrdom of Polycarp* that Polycarp delivered a similar kind of speech before the proconsul of Smyrna prior to
his martyrdom. Intriguingly, Hill can find a number of similarities between the
Epistle and Polycarp's speech in the martyrdom account. In both, for example,
the speaker addresses a benevolent civil ruler in order to offer a defense of and
instruction in Christianity. (The literary parallels seem stronger when laid out in
the Greek!) The unity of the *Epistle* is important because in the disputed chapters
the author claims to be a "disciple of the apostles." Polycarp comes immediately
to mind here, especially since the *Epistle* author's use of John and certain forms
of antiheretical argument mirrors what we already know about Polycarp from
Irenaeus.

Hill then turns to a number of literary parallels between the words of Polycarp
in the *Martyrdom* and specific passages in the *Epistle*. The number of these parallels is suggestive, and they provide the most compelling evidence for Polycarp as

the epistle's author, but this is probably the place where the argument as a whole is the weakest, because it depends on the historicity of the *Martyrdom*. It is possible, of course, that the *Martyrdom* does more or less accurately record Polycarp's actual words, but it is just as possible (as Hill acknowledges in the first part of the book) that the *Martyrdom* offers a stylized, genre account of Polycarp's death, with no bearing on what Polycarp said or did. For this reason, I think we must regard the parallels Hill adduces to be extremely interesting but no more than that, and this section of the work would have benefited from a discussion of the *Martyrdom*'s historicity.

While this may say as much about my own predilections as it does about the book itself, I still found this book refreshing. I enjoyed following a tightly reasoned, well-documented, close reading of a few specific texts. This is how I was trained to do scholarship, and it is always a pleasure to see one's own craft so expertly employed. I do not know what this means for the future of academic monographs, but I hope that it bodes well. This kind of monograph is the life-blood of scholarship, not least because the more synthetic, expansive scholarly works depend on these kinds of close readings. I commend Mohr Siebeck for their support of this text.

A Woman's Place: House Churches in Earliest Christianity, by Carolyn Osiek and Margaret Y. MacDonald, with Janet H. Tulloch. Minneapolis: Fortress, 2005. Pp. vi + 345. Hardcover. $35.00. ISBN 0800636902.

David Parris, Fuller Theological Seminary, Colorado Springs, Colorado

In this highly recommended work, Osiek and MacDonald examine the everyday lives of women in the New Testament. This includes all the diverse roles, responsibilities and stages of life that women experienced: birth, childhood, marriage, child-bearing, motherhood, wet-nurses, nannies, slaves, wives, widows, and grandmothers. The title for their book is highly indicative of its content and approach. The house-church movement is the lens through which they explore the lives of women in the early church, and it is through the lives of these women that we come to learn more about the nature of the primitive church. In fact, they argue that the earliest Christian documents give us certain insights into the lives of women during this period that are not found in other literature.

The two dominant themes that run through the book are as follows. First, as opposed to the current interest in female ascetic movements, Osiek and Mac-Donald focus on the lives of married women and widows in the house churches. They argue that the contributions married women made to the church have been overlooked and that the roles they played as married women made a more significant impact on the church than did single women. Second, the attention they give to the lives of ordinary women allows us to grasp "what women were doing most of their time and to savor the atmosphere of the communities" (247).

In the introduction, the authors position their work along three axes that have played a central role in feminist studies: patriarchy versus a discipleship of equals; public space versus the private domain of the house; and ascetic movements versus the domestic life led by most women. In each instance the authors thread a third way between these polarities. For example, instead of taking the side of legal scholars who claim that Greco-Roman culture was a patriarchal society or the opposing camp that argue Jesus instituted a community of equals, Osiek and MacDonald take the position that the church participated in a contemporary movement toward greater freedom for women (cf. Bruce Winter, *Roman Wives, Roman Widows*, 2003).

Chapters 2–10 can be roughly outlined as sketching the chronology of a woman's life from birth to maturity. The exception to this outline is chapter 2, which focuses on wives and may have been given this position of prominence due to the significant role marriage played in the first century. Even though the evidence we possess about women from that time frame is very limited, Osiek and MacDonald present a well-supported argument for the significant role that women played in the early church. In particular, they argue that we need carefully to differentiate between the ideal views on marriage presented in the New Testament and the complicated reality of marriage in the first century.

Chapters 3 and 4 concentrate on maternity, the rearing of children, and growing up as a child in a house church. In this regard the authors offer us a very important reminder as twentieth-century Westerners: "To a much greater extent than is the case for modern western women, ancient women's lives were determined by the realities of procreation" (50). If women are underrepresented in classical literature, female children are perhaps the most underrepresented group. In this regard the chapter on "Growing up in the House-Church Communities" is a welcome contribution to our understanding of the Greco-Roman world. The amount of attention, time, and energy that was given to childbirth and raising children within that culture suggests how highly valued a woman's ministry within the church as caregivers and educators would have been.

Chapter 5 reminds us of the tragic lives that female slaves led. According to Aristotle, a slave was to be ruled by a master and a woman was to be ruled by a man. Thus a female slave was doubly dominated and twice vulnerable! The life of a slave was characterized by having no ancestry, lineage, or hope of inheritance (since her family ties could be broken, and often were, at any time). Because females slaves stood outside the honor/shame value system of that culture, issues of sexual propriety simply did not apply to them. They were property and were completely sexually available to the people who owned them. This raises questions for Osiek and MacDonald concerning how Paul's admonitions for a slave to be obedient in everything and his sexual ethics would have been received by the house churches.

The marriage code in Eph 5:22–33 is examined in the sixth chapter through two lenses. The first is reading the larger text of Ephesians as a resistance document against Roman imperial ideology. The second is to read the section on marriage from the perspective that a married couple was often portrayed as a microcosm for the larger society. Thus the Christian couple should be seen as an apologetical ideal representing the unity, love, and purity of the church to the communities in which they lived. But this raises an interesting paradox. Marriage is presented in very conventional terms in a letter that is calling for a countercultural lifestyle.

Chapters 7–9 draw our attention to the roles women played as leaders and patrons in the church. Even though most of the ancient evidence in this area comes from male authors, they give us surprising insights into how much authority women exercised over their households. If the house was the woman's domain, then this has profound implications for a primitive Christian movement that was organized around households. Janet Tulloch's contribution (ch. 8, "Women Leaders in Family Funerary Banquets") inquires what we can learn from eight frescos depicting Christian funerary banquets from SS. Marcellino e Pietro in Italy. This chapter presents an interesting case study in how to read a work of art and the problems attendant in doing so. Tulloch contends that these frescos depict real women hosting banquets and leading those who attended in remembrance toasts and, as a result, portray the changing roles that women played within society and the images. The ninth chapter examines how the backbone of the Roman social system, patronage, provided means for women to exercise authority through informal social networks.

In the penultimate chapter, "Women as Agents of Expansion," the authors synthesize the various topics covered in the book into a composite picture of how women functioned within the early church. Based on a theory of social networking, they argue that it was their roles as wives, mothers, and widows that opened certain avenues for ministry for women that greatly enhanced the expansion of the church. It was through these conventional roles that women exercised unconventional ministries. "Among the most fascinating information emerging from this survey is the ever-present suggestion of danger. These women were clearly taking risks for the sake of the gospel" (228).

Before I discuss what I perceive as the strengths of this work, let me briefly mention two minor weaknesses. The first is that the authors often seem to reach conclusions based on common sense. This could simply be a stylistic feature of the book, since they often mention how there is not much by way of evidence for a particular topic they are discussing and the very meticulous manner by which they argue their case. The second is definitely a stylistic feature of the book: there is a fair amount of redundancy within the text.

Having said that, A Woman's Place provides a thorough and multifaceted portrait of the lives, roles, and ministries of women in the primitive church. But it accomplishes far more than that. Because Osiek and MacDonald examine the lives of women within the context of the larger Greco-Roman culture, the reader is exposed to many of the dominant elements within that culture: honor and shame, slavery, marriage, houses and household management, structure of the early church, and the common lives of everyday people. Their interaction with not only key biblical passages but a carefully chosen corpus of classical texts (e.g., Plutarch, Soranus, Celsus, Shepherd of Hermas, 1 Clement, *Martyrdom of Perpetua*, and *Acts of Thecla*) provides an introduction to those texts and also a model for how this material shapes our understanding of the house church. Finally, they do an excellent job presenting in a clear manner the complex lives of women within the house church. As such, *A Woman's Place* is especially well-suited to be a required textbook for a New Testament survey course, especially one that focuses on the book of Acts through the epistles.

HISTORY OF INTERPRETATION

Martin Noth—aus der Sicht der heutigen Forschung, edited by Udo Rüterswörden. Biblisch-theologische Studien 58. Neukirchen-Vluyn: Neukirchener, 2004. Pp. viii + 100. Paper. €19.90. ISBN 3788720018.

Steven L. McKenzie, Rhodes College, Memphis, Tennessee

This small volume is a collection of four papers presented on 2 November 2002 at a commemoration of Martin Noth's one hundredth birthday held at the Evangelisch-Theologisch faculty of the Rheinischen Friedrich-Wilhelms University in Bonn, where Noth once served.

The first essay, by Rudolf Smend, is entitled, "Martin Noth (1902–1968): Person und Werk." The essay contains three parts: a biographical sketch of Noth; a discussion of the personal and professional relationship between Noth, Albrecht Alt, and Gerhard von Rad; and an overview of Noth's bibliography and major contributions to Old Testament studies. The essay makes for enjoyable reading, not least because of several anecdotes that *Alttestamentler* will find delightful. These concern, above all, the relationship of mutual admiration and respect between the three giants, Alt, Noth, and von Rad. Smend recounts one such anecdote illustrating Noth's exuberance over his first trip to Palestine in 1925. A cousin who saw Noth come bounding up the stairs of one of the buildings of the University of Leipzig remarked that he must just have become engaged. "Much better!" Noth replied. "I'm going with Alt to Palestine."

The second entry in the volume, by Horst Seebass, treats the heritage of Noth for the study of the Pentateuch and Hexateuch. Recognizing that the trend in present-day scholarship (at least in the German-speaking sphere) is away from Noth's model of a Tetrateuch + Deuteronomistic History back to that of a Pentateuch or Hexateuch, Seebass sketches what he sees as Noth's most important contributions to subsequent study. First, Noth adopted certain principles for further development of Wellhausen's theory: abandon the attempt at further division of J into its sources; regard language as an ineffective tool for separating J and E; and understand P's reworking of J and E as the basis for further redaction of the Pentateuch. Second, Noth jettisoned the Hexateuch model. Third, Noth's main interest in his *Überlieferungsgeschichte des Pentateuch* was the use of Syro-Palestinian geography to reconstruct preliterary traditions. Fourth, Noth determined that the works of J and E were combined with P before the annexation of Deuteronomy.

Seebass then focuses on the book of Numbers, trying to show what features of Noth's pentateuchal theory may still be relevant. Numbers shows signs of being a distinct unit in its own right. It has its own frame, within which it infuses more recent legal materials into older narratives. Noth was correct, Seebass contends, to distinguish Deuteronomy from Numbers and the previous pentateuchal books. Noth's "fragmentary" model might be applied to the process of bringing together individual books into the Pentateuch rather than to his original idea of diverse traditions underlying the pentateuchal sources. The place of the book of Joshua remains an open question, but Noth's observation that there is no P foundation to Joshua, as there is to the books in the Tetrateuch, is still a valid reason not to incorporate it into a Hexateuch. Seebass regards Noth's tradition-historical approach as the next great phase in Old Testament study following Wellhausen and his interest in linking study of the text with that of geography and history as paradigmatic.

Christian Frevel's essay on "Deuteronomistic History or Histories? The Thesis of Martin Noth between Tetrateuch, Hexateuch, and Enneateuch" follows next. This article contains a description of Noth's Deuteronomistic History hypothesis and then a critical synthesis of its reception to the present. Frevel observes that in *Überlieferungsgeschichtliche Studien* Noth sought to solve the problem created in his Joshua commentary by his conclusion that the latter book did not contain the pentateuchal sources but that Deuteronomistic elements formed its basic structure. The question raised by Noth about the end of the pentateuchal sources in relation to the "conquest" remains a major crux today. Frevel notes that a corollary of Noth's theory involved the concept of Dtr as an author, by which he meant not a writer who created without the benefit of any source material but rather one who used sources yet was more than a mere collector.

Frevel critiques Noth's thesis in five areas. (1) He suggests that the idea of Dtr as a single author isolated (in Mizpah) from any cultic or institutional context reflected Noth's own situation in Königsberg. Scholarship on the authorship of the DtrH since Noth, above all the so-called "Smend" and "Cross" schools, indicates that the redactional situation within the DtrH is more complex than Noth admitted. (2) Noth's view of the "kerygma" or purpose of the DtrH as completely negative with no hope for the future was also reflective of Noth's own time. Subsequent research, beginning with von Rad and Wolff, questioned this notion and found indications of a positive outlook in the DtrH. These differing conclusions suggest the presence of different perspectives within the DtrH, again a more complex situation than Noth advocated. (3) But to give up the unity of the DtrH is really to give up its existence, and that is the step taken recently by an increasing number of scholars who argue for the existence of distinct books linked together in a developing corpus or the like. This is essentially a return to the situation in scholarship before Noth. Noth's observations about the role of Deuteronomistic texts and commonality of authorship are accommodated by positing a late level of Deuteronomistic editing that bound the originally separate books together. (4) The Hexateuch theory, thus, is a "thorn in the flesh" of the DtrH hypothesis. Newer hexateuchal models are not the same as those before Noth, because he proved that J and P do not continue in Joshua. However, in addition to the question of the conclusion to the narrative thread of the Pentateuch and the possession of the land, there is the matter of how to understand Josh 24, on which Noth himself vacillated. Recent scholarship has produced the "Jehovist" hypothesis, which espouses a pre-Dtr narrative thread in Joshua that stands in continuity with the Tetrateuch, to try to explain these problems. Frevel thinks that Josh 24 may be the conclusion of this thread and may come from J. He also sees Josh 13–21 as closely affiliated with Num 26–36 and thus intended to be understood in a hexateuchal context. (5) At the same time, the book of Deuteronomy is hardly suitable as the beginning of a work of history. Deuteronomy 1–3 fit best within a hexateuchal context, as they presuppose the tetrateuchal narrative and continue it with a review of the law on the plains of Moab—which makes perfect sense within a Hexateuch. Frevel favors Otto's theory (based on Lohfink) of an original "DtrL" source for this material running from Deut 1 to Josh 24, which was then combined with P into a Hexateuch.

Frevel summarizes: Noth's Deuteronomistic History hypothesis was a brilliant stroke; it lasted a long time and inspired much important scholarship. However, it has now become questionable for several reasons. Most of all, it does not explain the complexity of the evidence, especially outside of Kings, and it is no longer dominant, at least in the German-speaking sphere. The renewed Hexateuch theory poses a strong challenge to Noth's DtrH hypothesis. Still, the recent criticisms of Noth's theory are stronger than alternative syntheses proposed by the critics. There is no consensus explanation among recent critics for the overarching Dtr redaction in Deuteronomy and the Former Prophets nor for the development of the Pentateuch, which Noth's theory explained, albeit simplistically.

The final contribution, by W. H. Schmidt, is quite brief and focuses on Noth's role in founding the Biblische Kommentar series in 1950, also published by Neukirchener. Schmidt lauds Noth's ability to bring a variety of evidence—archaeological, topographical, historical, exegetical, and comparative—to bear on the biblical text and his insistence on that text as the source of theology rather than the reverse. At the same time, Schmidt suggests that Noth perceived Israel's uniqueness.

This volume is a worthy tribute to a scholar who has had a significant impact on the study of the Hebrew Bible. The essays by Seebass and Frevel are especially useful as indicators of the status quo in German-speaking circles of the field. Their perspectives are varied. Seebass is much more skeptical of recent trends toward a return to the Hexateuch. Frevel is clearly the youngest of the four and the only one who did not study with Noth or know him personally. Still, his respect for Noth and his work are well placed. Indeed, Frevel well recognizes the greatness and foresight of Noth when he closes his piece with Noth's own words acknowledging the need for constant reexamination of scholarly theories: "Denn wissenschaftliche Thesen, auch wenn sie weit verbreitet sind und mehr oder weniger einleuchtend zu sein scheinen, müssen immer wieder in Frage gestellt und an der Überlieferung überprüft werden." Of course, such a reexamination may just as well lead back to the theory with which it began, so that Seebass's reluctance to sign the Deuteronomistic Historian's epitaph may be well considered.

What Have They Done to the Bible? A History of Modern Biblical Interpretation, by John Sandys-Wunsch. Collegeville, Minn.: Liturgical Press, 2005. Pp. xx + 378. Paper. $39.95. ISBN 0814650287.

Jan G. van der Watt, University of Pretoria, Pretoria, South Africa

At the end of the preface Sandys-Wunsch makes reference to a saying by Winston Churchill concerning another politician: "He is a modest man; so much to be modest about." Sandys-Wunsch then applies this saying to himself because after thirty years of work on the subject he confesses that he is left with a strong sense of his own ignorance. To be honest, I think this is the feeling most of the readers will have about their own insights after reading this book. Sandys-Wunsch has opened up a world of activity surrounding the Bible and its interpretation that heightens one's awareness to the reality that biblical scholars today are just one small gear in a large machine. One quickly comes to realize that through the ages people were serious about their understanding of the Bible, had reasons for reading the Bible in the way they did, and always did it as children of their time. We realize that our roots of who we are and what we do as biblical scholars lie deeply imbedded in this history, but we also realize that we are not who they are—they rightly belong to the past, and we are children of our time.

This book gives an overview of the history of biblical interpretation stretching from 1450 to 1889, this being, of course, the period starting with the Renaissance and leading up to the critical nineteenth century. In an introductory chapter (ch. 1) the nature and concerns of biblical exegesis are discussed. The text of the Bible, language and translation, canon, exegesis and the factors influencing exegesis, and belief and unbelief in the history of biblical interpretation are, for instance, topics that receive attention. The most important elements are treated, but in some cases not with enough depth.

Sandys-Wunsch then systematically works through the different periods in history, tracing significant development in the field of biblical interpretation. He starts (ch. 2) with the period from 1450 to 1600 under the title of the Renaissance. During this period the influence of exegesis was wide-ranging. The Bible was seen as the central source of knowledge, not only for religious insights but on all other levels of society, such as the ethical, political, legal, and even scientific levels. Major events took place during this period that had a direct impact on the exegesis of the Bible, including printing as a technical innovation, the Reformation, the founding of major European universities as centers for academic study, and, of course unbelief as a phenomenon. The humanists were active during this period, not shying away from pointing out the difficulties in the Bible. In areas of textual criticism or philology, they laid strong foundations for what was to come.

Chapter 3 deals with the "Baroque" period (1600–1660). Before continuing with a description of the content of chapter 3, a remark must first be made about the way in which Sandys-Wunsch approaches his material. He starts his chapters with a discussion of the so-called "external factors." I regard this as the strongest characteristic of this book. Before jumping into discussions on what the biblical exegetes did, he provides a contextual framework for understanding the sociocultural and political atmosphere that prevailed during that particular period. This helps to explain why certain actions were taken during certain times and why certain solutions or positions were acceptable for their time, while later falling out of favor. Biblical exegesis is not practiced in a vacuum. Rather, children of a particular time, with the exegetical tools and insights of that particular era at hand, employ them. This is one central realization that one comes to when reading this book.

To return to the discussion of the "Baroque" period, the seventeenth century was a time during which the encyclopedic stronghold of the Bible on all levels of society was broken. Knowledge on different levels started to sideline the Bible as the central source of information. It was not immediately apparent, but cracks in the foundations began to appear. On the other hand, the Bible benefited from significant developments in language and semantics. This meant that the Bible and its text were studied with greater care than before.

Following the "Baroque" period came the early Enlightenment period (1660–1700). The Enlightenment had a direct influence on the understanding and status of the Bible and created a climate in which certain ideas and views were regarded as preferable to others. Questions were asked about the transmission of the Bible as well as on its view on creation and certain philosophical ideas. Radical thinkers attacked the origins and nature of the Bible. Its authority was rejected, although it was still defended by most scholars. The awareness of historical developments that could be studied in order to trace the development of ideas had a profound impact on exegesis. Philology and textual transmission were favorite and safe areas for biblical scholars to work in.

Considering these dense periods in history where major shifts took place, the difficulty of writing a history such as this become apparent. As Sandys-Wunsch himself acknowledges, selection plays a role, and, of course, there is also the presentation of the material that needs to be considered. For his selection he used criteria such as choosing biblical exegetes who offer interpretations open to reasonable discussion, and from these he made a reasonable selection, since not all exegetes of relevance can be discussed. This has both positive and negative outcomes: positively, he chooses a limited number of exegetes and discusses them in some detail (given the page restrictions); on the negative side, such selection naturally means that a somewhat limited picture emerges. This is not the fault of Sandys-Wunsch but rather a reality of writing any selective history. One is constantly confronted with choices—choices of which material to use and how to construct one's "story." All in all, I think Sandys-Wunsch writes a plausible account that makes sense and flows well. He combines his own interpretation effectively with the material he wants to present.

Chapters 5 and 6 cover the eventful eighteenth century, when the basis for the modern approach to the Bible was worked out. The focus falls mainly on the events in Germany, although England is not forgotten. In the context of the German university system, historical studies gained ground and significantly affected the approach to biblical studies. The development of historical-critical methods questioned treatment of biblical information in naïve ways. This section is the most detailed, and several scholars are treated in some detail.

Chapter 7 deals with aspects of biblical interpretation in the nineteenth century, showing how the questions formulated in the previous century were developed and worked out in the nineteenth century. As before, several scholars are scrutinized. Technical exegetical issues such as who the historical Jesus was and how he saw himself, the Synoptic problem, and the transmittal of the material came under discussion. Hermeneutical questions about the treatment of the material and the relation to faith were also addressed.

The book ends with an epilogue that to my mind could have been left out. It is more about the author than about the historical focus of the book. Sandys-Wunsch actually mentions that adding this epilogue was a suggestion of a reader of the first draft of the book. Perhaps he should not have followed this advice. His indexes are brief but effective.

As a historical text, this book is really well written and, as a result, relatively easy to read. I think most students will have no problems in drawing the necessary information from a reading of this book. The combination between information, explanation, and commentary is well done. I did come across a few small spelling errors (one in a German quote) that could receive attention in a future printing.

I am convinced that this book will be of value to both the student and the specialist. Anyone who wants to specialize in either the hermeneutics or the exegesis of the New Testament will greatly benefit from this history of modern biblical interpretation that Sandys-Wunsch has prepared for us.

Rediscovering the Traditions of Israel, by Douglas A. Knight. 3rd edition. Atlanta: Society of Biblical Literature; Leiden: Brill, 2006. Pp. xviii + 360. Paper/cloth. $45.95/$129.00. ISBN 1589831624/9004137653.

Steven L. McKenzie, Rhodes College, Memphis, Tennessee

It hardly seems appropriate to refer to a book by a youthful and vibrant scholar such as Doug Knight as a "classic," but that is how this volume is touted. And perhaps rightly so. In 1973 Knight performed an invaluable service for English-speaking biblical scholars by producing a critical synthesis of the traditio-historical research on the Hebrew Bible. Since much of this research had taken place particularly in Scandinavia, it was previously inaccessible to most English speakers. Knight's book was a remarkably useful contribution, all the more so considering that it was a dissertation.

Following introductory essays distinguishing *traditio* (process) from *traditum* (content) and characterizing tradition history as a method, the book consists of two main parts. The first traces the rise of traditio-historical research; the second focuses on the configurations of and debates over the method among Scandinavian scholars.

Knight begins his survey of tradition history with Richard Simon, who applied the Roman Church's position regarding tradition to the biblical period and thus came to emphasize the long process of transmission of biblical material. After touching on the contributions of a series of scholars, including Herder, Nachtigal, Wellhausen, Klostermann, and Eichhorn, Knight focuses on Gunkel as the chief pioneer of tradition history. Knight enumerates a series of fundamental principles of the method abstracted from Gunkel's *Schöpfung und Chaos* and his commentary on Genesis. Knight shows how Gunkel began with the smallest unit of a text and sought to retrace the total spectrum of historical development behind it. The text's *Sitz im Leben* provided the point of departure for tracing this development, and Gunkel took seriously the notion of oral tradition and oral composition. Gressmann and Alt furthered Gunkel's work in their efforts to recover the very earliest stage of traditions and their emphasis on the importance of the cult in their development. The latter was especially influential through his student, Martin Noth, and Noth's contemporary, Gerhard von Rad.

Von Rad and Noth ushered in a new era in Hebrew Bible research. Knight traces von Rad's theory of the development of the Hexateuch beginning with the ancient credo reflected in Deut 26:5b–9. The omission of Sinai from that credo led von Rad to posit two independent tradition complexes behind the Hexateuch. For von Rad, however, the Hexateuch was not the end result of a long process of fusion between these complexes. It was, rather, the work of a literary genius, the Yahwist, who inserted the Sinai tradition, organized and attached the patriarchal traditions, and led off with the primeval history behind Gen 2–11. Knight observes that for von Rad tradition history was something of a means to arrive at what was of theological significance.

Von Rad's theological objective represented a crucial difference from Noth, whose use of tradition history was aimed more at historical reconstruction. In both his *Überlieferungs-geschichte des Pentateuchs* and his *Überlieferungsgeschichtliche Studien* Noth focused not on credenda but on principal themes, which he sought to isolate. He saw these themes as furnishing the framework of the Pentateuch and Deuteronomistic History, respectively, and then tried to identify the traditional sources that had been used to fill in the framework in order to provide a complete picture of the way in which these two giant works had developed. In his *Geschichte Israels* Noth was primarily interested in what Israel's traditions might reveal about the settlement of Israel and the origin of the nation rather than in their prehistory. Knight stresses that for Noth questions were more important than answers and that he always sought to describe how Israel's traditions *could* have developed, recognizing that certainty was impossible. As a result, Knight points out that there was a certain arbitrariness in Noth's distinctions between primary and secondary traditions and that he may have overestimated the capability of tradition history in historical reconstruction.

Ironically, the second part of Knight's book on Scandinavian scholarship is actually briefer than the first. If the emphasis in the first part was on the contributions of von Rad and Noth, the second part builds toward a discussion of Ivan Engnell and the Uppsala circle. A chapter on "Beginnings" sketches Engnell's predecessors, including Mowinckel, Pedersen, Hylander, Nyberg (Engnell's teacher), Birkeland, and Lindblom. Knight's sketch well illustrates the issues that were debated and the diversity of opinion about them among these scholars. Of particular importance were attitude toward literary (i.e., source) criticism, the reliability ascribed to oral tradition, and the social affiliations of traditionalists behind various portions of the Bible.

Engnell basically sought to further and apply the viewpoint of Nyberg, his mentor, who advocated the predominance of oral tradition. In contrast to Mowinckel, he denied the usefulness of literary criticism. Knight points out that Engnell focused on the process of transmission *(traditio)* essentially to the exclusion of the *traditum*'s developmental history. What was important to him was the beginning stages and then the final form of the tradition in the present text. He avoided stratifying the tradition in between.

In the subsequent chapter on the "Uppsala Circle" Knight describes how scholars in conversation with Engnell in Uppsala modified and developed his ideas. Knight treats the works of Haldar, Widengren, Ringgren (Engnell's successor), Ahlström, and Carlson, in particular. In yet another chapter Knight surveys the work of Bentzen, Nielsen, Kapelrud, and Sæbø, who were in contact with and influenced in some way by the Uppsala circle. While Kapelrud and Nielsen stand relatively close to the circle in their work, Bentzen and Sæbø are much more eclectic, influenced as much by German scholarship as by Scandinavian.

An enduring contribution of Knight's book is the accessibility that it furnishes to Scandinavian scholarship. It is certainly important for scholars—both those entering Hebrew Bible studies and those who have been in it for some time—to be aware of or to refresh their memories about this branch of the field. Knight's book makes clear the diversity of perspectives among tradition historians and Scandinavians in particular, thus warding off any temptation to monolithic portrayal. It is these features that give this volume classic status and that warrant its republication.

At the same time, the present, third edition of this classic work raises an important question. It is a question addressed, although perhaps not entirely satisfactorily, in the book's epilogue: "Does Tradition History Have a Future?" The epilogue, a version of a lecture that itself is over a decade old, describes changes in five areas with which tradition history must come to terms: historiography, social history, ideological criticism, identification of and rivalries among ancient tradents, and the role of modern exegetes in the world of scholarship following postmodernism. Knight's identification of the need of tradition history to deal with these changing areas is well taken. But exactly how tradition history should evolve as a result is not addressed. There are also other questions that arise in the light of the development of Hebrew Bible studies over the last three decades. For instance, in view of the evidence at Qumran for the diversity and development of the biblical text, where exactly does one mark the "final form" or the end point of the *traditio* of a given book? Knight notes in the preface to the third edition that little by way of content has changed in this edition but that were he to write the same book now it would be quite different.

Of course, it is not fair to criticize Knight for the book that he *might* have written, especially since the basic purpose of this edition is to make available an enduring and classic work of scholarship. So perhaps the question of the last chapter is best addressed to the field as a whole. Where has tradition historical criticism come since the 1970s, and where will it go from here? Knight's work will be an important resource for fully addressing these questions.

HERMENEUTICS AND METHODS

Biblical Interpretation: History, Context, and Reality, edited by Christine Helmer, with the assistance of Taylor G. Petrey. Society of Biblical Literature Symposium Series 26. Atlanta: Society of Biblical Literature; Leiden: Brill, 2005. Pp. xii + 181. Paper/cloth. $24.95/$107.00. ISBN 158983089X/9004130748.

Tobias Nicklas, Radboud University of Nijmegen, Nijmegen, The Netherlands

Der vorliegende Band stellt die Ergebnisse eines Seminars der Biblical Theology Group der Society of Biblical Literature vor, das am 20. Juli 2002 im Rahmen des International Meetings in Berlin stattfand. Gesammelt sind neben einer Einleitung der Herausgeberin, Christine Helmer, insgesamt 10 Beiträge, die sich mit Fragen biblischer Theologie und Hermeneutik beschäftigen.

Ein erster Teil steht unter dem Titel „Historical and Theological Interpretation". Eine wichtige und souverän verfasste einführende Grundlage für das Folgende bietet bereits der eröffnende Aufsatz von Bernd Janowski, der einen guten Einblick in formale und materiale Aspekte Biblischer Theologie bietet. Dabei erweist Janowski zum Beispiel die Vieldeutigkeit des Begriffs „Biblischer Theologie" in einer Spannbreite zwischen „schriftgemäße[r]" und „in der Bibel enthaltene[r] Theologie" auf (17). Hilfreich sind auch die Gedanken des Autors zur Forschungsgeschichte, in denen er sich auf Fragen des Verhältnisses Biblischer Theologie zu historischer Kritik, religionsgeschichtlicher Forschung und *canonical approach* konzentriert. Gerade auf der Ebene der letzteren Dimension könnten inzwischen die gerade in allerneuester Zeit im deutschsprachigen Raum zu beobachtenden Aufbrüche im Zusammenhang mit „kanonisch-intertextueller

Lektüre" und „biblischer Auslegung" ergänzt werden. Im Rahmen der Frage nach gegenwärtigen Problemen beschäftigt sich Janowski mit der Diskussion um eine „Mitte der Schrift", um das Verhältnis zwischen Altem und Neuem Testament oder um die Bedeutung des Kanons.

Zu den Höhepunkten des Bandes gehört sicherlich auch Harold W. Attridges Beitrag zur Hermeneutik der Johannesexegese des Herakleon. Attridge arbeitet nicht nur die Qualität der (leider nur in Zitaten des Origenes erhaltenen) Exegese Herakleons heraus, sondern zeigt, dass beide antiken Autoren auf methodischer wie auch auf hermeneutischer Ebene deutliche Parallelen aufweisen. Attridge vergleicht besonders die Aussagen beider antiker Exegeten zum Johannesprolog und kommt zu folgendem Fazit: „Heracleon does no more violence to the text of John's Prologue than does Origen and in some particulars, appears to be trying mightily to give a consistent and coherent reading. At stake in their different readings of the text is a fundamental and theological disagreement, but the ‚heretic' seems to be defending a more exalted view of the Logos" (71).

Am Beispiel der Frage, auf welche Weise Origenes in seinen Exegesen mit dem Problem der Körperlosigkeit Gottes umging, macht Karen Jo Torjesen deutlich, inwiefern philosophische Konzepte in antiker Bibelrezeption verarbeitet und auch umgewandelt wurden: „What happens when the rarified beams of philosophical abstraction pass through the denser medium of scripture? Is their light bent? Scriptural language vivifies and, in a process of rhetorical involution, renders poetic the spare concepts of philosophical abstraction. In this process of rhetorical involution, scriptural language exerts a steady pressure on philosophical concepts and slowly reshapes them in its own image" (73). In der Problematik, die häufig anthropomorphe Sprache der Bibel mit dem philosophischen Konzept der Körperlosigkeit Gottes in Einklang zu bringen, habe Origenes eine Reihe von Strategien angewandt: Er habe immer wieder darauf gepocht, dass die Texte der Schrift als Offenbarungen Gottes zu verstehen seien, deren inspirierte Worte allegorisch aufgefasst werden müssten. Nur die biblische Sprache habe für Origenes die Potenz enthalten, sich für eine höhere, spirituelle Bedeutung zu öffnen. Das Problem, dass die Körperlosigkeit Gottes in biblischer Sprache nicht thematisiert werde, könne über ihre allegorische Deutung einer Lösung zugeführt werden: „Allegorical interpretation overlays new sets of meanings onto scripture and transforms spiritual meaning into a palimpsest of the original text. Unlike the palimpsest printed on papyri, however, the palimpsest created by allegorical interpretation is dynamic and fluid because the actual scriptures' words have a life and force of their own that exert a pressure on the meanings the allegorist has overwritten. The power of the actual words of scripture … should not be underestimated precisely because allegorical interpretation pays such minute attention to the actual words in their grammatical, literal, and historical senses" (79). Die Autorin macht zudem deutlich, wie Origenes in seinen philosophischen Argumentationen das Medium der Schriftsprache verwendet habe, sie verweist auf seine faszinierende Anwendung biblischer Intertextualität oder seine Praxis exegetischen Predigens.

Teil II des Bandes stellt Beispiele philosophischer Interpretation der Bibel zusammen:

Marvin A. Sweeneys Beitrag zeigt, wie Isaac Luria, Moses Mendelssohn und Asher Ginzberg (Pseudonym: Ahad Ha-'Am) Ideen eines „demokratisierten Jahwe-Bundes", wie sie sich besonders in Jes 55,1–5 finden, in ihre Messiaskonzepte einfließen ließen. Anknüpfend an Jesaja arbeiteten die genannten Autoren in je unterschiedlicher Weise heraus, dass *jeder* Mensch die Fähigkeit besitze, zusammen mit Gott an der Heiligung der Schöpfung zu wirken—eine Fähigkeit, die gleichzeitig als Verpflichtung zu verstehen sei. Eine Reihe von z.T. eher knappen Beiträgen setzt sich mit der Rolle der Interpretation biblischer Passagen bei Philosophen der Neuzeit auseinander: Nach einem Beitrag von Stephan Grätzel, der Johann Gottlieb Fichtes Interpretation des Johannesevangeliums unter die Lupe nimmt, sowie einer Arbeit der Herausgeberin, Christine Helmer, zu Friedrich Schleiermachers Exegese von Kol 1,15–20 bietet Joachim Ringleben einen Einblick in Georg Wilhelm Friedrich Hegels Interpretation von Gen 3. Hegel habe Gen 3 als einen Mythus aufgefasst, in dem die „Geschichte des menschlichen Geistes" (133) erzählt werde. Die Motive von „Unschuld" und „Fall" seien von Hegel als „wesentliche Momente in der Genesis von Subjektivität" (134) verstanden worden. Wilhelm Gräb arbeitet die Rolle des Johannesprologs für Friedrich Wilhelm Joseph Schellings Philosophie der Offenbarung heraus, während Garrett Green die These vertritt, dass Ludwig Feuerbachs Theorie der Religion eng mit seiner Theorie biblischer Hermeneutik in Zusammenhang stehe.

Das Buch ist durch eine knappe Bibliographie wie auch verschiedene Register gut erschlossen.

Der in seinen Themen sicherlich sehr breit gefächerte Band dürfte einerseits für Leser, die sich mit der Rezeptionsgeschichte biblischer Texte beschäftigen, interessant sein, andererseits bietet er wichtige Impulse für die hermeneutische Diskussion.

Rhetoric, Ethic, and Moral Persuasion in Biblical Discourse, edited by Thomas H. Olbricht and Anders Eriksson. Emory Studies in Early Christianity 11. London: T&T Clark, 2005. Pp. xiii + 401. Paper. $69.95. ISBN 0567028119.

Walter A. Vogels, Saint Paul University, Ottawa, ON, Canada

The present volume contains the papers presented at the Pepperdine University lecture hall facilities in Heidelberg, 22–25 July 2002. The meeting grouped scholars not belonging to an official organization but who are all interested in rhetoric. A first similar meeting was held at the same location in Heidelberg in 1992, and since then several meetings were organized in different parts of the world, with their papers always published. This time the conference "centered upon the ethos of the writer/speaker, but subthemes involved the ethos of those who teach biblical studies and the extent to which ideologies should replace

Enlightenment 'scientific' criticism. Certain participants heralded imperial criticism" (xii)

The book is divided into several sections. First is the keynote address: chapter 1, Elisabeth Schüssler Fiorenza, "Disciplinary Matters: A Critical Rhetoric and Ethic of Inquiry" (9–32). She defines an ethic of inquiry as "a new evaluative form of cultural practice and critical investigation that is no longer circumscribed by the positivist objectivism, subjectivism, liberalism, and nationalism of modernity or the masculine rationalism and European colonialism that have tended to relegate rhetoric to mere talk and to the dustbins of history" (13). The section on the Old Testament includes, chapter 2, Rodney K. Duke, "The Ethical Appeal of the Chronicler" (33–51). He argues that the persuasive appeal of the Chronicler is made through the character of the narrator as speaker, while other voices within the narrative add credibility to his work. The section on the Gospel includes chapter 3, Anders Eriksson, "The Old Is Good: Parables of Patched Garment and Wineskins as Elaboration of a Chreia in Luke 5:33–39 about Feasting with Jesus" (52–72), which contends that the parable, contrary to the classical interpretation, is not a rejection of Pharisaic Judaism to be replaced by Christianity but an invitation to the Pharisees to join the party. The section on ethos in general includes several papers. Chapter 4, Manfred Kraus, "Ethos as a Technical Means of Persuasion in Ancient Rhetorical Theory" (73–87), discusses how *ethos* was understood before Aristotle, by Aristotle himself, and later by Cicero and Quintilian. Chapter 5, John W. Marschall, "When You Make the Inside Like the Outside: Pseudepigraphy and Ethos" (88–102) demonstrates how Aristotle's view on *ethos* casts a new light on pseudepigraphy. Chapter 6, J. David Hester (Amador), "The Wuellnerian Sublime: Rhetorics, Power, and the Ethics of Commun(icat)ion" (103–18), argues that "the return of the sublime to rhetoric reminds us of the *goal* of our work as critics of the Bible … the bringing forth of the *healing* of the divine" (117). Chapter 7, Carol Poster's "Ethos, Authority, and the New Testament Canon" (118–37), shows how arguments from apostolic authorship rather than the intrinsic value of the writings played an important role in the debate over canonicity; this was similar to what was recommended in the rhetorical handbooks of the Hellenistic period.

The general section on Paul comprises six essays. Chapter 8, Thomas H. Olbricht's "The Foundations of the Ethos in Paul and in the Classical Rhetoricians" (138–59), contends that *ethos* in Paul is different from that of the classical rhetoricians, because of their difference in social location and their different views on the ideal person. In chapter 9, "Melody, Imagery, and Memory in the Moral Persuasion of Paul" (160–78). Roy R. Jeal tries to identify some of the melody, imagery, and memory in Rom 12 to show how it functions as part of the persuasive effect. Chapter 10, Fredrick J. Long, "From Epicheiremes to Exhortation: A Pauline Method of Moral Persuasion in 1 Thessalonians" (179–95), argues that Paul has conceived 1 Thess 4:1-5:11 as five *epicheiremes,* which correspond to the descriptions of *epicheiremes* in Cicero and Quintilian. Chapter 11, Mark D. Given's "On His Majesty's Secret Service: The Undercover Ethos of Paul"

(196–213), shows how Paul used the undercover *ethos* of an agent in God's secret service to infiltrate and destroy the strongholds of "the god of this world." Chapter 12, jointly authored by Todd Penner and Caroline Vander Stichele and titled "Unveiling Paul: Gendering Ethos in 1 Corinthians 11:2-16" (214–37), contends that Paul's major concern is the role of "the virile Greco-Roman male" and that this is the image he projected for himself and the "ideal" church. Chapter 13, "Authorial Ethos in Philippians: The Agōn Topos in Paul and Hellenistic Moralists" (238–54), by Russell B. Sisson, suggests that Paul uses an athletic analogy to describe his own "contest" and that of the Philippians in a manner similar to some Hellenistic moralists.

The section on the Pauline Epistles includes four papers. Chapter 14, Troy W. Martin's "Veiled Exhortations Regarding the Veil: Ethos as the Controlling Proof in Moral Persuasion (1 Cor 11:2-16)" (255–73), argues that praying with an uncovered head exposes the hair of the woman, which is part of her genitalia. Paul's *ethos* and that of the church determines the conduct of the Corinthians. Chapter 15, "Philippians 1:12–26 and the Rhetoric of Success" (274–83), by Johan S. Vos, contends that, to encourage the Philippians, Paul uses a rhetorical strategy similar to the ancient military rhetoric of success. Chapter 16, Rollin Ramsaran, "In the Steps of the Moralists: Paul's Rhetorical Argumentation in Philippians 4" (284–300) shows how Paul speaks as a moralist in his relationship to the Philippians. He writes a letter of friendship to them that contains guidance from a moral teacher to students but also draws upon Stoic-like meditation. In chapter 17, "The Function of Ethos in Colossians" (301–15), Jerry L. Sumney argues that the most outstanding aspect of Paul's *ethos* is his suffering, which plays an important role in convincing the Colossians to remain faithful to the teaching they have received. The section on Hebrews comprises chapter 18, Walter Übelacker, "Hebrews and the Implied Author's Rhetorical Ethos" (316–34). Übelacker contends that, because the letter to the Hebrews is anonymous, the implied author strengthens his *ethos* by several techniques, such as by showing respect for commonly acknowledged virtues. The concluding address: Vernon K. Robbins's "From Heidelberg to Heidelberg: Rhetorical Interpretation of the Bible at the Seven 'Pepperdine' Conferences from 1992 to 2002" (335–77), summarizes the evolution of rhetorical interpretation over these ten years: "The seven rhetoric conferences from 1992 to 2002 exhibit remarkable movement from the application of formal categories from Greco-Roman literary rhetoric to modes that interweave multiple practices informed by strategies of people as they interact with one another both within bounded social, cultural, and political spheres and across ethnic, national, cultural, and religious boundaries" (336).

As with all collective works, one notices great differences between the contributions. Some are very technical, especially in the section on the theme of *ethos* in general. Only a reader well informed on rhetoric will enjoy reading them. At times one wonders about the usefulness of some studies for biblical discourse. One is struck by the fact that the vast majority of these studies are on Paul. Only one article is on the Old Testament and one on the Gospels. Is this only because of the personal interest of the researchers in rhetorical interpretation, or does it mean that the method is only applicable to a certain number of texts? It is not clear why some articles on Paul are classified in the section general Pauline section and others in Pauline Epistles section. The study by Penner and Vander Stichele on 1 Cor 11:2–16 is put in the general section, while that by Martin on the same text is placed in the section on Pauline Epistles. In both sections one finds studies on Philippians. It is also interesting to note that the interpretations of the authors on the same biblical text can vary greatly. Sisson characterizes the rhetoric of Philippians as athletic, while Vos considers it military. The two studies on 1 Cor 11:2–16 also come to different conclusions. Rhetorical interpretation apparently does not provide the last and final word on biblical texts; in that aspect, this approach is thus not different from all other methodologies now used in biblical studies.

The concluding address by Robbins shows how rhetorical analysis, which is a rather new method, has come a long way: how it started, how it changed. In a very short time it has gained its place among other established methodologies to study texts.

Ancient Fiction: The Matrix of Early Christian and Jewish Narrative, edited by Jo-Ann Brant, Charles W. Hedrick, and Chris Shea. Society of Biblical Literature Symposium Series 32. Atlanta: Society of Biblical Literature; Leiden: Brill, 2005. Pp. xvii + 372. Paper/cloth. $39.95/$170.00. ISBN 1589831667/9004137684.

Loveday Alexander, University of Sheffield, Sheffield, United Kingdom

As Gareth Schmeling points out in his preface to this volume (xvii), "the working relationships between religious storytelling, whether Egyptian, Jewish, or Christian, and classical narratives are not in question." Nevertheless, the study of these relationships has been obscured for many years by artificial disciplinary distinctions: "For more than a century the academic disciplines responsible for studying these narratives, classics and religion, have been divided, gone their separate ways, and failed to discuss with each other on a regular basis common material." One of the major achievements of the SBL's Ancient Fiction and Early Christian and Jewish Narrative Group (now a Section) has been to explode these distinctions, facilitating a lively and interactive dialogue between exponents of "classical" and "biblical" studies and "putting back together fragmented academic disciplines, which had ceased to present an understandable picture of the mosaic that is the ancient world." The essays in this volume represent a selection of papers offered to the Ancient Fiction Group over the past decade, ably edited by Jo-Ann Brant, Charles Hedrick, and Chris Shea, and with a new introduction by Richard Pervo. The volume thus complements the Group's earlier excellent publication edited by Ronald Hock, Bradley Chance, and Judith Perkins (*Ancient Fiction and Early Christian Narrative* [SBLSymS 6; Atlanta: Scholars Press, 1998]). It is not in any sense a themed volume; its contents illustrate the variety and diversity of the

Group's work, the ways it has shaped a discipline as well as some of the divergent trajectories it has opened up.

Despite this exemplary commitment to interdisciplinarity, there is a sense in which the act of "putting back together fragmented academic disciplines" is here simply an act of juxtaposition: it is the Group itself, and the discussions it has generated, that provide the matrix for interdisciplinary reflection. The essays are divided neatly into the three familiar categories of Greco-Roman, Jewish, and early Christian narrative, and while some are explicitly comparative, others simply offer insights into discrete fragments of the mosaic, leaving it to us to make sense of the bigger picture. Part 1, "Ancient Greco-Roman Narrative," moves from familiar intertexts (Chariton, Homer, Vergil) to the less familiar (the encomiastic biography of Aspasia in Aelian's *Varia Historia*). Ron Hock's rich and stimulating essay on "The Educational Curriculum in Chariton's *Callirhoe*" (15–36) draws on the essential work of Morgan and Cribiore on the educational papyri to show how Chariton's work reflects the patterns of Hellenistic *paideia,* from the schoolroom maxims of the primary level through to the textbook deployment of the techniques of *ethopoiia* taught in the *progymnasmata.* Chris Shea's "Imitating Imitation: Vergil, Homer, and Acts 10:1–11:18" (37–59) argues for Vergil's *Aeneid* as a conscious model for the composition of Acts, using the Cornelius episode as an example of "striking similarities" (58) in plot structure and motif. Richard Pervo's "Die Entführung in das Serail: Aspasia: A Female Aesop?" (61–88) takes a much less familiar text and draws from it some typically tantalizing and provocative pointers for the reading of New Testament narrative. The story of Aspasia, courtesan and confidant to two Persian monarchs, forms one of the largest sections in Aelian's *Varia Historia,* drawing on a kernel of historical notices found in Xenophon, Plutarch, and Athenaeus. Aelian's encomiastic biography of this shadowy figure uses familiar schoolroom techniques to elaborate the bare bones provided by the tradition (84) and in the process effectively problematizes the relationship between fiction and history (84–86). Gerhard van der Heever, finally, takes a broader theme in "Novel and Mystery: Discourse, Myth and Society" (89-114), arguing that Merkelbach's thesis of an integral connection between the novels and the mystery religions is worth taking seriously, "provided one reinterprets both literature/fiction and religion" (114).

Part 2, "Jewish Narrative," explores a variety of potential intertexts, although with little attempt at explicit comparison. Chaim Milikowsky's "Midrash as Fiction and Midrash as History: What Did the Rabbis Mean?" (117–27) opens up a recurrent theme of the volume, the relation between fiction and history in ancient narrative. Milikowsky argues that rabbinic midrash operates with a clear distinction between "history" (represented by the biblical text) and "fiction" (represented by the exegetical expansions that are always contestable and never accorded the same status as a "given" within the developing tradition. Jo-Ann Brant's "Mimesis and Dramatic Art in Ezekiel the Tragedian's *Exagoge*" (129–47) shows what happens when a Jewish writer consciously and explicitly sets out to recast biblical narrative into Greek poetic form, killing off the narrator (129) and achieving in dramatic form "what the biblical narrative does not do, that is, to bring to exterior expression the pathos that lies in the background of the Hebrew narrative" (147). Conversely Tawny L. Holm's study of "Daniel 1–6: A Biblical Story-Collection" (149–66) argues that the closest and most illuminating parallels to the sequence of tales in Dan 1–6 lie not in Hellenistic but in ancient Near Eastern literature, specifically in Egyptian court tales. Two studies of 3 Maccabees illuminate different facets of this neglected work. In "3 Maccabees: An Anti-Dionysian Polemic" (167–83) Noah Hacham reads the fictions of 3 Maccabees as a polemic against the cult of Dionysus, aimed in all probability at Alexandrian Jews tempted to buy into the social advantages offered by the state-supported cult of Dionysus. Similarly Sarah Johnson, in "Third Maccabees: Historical Fictions and the Shaping of Jewish Identity in the Hellenistic Period" (185–97), as one of a group of polemical writings (in a variety of genres) that "employ fictions about the past in order to make a didactic point about 'identity'" (191) and model a form of assimilation that "will allow Greek-speaking Jews to preserve their traditions and their laws, while at the same time participating fully in the wider Greek world" (192). For this author, "history is not an end in itself, but simply raw material to be mined and shaped in the service of a particular ideology" (197). The *Testament of Abraham*, on the other hand, in Jared Ludlow's study of "Humor and Paradox in the Characterization of Abraham in the *Testament of Abraham*" (199–214) finds an unexpected element of paradox in this retelling of the Genesis account, stemming from a milieu "where the community felt comfortable enough with its identity that it could poke fun at some of its heroes without risking alienation" (213)—although this proved too risqué for the later Christian readers responsible for Recension B (213).

Part 3, "Early Christian Narrative," opens with Judith Perkins's rich and nuanced study of "Resurrection and Social Perspectives in the Apocryphal *Acts of Peter* and *Acts of John*" (217–37). These two *Acts*, Perkins argues, exemplify two poles of the second-century debate about the status of the body in Christian belief, a debate that also had marked social implications. Christians who maintained a "spiritual" view of resurrection, minimizing traditions of physical resurrection, were also "less resistant to the traditional social hierarchies based on the dichotomy of mind-soul and body" (219). Conversely, "those second-century Christians advocating for a resurrection of the fleshly body were refusing Greco-Roman culture's inscription of the body and those associated with it as base and sordid" (218). Dennis Ronald MacDonald covers more familiar ground in "The Breasts of Hecuba and Those of the Daughters of Jerusalem: Luke's Transvaluation of a Famous Iliadic Scene" (239–54), arguing that Luke 23:27–31 exhibits conscious *imitatio* of one of the most famous scenes in the *Iliad*, Hecuba's maternal appeal to Hector not to take on the conflict that will lead to his certain death and the destruction of the city at *Iliad* 22.25–89. J. R. C. Cousland goes to Greek tragedy for his intertext in "The Choral Crowds in the Tragedy according to St. Matthew" (255–73), while Rubén Dupertius finds a conscious evocation of the Guardians of Plato's *Republic* in the "utopian" summaries of Acts in "The Summaries of Acts 2,

4, and 5 and Plato's *Republic*" (275–95). Finally, Andy Reimer revisits Glen Bow-ersock's *Fiction as History* (Berkeley and Los Angeles: University of California Press, 1994), to look at the literary transformations of the empty tomb motif from Chariton to Shakespeare in "A Biography of a Motif: The Empty Tomb in the Gos-pels, the Greek Novels, and Shakespeare's *Romeo and Juliet*" (297–316).

This is a rich collection, then, with much to stimulate and inform. What precisely you *do* with this comparative material, and how it may (or may not) throw light on the narrative world of the New Testament (if that happens to be your interest), is less clear. In many ways the most successful papers are those that simply open up new literary horizons or offer new insights into the cultural world of the early Christian storytellers and leave us to draw our own conclu-sions. I would particularly single out here Hock's fine study of Chariton, which offers a cool, hard look at precisely *how* the praxis of Greek *paideia* impacts on the surface construction of Chariton's narrative and throws into relief the lack of such surface detail in most New Testament texts. Hock's study amply confirms the current consensus that even this earliest (and on the face of it simplest) of the novel texts deploys the resources of a highly sophisticated education. Neverthe-less, he closes with an important caveat that Chariton's education "must not be overestimated": it "tends to go no farther than the core authors and moreover betrays a knowledge of them that derived in many instances from quotations already selected by his teachers" (35–36). If this is true of Chariton, *a fortiori* the educational resources of the New Testament writers (whose explicit quota-tions account for little more than the maxims encountered at the primary level of education) must not be overestimated, or at the very least we need a coherent strategy to account for the avoidance in New Testament discourse of the parade of intertextual allusion that was taken for granted by the *pepaideumenos* of the Greek East. In this respect, as Richard Pervo puts it, "similarities place the differ-ences in relief" (84), and for students of early Christian narrative there is much food for thought in the Jewish narrative texts discussed in this volume (Brant, Holm, Hacham, Johnson) and their complex negotiation of the politics of identity and hybridity within a global empire.

There is in fact relatively little explicit comparative analysis of New Testament texts in this volume. What there is, interestingly, focuses largely on Luke-Acts (Shea, MacDonald, Dupertius), and it would be instructive to compare the essays in the companion volume in the Symposium series, Todd Penner and Caroline Vander Stichele, eds., *Contextualizing Acts: Lukan Narrative and Greco-Roman Discourse* (SBLSymS 20; Atlanta: Society of Biblical Literature, 2003). For my own part, I remain obstinately unconvinced by the assumption of conscious *imitatio* of the poetic texts of the high literary culture (especially Latin culture), as argued by Shea and MacDonald (a position I have argued more fully in "New Testament Narrative and Ancient Epic," in *Raconter, interpreter, annoncer: Parcours de Nou-veau Testament. Mélanges offerts à Daniel Marguerat pour son 60e anniversaire* [ed. Emmanuelle Steffek and Yvan Bourquin; Le Monde de la Bible 47; Genève: Labor et Fides, 2003), 239-49; now reprinted in my *Acts in Its Ancient Literary*

Context: A Classicist Looks at the Acts of the Apostles [Library of New Testament Studies 298; London: T&T Clark, 2006], 165–82). Much more suggestive, it seems to me, and potentially immensely fruitful, is Pervo's evocation of similarities and differences in plot and motif in the "border and shadowland between history and romance" (84) or van der Heever's nuanced exploration of the social and communitarian aspects of mythmaking and storytelling—an activity that is at once romantic, political and religious—within the broader framework of empire. Averil Cameron remarked long ago that the importance of narrative in early Christian literature, "at the very time when story was enjoying a prominence unusual in the ancient world ... cannot be without significance for the diffusion of Christianity as a whole" (Averil Cameron, *Christianity and the Rhetoric of Empire: The Development of Christian Discourse* [Sather Classical Lectures; Berkeley and Los Angeles: University of California Press, 1991], 89–93). The publication of this volume, and the continued existence of the Ancient Fiction Section, demonstrates that there is still much valuable work to be done in exploring the matrix of early Christian and Jewish narrative.

The Passion of the Lord: African American Reflections, edited by James A. Noel and Matthew V. Johnson. Facets. Minneapolis: Fortress, 2005. Pp. x + 190. Paper. $6.00. ISBN 0800637305.

Fernando Segovia, Vanderbilt University, Nashville, Tennessee

This volume brings together seven essays by African American Christian scholars of religion on the passion, the suffering and death of Jesus conveyed by the "Gospel story." Its immediate rationale, the preface explains, lies in the controversy generated by Mel Gibson's film *The Passion of the Christ*, given the stark absence of African American voices in such debates, despite the centrality of the passion for African Americans—the "passionate engagement" and "distinctive resonance" of black Christians with the Gospel story in light of "their unique historical trajectory." The project thus seeks to address this vacuum. Toward this end, a more fundamental rationale is identified as well. In so doing, the preface adds, the volume seeks to revisit the meaning of Jesus' death in African American consciousness, historical as well as contemporary, and rethink thereby African American theology in light of the common beliefs and practices of the Black church. The project involves, therefore, a critical revisioning of the tradition.

While their actual relationship to the movie varies considerably—from the nonexistent (Johnson; Baker-Fletcher), through the tenuous (Franklin) and the tactical (Ross; Williams), to the engaged (Noel; Terrell)—the essays, written from a broad variety of disciplinary and theological perspectives, yield rich insight into ongoing African American reflections on the passion. From the standpoint of biblical criticism, the volume may be seen as a contribution to cultural analysis of the Bible.

Robert M. Franklin ("The Passion and African American Pilgrimage") provides a framework for such reflections by unfolding a historical overview of African American faith and history. This "grand narrative" is constructed as a "drama in three parts": self-determination amid societal stability on the African continent (through the fifteenth century); collective struggle amid the sorrows of slavery (from the sixteenth century through the Civil Rights era); and striving amid celebration (beyond the 1960s through today). It is a drama involving suffering, struggle, resurrection—parallel to that of Jesus and by no means finished. Gibson's *Passion* should be approached as an opportunity for African Americans to learn their "big story" and use it, as "transformed nonconformists," toward the exercise of moral agency.

For such reflections on this analogous drama of Jesus and the community, Demetrius K. Williams ("Identifying with the Cross of Christ") advances a biblical foundation. Gibson's view of Jesus' death as unmerited and redemptive is in line with much of Christian tradition, including the African American. Such a view, however, has often served hegemonic purposes: the promotion of innocent suffering and passive humility. The solution is not to play down the foundational symbols of the passion, as proposed by various African American theologians and thinkers, given their appeal to oppressed groups, but to turn to an alternative view of the passion in the New Testament. While preserving the language of "redemption" from the tradition, Paul offers an "anti-imperial" reading of the passion: a symbol of struggle against oppression and the foundation for an alternative human community. This view is actually much closer to the African American tradition of resistance and liberation.

Various essays continue such revisiting and rethinking of the passion as redemptive by broadening the terms of the analogous drama in different directions. Rosetta E. Ross ("Passionate Living") and JoAnne M. Terrell ("What Manner of Love?") amplify the understanding of the passion within the Gospel story itself, while Matthew V. Johnson ("Lord of the Crucified") and James A. Noel ("Were You There?") expand the sociocultural context of the African American community.

Ross regards the redemptive view of the passion, espoused by Gibson, as unnecessarily restricted to the last days of Jesus' life, whereas a broader understanding of "passion" as a "reflection of deep feelings" would bring into play his entire life and driving commitments, namely, respect for the dignity of all and bringing life to all, especially the dispossessed. Such "passionate living" is directly tied to his death, insofar as it led to conflict and opposition with those in power. Jesus emerges thereby as an ethical model for committed living in the Christian tradition. Such a way of life lay at the heart of many in the Civil Rights Movement (Fannie Lou Hamer, for example) and should drive the African American community today in the ongoing quest for dignity and life for all. Terrell charges Gibson with following the customary portrayal of Jesus as "white," playing into the base values of sexism, racism, and classism and using violence to get "Jews" and "sinners" to accept guilt for the crucifixion and salvation by proxy and propitiation. Instead, it is the whole story of Jesus that makes people whole—a story of love for us, a love embracing neighbors and enemies and bringing about our own love for Jesus. From its matrix of slavery and oppression, Black faith saw in Christ complete redemption and a love ethic yielding human dignity and political resolve. From their own situation of multiple oppression, Black women see in Christ the need for love with justice. Consequently, Jesus' love in the passion is a love that identifies with human suffering and seeks to put an end to it.

Johnson argues for the centrality of the passion in African American "Christian consciousness" as a "metanarrative" comprising both death and resurrection. Such engagement points to a fundamental "congruity" between the Gospel story and the African American story: mutual origins in trauma and parallel visions of life as tragic. A community marked by ongoing traumatic experience comes to see a reflection of itself in Christ's own traumatic experience. Out of this "mytho-poetic mirror," a tragic understanding of life and faith emerges, embracing the reality of violence and oppression (profound homelessness) as well as divine solidarity and ultimate transformation (power to go on). Such complex consciousness neither Black liberation theology nor Black charismatic or prosperity theology has grasped, yet it constitutes the essence of the Black church. Noel seeks to explain why—in distinction to liberal white Protestants, with whom they share ideals of racial equality and social justice—African Americans stand alongside evangelical white Protestants in liking Gibson's vision of the passion. In the aftermath of modernity, the atonement became unpalatable for Northern liberalism while remaining intelligible for Southern evangelicalism, who saw defeat in the Civil War as victimization by Northerners and blacks and turned increasingly to the Bible as a proslavery text. African Americans encountered modernity through its "underside" of slavery. The passion became the central symbol of their "religious imagination," expressed in rituals (e.g., the spiritual "Were You There?"). In its portrayal of a God who shared their fate of crucifixion, they saw a reflection of their own traumatic experience and found orientation and meaning for their lives of suffering and survival. Black liberation theology has paid no importance to the passion, opening up thereby a gap between its ideal of racial justice and the tradition of the Black church.

Baker-Fletcher represents a logical conclusion to this project of revisiting and rethinking the passion by advancing a sustained theological interpretation of Jesus' death, grounded in both womanist and process theology. God is love but not all-powerful: God aims for the well-being of all creation, but God also shares power and allows for freedom; consequently, destruction and suffering are ever-present in the world. God also experiences the world in an omnipresent fashion through the Spirit, seeking the right relationship of all and giving hope to creation. Such love becomes fully manifest in the "God/man" Jesus, who, in bringing good news to the least in defiance of empire, becomes like the lynched of the world in his crucifixion. His death is not that of a sacrificial victim but one that seeks to overcome evil. The passion becomes thereby a "homeopathy," a symbol of life and hope and the foundation for love in the power of the Spirit toward the eradication of all oppression.

The volume represents a very fine and very welcome contribution to cultural analysis of the Bible. Its twofold objective is well accomplished: bringing an over-looked yet crucial perspective to bear on the public discussion of the passion by way of a critical rereading and reimagining of and from the African American tradition. Individually, the essays are all well argued and to the point. As a collection, however, they come across as rather disperse. An extended and integrative introduction was in order: setting forth the context, rationales, and aims at length; bringing the essays into conversation with one another; mapping a critical path for the future. As it is, too many angles remain loose: the wide range of reactions to the film; the particular contribution brought to the public controversy; underlying approaches to the reading of biblical texts; the critique of other African American theological traditions; the specific import of womanism; the overall assessment of Jesus' death. Nevertheless, key conclusions are evident across the board: acceptance of a fundamental congruence between the Gospel and the African American stories; rejection of the traditional interpretation of Jesus' passion as redemptive, as reflecting neither the Gospel nor the African American story. In one way or another, therefore, all these essays argue for a broader sense of the congruence, with emphasis on moral commitments and political transformation. In conclusion, this is not only a keen contribution to the public debate but also a sharp revisioning of the African American religious and theological tradition.

An Unsuitable Book: The Bible as Scandalous Text, by Hugh S. Pyper. The Bible in the Modern World 7. Sheffield: Sheffield Phoenix Press, 2005. Pp. viii + 186. Hardcover. $85.00. ISBN 1905048327.

Rannfrid Thelle, Luther College, Decorah, Iowa

This book is a collection of ten essays, seven of which have been previously published in an earlier form between 1993 and 2003. The essays are collected under the common heading of *An Unsuitable Book: The Bible as Scandalous Text*.

In the introduction (ch. 1) Pyper sets out the two main concepts that run through the essays, those of *unsuitability* and *scandal*. In various ways the idea of biblical literature as unsuitable—to its readers, ancient and modern, to its environment, to the religious community that canonized it and those that continue to interpret it as scripture—is explored throughout the collection. The application of scandal as a category is explained in moral terms, appealing to Kierkegaard: "We *should* be scandalized by the Bible—only then, [Kierkegaard] would argue, is there any chance that we might be taking it seriously" (2). Acknowledging his indebtedness to Kierkegaard, Pyper sets out scandal as a moral duty in reading biblical texts. The Bible is unsuitable, potentially dangerous, and encounter with it is risky. It will turn against those who attempt to control it, Pyper claims. But for those readers who recognize that it is unsuitable, understand its danger and power, and are properly scandalized, there is the reward of an "encounter with life" (8). So, reader, what will you choose?

In chapter 2, "Selfish Texts: The Bible and Survival," the Bible and the relationship to its reading community is analyzed in the language of evolutionary biology, Darwinian language of "survival of the fittest," and *memetics* (a way of talking about cultural units of information in a way analogous to genetics). Here the observation is that it is not always the most well-adapted species that survives, because if it is too well-suited to its environment it is less likely to survive sudden changes. Human beings, for example, are not really well-adapted and need care for many years after birth. Because of this, they have had to develop strategies for survival in many different environments and have thus survived. The same goes for the Bible. Because of its unsuitability, it has continued to resist becoming the text for *one* community and, by selfishly maintaining its identity, has survived through different communities. The Bible is dependent on the reading community for its survival, for being copied, but it also resists full appropriation by any one community in order to survive a change of environment, managing even to act as the authoritative text for totally opposing communities. Paradoxically, the survival of the text also depends on its domestication and propagation by specific communities, and the survival of specific communities seems to depend on their relationship to the Bible as identity-forming. This tension between the need for domestication and a striving toward the unleashing the wild is thematicized here for the first time and comes up again in later essays.

I would like to comment on the idea that the "traditional communities of interest in the Bible may be thought to be in danger of collapse" (28). This is part of the Western-centeredness that bothers me occasionally in this book. The assumption is that when those traditional communities lose interest, the Bible will perish. But I disagree that an iconic status for the Bible is its only option for survival, as Pyper seems to suggest, or his reassurance that the Bible cannot be "eradicated" from Western culture. The success of the Bible in other parts of the world, such as Africa or China, might suggest otherwise. This development would be very interesting to have in mind in a work about the Bible in the modern world. Will it turn on its original community in ways unimaginable to us today?

The second essay is entitled "Speaking Silence: Male Readers, Female Readings and the Biblical Text." Through various texts, ancient and modern, it explores how, in framing women's silences, male impotence is exposed. While framed silence becomes female utterance, the male response, in the failure to face up to this, is a silencing that leads to emotional muting. I am not totally convinced by this essay and need more explanation (this might betray me, of course, but I am taking the chance) in order to follow the leaps between biblical texts, modern Danish writers, and contemporary critics. In a strange way, I feel, as a woman, excluded from the *project* of this essay, and this may be Pyper's intention. After all, the essay seems to be, as I understand it, a call to male readers to face up to the biblical text and what it does to *them*.

"Readers in Pain: Muriel Spark and the Book of Job" (ch. 4) toys with the idea of the effect of a book on a reader and the idea that reading is (or should be?) *painful*. Pyper discusses Muriel Spark's novel *The Only Problem* and comments on the experience of pain that a reader feels when she or he cannot make sense out of a work. It addresses the curse of blessing, so to speak, inspired by both the biblical book of Job and readers' attempts to come to grips with it. Pyper brings up the power of the text in changing the reader and sees this as the way to go (64–65). If readers open themselves up to the text, they will be changed, maybe even wounded by it. Of course, this view of the power of the text to change the reader is not an invention of modern criticism but was the aesthetic of the ancient world, something that is very applicable to the biblical text. Pyper does not go into this, but it would be interesting to follow up on the idea that when a reader opens herself or himself up to the text and risks being wounded, she or he is using the text in a way that ancient aesthetics might have intended for texts to work. Could this help explain why such an ethics of reading might be the most appropriate for biblical texts?

In chapter 5, "The Bible in Bloom" (not previously published), Pyper thematicizes canonicity through a discussion of Harold Bloom's work. Concepts of struggle between texts are explored here: the ways in which writers attempt to avoid the influence of previous texts through misreading and the analogy of both the Darwinian struggle for survival and the Freudian concept of rivalry between a "father" text and later texts. This is basically an essay in support of Bloom and his views on canonization, especially on how such seemingly nonnormative biblical texts as Ruth, Esther, Ecclesiastes, Song of Songs, and what he calls the J material found its way into the canon. Canonization, something that seems to entail a process of limiting and containing, might paradoxically produce more texts. The discussion of canon and canonization is interesting and important, but do we need Bloom to remind us of the strangeness of texts or that there is a jungle out there? Do not the biblical texts themselves tell us this? On the other hand, this piece was enjoyable and fun to read, so why not allow it in our universities' gardens and "carefully weeded lawns."

Chapter 6, entitled "Modern Gospels of Judas: Canon and Betrayal," was published before the sensationalized publication of the *Gospel of Judas* in the spring of 2006, but the rumors of its existence were already circulating. In this piece Pyper explores the process of canonization and the effects of canonization from another angle, through a look at the texts inspired by the testimony about a Gospel of Judas. Judas the betrayer survives through noncanonical (or anticanonical) texts as Judas the betrayed or misunderstood. Judas has become the hero of those who mark resistance to the power of the church, those who feel left out, excluded. Pyper cites the work of Frank Kermode, who observes how the Judas character is constructed in the New Testament by filling out the narrative gap created by the Pauline text of 1 Cor 11:23, which reads, "In the night that the Lord Jesus was betrayed, he took bread...." A reference to some of the literature on this material would have been very helpful here. The essay continues into a discussion of the links between literature, canon, betrayal, and death and introduces modern texts on Lazarus also. I do wonder, however, how central the Judas literature really is to Western culture, and is it not perhaps too big a claim to say that Judas is the "figure through whom Western culture has worked out its anxiety over mortality, election and rejection" (86)?

The essay entitled "Reading Lamentations" (ch. 7) takes the discomfort of reading as its point of departure, as we saw in chapter 4, "Readers in Pain." Again, as in earlier essays, much of the focus is on the reader and on the idea of the pain of survival. Pyper introduces the idea of melancholia (taken mainly from the work of Tod Linafelt) as the appropriate explanation for the ambivalence "between compassion for Zion as a victim and yet justification of the punishment for her lasciviousness" (89–90). The argument runs along several lines, but basically Pyper explores some of the dynamics he sees as underlying the imagery and personifications in the text of Lamentations, to illuminate how the text serves as a vehicle for survival of the community and the survival of God the expense of Zion, ensuring the text's continued use and thus also its survival. Though this piece raises many significant questions and provides several interesting observations, it makes me wonder why there is no mention whatsoever of the ancient genre of city laments in trying to understand the function and workings of the text of Lamentations, or why, despite opening with an observation about the ritual reading of the book, there is no consideration of the place of ritual in human society that might help provide a context for understanding the dynamics of this text.

Chapter 8, "The Rebellious Son: Biblical Family Values," goes through various aspects of views on family that can be found in the Bible. Pyper shows first how the views on family values are diverse and not uniform. He then makes a case for how the preaching of Jesus brings in a new worldview when it comes to family; whereas family in the Old Testament was designed to secure survival, Jesus' teaching is predicated on resurrection. The essay continues to explore how the figure of Jesus in the Gospels challenges the tensions present in the biblical literature regarding family. This all serves to demonstrate to modern readers that the biblical literature contains "tensions and irreconcilabilities" (113), thus challenging those who attempt to use the Bible as a guideline for contemporary family values. This essay is clear and easily applicable to contemporary debate; however, it is very unfortunate that there are no references whatsoever to the fast-growing corpus of literature on the family in antiquity, something that would have situated the contribution within a very productive, ongoing debate.

In the ninth chapter, "Fleshing Out the Text: Re-reading Circumcision," Pyper explores the connections in contemporary debate between circumcision and the idea that violence might be intrinsic in biblical language. He does this, in part, by juxtaposing a warning Gershom Scholem is said to have uttered against secularizing Hebrew language by using it in Israel because of its potential violent power (cited in a letter by Derrida) with the fact that circumcision is performed almost universally in the United States, in a desacralized, deritualized context, a practice that is sharply criticized by certain groups. This is followed by a discussion of various contributions in the discussion of biblical tropes in contemporary discussions on violence.

Chapter 10, "What the Bible Can Do to a Child: The Metrical Psalms and *The Gammage Cup*" (not previously published), returns to the question of the introduction: Is the Bible suitable for children? The fact is that in Western Protestant culture the Bible is (or perhaps *was*) read by children. Indeed, going back some decades, the Bible was often used in teaching reading. In this piece Pyper recounts some of his own significant early encounters with literature and reflects on how these have shaped the way he reads the Bible. His recollections of reading the metrical psalms of the Scottish Psalter and, particularly, *The Gammage Cup* are enjoyable and offer valuable perspectives on the nature of reading and interpreting biblical texts that I think many readers can recognize in their own experience.

The final chapter, "The Bible as Wolf: Tracking a Carrollian Metaphor" (not previously published), is a tribute to Robert P. Carroll, the author's mentor. In this essay Pyper uses Carroll's book *Wolf in the Sheepfold* as a point of departure for an exploration of the ambivalent nature of the wolf as symbol. The piece takes up again some of the ideas from chapter 2 on wildness and domestication and on the nature of the symbiotic relationship between hunter and prey, applying this to the text and the reader. The book concludes with a bibliography and indices of scriptural references and authors.

One of the underlying features of this collection is that the author seems to presuppose the idea that human nature remains basically unchanged and does not seem to take into account cultural differences in time and place that might explain human behavior, reactions, values, and judgments. In one way or another, all characters and issues in the texts are understood in modern West-European terms, so to say. This is not necessarily wrong, and Pyper makes it plain that he is doing his reading within a Western matrix. It does make me wonder once in a while, however, whether or not this tendency might undermine some of the arguments. In some cases, contingent historical information or historical literary comparisons might have been useful to explain certain seeming incongruities. At least there could have been more room to *wonder* whether or not our problems with a text might not have to do with the gap between the world that the text came out of and our world as readers today. For example, there is nothing in the book of Job about him having trouble with the blessing of restoration and long life at the end. The text does not tell us this. Do we know that we understand the idea of the double blessing in the same way as ancient readers did? or as those who wrote the book of Job? Maybe we cannot know the answer to this, but these musings would have been good to include. Similarly, in the discussions on circumcision, I miss some clearer distinctions between circumcision as a historical practice (and information that might be available for the reconstruction of this phenomenon both in the past and in other cultures), and circumcision in a more abstract treatment by modern and postmodern thinkers such as Freud and Kristeva. A final example is from the discussion of the metaphor of mother in Lamentations (ch. 7). Here there is a discussion of the Levitical provisions on eating that is very exciting but that would have been greatly strengthened, in my view, by a clearer distinction between a reading of these within the context of biblical and ancient Near Eastern law and a contemporary theoretical discussion of the body and taboo, especially when the purpose of the essay is to understand the *writer* of Lamentations.

As a whole, the collection contains much valuable material, and I sympathize in many ways with Pyper's observation of the nature of the Bible as wild, potentially dangerous, unsuitable, and so forth. My last remark, however, has to do with the moralizing tone of the book. Pyper might not be so different from those groups of Bible users from whom he seems to want to distance himself, those who have domesticated the Bible and made it into cuddly wolf. There is a *right* and *good* way to be a reader, according to Pyper, though it might not be what the theologians or politicians want. It is to this purportedly good cause that Pyper rallies. Paradoxically, Hugh Pyper ends up making a case for the Bible as *suitable*. Its unsuitability is its suitability. It is suitable if read rightly, if used for the *good* reading, a reading that leaves the reader burned, wounded, scandalized, thus providing the opportunity for an "encounter with life."

The Bible and Empire: Postcolonial Explorations, by R. S. Sugirtharajah. New York: Cambridge University Press, 2005. Pp. vi + 247. Paper. $27.99. ISBN 0521531918.

Jason T. Larson, Syracuse University, Syracuse, New York

Professor R. S. Sugirtharajah, well-known for his stimulating work in postcolonial "Third-World" biblical hermeneutics through his *Postcolonial Reconfigurations* (2003), *The Bible and the Third World* (2001), and the collection *Voices from the Margin: Interpreting the Bible in the Third World* (1995), among other works, now presents a provocative and engaging collection of essays describing the use, abuse, and (dis)function of the Christian Bible in the context of the nineteenth-century British Empire. *The Bible and Empire* primarily seeks to point out what happens to the Bible when it is imposed on "natives" or offered to them for their ostensible benefit (1). Sugirtharajah is equally interested in the effects of this imposition on the colonized and in the colonizers' defense and justification of imposing the Bible on their colonial subjects. In a word, Sugirtharajah attempts to lay out how the Bible gets used by both the colonizers and the colonized. However, Sugirtharajah recognizes that this topic, by itself, is an enormous one, and he restricts himself to one century (the nineteenth) in the history of one colonial empire (the British), and, for the most part, to one geographical area (India), although there are important discussions within the African context as well.

In this, Sugirtharajah is remarkably successful. Even in places where he could conceivably be tempted to launch tangential discussions, Sugirtharajah sticks to the limits of the British Empire, to the English Bible (specifically, to the King James Version as the colonial Ur-text), and to how contemporary postcolonial theory can be a useful entrée into the general subject. Indeed, Sugirtharajah's postcolonialism is the guiding force behind each of the five chapters in the book. He defines postcolonialism as an "interventionist instrument that refuses to take the dominant reading as an uncomplicated representation of the past and introduces an alternate reading" in order to permit silenced and marginalized voices to speak out (3), which will be recognizable to those familiar with Sugirtharajah's other work. This operates on two levels in *The Bible and Empire*: on the one hand, Sugirtharajah reveals that many nineteenth-century interpreters of the Bible were already creating alternative readings against a dominant one. On the other hand, he presents these readings in today's postmodern context as models for new postcolonial work in biblical interpretation that can inspire the critical work of academic scholars as much as the poetic and prophetic work of contemporary postmodern ecclesiastics and "emergent" spiritual visionaries.

There are five essays in the book, with an average length of about fifty pages apiece, with an introduction and an afterword bookending the collection. In chapter 1 ("Textually Conjoined Twins: Rammohun Roy and Thomas Jefferson and Their Bibles"), Sugirtharajah examines how the Bible was appropriated to justify moral and ethical corrections in colonial India and in the newly independent United States. Sugirtharajah employs two early nineteenth-century distillations of the four Gospels into specifically ethical codes of conduct to illustrate this point. Raja Rammohun Roy's *Precepts of Jesus: The Guide to Peace and Happiness: Extracted from the Books of the New Testament, Ascribed to the Four Evangelists* (1820) and President Thomas Jefferson's *Life and Morals of Jesus* (1820) were both written as counternarratives to the dominant readings of the Gospel texts pronounced by the established clergy. In particular, both men rejected religious dogmatics as being one of the most divisive elements in already fractured societies and argued that religious ethics, as being essentially the same in every culture regardless of authoritative texts, could usefully be employed as social and political unifiers. Both men sought to accomplish this by simultaneously appealing to the Bible as their authority even while they sliced and diced it apart to reveal what the real Jesus said as opposed to what the institutional church wanted him to say, which according to Jefferson was "as easily distinguishable as diamonds in a dunghill" (14). For the Raja, his *Precepts* was part of his larger program to unite Hindus, Christians, Jains, Buddhists, and Muslims under one ethical imperative. By showing the consistency in Jesus' ethics and eliminating all elements of superstition and polytheism that he found present in the message of Baptist missionaries, the Raja sought to place Scripture on a par with the Qur'an and especially with the Vedas. Similarly, Jefferson initially examined Jesus' ethical teachings against the teachings of the Roman Stoics and ultimately came to the conclusion that the moral teachings of the Gospels, once stripped of two millennia of ecclesiastical accretions that encrusted the pure ethical words of Jesus, were superior to the classical philosophers. He hoped that Jesus' ethics as he understood and presented them would become a Christianity that would be widely practiced in the United States, not as a "religion" per se but as an ethical life of moral love and brotherhood that would promote unity even in diversity. The point here, for Sugirtharajah, is that both men in their contexts operated under the intellectual mood of the time, which sought to classify, codify, and investigate everything in order to somehow gain a bit more control over the subject. The Bible was used by both the Raja and the President to form a vision of society that suited their own governing purposes, which would be an alternative version to the official church-sanctioned one. However, as Sugirtharajah points out, this alternative was still an elitist vision, one that denied the possibility of India to exist independently of Britain, in the case of Roy, and that denied the ability of Native Americans and Black Americans to live as full members of society, in the case of Jefferson. Sugirtharajah closes this chapter by offering his reflections on how these two leaders in two vastly different geographic, cultural, and colonial environments could have possibly been motivated to answer their questions of policy by undertaking nearly identical projects.

Chapter 2, "Salvos from the Victorian Pulpit: Conscription of Texts by Victorian Preachers during the Indian Rebellion of 1857," pursues the issue of how the Bible and Christian sermons were used to prop up British *imperium* during the Indian Revolt of 1857. The author surveys the backgrounds and causes of the insurrection, which united both Hindus and Muslims against the common enemy of the British East India Company, and describes the general "cultural arrogance" of the British intelligentsia and ecclesiastics toward Indian culture. The event was fairly localized, and Sugirtharajah subtly notes that the revolt and the British public response to it has more connections to contemporary terrorism and the so-called "war on terror" than an actual full-scale war. It is also interesting to note, although Sugirtharajah does not, that the cultural processes of integration and assimilation that were introduced in the previous generation were now held in deep suspicion and even resentment bear striking similarity to Hellenist-Jewish cultural interaction in the second-century B.C.E. and to first-century Roman political-economic policy in Palestine in the first century C.E. Following this survey, Sugirtharajah turns his attention to over a hundred of Britain's "Day of Humiliation" sermons preached and published in response to the revolt. The vast majority of the sermons employ prooftexts from the Old Testament to justify Britain's self-perception of itself as God's chosen people, commissioned to wage war against God's heathen adversaries. Attentive readers will find numerous parallels to contemporary political and evangelical war rhetoric here, and in several instances Sugirtharajah makes these parallels explicit.

Sugirtharajah introduces the third chapter, "Thorns in the Crown: The Subversive and Complicit Hermeneutics of John Colenso of Natal and James Long of Bengal," as the fulfillment of a promise he made in his *The Bible and the Third World* (98). These men, both Anglican missionaries, made extensive use of Scripture to critique colonial policies and "the predatory nature of imperialism" (144), while supporting the causes of the indigenous populations of their respective mission fields, even while they defended Britain's ostensible program of bringing "civilization" to these other lands. The chapter has much to recommend it and, like the previous chapter, offers numerous parallels to contemporary mission work, national politics, and especially hermeneutical and exegetical academic work on the Bible itself. Colenso adhered to the then-emerging standards of historical-critical exegesis to draw parallels between biblical Jews and contemporary Zulus; Long pursued the text as an oriental work that, through narrative, poetic, and metaphoric analysis could be shown to be relevant to Bengalis as much as to Englishmen. Despite their different hermeneutical approaches, both missionaries worked within what would today be called a postmodern and postcolonial rubric that challenged Britain's racism and cultural bigotry and offered an alternative version of Christianity that left no room for imperial prejudices. Scholars and ministerial leaders looking for examples of subaltern readings of religious texts to engage the status quo in alternative presentations of textual interpretations for contemporary needs, demands, and issues will find this chapter especially rich.

The fourth chapter, "Texts and Testament: The Hebrew Scriptures in Colonial Context," intends to fill a void in Old Testament interpretive studies by focusing on how the Hebrew Bible functioned in Asia and Africa for orientalists, Christian missionaries, and even indigenous intellectuals in Hindu and African traditions. The postcolonial emphasis here is how the colonized turned repeatedly to the Old Testament to "challenge their cultural and religious defamation" by the colonizing powers and "to strengthen indigenous religious customs and traditions and to redefine their identity" in confrontation with the colonizers (6). It is a fascinating study of how many such indigenous interpreters of what became an imperial Bible remained faithful to their own indigenous customs even while professing and maintaining Christian identity through emphasizing the Jewish scriptures. Sugirtharajah concludes this chapter with his own all-too-brief survey of what the Old Testament says about empires and presents these thoughts in the context of the neo-imperialism of the post-9/11 world. While many readers will undoubtedly take issue with many of the sweeping generalizations made here and voice some nitpicking concerns over some of the details, it nevertheless should serve as a useful springboard for new studies and discussions about the Old Testament (and the New Testament as well) as a by-product of empire, a position with which I can scarcely disagree.

The fifth and final chapter is entitled "Imperial Fictions and Biblical Narratives: Entertainment and Exegesis in Colonial Novels." Here Sugirtharajah presents a postcolonial reading of Sydney Owenson's *The Missionary* (1811) and Akiki K. Nyabongo's *Africa Answers Back* (1936). In the former novel, a love story that describes the struggle of a Spanish Jesuit's ultimately unsuccessful attempts to convert Luxima, the Brahminic idol of his affection, to Christianity, biblical allusions are assumed, and much of the central character's development mirrors the biblical and traditional portraits of Saint Paul (this reader is particularly reminded of the apocryphal *Paul and Thecla* from Sugirtharajah's descriptions of *The Missionary*). The novel is a subversive description of the failure of the missionary's appeal to the Bible as the central authority of his life, not only to deliver the woman he loves into salvation, but even more its failure to deliver her into his own embrace. In Nyabongo's novel, however, the Bible assumes a much more central role. Here the protagonist is educated in the best education the West can offer in Buganda at the turn of the nineteenth century and receives a thoroughly biblical indoctrination to Western civilization. Like the former novel, *Africa Answers Back* describes the ultimate failure of the African mission and describes the story of how the protagonist uses his missionary education to champion his own people and struggle to emancipate from their colonial overlords.

The Bible and Empire concludes with an "afterword" that this reviewer found wanting. Given the general subject, Sugirtharajah's approving use of Edward Said's stated purpose of the intellectual to present alternative readings to counter official ones (8) and his introduction of the "afterword" with Donald Rumsfeld's infamous "We don't do empire" statement (222), I had expected some remarks on contemporary Anglo-American political rhetoric and official appropriation of Scripture to justify the neo-conservative imperial enterprise. Instead, Sugirtharajah surveys a number of recent books on "the new imperium" that offer little more than "restatements of a traditional, conservative, and highly romantic history of empire" (225). Sugirtharajah then comments on a number of new versions *of* the Bible and new books *about* the Bible. Here Sugirtharajah simply raises the rather Marxist specter of the materiality of "the book" and especially "questions about the social, class and economic functions of its production" in all these new versions, editions, and translations. In other words, the old colonial issues that surrounded the Bible as "the Englishman's book" are apparently no less present today than they were 150 years ago. Finally, the Bible remains "an establishment" book, despite all the various permutations of it (such as *The Green Bible*, the *Gay and Lesbian Bible,* and numerous "street Bibles"), by virtue of its appeal as the "final authority" to so many diverse groups.

These comments notwithstanding, *The Bible and Empire* is a work that should find a place on the shelves of academics, seminary students, church officials, theologians, and ministerial leaders. The prose is lively and eminently readable, and the various articles draw too many thought-provoking parallels to contemporary political and religious rhetoric to enumerate here. I trust that Dr. Sugirtharajah will continue this line of work and blaze new postcolonial or, perhaps better, "postimperial" trailways in biblical hermeneutics.

The Language of Symbolism: Biblical Theology, Semantics, and Exegesis, by Pierre Grelot. Translated by Christopher R. Smith. Peabody, Mass.: Hendrickson, 2006. Pp. vii + 238. Paper. $19.95. ISBN 1565639898.

Craig R. Koester, Luther Seminary, St. Paul, Minnesota

Underlying this study of symbolic language is the question, "How can we speak of God?" Pierre Grelot understands that God is not an abstract concept but a living presence, a being with whom people have a relationship. Speaking of this relationship is challenging because no one has a direct perception of God. Moreover, human language is rooted in sensory experience, which means that it cannot actually define God but must evoke the presence of One who cannot be seen. Symbolic language is the way that the Bible does this. According to Grelot, symbols do not constitute a particular literary genre. Rather, they are a means of evoking a sense of the divine presence while providing vehicles for reflecting on the divine reality that faith senses by intuition. The body of this book considers ways in which authors in both Testaments construct symbols that correspond to their faith experience. Discussion is organized into four categories.

Analogical symbols constitute the first category. These symbols refer to God in ways that are analogous to human beings. Theologically, it is possible to speak of God in the image of humanity because human beings are created in the image of God (Gen 1:27). For example, God is said to have a face, hands, and feelings much as human beings have. Analogical symbols are also used for Jesus—not for aspects of his earthly life that are accessible to historical inquiry but for the mysterious aspects of his person. For example, Christ is said to appear before the face of God in the heavenly sanctuary, an image that is not a physical description but a way of suggesting something about his present condition and activity in glory (Heb 9:34). Other symbols come from family relationships, such as depicting God's relationship with people as one of marriage or calling God "Father" and Jesus his "Son." Such images are not simply transferred from the human to the divine sphere but are transformed, so that they communicate intimacy rather than physical relationship. Similarly, God can be depicted as king and warrior, yet a crucial element of transcendence remains, since the Scriptures recognize that God's designs cannot be equated with the political aspirations of his people.

Mythical symbols are the second category. These pertain to two domains that are radically inaccessible to human experience: the world of God and the world of evil. The world of God pertains to goodness, joy, and life, whereas evil relates to illness, death, and moral failure. Mythical symbols also have to do with the beginning and ending of things, since it is in between these two poles that present experience unfolds. To answer questions such as Where is God? and How does God reveal himself? writers must use symbolic language. Because God is radically inaccessible, people speak of God being "up above" or "in heaven" in order to underscore his transcendence. They also picture heavenly messengers who help to communicate with people on earth.

Speaking of evil is similarly challenging, because so much about it is obscure. If God is from above, then evil is from below, from a realm that is as inaccessible as the realm of God, but for opposite reasons. If one can speak of divine messengers from the realm of goodness, it is natural to speak of evil spirits that bring suffering, illness, and death. The evil forces within human beings can also be personified as powers of sin, flesh, and death, using symbolic language. Some of the biblical portrayals of the conflict between good and evil echo myths from surrounding cultures, as God is said to have battled the monsters of chaos at creation (Isa 51:9–10), and heavenly powers are depicted defeating Satan the Dragon (Rev 12:1–17). Portrayals of the day of judgment also make use of mythic symbols, pointing to the future consummation of God's action in the present.

A third category consists of the figurative symbols that disclose the meanings within human history, showing how people and events contribute to the realization of God's designs. The narratives in the Bible are interpretations of history that are designed to show the dynamics of Israel's distinctive relationship with God. The stories of Israel's ancestors illustrate the faith to which people must hold. Accounts of successes and failures are seen in light of the people's faith and faithlessness and God's promises and judgments. New Testament reflections on Jesus' identity reinterpret earlier texts and traditions. Titles such as Son of David, Messiah, and Son of God, for example, are ways of affirming his unique relationship to God. Passages that speak of events in Jesus' life fulfilling the Scriptures show how Jesus fits into the larger story of Israel, allowing passages from older texts to disclose new dimensions of meaning. The church is also given a meaningful place in the broader story of Israel as Christian communities are considered to belong to the people of God and to share in the new covenant.

The fourth category is comprised of relational symbols. In these cases, aspects of people's experience in the world are transposed onto the plane of relationships with God. People speak of relating to God by using analogies from their relationships with people. Grelot recognizes that such analogies can obscure as much as they reveal and that the Scriptures must move beyond the limits of these relationships in order to suggest the indescribable. In the First Testament, those who believe in the divine revelation are able to respond to God's initiative and enter into a conscious relationship with him. Some of the relational language used in the First Testament includes that of searching and waiting for God, of seeing God and being seen by God, thirsting, loving, and being "with" God.

Jesus came within this framework, disclosing new dimensions of what this means for Christian faith. Jesus directs others to seek God's kingdom and righteousness, although God—like a woman searching for a lost coin—has already begun the process of seeking for them. Seeing is a verb that has different dimensions of meaning, and it can include the visions seen by Jesus and by others. In a vision, the essential thing is not sensory perception but the interior communication that results from it. Being "with" God is part of the First Testament's witness, but in the New Testament the relationship acquires a new dimension of meaning through the mediation of Christ.

The final chapter explores the meaning of Scripture in terms of literal exegesis and symbolic exegesis. For Grelot, the primary principle of biblical interpretation, from the perspective of Christian faith, is the contemplation of Christ Jesus in the totality of his mystery (201). In this process he is guided by the medieval theologians who discerned multiple meanings in Scripture. The Fatherhood of God took on new meaning when Jesus called God "Abba." The significance of social analogies is disclosed when Jesus' divine sonship is understood in light of his crucifixion and resurrection. The figurative dimensions of the First Testament writings, including the prophetic promises, are reread in light of the story of Jesus and his resurrection.

In this study Grelot has rightly identified the problem inherent in all theological discourse: speaking of the unseen God in human language. He articulates the issue well and generally relates the parts of his book to this central question. Treating symbols as elements that suggest and evoke rather than defining diving reality is also helpful. Some of Grelot's categories are more helpful than others. The section on analogical symbols rightly points out how many elements in human speech about God reflect social realities, but the section on figurative symbols, which explores issues of revelation in history, seems less germane to the subject. Each chapter of the book gives many examples from various parts of Scripture to illustrate a given category, but the examples do not always yield a clear sense of progression or argument.

A major issue is whether Grelot's use of the category of "symbolism" has become too broad to be useful. He seems to refer to any form of language that makes use of analogy as symbolism. Grelot is clear in articulating the way that Christian faith and the tradition of the church inform his reading of Scripture, and this provides a basic insight into his perspective. Readers who understand the medieval church's fourfold interpretation of Scripture—literal, tropological, allegorical, and anagogical—will find it easier to grasp what Grelot means by symbolism and theological interpretation than readers who are not familiar with the categories of spiritual exegesis. Readers working with recent scholarship on symbols and metaphors may find points worth pondering in this book, but many will want a more focused use of the category of symbolism.

Studies in Bible and Feminist Criticism, by Tikva Frymer-Kensky. JPS Scholar of Distinction Series. Philadelphia: Jewish Publication Society, 2006. Pp. xxvi + 436. Hardcover. $40.00. ISBN 0827607989.

Jason R. Tatlock, Morgan State University, Baltimore, Maryland

Following the author's endearing reflections upon her life and academic pursuits in a preliminary chapter, "Introduction: A Retrospective," the anthology officially begins with a section entitled "Comparative Culture I: Ancient Near Eastern Religions," which primarily focuses upon Mesopotamian and biblical accounts of the creation of the world and the subsequent deluge that threatened to eradicate humanity. Frymer-Kensky's interaction with such mythic literature characterizes a key facet of her early publications following the completion of her doctoral studies at Yale. Of particular importance in the first section, as well as later in the book (ch. 23), are the discussions that, as Frymer-Kensky's indicates, "represent my lifelong interest in biblical metaphysics and especially in Genesis 1–11, which has fascinated me ever since I first began to learn it seriously" (xv). The *Atrahasis* myth, for which a translation and an overview are provided in chapter 1 ("*Atrahasis*: An Introduction") is significant for her understanding of Gen 1–11, for the epic situates the Mesopotamian flood within a wider context, that of the creation of humanity, the problem of overpopulation, the attempted solutions to this problem, and the final resolution of the issue. The biblical account has a similar "Creation-Problem-Flood-Solution" (64) structure, but the dilemma faced by the Israelite God is not one of the earth's overpopulation; rather, God brings about a flood in order to purge the earth of the impurity brought about by iniquity, especially the contamination resulting from shedding innocent blood. Following the purification of the earth, capital punishment is inaugurated to counter the polluting effects of murder. These concepts are treated in chapters 3 and 4: "Israel and the Ancient Near East: New Perspectives on the Flood" and "The *Atrahasis* Epic and Its Significance for Our Understanding of Genesis 1–9." Regrettably, the wording is very similar between the two chapters, making the inclusion of both redundant. The reader would be advised to consult chapter 3, as it seeks to move the discussion beyond the material presented in chapter 4 (37–38). The other chapters, "The Planting of Man: A Study in Biblical Imagery," "Goddesses: Biblical Echoes," and "Lolita-Inanna," round out the first section by dealing with matters that are also important for treatments found later in the book, such as the biblical portrayal of Israel's relationship with God, the role of women and goddesses in the ancient Near East, and the significance of Inanna in Sumerian literature.

Section 2, "Comparative Culture II: Judaism and Christianity," begins in chapter 7, "The Image: Religious Anthropology in Judaism and Christianity," with a survey of Jewish and Christian perspectives on the ways in which humanity reflects the divine image, both physically and immaterially, concluding that the belief in this reflection should compel humans to respect the sanctity of life in all people, even if they do not believe in such a view. Christianity is again encountered in chapter 9, "Jesus and the Law," where Frymer-Kensky pursues an understanding of the nature of Jesus' interaction with the Torah. She deduces that, although Jesus did not teach the abolishment of the entire Torah, his emphasis upon the need to be perfect beyond what the Torah legislates left little practical advice on living out specific laws. This, coupled with the church's later desire to remove obstacles to Gentile conversion, resulted in the dismissal of the law in Christianity.

In chapter 8, "Biblical Voices on Chosenness," Frymer-Kensky dredges the biblical texts to examine an issue that the writers never truly resolve: Israel's exclusivity as the chosen people appears to be in contrast to God's universal mandate. A discussion of the inclusion of non-Israelites into a divine relationship is also found in chapter 10, "Covenant: A Jewish Biblical Perspective." In this chapter the author surveys the covenants of the Hebrew Bible to glean data for constructing a modern theology, concluding that the Abrahamic covenant can be a model for the contemporary world, a world in which we must live in peace with each other, not in war and turmoil, while acknowledging that God has children of diverse nationalities—an Abrahamic covenant for all peoples, so to speak. The general tenor of this piece corresponds well to Frymer-Kensky's treatment of biblical ecology presented later in the volume.

While the third section, "Feminist Perspectives I: Gender and the Bible," might formally begin the anthology's treatment of women's studies, the issues raised therein are not limited to this section and to section 4, "Feminist Perspectives II: Gender and the Law," for Frymer-Kensky's focus on bringing women's issues to the fore is evident at the beginning of the anthology and continues until its conclusion. Nevertheless, section 3 is significant in its own right, given its emphasis on introducing the reader to the field of women's studies and its attempts to outline the methodologies of feminist literary criticism in chapter 11, "The Bible and Women's Studies." Certain of these critical techniques are then illustrated in several of the other chapters included in the anthology. Yet prior to surveying these additional chapters, chapter 11 merits additional comment, especially in reference to its beginning, at which point Frymer-Kensky examines the primary justification for the new readings that scholars in women's studies have been offering. That is, feminist criticism is one of several approaches to literature that arose out of the transition from a modern to a postmodern world. According to this newer worldview, texts are open to multiple interpretations that are relative to the presuppositions of the individual readers. Hence, what was once considered objective in biblical studies came to be understood as readings essentially derived from a Protestant male perspective. Wrestling the texts away from such myopic interpretations has opened the door for marginalized people, such as women and minorities, to gain new insights from the texts. It is clear that reader-response criticism has greatly influenced Frymer-Kensky's appreciation of the exchange between text and reader, but she does not explicitly reference the impact it has had upon her work. The curious reader would benefit from exploring this school of thought further (see the slightly dated but relevant discussion by The Bible and Culture Collective in *The Postmodern Bible* [New Haven: Yale University Press, 1995]; for a general introduction to multiple forms of literary criticism, consult Bressler's *Literary Criticism: An Introduction to Theory and Practice* (4th ed.; Upper Saddle River, N.J.: Prentice Hall, 2007).

As for the techniques of women's studies that are applied in both the feminist sections of the anthology, chapter 12, "The Ideology of Gender in the Bible and the Ancient Near East," provides a biblical basis for the elevation of women to equal status with men given the ancient Israelite understanding of gender unity. That is, according to the Hebrew Bible, there is no innate distinction between male and female beyond physical characteristics, a view that is absent in Mesopotamian, Greek, later Jewish, and Western thought. Chapter 14, "Reading Rahab," embodies the technique of emphasizing the significance of female characters and concludes that one can read Rahab in either a positive (e.g., as a model proselyte and symbol of Israel) or a negative fashion (e.g., as a foreigner who will lead to the eventual apostasy of Israel). Frymer-Kensky, like the later Jewish and Christian writers, accentuates Rahab's positive characteristics. Chapter 15, "Patriarchal Family Relationships and Near Eastern Law," illustrates the principle of reconstructing the context in which women (and men) lived by examining the legal relationships represented by the patriarchal narratives of Genesis in light of cuneiform legal documents. Chapter 16, "Law and Philosophy: The Case of Sex in the Bible," continues the discussion of the laws that governed women's lives, particularly in the area of intercourse. Here Frymer-Kensky uses biblical law in order to evaluate the Israelite philosophy of sex. She finds that the Israelites recognized the disruptive power of sexuality if given free reign and sought to limit sexual activity to appropriate relationships with the primary purpose of enforcing the boundaries between familial units.

Chapter 13, "Sanctifying Torah," discusses the issue of "feminist consciousness" (195), which is the moment when women come to realize that their faith traditions have inadequately addressed their experiences. For Jewish women, Frymer-Kensky argues, the Torah should not be abandoned due to its inadequacies but engaged in a critical fashion to point out its oppressive nature while embracing its positive aspects. Frymer-Kensky's foray into Exodus results in the message that contemporary women must embody the strength of early Israelite women and no longer be silenced by oppressive behaviors that are not of divine origin. In this way, women can reclaim the Torah. But the reclamation of the Bible for female readers does not go far enough in repairing the disjunction created by patriarchal misappropriations of the divine message in the Jewish tradition. Women must make their voices heard in order to reclaim (or revise) postbiblical halakah as well. This is the focus of chapters 17 and 18, "Halakhah, Law and Feminism" and "The Feminist Challenge to Halakhah." These chapters could have been placed in the final section of the anthology, given their emphasis on engendering change in modern Judaism, but their inclusion in a feminist section highlights Frymer-Kensky's efforts to fight for female justice within her faith tradition rather than to allow herself to be alienated from it. While both chapters share the central theme that halakah must be changed to meet the needs of contemporary Jews, especially those of women, who have been marginalized by traditional halakah, chapter 17 is a more limited treatment, essentially a shorter version of what follows. Of the two, chapter 18 is a much more dramatic piece. It is a protest against Judaism's exclusion and oppression of women and a call to action for women to be the vehicles of change. One can sense the energy in the piece, and, for those of us not in attendance, one can only image the passion with which Frymer-Kensky must have delivered the paper in 1994 as part of The Gruss Lectures sponsored by The Harvard Law School Program in Jewish Studies (www. law.harvard.edu/programs/Gruss). This is one of the most compelling chapters in the collection.

The fifth section, "Theologies I: Biblical Theology," appropriately begins with a chapter entitled "Revelation Revealed: The Doubt of Torah," for it continues in the vein of the preceding feminist sections and returns to Moses at Sinai, to the scene where he misrepresents the divine message and excludes women from the Israelite congregation. The piece essentially examines the relationship between divine revelation and prophetic intermediacy, concluding that the biblical authors themselves were suspicious of messages claimed to have originated from God. Not only this, but the writers also convey the notion that God could provide deceptive and harmful revelations. The chapter ends with the comment that it was a later development in Judaism that resulted in the "absolute acceptance" of the written text (294). In light of Frymer-Kensky's other treatments on authority, one cannot help but surmise that there is an implicit critique of postbiblical writings that have been taken as authoritative in Judaism but that may not accurately represent divine intention. Her discussion of Moses continues in chapter 20, "Moses and the Cults: The Question of Religious Leadership," by explaining that the Israelites of the exodus generation were well on their way to becoming fixated upon Moses in the same way that modern cult members are attached to a central religious leader such as Jim Jones. The Israelites were spared such an existence because Moses' role as divine intermediary was displaced by the development of additional religious institutions, such as the law, the tabernacle, and the priesthood.

Concerning the rest of section five, chapters 21 and 23, "The Theology of Catastrophe: A Question of Historical Justice" and "Pollution, Purification, and Purgation in Biblical Israel," concentrate upon the way in which the effects of sin eventually reach a point of no return that results in imminent and indiscriminate catastrophic judgment. Chapters 22 and 24, "The End of the World and the Limits of Biblical Ecology" and "Ecology in a Biblical Perspective," investigate the biblical understanding of humanity's relationship to the earth, and though the chapters are similar in focus and wording, each has its own agenda. Chapter 22 primarily examines the biblical roots of apocalypticism, and 24 is concerned with our need to preserve the earth by being more responsible in how we treat it and our fellow human beings.

Whereas the start of the fifth section implicitly criticizes postbiblical traditions, the beginning of the sixth, "Theologies II: Constructive Theology," explicitly does so. Chapter 25, "The Emergence of Jewish Biblical Theologies," is suspicious of authoritative readings of the biblical texts, be they from the rabbis or modern academics, that have not allowed diversity in interpretation, arguing that Jewish theology must be grounded in the Bible, not secondary authoritative readings that have superseded it. This chapter also recognizes that the Bible itself is filled with competing theological perspectives. Thus, this chapter lays the foundation for constructing contemporary theologies that make the Bible relevant for today. A sampling of Frymer-Kensky's contributions to current Jewish theology is provided in the chapters that close out this section and the entire anthology. Chapter 26, "Constructing a Theology of Healing," provides practical advice on how those who suffer might become reintegrated into their faith communities. Chapter 27, "On Feminine God-Talk," recognizes that although God is not male, *he* is expressed in grammatically masculine ways. Such male-oriented imagery tends to alienate women, and Frymer-Kensky seeks to assist in connecting women to God through examining the possibility of using feminine, gender-neutral, or gender-random language to refer to God. Chapter 28, "Woman Jews," traces the history of women in Judaism from the rabbinic era, in which women were limited to the private sphere of Jewish life, to the late twentieth century, at which point women such as Frymer-Kensky have emerged to participate more fully in the public realm that was once denied them. The poetry presented in chapters 29 and 30, "Like a Birthing Woman" and "Shaddai," represents one of the ways in which the author embodies this transition in Judaism, that is, by contributing to Jewish liturgy.

Studies in Bible and Feminist Criticism illustrates the major themes that characterize Tikva Frymer-Kensky's distinguished career, and it complements her other published books, especially *In the Wake of the Goddesses: Women, Culture, and the Biblical Transformation of Pagan Myth* (New York: Macmillan, 1992). Several of the discussions in the current work grew out of the research connected to this earlier study, although *Studies in Bible and Feminist Criticism* certainly moves well beyond her work on goddesses in ancient Near Eastern culture. There are so many diverse issues raised in this anthology that individual readers will be intrigued and inspired by a myriad of insights. Frymer-Kensky's contributions cover a vast spectrum of disciplines from Sumerology through biblical studies and rabbinics to contemporary Jewish philosophy. It is her attempts to reform Judaism from within and her efforts to reclaim the Bible for women that will be among her most enduring contributions. The reader of this anthology will also notice that she was not only concerned about changing the lives of women and her fellow Jews, but she fervently sought to promote respect for all human life and wished to foster a more peaceful coexistence among all of God's creations.

Criticisms of the book will revolve around the specific content contained in any of the thirty chapters, but these will vary according to the individual readers who engage Frymer-Kensky's discussions. My own disagreements with particular conclusions need not detain us at this point.[1] More important for this review, however, are a few comments regarding some stylistic and methodological difficulties. First, there are very few infelicities in the four-hundred-plus pages, such as the change from Micaiahu to Micaiah (293) and Zaphaniah to Zephaniah (323), or the incorrect date for chapter 4, which was published in 1977, not 2004, but these are mainly minor and do not detract from the overall presentation. Yet there is one that does present some confusion to the reader. At the bottom of page 287 the heading of "Pentateuch" is provided and then followed by the statement: "The chaotic impression of this chapter is purposeful." The reader is unsure as to which chapter from the Pentateuch is under discussion here, though it is Exod 19. This difficulty is not encountered in the earlier publication of the chapter in *Textual Reasonings: Jewish Philosophy and Text Study at the End of the Twentieth*

---

1. Space does not allow for an extensive treatment of Frymer-Kensky's perspective on pollution. Overall, her analysis is sound and compelling, but in one area she does not take her argument to its logical conclusion. Throughout Frymer-Kensky repeats the notion that there are no rites in the Israelite tradition for the purification of the land, but she also notes that the blood of the murderer is the only element that can expiate the impurity that results from the contamination of innocent blood (60–64, 309, 342, 357, 360). Despite going this far, Frymer-Kensky fails to recognize that executing the murderer is itself a ritual of purification for the land, what should rightly be called a human sacrifice (see my "How in Ancient Times They Sacrificed People: Human Immolation in the Eastern Mediterranean Basin with Special Emphasis on Ancient Israel and the Near East" [Ph.D. diss., University of Michigan, 2006], esp. 175–81).

Century (Grand Rapids: Eerdmans, 2003), inasmuch as the heading "Exodus 19" is provided instead.

Second, Frymer-Kensky's presentations in this anthology suffer from two methodological complications: there exists a tendency to make sweeping generalizations and to leave several statements unsubstantiated. For example, she notes, "erotic attraction is also absent from the biblical tales of women's persuasion.... it [sex] is never a woman's strategy in order to gain power, influence, or information; never a woman's weapon by which she seeks to disarm or weaken men" (187–88). While this might be true of the Hebrew Bible in general, it is not absolutely the case. Perhaps this writer is reading too much into the narrative, but it seems rather clear that erotic attraction is very much at play in the story of Samson and Delilah. Samson is portrayed as especially weak when it comes to women, and the chapter in which he meets Delilah even begins with his visit to a prostitute in Gaza (Judg 16). While Samson may have finally given in to Delilah and told her his secret because of her incessant pleading, his eventual demise is brought about when his head is shaven after having fallen asleep on Delilah's lap. This is clearly not a platonic relationship. In fact, the verb (פתה) used when the Philistines initially ask Delilah to entice Samson to find out his secret can have sexual connotations (cf. Exod 22:15). As for the discussions in which Frymer-Kensky leaves statements unsubstantiated, a glaring example is found in her treatment of Phinehas's actions in Num 25. In this story Phinehas kills Zimri and Kozbi after they entered into a tent, or *kubbah*, and he thereby brings an end to the divine wrath afflicting the Israelites. Frymer-Kensky is inclined to accept an interpretation of the passage that understands the slain individuals as having performed some sort of idolatrous (not sexual) act in the tent because there exists pre-Islamic evidence from Arabia for the use of such *kubbah* for divinatory purposes and possibly also for white magic. Regrettably, Frymer-Kensky neither presents this evidence nor points the reader to an appropriate academic treatment of it (292). Other unsupported comments can be found elsewhere in the work (e.g., 115, 161, 167, 216, 290, 296, 309).

In closing, I wish to return to chapter 26, which deserves special attention, given Tikva Frymer-Kensky's recent departure (31 August 2006), after struggling with cancer for several years (http://www-news.uchicago.edu/releases/06/060905.frymer-kensky.shtml). In this chapter she concludes that pain and misery cannot be reduced to a simple theological understanding that suffering is equated to divine punishment. Such a perspective leads the sufferer to self-blame and deeper introversion, which is already a natural response to illness. That is to say, illness tends to alienate us from our friends, our religious communities, our God, and even our bodies. To counter this introversion, we must open ourselves up to community, to a complex deity, and to a complicated cosmos. Frymer-Kensky suggests that new rituals might be helpful in bringing about such openness, especially since normal practices work best when we feel physically normal but are inadequate when we are ill. In the end, however, the good health that we might experience at the immaterial level through our openness may not lead to physical restoration. It is truly regrettable that this proved to be the case in Frymer-Kensky's own life, but we can take consolation in the fact that she continued to work in the midst of her illness, which, as she states, can assist in the healing process:

> What else can help us open ourselves to God, to community, and to cosmos? If we are very, very lucky, we can study Torah. The Talmud states, "If he has a backache, let him study Torah; if he has a toothache, let him study Torah" (BT *Eruvin* 54a). Those of us who are blessed with the gift of Torah can lose ourselves in study no matter how contracted our ego, lose ourselves in the words of a page and the pages of the Word. This study connects us beyond ourselves, into the past, into the minds of others, and to God. For us, Torah is the way to the world. (390)

We are very, very lucky that Frymer-Kensky did study Torah, becoming the first female undergraduate to major in Talmud at the Jewish Theological Seminary (416) and the first woman to join the ranks of the Jewish Publication Society's Scholars of Distinction (x), the latter being the impetus for the creation of *Studies in Bible and Feminist Criticism*. Through this text we connect with Frymer-Kensky as she leads us through her thought-provoking analyses. Having never met her, this reviewer cannot possibly speak about her personality in great detail. Nevertheless, one catches glimpses of her character as it filters through the pages of this volume. In addition to her aforementioned passion, her sense of humor is easily recognized throughout the book, especially in chapter 5. It is no wonder, then, that a classmate of hers, Bruce C. Birch, wrote the *SBL Forum* to state (http://www. sbl- site.org/Article.aspx?ArticleId=587):

> Tikva's death is a terrible loss to biblical and ancient near eastern scholarship, but more importantly the loss of a wonderful human being. We were in graduate school at Yale together in the late 1960s and the many conversations and good times in her company are among my most cherished memories of those years.... She will be missed.

Indeed!

Faithful Interpretation: Reading the Bible in a Postmodern World, by A. K. M. Adam. Minneapolis: Fortress, 2006. Pp. x + 193. Paper. $20.00. ISBN 0800637879.

Joel B. Green, Asbury Theological Seminary, Wilmore, Kentucky

Adam's latest book rests at the confluence of a number of streams, including advances in reader-reception theory, dissatisfaction with historical criticism's claim to provide the singular and definitive meaning of biblical texts, the regnant hermeneutical model's insistence that a text houses its own meaning, and renewed interest in the theological interpretation of the Bible within those communities that turn to it for religious sustenance. To those who fear that the inescapable alternative to "technical biblical interpretation" (a.k.a. historical-critical scholarship) is hermeneutical chaos or barbarism, Adam observes, first, that historical criticism has proven itself unequal to the task of promoting theological readings of Scripture. Second, he avers that, given the misleading presuppositions of the standard biblical hermeneutics characterizing the twentieth century, this failure is only to be expected. Third, the way forward for Adam is marked by admitting that readers, not texts, produce meaning; by making room for a plurality (although not an infinite number of) plausible interpretations of a text; and by recognizing that "the legitimacy of an interpretation is determined by the body of readers evaluating it" (60). Good interpretation is thus known by its ethics rather than by its "cool reason."

Those who have followed Adam's publications elsewhere will find few surprises here, as each of the book's eight chapters has already appeared in print, whether in journals or edited volumes. What is remarkable, though, is the way these chapters participate in a common conversation, demonstrating the lengthy incubation of Adam's focused thinking on these matters. Chapter 1 is programmatic in its hard-hitting criticism of "modern biblical theology," particularly its defining premises, not the least of which are its presumption of discontinuity between the biblical past and the church's present (which overlooks "the fact that when a text has been interpreted every day for over nineteen centuries, there will be important continuity of interpretation" [28]) and its paradoxical aversion to theology. Biblical theology must be rethought from start to finish, according to Adam, substituting ethical criteria ("Can we live by this biblical theology?") for historical criticism as its definitive authority. Chapter 2 carries forward this assault on the supposed historical foundations for biblical theology by countering Ernst Käsemann's argument that historical criticism is required as a prophylactic against christological docetism. Historical inquiry, according to Adam, cannot speak to us about the divinity of Christ, so the antidote to docetism is "a resolutely Chalcedonian Christology" (13). Adam concludes, "One may have intellectual reservations about the value of historical criticism without thereby running the risk of heresy" (55). Chapter 3 comprises a third foray into hermeneutics, with its two-edged argument that readers, not texts, make meaning and that the inherently social and ethical character of interpretation shields against willy-nilly readings of texts. Set against the backdrop of a century or more of hermeneutical theorizing, Adam's claim is breathtaking: "The constraints upon textual interpretation do not derive from the nature of understanding, or of texts, or of language, or of communicative intent, or of truth, or of speech-acts, but always only from the sundry collocations of circumstances within which we formulate interpretations and judgments" (59).

The fourth chapter concerns itself with the supposed anti-Jewish character of the Gospel of Matthew, providing Adam with an effective case study for his emphasis on the readerly generation of meaning (and the responsibility this entails). In the fifth chapter he returns to a more theoretical focus, arguing for a "differential hermeneutics" (which locates meaning in human interaction, with the result that different interpretive outcomes are only to be expected as signs of the pluriform character of the human imagination) over against an "integral hermeneutics" (which assumes for each text a singular, correct meaning). "As parts of the body are not all eyes, feet, hands, or nose, so interpretations of Scripture are not all historically warranted assertions about the original intent of a human (or divine) author, nor is interpretive differentiation any more a result of sin than is corporal differentiation" (99). Chapter 7 exemplifies Adam's "differential hermeneutic" with its examination of the interpretation of the "sign of Jonah" in the sayings of Jesus in the Gospels. Chapter 6, on the other hand, spells out further the ethical focus of the church's interpretive work, emphasizing interpretations that generate forms of Christian discipleship resembling the life of Jesus, whereas chapter 8 engages a similar agenda, this time with reference to human sexuality and hallowed relationships.

For this book, Adam has provided a newly written epilogue, which serves to draw together the various emphases of the preceding chapters by introducing the language of "signifying practice" to describe theological exegesis. Interpretation accordingly points beyond itself to "the end of articulating the understanding of the gospel in a lived expression" (156). Such interpretation would find a home in diverse media (art and drama, for example, as well as texts), concern itself with the pastoral implementation of exegetical work, be open to the whole people of God and not only to its most trained students of the Bible, and account for the multiple influences from the whole of lived experience on our exegetical work.

The significance of Adam's work lies especially in two areas. First, he is unrelenting in his confrontation with "technical biblical interpretation," against which he has assembled a vigorous phalanx of pointed and well-honed questions. The effect is not necessarily to undo the work of historical inquiry in biblical studies but rather to unseat historical study in its role as the only or decisive criterion for legitimating a particular reading of a biblical text. Second, Adam has lent considerable support to an emerging interest in taking seriously the effects of our hermeneutical work, that is, the importance of embodiment and ethical comportment.

As important as these contributions are, I cannot help but wonder where Adam's proposals leave us on any number of issues. Let me mention four. (1) We might appreciate his securing so central a place for the reader and readerly community in biblical interpretation but still wonder what status is to be given biblical texts. What role will Adam allow for philology, grammar, and the bread and butter of discourse analysis? To put it differently, in the adjudication of possible interpretations, what status do "the words on the page" have? (My guess is that Adam would answer, "Much, in every way," with the caveat that these words have only the status granted them by readers and readerly communities, but in conversations about validity in theological interpretation I doubt that this is enough.)

(2) What role, if any, does historical analysis have in biblical interpretation? We might agree that the work of historians is neither sufficient nor decisive but

still wonder in what sense might Adam say that historical work is necessary, if at all. Does our recognition of these texts as in some sense cultural products constrain how (or what) they might be made to mean? (3) The same set of questions can be raised regarding the status of these texts—say, Obadiah or Matthew—on account of their home for Christians within the two-Testament canon. Does "canonical location" constrain meaning in any discernable way?

(4) What is for me one of the most ambiguous aspects of Adam's hermeneutical proposal is the identity of the community whom he endows with the interpretive task—and, indeed, with interpretive authority. I *think* he is concerned especially with particular, local communities. Sometimes, though, he seems to want to talk about what we might call a communion of churches (thus his reference to the Episcopal Church and House of Bishops in his discussion of human sexuality), and in a handful of places he apparently thinks of the one church across time and around the globe. My sense is that Adam's proposal as a theological hermeneutic cannot afford ambiguity on this point. If, as he says, "the legitimacy of an interpretation is determined by the body of readers evaluating it" (60), what are we to make of the fact that the constraints placed on interpretation on any number of points are altered in substantial ways depending on the identity of the "body of readers" evaluating a particular interpretation. If the "body of readers" is the "one, holy, catholic, and apostolic church," for example, then we find room for "differential interpretation" on a wide array of matters but at the same time recognize that certain readings championed by a more "local body of readers" have been and are excluded. How can Adam account for the reality that the "bodies of readers" that comprise the church are many but one?

In short, there is much to commend in Adam's diagnosis of the situation faced by persons and communities interested in theological interpretation. For someone who aims in his theological hermeneutic "to tell the truth about God and humanity" (3), however, Adam has not satisfactorily addressed the problem of how to adjudicate among not merely different but indeed competing and mutually exclusive interpretations.

TEXTUAL CRITICISM AND TRANSLATION

New Testament Greek Manuscripts: Variant Readings Arranged in Horizontal Lines against Codex Vaticanus: 1 Corinthians, edited by Reuben Swanson. Wheaton, Ill.: Tyndale House, 2003. Pp. xli + 503. Paper. $49.99. ISBN 0865850720.

Claudio Zamagni, Université de Lausanne, Lausanne, Switzerland

Depuis 1995, Reuben Swanson poursuit la publication très régulière de sa magnifique édition des principaux manuscrits du Nouveau Testament. Celui-ci est le huitième volume paru, après les quatre comprenant les évangiles, publié en 1995, le volume des Actes des apôtres (1998) et les volumes des épîtres aux Galates (1999) et aux Romains (2001). Ces livres ont déjà fait l'objet d'une longue série de comptes-rendus, tous largement positifs, et le miens ne pourra que s'aligner sur ceux-ci, car l'ouvrage de Swanson comble un vide important dans champ de la critique textuelle néotestamentaire.

Pour la présenter brièvement au lecteur francophone qui n'aurait jamais eu entre ses mains l'un de ces volumes, l'œuvre de Swanson édite les manuscrits grecs des différents livres néotestamentaires de manière quasiment diplomatique, en reproduisant intégralement leur texte. Le manuscrit Vatican («B») est pris comme texte de base, auquel fait suite une collation complète des autres témoins considérés, présentée de manières synoptique. Il s'agit d'une synopse composée sur des lignes et non sur des colonnes, comme pour les synopses plus courantes. De cette manière, il est possible di lire intégralement le texte de tous les manuscrits considérés, de voir immédiatement leurs variantes et leurs lacunes éventuelles, de comprendre à coup d'œil quelle est la leçon la plus attestée ou celle qui a le plus de chances d'avoir engendré les autres. Ce n'est pas une véritable édition diplomatique, car les textes sont publiés critiquement, sauf pour quelques-uns des caractères propres aux différents manuscrits, comme les abréviations des nomina sacra. Chaque volume est donc beaucoup plus de ce que le titre promet, car ce ne sont pas simplement les variantes qui sont éditées par rapport à un texte de base, mais c'est plutôt une édition complète des principaux témoins néotestamentaires. Évidemment, le choix de mettre le manuscrit Vatican comme base d'une telle «collation» est un choix purement conventionnel, même si il a un grand argument dans la qualité de ce témoin et dans son étendu, qui couvre presque l'ensemble du Nouveau Testament.

Naturellement, pour chaque volume, la liste des manuscrits publiés varie. Sont évidemment toujours édités les grands onciales, tandis que l'ensemble des autres témoins montre des variations somme tout assez considérables, en vertu des différents manuscrits couvrant les différents livres néotestamentaires. Dans le cas du présent volume, le groupe des témoins comprends 2 manuscrits sur papyrus, 16 en onciale, 65 en minuscule, le témoignage indirect de Clément d'Alexandrie, ainsi que quatre éditions critiques modernes (l'*editio princeps* d'Erasme, une édition du *receptus*, l'édition de Westcott et Hort et la dernière édition de Kurt Aland et collaborateurs, qui est actuellement le texte critique de référence). Un travail de ce type demande beaucoup d'espace et l'édition couvre un total de 289 pages, dans le cas du présent volume sur la première épître aux Corinthiens. La présentation synoptique par lignes est la même dans tous les volumes de cette série, tandis que les apparats en bas de la page, apportant des informations complémentaires, proposent quelques différences d'une édition à l'autre.

Le livre comporte aussi une série d'appendices, dont la plupart nouveaux par rapport à l'usage des autres volumes de Swanson. Un premier appendice comporte une liste des passages du manuscrit Vatican signalés par des *Umlaut* (dièrèses), signifiant sans doute la présence de variantes connues par le scribe (293–304). Un deuxième appendice propose des exemples de titres de chapitres que l'on peut trouver dans les manuscrits (305–7). Le troisième appendice répertorie les erreurs de lecture des manuscrits que l'on trouve dans la huitième édition de Tischendorf et dans les deux dernières éditions de Kurt Aland et collabora-teurs, c'est-à-dire le «Nestle-Aland» et le *Greek New Testament* (éditions de 1993), ainsi que quatre variantes de l'édition Kenyon du Papyrus 46 (309–18). Le qua-trième propose les erreurs trouvées dans le volume de la série *Text und Textwert der griechischen Handschriften des Neuen Testaments* dédié à Paul (319–22). Dans ces deux appendices, en plus des véritables fautes de lecture ou des erreurs dans la présentation des apparats critiques, il s'agit souvent des variantes concernant des formes d'itacisme ou d'autres variations apparemment mineures (s'il y a des détails qu'il faut considérer comme tels dans une édition critique !). L'appendice principal est cependant celle concernant la liste des variantes principales de la première épître aux Corinthiens, couvrant plus de cent pages (323–457). Le texte de la lettre y est repris intégralement, selon la leçon fixée dans la dernière édition du *Greek New Testament* d'Aland et collaborateurs, il est divisé en unités de sens et toutes les variantes faisant sens y sont reproduites (en laissant tomber la plupart des variantes graphiques, mais pas vraiment toutes). A mon avis, ce type d'appen-dice, nouvel par rapport aux autres volumes, n'est pas vraiment nécessaire. En effet, toutes les informations qu'il donne sont déjà dans le corps du texte (et dans une forme plus complète). Mais bien douteuse est surtout l'idée de faire une col-lation fondée sur un texte choisi à l'avance. Il suffit de considérer l'accueil moins que tiède réservé à la somptueuse édition de Luc des *American and British Com-mittees of the International Greek New Testament Project* (1984–1987), qui utilisait le textus receptus comme base de collation. L'intérêt principal de cet appendice est toutefois, je crois, d'une énorme portée «publicitaire», car c'est certainement l'outil qui est finalement capable de convaincre l'exégète le moins intéressé aux questions textuelles que le texte de «Nestle-Aland» est loin, mais vraiment loin, de représenter un apparat correct pour le texte néotestamentaire. Avec son option de ne pas présenter intégralement les variantes, même pas pour les manuscrits de première importance, le «Nestle-Aland» est en effet en mesure de rendre peu transparent l'établissement du texte (alors qu'il présente une grande quantité de variantes peu significatives quant à la leçon proposée). Cet appendice de Swanson montre alors d'un coup d'œil combien de variantes, souvent intéressantes, n'ont pas de place dans les éditions courantes du Nouveau Testament. Et de même fait l'appendice suivant, comportant les variantes attestées par un seul manuscrit, qui ne sont pratiquement jamais considérées dans les éditions courantes par la seule raison qu'il s'agit d'attestations uniques (459–87). Les deux derniers appendices comportent la liste des lacunes attestées dans les différents manuscrits considé-rés (489–95) et l'ordre des livres bibliques dans les manuscrits utilisés, comparé à celui de l'édition de Erasme (497–503).

　　Comme il arrive dans toutes les autres volumes de la série, ce tome contient une introduction (précédée par une présentation de Bruce Metzger) qui décrit l'édition concernée et son appendice dans les détails et qui permets ainsi de se familiariser rapidement avec son utilisation (de toute manière beaucoup plus simple que celle de n'importe quelle édition critique, car la présentation en synopse n'est pas un luxe courant). Comme les introductions des autres volumes, celle-ci aussi contient des informations valables pour l'ensemble de l'œuvre de Swanson. Certes, les principes ecdotiques de Swanson sont largement questionnables. Car souligner, comme il le fait, que tout manuscrit néotestamentaire a eu une dignité ecclésiale et communautaire (cf. xxix) face au texte «éclectique» des éditions critiques, qui n'a jamais existé en tant que tel dans le christianisme ancien, est sans aucun doute une grande (et évidente) vérité (cf. xvi–xviii et xxix–xxxv). Mais c'est un discours qui apparaît déplacé et incroyablement daté si la question qu'on se pose est d'aller plus loin que chaque manuscrit existant, en se demandant quel est l'original qui explique les différentes variantes existantes. A l'intérieur de cette problématique, qui est strictement théorique, les arguments de Swanson ne font à mon avis pas de sens. Comme il ne le fait pas vraiment l'option d'inclure dans cet apparat quatre éditions modernes ni celle d'inclure un seul auteur ancien comme témoin indirect (en dépassant d'ailleurs toute la bibliographie récente sur l'usage des sources indirectes pour la reconstitution du texte néotestamentaire). Ceci dit, les mêmes critiques théoriques s'adressent aussi, *mutatis mutandis*, à bien d'autres éditions, comme c'est bien le cas du «Nestle-Aland» (cf. notamment les remarques, largement partageables, données à la p. xviii).

En conclusion, comme il arrive dans toute édition critique, Swanson suit des principes questionnables, mais le résultat de son travail est cependant réellement extraordinaire par rapport aux éditions néotestamentaires courantes, notamment parce qu'il n'essaie pas de constituer un texte critique, mais il offre par contre ce qu'aucune édition courante est à mesure d'offrir: pour les manuscrits donnés, il donne *toutes les variantes* et dans une forme réellement lisible. Un de grands défauts des éditions d'Aland et collaborateurs (du moins jusqu'à la publication complète de l'*editio maior* qui a déjà ses dizaines d'années de retard), est que le choix des variantes de l'apparat est fait arbitrairement par les éditeurs, qu'aucun témoin est présenté intégralement (même pas les manuscrits Vatican ou Sinaïtique) et que l'utilisateur ne peut donc pas réellement vérifier les fondements critiques qui ont emmené à l'établissement du texte. Or, ceci est le principe fondamental de l'édition critique, s'il y en a un. Les volumes de Swanson le suivent irréprochablement, car ils peuvent être utilisés sans partager d'aucune manière les critères ecdotiques de l'éditeur. S'ils abdiquent au premier devoir de l'éditeur (constituer le texte), ils deviennent cependant le complément idéal et nécessaire au «Nestle-Aland» actuel. Du moment qu'ils existent et qui sont d'utilisation si simple, les tomes de Swanson sont simplement irremplaçables. De plus, ils paraissent avec un rythme de publication qui est presque stupéfiant si l'on considère qu'ils représentent le travail d'une personne pratiquement seule. Somme tout, il y a plus d'une raison s'il n'est pas facile de se les procurer, car ces volumes s'épuisent très rapidement peu après leur parution. C'est parce qu'il s'agit d'une œuvre exceptionnelle dans sa simplicité.

Beyond What Is Written: Erasmus and Beza as Conjectural Critics of the New Testament, by Jan Krans. New Testament Tools and Studies 35. Brill: Leiden, 2006. Pp. x + 390. Cloth. $173.00. ISBN 9004152865.

J. K. Elliott, University of Leeds, Leeds, United Kingdom

Krans's book is based on a detailed and carefully executed piece of research at the Vrije Universiteit, Amsterdam. In his work Krans examines the conjectural emendations proposed by Erasmus and Beza in their respective work on the Greek text of the New Testament. Conjectural readings have been introduced into the New Testament since the beginning. Most deliberate changes inserted by scribes into the manuscripts they were copying may be described as conjectural emendations of those texts. Modern scholars have also speculated about difficult readings found in the Greek New Testament, and some have proposed alternative readings that are not in the manuscripts. The United Bible Societies' Greek New Testament text followed by the Nestle edition has one such conjecture in the text printed at Acts 16:12. The *Editio Critica Maior* has recently printed a conjecture at 2 Pet 3:10. The siglum *cj* is found some 220 times in the apparatus of Nestle-Aland 25th edition, although the number of such occurrences has been pruned somewhat in the editions following (about 130 conjectures survive in the apparatus).

But under what circumstances did Erasmus and Beza make their emendations? Krans carefully traces where and how these scholars proposed changes to the Greek text. Krans emphasizes that both scholars' concerns were primarily with the *Latin* Bible, and here he is thus following H. J. de Jonge's perceptive opinion that what it was that Erasmus was doing when he published his *Novum Instrumentum* in 1516 was the promotion of a new Latin New Testament, the readings for which were verified by an accompanying Greek text. So when Erasmus and later Beza commented on readings in the Greek, they were doing so in order to establish rather than to revise the Greek. Both had comparatively few Greek manuscripts at their disposal: Erasmus only the ten or so to hand in Basle, and Beza the sixteen found in Stephanus, supplemented by the bilinguals 05 (subsequently named Codex Bezae) and 06.

"Whereas for Erasmus, the Greek text of the New Testament is first of all a source, which he treats in essentially the same way as any other classical text, for Beza, it is first of all (holy) scripture, which has to be treated with the utmost reverence." That sentence by Krans, found toward the end of his thesis (332), could well serve as a caricature undergraduate examination question, followed by the ubiquitous "Discuss," but it demonstrates Krans's careful judgment on the two scholars under his microscope. Understanding the context of conjectures and the historical circumstances of the writers confirms Krans's guiding principle from the outset that judgment of conjectures should be preceded by knowledge of their authors (3). A bald "*cj*" or even a "*cj* Erasmus" in an apparatus is useless in itself and reinforces my oft-stated opinion that the apparatus is no place for modern deliberate conjectures. If they belong anywhere, it is in a commentary.

Krans sets the record straight regarding Erasmus, often accused of being a scholar who irresponsibly tried to rewrite the New Testament text. In practice, many of the alleged emendations were arbitrary corrections (some subsequently verified) of the few manuscripts he had at his disposal. Other "emendations" of the Greek text were actually founded on the Vulgate. And, in any case, most of the proposed emendations are found, not in the printed text, but in his copious annotations. There are very few pure conjectures (those that may be so described are given on pp. 108ff.), although in several instances Erasmus provides reasons for an emendation without actually proposing a change to his text. The conjecture "her" at Luke 2:22 made its way into the King James English version.

Erasmus's working methods are exposed, and Krans puts us in his debt by detailing the nature of his annotations. In several Erasmus is shown as a perceptive textual critic and scholar of Koine Greek grammar well ahead of his time, and as only a reluctant emendator of the biblical text. Erasmus was alert to principles such as the acceptance of a harder reading as the original, of homoioteleuton, and of itacism, topics that resurfaced in New Testament scholarship two centuries later than Erasmus after a comparative lull in such editorial activities in the eighteenth century. We are shown how Erasmus discussed cruces such as Mark 7:3; 1 Cor 1:6–7; 1 Thess 2:7; Jas 4:2 (an emendation noted in the current Nestle edition); and 1 Pet 3:20. Krans provides us with telling examples wisely commented upon. Chapter 6 is a useful survey of how Erasmus reacted to others' conjectures (e.g., Jerome and Origen from the early Christian centuries or Valla from nearer his own day). Full and useful footnotes and cross-references to a wide range of appropriate secondary literature are provided. Krans's enviably fluent English style is to be congratulated. The only howler I spotted was a French term (*en bloque* on 196)! The welcome and ongoing series of scholarly publications of Erasmus's oeuvre (*Opera Omnia*) makes the appearance of this part of the published thesis particularly appropriate and timely.

Beza too was reluctant to make conjectural emendations. Like Erasmus, he discussed possible conjectural changes in his notes, and many of those have found their way into later discussions. There are ten emendations attributed to Beza in the Nestle-Aland 25th edition (the number is reduced in the following editions). Beza showed an interest in the readings of the manuscripts he adopted (from Stephanus) as well as betrayed a reluctance to accept many of the singular readings of Codex Bezae, which he regarded as an unreliable and maverick witness. (Beza's famous letter on this topic is translated on 229–30.)

This is a very thorough but readable thesis, displaying careful scholarship at its best: well–documented, judiciously analyzed, and logically presented and evaluated. In short, it is a richly deserved doctorate that we are now privileged to benefit from in the latest volume in this prestigious series.

Sôfer Mahîr: Essays in Honour of Adrian Schenker, edited by Yohanan Gold-man and A. P. Arie van der Kooij, and Richard D. Weis. Supplements to Vetus Testamentum 110. Leiden: Brill, 2006. Pp. x + 310. Hardcover. $147.00. ISBN 9004150161.

Dany Nocquet, Institut Protestant de Théologie de Montpellier, Montpellier, France

Cet ouvrage est dédié à Adrian Schenker président du comité éditorial du projet international: *Biblica Hebraica Quinta (BHQ)*. Ce livre est une vibrante reconnaissance pour l'érudition et le rayonnement amical qui l'ont animé dans la conduite de cet immense projet dont un premier volume sur les *megillôt* est paru en 2006.

R. Althann éclaire le texte de Job par quelques réflexions sur les raisons des différences entre M et G. Au delà de l'argument d'une *Vorlage* différente, la brièveté du texte G par rapport à M serait due aux techniques de traduction qui para-phrasent le texte hébreu lorsque celui-ci est incompréhensible, et qui le traduisent littéralement lorsqu'il n'y a pas de problèmes. Pour l'auteur il serait hasardeux d'user du texte grec pour corriger l'hébreu de Job. Par des exemples l'article plaide plutôt pour une compréhension plus approfondie de la poésie hébraïque avec ses techniques propres (métonymie, ellipse, omission volontaire: absence du pronom suffixe de la 2ème personne au 2ème stique de Jb 36,17 דין משפט יתמכו) pour jeter une nouvelle lumière sur les leçons du texte hébreu.

P. B. Dirksen se place du côté de l'utilisateur pour évaluer le nouvel appa-rat critique de la *BHQ* sur le Cantique des Cantiques. Il y a fort peu de témoins hébraïques, seuls G et S sont à prendre en compte. l'auteur mesure les écarts par le biais de quatre situations: (1) G diffère de M et de S, (2) S diffère de M et de G, (3) G et S sont en harmonie contre M, et (4) G et S sont différents de M et entre eux. A l'aide d'exemples l'auteur conclut que M offre un texte avec peu d'erreurs et qu'il n'y a pas de raison de le soumettre à G ou S. Dans quelques rares cas, les versions offrent une possibilité d'alternatives à M en 1,3.7; 4,9.12; 7,7.10.

Concernant le livre des Juges N. F. Marcos présente une réflexion sur le rap-port entre le texte hébreu et les différents témoins disponibles. Dans une première partie il présente les différents témoins: G et les fragments de Qumrân. Il constate que ces fragments renforcent en général le texte M. Pour les variantes, 4QJudg^a ne contient pas Jg 6,7–10 par rapport à M, l'auteur s'interroge: s'agit-il d'une omis-sion ou d'un texte initial plus court? En faisant l'histoire du texte, l'auteur constate que M propose un texte exempt de corruptions majeures. G ne remonte pas à une *Vorlage* trop différente de M mais explicite des mots difficiles et rares. G, T, S et V appartiennent à une tradition massorétique. L'absence d'un texte protomassoréti-que constitue la principale difficulté pour l'édition critique du texte du livre des Juges. La *BHQ* prend ici une autre option (complémentaire) que celle de *l'Oxford Hebrew Bible*.

A. Gelstone s'arrête sur les difficultés de traductions rencontrées par les anciennes versions à propos du livre des douze prophètes. Les difficultés de traduction sont liées aux homonymes, aux différences de vocalisation et aux confusions de racines entre verbes ayant en commun deux consonnes: אשם et שמם. Ces observations expliquent pourquoi l'ancien traducteur G a eu plus de difficultés à traduire que les traducteurs des versions plus tardives. L'influence de l'ancienne version G reste cependant forte puisque S donne aussi les erreurs de G.

En ce qui concerne l'édition de Daniel pour la *BHQ* A. Gianto note qu'un certain nombre de difficultés textuelles peuvent trouver une solution ou une explication par l'étude littéraire et stylistique de la tradition textuelle dans laquelle se trouve cette difficulté. Il en fait la démonstration sur l'étude de Dn 2.

Pour A. P. Goldman M s'avère un témoin assez fiable pour le livre de Qohéleth.

L'auteur montre avec finesse comment le texte fut «retouché» pour satisfaire aux critères de l'orthodoxie du judaïsme rabbinique et lui permettre de trouver sa place dans le Canon. Après avoir présenté les différentes sources qui mettent en cause la canonicité de Qohéleth, l'auteur étudie trois passages en 7,19; 7,23-24; 8,1 (différence de vocalisation et d'interprétation entre G et M sur ועז et ישנא) dans lesquels la distance entre G et M témoigne d'un texte retouché. Les positions de Qohéleth sur la Sagesse dans l'édition protomassorétique portaient en effet le risque de rendre illusoire l'obéissance à la Torah, essence même de la Sagesse pour le judaïsme rabbinique. M est donc à la fois le témoin privilégié du livre, mais M est aussi témoin de retouches qui répondent à un compromis théologique et au projet global d'édition de Tanakh.

Sur le livre du Lévitique I. Himbaza étudie les difficultés des traducteurs de G, des Targumim, de S, et de V devant la terminologie sacrificielle de Lv 1–7. Le traducteur grec utilise parfois le même mot pour traduire deux racines hébraïques différentes ou bien deux mots différents pour la même terminologie hébraïque. Si V semble avoir bien harmonisé sa traduction, les mots de אשה et de מנחה ne sont pas l'objet d'une appropriation assurée. En conséquence l'auteur estime que la textualité de M semble la mieux établie en Lv 1-7.

S'appuyant sur les travaux d'A. Schenker qui a montré l'antériorité de la *Vorlage* de la LXX sur le texte protomassorétique de M, Ph. Hugo fait une histoire de la recherche textuelle sur le Grec ancien des livres des Règnes. La recherche aboutit à la conclusion que G[L] (recension de Lucien d'Antioche, 3ème siècle de notre ère) fait une traduction d'un texte hébraïque antérieur à l'unification du texte consonnantique. G[L] est un des témoins les plus sûrs du grec ancien, même si la nature de ce témoin fait encore l'objet de débat. Ceci est corroboré par La, *Vetus Latina*, proche de G[L]. Les témoins privilégiés les plus importants du Grec ancien sont donc G[L] et le codex Vaticanus, G[B].

A. van der Kooij étudie la place des anciens témoins en hébreu du livre d'Esaïe qui proviennent de Qumrân et de la Mer morte. Par différents exemples l'auteur étudie les variantes entre les témoins anciens et M: lorsque 1QIsa[a] et 1QIsa[b] sont équivalents mais différents de M, lorsque 1QIsa[a] et 4Q sont équivalents mais diffèrent de M, et lorsque 1QIsa[a] et deux Mss de Qumrân sont équivalents mais diffèrent de M. Son analyse reconnaît en maints lieux la primauté des leçons de M par rapport aux nombreuses variantes. M atteste d'une tradition textuelle qui fut donc transmise depuis le 3ᵉᵐᵉ siècle avant l'ère chrétienne.

Pour Ezéchiel, la critique textuelle s'est souvent positionnée en faisant de la *Vorlage* de G une version plus ancienne que le texte protomassorétique de M. J. Lust confronte cette position que reflètent plusieurs commentaires en montrant le caractère hasardeux d'une correction de M par G. Après une présentation des principaux témoins de Qumrân et de G, il montre que M et G représentent des étapes rédactionnelles du texte d'Ezéchiel, ce sont «des rameaux issus d'une même souche». Les différences entre M plus long et G plus court relèvent de la critique littéraire. En effet en maints lieux, G offre un haut degré de littéralité par rapport à M. Si le texte de M est plus long que G, il ne s'agit pas de gloses ou d'ajouts postérieurs, ils peuvent appartenir à une édition originale. Ainsi l'usage du double nom de Dieu יהוה אדני remonte à la tradition protomassorétique. Si le texte de G est plus court que M, il ne s'agit pas d'omission, mais G est témoin de sections différentes de M. Le texte d'Ezéchiel est aussi le témoin privilégié d'un hébreu tardif qui se manifeste par l'usage de consonnes supplémentaires: «David», דויד.

D. Marcus permet au lecteur de se rendre compte concrètement des différences entre la *BHQ* et essentiellement la *BHS* sur les livres d'Esdras-Néhémie. Les différences sont la mise à disposition de nouvelles ressources (nouveau facsimilé de Mᴸ, fragments de Qumrân...), la comparaison de Mᴸ avec deux manuscrits du système massorétique de Tibériade (Mˢ¹ et Mʸ), la présentation nouvelle des deux Massores, l'inclusion de I Esdras, et de propositions textuelles circonscrites.

Sur le Deutéronome, C. McCarthy compare la Massorah parva et la Massorah magna de Mᴸ et à celle du manuscrit de Madrid (M¹). La comparaison conduit à mesurer les grandes variations entre les deux massores sur la quantité et le contenu des notes. L'auteur constate la spécificité de chaque massorah, et conclut qu'il ne convient pas «d'habiller un manuscrit avec la massorah d'un autre».

G. J. Norton s'attache à expliquer l'édition diplomatique du Psautier dans la *BHQ* et sa présentation dans Mᴸ. Le texte du psautier en Mᴸ fait apparaître des espaces qui ne sont pas à considérer comme des *setûmôt*. Les espaces laissés par les éditeurs des psaumes ne correspondent pas à des ruptures de sens dans le texte, mais ils ont plutôt une fonction ornementale. L'auteur constate un double arrangement ornemental des lignes qu'il nomme «un plus deux»: une ligne pleine et deux lignes avec espaces, et un arrangement en zigzag. La présentation de la *BHQ* fait place à un espace qu'au moment de la rupture accentuée et majeure de la ligne.

En s'intéressant à l'histoire de Balaam, Nb 22–24, l'intention de M. Rösel est de fournir à son lecteur les caractéristiques des témoins les plus importants du livre des Nombres: Mᴸ, 4QNumᵇ, Smr, et G. Pour Mᴸ il constate un certain manque de soin dans l'écriture de la Mp et pense qu'elle proviendrait d'une autre tradition textuelle. Elle est plus ancienne que le codex lui-même. Concernant les textes de Qumrân il constate que la spécificité des apports de 4QNumᵇ sur Nb

24,17 ou Nb 6 n'ont pas été assez prises en compte, alors qu'elles introduisent des formules de citations. Pour le témoin Smr, sa leçon (מגוג au lieu de מאגג de M) en Nb 24,7 est d'une grande importance pour le traducteur grec qui en fait une interprétation eschatologique. G porte des variantes qui font référence à une plus ancienne étape de transmission de l'hébreu ou qui sont originelles. L'étude aboutit cependant au constat que M a été tout à fait bien transmis. Chaque variante doit être interprétée dans son contexte.

Après avoir tracé l'évolution de l'interprétation du *paseq* entre Gesenius et Himmelfarb, M. Saebo examine son usage dans le livre d'Esther et conclut que le *paseq* est lié à la signification spécifique de certains mots. Il sert à sécuriser la compréhension et la lecture du texte. Il a dans ce cas un rôle emphatique et de distinction.

R. Schäfer étudie la structure du texte poétique de Lamentation 1 dans ses différentes variantes textuelles. Il montre l'importance de l'étude structurelle pour la critique textuelle. En examinant 4QLam, il offre une reconstruction du texte original des v.7 et 16-17 qui permet d'établir une structure poétique plus équilibrée et plus harmonieuse que celle offerte par le texte M.

Sur le livre des Proverbes J. de Waard s'intéresse au phénomène d'ignorance lexicale qui se trouve dans les anciennes versions derrière des *hapax legomenon* ou l'interprétation de métathèse. L'auteur étudie ce phénomène autour du mot rare קֶרֶת et d'une forme *hitpael* de la racine עלג. L'ignorance de G est parfois suppléée par la connaissance de V.

Enfin, au regard de la complexité de la situation textuelle du livre de Jérémie, R. Weis propose une première étape de critique rédactionnelle des péricopes en M et en G. Une deuxième étape consiste en une analyse des techniques de traductions de G afin d'établir une *Vorlage* hébraïque avec un certain degré de probabilité. C'est avec cette méthode que l'auteur analyse M (Jr 37–38) et G (Jr 44–45). Cela permet de distinguer au sein des différentes leçons ce qui relève de la «rédaction» et ce qui relève de la «transmission». Sans pouvoir encore dresser un bilan général, l'auteur estime que G et M préservent l'un et l'autre le texte le plus ancien. Mais M semble plus hétérogène et se caractérise par une diversité considérable.

En conclusion, cet ouvrage prépare le lecteur à accueillir l'édition complète de la *BHQ* qui le fera bénéficier des recherches et des découvertes récentes.

En faisant le point sur l'état du texte hébreu de 3o livres sur les 39 que compte la Bible hébraïque (près de 8O/100), ce volume est aussi une sorte de bilan intermédiaire sur l'immense travail en critique textuelle que représente l'édition de la *BHQ*. Deux faits au moins sont à noter. D'une part M représente dans la plupart des livres une tradition de transmission textuelle relativement fiable et ancienne. D'autre part les limites entre critique textuelle et critique littéraire sont perméables, les deux approches s'avèrent complémentaires l'une de l'autre.

New Testament Manuscripts: Their Texts and Their World, edited by Thomas J. Kraus and Tobias Nicklas. Texts and Editions for New Testament Study 2. Leiden: Brill, 2006. Pp. xii + 348. Hardcover. $181.00. ISBN 9004149457.

Christopher Tuckett, University of Oxford, Oxford, United Kingdom

New Testament textual criticism can, if one is not careful, operate as if textual variants and different readings in manuscripts are almost like disembodied platonic ideals floating in cyberspace. The underlying assumption of this book is that manuscripts themselves, in their concrete forms, can be just as interesting and worthy of study in their own right. Thus the essays collected here focus for the most part on concrete manuscripts and on what a consideration of these might have to tell us when we look at them more closely. In the words of the subtitle of the editors' introduction to the volume, "every manuscript tells a story," and the aim of the essays here is to seek to tell some of those stories.

Inevitably the collection is a little disparate, and some of the essays relate to the general focus only somewhat tangentially. For example, the first two essays focus more on places and/or broader geographical (and social) contexts in which Christian manuscripts were written and preserved. Eldon Epp continues his long-standing interest in the site of Oxyrhynchus, which has been famous for providing us with such a wealth of material in the form of papyri from its rubbish heaps, with his essay on "The Jews and the Jewish Community in Oxyrhynchus." He discusses the methodological problems in seeking to identify clearly Jewish personnel mentioned in the papyri (e.g., via their names) and shows how little remains, indicating perhaps the demise of the Jewish community at Oxyrhynchus for some considerable period in the second-third centuries. Marco Frenschowski provides an analysis of the evidence concerning the famous ancient Christian library at Caesarea, especially the problems about its disappearance in the fourth-fifth centuries, arguing that it may have been more of a private collection of books that was simply dispersed gradually after the death of Eusebius.

A number of studies address problems associated with specific manuscripts. Peter Head writes about a newly discovered fragment of Luke's Gospel (with the Gregory-Aland number 0312). Probably to be dated some time in the fifth century, it has small parts extant from Luke 5 and 7. No startling new readings are contained here, but any new early manuscript is inherently interesting. Dirk Jongkind provides an in-depth study of features of Codex Sinaiticus, considering the phenomenon of the three scribes who probably worked on the manuscript and looking at some irregularities in the make-up of the quires and the changes in the scribal hands at some places. Some of the evidence may suggest that the codex was produced "at a locality where there was demand for a large Bible but where one lacked the experience to produce one" (135). Tommy Wasserman discusses the text of P78 (POxy 2684), which may have contained the text of Jude 1–13 (only) as an amulet. Wasserman seeks to provide reasons why just this particular section of text might have been thought appropriate to use for this context. Tobias Nicklas and Tommy Wasserman provide a jointly written essay looking at the problems posed by the collection in one of the codices from the Bodmer collection (here Codex Bodmer Miscellani, the codex containing the texts of 1–2 Peter and Jude generally known as P72). Rather than focusing on the biblical texts alone, they ask what might have been the rationale that led to this particular collection of (apparently somewhat miscellaneous) texts. No clear answer is given: their conclusion is that the manuscript "bleibt rätselhaft" (188), but they provide valuable insights into the various (often little discussed) texts contained in the codex. Michael Holmes contributes a very detailed study of some of the readings in P46, especially those agreeing with those that appear in D F G, and argues that some may indicate a process of "commenting" on, or clarifying, the text where it may have been felt to be slightly unclear or obscure. Thomas Kraus writes a detailed account of manuscripts that contain the Lord's Prayer in "noncontinuous" manuscripts (i.e., not containing the full text of either Mathew or Luke but simply the prayer on its own or with other excerpts).

Slightly more general considerations are provided in the essay by Larry Hurtado, who discusses the sue of the staurogram (tau-rho) in early Christian manuscripts, arguing that it may be very early (it is present already in P45, P66, and P75) and may provide the earliest example of a kind of iconography, being a possible visual reference to Jesus' crucifixion. As such it would predate by some 150–200 years what had otherwise been thought to be the earliest representations of the cross (in late fourth- or fifth-century depictions). Malcolm Choat provides a valuable survey of possible echoes and allusions to New Testament texts in documentary papyri from Egypt to the end of the fourth century. Kim Haines-Eitzen considers the phenomenon of the papyri manuscripts of some apocryphal Acts literature, noting that they are often quite high-class productions, suggesting (perhaps more controversially) that this might tell us something about the original target audience or readership of these text. Finally, Stanley Porter offers some thoughts on the whole practice of textual criticism and the construction of the critical apparatus in the light of modern theories. He suggests (not unreasonably) that perhaps distinctions should be made between "continuous" and "noncontinuous" texts and that the latter may have no more (and no less!) right to be used as evidence as, say, lectionaries; he also suggests (more controversially) that apocryphal texts should be used to provide evidence of New Testament readings (although here there are immense problems in being certain that New Testament texts are actually being "cited" and if so which ones).

This is a fascinating collection of essays showing how much light can be shed from a consideration of concrete manuscripts and taking seriously the evidence they provide for illuminating the social and religious world in which early Christians lived out their faith and produced their written texts.

BIBLE AND CULTURE

The HarperCollins Study Bible Fully Revised and Updated: Including Apocryphal Deuterocanonical Books with Concordance, edited by Harold W. Attridge. San Francisco: HarperSanFrancisco, 2006. Pp. lxvi + 2204. Paper. $39.95. ISBN 0061228400.

Timothy A. Friedrichsen, The Catholic University of America, Washington, D.C.

The fully revised and updated version of *The HarperCollins Study Bible* became available in September 2006 in both hard and trade paperback covers, with the handy trim size of 6 1/4 × 9 3/16 inches. This reviewer received the paperback version, which appears to be quite sturdy and should have reasonable longevity. In addition, it lies nicely open on a desk, except when consulting the last eighteen pages, which are stiffer for the purposes of presenting eighteen color maps (see below). It is beyond the scope of this review to compare this edition with the earlier one and/or with other study Bibles. Rather, it will discuss the edition's strengths and weaknesses by focusing on the claims made about it (see back cover). Despite weaknesses noted herein, overall *The HarperCollins Study Bible* has much to offer and is strongly and happily recommended by this reviewer.

Like the original edition, a great plus of this study edition is that it continues to be "as inclusive as possible"; it contains "the most complete range of biblical books representing the several different canons of scripture" (Wayne A. Meeks, xiii): the canonical books of "the Hebrew Scriptures"; the apocryphal/deuterocanonical books accepted in the Roman Catholic, Greek, and Slavonic Bibles, as well as those books included in the latter two but not in other canons; and the books included in the appendices of the Slavonic Bible, the Latin Vulgate, and the Greek Bible. Given this inclusiveness, it is unfortunate that there is no article that provides an overview of the issues that gave rise to the varying canons of these traditions, save a few brief comments in the introduction (xvii–xviii). Nevertheless, it is helpful that "Names and Orders of the Books of the Bible in Several Traditions" (xxxi–xxxiii) are provided for "Jewish Bibles," which "include the books of the Hebrew scriptures (Tanak)," "Protestant Bibles," "Orthodox Bibles," and "Catholic Bibles." To conclude the introductory matters, there is a historical table (xxxiv–xxxv) from the beginning of the Chalcolithic age (4500 B.C.E.) to the Roman destruction of Jerusalem (70 C.E.).

This edition then moves to the "newly commissioned introductory essays" (back cover). John Barton lays out "Strategies for Reading Scripture" (xxxix–xliii). He first treats the "canonical approach" that is used by "most Christians" and is "not involved in technical biblical study" (xxxix). These readers expect that the texts "will be *true*" (xxxix), "*relevant ... important* and *profound*," and "*self-consistent*" (xl). Biblical criticism, on the other hand, "approaches the biblical text from a *literary* ... perspective," which concerns itself with the genre of each book and the historical questions surrounding its writing. This type of reading "brackets the question of the truth of the text until it establishes what the text means" (xli).

None of the introductions to the books shies away from the critical reading of the text, which is a commendable strength of this study Bible. The "canonical reader" is nevertheless assured: "The majority of critics do not deny the assumption that the Bible is important and profound; most of them would not bother to study it if they thought it trivial or insignificant" (xliii). The users of this work, however, will have to bridge the "compromise between critical and canonical readings" (xlii) on their own, which will no doubt be difficult for those who hold any critical reading of the text in high suspicion.

Ronald Hendel provides an informative essay on "Israelite Religion" (xliv–xlviii) that covers "some of the major themes in the Israelite religion from its hazy origins in the beginning of the Iron Age (ca. 1200 BCE) through the crystallization of the Bible as a sacred text during the Second Temple period (ca. 530 BCE–70 CE)" (xliv). David E. Aune follows this with "The Greco-Roman Context of the New Testament" (xlix–lvi), which helpfully outlines "the convergence of two great political and cultural empires that together exercised a profound effect on Western civilization and on Christianity" (xlix). He discusses the Greek and Roman conquests, the spread of Koiné Greek, and the religious and philosophical approaches taken by them.

The essays on "The Bible and Archaeology" by Eric M. Meyers (lvii–lxi) and "Archaeology and the New Testament" by Jürgen Zangenberg (lxii–lxvi) show the development of these disciplines. They highlight important events and personages, such as "the establishment of the American Schools of Oriental Research [ASOR] in Jerusalem in 1900" (lviii) and the "pioneering work … by [Sir] William M. Ramsay (1831–1939)" (lxiii; mistyped "Ramsey" in the same line). Both essayists clearly believe that archaeology, much like the reading of biblical texts, must be done critically and that "each discipline quite certainly needs the other" (lxi), or put another way, that disciplined archaeology "will continue to be an essential partner for NT scholars" (lxvi).

The translation text of this edition is "The New Revised Standard Version, the most accurate English Bible translation" (back cover). It is unclear to this reader how one really substantiates that claim. A better way to proceed would be to highlight the major reasons for using the NRSV: "a translation 'as literal as possible' makes this version well adapted for study"; "designed to be as inclusive as possible" in terms of the number of books (noted above) but also in that "it avoids language that might inappropriately suggest limits of gender" (Meeks, xiii). A "literal" translation is helpful for readers who are not familiar with the original languages but who wish to compare similar or parallel texts among books. That translation, however, may not always be the "best" *translation*. One can also wonder about how well the sensitivity to gender is carried off. A couple of examples can be offered. The translation of Gen 2:7, "then the LORD God formed man from the dust of the ground," is explained with a note: "Or *formed a man* (Heb *adam* [sic: *ha'adam*]) *of dust from the ground* (Heb *adamah* [sic: *ha'adamah*])." A more gender-neutral and accurate English translation that retains the inherit pun might read: "then the LORD God formed the human from the dust of the humus."

In Mark 2:27 "humankind" strikes this reader as an overwrought rendering of ἄνθρωπος; the note on this translation, namely, "lit. 'man,' referring to Adam," could also be differently worded.

Some of the introductions to the books are "completely new," while others have been fully revised and updated with "over 25 percent new or revised material" (back cover). As noted, none shy away from the critical reading of the text. They address the historical questions for each book's development and various theories that have been proposed, usually offering a judgment of the more/most likely theory. At times readers are directed to issues already covered in earlier introductions (and notes), which is helpful. Nevertheless, the edition is uneven in this matter, because at times there is a lack of such coordination, and there are even occasions where differing positions are taken. For example, while the "sources" of Genesis, "the Yahwist (J), Elohist (E), and Priestly (P)," are treated in the introduction to Genesis, the reader is not referred to the treatment of these sources in the "Introduction" (xv). Moreover, the introductions to the other books of the Torah/Pentateuch do not refer back to either of these treatments when it would have been appropriate to do so. In a similar vein, while the introduction to Mark notes that "the best (though not perfect) explanation for the relationships between Mark, Matthew, and Luke (the Synoptic Gospels) is the Two-Source Theory" (1724; the theory is then explained), the reader is not pointed to this treatment when the introduction to Matthew notes that the Evangelist "generally follows the largely geographical outline of Mark" (1667) or when the introduction to Luke notes that the Evangelist "revises and incorporates preexisting Christian sources (e.g., Mark and the 'sayings source' Q)" (1759). The introduction to Mark also addresses the very different presentation of the Gospel narrative in John when compared to the Synoptics but also notes the similarities between Mark and John, concluding that "although the author of John may not have used Mark as a written source, he was familiar with the content of Mark as a widely used Christian text" (1724). There is no mention at all of this possible/likely familiarity in the introduction to John (1814–15), unless the few opening observations on how "John differs significantly from the other Gospels" were supposed to suffice. Finally, this lack of coordination among introductions can also be seen in the treatment of the Pauline Letters. A helpful table, "Possible Chronology of the Pauline Letters" (1908), indicates that seven of the thirteen letters attributed to Paul are clearly from him, while 2 Thessalonians and Colossians receive an "if authentic" hesitance, and Ephesians, 1–2 Timothy, and Titus are presented "assuming pseudonymity." Some of the issues raised in this table are not taken up in individual introductions; some possible dates for composition discussed in introductions are not noted in this chronology. For example, the table dates Romans to 56–57 c.e., but the first line of the introduction to Romans—on the opposing page to this table—opens: "By 58 CE Paul thought that his mission in the Aegean region was completed (15.23)" (1909).

The claim that this edition has "twice as many notes as the leading study Bible" (back cover) may well be true, because the notes in this edition are, in a word, impressive. It seems safe to say that on average a third of every page is taken up with notes. In those notes—at least in the ones consulted by this reader—there are guides to the overall narrative of the book, references to other parts of the book and/or parallels in other works, historical information, textual and translation comments, interpretative options, and the like. Students will be informed about relevant information for understanding the text and its context; preachers/ prayers will find at times jewels that inspire reflection; scholars will learn things about books outside their specializations. At times, however, this reader was surprised by some silences; to illustrate this, these few New Testament examples are offered: no note on κενόω ("to empty") in Phil 2:7; no comment on ἁρπάζω ("to catch/snatch up") in 1Thess 4:17; no explicit connection of 42 months/1260 days in Rev 11:2–3; 12:6; 13:5 to the three and a half years of Antiochus IV Epiphanes' ban of Jewish observances—unless the reader acts on the parenthetical "see Dan 7.25…" in the note on Rev 11:2.

"Extensive maps, tables, and charts" (back cover) are provided. The eighteen color maps at the end of this volume are clear, helpful resources for the reader, especially given the exhaustive index to them (2197–2204). All the maps within the biblical texts, however, are blurry; perhaps it would have been better to have only the color maps and refer the reader to the relevant map(s) in the notes. Despite the many maps, I found no map that indicated possible exodus routes. The map at Exod 13:17–22, which shows the "setting of the narratives in Exodus and Numbers," including the major roads, seems to be a logical place to have done so. Many of the tables and illustrations are also blurred, but they remain helpful to the reader. (The table on 2107 indicating eight "Alternate Ways of Counting the Roman Emperors Signified in Rev 17.10–11" can be corrected: column F begins with Nero, not "Gaius," who is rightly indicated in the explanation of column E.)

The last claim on the back cover refers to "a handy, easy-to-read concordance" (2121–96). It is not intended to be comprehensive, although words for which "every reference in the NRSV" is given are marked with an asterisk; these, of course, tend to be rare words and names. The editorial choices for the limited references are not always clear (the entire concordance could not be perused). For words that appear in both the Old and the New Testaments, it seems advisable to include at least one reference from each Testament. For "aroma," 2 Cor 2:15 is noted, but not Jer 48:11, whose inclusion would have allowed for an asterisk. Of the thirty uses of "disciple" in the NRSV, only Matt 10:24 and Luke 14:26 are noted; why not at least one reference from John and from Acts? For "disciples," Mark is short-changed, but Matthew is given two references: 26:56; 28:19; the latter refers to the imperative μαθητεύσατε, for which an entry "disciple(s), to make" might have been included. As an aside, the concordance follows the American convention of a colon between chapter and verse, whereas elsewhere the British convention of a period is used (one slip of the colon was noted: introduction to Deuteronomy [255]). This reader finds the use of the en-dash between verse numbers unnecessarily heavy (at times in hyphenated words, too); a hyphen does nicely, and then the en-dash can be reserved for a citation that crosses two or more chapters.

As for "easy-to-read," the concordance suffers from what the entire edition suffers. HarperCollins' website notes that this publication is for readers twelve years of age and older, but much like cell phone ring tones that can be heard (only) by those younger than thirty, the print size in this edition seems aimed at that group. For this tri-focaled reader, the print was uncomfortably small. The print allows for the handy trim size noted above, but that also leads to pages with mere 1 cm margins, which is nearly antithetical to a "study Bible"—there are two endpages for "NOTES"!

Of course, there is no way any study Bible can be "all things to all people" (1 Cor 9:22). Nevertheless, for the targeted readership, it does seem that a glossary of technical terms would have been helpful, perhaps even more so than the (limited) concordance. The following alphabetically ordered examples—out of many possible examples—could have been noted with some sign (*, ¦, †, or ᵍˡ) to alert the reader to a definition in the glossary: antediluvian, anthroporphism/-phic, (warrior) ethos, etiology, Hellenism/-istic, Paulinist, peroration, recension. At times less technical wording is used, such as "intertwinings" rather than "intercalation" in the note on Mark 2:1–12 (with reference to other examples); the chosen word here seems to image more weaving than is the case.

In the end, even with the nits that have been—and still could be—picked, this fully revised and updated *HarperCollins Study Bible* has much to offer to a variety of readers and for a variety of contexts in which the Scriptures are read, studied, and reflected upon. The essays, introductions, and notes will inform and enlighten any reader and will challenge the faithful readers—if it does not upset them first—to bridge the gap between critical and canonical readings. This challenge is all too necessary wherever the sacred texts are used and abused by preachers and public figures who approach these texts ahistorically and uncritically.

Raising Cain, Fleeing Egypt, and Fighting Philistines: The Old Testament in Popular Music, by Mark McEntire and Joel Emerson. Macon, Ga.: Smyth & Helwys, 2006. Pp. xii + 115. Paper. $15.00. ISBN 1573124648.

Joachim Vette, Ruprecht-Karls Universität Heidelberg, Heidelberg, Germany

Raising Cain, Fleeing Egypt, and Fighting the Philistines, by Mark McEntire and Joel Emerson, raises a timely and highly intriguing question: How and where have Old Testament texts been received in popular music? Where do pop songs make reference to Old Testament material, and what is the nature of these references? As the authors point out, studying how biblical texts have been received throughout history is as interesting as studying how these texts have been produced and transmitted (viii). It is high time that reception history also take popular forms of cultural expression into account. The authors should be commended for not merely adding to the many voices lamenting that our knowledge of biblical texts and their contents is continually decreasing. Instead, they show that, as in times past, this material is a source of inspiration to contemporary art forms. McEntire and Emerson do well to sidestep the discussion of "high culture" versus "popular culture" in order to focus on the question of where Old Testament references appear at all in popular music. This approach has the potential to shed light both on central issues of contemporary cultural discourse and on the scope of creative use to which Old Testament material is still being put. At a minimum, popular music can serve as a heuristic tool, highlighting questions to the text that may not be emphasized in other areas of Old Testament reception.

While establishing their data base, the authors discovered that not all Old Testament topics are received in equal measure by popular music. This unsurprising fact led to the decision to group the references according to specific thematic clusters, which then created the structure of the book. The chapters resulting from these thematic clusters are titled: "The First Family: Singing about Paradise and Pain"; "Surviving the Storm: Singing about the Flood"; "Family Matters: Singing about the Ancestors"; "Let Me Out: Singing about the Exodus"; "The High and the Mighty: Singing about Warriors, Kings, and Queens"; "The Poet's Poets: Singing about Psalms and Wisdom Literature"; and "Shouting in the Wind: Singing about the Prophets."

Each chapter begins with a brief overview of the biblical content in question, including pertinent exegetical issues and canonical interconnections. As these clusters are of very different size, ranging from a few chapters (e.g., Gen 1–3) to several books (e.g., the entire Deuteronomistic History), these introductory summaries are helpful to various degrees. The introductions to the larger clusters cover so much material in so little space that the result must remain unsatisfactory. A small corrective is provided by the additional reading listed for each topic. The chapter then lists pop songs that make reference to material from these thematic clusters and adds short interpretations of how the reference is used in the respective song. Each discussion leads to a series of study questions exploring some of the issues raised by the songs presented. The book ends with a personal retrospective and several appendices providing access to the data base by song title, artist, and biblical reference.

The authors' presentation is at its best when the song under discussion is particularly creative in its use of Old Testament material. This is the case, for example, with "Man Gave Names to All the Animals," by Bob Dylan, where a discussion of the song leads to the interesting exegetical question of whether Adam had encountered the serpent before the serpent is explicitly introduced in Gen 3; or "My Brother Esau," by the Grateful Dead, which highlights the themes of estrangement and reconciliation central to the biblical narratives; or "Creeping Death," by Metallica, where the angel of death from the exodus story voices his thoughts during his rampage through the firstborn of Egypt; or also "Hallelujah," by Leonhard Cohen, where, as McEntire and Emerson state, Cohen's attempt "to rewrite a failed story with claims of 'I did my best' and 'I've told the truth' fits the long tradition within Judaism and Christianity of remaking David that began with the cleansing of his image in the book of Chronicles" (56).

As these examples show, readers will find many interesting and thought-provoking pieces of information when reading this book. As with many good questions, however, the question behind this book opens a wide field of possible additional questions that quickly show the limitations of what this book is able to accomplish. Thus the range of the data base and the criteria used in establishing it are not clear. Even though the authors deliberately choose not to distinguish between musical styles, indicating that many such styles are "created as much for marketing purposes as anything else" (x), more discussion is needed on what belongs to this inquiry and what does not. It is hard to understand, for example, why McEntire and Emerson mention Andrew Lloyd Webber's musical *Joseph and the Amazing Technicolor Dreamcoat* but not the songs from the soundtrack to the DreamWorks animated feature *Prince of Egypt*. What belongs to "popular music," and what does not? Further studies in this area may also find it helpful to include popular music in languages other than English.

A second area that needs to be expanded is the large topic of intertextuality. Even though the authors mention some of the issues pertinent to this area, more discussion is needed on the question of what constitutes a reference. Whereas the intertextual references contained in the songs mentioned above may be beyond doubt, this is not always the case. With Billy Joel's song "River of Dreams," the authors state: "Whether it is deliberate or not, the gazing across the river to the promised land evokes the life of Moses" (41). Standing at a river and gazing at the other side with a sense of longing may evoke many connections besides the life of Moses. With "Jeremiah Blues," by Sting, the authors state: "[The song] makes no direct reference to the book of Jeremiah other than the title. The tone of the entire song has much in common with the lament poems found in the book of Jeremiah" (86). Whether "tone" constitutes a criteria for an intertextual reference or not would have to be addressed in greater detail. In both cases, the question is warranted whether these two songs belong in this collection.

The book's major handicap, of which the authors are quite aware, is created by copyright legislation that prevents the reprinting of the song lyrics under discussion. This requires the reader simultaneously to access three sources (McEntire and Emerson's book, the Bible, and the Internet) in order to get the most out of this book. While the authors give some helpful advice how to locate the lyrics in question, it would have been a great service to the reader at least to provide more partial quotes from these lyrics, which are included with some discussions but not with others.

In a book concerned with the Old Testament in popular music, it is somewhat odd that the study questions accompanying each chapter move away both from the Old Testament texts and from the song lyrics to focus explicitly on the personal life of the individual reader (see, e.g., 29: "If you had to define a covenant between God and your family, what would that look like?"). Although good pop songs often elevate personal questions to the level of paradigmatic issues common to the human predicament in general, the study questions consistently reduce the issues posed by the Old Testament texts and the song lyrics to the personal experiences of each reader.

McEntire and Emerson's book introduces a fascinating subject matter to a wide audience. It offers many interesting insights and provides a first step into a field of study that will, I hope, receive further attention. It would be wonderful if the initial data base provided by the authors could be expanded, perhaps as a collaborative Web-based project.

English for Theology: A Resource for Teachers and Students, by Gabrielle Kelly. Hindmarsh, Australia: ATF Press, 2004. Pp. 240 + CD. Paper. $35.00. ISBN 1920691154.

Peter J. Judge, Winthrop University, Rock Hill, South Carolina

In the words of the author, this is "a resource workbook for the development of English language skills in theology and related disciplines for teachers and students of the Asia-Pacific region from language backgrounds other than English." It presupposes enough proficiency in English to conduct upper-level study. "A sound grasp of the basic structures and grammar of English is therefore assumed, but the need for ongoing revision and practice is also recognized" (xiii). A rather good vocabulary is also needed.

Section 1 (units 1–11) is devoted to providing instruction and developing practice in skills for academic reading comprehension in English, using real theological texts of various genres. The opening unit is a reflection on the reading process and the unique challenge of reading *theological* language, recognizing its metaphorical/connotative nature rooted in the mysterious experience of faith and *religious* language (whether verbal or nonverbal). The challenge for the theology student is thus not just one of comprehension but of entering into the various modes of theological discourse (with its unique vocabulary and syntax) to discover how they convey meaning. This is true and useful food for thought whether reading in a second language or not. After this first, rather theoretical, chapter, the book becomes a real workbook, immersing students in hands-on exercises through which they can progressively demonstrate and check their grasp and use of the particular concept introduced in each unit.

Unit 2 familiarizes users with various types of publications for theological texts, from scriptures to popular articles, and has them work at focusing on various physical elements of a text to promote efficient and appropriate use and citation. Unit 3 returns to the somewhat theoretical discussion of the first unit by examining modes of theological discourse, based on J. Macquarrie's 1967 work, *God-Talk*. Rather than simply read about these, however, students must work with short selections from real texts to identify features and characteristics of the various modes: mythical, symbolic-analogical, metaphysical, existential, and empirical.

Units 4–11, then, are each dedicated to teaching how texts "work" and how students can learn and use different types of reading comprehension skills to make the most efficient use of time and effort. Unit 4 concentrates on the way ideas are organized by genres and patterns. Recognizing the genre of a text is the student's first clue to comprehending its purpose and point, while learning to identify language patterns such as definitions, examples, contrasts, and so forth (often marked with "signpost" words and adverbs) help the student organize the logic of the text for understanding. Unit 5 gives the student practice in consciously "predicting" what might come from a text by connecting previous knowledge with clues in the opening sentence or paragraph of a text. In units 6 and 7, students learn to scan word lists, bibliographies, tables of contents, indices, and prefaces effectively and to skim texts efficiently to maximize time and comprehension and move research along. Building on those skills, unit 8 prompts students to understand and analyze the structure of a paragraph (ideally, a well-written one) in order quickly to comprehend the main and supporting ideas. Unit 9 then moves to the finer points of sentence structure, even having students practice diagramming sentences (progressively rather complex) and identifying main clauses in longer texts. Unit 10 teaches how to recognize the cohesive devices that are used in good English writing to tie a text together: things such as the use of key words, pronouns, and references to antecedents, substitute words and phrases, ellipsis, and so on. Finally, unit 11 returns to the topic of how sentences convey meaning and what kinds of meaning they convey by having students identify and interpret conceptual and propositional meaning, the influence of context on the meaning of a sentence, the use of rhetorical questions, pragmatic statements of feeling or attitude, and making inferences from literal meanings. Students also practice recognizing authorial voice or point of view in this closing unit of section 1.

Section 2 (units 12–24) offers the opportunity to practice the skills learned and apply them to Asian-Pacific culture and religion as well as twelve other specific topics relevant to the study of theology: "Theology and Spirituality"; "Theology and Language"; "Religion and Culture"; "Revelation and Theologising"; "Christology"; "The Problem of Suffering"; "Grace"; "Justice, Development and Good News"; "Understanding Scripture"; "Ecological Theology"; "Genes, Ethics and Theology"; and "Christianity and Religious Pluralism." For this section, a CD is provided with twenty-nine "Listening Texts" to help students practice their comprehension as well as improve their pronunciation, if desired. The workbook is meant ideally to be used in a group or classroom situation where students work through the texts and discuss and organize their learning together.

Each unit in this section is presented in four parts: part 1 introduces the specific theological theme, centered on a fairly easy-to-read text, and reviews some particular point of English grammar that can be exemplified in the text. Students thus work through a number of revision exercises designed to hone their understanding of verb tense and voice, articles, prepositions, relative clauses, noun and adverbial clauses, gerunds and gerund phrases, conditional clauses, participles and participial phrases, and apposition. Parts 2, 3, and 4 of these units build on comprehension and vocabulary using increasingly complex texts for reading and listening. Each of the four parts begins with a "Preparatory Discussion" designed to get students thinking and talking in small groups or as a whole class about what they already know of the theme and to anticipate the readings. The texts are well chosen and represent different genres; they are printed against a grey background, which sets them off nicely from the rest of the exercise tasks, and each line of text is numbered for quick reference while doing the exercises. Each unit concludes with a vocabulary list arranged by parts of speech on a full, otherwise blank page with an invitation to note other words from the unit or the topic that the student wants to remember and learn.

The book is equipped with linguistic and theological glossaries, appendices with both printed texts of all the "Listening Readings" and the answers to all the exercises so students can check their work, and a bibliography of all the texts used for reading comprehension. The material is arranged and printed so that note taking and writing for the exercises are easy to do right in the book itself, and there is a sturdy spiral binding that makes the book easy, actually pleasant to use.

This is a very useful and usable resource workbook, primarily of course for theology students for whom English is a foreign language, but I can think of situations where this book would work very well for native speakers who are beginning their studies in theology. (I daresay I know plenty of native English-speaking students who could benefit from practice in reading comprehension and points of grammar!) It is by no means a basic introduction to English; as mentioned above, a working proficiency in the language is presumed. Published in Australia, it does have Asian-Pacific students in mind, so there are a few spelling and bibliographic features, as well as accent and pronunciation idiosyncrasies on the CD, that might be foreign to some users in an American context, but these are hardly real impediments in my mind.

As Gustavo Gutiérrez mentions in his preface to this work, English has increasingly become the international language of theology. It behooves non-English speakers to be able to read (and ideally speak) the language and so participate in greater international and cross-cultural dialogue. This workbook, not only about reading theology in English but about comprehending theological writing itself, makes a fine contribution to the discipline and to international/intercultural understanding.

Index

AUTHORS AND EDITORS

REVIEWERS